STRATEGIC ASIA 2007–08

STRATEGIC ASIA 2007–08

DOMESTIC POLITICAL CHANGE AND GRAND STRATEGY

Edited by

Ashley J. Tellis and Michael Wills

With contributions from

Nick Bisley, Shahram Chubin, Svante E. Cornell, Lorraine Elliott, Frédéric Grare, Samuel S. Kim, Kenneth Lieberthal, Mike M. Mochizuki, C. Raja Mohan, Celeste A. Wallander, and Donald E. Weatherbee

 THE NATIONAL BUREAU *of* ASIAN RESEARCH
Seattle and Washington, D.C.

THE NATIONAL BUREAU *of* ASIAN RESEARCH

Published in the United States of America by
The National Bureau of Asian Research, Seattle, WA, and Washington, D.C.
www.nbr.org

This material is based upon work supported in part by the Department of Energy (National Nuclear Security Administration) under Award Number DE-FG52-03SF22724.

This report was prepared as an account of work sponsored by an agency of the United States Government. Neither the United States Government nor any agency thereof, nor any of their employees, makes any warranty, express or implied, or assumes any legal liability or responsibility for the accuracy, completeness, or usefulness of any information, apparatus, product, or process disclosed, or represents that its use would not infringe privately owned rights. Reference herein to any specific commercial product, process, or service by trade name, trademark, manufacturer, or otherwise does not constitute or imply its endorsement, recommendation, or favoring by the United States Government or any agency thereof. The views and opinions of authors expressed herein do not necessarily state or reflect those of the United States Government or any agency thereof.

NBR makes no warranties or representations regarding the accuracy of any map in this volume. Depicted boundaries are meant as guidelines only and do not represent the views of NBR or NBR's funders.

Publisher's Cataloging-In-Publication Data
(Prepared by The Donohue Group, Inc.)

Domestic political change and grand strategy / edited by Ashley J. Tellis and Michael Wills ; with contributions from Nick Bisley ... [et al.]
    p. : ill., maps ; cm. -- (Strategic Asia, 1933-6462 ; 2007-08)
    Based upon work supported by the Department of Energy (National Nuclear Security Administration) under Award Number DE-FG52-03SF22724.
    ISBN: 978-0-9713938-8-2
    ISBN: 0-9713938-8-5

    1. Asia--Politics and government--1945- 2. Asia--Economic conditions. 3. Asia--Commercial policy. 4. Asia--Defenses. 5. Asia--Strategic aspects. 6. Asia--Foreign economic relations--United States. 7. United States--Foreign economic relations--Asia. 8. National security--Asia. I. Tellis, Ashley J. II. Wills, Michael, 1970- III. Bisley, Nick, 1973- IV. National Bureau of Asian Research (U.S.) V. Series: Strategic Asia, 1933-6462 ; 2007-08

DS33.3 .D66 2007
320.95

Design and publishing services by The National Bureau of Asian Research

Cover design by Stefanie Choi

Printed in Canada

The paper used in this publication meets the minimum requirement of the American National Standard for Information Sciences—Permanence of Paper for Printed Library Materials, ANSI Z39.48-1992.

Contents

Strategic Asia: Regional Studies

Strategic Asia: Special Studies

Shahram Chubin
> An examination of the domestic sources and dynamics of Iran's
> nuclear program and the implications for Iran's future political
> orientation.

Nick Bisley
> An examination of the current status and possible evolution of
> Asian efforts to develop cooperative multilateral approaches to
> regional security.

Lorraine Elliott
> An examination of the implications of environmental degradation
> and resource decline in Asia for U.S. security interests and policy
> in the region.

Strategic Asia: Indicators

Preface

Richard J. Ellings

Strategic Asia 2007–08: Domestic Political Change and Grand Strategy is the seventh in the series of annual reports produced by NBR's Strategic Asia Program. This year's volume investigates the internal transformations taking place in pivotal Asian states and how these changes are affecting, or could affect, their respective grand strategies and foreign relations. Although it is generally understood that domestic politics plays an important role in how nations interact, this topic has been under-studied in the Asian regional context. The Asia-Pacific's emergence as the center of world economic, political, and military power makes such an analysis long overdue. It is unclear whether the dynamic social and political forces at work in the region will ultimately challenge or support the current structure of international relations, but there can be no doubt that the global impact of such forces will be profound.

A close examination of the domestic circumstances in Asia reveals multiple factors that act to constrain or reinforce states' strategic objectives and governments' decisionmaking options. Economics is a prominent factor, most notably for China. Upon its extraordinary economic development, China is building a powerful international presence. Indeed, achieving great power status in the region and the international community is a vital concern to China's leaders in order to satisfy popular demand and mitigate pressure on the Chinese Communist Party's (CCP) legitimacy. Before China can feel secure as a great power, however, it must solve significant internal challenges. The CCP faces complex and daunting socio-economic issues, the continuing task of economic reform, and inevitably political reform.

Asian states are experiencing significant and varying domestic political transitions. Japan and India are seeing their democratic political systems mature, while South Korea and Indonesia are beginning to consolidate democracy and realize its gains. Although a leadership transition may not be likely in the near term, the CCP is slowly implementing political reforms and loosening strict control over China's populace in response to the internal and external pressures of being a major power. Russia is reemerging as a regional power, but under Putin's increasingly centralized and patrimonial rule, once again the country's elite is using politics, as opposed to markets, for personal gain. In Pakistan and Bangladesh, weak political institutions are creating space for both the rise of a radical Islamist minority and an increasingly active role for their respective militaries. Central Asian governments are struggling to build genuine political institutions and defend simultaneously against the revival of communism and new ideological challenges from radical Islam.

Islam and other symbols of identity politics are important factors in Asia's political environment. In some states the rise of subnational groups organized along religious and ethnic lines is creating fissures that threaten domestic stability. In Pakistan and Bangladesh, for example, volatile ethnic, religious, and national identities—especially when taken together with the growing voice of radical Islamist groups—spill dangerously into South Asia and beyond. The conflict between the Thai government and the separatist insurgency in Thailand's Muslim southern provinces has severe implications for Southeast Asia. Other states, however, are coalescing around national identities and drawing upon them to act more decisively in the international arena. Nationalism is on the rise across Asia. Chinese nationalism reflects the aspirations of a people who see their country once again being a great power, but it is tinged with grievances from perceptions of past Japanese, European, and American imperialism. Largely in response to China's rise, Japan is increasingly assertive in global affairs. South Korea's emerging national identity is shaping its decisions as a pivotal actor in Northeast Asia. India, also sensitive to China's tremendous growth, is reasserting itself in international affairs. Frequently nationalism is manifested in energy politics as well: China's global reach for energy supplies, Russia's renewal with resurgent energy diplomacy, and Iranian oil and nuclear policies.

Although traditional security concerns remain central in the grand strategies of Asia's major powers, non-traditional security is increasingly relevant. Declining environmental health indices and increasing economic disparities have accompanied the region's rapid development and modernization. Many governments in Asia, most notably that of China, are challenged to ensure that economic growth continues at a significant pace and is widely shared in society in order to remain a political asset. Moreover, the prospect of democratization throughout the region is challenged by new or resilient patterns of militarization or social control in countries such as Bangladesh, Pakistan, Thailand, Russia, and China. Other states with a balance of democratic politics and rising economies, such as India and South Korea, are finding new strategic opportunities beyond their borders.

The convergence of these factors—spectacular but uneven economic growth, the political transitions underway, and traditional and non-traditional security concerns—suggests that the challenge of balancing internal and external factors will become increasingly complex. It is within the realm of this regional and great power interaction that the effects of domestic changes on grand strategies need close examination, particularly as the global center of gravity continues to shift toward Asia.

The National Bureau of Asian Research developed the Strategic Asia Program to fulfill three objectives: (1) to provide the best possible understanding of the current strategic environment in Asia;[1] (2) to look forward five years, and in some cases beyond, to contemplate the region's future; and (3) to establish a record of data and assessment for those interested in understanding the changes taking place in the Asian strategic landscape.

Within this framework, *Strategic Asia 2007-08: Domestic Political Change and Grand Strategy* is designed to be an integrated set of original studies that aims to provide the most authoritative information and analysis possible. Through a collection of country, regional, and special studies, this volume discusses significant political patterns and developments within key Asian states, alongside broader analyses of states' grand strategies. The implications for the United States are assessed in the hope that identifying the potential consequences of these internal developments and external strategies in the region will assist U.S. decisionmakers in their efforts to craft effective policy toward Asia. A companion website provides free access to the comprehensive Strategic Asia database, which contains a wealth of indicators for Asian demographic, trade, communication, and financial trends; measures of states' economic and military capabilities; and information on political and energy dynamics. Drawing together data from disparate sources, the database allows users to compare these statistics across a range of years, countries, and indicators, providing an invaluable resource to illustrate and assess the momentous changes underway in Asia.

---

[1] The Strategic Asia Program considers as "Asia" the entire eastern half of the Eurasian landmass and the arc of offshore islands in the western Pacific. This vast expanse can be pictured as an area centered on China and consisting of four distinct subregions arrayed clockwise around it: Northeast Asia (including the Russian Far East, the Korean Peninsula, and Japan), Southeast Asia (including both its mainland and maritime components), South Asia (including India and Pakistan, and bordered to the west by Afghanistan), and Central Asia (Kazakhstan, Kyrgyzstan, Tajikistan, Turkmenistan, Uzbekistan, and southern Russia). The Strategic Asia Program also tracks significant developments across the Asia-Pacific to the United States and Canada.

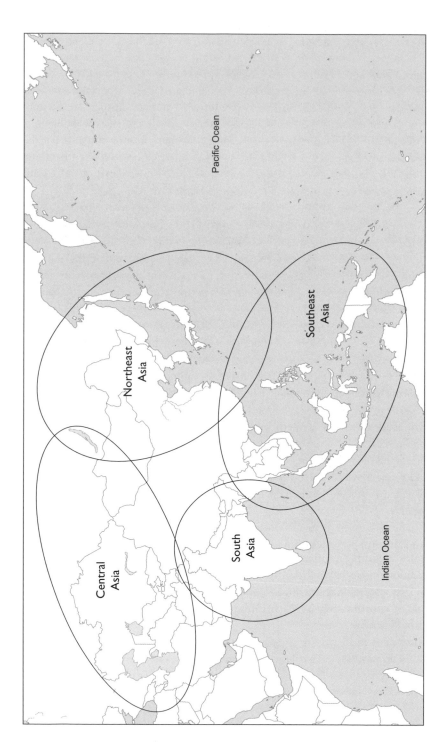

Acknowledgments

Against a backdrop of significant changes here at NBR this year, I have been impressed with the Strategic Asia team's ability to shepherd another high quality volume into print. Not only did we move our main office to a new location in the heart of downtown Seattle, but we also undertook a major institutional reorganization that is bringing new leadership to the Strategic Asia Program. None of this would have been possible without the commitment, energy, and constant support of a vast network of NBR staff and associates.

As in past years, our two senior advisors—General (ret.) John Shalikashvili, former Chairman of the Joint Chiefs of Staff, and the program's founding research director Aaron Friedberg, Professor of Politics at Princeton University and former Deputy National Security Advisor to the Vice President—have provided essential guidance and critical oversight to ensure the quality and relevance of this year's publication. I am deeply indebted to John's and Aaron's contributions to Strategic Asia as well as many other research initiatives across NBR. I look forward to welcoming this year the inaugural Shalikashvili Chairholder for National Security Studies, dedicated in John's name to honor policy-relevant scholarship in the field of national security studies. This new position will honor John's legacy, and the chairholder will play an important advisory role to the Strategic Asia Program.

Research Director Ashley Tellis and Program Director Michael Wills designed the research theme and agenda for this year's publication. During the research, writing, and editing processes, Ashley and Michael helped the research team explore the volume's underlying analytical questions. In light of the inordinate number of responsibilities that Ashley manages beyond his work with NBR, I am extremely grateful for his steadfast commitment to the Strategic Asia Program. Drawing on a wealth of insight and experience, Ashley's understanding of the major policy issues facing Asia and the United States is simply unmatched. During the past year, Michael has assumed additional responsibilities as Director of Research and Operations and has put his exceptional organizational and managerial skills to the exhaustive task of coordinating NBR's institutional reorganization. As Michael steps down from his role with the program, I am pleased to welcome Mercy Kuo as our new Strategic Asia Program Director.

Additionally, I want to acknowledge the important role that NBR staff and program associates have played behind the scenes. Working closely with Ashley and Michael, Jessica Keough, Strategic Asia Program Manager, provided vital research, logistical, and production support for this year's publication. Strategic Asia's good internal and external relationships owe much to Jessica's professional demeanor and attitude. Andrew Marble, NBR's Editor, and Sandra Christenson, Managing Editor, directed the review and technical editing of the volume and helped ensure the book's high caliber content and consistent readability. Andrew's and Sandra's editorial talents and keen eye for language and detail are a great source of pride for us here at NBR. Jannette Whippy did a superb job laying out the entire volume. Programmer Ben Andrews provided essential IT support and maintained the Strategic Asia database.

Much of the leg-work undertaken in the Strategic Asia Program has relied on the talents and dedication of this year's program associates and Next Generation research fellows. Program Associates Michael Jones and Stephanie Renzi and Next Generation Research Fellow Tim Cook provided superb research assistance to the authors, screened drafts, compiled the appendix, and supported the program throughout the year. Michael Jones, Next Generation Research Fellow Michael Cognato, and publications interns Casey Parks and Katherine Rosow provided invaluable assistance in the intensive editing, indexing, proofreading, and typesetting process.

I am also grateful to many other individuals who contribute to the Strategic Asia Program throughout the year. Our Board of Directors, in particular its Chairman George Russell, have led the way by providing insightful counsel and generous support for all of NBR's projects. With their guidance, we have worked to integrate our research initiatives to address salient policy issues in more meaningful ways. Senior Vice Presidents Brigitte Allen and Karolos Karnikis have provided essential assistance to sustain the development of the Strategic Asia Program.

Members of our Washington, D.C., office have diligently sought the ear of our nation's policymakers and helped raise the profile of all of NBR's activities, Strategic Asia in particular. Consistent with the changes that characterized the year, Daniel Wright left NBR in the spring to accept a position at the Department of Treasury as Managing Director for China and the Strategic Economic Dialogue. Needless to say, we are hugely appreciative of Dan's leadership and effectiveness in growing NBR's Washington, D.C., operations. We will miss him greatly, yet at the same time, we are excited that he has been asked to serve our nation in such a prominent way. We are also delighted that Roy Kamphausen has so masterfully assumed Dan's former responsibilities as Director of the Washington, D.C. office and look forward to the more prominent role Roy will play with Mercy in expanding the Strategic Asia Program. Special thanks go to Dan, Roy, and Raelyn Campbell for their outreach efforts. I would also like to acknowledge

Deborah Cooper, who provided logistical support for many of the Strategic Asia meetings and events in Washington, D.C.

Of course the most critical work fell to the authors who took on the challenging feat of exploring the relationships between domestic politics and grand strategies to produce a policy-relevant and superbly researched volume. I would like to acknowledge their hard work, dedication, and flexibility in meeting NBR's tight deadlines and requirements—a difficult feat for which they deserve much credit. These authors join a list of more than sixty other leading specialists who have written for the series, adding their unique talents to each volume and ensuring that Strategic Asia maintains a fresh perspective on the region. The anonymous reviewers, both scholarly specialists and government analysts, deserve thanks as well for their important task of reviewing the draft chapters. Their insightful critiques contributed to the high quality of this year's book.

Last but certainly not least, I would like to extend my deep appreciation to the sponsors of Strategic Asia—the Lynde and Harry Bradley Foundation, the National Nuclear Security Administration at the U.S. Department of Energy, and the GE Foundation. Their generous support and long-standing commitment has allowed us to strengthen and enhance Strategic Asia over the last seven years.

Richard J. Ellings
President
The National Bureau of Asian Research
August 2007

STRATEGIC ASIA 2007–08

OVERVIEW

EXECUTIVE SUMMARY

This chapter looks at domestic political developments in Asia and their implications for international relations and grand strategy in the region.

MAIN ARGUMENT:

Nearly all the major countries of Asia are undergoing important domestic political transitions that are affecting their governments. At the same time globalization, modernization, and a changing global balance of power are transforming the international environment. Understanding how internal developments shape regime responses to this shifting external environment is essential to properly assess changing strategies in the region. Responding effectively to any of these developments will necessitate responding to the underlying domestic political factors that are driving state behavior.

POLICY IMPLICATIONS:

- Economic change is driving the behavior of many critical Asian states, such as China, India, and Russia. Where maintaining economic success is a primary objective, grand strategies can in some ways be best understood as components of broader economic policies.

- Internal political transformations are drivers of international behavior in some other Asian states, such as Japan, South Korea, and Indonesia. Where democratization has deepened, political leaders more responsive to popular opinion have emerged to chart more assertive security approaches.

- The challenges of building institutions or arresting their decay dominate the agendas of still other Asian states, such as those in South and Central Asia. The informal social groups and militaries that control a growing share of political power in these countries define their grand strategies primarily in terms of maintaining regime survival and stability.

- Changing domestic political factors are also relevant in the pursuit by Iran of nuclear weapons, the growing plausibility of an Asian regional security architecture, and the increasing challenges posed to Asian countries by regional environmental problems.

Domestic Politics and Grand Strategy in Asia

Ashley J. Tellis

Domestic politics has long been viewed as a critical driver of a nation's grand strategy. From Thucydides in the west to Kautilya in the east, the character of a state's domestic politics—understood as encompassing everything from its history, ideology, economic arrangements, and governing institutions—was perceived to be the principal determinant of its national goals. To the degree that these goals could be realized only in reference to the objectives of other states—which, in turn, were conditioned by their own history, ideology, economic arrangements, and governing institutions— domestic politics was seen to shape the character of the international system as well. This articulation was masterfully sketched out in Thucydides' great work, *The Peloponnesian War*. Because of its assertion that "the real cause" of the conflict between Athens and Sparta was "the growth of the power of Athens, and the alarm which this inspired in Lacedaemon," this opus is often viewed as the acme of "systemic" realism. Yet, often overlooked is that Thucydides, despite having provided the most celebrated "structural" explanation for this collision, discerned its causes in the core conditions of domestic politics, in particular, the spiritedness of Athens and the passivity of Sparta. These internal characteristics defined the "grand strategies" of the two states and, together, created conditions for the combustive struggle that Thucydides would describe "as a war like no other."[1]

Ashley J. Tellis is Senior Associate at the Carnegie Endowment for International Peace and Research Director of the Strategic Asia Program at NBR. He can be reached at <atellis@carnegieendowment.org>.

[1] For an analysis of Thucydides' explanation of the Peloponnesian War from the perspective of social science, see Ashley J. Tellis, "Reconstructing Political Realism: The Long March to Scientific Theory," in "Roots of Realism," ed. Benjamin Frankel, special issue, *Security Studies* 5, no. 2 (Winter 1995): 3–100.

This approach to understanding international relations and grand strategy as outcomes of domestic politics has been part of a long tradition of political inquiry that, until the advent of neo-realism, was the dominant mode of explaining the actions of states. After Thucydides, a long and distinguished list of Western political theorists—such as Aristotle, Cicero, Augustine, Machiavelli, Hobbes, Kant, and Burke—and Eastern theorists such as Kautilya all in different ways argued that domestic and international political life cannot be understood except through the prism of the "regime." The regime writ large—meaning the values and structures associated with the distribution of power within a country—provided the medium for human nature to express itself.[2] This human expression invariably found a distinctive manifestation in the country's "grand strategy," which could be understood as the device by which statesmen organize the whole gamut of domestic and international resources to produce, at the very least, security for their country. Such a grand strategy would, no doubt, be shaped by the perceptions of the power, interests, and objectives of one's neighbors; these realities would, however, also be comprehensible only as products of their own domestic politics or, in other words, the strategic choices of those regimes.

This introductory chapter is divided into three sections. The first section argues for incorporating "domestic" politics into theories of international politics, especially realist theories of international politics. Such incorporation is beneficial for explanatory comprehensiveness and on the grounds of fidelity to the larger tradition, which has always been concerned over how power has been exercised both within and outside states. The second section surveys the key currents of contemporary domestic politics in Asia as analyzed by the various authors whose work is included in this volume. The third and concluding section highlights the key issues for policymakers that are suggested by the various country, regional, and topical studies found in this book.

Restoring Domestic Factors and Grand Strategy to International Politics

This volume, *Strategic Asia 2007–08: Domestic Political Change and Grand Strategy*, explores how domestic politics and the changes occurring therein in key Asian states affect their grand strategies. Although every

---

[2] Eugene F. Miller, "Leo Strauss: Philosophy and American Social Science," in *Leo Strauss, the Straussians and the American Regime*, ed. Kenneth L. Deutsch and John A. Murley (Lanham: Rowman and Littlefield, 1999), 91–102; and Steven Lenzner and William Kristol, "What was Leo Strauss up to?" *The Public Interest* 153 (Fall 2003): 9–39.

volume of the Strategic Asia series since its inception has implicitly engaged issues of domestic politics in the context of exploring the annual main theme, this year's effort makes domestic politics the explicit center of analytical attention. The goal of the research, as always, is to explain a nation's "grand strategy," meaning the objects and instruments by which a given country produces national security, and to understand the international consequences of these strategies and other driving forces for the country itself, the larger region, and the United States. The volume therefore focuses on grand strategy as the dependent variable. The goal is twofold: first to describe the national security goals of various Asian states, and second, and more importantly, to explain how these states have gone about securing their interests in the context of the larger changes in their domestic environment.

This focus on domestic politics and the changes occurring in the key Asian states is of particular interest because almost all the major countries of Asia are undergoing significant internal political transitions, either in terms of leadership change, ideological flux, institutional alteration, or societal transformation. In political history such dramatic transitions rarely occur synchronically within a given region, especially one that is as diverse and important as Asia. By all accounts, the Asian continent is clearly becoming the most important concentration of power within the international system; how this power will be employed in the years and decades ahead remains an issue of considerable significance. Because this exercise of power will arguably depend greatly on the nature of the regimes found in various Asian states, an examination of the transformations taking place in their domestic politics and how these changes are affecting or could affect their respective grand strategies is worthwhile.

Such an effort has particular merit because a wide range of contemporary scholarship in political science and international relations theory has demonstrated that domestic politics plays an extraordinary role in how states respond even to those challenges which ordinarily appear to lie outside the bounds of domestic politics as conventionally understood. Thus, for example, Jack Snyder has shown how domestic struggles within states shape their international ambitions. Bruce Bueno de Mesquita and David Lalman have demonstrated how domestic politics affects choices involving interstate war, while Susan Peterson has shown the same with respect to crisis bargaining. Bruce Russett has cogently argued the case for why certain domestic political structures and regimes, such as democracy, have significant pacifying effects even in an otherwise anarchic international political system. Daniel Verdier, Sharyn O'Halloran, and Helen Milner have made seminal contributions on how domestic politics affects national economic choices, particularly in respect to trade policy. Paul Huth has explored how domestic politics shapes a country's approach to resolving territorial disputes, while Jeffery Legro and Elizabeth Kier have investigated the same in the context of military doctrine, and Allan Stam has demonstrated how domestic politics can in fact shape the very outcome of war. These, and many other scholars—such as Robert Putnam, Andrew Moravscik, Roger Rogowski, and David Lake—have thus contributed to clarifying the critical relationship between domestic politics and state strategies in international politics.[3]

While the literature on this relationship is indeed vast and beyond easy synopsis, the proposition that domestic politics shapes a nation's grand strategy ordinarily would have been trite and banal were it not for the fact that the most prominent contemporary academic theory of international politics—neorealism or structural realism—is often understood as claiming that domestic politics is irrelevant to the explanation of state decisions. Such a reading derives largely from Kenneth Waltz's insistence that unit-level factors must be excluded from structural explanations pertaining to the large-scale uniformities in international politics. As Waltz argues, "a system theory of international politics" must not include variables in play "at the national level, and does not imply or require a theory of foreign policy any more than a market theory requires a theory of the firm."[4] In the sparsest version of his formulation, the presence of "anarchy" (meaning the absence

---

[3] See, for example, Jack Snyder, *Myths of Empire: Domestic Politics and International Ambition* (Ithaca: Cornell University Press, 1991); Bruce Bueno de Mesquita and David Lalman, *War and Reason* (New Haven: Yale University Press, 1992); Susan Peterson, *Crisis Bargaining and the State: Domestic Politics and International Conflict* (Ann Arbor: University Michigan Press, 1996); Bruce Russett, *Grasping the Democratic Peace* (Princeton: Princeton University Press, 1993); Daniel Verdier, *Democracy and International Trade* (Princeton: Princeton University Press, 1994); Sharyn O'Halloran, *Politics, Process, and American Trade Policy* (Ann Arbor: University of Michigan Press, 1994); Helen V. Milner, *Interests, Institutions, and Information: Domestic Politics and International Relations* (Princeton: Princeton University Press, 1997); Paul Huth, *Standing Your Ground: Territorial Disputes and International Conflict* (Ann Arbor: University of Michigan Press, 1996); Jeffery Legro, *Cooperation Under Fire: Anglo-German Restraint During World War II* (Ithaca: Cornell University Press, 1995); Elizabeth Kier, *Imagining War: French and British Military Doctrine Between the Wars* (Princeton: Princeton University Press, 1997); Barry R. Posen, *The Sources of Military Doctrine* (Ithaca: Cornell University Press, 1984); Allan Stamm, *Win, Lose, or Draw: Domestic Politics and the Crucible of War* (Ann Arbor: University of Michigan Press, 1996); Robert D. Putnam, "Diplomacy and Domestic Politics: The Logic of Two-Level Games," *International Organization* 42 (1998): 427–60; Andrew Moravscik, "Introduction: Integrating International and Domestic Theories of International Bargaining," in *International Bargaining and Domestic Politics*, ed. Peter B. Evans, Harold K. Jacobson, and Robert D. Putnam (Berkeley: University of California Press, 1993), 3–42; Roger Rogowski, "Institutions as Constraints on Strategic Choice," in *Strategic Choice and International Relations*, ed. David Lake and Robert Powell (Princeton: Princeton University Press, 1998), 115–36; and David Lake, "Powerful Pacifists: Democratic States and War," *American Political Science Review* 86, no. 1 (March 1992): 24–37. For a more exhaustive survey of works pertaining to the relationship between domestic and international politics, see James D. Fearon, "Domestic Politics, Foreign Policy, and Theories of International Relations," *Annual Review of Political Science* 1 (1998): 289–313.

[4] Kenneth N. Waltz, *Theory of International Politics* (New York: Random House, 1979), 71–72.

of super-ordinate authority in the international system) and the distribution of power among states (meaning the number of great powers existing at any given point in time) suffice to explain the recurrent regularities of international politics, the most important of which are repeated balancing behaviors by states.[5] Grand strategy in this scheme of things is reduced to a triviality that varies only in accordance with the differences in a state's geographic location and relative power.

This approach, when coupled with Waltz's own ambiguous formulations about the relationship between domestic politics and international behavior in his classic *Theory of International Politics*, has given rise to a large literature that implicitly or explicitly seeks to refute his claims. His critics counter either by asserting that many balancing behaviors cannot be explained without reference to domestic politics or, more interestingly, that what often appears as balancing behavior internationally is little other than the efforts made by some political groups to manipulate foreign policy in order to advance their own interests domestically[6] While this debate cannot be resolved here, worth noting is that Waltz's claim that domestic politics, a unit-level artifact, is unnecessary to explain the recurring regularities in international politics does not necessarily contradict the assertion that domestic politics is essential to understanding how states respond to the challenges posed by a competitive international system.

The neorealist desire to overturn the classical realist heritage on this issue is driven by both methodological and substantive concerns. At the methodological level, the neorealist effort can be viewed as still subsisting in the traditional realist paradigm to the degree that it is viewed primarily as a "thought experiment" that seeks to investigate how much the most parsimonious hypothesis, centered on systemic factors alone, can explain about international politics. Neorealism begins to deviate substantially from the traditional realist pattern of explaining political phenomena, however, when its methodological preferences begin to reflect a different substantive claim: that the domestic politics of a state, and specifically its political regime, does not matter fundamentally as far its national strategies are concerned. All states, irrespective of the character of their internal regimes, will behave similarly so long as they find themselves in comparable strategic environments.

---

[5] Waltz, *Theory of International Politics*, 79–128.

[6] For a useful survey of how different schools of international relations theory perceive international politics to be enmeshed with domestic politics, see Peter Gourevitch, "The Second Image Reversed: The International Sources of Domestic Politics," *International Organization 32*, no. 4 (Autumn 1978): 881–912.

Though whether this assertion is true remains a matter for empirical research, the problematic consequences of the neorealist position are worth recognizing. By asserting the essential irrelevance of domestic politics and the character of the regime (and, by implication, grand strategy), the neorealist argument divorces itself from both classical political philosophy and the traditional realist heritage. If the explanatory fruits of neorealism were in fact greater than that of its progenitors, this consequence might be dismissed entirely as an aesthetic casualty or one pertinent to the history of ideas rather than as a substantive loss. It is not obvious, however, that this is in fact the case. To begin with, neorealism's principle prediction about invariant balancing in the international system is neither deductively accurate nor empirically true. Thus, even within its own self-defined frame of reference, the explanatory value of neorealism's key conclusion is suspect. Further, its own methodology precludes neorealism from interrogating what was of great interest to both classical philosophy and traditional realism: the creation of political order *within* states and the implications of this process for international politics. Neorealism cannot explain the phenomenon of state formation and, by implication, cannot account for the fact that the genesis of international politics is rooted in the incomplete process of producing order from a primordial, albeit hypothetical, "state of nature." Thanks to this lacuna, neorealism cannot defend itself against its strongest critics. By asserting the primacy of domestic politics, these detractors are in effect arguing that the international realm is little other than an arena for national elites to contend with one another—even as these leaders might just as regularly collaborate across state boundaries to defend their privileged positions *within* their respective national hierarchies against other subaltern claimants to power.[7]

As a result of its methodological approach and substantive claims, the neorealist paradigm thus risks being unable to account for what is an important dimension of political life—both inside and outside states— and one that necessitates both grand strategy and its corollary, which is statesmanship. The best that neorealism can do in these circumstances is to admit that while the global distribution of power will define the challenges that states must meet if they are to survive in a competitive environment, there may still be room for analysis of domestic politics. Consideration for this non-system-level variable can be entertained because this arena invariably regulates how exactly states go about this task of decisionmaking and to what degree these states may in fact be successful, relative to other states. Neorealists should, no matter how grudgingly, concede this

---

[7] Tellis, "Reconstructing Political Realism"; and Ashley J. Tellis, "The Drive to Domination: Towards a Pure Realist Theory of Politics" (Ph.D diss., University of Chicago, 1994).

position, because even in terms of their own paradigm the differences in the objectives pursued by states, the capacity of others to confidently assess those objectives, the variation in effective national power, the ability of states to evaluate such variation, and the differential capabilities among states for increasing their power are precisely what make "domestic politics" so central to explaining various international outcomes. At the very least, therefore, explaining the recurrent regularities in international politics and the drivers shaping state decisions in the face of international pressures are thus complementary—and not competitive—analytical tasks. This insight, which remains the bedrock upon which the classical realist corpus was built, often appears at risk of being overlooked in crude formulations of the neorealist paradigm.

While explaining the repetitive patterns of international politics in the manner sought by Waltz may justify treating countries as differentially sized "black boxes"—at least as a methodological expedient in the first instance—understanding how and why states respond to international competition in the way they do requires prying open these bordered "power containers."[8] The analyst must look within the "country-as-a-black box" to understand how state structures, society, and the interstices of state-society relations bear upon the country's strategic objectives and its ability to successfully attain those objectives. This kind of analysis is necessary for at least two reasons, both of which would have been readily understood by the classical realist tradition.

The first is in response to the neorealist presumption that states can effortlessly transform their resource endowments into effective national power in response to changing systemic constraints—much as prices constantly shift in relation to changes in supply and demand in a perfectly competitive market. Nations actually invariably require conscious public policies that enable them to make such adjustments in practice. This, in turn, requires a "grand strategy," meaning an internal plan of action that enables a national leadership to navigate through all manner of domestic institutional, ideological, political, and economic constraints in order to reach its goal. Any action that changes the prevailing status quo in regard to mobilization and extraction of societal resources invariably creates new winners and losers; a state's grand strategy must therefore find ways of obliging various internal constituencies (and perhaps even accommodating other transnational constituencies in support of its aims) even before its

---

[8] Anthony Giddens, *The Nation-State and Violence* (Berkeley: University of California Press, 1987), 13.

worth is tested through contact with national competitors.[9] Eckart Kehr described the challenge in his masterful study of Weimar history:

> A foreign policy has—this may sound trivial but it is often overlooked—not only an antagonist in front of it but a homeland behind it. A foreign policy is contending with the adversary and also fighting for its own country; it is guided by its opponents' moves, but also—and even to a larger extent—by the will and needs of the homeland, whose concerns are primarily domestic.[10]

Managing this process is neither costless nor automatic but in most instances will determine how a country performs relative to others in coping with the challenges posed by the international environment.

Second, even as statesmen orchestrate their national responses to the larger strategic environment, they must be mindful of the consequences of their international policies for their own influence and authority at home. In this sense, leaders—even in the most authoritarian regimes—are condemned to play "two-level games."[11] The elite must constantly consider how their foreign policies are judged by various domestic stakeholders who can affect the elite hold on power. Recent scholarship suggests that political leaders are constrained by two factors at the domestic level: policy ratification and leadership selection.[12] Policy ratification, carried out through formal or informal means, refers to the fact both that domestic audiences evaluate the success of a statesman's foreign policies and that these evaluations condition their support for the governing dispensation. Leadership selection, in turn, is connected to the nature of the regime and is related to the kind of individual costs that statesmen bear should their preferred strategies or policies fail. The conventional wisdom on this issue is that democratic leaders face greater audience costs than authoritarian leaders and, hence, are more constrained in their choice of policies. The flip side, however, is that democratic leaders can also afford to take more risks because failures of grand strategy would "only" cost them their office, whereas any comparable fiascos accruing to authoritarian leaders could produce more devastating consequences for them personally. Important here is that the burdens of failed national strategies have an impact on leadership choices: because this reality shapes how states finally behave in

---

[9] Richard Rosecrance and Arthur A. Stein, "Beyond Realism: The Study of Grand Strategy," in *The Domestic Bases of Grand Strategy*, ed. Richard Rosecrance and Arthur A. Stein (Ithaca: Cornell University Press, 1993), 3–21.

[10] Eckart Kehr, *Economic Interest, Militarism, and Foreign Policy* (Berkeley: University of California Press, 1977), 23.

[11] Putnam, "Diplomacy and Domestic Politics."

[12] Ibid.; and Joe D. Hagan, *Political Opposition and Foreign Policy in Comparative Perspective* (Boulder: Lynne Rienner, 1993).

international politics, such "domestic" factors must be accommodated by any realist theory of international politics.

The Diversity and Challenges of Domestic Politics in Asia

Investigating how domestic politics impacts grand strategy is a challenging task that requires addressing diverse issues pertaining to the political system, political ideology, elite and mass politics, political economy, and international relations. The notion of "domestic politics" implicit in this volume is, therefore, a broad one that refers to the relationships between the "rulers" and the "ruled" in any given country. Since this compact is manifested in certain constitutional arrangements that describe the nature of the regime, each of the chapters in this volume considers (1) the structures of authority, i.e., the institutions that sanction political actions and (?) the structures of power, i.e., those critical social forces (or groups) having the capacity to shape decisions made by state authority in consequential ways. As appropriate, each chapter examines, explicitly or implicitly, what accounts for the particular compact between the rulers and the ruled in the state or region under focus; to what social, political, ideological, economic, and international forces the rulers and the ruled are responding; what external or internal factors could change the current structures and processes of domestic politics within a given state; and what the potential for significant change in domestic politics at either a structural or process level is over the next five years.

To the degree possible, each of the authors has also attempted to map the patterns of internal change in the country or region concerned against the backdrop of the three great transformations currently occurring in the global system:

- the phenomenon of globalization, understood as the growing share of global economic activity occurring between people who live in different countries and the increasing integration of economies around the world

- the phenomenon of modernization, understood as the increased capacity for social transformation on the part of both states and societies through the growing rationalization of human action

- the phenomenon of the changing balance of power globally, presaged
  by the shifting core of the international system from the United States
  and Europe to Asia and as witnessed most acutely in the form of new
  rising states such as China and India

The analysis of domestic politics herein, as in all previous volumes
of Strategic Asia, is undertaken ultimately with a view to understanding
how transformations underway in key states in Asia affect their strategic
behaviors. Toward that end, each of the country or regional chapters in
the volume concludes with an assessment of the implications of internal
political change for the relations that these key states in Asia have with
their neighbors and the United States, specifically with respect to the
following issues: (1) questions of war and peace; (2) questions pertaining
to internal versus external balancing, that is, the choice between relying
on one's own resources for producing security versus seeking new foreign
allies; (3) questions relating to military modernization, arms races, and
the development of weapons of mass destruction; and (4) questions
relating to the reality or prospect of cooperative security relations with
the United States.

By thus engaging a wide range of issues in a manner pertinent to each
country, this volume provides a synoptic view of how the evolving internal
changes and domestic political trends in different states or regions in
Asia condition their individual ability to pursue grand strategies that are
otherwise broadly shaped by their location and relative strength in the
international system.

Given that the Asian continent today is synonymous with rapid
economic growth, it is no surprise that several of the chapters in this
volume describe the management of economic change as being one of the
central issues of domestic politics. This certainly is the case for the three
major Asian actors: China, India, and Russia—though the challenges posed
to each of these states differ considerably.

Kenneth Lieberthal's study of China represents the clearest explication
of the view that domestic politics in China today is fundamentally about
sustaining the prevailing high rates of economic growth in order both to
recover the great power status that Beijing had enjoyed historically and to
avert the domestic political instability that would arise if economic growth
were to falter. Because China is, and will likely remain, an authoritarian state
for some time to come, the compact between rulers and ruled is ultimately
enforced through the coercive power wielded by the former over the latter.
The costs of enforcing this compact on a routine basis, however, are lowered
considerably by the implicit social contract that exists between the Chinese

Communist Party and the people of China—a contract wherein the population appears to accept the Party's rule so long as growing personal freedoms and economic prosperity become increasingly available. Because preserving this arrangement requires continued high economic growth, Lieberthal persuasively describes how the Communist Party has liberated provincial and local governments to create what has become an economic juggernaut that even the central government now has difficulty controlling. In order to protect the possibilities for continued economic expansion, Beijing has altered its international diplomacy to "tamp down looming fears of a China threat." The success of this strategy, however, has sustained an even more vigorous domestic economic dynamism than expected, leading in turn to a trail of new problems such as corruption, individual exploitation, regional disparities, rising inequality, depletion of natural resources, and severe environmental degradation. Although some of these problems have contributed to significant internal unrest in China, this phenomenon does not yet appear to pose an imminent threat to Communist rule. As Lieberthal notes, the still-strong Chinese ruling elite is willing to permit its citizenry to expand their zone of political indifference to pursue personal interests, but will "simply…not tolerate active opposition to the state." Only time will tell whether continued prosperity will change this dynamic, both at the level of what citizens demand and what the state permits. Until that point, however, China will continue to remain a fascinating example of how the challenges of managing rapid economic growth continue to constitute the central pivot of its domestic politics.

In different ways and in a different context, managing economic growth is also one of the central issues facing domestic politics in Asia's other emerging power, India. As C. Raja Mohan elaborates, the increased pace of economic growth in India over the last decade has raised India's standing in the international system considerably and brought the country within reach of realizing its traditional post-independence dream of once again becoming a great power. In that sense, there is a remarkable similarity between the ambitions of India and China: both countries were major powers before the colonial era and both seek to resurrect their traditional greatness once again by exploiting the opportunities offered by market economics and globalization. In India's case domestic politics plays a crucial role, but in a manner very different from China. Because India is a strong democratic state, all public policies—including those related to economic reform and liberalization—must comport with the test of political acceptability. The fragmentation of India's political parties after the demise of the "Congress system," coupled with the presence of a weak national leadership and a defensive political culture, has resulted in a situation where even though there is a general national conviction that economic reforms must continue, there are sharp divides about the specific policies to be pursued. This contestation is inevitable because all economic reforms create winners and losers, and in a democratic system losers in the economic marketplace will seek to avert, or compensate for, losses through the political market, which regulates the distribution of power. Consequently, what may be most surprising is that India can sustain high double-digit growth rates despite lapsing into its new "Hindu rate of reform." The Indian case, in Mohan's analysis, is telling because it illustrates not only how the management of economic processes has become central to domestic politics in yet another critical Asian state, but more importantly also because his conclusion that "even suboptimal outcomes for India's grand strategy still might be large enough to make a difference to the evolution of the international system" has significant consequences for the future Asian balance of power and for the United States.

Celeste Wallander's chapter on Russia also highlights the centrality of economic growth and political economy to domestic politics, but in a manner that is quite different from the challenges witnessed in China and India. There are some similarities, to be sure: the Russian renaissance, which has attracted much attention of late, is intimately linked to the economy rebounding in a manner that was unanticipated after the collapse of the Soviet Union. The analogy also has limits, however. True, the production of economic power in China and India is very much driven by national imperatives, which in the latter case are actually ratified by formal consent of the ruled. The Russian objective of securing economic growth appears to be driven, however, by the objective of bolstering a state that consists of a narrow set of corrupt patron-client relationships that involve current or former members of the intelligence services who are umbilically connected to the presidency of Vladimir Putin. Therefore, even though Russia's governing institutions are intended to be at least formally responsive to its polity, in practice these institutions exist mainly, as Wallander summarizes, to "manage the political, economic, and social system" for an "elite that is not accountable to Russian society." Both the present resurgence of Russia and the structures of its domestic politics are, therefore, quite fragile: the former is based primarily on energy and raw material exports whose production infrastructure has not been appropriately modernized, while the latter revolves mainly around a corrupt patrimonialism in which patrons and clients continually trade power and wealth and by so doing "capture" the state to serve their own narrow political ends. The general populace appears to countenance these predatory governing arrangements only because the Russian people are objectively better off than they were in the aftermath of the Soviet collapse and because their expectations of improving economic conditions make them less sensitive to the abuses of "managed democracy." Wallander summarizes the situation succinctly:

> The legitimacy of the political system…is based on what the system provides, not what it is. Should the system fail to produce, the lack of accountability and responsiveness, as well as the pervasive cynicism of Russian citizens about their leaders, may expose the weakness underlying Putin's supposedly strong state.

Precisely because Moscow continues to possess islands of technological excellence, any significant Russian failures that materialize in the context of rising Chinese power could have significant geostrategic consequences for the region and for the United States.

While this volume depicts managing economic transformation as being the central domestic political issue in at least three great Asian powers, the importance of economic change is witnessed in many of the smaller Asian states as well. In at least three instances in Southeast Asia—in Indonesia, Vietnam, and Singapore—positive economic developments remain critical to the management of domestic politics. In Indonesia, in particular, as Donald Weatherbee describes in his regional study of several key Southeast Asian states, improved economic performance has intersected virtuously with reform of domestic governance. The traditional arrangements between rulers and ruled in Indonesia—the most important state in Southeast Asia—are undergoing dramatic changes for the better. As Weatherbee succinctly states, "Indonesia stands out as a democratic success in Southeast Asia." In a region where authoritarian regimes are legion and military authoritarianism is not uncommon, Indonesia—with its large Muslim population, critical geographic location, and the locus of traditional regional leadership—seems to be redefining itself as a "normal developing democracy with a vibrant and free civil society,…an elected parliament,… a reform agenda,…[and] a civil-military culture in transition." Though these developments have no doubt been aided by external assistance, the domestic civilian leadership of President Susilo Bambang Yudhoyono has been the most important factor insofar as his reform agenda has helped the country achieve its targeted growth rates after many years of languishing in an economic morass. Although domestic transformations of the sort visible in Indonesia are not comparably evident in Vietnam, Hanoi has done even better than Jakarta in terms of economic performance. By rapidly expanding trade with the United States and others, Vietnam has chalked up dramatic improvements in economic performance that enable the country to both balance China successfully and maintain authoritarian structures of domestic rule. Whether continued high rates of economic growth will lead to political liberalization in Vietnam is uncertain, but this case—like others discussed above—exemplifies the centrality of economic factors to domestic politics in many Asian states.

While these examples illustrate why Asia continues to remain the home of economic miracles, the sheer diversity of the continent creates room for drivers other than economics. Interestingly, internal political transformations dominate domestic politics in the largest Asian economy today, Japan. This phenomenon appears ironic given that for many decades Tokyo exemplified the proposition that "all politics was economics by other means." The fact that institutional political change is now the most prominent element of Japanese politics highlights two important realities. The first is that Japan has convincingly pulled itself out of the economic doldrums of the past decade and is slowly moving toward accommodating the kinds of structural changes that most Japanese have long recognized as overdue. The second is that amidst all the hyperbole about a rising China, Japan still remains the world's second largest economy and the most important center of technical innovation in Asia. As such, the country is confronted by all the problems associated with mature economies, including in Japan's case, unfavorable demographics. Although these problems will require careful tending, the Japanese economy today does not need dramatic external interventions any more to sustain its long-term viability and performance.

These two facts taken together imply that questions concerning the structure of Japan's governing institutions, the nature of its political regime, and its long-term international profile and interests can once again take center stage in its domestic politics. As Mike Mochizuki's superb chapter on Japan's "long transition" in this volume indicates, these issues appear to be precisely the ones that dominate Japanese domestic politics today. Mochizuki demonstrates persuasively how Japan's desire to gradually assume the status of a normal country is reflected in its domestic political transformations—the slow consolidation of a two-party system involving the Liberal Democratic Party (LDP) and the Democratic Party of Japan (DPJ) and the increasing power accruing to the Prime Minister and the Cabinet Secretariat where policymaking is concerned (in contrast to the old dispensation, which favored strong personalities drawing their strength from party politics and backroom deals). The all-powerful Japanese bureaucracy has been reformed in this context to become more responsive to the political leadership. In a new sign suggesting that the compact between rulers and ruled is being subtly redefined in the direction of greater sensitivity to the latter, the social bases of the political power of the major political parties is changing, even as the government itself is being compelled to take public sentiments into account when formulating public policies. These multiple transformations are leading inexorably to new efforts to redefine Japan's security approaches in Asia, which as Mochizuki points out implicate "values, national security, economics, and international order." His chapter provides a rich and fascinating analysis of the debates occurring in Japan on each of these issues but warns, in contrast to more breathless exclamations of imminent and revolutionary change, that Japan's transformations in national strategy will be slow and incremental, though generally convergent with U.S. interests.

Japan provides a good example of how the classic issues of domestic politics—the relations between rulers and ruled and the desires of rulers to enhance the external security environment in order to both advance the nation's interests abroad and their own power at home—are well and alive in Asia. The same also hold true, again in different ways, in the Korean peninsula as well. Samuel Kim's essay on domestic politics in North and South Korea explicates the thesis that "domestic factors [in both countries] are more determinative in the formulation of...grand strategy, whereas external factors take precedence in determining the successful outcomes of [these] grand strategy enactments." That this would be true in the case of North Korea is not hard to discern. In fact, it would not be an exaggeration to say that almost every state policy in Pyongyang is driven by one central consideration: protecting the survival of the rulers against both their external circumstances and their masses internally. In North Korea, more than in any other nation on earth, the interests of the state are identical to the interests of its deified tyrant. Kim aptly describes the Democratic People's Republic of Korea as a "relatively simple mono-organizational system with a low degree of institutionalization, where the boundaries among state, system, and regime have become blurred and overlapping—if not completely erased. The North Korean state is and becomes synonymous with the North Korean system as a whole." Domestic politics in such an environment essentially revolves around the bargains that the supreme leader strikes with the coercive apparatus that maintains their common power, with all other developments—whether political extortion abroad or economic "reforms" internally—orienting the country toward the achievement of "tangible concessions necessary for system maintenance and survival."

The contrasting South Korean example represents, in Kim's analysis, a remarkable tale of how genuine internal political transformations, especially the ever-strengthening consolidation of civil rule in the face of the past legacy of military domination, intersect with the success of Seoul's economy. This economic miracle was brought about by globalization and its desire to achieve a certain measure of strategic autonomy, given that it is surrounded by major powers such as China, Japan, Russia, and metaphorically, the

United States. Kim's illuminating analysis of the domestic currents in South Korean politics demonstrates that the continuing strengthening of democracy, which is by no means complete, has already changed the security *gestalt* in the peninsula. These changes have in turn driven Seoul toward affirming notions of mutual security and security multilateralism, at least as supplements to the older instruments of tight military alliances. The developments have also resulted in a deepening of civil society which, because of its early role in the restoration of democracy, has been further empowered to influence diverse areas such as the advancement of human rights, environmental protection, the rule of law, and even the terms of the U.S.-ROK security alliance. This process has resurrected various kinds of anti-American sentiments, though the depth and durability of these feelings is a matter of some debate. The churning of South Korean domestic politics finds expression in Seoul's concerted effort to construct a new grand strategy based on the conscious exploitation of globalization to further enhance South Korean national power. As Kim describes, this effort at reconstructing grand strategy integrates different actors—such as politicians, policymakers, business entrepreneurs, academicians, and journalists—in support of a comprehensive vision that embraces political, economic, cultural, and social dimensions. Only time will tell whether this vision will be realized in its most expansive forms. In the meantime, however, South Korea represents a good example of how internal changes in regard to the distribution of power have a direct impact not only on how grand strategy is formulated but also the substantive content of the strategy, to include efforts at reshaping the larger structure of strategic relations in and around the Korean peninsula.

Managing economic transformations constitutes the major challenge of domestic politics and grand strategy in one set of Asian states; successfully completing internal institutional transformation represents another type of challenge in some other Asian states. The issue of building institutions anew or arresting the decay of political frameworks already in existence then appears to form the third category of contemporary experience in Asia. A good example of the former phenomenon is domestic politics in Central Asia, especially in Uzbekistan and Kazakhstan, which are the focus of Svante Cornell's chapter in this volume. As Cornell frames the issue, the core problem in both these countries is "institutional weakness" deriving from "the immense economic and social problems that accompanied the transition from Soviet rule." This should not be surprising, he notes, because "no state, emirate, or principality had ever existed [historically] with the name, or roughly the same borders, of the current five post-Soviet Central Asian states." Given this fact, the formal institutions of authority that currently exist do not adequately reflect the true structures of power, which are a complex mixture of authoritarian or semi-authoritarian rulership connected to, or drawing sustenance from, various sub-statal "solidarity groups" organized around kinship, regional, or economic oligarchies. In such an environment, the core political challenge faced by the rulers is to sustain a "minimum winning coalition" that includes key power-producing groups such as the security forces and the revenue-producing resource base. With such foundations, each of the Central Asian states has had to cope with multiple strategic problems: consolidating a precarious national identity, protecting national autonomy in the face of larger and more capable neighbors from outside the region, warding off internal threats to rule, and protecting themselves against the formal resuscitation of old ideologies like communism and new ideological threats like resurgent Islam. Against this backdrop, Cornell explores why a state like Kazakhstan has turned out to be more successful than Uzbekistan. This outcome appears to be conditioned less by the presence or absence of natural energy resources and more by the Kazakh ability to reform the national economy better than the Uzbeks, a fact that is intimately linked in the latter case to the character of its state-society relations. The fact that Uzbekistan also has a problem with radical Islamist groups and shares a border with a still-unstable Afghanistan has not helped, thus leading to Cornell's unsettling conclusion that Uzbekistan appears to be "increasingly unstable—a development that holds important consequences for the region."

The problems of institutional inadequacy which are endemic to Central Asia also find reflection in two major South Asian states, Pakistan and Bangladesh, albeit for different reasons. As Frédéric Grare's dispiriting analysis indicates, both these South Asian states, which are intertwined by a long and painful history, now seem to be headed toward an unintended convergence, thanks to the progressive decimation of the political institutions in place since their founding. In both cases, the respective armies of the two countries carry the lion's share of the blame. The weaknesses of the political parties and successive civilian governments in both states has opened the door not only for the success of radical Islamist groups, which are now more prominent than ever, but also for various transient civil-military dalliances pursued by the former in order to secure their own narrow political goals. The armies in both countries have thus become the pivotal political institutions and are viewed, ironically, as the last bastions of stability—a view that they themselves are no doubt eager to promote but that, more problematically, has the effect of actually corroding stability to the degree that it becomes entrenched as the received wisdom in the minds of both the native populations in these countries and their international partners. As Grare points out in his analysis, the deepening centrality of the military in the political life of both countries is causally related to the rise of Islamist terrorist groups in South Asia: in Pakistan, these groups have become convenient instruments for the ongoing geopolitical struggles with India, and in Bangladesh, these groups serve both the army's interests in controlling the civilian political parties as well as harassing India. As Grare concludes, the upshot of these destabilizing evolutions is that "if complacency or complicity of the Bangladeshi and Pakistani elites continues, both countries risk allowing a tiny minority—those identifying political Islam as their primary political identity—to ultimately determine both the bilateral relationship and the stability of the region." For the United States, which is actively involved in prosecuting a difficult war against al Qaeda in South Asia, this conclusion merits careful reflection.

Domestic problems caused by institutional decay are obviously not peculiar to South Asia. In Southeast Asia, as Donald Weatherbee recounts, two historical U.S. allies—the Philippines and Thailand—owe many of their current internal problems to crises of legitimacy and failures of civil-military relations. Despite strong U.S. support to the Philippines in the war on terrorism, the post-Marcos structures of governance have proven to be considerably infirm, with issues of corruption, politically motivated efforts at constitutional revision, and fragile civil-military relations still undermining political stability. In Thailand, the man on horseback has returned again. Discontent with a popular civilian prime minister, whose social basis of support was drawn from marginalized and hitherto unrepresented sections of the ruled (i.e., rural Thais) led the traditional social and political elites (i.e., bureaucrats, military, royalists, and academics) "who tended to view their power in the country's governance as an entitlement rather than as a democratic reward," to acquiesce to a coup that has decisively threatened not only previous Thai progress in civil-military relations but also security relations with the United States.

When viewed synoptically, therefore, the country and regional studies in this volume provide a complex picture of the domestic changes that are currently occurring in key regions or states in Asia across at least three broad dimensions: management of economic growth, transformation of political institutions, and politico-social deinstitutionalization and decay. Each of these drivers then affect the strategic behaviors of the countries involved in consequential ways, and each of the chapters explores this reality with a view to understanding the impact on the United States.

Continuing a tradition begun in previous Strategic Asia volumes, this edition also includes three special studies on different issues of contemporary relevance. The first by Shahram Chubin on Iran focuses on exploring how domestic political factors affect Tehran's strategic choices with respect to pursuing nuclear capabilities. On the fundamental issue of whether Iran's nuclear ambitions are driven by internal forces or by the external environment, Chubin forthrightly declares that "Iran's quest for a nuclear capability is the product of domestic politics and the demands of revolutionary legitimacy rather than a strategic imperative." Equally importantly, however, he argues that the nuclear program has become a touchstone for two radically opposed domestic visions of Iran's strategic direction. All sides in the debate do appear to agree that Iran cannot surrender its sovereign right to acquire various nuclear competencies, which in a sense justifies the claim to the existence of a broad "national consensus" on the issue. One group within the domestic debate, however, views the nuclear issue primarily as leverage "to regularize Iran's relations with the world, [to include] embracing globalization and domestic reform." The opposing group, on the other hand, views the nuclear program as providing strategic capabilities that would immunize Iran against any countervailing power that may be brought against it, as Tehran continues to prosecute its revolutionary anti-Western agenda. The presence of such diametrically opposed social forces once again illustrates the importance of integrating domestic politics into the explanation of international political outcomes and as a policy matter in this instance in particular, leads Chubin to wonder whether there is any room for compromise short of permitting Iran to acquire full mastery of the nuclear fuel cycle.

The second special study, by Nick Bisley, addresses an issue that has received particular attention in the second term of the Bush administration, namely whether the United States should invest attention and resources in constructing an overarching regional security architecture in Asia as a means of sustaining stability over the long term. Noting the entrenched mistrust and suspicions that pervade many dyadic relationships and organizations in Asia, Bisley admits that the current "alphabet soup" of bilateral and multilateral regional institutions has not substantively mitigated the current security anxieties in the region. In part, this failure has come about because security organizations in Asia, unlike those in Europe, are neither overarching nor products of a common history, common values, and a common valuation of current and prospective threats. Despite these realities, Bisley argues that a security architecture—defined as a "reasonably coherent association of international institutions, dialogue forums, and other mechanisms that collectively work to secure a defined geopolitical space"—is worth considering from the viewpoint of the United States for two reasons. The first is that there appears to be in Asia a growing demand for some kind of multilateral institution, perhaps even one created by a restructuring of some existing body, if for no other reason than confidence building. The second is that a multilateral institution would enable the United States to better cope with the emerging collective action problems related to public health, the environment, and climate change and, as such, would not replace but supplement its existing bilateral alliances in Asia, at least in the near term. Whether U.S. policymakers agree with Bisley's recommendations or not, his analysis deserves careful consideration and certainly warrants a deep assessment of whether the benefits of creating a continent-wide security framework are worthwhile compared to their costs. His essay, therefore, ought to become important source material as policymakers ponder their next steps on this issue.

The third and final special study in this year's edition of Strategic Asia is Lorraine Elliott's illuminating essay on environmental degradation and its impact on security in Asia. The question of environmental health globally is a subject of acute contemporary interest, receiving great attention in important international fora, including the United Nations (which recently had its first ever debate on global warming in the Security Council) and even in traditional security documents like the U.S. National Security Strategy. While almost everyone agrees on the importance of protecting the environment as a question of planetary survival, the debate usually falters when its connections with the national security of specific states (or regions) are at issue. Elliott's paper makes a sterling contribution to this question in two specific ways. First, the chapter carefully surveys the types of environmental problems that challenge the Asian region as a whole by going beyond the issues of climate change to a more diverse and complex cluster of crises involving pollution, resource depletion, agrochemical abuse, deforestation, groundwater depletion, and the like. Second, her analysis anchors these issues in a defensible notion of environmental security that, although non-realist in orientation, provides a useful framework that explains how "environmental degradation could be a factor in social stress, communal violence, and political disaffection and instability," even if such degradation does not always provoke actual interstate conflict. In detailing how various Asian states have responded to these problems, Elliott makes a cogent case for a broader U.S. response than has been evident thus far. She argues that current trends in regards to environmental security in Asia are likely to undermine the U.S. security vision for the region "by making vulnerable the stability of political relationships between and among countries, by exacerbating social grievances and human insecurities within countries, and by the impact on economic development, trade, and resource security." Elliott thus urges the United States, first, to view itself in the Asian context "as a collaborative partner rather than pursuing its own policy interests" and, second and more generally, "to reduce the U.S. contribution to environmental degradation with global reach" as a means of contributing to regional stability.

Conclusion

When the chapters in this volume are read synoptically, it becomes quite apparent that the issues of internal change and domestic politics deeply condition the choices of states as expressed through their international behaviors. Put differently, while the issues of anarchy and the distribution of power shape the systemic context within which these behaviors are expressed, there is a pressing argument that these structural constraints ought to be conceived merely as one of many variables that account for how states behave in international politics. Thus, the chapters provide further evidence for reconceptualizing international relations theory, including neorealist theories, in the direction that takes them closer to their classical realist predecessors.

Beyond the issues of reframing theory, however, all the chapters that follow flag important issues that will be of great concern to policymakers. Whether considered separately or together, these issues will indeed shape the future not only of the Asian region but also of the stability of the international system and, hence, merit careful and continued scrutiny. These issues include:

- China: Will the current patterns of domestic political economy described by Lieberthal result in an unsustainable pattern of economic growth over the long term or in unmanageable demands for political change that threaten the success of the Chinese economy?

- India: Will the currently fractured features of Indian domestic politics described by Mohan prevent the Indian state from realizing its geopolitical ambitions either because of continued internal incoherence or because the distributionist impulses of populist politics trump the imperatives of growth?

- Russia: Will the rentier ethos of Russia's current governing regime described by Wallander prevent the country's successful resurgence as a great power over the long-term or could it precipitate a collapse that threatens regional stability?

- Southeast Asia: Will the steady Indonesian domestic consolidation described by Weatherbee propel it once again to a position of effective leadership of Southeast Asia? Will the continuing transformations in Vietnam move it toward increasing tacit strategic coordination with the United States?

- Japan: Will the internal changes in Japanese domestic politics described by Mochizuki continue inexorably along to the point where Japan genuinely becomes a "normal" country and accepts the strategic burdens usually accepted reciprocally by other American alliance partners?

- North and South Korea: Will the strengthening of South Korean civil society as described by Kim successfully lead to the increased autonomy sought by South Korean elites and a productive strengthening of the U.S.-ROK security alliance? Will the North Korean survival strategy be successful and if not, what are the alternatives and their impact on regional security?

- Central Asia: Will the Central Asian states be able to protect their security, autonomy, and resources, despite the pervasive state weakness described by Cornell, if their major regional neighbors— Russia, China, and India—alter their current national strategies toward the region?

- Pakistan and Bangladesh: Will Pakistan be able to transform itself into a successful state and effectively contribute toward defeating international terrorism if the infirmities described by Grare continue to afflict the body politic? Will Bangladesh become a new hub of international extremism and a new example of state failure in South Asia?

- Iran: Which faction in the internal Iranian political struggle identified by Chubin—i.e., the conservative revolutionaries or the progressive internationalists—will finally come out ahead in the current struggle for power and what can the West do to strengthen the latter in this fight? Furthermore, assuming that the West can in fact play a significant role, would its contributions have a quick enough impact to deflect Tehran's course before Iran acquires mastery of the enrichment process?

- Asia's security architectures: Will the enhanced production of public goods that Bisley identifies as being the key benefit of creating an Asian security architecture be deemed worth the private costs accruing to the United States as Washington contemplates its future involvement in the Asian continent?

- Asia's environment: Can the Asian states—whether individually or collectively (with or without U.S. cooperation)—find ways of stemming the environmental degradation that threatens to undermine the continent's otherwise impressive economic performance?

Understanding these issues in their multifarious consequences will undoubtedly occupy U.S. policymakers for years to come. These questions ought to provoke consideration by international relations theorists as well.

STRATEGIC ASIA 2007–08

COUNTRY STUDIES

EXECUTIVE SUMMARY

This chapter examines China's international goals and impact through the lens of domestic politics and internal changes and assesses how these factors shape China's grand strategy.

MAIN ARGUMENT:

China's grand strategy seeks to sustain rapid domestic economic development for another decade or more. Economic success has vastly enhanced the PRC's global importance. Internal requirements strongly affect the PRC's approach to and impact on the international arena. These concerns make credible China's declared need for long-term peace to achieve national development goals. The nature of China's development and the measures to sustain it, however, pose challenges for the U.S. and others.

POLICY IMPLICATIONS:

- Given the momentum of its development, barring major disruptions China's international importance will continue to grow rapidly in the next five years.

- The U.S. and China share fundamental interests in many traditional and nontraditional security and economic areas and have developed an impressive capacity for collaboration. Underlying mutual distrust is growing, however, with potentially costly future consequences.

- Traditional U.S. engagement of China is no longer sufficient. "Focused engagement"—according far greater importance to the extent to which Beijing partners with Washington on issues most critical to the future relationship—would be a more effective new approach.

- China will more likely act as an international stakeholder if the U.S. frames U.S.-China issues objectively, initiates serious efforts to address them, and credibly signals a willingness to engage in long-term bilateral cooperation.

- By resuscitating its regional diplomacy and addressing Asia's critical regional economic, environmental, and nontraditional security issues, Washington can strengthen the U.S. position in Asia and reduce the negative effects of China's growing role and influence there.

How Domestic Forces Shape the PRC's Grand Strategy and International Impact

Kenneth Lieberthal

Domestic factors explain only a part of China's foreign policy. Beijing's policies also seriously reflect threat perceptions and other international developments. To a remarkable extent, however, domestic concerns structure the strategic objectives of China's formal foreign policy, and the nature of the domestic system produces many of the outcomes that cause other countries to worry about China's impact and objectives.

China is in the midst of change and economic development that is unprecedented in scale and scope. Nearly three decades of efforts have produced an explosion of energy in a political system that, while authoritarian, is flexible, dynamic, and features vigorous competition between different localities. Economic growth has included accepting extensive FDI and promoting foreign trade.

After nearly thirty years of reform, the top leaders today harbor a contradictory pair of convictions. The first is that China has become a major country globally and should be treated as such. The second is that rapid growth must continue if China is to avoid massive domestic political instability. In Chinese terminology, the leadership feels they are successfully riding a tiger—but to dismount (from a program of dynamic growth) would risk being devoured by that tiger. Three factors—the leadership's mentality, Beijing's resulting grand strategy, and the actual spillover effects of the dynamics of China's domestic system—are profoundly shaping the international consequences of China's rise.

Kenneth Lieberthal is William Davidson Professor of Business Administration at the Ross School of Business, Arthur F. Thurnau Professor of Political Science, Distinguished Fellow and Director for China at The William Davidson Institute, and Research Associate of the China Center at the University of Michigan. He can be reached at <kliebert@bus.umich.edu>.

The contours of the situation as of 2007 primarily reflect developments since the end of the Asian financial crisis in the late 1990s. China's domestic economy since then has been growing at about 10% per year, and internal changes such as urbanization and privatization have accelerated to an unprecedented pace. The leaders have declared that the country has a strategic opportunity to utilize a period of relative international peace to become a "relatively well-off society" by the year 2020. Since the late 1990s the People's Republic of China (PRC) has developed a sophisticated foreign policy and new security concept to realize this strategic opportunity.

After providing an initial overview of China's strategic objectives and grand strategy, this chapter then explains the key issues in China's domestic politics, political economy, and society that affect the PRC's strategic objectives and broader international impact. The concluding section examines the implications for U.S. policy.

China's Strategic Objectives

China's leaders regard the time between now and the year 2020 as a strategic opportunity to develop the economy and achieve "relatively well-off" (*xiaokang*) status.[1] They appreciate that continued rapid economic development and an improved capacity to generate new technologies will not only enhance the PRC's international stature but also raise concerns in other countries regarding China's capabilities and intentions. Leaders in Beijing have therefore shaped China's foreign policy around the goal of discrediting what they term the "China threat theory," in part by affirming their unswerving commitment to "peaceful development."[2] Fear that seriously faltering economic growth could result in major domestic turmoil makes support of ongoing economic development the core goal of Beijing's foreign policy. China's economic development strategy, moreover, fully leverages opportunities for international engagement.

To tamp down looming fears of a China threat arising from the rapid expansion of its capabilities, Beijing has significantly changed its diplomacy since the late 1990s. Until then, the PRC had typically articulated broad principles rather than engage in pragmatic efforts to build institutions and

---

[1] "China to Quadruple GDP in 2020 from 2000: Jiang," *People's Daily*, November 8, 2002; and Qingfang Zhu, "Development Indicators for a Comprehensive Relatively Well-off Society in 2020," *Xueshu Dongtai Journal*, no. 3 (2003). The year 2020 is used symbolically. There are no writings that posit a sudden change as of 2021.

[2] The PRC is so sensitive to the perception of China's growth posing a threat to others that Beijing dropped its earlier formulation of the "peaceful rise of China" in favor of affirming the "peaceful development of China." Critics in China had noted that use of the term "rise" (*jueqi*) might provoke fears on the part of others.

resolve problems. The PRC's stances often sought to place interlocutors at a moral disadvantage. During the U.S.-China negotiations on a bilateral accession agreement for China's entry into the World Trade Organization (WTO), for example, the Chinese side explicated with moral fervor the long history of imperialist aggression against China, intimating that as a consequence the United States owed China special consideration.[3]

The changes since then have been remarkable.[4] In Asia and elsewhere Beijing is seeking various forms of bilateral partnerships that are less than alliances but more than simple friendships. Multilaterally, Beijing is supporting the development of various forums and cooperative efforts that are not fully institutionalized but that do involve substantial interaction around defined issues and goals.[5] In both dimensions, the Chinese approach differs significantly from American tradition and practice. China dubs this approach a "new security concept."

Especially in regard to Southeast Asia, China has become an enormously active and generally astute actor, promoting multilateral efforts, playing to the sensitivities of interlocutors, encouraging regional cooperation, and inviting investment into China. China has taken the lead to propose regional initiatives[6] and has agreed to meet various concerns among Southeast Asian countries, such as pledging to adhere to the Treaty of Amity and Cooperation[7] and signing a declaration of a code of conduct with the Association of Southeast Asian Nations (ASEAN) in 2002.[8]

---

[3] Personal observation of the author.

[4] Evan S. Medeiros and Taylor Fravel, "China's New Diplomacy," *Foreign Affairs* 82, no. 6 (November/December 2003): 22–35; David Shambaugh, ed., *Power Shift: China and Asia's New Dynamics* (Berkeley: University of California, 2005); and Alastair Iain Johnston and Robert S. Ross, eds., *New Directions in Chinese Foreign Policy* (Stanford: Stanford University Press, 2006), especially part II, 217–308.

[5] The PRC Ministry of Foreign Affairs website provides information on the numerous bilateral partnerships of various types that China has formed since the early 1990s: http://www.fmprc.gov.cn/chn/gjhdq/default.htm. For the best available discussion of this issue and of changes in China's policy over time, see Avery Goldstein, *Rising to the Challenge* (Stanford: Stanford University Press, 2005). See also Evan S. Medeiros, "China's International Behavior: Activism, Opportunism, Diversification" (paper presented at the U.S.-China Relations Ninth Conference, March 31–April 8, 2007).

[6] In 2003 China proposed a new ASEAN Regional Forum (ARF) "Security Policy Conference" of military officers and defense officials to promote greater collective security. At China's initiative, in 2004 China and ASEAN signed an agreement of comprehensive economic cooperation that will build a China-ASEAN free trade zone by 2010. See Sheldon Simon, "Southeast Asia: Back to the Future?" in *Strategic Asia 2004–05: Confronting Terrorism in the Pursuit of Power*, ed. Ashley J. Tellis and Michael Wills (Seattle: The National Bureau of Asian Research, 2004), 261–99; and "China, ASEAN Start Building Free Trade Area," Xinhua News, November 30, 2004.

[7] Sheldon Simon, "Southeast Asia: Back to the Future?" 261–99.

[8] John Daly, "Energy Concerns and China's Unresolved Territorial Disputes," Jamestown Foundation, China Brief 4, no. 24, December 2004; and "Wen, Arroyo Express Satisfaction with China-ASEAN Ties," Xinhua News, January 16, 2007.

In South Asia Beijing has with regard to India promoted border talks, agreed to military-to-military exchanges and even joint naval exercises, signed a memorandum of understanding (MOU) on joint bidding in areas where the two countries' national oil companies compete for the same blocs in third countries, and encouraged substantially higher levels of trade. None of this has completely removed mutual distrust, but the efforts are remarkably forward-looking in the context of the history of the Sino-Indian relationship before 2000.[9] China has also counseled Pakistan to reduce tensions with India and cooperate with the United States on counterterrorism efforts.[10]

Chinese diplomacy toward Northeast Asia has not evolved as significantly. High level contacts with Japan withered during Prime Minister Koizumi's tenure, with his visits to the Yasukuni Shrine providing the specific justification for refusals by Chinese leaders to meet with him.[11] Since 2000 China has continued a process, begun in the early 1990s, to improve relations with the Republic of Korea (ROK). Despite some tensions over issues of ancient history, on balance the Chinese-ROK relationship has flourished to the point where Korean popular culture is all the rage in China and public opinion polls in South Korea reveal enormous admiration for China. China is also becoming a very popular destination for South Korean students to study abroad.[12] These developments have raised the possibility of future divisions in Northeast Asia that might see Seoul more closely aligned with Beijing and Tokyo more strongly tied to Washington.

There is also evidence of serious efforts by China to reduce regional tensions in Northeast Asia. Beijing welcomed Prime Minister Abe's visit immediately after he assumed office and followed up to reestablish regular high-level visits.[13] More importantly, Beijing has played an increasingly active role in promoting a solution to the North Korea nuclear issue via the six-party talks. The September 2006 statement of principles signed by all sides was drafted by China to break an impasse that threatened to derail the

---

[9] "China and India Unveil Plan for Trade and Cooperation," *International Herald Tribune*, November 21, 2006; "India, China MOU on Military Ties," *The Hindu*, May 30, 2006; Kenneth Lieberthal, "Energy Security and the Future of Energy Cooperation: China" (paper presented at Power Realignments in Asia: China, India, and the United States, New Delhi, December 14–17, 2006); and Derek Mitchell and Chietigj Bajpaee, "China and India," in *The China Balance Sheet in 2007 and Beyond*, ed. C. Fred Bergsten, Bates Gill, Nicholas R. Lardy, and Derek Mitchell (Washington, D.C.: Center for Strategic and International Studies and Peter G. Peterson Institute for International Economics, 2007), 151–70.

[10] Michael Swaine, "China: Exploiting a Strategic Opening," in Tellis and Wills, *Strategic Asia 2004–05*, 67–101.

[11] "China-Japan Talks 'Expect No Breakthrough," *China Daily*, February 9, 2006.

[12] "Young Students Head for China, SE Asia," *Chosun Ilbo*, January 9, 2007.

[13] "President Hu to Make Plans for Japan Visit," *China Daily*, November 19, 2006.

entire venture.[14] Moreover, China has encouraged trilateral meetings among defense ministers and foreign ministers from Japan, the ROK, and the PRC. While these meetings have not yet produced serious results, they may create the basis for more serious consultative mechanisms in the future.

China has also significantly shifted its policy on the crucial Taiwan Strait issue. In a series of steps in 2005–06, Hu Jintao led the way to a new Chinese posture that essentially focuses on building bridges to Taiwan and deterring Taiwan independence. This differs critically from the earlier posture of actively promoting unification with Taiwan—Hu evidently concluded both that peaceful unification is impossible to achieve during his tenure in office and that pursuing that impossible goal in reality strengthened the forces for independence in Taiwan. This new posture brings Beijing's operational policy far closer to the long-standing center of gravity of Taiwanese public opinion, which consistently shows roughly 70% of the populace opting for continuation of some form of the status quo. Hu Jintao also counts on the United States both to support this approach and to help rein in any activities in Taiwan that might upset the status quo. President Bush has proven to be supportive of this approach.[15]

Beijing evidently viewed the September 11 attacks as an opportunity to improve China's strategic relationship with the United States. Beijing initially helped draft the terrorism resolution adopted by the UN Security Council (UNSC) and encouraged Pakistan to side decisively with the United States.[16] Despite serious misgivings about various aspects of U.S. policy, China has since September 11 generally muted criticisms and been cooperative. In the wake of September 11, for example, the Federal Bureau of Investigation received permission to have an office in Beijing, and China has cooperated in prior inspections of containers before departing PRC ports for the United States.[17]

In sum, China has in recent years adopted a set of relatively pragmatic approaches to tamping down potential disquiet over the meteoric rise in the PRC's strength and impact. Beijing continues to stress the paramount importance of respecting national sovereignty, which often translates into reluctance to support sanctions and indifference to the domestic governance of the states with which it deals. Beijing also continues to take an extremely

---

[14] Jing-dong Yuan, "China's New North Korea Diplomacy," *Asia Times*, November 14, 2006.

[15] The shift in Hu Jintao's policy toward Taiwan can be seen through his pronouncement of the four-point guidelines on cross-Strait relations in March 2005. See "Four-point Guidelines on Cross-Straits Relations Set Forth by President Hu," Xinhua News, March 4, 2005.

[16] Swaine, "China: Exploiting a Strategic Opening," 67–101.

[17] "China, U.S. Strengthen Anti-terrorism Cooperation in Container Security," *People's Daily*, July 30, 2003; and "FBI Office Opened in U.S. Embassy in Beijing," *People's Daily*, October 24, 2002.

unyielding approach to all issues that touch on Taiwan's international political standing. Within these parameters, however, China has focused its increasingly sophisticated and wide-ranging diplomatic activities on securing the conditions necessary for continued rapid economic development.

The discordant note in the above picture is a rapid, ongoing upgrading of People's Liberation Army (PLA) capabilities, buttressed by annual double-digit increases in the announced defense budget.[18] The PLA shoulders the responsibility to protect the political system from internal challenge. The members of the PLA take an oath of office that binds them to protect not only the PRC but more specifically the Chinese Communist Party (CCP). The PLA is headed by the Military Affairs Committee of the CCP, not by the government. Hu Jintao chairs the CCP's Military Affairs Committee.

Until the 1980s the PLA focused especially on maintaining domestic order and enforcing the will of the CCP. Starting in the mid-1980s, however, the reformers in the CCP initiated wide-ranging programs to create a more professionalized PLA with upgraded border protection and force projection capabilities and also gradually decreased the military's role in domestic affairs. By 2007 the PLA has become a basically professional military force that, though having residual domestic political tasks, is primarily focused on national security issues and defense modernization. Uniformed military representation at the top of the political system has been drastically reduced.[19]

Estimates of actual defense spending in China vary a great deal, with the U.S. Department of Defense numbers toward the high end of the scale.[20] Despite several defense white papers, lack of PRC transparency on this issue makes all figures no better than rough approximations. Nobody is in doubt, however, that defense spending since the late 1990s has gone up at a rate that substantially exceeds growth of GDP.

The new increase in spending has focused on transforming the nature of the PLA, rather than simply adding more of the same. The broad directions of change include greater stress on information warfare, strengthened "joint" capabilities, and improved force projection via enhancements in

---

[18] David Shambaugh, "China's Military Modernization: Making Steady and Surprising Progress," in *Strategic Asia 2005–06: Military Modernization in an Era of Uncertainty*, ed. Ashley J. Tellis and Michael Wills (Seattle: The National Bureau of Asian Research, 2005), 67–103. The official defense budget climbed to 350.92 billion *renminbi* (RMB) in 2007, an increase of 17.8% over the 2006 figure; see *People's Daily*, March 4, 2007.

[19] David Shambaugh, *Modernizing China's Military: Progress, Problems, and Prospects* (Berkeley: University of California Press, 2002).

[20] Office of the Secretary of Defense, *Military Power of the People's Republic of China: A Report to Congress Pursuant to the National Defense Authorization Act, Fiscal Year 2007*, 110th Congress, 2nd sess., http://www.defenselink.mil/pubs/pdfs/070523-China-Military-Power-final.pdf.

naval, air, and missile capacities. The PRC has imported key technologies and systems from Russia and Israel and has sought to enable the military to reap benefits from development of new technologies in the civilian sector. All of these efforts have been accompanied by significant organizational changes designed to produce leaner, more agile, and lethal armed forces.[21]

The initial focus of these changes was directed toward enhancing the capacity to make good Beijing's threat to use force against Taiwan should Taipei step over an ill-defined line toward independence. Beijing now apparently feels on track to achieve that goal, and there is serious debate in China's military and think-tanks about the broader and longer-term goals that should structure future military development.[22]

The PLA has become more open and transparent in the course of these changes. The Chinese military now holds exercises with various other militaries, frequently hosts other military leaders and accepts foreign military officers into its National Defense University programs, and in other ways tries to present a constructive image to the United States and others in the region.[23] The speed and scale of the PLA's development, however, is causing concerns in the region, not least among the Japanese. Furthermore, the PLA remains on balance the least transparent of any of the major militaries in the region outside of North Korea.

China's Grand Strategy

China's grand strategy is designed both to sustain high speed economic development and to blunt any concerns that other countries may have about rapidly growing PRC capabilities. This strategy seeks to reduce to a minimum the chances that conflict abroad will disrupt the path to development at home; assure access to the raw materials, parts and components, and technology necessary to sustain China's unprecedented economic growth; and prevent developments in Taiwan from provoking either cross-Strait military conflict or a domestic political crisis in the PRC.

Although scholars and officials in China debate many particulars about foreign policy, programmatic differences between various elite groups on

---

[21] Harold Brown, Joseph Prueher, and Adam Segal, *Chinese Military Power: Independent Task Force Report* (New York: Council on Foreign Relations Press, 2003); David Shambaugh, *Modernizing China's Military*; and Anthony Cordesman and Martin Kleiber, *Chinese Military Modernization* (Washington, D.C.: Center for Strategic and International Studies, 2007).

[22] For detailed information on trends and debates regarding China's war fighting concepts that include but also go far beyond cross-Strait scenarios, see James Mulvenon and David Finkelstein, eds., *China's Revolution in Doctrinal Affairs: Emerging Trends in the Operational Art of the Chinese People's Liberation Army* (Alexandria: CNA Corporation, 2005).

[23] Information Office of the State Council of the People's Republic of China, *China's National Defense 2006* (Beijing, December 2006).

the major components of this grand strategy appear non-existent. The Politburo-level leadership in Beijing believes that in order to achieve priority domestic objectives China's foreign policy should adhere to the following framework:

- regard the United States as the world's most important country and not allow the U.S.-China relationship to turn significantly negative

- recognize that over the long run the United States does not want China to achieve its full national potential and will take measures to inhibit China's success—China should, therefore, simultaneously encourage development of centers of power that reduce U.S. dominance while carefully refraining from giving such efforts an explicitly anti-U.S. flavor

- enhance ties with countries (such as India and Australia) that the United States appears to be lining up with to constrain China

- encourage strong bilateral economic and political relationships in Asia and buttress these relationships with initiatives to create subregional and regional multilateral capabilities, preferably with little or no U.S. role

- manage diplomatic relations so as to maintain access to key export markets

- assure access to and preferably have ownership over raw materials and energy in order to supply China's growing economy

- increase China's voice and roles in multilateral organizations and activities

- strengthen ties to Taiwan and develop the capacity to wreak unacceptable damage with conventional arms should Taiwan take measures that are seen in the PRC as declaring *de jure* independence

- seek to be treated as a country of major power status while limiting the costs of China's international system maintenance responsibilities and maintaining a self-identification as a developing country

In short, China has a need for a peaceful environment and relatively open world economy in order to sustain its economic trajectory. This need constrains China to work constructively with the United States while at the same time on the margins to encourage trends that reduce U.S. global dominance. China's need to sustain its economic trajectory also requires Beijing to lessen frictions with countries that are major suppliers and markets, limit the PRC's international responsibilities while enhancing its prestige, and deter Taiwan's achieving formal independence.

Domestic Factors Shaping China's International Impact

China's national elites have developed a foreign policy to help sustain the country's rapid domestic growth and political stability. As noted above, evidence suggests that, despite rigorous debates about various foreign policy issues in the academic literature in China, Beijing's fundamental grand strategy is not seriously contended at the top.

The consensus on broad strategy seems to apply as much to the domestic system as to grand strategy in foreign policy. Since the 1990s China has achieved a relatively settled overall arrangement of its political system. As such, the political elite see economic growth as providing legitimacy, buttressed by the notion that China is pursing a unique path to realize national aspirations. The emerging economic elite draw close to the political elite in order to enhance their status and business prospects. The intellectual elite accept that political instability would threaten China's overall progress and in general support the notion that Western models are not adequate to guide the development of such a large and distinctive country.

The political elite are willing both to loosen up restrictions on lifestyle choices and to encourage rampant consumerism and a vibrant popular culture—as long as these do not touch on dissident political themes. Although the political elite are happy to have people focus on personal interests rather than politics, they simply do not tolerate active opposition to the state. With economic growth as a lynchpin of this entire system, those at the bottom can suffer from serious exploitation, especially as local levels of the state collude with local businessmen for mutual profit. This problem has in turn focused political reform efforts largely onto attempts to improve both local governance and the well-being of those at the bottom. Encouraging nationalist sentiment to bolster support for the state is also a part of this strategy for keeping a potentially restless populace in line.[24]

Elite competition, therefore, seems to be more for power and privilege than for competing programmatic or ideological goals, either domestically or internationally.[25] The political elites are not contending over fundamentally different programs—all regard continuing strong economic growth as critical and fear widespread popular unrest. All the leaders also

---

[24] Joseph Fewsmith, "The Politics of Economic Liberalization: Are There Limits?" in *China's Rise and the Balance of Influence in Asia*, ed. William W. Keller and Thomas G. Rawski (Pittsburgh: University of Pittsburgh, 2007), 74–94.

[25] Having a distinct formulation canonized as a guiding principle is a source of domestic prestige and power. Hu Jintao has, for example, promoted the notion of a "harmonious society" and is touting the idea of a "harmonious world," buttressed by ancillary ideas such as "taking people as the base" and "scientific development." Jiang Zemin promoted adoption of the notion of the "Three Represents" and of a "New Security Concept." The substantive content of these broad slogans, however, remains flexible and vague, and adjustments in direction are very much evolutionary.

recognize that the nature of the system is such that those at the very top must maintain a facade of collective unity or otherwise risk underlying tensions welling up to produce widespread disruption of public order.

Nationalism is a double-edged sword in this system. The top leaders cultivate nationalism in order to shore up support but fear that popular unrest could be ignited around allegations that Beijing is not sufficiently protecting the PRC's dignity and interests. Should the leaders sense this situation developing, their response would prioritize restoring their nationalist credentials domestically over their normal foreign policy goals.[26]

In short, the most important factors shaping China's international impact are not the ebb and flow of elite politics and factional disputes. These dynamics may affect particular responses to occasional tactical issues but pale in importance when compared to the international repercussions of the PRC's domestic systemic features and challenges.

China's overall international footprint, moreover, extends well beyond Beijing's formal foreign policy. For example, the dynamics of the PRC's internal system are creating huge export surpluses, regional integration of an East Asian manufacturing system, and serious transnational environmental problems and public health threats. Understanding the domestic system's key present driving forces is therefore necessary to understand the present and likely future international challenges stemming from domestic developments.

In sum, major domestic goals and concerns set Beijing's overall priorities, elite politics affect tactics around the margins, and the structure of the PRC's political economy and social dynamics determine many of the actual outcomes of international consequence. The following analysis, therefore, focuses first on China's current internal system dynamics and then on the resulting effects on the PRC's regional and global footprints.

The PRC's Political Economy

China's underlying political economy explains many of the developments that most concern international observers. Once reforms began in the late 1970s, China's leaders confronted the vexing problem of how to transform a Maoist totalitarian system into a different type of authoritarian polity without occasioning the collapse of the system in the process. China's leaders had no grand strategy of reform, and operational goals of the reforms evolved over time as leaders gained more experience and resolved internal political disagreements. Tactically, these leaders

---

[26] Susan Shirk, *China: Fragile Superpower* (New York: Oxford University Press, 2007), 1–13.

pursued a policy of trial and error, encouraging experimentation and then deciding which local experiences to popularize and support centrally—a strategy described as "crossing a river by feeling for stones on the bottom."[27] This strategy eventually produced a set of system dynamics of enormous consequence.

A key component of the reform approach was to strengthen territorially based political organs at the overall expense of line organs whose power emanated from Beijing. China has a political system of five territorial levels of political power: center (national), province, city, county, and township. The strategy that developed was that the leaders of each of these territorial units would say to the units directly below them (e.g., the provincial leaders to the leaders of each city within the province): "We will give you the policy flexibility necessary for you to take measures to make the economy under your jurisdiction grow. You can benefit from that growth through both good annual performance reviews and in various less formal ways. You must, however, keep your policies within broad outlines that come down to you from above, and we will retain the power to promote, retain, dismiss, and punish you."

The national level retains considerable power under this system by allocating many key resources, adopting laws and regulations, providing specific exemptions from regulations to particular localities, and using investigative and coercive powers to discipline localities. This is thus a system in which the center establishes overall priorities and major strategies, but generally encourages and (if successful) rewards local initiative and creativity.[28]

The results of this basic approach have been startling. Although China has a one-party authoritarian political system, there is dynamic competition among localities for everything from infrastructure to foreign direct investment. Localities by now differ in terms of the fundamental structure of their economies, with some entire provinces having become overwhelmingly dominated by private enterprises even as others retain

---

[27] There are many good overviews of the politics and changes during the reform period, including: Joseph Fewsmith, *Dilemmas of Reform in China: Potential Conflict and Economic Debate* (New York: ME Sharpe, 1994); Merle Goldman and Roderick MacFarquhar, eds., *The Paradox of China's Post-Mao Reforms* (Cambridge: Harvard University Press, 1999); Kenneth Lieberthal, *Governing China: From Revolution through Reform*, rev. ed. (New York: W.W. Norton, 2004); and Barry Naughton, *The Chinese Economy: Transitions and Growth* (Cambridge: MIT Press, 2007).

[28] Lieberthal, *Governing China*, 186–96.

many state-owned enterprises (SOE) at the core of their economies.[29] Generally, the east coast provinces have fared best in this system.[30]

The enormous overall growth that this system has generated has played a fundamental role in sustaining political stability through the reform effort. Poverty alleviation, income growth, social mobility, and increased access to the accoutrements of middle-class life (communications, entertainment, travel, private housing, and so forth) have been major developments in China under the reforms, especially since the mid 1990s. Young peasants increasingly have the opportunity to seek opportunities in the major cities, and both intellectuals and capitalists have become part of the CCP's political base.

This political economy has also enabled the CCP to transition from a Maoist mobilization-type party to something vastly different without experiencing a fundamental collapse in the process. By 2007 the CCP had become a bureaucratic capitalist entrepreneurial juggernaut, with party officials throughout China wielding political power on behalf of various enterprises in their localities to increase local GDP. The political system is thus sustaining internal cohesion in substantial measure by enabling party officials to prosper by sharing in the local wealth fostered by their political power. As noted above, contestation in this system is more over power and position than over competing programmatic platforms.

In many ways, the party is both the major strength and the key weakness of the Chinese system. The party has devised the strategy that the country has followed during its decades of reform and, by restricting popular power, is able to impose sacrifices in order to promote development. At the same time, the party suffers from the ills of corruption and inbreeding, and its monopoly of power may make the party too unresponsive to popular concerns to sustain political stability during the coming years of ongoing wrenching social and economic changes.[31]

China's leaders have nevertheless determined that only the ongoing concentration of power in the hands of the CCP will provide a sufficiently secure basis for sustaining the socially difficult measures necessary to develop a relatively well-off economy by the 2020s. The CCP elite is convinced that a more democratic system would fall short because too many people would vote to attenuate necessary measures.

---

[29] For example, the private sector dominates Zhejiang's economy while the state sector dominates Shanghai's.

[30] Loren Brandt, Thomas Rawski, and Xiaodong Zhu, "International Dimensions of China's Long Boom," in Keller and Rawski, *China's Rise*, 14–46; and James Fallows, "China Makes, The World Takes," *The Atlantic Monthly* 300, no.1 (July/August 2007): 48–72.

[31] Lieberthal, *Governing China*, 240–42; and David Shambaugh, *China's Communist Party: Atrophy & Adaptation* (forthcoming, 2008).

The party is thus likely to continue to dominate Chinese politics for the coming decade or more. This in part reflects the enormous scope of the CCP's reach—having more than 70 million members and appointing virtually every individual in a position of any power in the government, media, education, health, and economic sectors.[32] In China organized politics is by definition intra-party politics, and the CCP alone makes all major decisions regarding government action.

Politics in China therefore tends to center around three issues: which individuals will be promoted to coveted posts, which localities will be favored with state investments or various other incentives that permit greater growth and enrichment, and what measures must be taken to prevent social strains and resentments from becoming the source of large-scale unrest.

CCP General Secretary and State President Hu Jintao and Premier Wen Jiabao can encourage their preferred overall directions on each of these issues but are in fact limited in what they can accomplish. At least until the 17th Party Congress is convened in the fall of 2007, the two leaders must contend with a majority of members of the Politburo Standing Committee who are stalwarts of former party head Jiang Zemin. Hu will very likely be able to command a Standing Committee majority after the 17th Congress, but even then the system will continue to permit a great deal of policy flexibility by subnational leaders. The capacity of localities to tap local resources for growth means inevitably that the socio-economic gap between the rich coastal provinces and the interior will continue to widen. Measures taken to promote greater social equity and take some of the hard edge off of wrenching social changes are also subject to substantial distortion when filtered through the multilayered Chinese political system.

Hu's slogans of "harmonious society," "taking people as the base," and "scientific development," therefore help to set a tone and general direction but have not seriously changed the realities most citizens face.[33] Those realities result more from the dynamics of the system than from the dictates of any single individual or group at the top.

As of 2007 the same political economy that has produced China's dynamic growth has also produced obvious problems. The incentives for subnational territorial political leaders to increase local growth have led to systematic and pervasive local state interference in individual enterprises, both state-owned and private. While markets largely determine retail sales,

---

[32] This is with the partial exception of entrepreneurs in the private sector, although even some of them are party members.

[33] The discovery of widespread use of slave labor in the brick kilns of several north China provinces is a recent example of such realities. See David Lague, "China Tries to Contain Scandal Over Slave Labor with Arrests and Apology," *New York Times*, June 23, 2007.

local political considerations often guide decisions concerning credit, business licenses, site allocations, and so forth. Local territorial leaders also generally control local courts and local regulatory bodies such as the Environmental Protection Administration (EPA).

This distribution of power has, among other things, made it almost impossible to address effectively the massive problems of environmental degradation, piracy of intellectual property, local corruption, and protectionism, as local leaders give local growth priority over other considerations. This transformation has also made the political system a virtually unstoppable growth machine. Every year the national leaders seek steady growth but fail to prevent local governments from expanding GDP more rapidly than Beijing desires. The underlying incentives are simply too strong to fully overcome through broad measures from above.[34]

These problems are difficult to address significantly without sharply reducing the extent of local state interference at the level of the enterprise, but apparently the leadership in Beijing currently does not view separating the state from enterprise affairs as a priority agenda item. Tackling this issue would require expending enormous political capital to enforce a change that would run counter to the personal interests of territorial political leaders throughout the political system. China's leaders are instead attempting to improve the quality of the political system, and the CCP has in fact devoted significant attention to this effort.[35] The current political leaders, however, do not view either fully independent supervision of the CCP or competition for power with other independent political parties as part of the solution to China's difficulties.[36]

Though having become a huge generator of economic growth, this dynamic political system thus has serious institutional deficiencies. The system is, for example, far better at building than regulating. As activities in China increasingly feed into global supply chains, this set of domestic characteristics is generating increasingly serious consequences.[37]

China's leaders evidently look to the experiences of the ROK and Taiwan as being of reference value. Both countries pushed through development under tough authoritarian governments and then democratized in the wake

---

[34] Lieberthal, *Governing China*, 246–48; and Elizabeth Economy and Kenneth Lieberthal, "Scorched Earth: The Risks and Opportunities for Business in China," *Harvard Business Review* 85, no. 6 (June 2007): 88–96.

[35] "Full Text of Jiang Zemin's Report at the 16th Party Congress," *People's Daily*, December 10, 2002, http://english.people.com.cn/200211/18/eng20021118_106983.shtml.

[36] See Edward Cody, "China's Premier Calls Democracy a Distant Goal," *Washington Post*, February 28, 2007.

[37] See, for example, Walt Bogdanich and Jake Hooker, "From China to Panama: A Trail of Poisoned Medicine," *New York Times*, May 6, 2007.

of their respective economic successes. This approach is understandable and implies that some form of democratization will move onto the active political agenda once the economy has reached a considerably higher stage of per capita GDP. This approach, however, raises two major concerns in terms of China's international footprint in the coming years.

First, as long as Beijing insists on authoritarian one-party rule, China will not enjoy whole-hearted ties with any of the advanced industrial democracies, including the United States. The obvious difference in values is too palpable to avoid remaining a serious problem in these relationships.[38] In addition, an authoritarian government inevitably resorts to measures that become the targets of human rights charges, creating further problems for China's relations with the advanced industrial countries. This both has broad consequences and poses specific problems. For example China's full membership in the International Energy Agency (IEA)—a potentially important organization for managing future problems in international oil supplies—is likely to be denied until China transitions further to more democratic governance.

Second, the situation facing the PRC differs fundamentally from that managed by the ROK and Taiwan. Both of the latter polities encompass populations the size of but one Chinese province. China is so large and diverse that it is simply unclear whether a single political party can prove adequately responsive to maintain social and political stability in the years going forward. Governing China is made additionally complicated by the veritable tsunamis of urbanization, privatization, marketization, and globalization that are unsettling Chinese society. Moreover, all of these developments are occurring during the age of the information revolution in the PRC, a new factor that did not figure into the authoritarian phases of development in the ROK and Taiwan.

China is thus placing a major bet that commitment to a one-party authoritarian form of governance will prove key to holding the society together over the coming decade and beyond of wrenching transition. The situation is too complex, however, for any analyst to have real confidence as to whether this bet will pay off. If Beijing proves conspicuously wrong, the spillover effects for the international arena will be very large.

Political responsiveness is a critical issue in view of China's incipient creation of a civil society. The state has tolerated the formation of NGOs, which now number in the hundreds of thousands. Numerous restrictions, however, reduce the autonomy of these organizations, subject them to

---

[38] The United States, for example, does not criticize democratic India for types of behavior—such as pursuing energy ties with rogue states such as Iran and the Sudan—that it cites as evidence of authoritarian China's worrisome foreign policy values.

state supervision, and prevent them from competing with each other for support. Religious organizations have also sprung back, again under substantial state limitation, and other forms of professional, social, and clan organizations have likewise mushroomed in recent decades. In addition, the Internet, e-mail, mobile phones, and the blogosphere have exploded and seriously impacted the lives of most urban and many rural citizens.[39] These developments have created an extremely lively sphere of social organizations that now extends even to property owners associations in urban gated communities. Nobody has developed good measures to capture either the scope or the dynamic potential of the progress toward development of China's civil society. Moreover, the political leadership is schizophrenic, not only seeing the necessity of increasingly turning to non-state actors to solve problems and manage issues but also at the same time fearing the potential that some sort of "color revolution" will grow out of these developments.[40]

In sum, China is in the midst of ongoing massive transition. Dynamics of the political system, relations between state and society, developments within society itself, and the growth of the economy are all characterized by rapid and often unsettling change. The leaders are focused on the challenge of maintaining stability while promoting ongoing rapid economic growth that fully leverages the opportunities afforded by globalization. Foreign influences are woven through the fabric of this complex domestic tapestry, and countless domestic policy discussions bring in foreign references, benchmarks, and actions as part of the debate. The model that has brought success to this point—China's underlying political economy as described above—is now showing serious strains that require major changes. Beijing's capacity to maintain overall social and political stability, while simultaneously continuing to pursue goals of wealth and power, will significantly impact China's future international footprint.

The mind-set of China's leaders combines general confidence with a note of caution. Given the recent record, they understandably feel that they have set China onto the right path and are achieving extraordinary success. They recognize that they remain years away from their goal of making China into a relatively well-off society. Although acutely aware of the enormous environmental, social, and other domestic challenges

---

[39] Elizabeth Economy reviews many of these restrictions as they have affected environmental NGOs in her book *The River Runs Black* (Ithaca: Cornell University Press, 2004). See also C. Fred Bergsten, Bates Gill, Nicholas R. Lardy, and Derek Mitchell, *China: The Balance Sheet* (New York: Public Affairs, 2006), 40–72; and James Mulvenon, "Breaching the Great Firewall?" in Bergsten, Gill, Lardy, and Mitchell, *The China Balance Sheet in 2007 and Beyond*, 79–92.

[40] Carl Minzer, "Social Instability in China: Causes, Consequences, and Implications," in Bergsten, Gill, Lardy, and Mitchell, *The China Balance Sheet in 2007 and Beyond*, 55–78.

confronting the country, China's leaders feel that they must be very cautious in making serious changes to the formula that has been serving them so well.

Sustaining Stability

China's leadership has adopted major policies intended to provide a cushion sufficient to maintain domestic political stability through a period of ongoing rapid, wrenching changes. These policies are posited on the core requirements of continuing rapid GDP growth, maintaining a unified political system, and avoiding major failure on issues of nationalism, especially the Taiwan issue. To the extent possible, these policies also entail efforts to develop a more effective social safety net, allow for fast-paced urbanization to reduce rural discontent and poverty, and nurture ongoing expansion of the middle class.

The shift toward a market-oriented system eroded the former urban and rural safety nets, which were based both on SOEs in a planned economy and on collective agriculture. Failure to adequately reconstitute a social safety net in either urban or rural areas has forced Chinese citizens to save money to cover potentially crippling future obligations—e.g., a health crisis, education for children, and unemployment and retirement funds. These security measures hold down personal consumption and impel Chinese citizens to deposit very large proportions of their income into low-interest bank accounts.

A great deal of effort is now being made to develop adequate systems of support to reduce the vulnerabilities of those who have lost out under the market reforms. Health care reform, reducing the real costs of public education, and development of new pension, welfare, and unemployment systems are all on the national agenda.[41] The incompleteness of the effort to develop a social safety net, however, is both challenging China's domestic social stability and complicating the efforts of the PRC to be responsive

---

[41] For a Chinese language version of the Central Committee of the Communist Party of China's "Resolutions on Major Issues Regarding the Building of a Harmonious Socialist Society," see *Sina News*, October 18, 2006, http://news.sina.com.cn/c/2006-10-18/125711271474.shtml. See also Wen Jiabao, "Report on the Work of Government," report delivered to the 5th Session of the 10th National People's Congress, Beijing, March 5, 2007, http://www.china.org.cn/english/government/90522.htm.

to concerns in the United States and elsewhere about China's enormous trade surplus.[42]

China has adopted a policy of permitting urbanization on a huge scale. Since 1992 more than 160 million Chinese have shifted from rural to urban existence. Beijing anticipates that the total number of migrants as of 2010 will exceed 240 million and that by 2020 will be in the range of 300 to 350 million.[43] In short, China is domestically experiencing what is likely the largest-scale sustained migration in human history, and this process will continue for another decade or more.

The consequences of these migration trends are enormous and complex.[44] This massive movement to the cities is sustaining very high levels of demand for infrastructure development and increased provision of services. Under these circumstances, reducing per capita energy and raw materials consumption in the foreseeable future is virtually impossible.[45] The international natural resource and environmental consequences are therefore substantial.

Urbanization also promises to maintain a reasonable demographic pyramid in urban China long after the country as a whole takes a decided turn toward becoming an aged society in 2015.[46] This should enable the PRC to maintain manufacturing competitiveness in the global economy far longer than its national demographic structure might otherwise suggest. China's key urban planners note, moreover, that as of 2002 the three major urban regions—the Pearl River Delta, the Yangtze River Delta, and the Beijing-Tianjin-Tangshan area along the Gulf of Bohai—produced 38% of China's total GDP. These experts expect that as of 2020 these same three areas will produce 65% of China's much larger national GDP.[47] That is very significant in terms of China's future posture with the international arena: these three regions are the most important nodes of China's interaction with

---

[42] At nearly 9% of GDP in 2006, China runs an extraordinarily high global trade surplus. One of the key elements of this trend is Beijing's inability to boost domestic consumer demand. In global terms, China's GDP has a higher investment component and lower personal consumption component than almost any other country in the world. Without major progress on reconstructing the social safety net, this situation is unlikely to change. See Nicholas Lardy, "China: Rebalancing Economic Growth," in Bergsten, Gill, Lardy, and Mitchell, *The China Balance Sheet in 2007 and Beyond*, 1–24.

[43] Author's conversations with pertinent Chinese officials and scholars.

[44] Ping Huang and Frank N. Pieke, "China Migration Country Study," in *Migration Development: Pro-Poor Policy Choices in Asia* (London: UK Department for International Development, 2003).

[45] Average urban energy consumption in the PRC is 2.5 times average rural energy consumption.

[46] After the year 2015 the ratio of working age population to dependents will rise sharply on a national basis. See Ross Garnaut, Ligang Song, Stoyan Tenev, and Yang Yao, *China's Ownership Transformation: Process, Outcomes, Prospects* (Canberra: Australian National University, 2005).

[47] *Zhongguo chengshi fazhan baogao* (2002–2003) [China Urban Development Report, (2002–2003)] (Beijing: Commercial Publishing House Press, 2004).

the international economy and are also coastal regions that are potentially highly vulnerable to U.S. military power. Ongoing urbanization along these lines highlights the major structural bets China is placing both on ongoing participation in global interdependence and on avoiding military conflict in Asia.[48]

Expansion of the middle class and assuring ongoing upward social mobility are also important pillars of the overall effort to maintain political and social stability. According to the director of the Research Office of the State Council, as of June 2007 China had over 80 million middle class households.[49] Most important, nearly all members of the middle class only achieved that status in the past decade or less.

China's leaders are determined both to provide the accoutrements of a good life to those who have made it into the middle class and to maintain the perception that avenues of upward mobility remain open to those who have not yet succeeded. Leaders fear that any serious change in this perception could cause severe social unrest. These concerns drive the leadership to invest increasingly heavily in education in order both to enable the economy to shift toward higher value-added activities and to accommodate the enormous demands for educational opportunity. China's higher education system has quadrupled enrollments since the Asian financial crisis in the late 1990s.[50]

China has developed the most rapidly growing automobile market in the world, which in turn is requiring additional investments in roads, parking areas, wholesale and retail fuel networks, and so forth. High quality consumer goods and services are also in enormous demand, and even personal financial services are now sought after. Ongoing development of an ever-larger middle class is, in sum, a political requirement that brings with it enormous consequences for China's energy, environment, and international trade postures.[51]

As noted above, China's leaders are nurturing popular nationalism to buttress their capacity to rule this rapidly changing society. Nationalism,

---

[48] Also noteworthy is the fact that China is building strategic petroleum reserves in the form of above-ground tank farms located near the coast.

[49] Middle-class household defined as households with an income of between about $7,800 and $65,800. See "China Has 80 Million Middle Class Members: Official," *Xinhua News,* June 18, 2007.

[50] On the expansion in particular of China's technical education capacities, see William Keller and Louis Pauly, "Building a Technocracy in China: Semiconductors and Security," in Keller and Rawski, *China's Rise*, 47–73.

[51] Diana Farrell, Ulrich A. Gersch, and Elizabeth Stephenson, "Lessons from a Global Retailer: An Interview with the President of Carrefour in China," *McKinsey Quarterly 2006 Special Edition: Serving the New Chinese Consumer* (2006): 70–81; and Peter N. Child, "The Value of China's Emerging Middle Class," *McKinsey Quarterly 2006 Special Edition*, 60–69. On the anticipated growth of the middle class, see "The Middle Kingdom's Middle Class," Chart Focus Newsletter, member edition, *McKinsey Quarterly* (June 2007).

however, is a two-edged sword. On the one hand, if managed properly, it can reduce pressures that might stem from comparisons of China's performance to those of other countries. On the other hand, if the leaders are seen to fail to defend national dignity or properly manage national interests and security, nationalism can cause China's leaders to be swept aside by the nationalist emotions they have encouraged. The top leaders are deeply sensitive to this possibility and will, in a period when they perceive such a challenge, focus their domestic and international responses on preserving their nationalist bonafides.

The Taiwan issue is the most sensitive nationalist issue in China. The PRC claims Taiwan as a part of China and is absolutely serious about the centrality of this claim to its nationalist credentials. The PLA, as noted above, has focused its modernization effort primarily around the task of deterring or, if necessary, defeating a Taiwan bid for formal independence. Beijing has been willing to expend extraordinary diplomatic effort to isolate Taiwan in the international arena.[52]

This Taiwan policy runs the risk for Beijing that Taipei will, likely inadvertently, cross a red line that is seen in China as constituting an unacceptable bid to turn Taiwan's present autonomy into formal independence. If all else fails, there is little doubt that Beijing's response would include military action, risking the possibility of military conflict with the United States.[53] In China, therefore, there is a real need to prevent this potential catastrophe from coming about. Beijing seeks to do so through a combination of credible increments to China's military capabilities, determined efforts to isolate Taiwan internationally, and increasingly creative approaches to building ties across the Taiwan Strait that are designed to reduce the chances of any real bid for Taiwan independence.[54]

China's domestic need to cultivate nationalism, therefore, has somewhat ironically led to a cross-Strait policy that seeks to reduce tensions and build long-term ties strong enough to prevent a future rupture. These ties have long included attracting Taiwan investment into the mainland, thus facilitating China's goal of rapid GDP growth while enhancing the interests in long-term cooperation on both sides of the Taiwan Strait. Chinese leaders will not, however, acquiesce to actions in Taipei that undermine their own nationalist credentials.

---

[52] Alan Romberg, *Rein In at the Brink of the Precipice: American Policy toward Taiwan and U.S.-PRC Relations* (Washington, D.C.: Stimson Center, 2003).

[53] Richard C. Bush and Michael O'Hanlon, *A War Like No Other: The Truth About China's Challenge to the U.S.* (New Jersey: John Wiley & Sons, 2007).

[54] Kenneth Lieberthal, "Preventing a War Over Taiwan," *Foreign Affairs* 84, no. 2 (March/April 2005): 53–63.

Foreign Policy Repercussions

Fundamentally, China's domestic system needs a foreign policy that maintains open access to markets, enables the PRC to acquire needed technology and natural resources, and avoids international conflict, especially with the United States. China has sought to do this in part by creating a web of interlocking regional and global trade and investment flows that provide some protection from trade-distorting measures from other countries.

China's approach to economic development since 1978 has built in significant roles for foreign investors and foreign trade. Initially, the investors were primarily overseas Chinese in Hong Kong and Southeast Asia, and investment targets were sharply limited in terms of geography, type of investment, and sector. With full implementation of the PRC's WTO accession, however, these restrictions were gradually relaxed. China now has one of the world's most open major economies.

The process of encouraging FDI has in turn had wide-ranging ripple effects in China's domestic economy, contributing mightily to the country's economic and job growth, providing a wealth of knowledge about international standards and requirements, and unleashing competitive forces that have impacted significantly the dynamics of China's urban economic reforms.[55]

Since the end of the 1990s Beijing has developed a free trade agreement (FTA) with the countries of ASEAN, in part to demonstrate that China's development could produce major benefits for ASEAN countries and thus reduce the likelihood that they would adopt countermeasures. Changes in China that have resulted from the country's acceptance of an extraordinarily wide-ranging and intrusive agreement to enter into the WTO have also opened up major new areas for foreign participation in the Chinese economy.[56]

Beijing's initiatives regarding both ASEAN and WTO entry have produced wide ranging changes in the manufacturing supply chains in Asia and resulting global trade flows. Since 2000 the PRC has increasingly become the point of final assembly of a newly emerged Asian regional manufacturing system. The "dragon" economies of Asia—Japan, the ROK, Taiwan, Hong Kong, and Singapore—are producing high value-added parts and components and then shipping them to China for final assembly, packaging, and export. Many of the firms in China that work on the parts

---

[55] On these issues, see Mary Gallagher, *Contagious Capitalism: Globalization and the Politics of Labor in China* (Princeton: Princeton University Press, 2005); Nicholas Lardy, *Integrating China into the Global Economy* (Washington: The Brookings Institution, 2002); Naughton, *Chinese Economy*; and (for a different perspective) Yasheng Huang, *Selling China* (Cambridge: Cambridge University Press, 2003).

[56] Lardy, *Integrating China*, 1–27, 106–33.

and components are subsidiaries of the foreign firms that exported the intermediate products to China. Most exports of the finished products from China go to the North American and European Union (EU) markets. In this set of transactions, typical value added in China is roughly 25–35%. In addition, more than 65% of China's exports to North America and the EU come from foreign-invested enterprises in the PRC.[57] This set of transactions has several important effects.

China has now become the largest trading partner of nearly every country in East and Southeast Asia. Up until the year 2000, this status belonged to the United States, not China. With this enormous shift, China's weight in the region has increased. As a consequence, the economic fortunes of the more developed East Asian economies are linked ever more closely with China's continuing economic growth.

The FTAs that Beijing is promoting with ASEAN and others are not of the type that the United States generally wants to see. The United States usually seeks FTAs that are relatively comprehensive and deep. China, by contrast, more readily opts for politically driven FTAs that are neither comprehensive nor deep. Washington has reason for concern that the Chinese approach will gain increasing legitimacy and favor.[58] The political dimension of China's FTA approach, however, is quite effective in reducing trade barriers that the PRC might otherwise encounter.

In sum, although there is no regional economic bloc in Asia, China's core foreign policy has combined with regional market forces to create a high level of integration in the region's manufacturing supply chain, a chain that produces products destined primarily for the North American and EU markets. This set of developments has been integral to China's efforts to expand its GDP and absorb foreign management skills and technology. China's own role in this supply chain has grown very rapidly, and Beijing uses this enhanced influence to encourage development of FTAs that apparently are designed for both political and trade purposes.

Beijing is also very much focused on using diplomatic capabilities to develop access to the natural resources necessary to sustain rapid growth. China is seriously short of natural resources (see **Table 1**). In terms of global averages of oil, arable land, grasslands, forests, water, and most minerals, the PRC has less than one-half of the per capita availability of each resource typical elsewhere. This statistic is particularly notable because China's

---

[57] Brandt, Rawski, and Zhu, "International Dimensions"; Guillaume Gaulier, Françoise Lemoine, and Deniz Ünal-Kesenci, "China's Emergence and the Reorganisation of Trade Flows in Asia," Centre d'Etudes Prospectives et d'Informations Internationales (CEPII), Working Paper, no. 2006–05, March 2005; and "Export Mix Adjustment Urged," *China Daily*, December 21, 2004.

[58] C. Fred Bergsten, "China and Economic Integration in East Asia: Implications for the United States," in Bergsten, Gill, Lardy, and Mitchell, *The China Balance Sheet in 2007 and Beyond*, 171–86.

TABLE 1   China's natural resource use per capita

Land and water resources	Global	China
Renewable water (m³/ person) (2004)[1]	8549.00	2206.00
Population density (people/ km²) (2000)	45.00	133.00
Agricultural land (hectares/ person) (2002)[2]	0.25	0.12
Forest area (hectares/person) (2000)[3]	0.64	0.13
Fossil fuel reserves (2003)[4]	**Global**	**China**
Coal reserves (metric tons of oil equivalent/person)	79.40	45.70
Oil reserves (metric tons of oil equivalent/person)	24.80	2.51
Natural gas reserves (metric tons of oil equivalent/person)	25.10	1.27

SOURCE: Unless otherwise cited, data is from United Nations Development Programme; United Nations Environment Programme; World Bank; and World Resources Institute, *World Resources 2005—The Wealth of the Poor: Managing Ecosystems to Fight Poverty* (Washington, D.C.: World Resources Institute, 2005), http://www.wri.org/biodiv/pubs_description.cfm?pid=4073.

[1] Renewable water statistics indicates the maximum per capita theoretical amount of freshwater resources available for each country.

[2] Agricultural land data is from *World Resources 2005*; and 2002 population data from "2002 World Population Data Sheet," Population Reference Bureau, http://www.prb.org/pdf/WorldPopulationDS02 Eng.pdf.

[3] Forest area data from Food and Agriculture Organization of the United Nations, *Global Forest Resources Assessment 2000* (Rome: Food and Agriculture Organization of the United Nations, 2001), http://www.fao.org/forestry/site/fra2000report/en/. World population data for 2000 is from Population Division of the Department of Economic and Social Affairs of the United Nations Secretariat, *World Population Prospects: The 2004 Revision* (New York: United Nations, 2005), http://www.un.org/esa/population/publications/WPP2004/wpp2004.htm. China's population data for 2000 is from United Nations Economic and Social Commission for Asia and the Pacific, *Asia Pacific in Figures 2004* (New York: United Nations, 2005), http://www.unescap.org/stat/data/apif/.

[4] Fossil fuel data is from *World Resources 2005*; and population data for 2003 is from Carl Haub, "2003 World Population Data Sheet," Population Reference Bureau, 2003.

resources are figured into these global averages—if China's own resources were to be taken out, China would actually have less than 25% of the global per capita average of most natural resources.

Since the early 1990s GDP growth has made acquisition of natural resources a major driver of the PRC's foreign policy. While this focus is especially obvious with respect to China's policies toward Africa, the

Middle East, and Latin America, it is also clearly evident in policies toward countries in Asia such as Australia and Indonesia. [59]

In recent years Beijing has proven willing to focus enormous diplomatic activity around natural resource acquisition. Since 2005 Hu Jintao and Wen Jiabao have visited seventeen African countries. From 2001 to 2006 Hu spent a total of sixteen days in five Latin American countries, which was more time than President George W. Bush spent in the region during that period. Virtually every one of these trips has produced a combination of deals to provide Chinese firms with access to local raw materials in exchange for some combination of Chinese subsidized loans, grants, infrastructure projects, and debt forgiveness.[60] Indeed, given the lack of conditionality of the typical Chinese offer, the loan and grant activity has reached proportions that are worrying officials at the World Bank.[61]

Notably, Beijing evinces distrust of international market forces in this resource acquisition effort. China therefore opts in many cases to purchase equity stakes in resources abroad in the evident belief that ownership will provide greater supply security and price stability.

The oil sector illustrates the problems that ensue. Beijing's three national oil companies are generally not competitive with the Western majors in terms of technology and business skills. The Chinese companies therefore typically acquire equity investments in foreign oil reserves in those countries where, for political reasons, Western majors are prohibited by their governments to operate. This leads to Chinese investments in places like the Sudan, Iran, and Burma. As Washington considers these rogue states, and generally seeks to pressure such states to be more responsible, this resource-acquisition effort is creating unwanted tensions with the United States. The United States, in addition, regards this equity approach to oil supplies as China's "taking oil off the market." While conceptually mistaken, this view

---

[59] For policies on Africa, the Middle East, and Latin America, see Bates Gill, Chin-hao Huang, and J. Stephen Morrison, "China's Expanding Role in Africa: Implications for the United States" (a report of the CSIS Delegation to China on China-Africa-U.S. Relations, November 28–December 1, 2006); Mauro De Lorenzo, "China and Africa: A New Scramble?" American Enterprise Institute (AEI), Short Publications, April 2007, http://www.aei.org/publications/filter.all,pubID.25912/pub_detail.asp; and Esther Pan, "China, Africa, and Oil," Council on Foreign Relations, Backgrounder, January 26, 2007, http://www.cfr.org/publication/9557/.

[60] Wenping He, "Partners in Development," Beijing Review, November 2, 2006; "Chinese FM Says President Hu's African Tour Successful," Xinhua News, February 11, 2007; Gill, Huang, and Morrison, "China's Expanding Role in Africa"; and Peter Hakim, "Is Washington Losing Latin America?" Foreign Affairs 85, no. 1 (January/February 2006): 39–53.

[61] "China Loans Create 'New Wave of Africa Debt,'" Financial Times, December 7, 2006.

adds to the growing distrust in the oil sector between the governments in Washington and Beijing.[62]

China's drive to acquire natural resources abroad is deeply affecting Beijing's overall diplomacy. China assiduously cultivates the leaders of countries of interest and, when necessary, protects them from the UNSC-mandated sanctions. China's extraordinary November 2006 conference of the leaders of 48 African countries (out of the continent's total of 53) in Beijing highlights this diplomatic focus.[63] These initiatives are also in many instances providing entree to Chinese firms and products in the markets of the foreign countries concerned and, at the same time, are closely identifying China with governments that are often brutal and corrupt, negatively affecting the PRC's reputation in the West. All of these dynamics risk both creating popular animosities that could complicate China's plans and raising tensions with the United States.[64]

There are opportunities for China to take a different approach to resource acquisition abroad, especially in the oil sector. Real supply security and price stability can be attained more effectively through becoming a sophisticated market player—and cooperating with other importers through mechanisms such as that developed by the IEA—than via the more mercantilist instincts that Beijing currently follows.[65] There is no indication to date, however, that China's basic approach to meeting its resource concerns is changing. That approach is affecting both the PRC's reputation and its impact on everything from World Bank lending to forest degradation in Malaysia and Indonesia[66] to the genocide in Darfur.

China's foreign policy thus prioritizes the elements needed to sustain the country's rapid economic growth. Beijing prefers to pursue these efforts in ways that do not raise tensions with the United States. In respect to FTAs and resource acquisition strategies, however, Beijing is willing to rankle Washington where necessary in order to achieve China's core goal of continuing on the path to becoming a relatively well-off society by 2020.

---

[62] Kenneth Liberthal and Mikkal Herberg, "China's Search for Energy Security and Implications for U.S. Policy," *NBR Analysis* 17, no. 1, April 2006; and Daniel Rosen and Trevor Houser, "What Drives China's Demand for Energy (and What It Means for the Rest of Us)," in Bergsten, Gill, Lardy, and Mitchell, *The China Balance Sheet in 2007 and Beyond*, 25–54.

[63] Forum on China-Africa Cooperation, *Forum on China-Africa Cooperation Beijing Action Plan (2007–2009)*, available on the website for the Chinese Ministry of Foreign Affairs, http://www.fmprc.gov.cn/zflt/eng/zyzl/hywj/t280369.htm.

[64] "China Acknowledges Downside in Africa," *Washington Post*, February 8, 2007.

[65] Liberthal and Herberg, "China's Search for Energy Security."

[66] Elizabeth Economy, "The Case of China and the Global Environment Dizzying Growth, Devolution of Power, Environmental Disaster" (paper presented at Power Realignments in Asia: China, India, and the United States, New Delhi, India, December 14–17, 2006).

International Impact

China's domestic political economy described above naturally has a significant impact on the international arena. The effect extends beyond the state's formal foreign policy that centers around buttressing the PRC's economic prospects and spills over into a set of broader but arguably equally important international repercussions. Three such issues that warrant particular attention are environmental degradation, public health threats, and intellectual property rights problems.

Environmental Issues

The PRC is experiencing extremely severe environmental problems that impact on the international arena. China's political economy, moreover, warrants major concern about the level of success that the world should expect from the efforts Beijing is now pouring into environmental amelioration.[67] Ironically, environmental degradation poses perhaps the most severe threat to China's capacity to sustain recent levels of economic growth and even to maintain social stability.

The domestic political economy provides strong incentives to territorial leaders to increase GDP each year, even at the expense of severe environmental deterioration. Note that EPA officials in each locality are under the thumb of that locality's leaders, and the same territorial officials also control the local courts. As a result, for example, in 2006 the national EPA announced that, because of interference by the relevant local officials, only 500 of the 70,000 reported cases of violations of environmental laws and regulations from 2003 to 2005 had been dealt with.[68]

The spillover effects of China's environmental deterioration are numerous. More than one-third of the country's arable land now suffers from acid rain, and prevailing weather patterns mean that acid rain is imposing substantial harm on agriculture in Korea and Japan. China's carbon emissions are at a level that has made it second only to the United States as a contributor of greenhouse gases. By the end of 2007 China may become the world's largest contributor to global warming. These impacts occur despite the fact that China's economy is a relatively small fraction of

---

[67] China's present 11th Five Year Program allocates roughly $175 billion for environment-related projects. See Economy and Lieberthal, "Scorched Earth," 6.

[68] Economy and Lieberthal, "Scorched Earth," 3.

the size of the U.S. economy. China has also become a huge contributor to coastal maritime pollution.[69]

The two largest potential international problems posed by China's domestic environmental situation revolve around the declining availability of usable water and problems in limiting carbon emissions. Each is deeply affected not only by the PRC's natural resource base but also by Beijing's pursuit of developmental goals within the current political economy.

China's fundamental water profile would pose difficulties for any government. Overall national availability of water per capita is only 25% of that of the United States or Europe. In addition, the internal distribution of water is uneven. The north China plain, home to about 40% of the country's population and GDP, has per capita water availability of only 1,100 cubic meters per year. By global standards this is slightly over half the amount that is considered to mark an area that is severely water short; the water table in north China, moreover, is dropping precipitously. In addition, the quality of available water is very poor. Pollution has resulted in less than 20% of river water nationally being treatable to the level of inferior drinkable quality and another 35% only being of use, at most, for industry or agriculture. The remainder is too polluted for any use. Overall, well over half of China's approximately 650 cities are considered chronically water short and more than one hundred have critical water deficiencies.

The political economy works against successful management of this problem. True, economic might enables China to construct pertinent facilities at a pace that is likely unmatched anywhere else in the world. During 2000–04, for example, Beijing supported the construction of five hundred water treatment plants in cities around the country. The PRC is now embarked on the largest water transfer project in human history, seeking to bring water from central China to the Beijing-Tianjin area via two major routes at a budgeted cost of approximately $45 billion. Local territorial leaders generally react to such construction—which means funds from the center, jobs, and prestige—with alacrity.

This same political economy, though, creates strong disincentives to incur the cost of operating the facilities effectively once they are constructed. Of the five hundred urban water treatment plants built in 2000–04, a follow-on inspection indicated that more than half were not operating. The same is very likely to be true of numerous water treatment plants that are scheduled to be built along the eastern channel of the south-to-north water transfer project now under construction. The basic reality is that once facilities are constructed, money is needed to run them, and local territorial leaders

---

[69] Elizabeth Economy, "The Case of China and the Global Environment"; and Economy, *The River Runs Black*, 1–90.

are loathe to spend the funds that might otherwise contribute directly to increasing GDP.[70]

The water problem could also impact China's potential ability to sustain economic growth. Growing shortages on the north China plain call into serious question the ability to sustain even current population and economic activity levels more than five to ten years into the future, and the repercussions—social, economic, and political—of a fundamental water crisis in north China could be severe. So much of China's foreign policy and broader international impact, however, stem from a continued capacity to sustain rapid economic growth that the international policies and impact of the PRC will be deeply affected should the water crisis intensify instead of abate.

The issue of greenhouse gases is comparable to the water problem, and the international repercussions are even more direct. China's economy relies on burning coal for over 65% of the country's energy demand, and domestic coal sources generally have high sulfur content. Because the major coal basins are in the water-starved areas of north China, most coal is shipped from the mines unwashed and burned that way by end users, resulting in pollution that is more severe. Beijing has serious programs underway to diversify from coal to nuclear, hydro, petroleum, wind, solar, and biomass power. Even success with these programs will still leave coal as the source of more than 60% of China's energy in 2020, a time when China's GDP will be vastly larger.

In response to this dependence on coal, the national government is adopting policies and investing funds to ameliorate the damage. As with the water problem, however, the underlying political economy produces a situation in which scrubbers are installed in power plants but then not turned on, and energy efficiency considerations are downplayed at the local level when they interfere with maximizing GDP growth.[71]

China is poised to suffer greatly as the climate changes. The PRC's own computer models indicate that north China will experience accelerated loss of water, while the coastal cities that are the biggest centers of growth will be threatened by rising sea levels.[72] Both economic growth and social stability are, therefore, under growing threat.

The international implications of the above are potentially severe. Regarding global climate change, Beijing's current international posture is that China is prepared to accept technological assistance from abroad

---

[70] Economy and Lieberthal, "Scorched Earth," 6.

[71] Ibid.

[72] Ministry of Science and Technology, China Meteorological Administration, and Chinese Academy of Science, *National Assessment Report on Climate Change*, December 6, 2006.

and to invest in some ameliorative activities. But Beijing argues that the fundamental problem of global warming stems from the development strategies pursued over many years by rich Western countries and Japan, and that therefore those countries must take the lead in solving the issue. China cannot adopt measures that would slow down its ability to expand its economy.[73] China is becoming such an important producer of greenhouse gasses, however, that failure to bring this problem under better control will have very pernicious consequences for any global efforts to address the climate change issue. If the climate change issue becomes more integral to U.S. foreign policy after a new administration takes office in 2009, the potential for this issue to move to the center of U.S.-China relations is significant.

Public Health Threats

The decline of the public health system in China, most notably in the rural areas, has diminished the country's capacity to quickly identify and isolate new public health threats, such as an avian flu that becomes easily transmissible to and among humans. Southeast China has almost the perfect combination of large numbers of domestic fowl, pigs, and people living in close proximity to become a starting point for a global flu pandemic.[74]

China's underlying political economy, moreover, provides local officials with strong incentives to cover up any outbreak of avian flu (or other potentially serious disease) in order to protect the ability of the locality to grow the economy and attract investment. This set of considerations may have played a significant role in the early gestation of SARS (severe acute respiratory syndrome) in Guangdong province in 2002.

Only if caught and contained quickly can a highly contagious form of avian flu be stopped from spreading, as the scope of the problem increases exponentially rather than arithmetically. Early detection and reporting is, therefore, crucial to preventing a pandemic from starting. The Chinese system can be extraordinarily effective in taking the measures necessary to contain an outbreak, but unfortunately the underlying political economy makes early reporting of a problem less likely. Reporting time could prove crucial in determining whether authorities would detect a local avian flu outbreak early enough to gain control and prevent the outbreak from

---

[73] Lailai Li, "Work With, Not Trash, China on Climate Change," *China Daily*, June 13, 2007, 10.

[74] Ann Marie Kimball, "When the Flu Comes: Political and Economic Risks of Pandemic Disease in Asia," in *Strategic Asia 2006–07: Trade, Interdependence, and Security*, ed. Ashley J. Tellis and Michael Wills (Seattle: The National Bureau of Asian Research, 2006), 365–89.

sparking a global pandemic.[75] Deterioration of the rural public health system thus has potentially extremely serious international repercussions.

Intellectual Property Rights

Theft of intellectual property (IP) is a problem of monumental proportions in China. Many factors contribute to the seriousness of the issue including: China's lack of a tradition (and therefore of a norm) of IP protection, the country's desire to master more advanced technologies and resentment of what Beijing often sees as exorbitant foreign license fees to use that technology, improvements in digital scanning technology that have made reverse engineering a more viable approach to moving up a manufacturing technology ladder, and a lack of relevant business ethics. The underlying political economy is an additional major contributor both to the existence of and to the difficulty in gaining control over the problem.

Experience elsewhere suggests that virtually every current industrialized country at an earlier development stage engaged in massive IP theft. Typically, over time the country had some domestic firms that developed indigenous IP and used their influence in the political system to shift government policy toward greater protection. The same process is observable in China: the city of Shanghai, which hosts some of China's most advanced firms, has established an IP court and is relatively serious about reducing IP theft.

China's political economy, however, makes pirate firms in some localities every bit as valuable to the local territorial leaders as legitimate firms are in other localities. Counterfeiting and piracy are becoming core competitive advantages of some places in China, and the political power of local governments is being employed to protect those offenders who provide jobs and income. Without serious changes in the country's political economy, it is unclear whether China as a whole will follow the trajectory of other countries on this issue and bring the national problem under control.

Fake Chinese goods are now flooding the international markets not only in simple products like CDs and Nike shoes but also in complex pharmaceuticals, spare parts of aircraft, and even entire automobiles. If China does not improve its record on IP protection, the private sector globally will have far fewer incentives to invest in development of new technology. The facts that the vast majority of the counterfeit goods caught by U.S. Customs originate in China and that many Chinese pirates compete

---

[75] Margaret A. Hamburg, "Public Health in China: Emerging Disease and Challenges to Health," in *China's March on the 21st Century*, ed. Kurt M. Campbell and Willow Darsie (Washington, D.C.: The Aspen Institute, 2007), 61–73; and Laurie Garrett, "The Next Pandemic?" *Foreign Affairs* 84, no. 4 (July/August 2005): 3–23.

with legitimate American firms for markets for their proprietary products help explain why IP protection has already become a serious and highly contentious issue in U.S.-China relations.[76]

Conclusion

The various dimensions of China's internal development examined above account in major part for some of the most consequential dimensions of China's overall impact on the international arena to date and will continue to do so over the coming five years and beyond. These include how China contributes to global climate change, has the potential to become the starting point for a global public health pandemic, and is negatively impacting the fundamental framework for global IP development. All of these issues are in significant part consequences of the underlying political economy that has produced such startling economic growth and system stability to date, and yet at least the first two also call into question the prognosis for future growth and stability, even as they exacerbate international problems.

All of the above is compatible with Beijing's ongoing assertions that China is committed to "peaceful development." The interests and issues laid out above give credibility to Beijing's declaration that China needs a long term period of peace in order to achieve the country's highest priority goals. These same issues, however, highlight that the nature of both the country's core domestic challenges and the CCP's responses themselves create issues of major consequence for the international arena.

Implications

China's fundamental foreign policy strategy is shaped by strong domestic drivers and a basic consensus among the country's top political leaders. The major changes that can be anticipated, therefore, are those made necessary by the PRC's growing need to import resources, responsibilities as an increasingly important power, and reactions to developments beyond China's control in the international arena. The PRC leadership is likely to remain focused as much as possible on using foreign policy measures to

---

[76] Kenneth Lieberthal, "The Coming Crisis Over Intellectual Property Rights," *Harvard Business Review* 83, no. 2 (February 2005): 44–47; Lu Wei and Dong Tao, "China's Intellectual Property System: Challenges and Policy Trends," *Governance in China* (Paris: Organization for Economic Co-operation and Development, 2005), 43–57; Andrew Mertha, *The Politics of Piracy: Intellectual Property in Contemporary China* (Ithaca: Cornell University Press, 2005); Anne Stevenson-Yang and Kenneth DeWoskin, "China Destroys the IP Paradigm," *Far Eastern Economic Review* (March 2005): 9–18; and Judith Lee and James Slear, "Doing Business in China: Unique Corruption Compliance Concerns and Strategies," Washington Legal Foundation, 2006, 1–20.

provide the conditions necessary—e.g., access to materials and markets, and avoidance of actual conflict—to sustain rapid economic development.

Beijing is also trying to enhance the country's soft power internationally. China's leadership avoids using the term "Beijing consensus" to differentiate China's development model from that of the "Washington consensus"[77] promoted by the United States since the early 1990s. Beijing's policies that have produced such remarkable growth to date overlap, however, in only minor ways (primarily, relatively open economy) with the Washington consensus, and China does not mind having others notice and learn from its distinctive approach to development. Beijing is also not shy about advocating the need for each country to find its own path to development—i.e., not to follow a Western democratic free market model.[78]

China is thus likely to build on its existing foreign policy efforts in the coming half decade. First, China will likely continue to promote the development of Asian regional organizations, while exhibiting little enthusiasm for incorporating the United States in these efforts. These regional organizations, from Beijing's perspective, should reduce the chances that other countries will perceive China as a threat and coalesce to oppose PRC interests. Such organizations will also facilitate further integration of China into the developing regional economy, thus reducing the chances of trade barriers that could impact China's economic trajectory and strategy.

Second, China will seek to reduce the threat of disruption posed by North Korea's nuclear program. Since the early 1990s China has acted on the premise that ultimately the ROK will dominate the Korean peninsula, and since 2003 Beijing has brokered a multilateral process in order to reduce the chances that North Korea's nuclear program will do serious damage to the PRC's interests. China's approach to the North Korea issue is closest to that of the ROK, and there is some risk that over time this issue will lead in the direction of distinctive China-ROK and U.S.-Japan alignments, even in the context of ongoing U.S. alliances with both the ROK and Japan.[79]

Third, China will continue a strategic approach of seeking to build bridges to Taiwan in the hope of producing long-term stability in cross-Strait relations and avoiding a crisis over Taiwan independence. Only developments in Taiwan toward formal assertion of independence that

---

[77] The "Washington consensus" postulates that developing countries can develop more rapidly and steadily if they adopt open markets and financial systems, develop strong financial and other governing institutions, establish strong court systems, and implement democratic governance.

[78] Joshua Ramo, *The Beijing Consensus: Notes on the New Physics of Chinese Power* (London: The Foreign Policy Centre, 2004), http://fpc.org.uk/fsblob/244.pdf.

[79] Kenneth Lieberthal, "China's Strategies and Goals toward Northeast Asia," *Asia Policy* 3 (January 2007): 65–70. Decisions by the Bush administration in the spring and summer of 2007 have moved U.S. policy on North Korea closer to that of Beijing.

would call into question Hu Jintao's nationalist credentials would put this basic strategy at risk.

Fourth, China will seek to reduce tensions in Sino-Japanese relations, although Beijing will continue to monitor closely the posture of Japanese leaders regarding sensitive historical issues. Growing Sino-Japanese economic ties should inhibit a fundamental escalation of bilateral tensions, while mutual unease over respective positions in Asia will keep tension from being fundamentally reduced.

Fifth, China will continue to develop the PLA's capabilities. The PRC's effort to gain sufficient military advantage over Taiwan is far advanced, and Beijing is now working to configure PLA forces for missions beyond that core task. Apparently the PLA is designing a three-tier (land, sea, and air), three perimeter system of outer detection and implicit warning (followed by demonstration of detection), intermediate interception (accompanied by demonstration of the capability to interdict with force), and inner denial (including the lethal use of force against intruders). This set of goals has produced a focus on ground force mobility to meet threats at the country's borders and on better capacity to patrol adjacent seas and air space. An additional focus is on the modernization of China's strategic deterrent and development of the ability to neutralize the superior command, control, communications, computers, intelligence, surveillance, and reconnaissance (C4ISR) capabilities of more advanced and formidable foes, particularly the United States and Japan. China's military programs do not include, as yet, the development of capabilities for longer-range force projection.

Sixth, China will demonstrate its sensitivity to environmental concerns while likely trying to avoid formal international commitments regarding emission goals that might constrain its own economic development.

Finally, China may increasingly promote a set of approaches to economic development that run counter to the core principles of the Washington consensus and thus serve as counterpoints to America's more liberal democratic recommendations.

There are developments that could alter significantly this set of expectations of China's future policy as outlined above. Major domestic unrest could prove deeply disturbing, as the measures taken to restore order might be brutal enough to trigger serious international repercussions. Analysis of the sources of potential unrest might move the elite consensus away from supporting a more open economy and in the direction of imposing tighter restrictions and a more disciplined system. Serious, prolonged breakdown of the political order would produce far more wide-ranging international consequences, potentially extending to massive refugee flows, nuclear weapons trafficking, and making territory and resources inside China accessible to international non-state bad actors. The end to China's economic boom that would likely result would have massive repercussions in Asia and beyond, triggering major political and economic readjustments throughout the region.

As China's exports grow, outward investment by Chinese firms increases, and Beijing continues to deal extensively with countries viewed by the United States and others as rogue states, there is a risk that international openness to Chinese exports and overseas investments will come into serious question. Beijing is likely to try to adapt as necessary to reduce the dangers that foreign protectionism pose to China's development model, but there is considerable room for increased friction in this set of issues. If protectionism—especially in the major markets of North America and Europe—grows to significant levels, Beijing will likely interpret this development as a concerted effort to prevent China from realizing its legitimate goal of becoming a relatively well-off society. At a minimum, the results would likely include both an increased degree of fractiousness on major issues at the United Nations and elsewhere and potentially closer ties between China and Russia.

Implications for U.S. Policy

The U.S.-China relationship is critical to most of the issues above. The United States is far more important than any other country for China's core security concerns, including the PRC's ability to avoid cross-Strait conflict, assure access to energy supplies, and reduce balancing against China's power by Japan and other countries in Asia. The United States is the single largest export market for Chinese products. China, therefore, will try to nurture a basically constructive relationship with the United States even as Beijing indicates less than full agreement with many U.S. policies, seeks military capacities to blunt key U.S. capabilities, and encourages the development of multilateral dialogues and organizations that do not include U.S. participation.

The United States has come to recognize China as a major power, one that could prospectively become either a serious partner or major rival. This relatively new perception acknowledges the potential opportunity to work together with China to achieve goals that are very much in U.S. interests. Issue areas for possible cooperation include counterterrorism, energy security (the United States and China are and will remain the world's two largest importers of oil), and environmental protection, as well as working together to assure peace and prosperity in Asia, strengthen a relatively open global trading system and related multilateral economic regimes, and deal with an array of nontraditional security threats such as piracy, counterfeiting, drug smuggling, human trafficking, and disease prevention.

This potential for wide-ranging cooperation undergirds the September 2005 assertion by then deputy secretary of state Robert Zoellick that the United States wants China to act increasingly as a "responsible stakeholder" in the international system.[80] This vision, along with the reality that the Chinese and U.S. economies have become deeply interdependent, have led to extraordinarily wide-ranging and frequent contacts between government departments in Beijing and Washington. In short, the United States and China now have a relationship that is operationally mature and complex. Each side knows how to deal with the other on many issues, and no single issue other than a war across the Taiwan Strait can upset U.S.-China ties across the board.

All, however, is not well. There is deep and growing distrust on each side concerning the long-term intentions of the other. Almost all Chinese elites feel that the United States, having a zero-sum perspective, will not permit China to develop to its potential—an outcome that would effectively reduce the relative dominance of the United States in the world. This perception makes China's leaders and elites interpret issues—such as calls by the United States for China to reduce greenhouse gas emissions to reduce global warming—as U.S. ploys to hold China back rather than as genuine efforts to reach out to address common problems.[81]

The United States harbors equally strong suspicions. Numerous U.S. officials are convinced that China will eventually use its growing power to marginalize the United States in Asia, the most important region in the world. More broadly, U.S. leaders do not trust the intentions of an authoritarian country whose values appear to differ so palpably from those that the United States espouses. In U.S. politics China has increasingly become the poster child for what are perceived as the ills of globalization, especially in terms of the loss of manufacturing jobs.

Concerns of U.S. policymakers and government officials are expressed in many ways. Some U.S. officials assert that China engages in unfair competition that has resulted in a historically unprecedented bilateral trade deficit and related IP problems. According to those officials, these problems stem both from China's cynical failure to implement national laws and

---

[80] Robert Zoellick, "Whither China: From Membership to Responsibility?" (remarks before the National Committee on U.S.-China Relations, New York, September 22, 2005), http://usinfo.state. gov/eap/Archive/2005/Sep/22-290478.html. See also Deputy Assistant Secretary of State Thomas Christensen, "China's Role in the World: Is China a Responsible Stakeholder?" (remarks before the U.S.-China Economic and Security Review Commission, Washington, D.C., August 3, 2006), http://www.state.gov/p/eap/rls/rm/69899.htm.

[81] Author's conversations with Chinese officials and scholars.

regulations and state intervention in currency markets for the purpose of holding down the value of the *renminbi* vis-à-vis the U.S. dollar. Some U.S. officials condemn what they view as China's support for bad regimes such as North Korea, the Sudan, Burma, and Iran. Additionally, some feel that China potentially poses long-term, very serious security challenges to the United States simply because in the coming decades the PRC is the only country that has the potential to become a "peer competitor" of the United States.

The coming half decade will exert tremendous influence on the longer-term directions of the U.S.-China relationship, and the stakes are extremely high. Fundamental failures will lay the groundwork for long-term competition of a very serious nature, increasing the chances of tension and conflict while reducing the potential for cooperation to increase both regional and global economic prosperity and the capacity to deal with nontraditional security threats.

Policies to date have created a dense network of relations but have not resolved the issue of growing mutual distrust. The United States should therefore modify its traditional notion that simply engaging China on a wide variety of issues is sufficient and instead adopt a more results-oriented standard. "Focused engagement"—according greater importance to achieving active cooperation on specific critical issues—should become the new approach. This shift will require specifying more clearly the major areas of mutual interest that are most critical to long-term cooperation. If successful, this strategy will enhance mutual trust and achieve China's active cooperation in working toward mutual goals that concurrently maximize benefits to the entire international community.

Focused engagement with China will require that the United States be objective in analyzing issues in the bilateral relationship, which currently is not always the case. For example, too few U.S. officials understand the extent to which the U.S.-China bilateral trade deficit reflects the reality that China has become the point of final assembly for a newly integrated East Asian regional manufacturing system. Better understanding of this issue could potentially shape a different and more efficacious U.S. approach. Few in the United States appreciate that China ends up supporting some questionable regimes not out of a global strategic plan but rather in part because China is a latecomer to the international oil markets and feels sharply constrained by the competitive dynamics of the international energy sector.[82] Again, more careful consideration of China's realities might produce more effective U.S. approaches.

---

[82] Lieberthal and Herberg, "China's Search for Energy Security," 22–23.

The United States should also address domestic problems that have become entangled in its relationship with China. The global U.S. trade deficit, for example, has mushroomed due to the combination of extremely low personal savings rates in the United States and the U.S. government's large fiscal deficit. Asia as a whole—including China—accounts for a far lower share of that global deficit now than during the 1990s.[83] No unilateral U.S. actions toward imports from China will seriously affect the deficit with China unless the United States also addresses those underlying problems regarding domestic savings and fiscal shortfalls.[84]

In seeking China's cooperation, a key challenge is to devise concrete policies that engender China's trust by demonstrating that the United States does not seek to hobble China's long-term development. Seeking ways to bring China into a reconstituted G-8 or into the oil sharing regime devised by the IEA for coping with disruptions to international oil supplies are the types of measures that could credibly signal the U.S. intention to engage in long-term cooperation with a powerful China to address issues of bilateral and of global concern.[85] These are actions that would benefit the interests of both China and the United States. Washington should make clear to Beijing that China's impact on the international system is now so large that the PRC must take more seriously than ever before China's obligations as a responsible stakeholder.

The United States cannot neglect the possible problems that might be encountered with China, and the two countries' interests are not aligned on all major issues. To some extent the U.S. military will develop capabilities and working relationships with third countries with China's potential to become a peer competitor very much in mind. An important aspect of this type of engagement, however, should be to not create the problems that the United States is seeking to avoid. The U.S. military is currently enormously more powerful than is the PLA, and therefore China pays careful attention to long-term directions of the U.S. military. Beijing will almost always devise means to push back when U.S. actions appear to pose a serious threat to China—e.g., when the United States asserts a unilateral right to develop military capabilities in space.[86]

---

[83] Brandt, Rawski, and Zhu, "International Dimensions," 32–35.

[84] Stephen Cohen, "The Superpower as Super-Debtor: Implications of Economic Disequilibria for U.S.-Asian Relations," in Tellis and Wills, Strategic Asia 2006–07, 29–63.

[85] Lieberthal and Herberg, "China's Search for Energy Security," 31–35.

[86] For the official U.S. National Space Policy of August 31, 2006, see Office of Science and Technology Policy, U.S. National Space Policy, http://www.ostp.gov/html/US%20National%20S pace%20Policy.pdf.

To a considerable degree, limiting the extent to which China's development produces changes in regional dynamics that are adverse to U.S. interests primarily requires the United States to become more involved again in Asian regional issues. Since September 11 the focus of the United States has tilted so strongly toward counterterrorism that matters of greater concern within Asia have received short shrift. China has focused on addressing those regional concerns that the United States has retreated from. A broad shift toward more intensive engagement in Asia, keyed to the major economic, environmental, and nontraditional security threat concerns in Asia, would both catch China's attention and greatly increase U.S. standing and influence in the region. In the process, Washington should make every effort to clear the hurdles necessary to participate fully in the newly emerging Asian regional organizations—such as the East Asia Forum—and begin to promote steps toward the development of a Northeast Asia security community.[87]

China's enormous accomplishments have catapulted the country into a central role in Asia and a preeminent role in U.S. foreign policy concerns. The United States and China share fundamental interests in many traditional and nontraditional security and economic areas, and the two countries have developed an impressive capacity to work together. Underlying mutual distrust is growing, however, with potentially costly future consequences. Given its traditions and extraordinary capabilities, the United States should take the lead in structuring issues objectively, initiating efforts to address those issues, and finding ways to credibly signal a willingness to cooperate over the long run with China as a major power. These efforts should encourage China to play an active and constructive role in the international system. Simple engagement is no longer sufficient; focused engagement should become the new standard.

---

[87] See Nick Bisley's chapter in this volume.

EXECUTIVE SUMMARY

This chapter examines political developments in Japan and analyzes how domestic politics affects the country's strategic response to the changing international environment.

MAIN ARGUMENT:

- Japan has moved toward a two-party system, and political leadership and the mobilization of public support matter more for governance than before. The prime minister and the cabinet secretariat together now wield greater executive power, and the bureaucratic state has been reformed to respond more effectively to security as well as economic challenges.

- Japan has become more willing to contribute to its alliance with the U.S. and various international security activities; anti-militarism norms and domestic politics, however, are likely to restrain Japan from using military force abroad.

- Japan's grand strategy will evolve incrementally rather than change dramatically. Japan will continue to balance between the security imperative of its alliance with the U.S. and the economic imperative of developing a favorable Asian environment for its long-term commercial interests.

POLICY IMPLICATIONS:

- The recent revival of Japan's economy and Japan's trend toward greater security and diplomatic activism are generally consistent with U.S. interests. The U.S. benefits from a Japan that is more capable, proactive, and influential in Asia.

- Although the U.S. and Japan converge strategically, there will continue to be tactical differences stemming from different priorities and perspectives. Such tactical differences require U.S. policymakers to remain attentive and not complacent about the alliance. Sensitivity to the risks of inflated expectations and entrapment as Japan recalibrates its grand strategy will prove useful to the U.S.

Japan's Long Transition: The Politics of Recalibrating Grand Strategy

Mike M. Mochizuki

The changing international environment presents Japan with strategic challenges and opportunities in both the traditional security and economic realms. On the one hand various security uncertainties (e.g., North Korea's nuclear and missile programs, the rise of China, and international terrorism) are testing Japanese defense policies; on the other hand the end of the Cold War has also given Japan an opportunity to help create a more stable regional security order. Economic globalization provides Japan an opportunity to extend and deepen its overseas commercial reach but also challenges Japan to maintain its industrial and technological competitiveness. Although shaping Japan's calculations, these developments do not by themselves ordain the country's strategic response. As with any other major power, Japan's grand strategy is not determined entirely by its external environment, geographic position, and natural resource endowments. Domestic forces do play "a pivotal role in the selection of a grand strategy."[1]

Mike M. Mochizuki holds the Japan-U.S. Relations Chair in Memory of Gaston Sigur at the Elliott School of International Affairs in George Washington University. He can be reached at <mochizuk@gwu.edu>.

The author would like to thank the two anonymous reviewers for their insightful comments and suggestions on an earlier version of this chapter and Stephanie Renzi for her preparation of figures 1 and 2. He is also grateful to Ellis Krauss for sharing his knowledge of Japanese politics and for helping clarify the author's own thinking.

[1] Richard Rosecrance and Arthur A. Stein, "Beyond Realism: The Study of Grand Strategy," in *The Domestic Bases of Grand Strategy*, ed. Richard Rosecrance and Arthur A. Stein (Ithaca: Cornell University Press, 1993), 5. In line with Rosecrance and Stein, this chapter considers "grand strategy" in terms of a state's adaptation of non-military as well as military resources to achieve security but also treats security in a broad sense to include both military and economic security. This broad conception of security, which has strong historical roots in Japan, is exemplified by the notion of "comprehensive security."

This chapter examines how domestic political developments after the end of the Cold War have affected Japan's grand strategy, which was institutionalized after World War II. The chapter argues that, despite significant changes in the external environment, domestic factors are steering Japan to incrementally recalibrate rather than radically alter its grand strategy. After briefly summarizing the main parameters and evolution of Japan's grand strategy during the Cold War era, the chapter analyzes change in political institutions and processes since the early 1990s by focusing on the following: party system and electoral politics, the bureaucratic state and executive power, and interest intermediation and civil society. The chapter then examines Japan's contemporary strategic discourse and the way this discourse is linked to elite politics and public opinion. The chapter next delineates the incremental policy responses in Japan that are emerging through this filter of domestic politics and discourse. The chapter concludes by drawing implications for U.S. policy toward Japan.

Strategic Evolution: Toward a Regime Shift?

Prime Minister Yoshida Shigeru established the basic parameters of Japanese diplomacy during the U.S.-Japan peace talks after World War II. Yoshida resisted U.S. pressures to rearm Japan, insisting that his country must focus on economic reconstruction. He struck a shrewd strategic bargain with the United States whereby Japan would host U.S. forces and bases on Japanese territory and the United States would provide Japan with security protection and facilitate Japan's reintegration into the world economy. This bargain was later institutionalized into a grand strategy that scholars have called the "Yoshida Doctrine."[2] Under this strategy Japan prohibited exercising the right of collective self-defense and restricted the use of force to what was "minimally necessary" to defend the home islands. While relying on the United States for security and deferring to Washington on major strategic issues, Japan concentrated on economic development by pursuing a neo-mercantilist foreign economic strategy. This strategy optimized access to export markets, natural resource supplies, and frontier technologies; used government-business cooperation to facilitate industrial and technological innovation at home; and minimized the domestic negative social effects of economic and industrial change.

This grand strategy enjoyed sturdy domestic political foundations. The political stalemate and later *modus vivendi* between pacifist political

---

[2] Kenneth B. Pyle, *Japan Rising: The Resurgence of Japanese Power and Purpose* (New York: Public Affairs, 2007), 210–77; and Richard J. Samuels, *Securing Japan: Tokyo's Grand Strategy and the Future of East Asia* (Ithaca: Cornell University Press, 2007), 38–59.

forces on the left and realists and nationalists in the center and on the right constrained Japanese defense policy despite U.S. pressures. A tacit consensus between conservatives and progressives in favor of economic growth with social equity provided both the political cover and motivation for Japan's neo-mercantilist economic strategy.[3] The priority on economic development was reflected in the power of the economic ministries (e.g., the Ministry of Finance and the Ministry of International Trade and Industry) and their extensive network of ancillary policy organizations. By contrast, the Defense Agency lacked full ministerial status and was colonized by bureaucrats from other ministries. Insofar as the alliance with the United States was the key pillar of defense policy, the Foreign Ministry often had more influence on security-related matters than the Defense Agency.

As its position in the global economy rose and the international environment changed, Japan made adjustments to the original version of the Yoshida strategy. In response to U.S. requests for greater defense burden–sharing during the Cold War, Japan enhanced bilateral cooperation for homeland defense and contributed more host-nation support for U.S. forces deployed in Japan. After the end of the Cold War, Japan began both to contribute to rear-area support on U.S.-led missions that were not directly related to defense of the home islands (in what was termed "situations in areas surrounding Japan") and to deploy defense forces in UN peacekeeping operations.[4] On the economic front, Japan gradually shifted its neo-mercantilist strategy to a more liberal direction by encouraging FDI, relaxing protectionist practices and policies, and pursuing moderate market-oriented reforms at home. Finally, Japan actively encouraged the development of regional multilateral dialogues and processes in both the economic and security realms in order to manage regional economic integration and to mitigate potential regional security dilemmas.

In 1993 Japan experienced a political earthquake. Defections from the ruling Liberal Democratic Party (LDP), a successful no-confidence motion in parliament, and a subsequent LDP loss of its Diet majority in a general election toppled the venerable conservative party from power for the first time since its formation in 1955. Many factors were behind the stresses that triggered this upheaval: discontent about corruption scandals and uninspirational leadership, security uncertainties after the end of the Cold War, international humiliation because of Japan's underappreciated

---

[3] Terry MacDougall and Ikuo Kabashima, "Japan: Democracy with Growth and Equity," in *Driven By Growth: Political Change in the Asia-Pacific Region*, ed. James W. Morley (New York: M.E. Sharpe, 1999), 275–309.

[4] Christopher W. Hughes, "Japanese Military Modernization: In Search of a 'Normal' Security Role," in *Strategic Asia 2005–06: Military Modernization in an Era of Uncertainty*, ed. Ashley J. Tellis and Michael Wills (Seattle: The National Bureau of Asian Research, 2005), 112–14.

response to the Persian Gulf War of 1990–91, and the bursting of the bubble economy. As a non-LDP coalition government formed around political maverick Hosokawa Morihiro, many observers heralded the end of the so-called 1955 system and the birth of a new political order under which would emerge a new international orientation and strategy. This unwieldy non-LDP coalition government, however, collapsed after less than ten months, and the LDP returned to power in June 1994 by forging a coalition with its erstwhile political and ideological adversary, the Japan Socialist Party (JSP). The LDP remains in power, albeit in coalition with the middle-of-the-road Komeito, and Japan may still be in the midst of its long political transition.

One of the chief protagonists of the 1993 political realignment was Ozawa Ichiro. After serving as its secretary-general Ozawa bolted the LDP and authored a bold vision for restructuring Japan so that the country would contribute more vigorously to international security and wean its citizens from overdependence on the state and instead exercise greater individual responsibility and initiative.[5] Ozawa currently leads the largest opposition party, the Democratic Party of Japan (DPJ). Rather than Ozawa, however, the person who now appears to be driving the quest for a new regime and strategy is Abe Shinzo, who ironically was first elected to the National Diet as an LDP member in the July 1993 general election that pushed the LDP temporarily out of power. The first postwar-born prime minister, Abe has called for a bold review of "postwar regimes" because they "have become incapable of adapting to the great changes taking place in the 21st century." By setting sail on a "new course," he has ambitiously vowed "to draw a new vision of a nation which can withstand the raging waves for the next 50 to 100 years to come."[6]

Prime Minister Abe has benefited from the legacy of his predecessor, Koizumi Junichiro. By calling for reform without sanctuaries and threatening to break up the LDP if need be, Koizumi magically transformed the LDP's image from that of a dysfunctional party that impeded reform to one that could be the vanguard of change. When Koizumi dissolved the House of Representatives and called a snap election after LDP rebels blocked his postal system privatization legislation, voters gave the LDP a landslide electoral victory in September 2005. With the LDP winning over 60% of the lower house seats and the LDP-Komeito coalition controlling a two-thirds majority, some Japanese commentators declared the birth of

---

[5] Ozawa Ichiro, *Blueprint for a New Japan: The Rethinking of a Nation* (Tokyo: Kodansha International, 1994), 93–121, 153–58.

[6] "Policy Speech by Shinzo Abe to the 166th Session of the Diet," Prime Minister of Japan and His Cabinet website, http://www.kantei.go.jp/foreign/abespeech/2007/01/26speech_e.html.

a "2005 system" displacing the old 1955 system.[7] Since becoming prime minister in September 2006, Abe has already used the parliamentary majority that Koizumi bequeathed him to push through controversial legislation on education and a bill establishing the national referendum procedure for constitutional revision. The LDP's historic defeat in the July 2007 upper-house election has, however, dramatically altered the political equation. Although Abe is determined to stay in office and continue to "construct a new country," he will need to quickly revive his popularity and political capital if he is to survive as prime minister, much less pursue his ambitious agenda.

Ultimately, a shift to a new regime in Japan would need to entail a change that transcends not only specific leaders or governments but also particular election results. Following T.J. Pempel's conceptualization, this chapter views a regime as involving the integration and mutual reinforcement of three essential elements: institutions, societal alliances, and a public policy profile. Accordingly, Japan's postwar regime consisted of the following: a dominant party system led by the LDP, a powerful state bureaucracy, a conservative ruling social coalition encompassing big and small business and the agricultural sector, and a public policy profile of "embedded mercantilism" and a "minimalist security posture."[8] A regime shift would then require a transformation in all these elements, a domestic change that could have profound implications for grand strategy.

Writing in the 1990s Pempel saw Japan caught between protection and erosion of the old regime but concluded that the conservative regime was indeed unraveling.[9] Almost a decade later, Kenneth Pyle is predicting "a comprehensive revision of the Japanese system" and asserts that the "Yoshida Doctrine, once proclaimed as Japan's 'permanent' (eien) strategy, is a dead letter."[10] External developments—such as the rise of China, security uncertainties regarding the Korean Peninsula and Taiwan, globalization and regional economic integration, and even potential shifts in U.S. foreign policy—have certainly provoked Tokyo to re-examine Japanese foreign policy and to debate openly the question of national strategy. The evolution of domestic political institutions and strategic discourse suggest, however, that Tokyo will not make a sharp break with the Yoshida Doctrine. While recalibrating once again this strategy to yield an updated and perhaps more

---

[7] See for example Tanaka Naoki, *2005-nen Taisei no Tanjo* [Birth of the 2005 System] (Tokyo: Nihon Keizai Shimbunsha, 2005), 13–54.

[8] T.J. Pempel, *Regime Shift: Comparative Dynamics of the Japanese Political Economy* (Ithaca: Cornell University Press, 1998), 20–26, 42–80.

[9] Ibid., 169–205.

[10] Pyle, *Japan Rising*, 374.

effective version, Japan is unlikely to abandon the strategy's basic parameters, which include: (1) restrictions on the use of military force primarily limiting it to homeland defense, (2) the primacy of Japan's alliance with the United States and the hosting of U.S. forces, and (3) neo-mercantilist policies and practices to maximize economic opportunities and minimize economic vulnerabilities.[11]

Party System and Electoral Politics

Corruption scandals during the late 1980s sparked a movement to revise the electoral system. Reformers argued that Japan's system of medium-sized multi-member districts with single non-transferable votes perpetuated clientelistic politics by forcing intraparty electoral competition for any party with majoritarian ambitions.[12] These proponents of electoral reform advocated the adoption of a single-member district electoral system that would facilitate the development of a two-party system that would see an alternation of the party in power, discourage clientelistic voter mobilization, and encourage election campaigns centered around policy debates. The failure of the electoral and political reform bills in the summer of 1993 triggered a political realignment that involved LDP defections, a no-confidence vote against the Miyazawa government, the LDP's loss of a parliamentary majority in the subsequent election, and the formation of a non-LDP coalition government. This six-party coalition was short-lived but managed to alter the electoral system drastically. Japan adopted a hybrid system for the more powerful House of Representatives that combined single-member districts and proportional representation (PR) in regional bloc constituencies. This change not only pushed Japan toward a two-party system but also altered the political dynamics within the ruling LDP.

Movement toward a Two-Party System

By participating in the non-LDP coalition government from August 1993 to June 1994, the JSP was compelled both to disavow its advocacy of

---

[11] For example, Soeya Yoshihide of Keio University argues that Japan will more fully consolidate rather than abandon the foreign policy line originally charted by the Yoshida Doctrine. See Soeya Yoshihide, *Nihon no Miduru Pawa Gaiko* [Japan's Middle Power Diplomacy] (Tokyo: Chikuma Shobo, 2005), 198–210.

[12] On the impact of intraparty electoral competition, see Frances McCall Rosenbluth, "Internationalization and Electoral Politics in Japan," in *Internationalization and Domestic Politics*, ed. Robert O. Keohane and Helen V. Milner (Cambridge: Cambridge University Press, 1996), 137–56. On Japanese clientelistic politics, see Ethan Scheiner, *Democracy without Competition in Japan: Opposition Failure in a One-Party Dominant State* (Cambridge: Cambridge University Press, 2006), 64–89.

an "unarmed neutrality" security policy and to accept an electoral reform that undermined the party's ability to win at least one seat in many of the medium-sized districts. The party then clung to power by switching to an "unholy" alliance with its long-term adversary, the LDP, in 1994–96. Although the Socialist leader Murayama Tomiichi even served as prime minister for about eighteen months, soon thereafter his party disintegrated and many of its Diet members joined the newly formed DPJ. With the JSP losing its status as the largest opposition party, the most vigorous parliamentary voice for a pacifist foreign policy all but vanished.[13]

The decline of the JSP (renamed the Social Democratic Party of Japan or SDPJ) into a minor party helped move Japan toward a two-party system. The DPJ emerged as the number-one opposition party by bringing under a single political roof LDP defectors, the Democratic Socialist Party (DSP), and former SDPJ members. By projecting an image of itself as a pragmatic centrist party, the DPJ sought to define itself as a viable alternative to LDP-led governments. A contentious diversity of views within the party and the substantial overlap in policy positions between the DPJ and LDP, however, impaired the DPJ's ability to inspire voters. The new electoral system's hybrid character also allowed for the survival of small parties like the Komeito, the Japan Communist Party, and even the SDPJ.

Despite the hope of some reformers that electoral reform would eventually bring about an alternation in the ruling party and an end to LDP hegemony, the LDP has managed to remain in power continuously since that brief ten-month period in 1993–94 during which the LDP was relegated to opposition status. Splits and amalgamations of groups that defected from the LDP prompted a number of the 1993 defectors to rejoin the LDP. Repeated attempts by some LDP defectors to trigger an LDP split even greater than in 1993 failed as most LDP politicians were willing to check their intraparty disputes in order to remain in power. In addition to forging coalitions with and even absorbing different conservative mini-parties, the LDP has since 1999 developed a partnership with the Komeito, the political arm of the religious group Sokagakkai with a strong base in Japanese cities. The LDP has used clientelistic vote mobilization to win about 75% of the single-member lower-house seats in rural districts.[14] Despite the emergence of an anti-clientelistic backlash in many urban electoral districts, the DPJ effort to dominate the urban vote as a counter to the LDP's grip on the rural vote has been blunted by the Komeito's support for the LDP. The Komeito has succeeded in getting most of its loyal city-based supporters to vote for LDP

---

[13] Ito Atsuo, *Seito Hakai: Nagata-cho no Ushinawareta Ju-nen* [Political Party Collapse: the Lost Decade of Nagata-cho] (Tokyo: Shinchosha, 2003), 80–103.

[14] Scheiner, *Democracy Without Competition in Japan*, 177.

candidates in single-member urban districts and for Komeito candidates in the PR regional blocs.

The LDP's grip on power is, however, not inevitable. While public support for the LDP tends to be ahead of the DPJ, polls indicate that more Japanese are inclined not to identify with a particular party (see **Figure 1**). This large pool of non-aligned voters presents an opportunity for an opposition party like the DPJ to mobilize these citizens with attractive leaders and policies as well as to capitalize on LDP missteps and weaknesses.[15] In the July 2007 upper-house election, the DPJ defeated the LDP by taking advantage of the Abe government's inept response to the loss of pension records for about 50 million people and various scandals and misstatements by cabinet members. If the DPJ can translate this anti-LDP vote into more lasting support for the DPJ, then this opposition party might be able to repeat its 2007 victory in the next election for the House of Representatives which must be held by fall 2009. This lower house is decisive in electing the prime minister. Even if the DPJ fails to win a single-party majority in the lower house, becoming the plurality party might be enough to pull the Komeito away from its coalition with the LDP and oust the conservatives from power. To become the governing party, however, the DPJ must avoid leadership troubles and scandals of its own as well as maintain internal unity and present an attractive and compelling policy program.

Change within the LDP

The 1994 electoral reform has also affected dynamics within the ruling LDP. Under the new hybrid system of single-member districts and PR regional blocks, LDP politicians no longer need to compete directly with each other in lower house elections. This change has weakened the role of LDP factions. Prospective conservative candidates no longer need to look to factions to obtain LDP endorsements. Furthermore, new regulations on political funding now prohibit financial contributions going directly to factions. Consequently, factions have become less important in the election of the LDP president and therefore of the prime minister—although factions still play a significant role in allocating posts in the party and the National Diet.[16]

After the 1993–94 political turmoil and electoral reform, three of the big four LDP factions have split. Of particular significance has been the

---

[15] Steven R. Reed, "Conclusions," in *Japanese Electoral Politics: Creating A New Party System*, ed. Steven R. Reed (London: RoutledgeCurzon, 2003), 198.

[16] Ellis S. Krauss and Robert Pekkanen, "Explaining Party Adaptation to Electoral Reform: The Discreet Charm of the LDP?" *Journal of Japanese Studies* 30, no. 1 (Winter 2004): 13–17.

FIGURE 1   Popular support for Japanese political parties

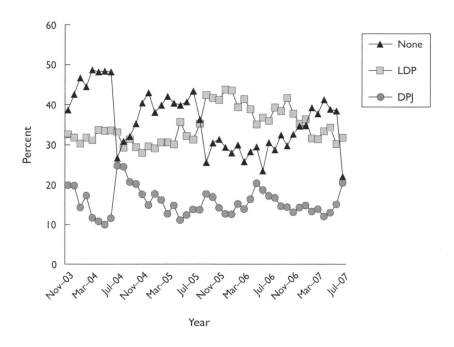

SOURCE: "Monthly Survey of Political Attitudes," NHK Broadcasting Culture Research Institute, November 2003–July 2007, http://www.nhk.or.jp/bunken/research/yoron/seijiishiki/list_seijiishiki1.html.

splintering of the huge Tanaka faction and its successors that had once dominated LDP politics from the 1970s into the 1990s. The one faction that has avoided such a split has been the factional lineage of Fukuda-Abe-Mori. Not coincidentally, the last three Japanese prime ministers (Mori Yoshiro, Koizumi Junichiro, and Abe Shinzo) have come from this faction. As factional cohesion has weakened and the number of factions has increased, negotiation among factional bosses no longer plays as key a role in achieving intraparty consensus on contentious policy issues.

The impact of electoral reform on other aspects of the LDP has been more limited. Although many reformers saw single-member election districts as a means to shift away from "personal-vote" strategies driven by the *koenkai* (individual support organizations of politicians), these organizations have survived. Koenkai help politicians mobilize enough votes to win in the PR regional bloc even though they may fail to win in the single-member districts. These organizations can also attract voters—especially non-aligned voters—who might not support the LDP in the PR blocs.[17] Electoral reform also has not eliminated the role of policy "tribes" (*zoku*) composed of veteran politicians who, because of their experience and connections with relevant state agencies and interest groups wield influence in a particular policy area.[18] By serving as a means both to influence policy and to raise political funds, policy specialization still can enhance a person's political career.

One indicator of the continuity in LDP politics is the re-entry of some of those who had rebelled against Koizumi's postal privatization legislation. Koizumi quickly ousted the rebels to gain the political high ground and lead the LDP to victory in the September 2005 election. Prime Minister Abe reversed this action in November 2006, however, by allowing eleven lower house rebels who had been re-elected in 2005 as independents to re-join the party. Although this unprincipled move caused Abe's public approval rating to drop sharply, the LDP wanted to use the strong koenkai of these politicians to mobilize votes for the July 2007 upper house election.[19]

Toward a Westminster Model?

What has been the net effect of these changes and continuities in Japan's party system and electoral politics? One standard for assessment might be the British Westminster model of parliamentary politics. This model involves a political system in which two strong parties compete for power, the prime minister exercises decisive leadership based on a clear electoral mandate, the parliament serves primarily as an arena of debate rather than as a legislature to transform the government's legislative program, and the governing party changes in response to shifting voter preferences over general policy choices. By that standard Japan offers a problematic and mixed picture.

With the persistence of electoral dualism between rural and urban areas, clientelistic politics still plays a major role in voter mobilization. The two largest political parties, the LDP and DPJ, are still not the cohesive organizations for interest aggregation and mobilization of public mandates that political reformers had envisaged. The survival of koenkai and of factions and policy tribes (albeit in a somewhat weaker form than before) limits party cohesion and constrains top-down leadership in the ruling LDP.

---

[17] Krauss and Pekkanen, "Explaining Party Adaptation to Electoral Reform," 10–13.

[18] Ibid., 17–23.

[19] Masami Ito, "LDP Seen Putting '07 Poll Interests above Voter Mandate on Postal Bills," *Japan Times*, December 5, 2006.

Due to its history as an amalgamation of disparate political groups with divergent policy positions, the DPJ also suffers from weak party cohesion and intraparty constraints on leadership.

Moreover, as long as neither the LDP nor the DPJ can win a majority in *both* houses of the National Diet the Komeito will remain a pivotal party and prevent the emergence of a clean two-party system that approximates the Westminster model. Even after its landslide victory in the September 2005 election the LDP needed the Komeito as a partner to maintain a majority in the upper house.[20] The LDP-Komeito coalition's loss of its upper-house majority after the July 2007 election, however, did not diminish the importance of the Komeito to the LDP. In order to override a potentially obstructionist House of Councilors led by the DPJ and its possible Diet allies, the LDP needs the Komeito to wield the required two-thirds majority in the House of Representatives. If the Komeito is willing to shift its coalition partner then the governing party could theoretically change independent of a particular election result. So far, however, the electoral complementarity between the LDP and Komeito (i.e., the LDP strength in rural areas and the Komeito base in urban centers) makes this political alliance resilient.[21] If there is a fundamental policy disagreement between the LDP and the Komeito or if the LDP should lose its parliamentary plurality to the DPJ in the more powerful lower house, then the possibility that the Komeito could shift coalition partners increases. Under such circumstances, however, the LDP itself could potentially split, provoking a new political realignment and the rise of a non-LDP government.

Despite these caveats, there are also signs of a new politics that leans toward a Westminster model. In the politics of old, LDP factionalism and decentralized decisionmaking processes within the ruling party yielded Japanese prime ministers that, compared to their counterparts in Britain, were relatively weak. The large pool of "floating" non-aligned voters and the introduction of PR blocs that require voting for a political party (rather than a particular candidate as in the single-member districts) have, however, enhanced the importance of party labels and thereby the image of the party leader in electoral politics. Because even within the LDP the role of factions in electing the party president has declined, the ability to garner public popularity is now more critical for a politician to become

---

[20] Following the September 2005 election, the LDP-Komeito coalition has controlled more than 69% of the seats in the House of Representatives.

[21] According to Aurelia George Mulgan, LDP candidates are increasingly dependent on the Komeito support base to win urban votes. Aurelia George Mulgan, "Where Tradition Meets Change: Japan's Agricultural Politics in Transition," *Journal of Japanese Studies* 31, no. 2 (2005): 271–72.

prime minister. A popular prime minister's public support can translate into electoral support for the governing party.

Koizumi personified this new politics by calling and winning a snap election in September 2005 after rebels within his own party attempted to block legislation to privatize the postal system. The public image of politicians also was a critical factor behind Abe Shinzo's rise, by leapfrogging more experienced leaders in the LDP, to the prime ministership in September 2006. Abe shot up to national prominence by mobilizing public sentiment against North Korea over the abduction issue. His personal popularity created a bandwagon effect in the LDP presidential race and prevented the second- and third- largest LDP factions (the Tsushima and Koga factions) from even fielding a candidate. Under the new politics of Japan, political leaders must play increasingly to the media in order to build and sustain public support. The traditional leadership style of prime ministers making backroom deals and practicing the politics of adjustment (*chosei-gata seiji*) no longer resonates with the public. As Ellis S. Krauss and Benjamin Nyblade have suggested, even Japanese politics may be moving toward "presidentialization" whereby governments are becoming increasingly personalized and the party leader becomes a more autonomous political actor.[22]

The Bureaucratic State and Executive Power

Ever since the Meiji era, an elite bureaucracy has played a central role in guiding Japan's modernization. The higher civil service attracted the best and brightest from the most prestigious universities. A large part of the civilian bureaucracy—especially the economic agencies—emerged with its power and prestige intact after World War II. With a strong esprit de corps, career bureaucrats worked long hours with modest pay on behalf of the national interest and were rewarded upon retirement by "descending from heaven" (*amakudari*) to lucrative positions either in the private sector or in one of the many public or quasi-public special corporations or institutions. According to Chalmers Johnson, Japan's political system was "one of bureaucratic domination in which the LDP reigns but the elite state bureaucracy actually rules."[23]

---

[22] Ellis S. Krauss and Benjamin Nyblade, "'Presidentialization' in Japan? The Prime Minister, Media and Elections in Japan," *British Journal of Political Science* 35, no. 2 (April 2005): 357–68.

[23] Chalmers Johnson, "The State and Japanese Grand Strategy," in *The Domestic Bases of Grand Strategy*, ed. Richard Rosecrance and Arthur A. Stein (Ithaca: Cornell University Press, 1993), 216.

Japan's bureaucratic state was not monolithic, however, and inter-ministerial rivalries often made government-wide policy coordination difficult. Moreover, the state could be divided between those agencies that were responsible for guiding and facilitating the nation's economic development and those that were responsible for distributing the fruits of that development to society. In other words, the "developmental state" worked to enlarge Japan's economic pie, while the "distributive state" managed the slicing of the growing economic pie. The two sides of the Japanese state complemented each other nicely to ensure that development occurred with minimal socio-political costs and conflict.[24]

By the 1990s, however, the aura surrounding elite bureaucrats had dissipated because of scandals involving senior officials. The media attacked the bureaucracy and called on elected politicians to control bureaucrats on behalf of the public interest. Even business interests that had heretofore cooperated with economic agencies on behalf of developmental policies began to argue that many of the practices of the interventionist state had outlived their usefulness. The bubble economy and its subsequent burst—leaving a finance sector drowning in bad loans—wrecked the reputation of the most prestigious ministry of all: the Ministry of Finance (MOF). Moreover, the growth of the national government deficit necessitated trimming distributive policies and downsizing the bureaucratic state in order to rally public support for tax increases.

Limited Reform of the Developmental and Distributive State

In 1996–98 Prime Minister Hashimoto Ryutaro pursued an ambitious administrative reform campaign to address some of the above complaints. In the largest government restructuring since the late 1940s, the number of ministries was reduced from 23 to 13, enabling a decrease in the number of officials.[25] The substantive outcome of this reform effort was, however, far from revolutionary. Despite some important institutional changes the essential features of the "developmental" and "distributive" state have survived.

The MOF forfeited its supervisory role over the banking sector to a newly created Financial Services Agency and yielded much of its influence over monetary policy to the Bank of Japan. With the ministry losing its exclusive jurisdiction over the financial sector, the regulatory system became

---

[24] For an analysis of how the Japanese state intervened to assist weak economic sectors as well as growth industries, see Aurelia George Mulgan, "Japan's Interventionist State: Bringing Agriculture Back In," *Japanese Journal of Political Science* 6, no. 1 (2005): 29–61.

[25] Ko Mishima, "The Failure of Japan's Political Reform," *World Policy Journal* 22, no. 4 (Winter 2005/06): 50–51.

based more on rules rather than informal relationships.[26] A Council on Economic and Fiscal Policy (CEFP) was also established as a special cabinet committee chaired by the prime minister. Although initially designed to weaken the MOF's grip on the government's budgetary process, this reform failed to achieve the original objective. The MOF obstructed attempts by the CEFP to seize control of the budget. During the Koizumi government, MOF officials ended up helping to run the council and used this body to push through what they have always sought: cuts in government spending.[27] Moreover, the MOF's loss of influence over the financial system did not impede the ministry's efforts to promote regional financial cooperation with China and other Asian countries after the 1997 East Asian financial crisis.[28]

The Ministry of International Trade and Industry (MITI), the famous pilot agency of industrial policy, emerged intact from this reform period under a new name: the Ministry of Economy, Trade, and Industry (METI). By shedding many of its old protectionist practices designed to nurture or restructure domestic industries, METI redefined its mission to cultivate a more hospitable international environment for Japan's commercial and industrial interests in an era of globalization. While encouraging both outward and inward FDI, METI has promoted a regional version of industrial policy in East Asia. METI has also embraced global and regional multilateralism and promoted bilateral free-trade agreements.[29] The ministry continues to take the lead in working with the private sector in securing stable and new energy resources, and METI shaped the 2002 legislative package to break up the debt-saddled Japan National Oil Corporation to protect its interests.[30] In some ways, METI has become more powerful relative to other economic ministries after METI's bureaucratic rival in the telecommunications and information technologies sector was weakened with the split of the Ministry of Post and Telecommunications (MPT).

---

[26] Jennifer Amyx, "Reforming Japanese Banks and the Financial System," in *Japan—Change and Continuity*, ed. Javed Maswood, Jeffrey Graham, and Hideaki Miyajima (London: RoutledgeCurzon, 2002), 62–63.

[27] Aurelia George Mulgan, *Japan's Failed Revolution: Koizumi and the Politics of Economic Reform* (Canberra: Asia Pacific Press, 2002), 143–44, 186–91.

[28] Saori N. Katada, "Japan's Counterweight Strategy: U.S.-Japan Cooperation and Competition in International Finance," in *Beyond Bilateralism: U.S.-Japan Relations in the New Asia-Pacific*, ed. Ellis S. Krauss and T.J. Pempel (Stanford: Stanford University Press, 2004), 176–97; and Jennifer A. Amyx, "Japan and the Evolution of Regional Financial Arrangements in East Asia," in Ibid., 198–218.

[29] Masaru Kohno, "A Changing Ministry of International Trade and Industry," in *Japanese Governance: Beyond Japan Inc.*, ed. Jennifer Amyx and Peter Drysdale (London: RoutledgeCurzon, 2003), 96–112.

[30] "The Devil Is In the Details," *Daily Yomiuri*, May 6, 2002; and "METI to Integrate Government Oil Firms by FY04," *Daily Yomiuri*, February 6, 2003.

Change of the agencies in the "distributive state" was even more limited because of the zoku politicians who allied with bureaucrats to resist reform. When threatened with a break up, the Ministry of Construction (the hotbed of clientelistic pork-barrel politics) countered by getting the backing of the LDP construction zoku, construction companies, and local governments. In the end, the ministry prevented the split and was merged with the Ministry of Transportation and the National Land Agency to form the new Ministry of National Land and Transportation.[31] The end result was an amalgamation of different agencies that had been notorious for their role in pork-barrel politics. The Ministry of Agriculture, Fishery, and Forestry—which was responsible for market-distorting subsidies and protectionist measures for agriculture—escaped major reforms.[32]

Another way to reduce wasteful public works spending was to go after the Fiscal Investment and Loan Program (FILP) and the special public corporations funded by the FILP. The FILP had served as the mechanism for allocating capital from postal savings and insurance accounts to fund public infrastructure projects managed by public corporations.[33] The amount of money channeled in this way was enormous—amounting to ¥418 trillion or 82% of Japan's gross domestic product in 2000.[34] To restrict the flow of FILP money, the initial reform target was the Trust Fund Bureau (TFB) of the Finance Ministry that collected postal savings and insurance premiums to supply the FILP. The elimination of the TFB failed to curtail the money flow, however, because under the new system the FILP could issue bonds that were then purchased by the post office.

Therefore, Koizumi decided to push his long-held objective: the privatization and breakup of the postal system itself. His bold dissolution of the House of Representatives to counter the anti-reformers in his own party did yield a sweet electoral victory for Koizumi, but the substance of the postal privatization package that eventually passed the National Diet fell short of his original ambitions because of compromises he had to make. Japan Post would be privatized and split into four separate companies— but there was a catch: even after privatization is completed by 2017 the government would still be able to keep one-third of the shares of the holding company overseeing the four privatized companies. Although the

---

[31] Ko Mishima, "The Changing Relationship between Japan's LDP and the Bureaucracy: Hashimoto's Administrative Reform Effort and Its Politics," *Asian Survey* 38, no. 10 (October 1998): 978–80.

[32] Aurelia George Mulgan, *Japan's Interventionist State: The Role of the MAFF* (London: RoutledgeCurzon, 2005), 140–46.

[33] This account relies heavily on Leonard J. Schoppa, *Race for the Exits: The Unraveling of Japan's System of Social Protection* (Ithaca: Cornell University Press, 2006), 137–43.

[34] Takero Doi and Takeo Hoshi, "Paying for the FILP," National Bureau of Economic Research, Working Paper, no. 9385, December 2002, 2.

government would be required to sell all of its savings and life insurance operations, the four postal firms are permitted to own each other's shares, thereby protecting the postal savings and life insurance firms from hostile takeovers.[35] Moreover, as Leonard Schoppa writes, "the reforms contain no provisions that guarantee that the flow of postal savings to the FILP agencies will stop, or even slow.[36]

Koizumi was even less successful in reforming another one of his key targets: the Japan Highway Public Corporation (JHPC). In an attempt to overpower resistance within the LDP he appointed a blue-ribbon panel to draft a thorough reform plan that would curtail highway and road construction and re-allocate road tax revenues to other more useful programs, but a sharp conflict within the panel's leadership sabotaged the effort. The JHPC privatization legislation that eventually passed in June 2004 was replete with so many compromises that it had no meaningful effect on highway construction plans.[37]

After the re-entry of rebels against postal privatization into the LDP sharply lowered his cabinet's approval rating, Abe saw the need to demonstrate that he was indeed a reformer like Koizumi by tackling the amakudari system. After retirement at an early age (often around the age of 50), career civil servants "descended from heaven" to high-paying and influential positions in the private sector and government-affiliated organizations. This system encouraged collusive relations between the public and private sectors and created a permissive environment for bid-rigging and price-fixing. According to a government study released in April 2007, government agencies assisted the re-employment of 1,968 central government officials from 2004 to 2006, and 1,346 of these officials were virtually forced upon private companies and government-related entities. Of these 1,346 officials, moreover, 500 came from the Ministry of Land and Transportation that oversees the construction industry.[38]

With an eye on the July 2007 upper house election, the Abe government hastily drafted legislation that creates a human resources center within the cabinet secretariat to manage the re-employment of retiring officials and abolishes by 2011 the role of ministries and agencies in brokering jobs for their own bureaucrats. Because of fierce resistance from bureaucrats, however, Abe compromised to allow the government ministries both

---

[35] Steven K. Vogel, *Japan Remodeled: How Government and Industry Are Reforming Japanese Capitalism* (Ithaca: Cornell University Press, 2006), 108–10.

[36] Schoppa, *Race for the Exits*, 141.

[37] Otake Hideo, *Koizumi Junichiro Popyurizumu no Kenkyu: Sono Senryaku to Shuho* [Study of Koizumi Junichiro's Populism: Strategy and Style] (Tokyo: Toyo Keizai Shimposha, 2006), 11–77.

[38] Hiroko Nakata, "'Amakudari' Too Entrenched to Curb?" *Japan Times*, May 29, 2007.

to provide the job center with information about their officials and to raise issues about "efficiency and feasibility." There is concern that these provisions might provide the bureaucracy with a loophole to get involved in the actual operation of the human resources center and make the practice of re-employing retiring officials even more opaque. The Abe reform plan passed the Diet in June 2007, but the government put off more fundamental issues of civil service reform—such as raising the retirement age of officials and instituting a merit-based evaluation system.[39]

Emergence of a Core Executive

Although the overall effect of bureaucratic reform has been mixed, Japan has taken significant steps to enhance the prime minister's power within the government structure. In 1982 Prime Minister Nakasone Yasuhiro got the ball rolling by appointing the political heavyweight Gotoda Masaharu to serve as his chief cabinet secretary (CCS) in order to strengthen the cabinet's coordination function over the bureaucracy. Thereafter, this post has evolved from a relatively low-ranking cabinet position to one of the most powerful positions in the Japanese government. As the role of the CCS grew in importance, so did the roles of the deputy CCSs, especially the administrative deputy chief cabinet secretary—an official from the bureaucracy who serves as the chief liaison between the prime minister and the various administrative agencies.[40] In 1986 Nakasone also attempted to concentrate executive authority by establishing within the cabinet secretariat the three offices of internal affairs, external affairs, and national security affairs with their directors coming from the Ministry of Finance, the Ministry of Foreign Affairs, and the Defense Agency respectively.

Since the Nakasone reorganization did not address the problems of inter-agency rivalries, Prime Minister Hashimoto revamped the cabinet secretariat by abolishing the above three offices established by Nakasone, creating in their place three assistant chief cabinet secretary (ACCS) positions who could be politically appointed by the prime minister and housing these three new officials (with a rank equivalent to vice minister) in one office (the Office of Assistant Chief Cabinet Secretaries or OACCS) with a large professional support staff. This overarching policy unit was

---

[39] Hiroko Nakata, "'Amakudari' Crackdown Called Toothless, Poll Ploy," *Japan Times*, April 14, 2007; Hiroko Nakata, "Cabinet OKs 'Amakudari' Bill, Bureaucrat Reform," *Japan Times*, April 25, 2007; and "Doubts Linger Over Reform Bills, Critics Question Effectiveness of New Law to Revamp Civil Service," *Daily Yomiuri*, July 2, 2007.

[40] According to Shinoda Tomohito, the Chief Cabinet Secretary is "at least equivalent to the combined functions of the U.S. administration's chief of staff and the White House spokesperson." See Tomohito Shinoda, "Japan's Cabinet Secretariat and Its Emergence as Core Executive," *Asian Survey* 45, no. 5 (September/October 2005): 801–6.

subdivided into various functional policy groups. The Hashimoto reforms also permitted the creation of ad hoc policy "rooms" within the OACSS. Most of the officials manning these policy groups come from the professional civil service, but the quality of these officials, who are seconded to the cabinet secretariat from their home ministries and agencies, has risen immensely as the secretariat has come to play a bigger role in policymaking.[41] As of 2007 the cabinet secretariat has a staff of 650 officials and encompasses seventeen ad hoc policy groups.[42]

Moreover, the Hashimoto administrative reforms that were eventually implemented in January 2001 clarified the legal authority of the prime minister and the cabinet secretariat to initiate policy. The revised cabinet law explicitly stated that the role of the cabinet secretariat is "to present policy direction for the government as a whole, and coordinate policy strategically and proactively."[43] Prime Minister Koizumi took full advantage of this new legal mandate to exercise top-down decisionmaking regarding a number of controversial policy issues, such as the Anti-Terrorism Special Measures Law of October 2001 that enabled Japan's rear-area support for U.S. military operations after September 11, 2001 and the Iraq Special Measures Law of August 2003 that permitted the deployment of ground self-defense forces to assist the reconstruction of postwar Iraq.[44] Regarding domestic economic issues, Koizumi on occasion used the cabinet-based Council on Economic and Fiscal Policy to push through his reform ideas in the face of resistance from his own party.

Strengthening the State in National Security Affairs

Perhaps the most profound institutional changes in the Japanese state have occurred in the realm of security affairs. During the Cold War era, the influence of government agencies in charge of security policy paled in comparison to the robust ministries and policy networks that dealt with economic policy. After the 1990–91 Persian Gulf War, Japan moved to rectify this imbalance by creating what some have called a "new defense establishment."[45]

---

[41] Shinoda, "Japan's Cabinet Secretariat and Its Emergence as Core Executive," 807–12.

[42] An organizational map of these groups is located on the website of Cabinet Secretariat of Japan at: http://www.cas.go.jp/jp/gaiyou/sosiki/index.html.

[43] Tomohito Shinoda, "Koizumi's Top-Down Leadership in the Anti-Terrorism Legislation: The Impact of Political Institutional Changes," *SAIS Review* 23, no. 1 (Winter/Spring 2003): 25–26.

[44] Shinoda, "Koizumi's Top-Down Leadership in the Anti-Terrorism Legislation," 28–32; and Tomohito Shinoda, "Japan's Top-Down Policy Process to Dispatch the SDF to Iraq," *Japanese Journal of Political Science* 7, no. 1 (April 2006): 71–91.

[45] Yuki Tatsumi and Andrew L. Oros, eds., *Japan's New Defense Establishment: Institutions, Capabilities, and Implications* (Washington, D.C.: Henry L. Stimson Center, 2007), 9–21.

To enhance its ability to integrate policy and develop a longer-term diplomatic strategy, the Ministry of Foreign Affairs (MOFA) created in 1993 the Foreign Policy Bureau (Sogo Gaiko Seisaku Kyoku) as a super-bureau in the ministry. Before this the Treaty Bureau had been the most powerful MOFA bureau, reflecting the priority on interpreting and explaining the relationship between international treaties (e.g., the U.S.-Japan Security Treaty) and policy.[46] Within the Foreign Policy Bureau the Security Policy Division was given the task of addressing all security issues—a departure from the traditional bilateral emphasis of the Security Treaty Division of the North American Bureau.

The Defense Intelligence Headquarters was established in 1997 to integrate the intelligence activities of the Defense Agency and the different branches of the Self-Defense Forces (SDF). Then in 2003 the National Diet enacted, with an overwhelming majority of about 90% of the parliamentary votes, a legislative package to strengthen the state's ability to respond to armed attacks. Among other things the legislation clarified the responsibilities of different government units and public institutions, called on local governments and citizens to cooperate with the national government, and mandated the establishment of a coordination task force headed by the prime minister to deal with emergencies.[47]

Whereas the Defense Agency was finally being elevated into a full-fledged ministry (the Ministry of Defense) in January 2007, Prime Minister Abe has sought to strengthen executive power by calling for an upgraded National Security Council modeled after the U.S. National Security Council.[48] His aim is to enhance the ability of the prime minister and the cabinet to deal with crisis situations both by insuring prompt delivery and analysis of information and by clarifying and streamlining the chains of command. If Abe's vision is realized, the professional staffing in the cabinet secretariat regarding national security matters will expand even more.

Interest Intermediation and Civil Society

The societal underpinnings of Japanese politics are best understood in light of the changing pattern of interest intermediation and the role of civil society. As T.J. Pempel has argued, the postwar Japanese regime of

---

[46] See Yakushiji Katsuyuki, *Gaimusho: Gaiko Ryoku Kyoka e no Michi* [Ministry of Foreign Affairs: Road toward Strengthening Diplomatic Power] (Tokyo: Iwanami Shoten, 2003), 74–87.

[47] National Institute for Defense Studies, *East Asian Strategic Review 2004* (Tokyo: Japan Times, 2004), 220–22.

[48] Hiroko Nakata, "Panel Endorses Formation of New Security Council," *Japan Times*, February 28, 2007.

LDP predominance rested on a dominant social coalition consisting of big and small business and agriculture.[49] Each of these societal sectors had their summit-like organizations that participated in interest intermediation processes in tandem with the LDP and relevant bureaucratic agencies. Although the Keidanren was the most influential voice of big business as a whole, on sectoral policies industrial associations were more central in working with ministries like MITI to formulate and implement industrial policies. The LDP helped to insulate this government-business partnership from political pressures that could undermine the economic rationality of industrial policy.[50] Small business and agricultural interests in turn appealed to both the LDP and the bureaucratic state for compensatory measures to mitigate the negative effects of economic change. This quasi-corporatist arrangement of "embedded mercantilism" provided the dual benefit of facilitating Japan's economic rise while preserving social stability and equity.

How labor organizations fit into this regime was more problematic. Unlike its counterparts in other functional sectors, the labor movement was fragmented into competing national centers and strong enterprise unions. The division of national labor centers contributed to the political fragmentation of the opposition camp and played into the hands of the ruling LDP. As a result political parties representing labor unions were, until 1993, formally excluded from power. Despite these weaknesses, however, labor unions were eventually able to negotiate social contracts with corporate management that provided employment security, generous benefits, and, eventually, well-deserved pay hikes for "permanent" workers.[51]

By the 1990s the political solidarity of the conservative social coalition began to fray. In face of strong international pressures (especially from the United States) to open up domestic markets, the LDP government was forced to shift away from the previous protectionist measures through which it had won the electoral loyalty of farmers and small businesses. The proportion of farm voters in the electorate has declined dramatically from 14.7% in 1990 to 7.7% in 2003. This demographic change, along with the introduction of single-member election districts, has made mobilization of the agricultural vote insufficient for LDP politicians to win elections, even

[49] T.J. Pempel, *Regime Shift: Comparative Dynamics of the Japanese Political Economy* (Ithaca: Cornell University Press, 1998), 63–65.

[50] Daniel I. Okimoto, *Between MITI and the Market: Japanese Industrial Policy for High Technology* (Stanford: Stanford University Press, 1989); and Mark Tilton, *Restrained Trade: Cartels in Japan's Basic Materials Industry* (Ithaca: Cornell University Press, 1996).

[51] Sheldon Garon and Mike Mochizuki, "Negotiating Social Contracts," in *Postwar Japan as History*, ed. Andrew Gordon (Berkeley: University of California Press, 1993), 155–64.

in rural areas.[52] This did not mean, however, that LDP candidates could ignore agricultural interests; farmers could punish the conservatives simply by not voting at all.[53] This calculus applied as well to small business voters who remained important to LDP politicians running in urban areas.[54] At the same time business interests became fragmented. While the internationally competitive industries and corporations favored deregulation and a less interventionist state, weaker industrial sectors and corporations sought state protection and resisted international liberalization pressures.[55] These tensions within the conservative social coalition weakened LDP cohesion. For the LDP these tensions also posed a vexing dilemma between economic liberalization on the one hand and state interventionism to ameliorate the dislocative effects of market forces on the other.

While the conservative social coalition confronted these challenges, a sense of crisis in organized labor prompted a drive toward unity. Not only was the rate of unionization declining but also many workers were abandoning the pro-labor JSP and DSP and instead voting for the LDP. Therefore, the only way to take advantage of the fissures in the conservative political camp was to reconfigure, if possible, the labor movement behind a single national center. Moderate but cohesive private-sector industrial unions spearheaded this consolidation drive and succeeded in creating Rengo (the Japan Trade Union Confederation) in 1987.[56] Rengo eventually succeeded in bringing together unions from all four of the competing national labor centers to become the largest union organization in Japan with about 6.7 million members. Rengo's formation helped to create the political conditions conducive for both the 1993–94 non-LDP coalition government and, ultimately, the formation of the DPJ. This national labor center now serves as one of the foundations of DPJ electoral support and restrains the DPJ's support for economic liberalization.

In addition to established interest organizations representing functional economic interests, modern Japan has experienced periods in which social organizations that are commonly associated with civil society have flourished. Despite their apparent voluntary nature, many of

---

[52] Mulgan, "Where Tradition Meets Change," 264–65.

[53] In the July 2007 House of Councilors election, the DPJ led by Ozawa Ichiro successfully appealed to economically anxious farmers by promising income support and, by doing so, managed to defeat LDP candidates in a number of rural single-member electoral districts.

[54] Robert Bullock, "Redefining the Conservative Coalition: Agriculture and Small Business in 1990s Japan," in *The State of Civil Society in Japan*, ed. Frank J. Schwartz and Susan J. Pharr (Cambridge: Cambridge University Press, 2003), 175–94.

[55] Pempel, *Regime Shift*, 164–67.

[56] Lonny E. Carlile, "Party Politics and the Japanese Labor Movement: Rengo's 'New Political Force,'" *Asian Survey* 34, no. 7 (July 1994): 606–20.

these organizations failed to assert and sustain their autonomy from the state, and some even became instruments of government intervention in society.[57] Nevertheless, others have managed to mobilize support to exert influence on public policy. During the late 1960s and 1970s, for instance, a coalition of religious organizations in cooperation with progressive political parties successfully blocked an LDP attempt to nationalize the controversial Yasukuni Shrine,[58] and citizens' movements successfully pressed the government to adopt more vigorous anti-pollution measures.[59] The grass-roots peace movement contributed to restraining Japan's rearmament and implanting antimilitarism norms in the country's strategic culture.[60]

The 1990s witnessed another surge of civil society activity. The failure of the state to respond effectively to the devastating Hanshin earthquake of 1995 brought an outpouring of volunteer assistance from citizens. This activity spawned the 1998 passage of legislation making it easier for groups to incorporate as non-profit organizations (NPO) with less government regulation.[61] The subsequent flowering of non-governmental organizations (NGO) has increased citizen pressure on local and national government to be more transparent and responsive.[62] Greater NGO activity has even affected Japan's foreign relations. For example, as Japan's foreign aid programs have shifted away from financing large-scale infrastructure projects ("hard aid"), NGOs are playing an increasing role in Japan's "soft aid" that employ human resources for welfare, health, educational, and environmental programs in developing countries.[63] Such organizations now put a more human face on Japan's international contribution.

---

[57] Sheldon Garon, "From Meiji to Heisei: The State and Civil Society in Japan," in Schwartz and Pharr *The State of Civil Society in Japan*, 42–62.

[58] Tanaka Nobumasa, *Yasukuni no Sengo Shi* [Postwar History of Yasukuni] (Tokyo: Iwanami Shoten, 2002), 105–7.

[59] Margaret A. McKean, *Environmental Protest and Citizen Politics in Japan* (Berkeley: University of California Press, 1981).

[60] Mari Yamamoto, *Grassroots Pacifism in Post-war Japan: The Rebirth of a Nation* (London: RoutledgeCurzon, 2004), 104–23, 152–81, 204–21.

[61] Frank Schwartz, "Introduction: Recognizing Civil Society in Japan," in Schwartz and Phar *The State of Civil Society in Japan*, 14–19.

[62] Jeff Kingston, *Japan's Quiet Transformation: Social Change and Civil Society in the Twenty-First Century* (London: RoutledgeCurzon, 2004).

[63] Keiko Hirata, *Civil Society in Japan: the Growing Influence of NGOs over Tokyo's Aid and Development Policy* (New York: Palgrave MacMillan, 2002), 128–53.

Changing Strategic Discourse

Institutions and organizations matter a great deal in shaping national strategic choices, but substantive ideas and visions are critical in giving flesh to these choices. Japanese debates about strategy after the Cold War have transpired along numerous dimensions that include the following: values, national security, economics, and international order.

Regarding the realm of values, Japanese leaders such as Prime Minister Abe and Foreign Minister Aso Taro have been trumpeting Japan's commitment to democratic norms. Japan's alliance with the United States is now frequently defined in terms of common values as well as common interests.[64] What this operationally means for foreign policy, however, is unclear. Japan still has a ways to go before fully embracing, as the United States has, the promotion of democracy abroad as one of its foreign policy objectives. The primary motivation for this "values-oriented diplomacy," may be to distinguish Japan from China and perhaps to promote a coalition of democratic states in the Asia-Pacific (e.g., the United States, Japan, Australia, and India) to counter China's rise.[65]

This use of democracy in foreign policy, however, has its skeptics and critics. Progressives see the conservative leadership's embrace of democratic values as hypocritical. They point to the government's moves to use legislation to revive national symbols like the *hinomaru* flag and the *kimigayo* anthem as harking back to an undemocratic and militarist Japan of old.[66] Prime Minister Abe's successful effort to revise the Basic Education Law by incorporating the promotion of patriotism is seen by the political left as a troubling step backward from the democratic ideals of postwar Japan. The controversy over revising the imperial lineage law to permit a woman to ascend to the throne exposed the gender discrimination that permeates Japanese society. Critics of the government's appropriation of democratic ideals for diplomatic purposes charge that many conservatives want to diminish and even deny Japan's war responsibility and wartime atrocities. Progressives also see state officials as provoking xenophobic public reactions to foreigners in Japan by exaggerating crime statistics.[67]

---

[64] Michael J. Green, "Democracy and the Balance of Power in Asia," *American Interest* 2, no. 1 (September/October 2006): 96–98.

[65] Abe Shinzo has in fact articulated this notion in his book. See Shinzo Abe, *Utsukushii Kuni e* [Toward a Beautiful Country] (Tokyo: Bungei Shunju, 2006), 158–60. What is striking, however, is how often the Republic of Korea is not mentioned when Abe and Aso discuss their diplomacy based on values.

[66] Takahashi Tetsuya, *Kyoiku to Kokka* [Education and the State] (Tokyo: Kodansha, 2004), 142–66.

[67] Apichai W. Shipper, "Criminals or Victims? The Politics of Illegal Foreigners in Japan," *Journal of Japanese Studies* 31, no. 2 (2005): 299–327.

A close look beyond the rhetorical flourishes about Japan as the embodiment of universal democratic values reveals that there is still much popular discussion of the need to preserve Japan's unique cultural traits that differ significantly from both the United States and the West as well as from China. For example, books about the "dignity" (*hinkaku*) of Japan not only have become huge bestsellers but also resonate with Prime Minister Abe's own vision of Japan as a "beautiful country."[68] As a counter to this cultural nationalism, Japanese liberals and progressives argue that Japan needs to become a more cosmopolitan and open society that does not discriminate against women, foreigners, and minorities and accepts a plurality of lifestyles. Japan will have much more "soft power" by becoming such a country than by merely repeating the rhetoric of democratic values.

Regarding national security, the debate has centered around the issues regarding the use of force and the nature of Japan's alliance with the United States. As Richard Samuels has argued, this strategic discourse has tended to divide into four general schools of thought.[69] Mainstream opinion embraces a close alliance with the United States but is divided regarding the use of military force. One mainstream group sees the need for Japan to contribute more to international security primarily through non-military means or through rear-area support while restricting the use of force primarily to Japan's own defense.[70] The other mainstream group is more supportive of "normalizing" Japan as a military power and exercising the right of collective self-defense so Japan can use force to defend allied countries like the United States.[71] The non-mainstream schools converge in terms of advocating greater autonomy from the United States yet disagree over the role of military power. One group argues that Japan should seek autonomy through greater military strength, even the development of nuclear weapons, because the U.S. security guarantee over Japan may be unreliable.[72] The other group prefers to achieve autonomy by refusing to support U.S. military options beyond Japan's defense.[73]

Concerning economics, the strategic discourse has tended to reflect three clusters of opinion. One view supports more thorough liberalization

---

[68] Fujiwara Masahiko, *Kokka no Hinkaku* [Dignity of the Nation] (Tokyo: Shinchosha, 2005).

[69] Richard J. Samuels, "Securing Japan: The Current Discourse," *Journal of Japanese Studies* 33, no. 1 (2007): 125–52.

[70] Soeya, *Nihon no Midoru Pawa Gaiko*; and Terashima Jitsuro, *Warera Sengo Sedai no "Saka no Ue no Kumo"* [Our Postwar Generation's "Clouds at the Hilltop"] (Tokyo: PHP Kenkyujo, 2006).

[71] Shikata Toshiyuki, *Mu Bobi Retto* [Defenseless Archipelago] (Tokyo: Kairyusha, 2006).

[72] Nakanishi Terumasa, ed., *"Nihon Kaku Buso" no Ronten* [Arguments about "Japan's Nuclear Forces"] (Tokyo: PHP Kenkyujo, 2004).

[73] Asai Motofumi, *Shudan-teki Ji'ei Ken to Nihon Koku Kempo* [Right of Collective Self-Defense and Japan's Constitution] (Tokyo: Shuei-sha, 2002).

of economic policies and business practices in order to maximize market-driven economic growth. Advocates of this view tend to downplay the problem of increasing economic inequality, believing that a more dynamic economy and a more fluid labor market would give Japanese more opportunities to get a slice of a new prosperity.[74] A second view supports maintaining as much as possible the traditional policies and practices that enabled Japan to have both economic development and social equity. This economic conservatism supports the continuation of government compensatory policies, the lifetime employment system, and even protectionist measures for weak economic sectors. Finally, a third view acknowledges that Japan needs to adopt more market-oriented reforms to meet the challenges of economic globalization but argues that such liberal reforms are inadequate. Proponents of this view believe that Japan must address more forthrightly the problem of growing economic inequality and must develop more extensive social safety nets.[75]

On the issue of international order, there has been a vigorous debate concerning the possibility and desirability of developing an East Asian community. Some believe that even while maintaining a robust alliance with the United States, Japan should work vigorously with Asian countries—such as China, South Korea, and the Association of Southeast Asian Nations (ASEAN) states—to harness regional economic integration for community-building.[76] Others caution that regional institutions and processes that exclude the United States will undermine the alliance; they therefore tend to favor either cultivating a coalition of maritime democratic states with the U.S.-Japan alliance at its core or revitalizing the Asia Pacific Economic Cooperation process. Finally, as a compromise, many support an East Asia community-building process that incorporates Australia, New Zealand, and India in addition to the East Asian countries belonging to the ASEAN +3 dialogue. The inclusion of these three countries would hopefully counterbalance Chinese influence as well as reassure the United States.

Disconnect between Politics and Strategic Ideas

The above strategic discourse poses significant political challenges. First, the contending views within each issue dimension do not line up

---

[74] Takenaka Heizo, who served in the Koizumi administration, is one of the most influential proponents of this view. Takenaka Heizo, *"Tsuyoi Nihon" o Tsukuri Kata: Keizai–Shakai–Dai Kaikaku no Kaizu* [How to Create a "Strong Japan": Chart for Great Reform of Economy and Society] (Tokyo: PHP Kenkyujo, 2001).

[75] Tachibanaki Toshiaki, *Kakusa Shakai: Nani ga Mondai na no ka* [Disparity Society: What Is the Problem?] (Tokyo: Iwanami Shoten, 2006).

[76] Taniguchi Makoto, *Higashi Ajia Kyodotai* [East Asia Community] (Tokyo: Iwanami Shoten, 2004).

across dimensions to yield a single spectrum of opinion that can crystallize political positions. Second, while there is some overlap between different issue dimensions, opinion leaders often focus on one dimension to the neglect of others. Therefore, it is impossible to reduce the strategic debate to a one-dimensional left-versus-right, progressive-versus-conservative competition. Finally, even within each issue dimension, the debate does not break up neatly along political party lines. For example, there are security hawks and doves in both the LDP and DPJ, although the Komeito tends to be uniformly dovish. Additionally there are proponents and opponents of more vigorous market-oriented reforms in both the LDP and DPJ, while the Komeito has tended to support market-oriented reforms that are sensitive to urban small businesses.

In his exploration of a potential regime shift in Japan, T.J. Pempel posited "an underlying socioeconomic bifurcation between deregulation and internationalism on the one hand, and regulation and nationalism on the other." Although this hypothesized bifurcation of basic policy choices is more simplified than the above portrayal of Japan's current strategic discourse, even his analysis was open-ended about whether the Japanese party system would eventually gravitate around these two sets of views and parties would compete for an electoral mandate in favor of one alternative or the other.[77]

What appears to be emerging in Japan is a quasi-two party system that tends to obfuscate rather than clarify strategic choices. The positive effect is that this situation could steer Japan toward both a moderate course and incremental change and prevent extremism—what Richard Samuels calls "Japan's goldilocks strategy," one that is neither too hard or too soft but gets security just right.[78] The negative effect, however, could be a Japan that muddles through without strategic clarity and vision. Muddling through may be sufficient when hard choices are unnecessary but may cause political paralysis in crisis situations. The trend in Japan toward "presidentialization" of the prime ministership and the concentration of executive power can help to overcome the log-jam as Koizumi did when he pushed through legislation on postal system privatization. This same trend, however, can also present opportunities for political leaders to mobilize and pander to populist nationalism to the detriment of sober strategic calculations and decisions.

---

[77] Pempel, *Regime Shift*, 216–17.

[78] Richard J. Samuels, "Japan's Goldilocks Strategy," *Washington Quarterly* 29, no. 4 (Autumn 2006): 111–27.

Role of Public Opinion in Strategic Discourse and Choices

How does public opinion matter for Japan's strategic discourse and choices? Paul Midford argues that LDP-dominant governments anticipate public reaction and tailor policies that "avoid provoking the emergence of opposing stable opinion majorities."[79] Although not necessarily determining concrete policy choices, public opinion can constrain policy outcomes enough to have general strategic consequences. Over the years the Japanese public has become more supportive of SDF involvement in overseas non-military humanitarian and reconstruction activities but has opposed participation in operations that entail the use of military force abroad. Consistent with this public preference, the government has carefully limited Japan's contribution to post–September 11 international security operations to non-combat logistical and humanitarian support. Strong opposition to the war on Iraq did not prevent the Koizumi government from deploying SDF ground units to Iraq but did restrict the mission of these units to humanitarian and reconstruction operations in a well-fortified and relatively secure area of Iraq, with the SDF relying on Dutch forces for protection.[80]

Public opinion may also affect the movement to revise the constitution. Although a sizeable majority now favors amending the constitution, there is little consensus in favor of revising Article 9—the so-called peace clause. According to an *Asahi Shimbun* poll conducted in April 2007, 58% saw the necessity of revising the constitution, but only 6% of this pro-revision group favored revision because of "problems with Article 9." The reason cited most by revisionists (84%) for changing the constitution was instead to incorporate new rights and institutions. The poll also indicated that only 18% agreed with the LDP proposal to change Self-Defense Force (*Ji'eitai*) into a full-fledged military (*Ji'eigun*), whereas 70% preferred keeping the SDF as is.[81] Opinion polls also show that there continues to be much public opposition to collective self-defense.[82] These results suggest that political elites seeking to change the constitution will need to tread cautiously

---

[79] For Midford's delineation of conditions that enable public opinion to shape policy outcomes, see Paul Midford, "Japanese Public Opinion and the War on Terrorism: Implications for Japan's Security Strategy," Policy Studies 27 (Washington, D.C.: East-West Center, 2006), 8–13.

[80] Midford, "Japanese Public Opinion and the War on Terrorism," 20–40.

[81] "'Abe Kaiken' Min-i to Kyori Kan" [Sense of Distance between 'Abe's Constitutional Revision' and Public Will], *Asahi Shimbun*, May 2, 2007, 5.

[82] According to an April 2006 survey conducted by the liberal *Asahi* newspaper, 53% favored the current policy of not exercising the collective self-defense right, while only 36% supported exercising that right. See *Asahi Shimbun*, May 3, 2006. Even a poll conducted by the conservative *Yomiuri* newspaper in March 2007 found 50% supporting the current policy of prohibiting collective self-defense, while less than 42% favored exercising the collective self-defense right by either revising or reinterpreting the constitution. See "Kempo 'Kaisei' Sansei 46%, 3-Nen Renzoku de Gensho," [Support for Constitutional 'Revision' 46%, Decline for the Third Consecutive Year], *Yomiuri Shimbun*, April 5, 2007.

in order to prevent the emergence of a stable and united public majority against the revision movement.

If the public's resilient antimilitarism helps to curb Japan's ambitions as a military power, does populist nationalism drive a more assertive foreign policy? The popular reaction against Chinese and Korean protests regarding Koizumi's visits to the Yasukuni Shrine certainly allowed Koizumi to repeat these pilgrimages without much domestic political cost. More importantly, the public outcry over North Korea's handling of the issue of abducted Japanese citizens effectively blocked Koizumi's engagement policy toward Pyongyang and encouraged Abe to sustain a hard-line policy toward North Korea even after the Bush administration shifted toward a more flexible approach after the November 2006 mid-term election.

Yet there are limits to Japanese populist nationalism. After the deterioration of Sino-Japanese relations under Koizumi, most Japanese favored stabilizing relations with China and applauded not only Abe's "ice-breaking" trip to Beijing soon after becoming prime minister but also his restraint on Yasukuni pilgrimages based on a policy of ambiguity. Although the Japanese strongly oppose providing bilateral assistance to North Korea until there is meaningful progress in resolving the abduction issue, the public is reluctant to support a militarily aggressive policy against North Korea.[83]

The prevalent view that the Japanese younger generation tends to be more nationalistic than the older generation is an assumption that needs to be given a more critical look. A December 2006 *Asahi Shimbun* survey showed that 63% believed that Japanese patriotism (*aikokushin*) needed to be strengthened while 27% did not.[84] The generational breakdown indicated that those in the younger generation were much less inclined to see the necessity of strengthening patriotism than those in the older generation.[85] Moreover, the younger generation tended to be less willing to fight than the older generation even if Japan was attacked by a foreign country. In an amazing result, more Japanese males in their twenties and thirties preferred to surrender or flee than to fight.[86]

---

[83] Midford, "Japanese Public Opinion and the War on Terrorism," 31–32.

[84] "Nihon ni Umare 'Yokatta' 9-wari" [90% Glad They Were Born in Japan], *Asahi Shimbun*, January 25, 2007, 20.

[85] For example, 46% of those in their twenties saw the need for greater patriotism, whereas 71% of those in their sixties saw such a need.

[86] The breakdown for males in their twenties was 24% for surrendering, 24% for fleeing, and 45% for fighting. The breakdown for males in their thirties was 20% for surrendering, 29% for fleeing, and 40% for fighting. By contrast, the result for males in their sixties was 13% for surrendering, 14% for fleeing, and 62% for fighting.

Implications for Japan's Grand Strategy

The continuity as well as change in political institutions and strategic discourse suggest that Japan's strategy will evolve incrementally—with much tugging and pulling by contending political forces and opinion—rather than depart fundamentally from the postwar strategy of military restraint and economic realism. Prime Minister Abe does want Japan to break out from its postwar regime and mentality; as doctrinaire as he may be, however, political constraints will compel him to be pragmatic and to rein in his ambitions. Abe has used the parliamentary majority inherited from Koizumi to push through some of his agenda during his first year in office, but the LDP's defeat in the July 2007 House of Councilors election entails a huge setback for him. This election was not about security policy or constitutional revision. It was primarily about domestic issues such as the government's mishandling of pension records, political corruption scandals, and economic uncertainties and inequality.

Political elites are now eyeing the next House of Representatives election that must be held by September 2009. Abe must revive his personal popularity quickly if he wants to remain prime minister and win a lower-house electoral mandate to pursue his regime transformation agenda. If Abe cannot do this, an intra-LDP movement will gain traction to dump him in favor of a more appealing leader to head the LDP before the next lower-house election. The opposition DPJ, in turn, must convert the anti-LDP sentiment expressed in the July 2007 upper-house election into durable support for the DPJ and force the LDP-led government to dissolve the House of Representatives and call an election before the LDP can recover politically. Much of the parliamentary jockeying is likely to center around domestic economic and social policy issues since those topics are now what most preoccupy the public.

Nevertheless, the LDP-Komeito coalition's loss of its upper-house majority has altered the political context for addressing foreign policy issues. DPJ leader Ozawa has signaled that his party will oppose an extension of the anti-terrorism law expiring in November 2007 that has enabled Japan to provide rear-area support (including refueling of naval ships in the Indian Ocean) in U.S.-led military operations against terrorism. This opposition could steer Abe's coalition government to override the upper house by wielding its two-thirds majority in the lower house. Such a Diet confrontation could transform security policy into a salient issue for future electoral competition and even expose disagreements *within* both the LDP and DPJ. Alternatively, the LDP-led government could compromise with the DPJ regarding an extension of the anti-terrorism law and be less daring regarding other security policy issues. Whichever course the government chooses, political hurdles to altering Japan's grand strategy remain formidable.

Constitutional Revision

Prime Minister Abe has made constitutional revision one of his central objectives. A thorough change of the postwar constitution would encompass a multiplicity of issues ranging from redefining the role of the emperor to articulating new rights and duties for citizens. Much of the attention, however, has focused on whether and how to revise Article 9, the war-renunciation article. Revisionists who, like Abe, want to relax most of the postwar restrictions on Japan's defense forces would like to transform the Self-Defense Force into a full-fledged self-defense military. If such a transformation were to take place, Japan's military forces would gain unequivocal constitutional legitimacy and the military would be subject to military law. Revisionists would also like to rewrite Article 9 so that, without much constitutional constraint, Japan can participate fully in international security missions (whether under the United Nations umbrella or as part of a multinational coalition) as well as exercise its right to both collective and individual self-defense.

Abe has engaged the revision movement in two ways. First, he is seeking to chip away at the long-standing constitutional interpretation of the Cabinet Legal Affairs Bureau (CLB) that Japan possesses the right of collective self-defense under international law but cannot exercise that right because doing so would exceed what is "minimally necessary" to defend itself. By appointing a blue-ribbon panel of scholars and former officials who are favorable to reinterpretation, Abe hopes to overpower CLB resistance. The panel is slated to address four situations in which Japan might use military force even if not directly attacked or threatened: (1) the shooting down of a ballistic missile headed toward the United States, (2) retaliation if a U.S. naval ship were attacked in international waters, (3) a military response if another country's military with which Japan was cooperating in an international reconstruction operation were attacked, and (4) rear-area support in terms of transporting ammunition and military equipment.[87] If the panel recommends that such actions would not violate the constitution, then the Abe cabinet may issue a new constitutional interpretation. Before such a reinterpretation can be implemented as concrete policy, however, a series of enabling bills would need to pass the National Diet. The passage of such legislation has become more

---

[87] "Shudanteki Jieiken Kaikin Saguru Shusho," [Prime Minister Seeking to Lift the Ban on Collective Self-Defense] *Asahi Shimbun*, April 25, 2007, 3.

difficult after the July 2007 upper-house election. Soon after the election, the secretary-general of the Komeito (the LDP's coalition partner) announced his opposition to reinterpreting the constitution.[88]

Second, the Abe government has laid the procedural groundwork for formal revision by pushing through legislation that establishes the procedure for a national referendum that is required by the constitution for any amendment. The referendum legislation goes into effect in June 2010, and concrete constitutional revision proposals can be formally submitted to the Diet starting that year. The challenge now for revisionists is to forge a national consensus on the substance of revision. As noted above, such a public consensus does not exist now—especially regarding Article 9. Revision requires a two-thirds majority in both houses of the Diet, something that the LDP lacks. Therefore, those in the LDP who want to amend the constitution will need to reach out and compromise with the Komeito and even the DPJ.[89] If a broad cross-partisan consensus cannot be reached or if the revisionists are unwilling to compromise, then the differences within the LDP and the DPJ on the constitutional question could trigger party splits and a political realignment.

Due to these political constraints, any constitutional amendment occurring in the next five or so years would likely need to be acceptable to a wide range of interests in order to be successful. This need will probably mean at the very least the incorporation of explicit language that limits the use of force. Ironically, if Abe succeeds in reinterpreting the constitution along the lines discussed above, then the urgency of pushing harder on the issue of the right to collective self-defense would decline. Under such circumstances the move to amend the constitution may focus on issues other than Article 9, and Japan could choose a relatively uncontroversial amendment just to test the revision process and to get the public accustomed to the idea of amending the constitution.

Security Policy and Military Modernization

In a process that many observers call Japan's "normalization" as a security actor, Japan is now engaging in security activities that were

---

[88] "Kempo Kaishaku Henko Konnan ni—Komei Gawa, Hantai o Meigen" [Modifying Interpretation of the Constitution Becomes More Difficult—the Komeito Side Declares Its Opposition], *Asahi Shimbun*, August 9, 2007.

[89] The Komeito leadership has expressed its opposition to collective self-defense, and a large majority of the Japanese public believe that Article 9 has contributed to Japan's peace. "Kyujo 'Heiwa ni Koken' 78%" [78% Article Nine "Contributes to Peace"], *Asahi Shimbun*, May 2, 2007; and "Ota Says no way to 'Collective Self-Defense,'" *Japan Times*, May 3, 2007.

unimaginable during the Cold War.[90] In addition to the traditional mission of defending the home islands against direct military threats, the Japanese self-defense forces have embraced a second mission of participation in "international peace cooperation activities" to improve the international security environment. Examples of such activities include participation in numerous UN peacekeeping missions, rear-area support for UN-sanctioned military operations against Afghanistan after the September 11 terrorist attacks, ground force deployments and airlifts to assist the reconstruction of postwar Iraq, and cooperation with the United States, Australia, and India to provide timely humanitarian assistance after the disastrous 2005 tsunami in Southeast and South Asia. To strengthen its alliance with the United States, Japan is both cooperating to develop more robust missile-defense systems and enhancing its potential to participate in joint operations with U.S. forces. Japan is cultivating security relationships beyond the bilateral U.S.-Japan security framework with countries such as Australia and India. Japan has also passed emergency legislation to facilitate more effective and timely responses to crises. In addition to acquiring new transport and refueling capabilities that will facilitate Japanese involvement in "international peace cooperation activities," Japan has enhanced its self-defense capabilities by procuring PAC-3 (Patriot Advanced Capability 3) batteries and the naval Standard Missile SM-3 air defense systems for its Aegis-equipped Kongo-class destroyers. Finally, Japan has upgraded the capabilities of the Japan Coast Guard, transforming it into what Richard Samuels calls "a de facto fourth branch of the Japanese military."[91]

As striking as the above developments are, important to highlight as well is what Japan is not doing. Despite all the talk about the North Korean threat and China's worrisome military modernization, Japan's defense budget has actually declined (not increased) during the last five years as a result of public finance constraints and the absence of political will to increase defense expenditures (see **Figure 2**). Even while participating more in overseas security activities, Japan has refrained from engaging in activities that involve the use of force or a direct integration with the use of force. Japan has avoided cooperating with the United States in operations that could be construed as violations of the prohibition on exercising the collective self-defense right. For example, the ground force deployment to Iraq was legitimated not within the framework of the U.S.-Japan alliance but rather as a UN-mandated peacekeeping and humanitarian operation. Chinese nuclear modernization and the October 2006 North Korean nuclear

[90] See Hughes, "Japan's Military Modernization," 112–29.

[91] Samuels, *Securing Japan*, 77.

FIGURE 2   Japan's defense expenditure, 1988–2005

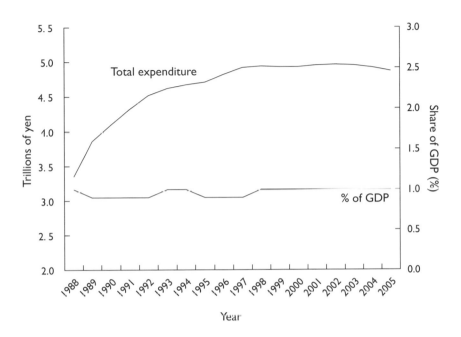

SOURCE: Stockholm International Peace Research Institute, SPRI Military Expenditure Database, http://first.sipri.org/non_first/milex.php.

test notwithstanding, Japan has not veered away from its non-nuclear policy because of the country's strong domestic norms against nuclear weapons, nuclear energy interests and commitment to the nuclear non-proliferation treaty, and realist security calculations.[92]

The Japanese public remains firmly opposed to the use of force except for the purpose of self-defense.[93] According to the government's interpretation of the constitution, Japan reserves the right to engage in pre-emptive or retaliatory strikes to defend itself; Japan has, however, so far refrained from possessing the military capabilities to launch such strikes. There are now open discussions within the Japanese defense establishment about seeking to acquire Tomahawk cruise missiles or the F-22 Raptor stealth fighters from the United States. Both systems would give Japan an offensive punch,

---

[92] Mike M. Mochizuki, "Japan Tests the Nuclear Taboo" *Nonproliferation Review* 14, no. 2 (July 2007): 303–28.

[93] Midford, "Japanese Public Opinion and the War on Terrorism," 40–45.

but the receptivity of the Japanese public to such a military buildup has not been tested yet. The next five-year defense procurement plan (FY 2009–13) may become a critical juncture for Japan in deciding whether to acquire offensive military capabilities.

Foreign Economic Strategy

Japan has responded in a multifaceted fashion to the strategic challenges and opportunities presented by economic globalization. While initially concerned over industrial hollowing out, Japan has used its renovated domestic policy institutions and corporate networks to seize regional and global commercial opportunities. Rather than adopting the "market fundamentalism" of the United States, Japan has adapted its former developmental policies and practices to nurture a region-wide integrated production system with much of the higher value-added aspects remaining at home.[94] By using this production network and by moving up the technological ladder, Japanese companies have been able, with government support, both to take advantage of the economic recovery of East Asian countries after the 1997 regional financial crisis and to maintain access to North American and European markets. The growing Chinese economy thus has become an engine for, rather than a threat to, Japan's own economic recovery.

This regional economic strategy has manifested itself in various ways. For example, to hedge against the United States in the telecommunications sector Japanese officials and corporate leaders have worked with their counterparts in China as well as South Korea to develop regional standards that would give Japanese companies privileged access to East Asian markets.[95] To prevent a recurrence of the 1997 regional crisis, Japanese finance officials have incrementally but methodically pursued regional financial cooperation with a long-term eye on a developing regional currency system.[96] After initially being a champion of the Asia Pacific Economic Cooperation (APEC) forum for managing and promoting regional economic integration, Japan worked with Singapore in 1999 to trigger the bilateral free-trade

---

[94] Samuels, *Securing Japan*, 159–61; and Watanabe Toshio ed., *Nihon no Higashi Ajia Senryaku* [Japan's East Asian Strategy] (Tokyo: Toyo Keizai Shimposha, 2005), 75–128.

[95] Mark C. Tilton, "Seeds of an Asian E.U.? Regionalism as a Hedge against the U.S. on Telecommunications Technology in Japan and Germany," *Pacific Review* 20, no. 3 (September 2007): 301–27.

[96] Shimizu Satoshi, "Higashi Ajia Kin'yu Kyoryoku no Naka no Nihon" [Japan within East Asian Financial Cooperation] in *Nihon no Higashi Ajia Senryaku*, ed. Watanabe Toshio (Tokyo: Toyo Keizai Shimposha, 2005), 43–74.

agreement (FTA) bandwagon in the Asia-Pacific region.[97] Although having lost some of the initiative to other players because of protectionist pressures from its agricultural sector, Japan now is even actively pursuing an FTA with Australia that poses a major challenge in agriculture.[98] To weave these various FTAs together into a regional economic order, METI unveiled in summer 2006 a proposal for an East Asian Economic Partnership Agreement (EPA) that encompasses the ASEAN states, Japan, China, South Korea, Australia, New Zealand, and India.

This emphasis on regionalism, however, does not prevent Japan from having a global economic perspective. Japan indeed is now using a variety of trade forums (bilateral, regional, and global) not only to check U.S. trade unilateralism but also to stabilize and make more predictable trading relationships in the Asian region and beyond.[99] Japan's quest for secure energy and other resources also remains global in reach.

Relations with the United States

There is indeed a broad political consensus in Japan that the alliance with the United States serves national interests. Despite strong Japanese misgivings over President George W. Bush's unilateralism and his problematic war against Iraq, most Japanese were pleased by Koizumi's close friendship with Bush. Koizumi's successor, Abe, has attempted to replicate some of that magic in order to bolster his political standing at home. For better or for worse, the Japanese understand the strategic importance of good relations with the United States. Therefore, Japan has extended by two years the Air SDF airlift mission to support UN and multinational forces in Iraq and passed legislation to implement the U.S. defense transformation plan for bases and forces in Japan.

At the same time, there is ambivalence in Japan about the United States. Recent polls suggest that Japanese trust of the United States is declining, although the Japanese tend to have more positive views of the United States than do Europeans.[100] Many Japanese are concerned that relaxing constitutional constraints on collective self-defense and furthering U.S.-Japan defense cooperation could entrap Japan in U.S.-led security operations that Japan would rather avoid. While welcoming the October

---

[97] Naoko Munakata, *Transforming East Asia: The Evolution of Regional Economic Integration* (Washington, D.C.: Brookings Institution Press, 2006), 110–12.

[98] For how the pursuit of FTAs can be used to pressure the Japanese agricultural sector to liberalize, see Mulgan, "Where Tradition Meets Change," 276–81.

[99] Saadia M. Pekkanen, "Bilateralism, Multilateralism, or Regionalism? Japan's Trade Forum Choices," *Journal of East Asian Studies* 5, no. 1 (2005): 77–103.

[100] Midford, "Japanese Public Opinion and the War on Terrorism," 45–49.

104 de Strategic Asia 2007–08

2000 Armitage-Nye Report for its emphasis on the importance of the U.S.-Japan alliance, Japanese have been wary of the report's advocacy of the U.S.-UK alliance as the model for the U.S.-Japan alliance.[101] The people of Japan are unprepared to fight side-by-side with Americans (as the British do) in overseas military operations that do not directly affect their own territorial security.

Japanese also find the fickleness of U.S. foreign policy aggravating and Washington's moralism self-righteous. So while maintaining and even strengthening the alliance with the United States, the Japanese frequently entertain thoughts of greater autonomy within the framework of the alliance. At the same time, however, they recognize that Japan lacks a more attractive alternative partner and that the costs and risks of true strategic autonomy are too great to bear. The Japanese therefore harbor some hope that by contributing more to the alliance Japan might gain a greater voice in that alliance.

Relations with Asia

Japan's policy toward Asia illustrates how domestic politics shapes and constrains Japan's quest for a more autonomous and assertive foreign policy. This policy also demonstrates how assertiveness has induced tactical jitters even while Japan has gravitated around relatively consistent strategic parameters.

Encouraged by a few career diplomats in the foreign ministry, Prime Minister Koizumi boldly explored the possibility of rapprochement with North Korea by making an extraordinary trip to Pyongyang in September 2002. By getting Kim Jong-il to apologize and come clean regarding the abduction issue, Koizumi hoped that Tokyo would gain diplomatic flexibility and leverage to engage Pyongyang and steer North Korea away from its threatening policies. Given the Bush administration's hard-line posture toward North Korea, this gambit was a remarkable display of Tokyo asserting autonomy vis-à-vis Washington. The move backfired, however, when North Korea announced that eight of the thirteen abductees that Japan was pursuing had died. This shocking news overwhelmed the "positive" North Korean gesture of allowing the remaining five to visit Japan. In May 2004 on a second trip to Pyongyang, Koizumi persuaded North Korea to allow the abductees' surviving family members to go to Japan. Due to the fiercely negative reaction of the Japanese public, however, Koizumi abandoned any further overtures toward Pyongyang.

---

[101] "The United States and Japan: Advancing Toward a Mature Partnership," National Defense University, Institute for National Strategic Studies, INSS Special Report, October 2000.

The failure of the Pyongyang initiative catapulted Abe Shinzo to national political prominence. As deputy chief cabinet secretary, Abe sharply criticized the foreign ministry's initiative, using nationalistic sentiments to increase his popularity. Without the North Korea factor, Abe would not likely have become prime minister so early in his political career, despite his pedigree. The October 2006 North Korean nuclear test played into Abe's hand by demonstrating how threatening North Korea was to Japan. In cooperation with the United States Abe used the test to push Japan toward a full-fledged containment—even squeezing—policy toward Pyongyang. After the U.S. mid-term election when the Democratic Party regained majorities in both houses of Congress, Bush shifted gears, however, and allowed the State Department to work closely with China on a much more flexible approach toward North Korea. This about-face irritated the Abe government and took some of the wind out of Abe's nationalistic sails.

Domestic politics has also complicated Japan's relations with South Korea. As a democratic ally of the United States, the Republic of Korea (ROK) ought to assume a central role in the Japanese government's strategy of cultivating a coalition of Asia-Pacific democracies. Yet Japan has been much less energetic in pursuing relations with South Korea than with Australia or India. Although part of the problem lies with the erratic political style of ROK president Roh Moo Hyun, Japan has also allowed (for domestic political reasons) disputes about past history and Takeshima/Dokdo to give political ammunition to South Koreans hostile toward Japan.[102] This situation unfortunately threatens both to undermine the positive interactions between the Japanese and South Korean defense communities that have developed during the last decade and to exacerbate potential security dilemmas between these two neighbors as Japan expands its regional security role.[103]

Although the rise of China may be Japan's most profound long-term strategic challenge, domestic politics has muddled the implementation of a consistent strategy toward China. After 1989 Japan gradually shifted from a conciliatory strategy toward China (the "friendship diplomacy" paradigm) to a mixed hedging strategy combining cooperative engagement and moderate security balancing.[104] During the Koizumi years, however, Japan appeared willing to risk a downward spiral in relations with China.

---

[102] Sung-jae Choi, "The Politics of the Dokdo Issue," *Journal of East Asian Studies* 5, no. 3 (September/December 2005): 465–94.

[103] Cheol Hee Park, "Japanese Strategic Thinking toward Korea," in *Japanese Strategic Thought toward Asia*, ed. Gilbert Rozman, Kazuhiko Togo, and Joseph P. Ferguson (New York: Palgrave Macmillan, 2007), 183–97.

[104] Mike M. Mochizuki, "Japan's Shifting Strategy toward the Rise of China," *Journal of Strategic Studies* 30, no. 4 (August 2007): 739–76.

This approach was ironic because Koizumi, who was not a doctrinaire nationalist, emphatically declared that China was an economic opportunity, not a threat, for Japan. To outflank former prime minister Hashimoto in the LDP presidential race in spring 2001, Koizumi made a campaign promise to visit the Yasukuni Shrine every year on August 15th. Although avoiding the August 15th date until 2006, Koizumi stubbornly followed through on this promise after becoming prime minister despite strong Chinese protests and the cancellation of high-level bilateral exchanges. China's complaints over Yasukuni only stoked Japanese nationalism. Even while admiring Koizumi's backbone to stand up to China, however, many Japanese were alarmed by the deterioration in Sino-Japanese relations. They were unwilling to abandon positive engagement with China and pursue a stridently confrontational policy, especially when the Chinese market and manufacturing base were playing such a critical role in Japan's economic recovery.

The inevitable election of Abe, who is much more of an ideological nationalist than Koizumi, to the prime ministership alarmed the business community, raising concerns that further worsening of Japan-China relations would place Japanese commercial interests in China at risk. There were strong voices in both the LDP and the DPJ calling on the next prime minister to repair the damage wrought by Koizumi. Abe heeded this advice. Contrary to his strong personal conviction, Abe temporarily defused the shrine issue by assuming an ambiguous stance about Yasukuni pilgrimages and succeeded in "breaking the ice" in bilateral relations by visiting Beijing within two weeks after becoming prime minister. China reciprocated with Premier Wen Jiabao's "ice-melting" visit to Japan and has refrained from aggressively harping on the history issue. The diplomatic atmosphere has improved enough to permit more serious bilateral discussions to address the dispute over conflicting EEZ (Exclusive Economic Zone) claims in the East China Sea.[105]

The rise of China has also prompted Japan to modify its energy strategy. After the oil shocks of the 1970s, Japan engaged in a policy of diversifying energy sources and improving energy conservation and efficiency. Although continuing to depend heavily on Middle East oil, Japan was encouraged by the global oil supply-demand equation to take a more relaxed attitude toward energy security as well as to focus on oil prices and see oil more in terms of being a tradable commodity in a global market. The steep increase in China's demand for energy has, however, caused Japan to be more

[105] James J. Przystup, "Japan-China Relations: New Year, Old Problems, Hope for Wen," *Comparative Connections* 9, no. 1 (April 2007): 117–32.

assertive, even mercantilist. Japan's decision to pursue the Azadegan oil field in Iran despite U.S. misgivings reflected this policy shift.[106]

In the last year, Japan suffered two major blows in its quest for greater energy security. First, as the international community (led by Europe and the United States) moved toward sanctions against Iran because of its nuclear program, Japan decided to reduce its stake in the Azadegan oil field.[107] This retreat along with the striking absence of efforts by Japan to use its good relations with Tehran to influence international policy toward Iran shows both the limits of Japan's proactive diplomacy and the need for Japan to temper its mercantile realism for the sake of security realism. Second, the Russian state gas monopoly Gazprom decided to gain control over Sakhalin-2, the world's largest integrated oil and natural gas project. The Japanese have tried to put the best face on this setback. While some Japanese strategic thinkers contemplate an entente with Russia to balance China's rise, most policymakers view Russia through the lens of energy security. Japan now competes vigorously with China in trying to get Moscow to decide on more favorable pipeline projects. Japan is also pursuing a nuclear energy agreement to tighten energy links with Russia.[108] In large part to counter China's mercantilist efforts to sign oil agreements around the world, Prime Minister Abe downplayed his talk about a values-oriented foreign policy during his spring visit to the Middle East, instead focusing on promoting his country's energy security interests.[109]

METI official Naoko Munakata has commented:

> The essence of Japan's grand strategy is, first, to maintain and strengthen, as necessary, the security alliance with the United States, and second, to capitalize on East Asian economic growth to revitalize its economy and eventually build an East Asian community to secure peace, stability, and prosperity in the region, in the interest of Japan's own economy and security.[110]

Munakata sees these twin goals as compatible. Although she is probably right, Japan over the next decade will face the challenge of keeping these two goals compatible. In other words, how can Japan make its alliance with the

---

[106] Raquel Shaoul, "An Evaluation of Japan's Current Energy Policy in the Context of the Azadegan Oil Field Agreement Signed in 2004," *Japanese Journal of Political Science* 6, no. 3 (2005): 411–37.

[107] Kanako Takahara, "Iran Oil Deal Gone, As Is Headache: Azadegan Setback Eases U.S. Strain, But at China's Gain," *Japan Times*, October 14, 2006.

[108] "Gazprom Gets Sakhalin-2 Control: Setback for Energy Security?" *Japan Times*, December 23, 2006; Hisahiko Okazaki, "Entente To Balance China," *Japan Times*, April 30, 2007; and Reiji Yoshida, "Japan, Russia Agree to Discuss Nuke Pact," *Japan Times*, March 1, 2007.

[109] "Abe Looking For Oil on Middle East Trip," *Japan Times*, April 29, 2007; and "Abe Blows Japan's Trumpet, Cautiously," *The Economist*, May 5, 2007, 53–54.

[110] Munakata, *Transforming East Asia*, 151.

United States robust without undermining Japanese economic strategy in East Asia? As Christopher Hughes and Ellis Krauss warn, by moving closer to the United States, Japan "further distanced it[self] from its Northeast Asian neighbors with whom it is so economically integrated."[111]

Back in the early 1990s Japan sought to harmonize the alliance with the United States and Japanese regional economic strategy by cultivating a regional order that would fuse the United States and East Asia together. Japan did this by promoting trans-Pacific regional dialogues, including the APEC forum and the ASEAN Regional Forum (ARF). After frictions arose with the United States over regional trade liberalization and the 1997 East Asian financial crisis, Japan lost enthusiasm for APEC. Moreover, with the rise of Chinese military power Japan became increasingly pessimistic about ARF as a potential region-wide institution to promote security cooperation.[112] As a consequence, Japan began to delink the economic and security dimensions of its regional policy. On the one hand, to promote regional economic cooperation Japan embraced the ASEAN +3 dialogue and entertained the concept of an East Asian community that excluded the United States. On the other hand, Japan enhanced defense cooperation with the United States in order to counter both a rising China and a threatening North Korea. The pitfall of this dualistic approach was that it gave China the initiative to push for an East Asian summit without U.S. participation and provoked concerns in Washington that Tokyo unwittingly might be facilitating regional institution-building that weakens U.S. influence in the region, with negative security consequences.

Recognizing these risks, Japan has recently recalibrated its regional policy to re-link the economic and security dimensions. Tokyo has pushed for the inclusion of India, Australia, and New Zealand in the East Asia Summit process and proposed a region-wide EPA as a counter to China's influence. During the May 2007 U.S.-Japan Security Consultative Committee, Japan re-embraced APEC by declaring with the United States the strategic objective of "increasing cooperation to strengthen APEC as the pre-eminent regional economic forum, recognizing its crucial role in promoting stability, security, and prosperity in the region."[113] Tokyo has been working with Washington and Canberra to promote trilateral Japan-U.S.-Australia security cooperation. In parallel with U.S. initiatives

---

[111] Christopher W. Hughes and Ellis S. Krauss, "Japan's New Security Agenda," *Survival* 49, no. 2 (Summer 2007): 163.

[112] Takeshi Yuzawa, "Japan's Changing Conception of the ASEAN Regional Forum: From Optimistic Liberal to a Pessimistic Realist Perspective," *Pacific Review* 18, no. 4 (December 2005): 463–97.

[113] "Joint Statement of the Security Consultative Committee Alliance Transformation: Advancing United States-Japan Security and Defense Cooperation," May 1, 2007, http://www.mofa.go.jp/region/n-america/us/security/scc/joint0705.html.

to enhance cooperation with India, Japan has been exploring security collaboration with India as well. To steer ARF in a more favorable direction, Japan succeeded in getting a quadripartite dialogue (involving Japan, the United States, Australia, and India) embedded in the ARF senior-officials meeting.[114]

Implications for the United States

Since embarking on a long political transition in the early 1990s, Japan has implemented significant institutional changes. With Japan's move toward a two-party system, governance depends much more than before on skillful political leadership and the mobilization of public support. The prime minister and the cabinet secretariat have come to wield greater executive power, and the bureaucratic state has been reformed to respond more effectively to security as well as economic challenges. Japan is also more willing and able to contribute both to its alliance with the United States and to various international security activities.

Despite the above changes, however, important continuities remain. Even while incorporating more market-oriented approaches to deal with economic change and social welfare, Japan continues distributive policies that sustain clientelistic politics and developmental practices based on close government-business cooperation. Notwithstanding the emergence of a "new defense establishment" and the movement to revise Article 9 of the constitution, anti-militarism norms and domestic political dynamics are likely to restrain Japan from using military force abroad. As it has done for much of the post-World War II period, Tokyo will also continue to balance between the security imperative of its alliance with the United States and the economic imperative of developing a favorable Asian environment for Japan's long-term commercial interests. During the next five years, as during the 1990s, Japan may experience political volatility due to party realignments that could trigger some jitters in foreign policy; the twin security and economic imperatives will, however, continue to define Japan's grand strategy.

Both the recent revival of Japan's economy and Japan's trend toward greater security and diplomatic activism are generally consistent with U.S. interests. Given the overall bilateral convergence regarding strategic goals and values, the United States benefits from a Japan that is more capable, proactive, and influential in Asia. Because of its preoccupation with the

---

[114] "Japan-U.S. Summit Meeting Summary," June 6, 2007, http://www.mofa.go.jp/region/n-america/us/summit0706.html.

Iraq quagmire, Washington may indeed look to Tokyo for help in Asia to compensate not only for overstretched U.S. capabilities but also for its inability to focus sufficient attention on the region. As the United States relies more on Japan as an ally, however, Washington also needs to be sensitive to the following considerations.

First, although the United States and Japan converge strategically, there are and will continue to be tactical differences that stem from different priorities and perspectives. Tokyo's recent reluctance to embrace fully the Bush administration's shift to a positive engagement policy toward North Korea is just one example. Japan's greater enthusiasm for bringing India into the emerging trilateralism of security cooperation among the United States, Japan, and Australia is another. Moreover, the persistent U.S.-Japan gap in perspectives regarding how to relate market forces to government-business relations yields somewhat dissimilar approaches to regional economic integration. Such tactical differences demand that U.S. policymakers remain attentive and not complacent about the alliance—especially since a sizeable constituency in Japan continues to favor more diplomatic autonomy from the United States.

Second, there is the danger of inflated expectations. Japan may indeed reinterpret the constitution to permit the shooting down of missiles headed for the United States or the protection of U.S. naval vessels operating in the high seas. Japan may even formally revise Article 9 of the constitution. As its recent track record demonstrates, Tokyo is becoming more comfortable with providing logistical rear-area support. Japan remains, however, far from becoming like the United Kingdom regarding joint participation in the use of force in overseas military operations. If expecting Japan to become such an ally, the United States is likely to be disappointed, and this disappointment could undermine political support for the alliance in both countries.

Finally, there is the risk of entrapment.[115] If Japan becomes more assertive or even simply more protective about its territorial claims and economic interests in the East China Sea, the United States might be drawn into a Sino-Japanese conflict where U.S. interests are secondary. Washington therefore has a keen interest in having Japan and China move both toward deeper historical reconciliation and toward reaching a compromise over the EEZ dispute. Due to this risk of entrapment, it would be shortsighted for the United States to attempt to harness anti-Chinese sentiments in Japan for the purpose of making Japan a more robust U.S. ally in order to contain China

---

[115] Hughes and Krauss, "Japan's New Security Agenda," 171–72.

militarily.[116] Moreover, if the issue of history continues to be problematic in Japan's relations with South Korea, then the United States could face a formidable task of managing relations with two key allies in Northeast Asia after Korean reunification. Therefore, just as Japan faces the challenge of balancing its strategic interests with regard to the United States and Asia, the United States confronts a comparable challenge of balancing its strategic interests concerning Japan and the rest of Asia.

---

[116] "Sino-Japanese Rivalry: Implications for U.S. Policy," National Defense University, Institute for National Strategic Studies, INSS Special Report, April 2007.

EXECUTIVE SUMMARY

This chapter explores the post–Cold War grand strategies of South Korea and North Korea with emphasis on the effects of external factors on domestic politics, the impact of domestic politics on grand strategies, and the policy implications for Northeast Asia in general and the U.S. in particular.

MAIN ARGUMENT:
Despite their historical "shrimp among whales" identity, both Koreas have found new opportunities to take strategic initiatives that would not have been possible during the Cold War. South Korea is now a pivotal player in Northeast Asian economics, security, and culture, while North Korea has pursued a survival-centered strategy well despite increasing challenges on both domestic and external fronts. Upcoming leadership changes within both countries and the growing influence of domestic political forces on strategy formation suggest the Koreas' strategic trajectories in the next five years will continue to evolve.

POLICY IMPLICATIONS:
- If the six-party process is allowed to continue, then there may be scope for Seoul's two-legged grand strategy of globalization and engagement with the North to continue.

- If the U.S. continues to view North Korea through a Manichean lens and the sanctions regime continues, then Pyongyang could accelerate its survival tactics or even step up its nuclear program.

- If the U.S. cooperates with Beijing, Seoul, Tokyo, and Moscow to address the issue of common security, then the chances for long-term stability on the Korean Peninsula will be increased.

The Two Koreas: Making Grand Strategy amid Changing Domestic Politics

Samuel S. Kim

This chapter explores the grand strategies of South Korea (Republic of Korea, ROK) and North Korea (Democratic People's Republic of Korea, DPRK) in the post–Cold War era. The chapter poses and addresses three key questions. First, what has been the interplay of external factors (three global transformations—the end of the Cold War, "the third wave" of democratization, and globalization) and the making of grand strategies in Seoul and Pyongyang? Second, what explains the dynamics of Seoul's and Pyongyang's domestic politics from which these grand strategies have emerged? Third, what are the policy implications of the two Koreas' evolving grand strategies for Northeast Asia in general and the United States in particular?

Despite the conventional realist wisdom about the security predicament of the weak in the region of the strong, both Koreas (albeit more for South Korea) have found new opportunities—and challenges—for taking new strategic initiatives and assuming new national roles and identities that would not have been possible during the Cold War years. The synergy of local, regional, and global transformations in the post–Cold War era has now brought to an end the proverbial identity and role as the helpless "shrimp among whales."

South Korea is now a pivotal middle-power player in Northeast Asian politics, economy, and culture, while North Korea has survived despite multiple external shocks and internal woes and has played the nuclear card to enhance its asymmetrical bargaining power. South Korea has made

Samuel S. Kim is Senior Research Scholar at Columbia University's Weatherhead East Asian Institute. He can be reached at <ssk12@columbia.edu>.

several subtle but significant policy shifts. Once fearing allied abandonment, Seoul now fears allied entrapment in the U.S.-ROK alliance. South Korea has also fundamentally shifted its policy toward North Korea, away from confrontation toward functional engagement. Pyongyang's strategy has *faute de mieux* been forced to shift from Kim Il-sung's "magnificent obsession" (i.e., the quest for absolute international legitimation and reunification on his terms) to a security-cum-survival strategy.

Although important in the successful enactment of preferred national roles or identities, capabilities convey little meaning unless they are parsed in the context of the domestic politics that define the parameters within which political leaders mobilize national resources in the pursuit of core national values, interests, and identities. Any assessment of the ultimate significance of the new roles adopted by Seoul and Pyongyang in the conduct of their post–Cold War international relations in Asia in general and Northeast Asia in particular therefore requires an understanding of their grand strategies.

"Grand strategy" is a concept associated with "great powers." As such the term is largely absent in the literature of Korean and small-state foreign-policy studies.[1] Nonetheless both Koreas can be said to have developed grand strategy by dint of both their pivotal geographical location and strategic behavior. Northeast Asia is one of the most important yet most volatile regions of the world, as evidenced by a map of the region and at the geopolitical furor from the latest U.S.-DPRK nuclear standoff. Each of the Big Four (China, Japan, Russia, and the United States) has come to regard the Korean Peninsula as the strategic pivot point of Northeast Asian security and therefore as falling within each country's respective geostrategic ambit.[2]

The grand strategies of both Koreas are closely keyed to and shaped by three overarching national objectives: security, development, and legitimacy. These objectives remain inseparably linked in the concept and conduct of the foreign relations of these two states. Put differently, the grand strategies of both Koreas are designed to enhance security in the broadest sense, embracing political, economic, and identity components. The relationship between domestic and external factors for the formation and enactment of these grand strategies is complex and evolving, but this chapter postulates that domestic factors are more determinative in the formulation of a grand

---

[1] The theory of international politics, as the leading structural realist argues, "is written in terms of the great powers of an era." Kenneth N. Waltz, *Theory of International Politics* (Reading: Addison-Wesley Publishing Co., 1979), 72.

[2] See Nicholas Eberstadt and Richard J. Ellings, "Introduction," in *Korea's Future and the Great Powers*, ed. Nicholas Eberstadt and Richard J. Ellings (Seattle: University of Washington Press, 2001), 1–2.

strategy, whereas external factors take precedence in determining the successful outcomes of grand strategy enactments.

In the post–Cold War era, the international and domestic factors have all worked in Seoul's favor yet in Pyongyang's disfavor, as shown in their contrasting responses to the changing requirements of strategic adaptation. Despite some gaps between promise and performance, semantic variations, and the turbulence of democratic politics, Seoul's globalization and engagement strategies have evolved in sync with South Korea's democratic consolidation process and growing national strength—from Kim Young Sam's *segyehwa* (globalization) drive to Kim Dae Jung's "informationization" strategy to Roh Moo-hyun's free trade agreements (FTA) strategy and, since 1998, from Kim Dae Jung's "Sunshine Policy" to Roh Moo-hyun's "Policy of Peace and Prosperity." Pyongyang's less-than-"grand strategy," on the other hand, has been hobbled by three megacrises: security, economic, and identity. These crises have shifted DPRK strategy from Kim Il oung's magnificent obsession to Kim Jong-il's "military-first" survival strategy. Yet the continuity and stability of grand strategies of the two Koreas remain subject to the changing dynamics of international and domestic politics.

In pursuit of these lines of inquiry, this chapter is organized in three sections that provide an assessment of the two Koreas' grand strategies in the post–Cold War era. The first section briefly appraises the extent to which the three global transformations affect the making of grand strategies in Seoul and Pyongyang. The second section offers an analysis of the changing dynamics of domestic politics from which grand strategies have emerged. The third and concluding section briefly outlines the policy implications of the evolving grand strategies of the two Koreas for Northeast Asia in general and the United States in particular.

The Interplay of External Factors and Grand Strategies

It is essential to step back a little to fully appreciate the momentous changes that have occurred in the grand strategies of the two Koreas in the post–Cold War era. Thanks to its geographical location and size, Korea as a whole has throughout its history experienced more than 900 foreign invasions. For more than a century, and especially between 1894 and 1945, the Korean Peninsula was a battleground that absorbed and reflected wider hegemonic struggles and even sanguinary wars. During this period, Korea as the hermit kingdom was conquered, colonized, liberated, and divided; Korea's stunted national identity as a shrimp among whales has evolved through a three-stage mutation process: from Chosun (Yi) Korea (1392–1910), Colonial Korea (1910–45), and then Divided Korea (1945–present).

In mid-August of 1945 Korea was simultaneously liberated and divided into two separate political entities, resulting in the creation of two separate systems, two incomplete nation-states, and two distinct identities. Such partial states and divided nations are primed for zero-sum, often violent politics of national-identity mobilization intended to maximize exclusive security and legitimacy.

Under the sponsorship of competing superpowers, the divided Korean Peninsula saw the beginnings of a politics of competitive legitimation and delegitimation. The divergent paths of the two Koreas in terms of state-making, identity, and legitimacy initiated a crisis that affected both domestic and international politics during the Cold War. The elements of this crisis have remained fairly consistent in both Koreas: leadership and succession have created a legitimation challenge, the perceived or actual threat from each other has created a national identity challenge, and the dilemmas of allied entrapment or abandonment have created a security challenge.[3]

Like conjoined twins attached at the hip, each half of Korea has operated with the knowledge that its actions and national identity are reflected in its ideologically opposed doppelganger. The two Koreas thus have no choice but to accommodate the other as an alter ego in the construction or reconstruction of a one-nation identity. Because the identity differences between the two Koreas are too deeply rooted to be simply merged into a common one-nation identity, an identity reconciliation is necessary for peace on the Korean Peninsula.[4]

During the long Cold War years, the grand strategies of the two Koreas were anchored in mutually antagonistic identities centered on alliance maintenance for security, development, and legitimacy. The DPRK's main security concern was less to balance against or bandwagon with the United States and more to maximize military and economic aid from both Moscow and Beijing. Ironically, it was the Sino-Soviet conflict, not the superpower rivalry, that enhanced "the power of the weak." Pyongyang's security behavior demonstrated a remarkable unilateral balancing strategy in its relations with Moscow and Beijing. If necessary, North Korea would take sides on particular issues while attempting to extract maximum payoffs in economic, technical, and military aid without clearly aligning with one country. To the South, Seoul's abiding worries had more to do with allied abandonment than allied entrapment.

---

[3] Samuel S. Kim, *The Two Koreas and the Great Powers* (New York: Cambridge University Press, 2006), 28.

[4] Ronald Bleiker, *Divided Korea: Toward a Culture of Reconciliation* (Minneapolis: University of Minnesota Press, 2005), xliii.

Against this backdrop, three global transformations—the end of the Cold War, "the third wave" of democratization, and globalization—have transformed the context and the conditions under which the two Koreas' grand strategies could be formulated in their respective domestic politics. Without the overarching structure of superpower conflict, local and regional dynamics become ever more salient, and the two Koreas have been experiencing greater latitude in shaping their grand strategies. All the same, the foreign policies of most states, including South Korea, have become increasingly mired in turbulent domestic politics. Foreign-policy decisionmakers are no longer constrained by the structure of the international system as they choose competing strategies from a wide and varied menu of feasible and desirable policy options.

Domestic Politics and Grand Strategy

Differences in internal political systems and resulting domestic politics have a greater impact than the structure of the international system on how state decisionmakers define threats and vulnerabilities.[5] In the post–Cold War world, the foreign policies of most states have become increasingly disoriented, as domestic special interest groups intervene more aggressively than ever in foreign policy. Consider the extent to which changes of political leadership amid turbulent domestic politics in South Korea (1998) and the United States (2001) have brought about remarkable role reversals in strategic or policy terms, with the unintended consequences of widening and deepening the alliance chasm.

South Korea

The South Korean political system. The Republic of Korea, one of the most remarkable and influential among third-wave democracies, began transiting to democracy in late 1987 and five years later elected the first civilian leader in three decades, Kim Young Sam. South Korea reached another milestone in its democratization process by gaining entry into the Organization for Economic Co-operation and Development (OECD) in 1996. This formerly war-ravaged country thus claimed a new identity as "an East Asian model of prosperity and democracy."[6] Although the 1997 Asian financial crisis brought this brief golden age to an end, another milestone was reached when South Korea became the first third-wave democracy

---

[5] Barry Buzan, "Security, the State, the 'New World Order,' and Beyond," in *On Security*, ed. Ronnie D. Lipschutz (New York: Columbia University Press, 1998), 187–89.

[6] "The Upheaval in South Korea," *New York Times*, December 26, 1995, A14.

in East Asia to experience a peaceful transfer of power to an opposition party.[7]

Under Kim Young Sam, democratic consolidation (the delegitimation of military authoritarianism) made great strides, as is evident in two cases of anti-corruption. First, *Hanahoi* ("One-Mind Club"), a secret kingmaking military clique, was dismantled. Second, in August 1996 Chun Doo Hwan and Roh Tae Woo, both former presidents, were prosecuted and imprisoned on charges of military mutiny, national sabotage, and political corruption. The conviction of the former presidents, which did not trigger a military backlash, constitutes one of the most far-reaching efforts at retroactive accountability in any third-wave democracy. These developments reveal a mutual evolution of security thinking and democratic consolidation in South Korea.[8] While the reduction of military involvement in politics has enhanced democratization, so has democratization changed the way South Koreans think about security, particularly under the administrations of Kim Dae Jung and Roh Moo-hyun. For example, in the South Korean security logic, self-help security has been replaced by the notion of mutual security, and security multilateralism has supplanted bilateralism.

Although South Korea experienced a number of political reforms during its first two decades of democracy, more far-reaching normative, institutional, and behavioral transformations are still required before a mature, fully consolidated liberal democracy is formed. Lingering parochial ties built on particularistic provincial identities still hinder meaningful national debate on national and global policy issues. The deeply embedded politics of fragmentation, as reflected in the dysfunctional party system, remains foremost among South Korea's impediments to democratic consolidation. As a result, political parties play no role in the making of grand strategy. This geographical, social, cultural, and political fragmentation is characterized by fratricidal provincial factionalism, infighting between and among political parties, labor-management conflict, and divides between the right- and left-wing ideologies. As such South Korea has yet to be unified within its own borders.

The rise of civil society and the anti-American movement. In democratic development the active participation of civil society typically diminishes, but in South Korea civil society groups have played an important role in the democratic consolidation process. Tellingly, South Korea's democratic

---

[7] For further discussion, see Samuel S. Kim, ed., *Korea's Democratization* (New York: Cambridge University Press, 2003).

[8] Victor Cha, "Security and Democracy in South Korean Development," in *Korea's Democratization*, ed. Samuel S. Kim (New York: Cambridge University Press, 2003), 201–19.

consolidation process developed in tandem with the "anti-American" movement.

South Korea's seemingly atavistic anti-American movement experienced a striking metamorphosis in the post-transition period. Unlike the movement of the early 1980s, the new anti-American movement of the late 1990s and early 2000s found a new identity that focused on the advancement of human rights, environmental protection, and the rule of law. The movement's broad agenda allowed disparate groups and interests to share information, coordinate political action, and mobilize resources in order to increase domestic and international public impact. The movement's overall aim has been both to influence Korean and U.S. government policies and to deal with issues of common concern that are typically absent from bilateral U.S.-ROK discussions, including environmental safety, land usage, and violence against women in the *kijich'on* (U.S. military camptowns).[9]

The rise of Korean civil society and the anti-American movement have served to open new pathways into the domain of foreign and security policy; this area of policymaking has tended to be the least democratic domain in South Korean politics, where participation having been actively suppressed by the national security managers of the Park and Chun governments. Owing to initiatives of the Kim Young Sam administration in the early 1990s and then by the Kim Dae Jung and Roh Moo-hyun governments, however, national security and foreign policy has been diversified and democratized, and political space for open debate and criticism of Korea's foreign and security relations (including the U.S.-ROK alliance) has been opened. Citizen activists who express anti-American opinions no longer fear jailing or harassment.

In 2002 more than one hundred South Korean civic organizations came together in a massive protest against the "unequal" Status of Forces Agreement (SOFA), a symbol of U.S.-ROK relations. Nationwide demonstrations broke out in response to the acquittal of two U.S. soldiers accused of killing two Korean teenagers in a June 2002 traffic accident. Additionally, just before the presidential election of December 2002 more than 300,000 Koreans gathered throughout the country in protest, singing and holding votive candles. The protesters announced a "day of the restoration of national sovereignty," demanding a fair and equal partnership between Korea and the United States. Roh Moo-hyun's victory in that election was due in part to his ability to capitalize on anti-U.S. sentiment. At that time, Roh's election was linked directly to the changing socio-cultural landscape in South Korea.

---

[9] Katharine H. S. Moon, "Korean Nationalism, Anti-Americanism, and Democratic Consolidation," in Kim, *Korea's Democratization*, 135–58.

Owning to an accumulation and combination of external strategic developments and domestic political changes in the ROK and the United States, the U.S.-ROK alliance is in greater danger of unraveling in the early 21st century than in the past two decades. As Hahm Chaibong writes, "the most important reason for the deterioration of the alliance is the sea change in South Korea's domestic politics that has taken place during the past 10 years, one that saw the rise of the 'progressives,' supported by a new generation with views of North Korea and the U.S.-South Korean alliance that are radically different from the view espoused by the older generation."[10] With the coming of a conservative Bush administration in 2001, differences—of worldview, strategic doctrine, and grand strategy—between the two countries have been "highlighted and intensified by the personal styles of the current U.S. and ROK heads of state," even as each country is widely and deeply polarized internally.[11]

Quite doubtful, however, is whether this movement can truly be considered anti-Americanism. The Pew Global Attitude Project surveys have shown that this movement is part of a more widespread and universal phenomenon of distaste for the new U.S. grand strategy of unilateral triumphalism than a broader opposition to Americans or American society."[12] Such sentiments are not frozen in time but are in flux and susceptible to shifts depending on political changes within either Seoul or Washington.

Despite the pressures from civil society, the United States remains a key economic partner for South Korea—especially in the sectors that are important for Korea's economic growth and development—and Seoul is limited in the degree to which it can back off from the U.S.-ROK alliance. Younger South Koreans consistently told pollsters their dislike of U.S. foreign policy, "even as most of them acknowledged appreciating aspects of U.S. society and culture."[13] Many of these young Koreans may be found studying in the United States. According to U.S. Immigration and Customs Enforcement figures, South Korea has nearly 100,000 students in the United States and ranks first in the number of foreign students studying in the United States in the past two years (2005–06).[14]

---

[10] Hahm Chaibong, "South Korea's Progressives and the U.S.-ROK Alliance," *Joint U.S.-Korea Academic Studies*, vol. 17 (2007): 188–89.

[11] See David Straub, "U.S. and ROK Strategic Doctrines and the U.S.-ROK Alliance," *Joint U.S.-Korea Academic Studies*, vol. 17 (2007): 166–67.

[12] Bruce Cumings, "Anti-Americanism in the Republic of Korea," *Joint U.S.-Korea Academic Studies*, vol. 14 (2004): 205–29.

[13] Straub, "U.S. and ROK Strategic Doctrines and the U.S.-ROK Alliance," 182.

[14] "Koreans Make Up Largest Foreign Student Presence in U.S.," *Hankyoreh*, April 6, 2007, http://english.hani.co.kr/arti/english_edition/e_national/201272.html.

South Korea's evolving globalization strategy. Since late 1994 grand strategy and the globalization drive have developed in tandem to such an extent that the globalization strategy is and becomes grand strategy. There is no illusion that Korea will ever become a great power, and this may explain why the term grand strategy is absent from Seoul's foreign policy pronouncements and presidential speeches.

What then is this globalization strategy? Not until November 17, 1994 did President Kim Young Sam formally outline his own vision for globalization strategy. Then throughout 1995 and 1996 a "globalization fever" swept the country: no other buzzword was more commonly used—and misused—among politicians, policymakers, business entrepreneurs, academicians, and journalists. Still, Kim Young Sam's globalization drive was primarily a cheap and easy way of projecting a new Korean national identity as a newly industrialized and democratized country deserving membership in the OECD and the United Nations Security Council.

President Kim Young Sam's *segyehwa* drive began with a bang but ended, owing to the Asian financial crisis that swept across East Asia in the latter half of 1997, with a whimper. President Kim Dae Jung continued the globalization drive with greater vigor, however, even as the new administration disassembled the Presidential Segyehwa Promotion Commission (PSPC) set up by the previous administration.

In his 1998 inaugural address President Kim Dae Jung spelled out a three-principle Sunshine Policy toward the North as well as envisioning the new millennium as an era of "informationization" in which "intangible knowledge and information will be the driving power for economic development"; hence the globalization of Korean culture and Korean diplomacy "will center around the economy and culture."[15] On January 3, 2000 President Kim pronounced a new millennium vision: "The new century will be categorized as a period of globalization, digitalization and time management. Whether Korea becomes a first- or third-rate country will be dependent, to a large extent, on whether Koreans are ready to adapt to changes." The vision statement includes several overarching goals, such as making Korea a top-ten information and knowledge superpower, developing the next-generation Internet and the information superhighway by 2005, and bridging the "digital divide" through productive welfare and balanced regional development.[16] For South Korea, there is no easy escape from globalization that would not lead to major economic disaster. The strategy for South Korea is not a choice between exit and embracement

---

[15] For an English text of the inaugural speech, see *Korea Herald*, February 26, 1998.

[16] See World Bank East Asia and the Pacific Region, "Republic of Korea: Transition to a Knowledge-Based Economy," World Bank, Report No. 20346-KO, June 29, 2000, i–ii.

but rather a constant adaptation to the logic of globalization dynamics and quickening economic, cultural, and social product cycles. President Kim Dae Jung repeatedly stressed in his proactive summit diplomacy the importance of culture, knowledge, and information in Korea's globalization-cum-grand-strategy.

In his inaugural address on February 25, 2003 President Roh Moo-hyun laid out what has come to be known as the "Policy of Peace and Prosperity." The president's address centered around three policy goals: participatory democracy, balanced development of society, and the opening of a new era for a peaceful and prosperous Northeast Asia.[17] Roh sees Northeast Asia ready for a new era: "In this new age, our future can no longer be confined to the Korean Peninsula. The Age of Northeast Asia is fast approaching. Northeast Asia, which used to be on the periphery of the modern world, is now emerging as a new source of energy in the global economy." Roh further noted that South Korea "is being equipped with all the basic requirements necessary to lead the Age of Northeast Asia in the 21st century. The country is well poised to emerge as an international logistics and financial hub in Northeast Asia."[18] Making a contrast with divisions of the past, Roh called for South Koreans both to embrace the growing regionalism in Northeast Asia and to play a leading role in defining the country as no longer being a shrimp caught between whales.

President Roh's willingness to open South Korea to the global economy and culture is, however, most visible in his tenacious pursuit of FTAs. These agreements are a key component of his grand strategic plans but are also a nightmare scenario for globalization opponents and his core group of supporters in the Uri Party. After experimenting with an FTA with a minor trade partner (Chile), the Roh administration signed a more important agreement with Singapore. Emboldened by its experience, the administration successfully concluded an FTA with the United States (KORUSFTA) on April 2, 2007 after a long series of often contentious and grueling negotiations lasting more than ten months.

Faced with the most massive anti-globalization opposition and the most serious challenge to his political leadership, President Roh in a television address to the nation offered the following justifications: (1) that the KORUSFTA negotiations were first proposed and initiated by the Korean government, as if to dispel the prevalent perception that this

---

[17] Roh Moo-hyun, "History, Nationalism and Community," *Global Asia* 1, no. 2 (Spring 2007): 10–13.

[18] For an English text of President Roh's February 25, 2003 inaugural address, see "Address by President Roh Moo-hyun at the 16th Inaugural Ceremony: A New Takeoff Toward an Age of Peace and Prosperity," Korean Office of the President website, http://english.president.go.kr/cwd/en/archive/archive_list.php?m_def=2&ss_def=1&meta_id=en_speeches.

was an imposition of the United States; (2) that the Korean government "sat down at the negotiating table with the insightful perspective of a big businessman looking ahead to the future of the economy as well as to the changes in the global markets, including China, so that it would not remain as a near-sighted merchant bent on only immediate interests"; (3) that the KORUSFTA is "not a matter of politics or ideology," and as such it should not be handled "with nationalistic emotions or political calculations"; and (4) that this was a necessary step toward developing Korea into "an advanced nation," though "the stark reality of today's world" is that "advanced status cannot be attained just by working hard."[19]

There were multiple stimuli for presidential initiative and intervention in the KORUSFTA negotiations. As a nation poor in natural resources, South Korea has few options other than to export its manufactured goods and import its necessities. Indeed, South Korea's economic advancement has paralleled the liberalization of international trade since Park Chung Hee launched an export-oriented developmental strategy in the early 1960s. If ratified by U.S. Congress and ROK National Assembly, the recently concluded KORUSFTA will produce winners and losers, but gains will be far greater than losses for a nation that depends on external trade for its survival.

Far from becoming a regional hub in Northeast Asia, South Korea finds itself caught between relentless twin pressures from China and Japan. The KORUSFTA is believed to be the only option that could resolve this predicament. Concerns about China's rapid economic rise, rather than worries about Japan, may have been what prompted the Roh government to initiate a bilateral FTA deal with the United States. While the total value of Korea's trade with the United States doubled from 1990 to 2006, the U.S. share of Korea's exports declined from 40% in the late 1980s to 14.5% in 2005, while China's share of South Korea's foreign trade increased from virtually zero in the late 1970s to about 22% in 2005. Having not only become a source of Korea's export-driven growth, China is conversely also rapidly becoming a competitor, chipping away at Seoul's export market share in third countries, especially in the United States and Japan.[20] Naturally, Korea seeks easier access to the U.S. market, the largest and the most sophisticated in the world. Paradoxically, the KORUSFTA would give a substantial boost to Roh's aspiration to make Korea the economic hub in Northeast Asia, with

---

[19] For an English text of President Roh's April 2, 2007 speech, see "Address to the Nation by President Roh Moo-hyun on the Successful Conclusion of the KORUS FTA Negotiations," Korean Office of the President website, http://english.president.go.kr/cwd/en/archive/archive_list.php?m_def=2&ss_def=1&meta_id=en_speeches.

[20] Kim, *The Two Koreas and the Great Powers*, 80–81.

China, Japan, and the European Union (EU) rushing to negotiate an FTA with South Korea.

The ROK's globalization-cum-grand-strategy is based on and proceeds from the three irreducible principles: security, development, and legitimacy. The underlying logic of this evolving globalization strategy is not to make Korea a "great power" but to engage in an intense status drive for developing Korea into "an advanced world nation." Such a status drive requires a long and stable peace on the Korean Peninsula. Although the transformation of South Korea's grand strategy in the post–Cold War era was an outgrowth of the ongoing interaction of domestic and external factors, in the end political leadership was the most significant factor in shaping Korea's grand strategy. In substantive policy terms, the momentous change in political leadership in late 1997 was equivalent to "regime change" in South Korean intermestic politics.

Engagement with the North: From the Sunshine Policy to Peace and Prosperity. With the coming of the Kim Dae Jung administration, Seoul's grand strategy became inextricably linked to the Sunshine Policy of engagement toward North Korea. The 2000 Inter-Korean Summit would not have been possible without the "regime change" in South Korea's domestic politics that occurred in late 1997. With President Kim Dae Jung's initiation of the Sunshine Policy in his inaugural address in February 1998 and his major policy speech in Berlin (known as the Berlin Declaration) in March 2000, the seemingly unthinkable happened in June 2000: South Korean President Kim Dae Jung and North Korean Chairman Kim Jong-il embraced each other at an inter-Korean summit in Pyongyang, symbolically signaling their acceptance of each other's legitimacy. Most remarkably, unlike all previous inter-Korean dialogues, this summit was initiated and executed solely by the Koreans. President Kim Dae Jung initiated a new grand strategy of opening to North Korea—the Sunshine Policy—with a pledge not to undermine or absorb the DPRK. The Sunshine Policy was based in part on explicit recognition of the fact that undermining the DPRK is not a viable policy option because of the disorder and destruction that would follow from a Northern collapse via external explosion or internal implosion. The Sunshine Policy aimed to create "a set of interdependencies that in the long run would discourage North Korea from external aggression and perhaps even promote the internal transformation of the regime."[21] Speaking to one of the remaining key fears in Pyongyang, President Kim Dae Jung's repeated pledges and pronouncements that the South has no intention "to undermine or absorb North Korea" stand out as one of the

---

[21] Marcus Noland, *Avoiding the Apocalypse: The Future of the Two Koreas* (Washington, D.C.: Institute for International Economics, 2000), 113.

most significant steps toward accepting identity difference as an integral part of the peace process.

Indeed, the summit seemed to have brought the two Koreas down from their respective hegemonic-unification visions to a place where peaceful coexistence of two separate states was possible. In the wake of the summit Pyongyang proclaimed publicly for the first time that "the issue of unifying the differing systems in the north and the south as one may be left to posterity to settle slowly in the future."[22] All the same, South Koreans have been increasingly wary of a German-style unification by absorption and have been more supportive of engaged interaction with North Korea. Although Kim Dae Jung proclaimed frequently that he did not expect Korean unification within his lifetime, the gradual and functional pathway to a peaceful unification of Korea seems more apparent today than ever.

With Roh Moo-hyun as president, the Sunshine Policy has shifted and mutated into the Policy of Peace and Prosperity—a shift also away from fear of allied abandonment toward fear of allied entrapment. While no longer fearing abandonment of its own security interests in Washington's pursuit of a separate deal with Pyongyang, Seoul's main security dilemma has been centered on entrapment by a U.S. strategy that could either suck South Korea into an escalated military conflict or a repetition of the great power rivalry of the late nineteenth century that resulted in Korea's colonization. In March 2005 President Roh publicly declared, "we will not be embroiled in any conflict in Northeast Asia against our will. This is an absolutely firm principle we cannot yield under any circumstances."[23] During the same month, Roh warned that Seoul may not side with the United States and Japan against China and North Korea.[24] While criticizing the traditional idea that Seoul should seek triangular security cooperation with Washington and Tokyo, President Roh asserted that, in the interests of a lasting peace on the Korean Peninsula and in Northeast Asia, South Korea needs not to contain China but to include it in a multiparty security regime.[25]

Another indication of a major shift in South Korea's grand strategy is the fact that the Roh government's position on the North Korean nuclear crisis is far closer to that of China than that of the United States. Roh's two-

[22] "Rwonpangche nun kachang hyongsil chok'iko haprichok'in chokuk tong'il pangto" [A Confederal System is the Most Practical and Rational Way for Fatherland Unification], Rodong Sinmun, June 25, 2000, 6; emphasis added.

[23] For an English text of President Roh's March 8, 2005 speech, see "Address at the 53rd Commencement and Commissioning Ceremony of the Korea Air Force Academy," Korean Office of the President website, http://english.president.go.kr/cwd/en/archive/archive_list.php?m_def=2&ss_def=1&meta_id=en_speeches.

[24] "Roh Hints at New East Asian Order," Chosun Ilbo, March 22, 2005.

[25] Ryu Jin, "Roh Seeks N-E Asian Security Regime," Korea Times, October 21, 2005.

legged grand strategy contains the organic linkage and interdependence of peace and prosperity. President Roh responded warmly to the breakthrough of February 13, 2007—"Initial Actions for the Implementation of the [September 13, 2005] Joint Statement"—and called for an agreement between the two Koreas for the creation of a permanent peace regime. Referring to a low credit rating that South Korea receives owing to security problems on the Korean Peninsula, Roh said that "the successful settlement of negotiations between South and North Korea on lasting peace as well as the nuclear problem would eliminate non-economic hurdles to South Korea's ascent to the top of the global credit rating ladder."[26]

In short, the principal source or determinant of South Korea's grand strategy is presidential leadership. The fundamental shift in Seoul's grand strategy—especially its strategy of functional engagement and cooperation with Pyongyang—is directly associated with the progressive Kim Dae Jung administration in early 1998 and another progressive administration, that of Roh Moo-hyun, in early 2003.[27] The other domestic factors—such as proactive civil society, party politics, public opinions, ideological cleavage or polarization, and external strategic changes—also can transform the context and conditions of domestic politics but cannot play the determinative role in the making of grand strategy.

North Korea

The North Korean system. The North Korean system cannot be understood without identifying and examining the characteristic features of the system as a whole and analyzing the interactive processes among its component units and overall system effects and outcomes. A serviceable answer to the question "What is North Korea?" requires an examination of an identity that the self attempts to secure but others do not bestow, as well as an identity that others attempt to bestow but the self does not appropriate. The official identity, the DPRK, stands out as a misnomer. North Korea is no longer, if it ever was, a people's government, much less a republican or democratic one. Other solipsistic terms—such as "our style socialism" (*urisik sahoe chuui*), "ideological superpower" (*sasang taeguk*), and "great power" (*kangsong taeguk*)—have become the more

---

[26] Cited in Donald G. Gross, "U.S.-Korea Relations: Unexpected Progress on All Fronts," *Comparative Connections* 9, no. 1 (April 2007): 46.

[27] In a similar vein, Robert Litwak sharply argued that "regime intention" (leadership intention) rather than regime type is the more accurate indicator of a country's decision to go nuclear. See Robert Litwak, "Non-Proliferation and the Dilemma of Regime Change," *Survival* 45, no. 4 (Winter 2003–04): 11.

recent nomenclatures in projecting a self-defined national role conception in the post–Cold War world.

Identity terms and badges bestowed by others have multiplied over the years, such as "monocracy," "totalitarian," "mono-organizational," "guerrilla dynasty," "rogue," "mendicant," "pariah," "autistic," "erratic," "terrorist," "reclusive," and, most frequently, "Stalinist." There is still a sense in which the North Korean system is both more than and less than Stalinist. As the first-ever socialist dynastic political system, North Korea may be better seen as a hybrid of modern Stalinism and traditional Korean authoritarianism. Hwang Jang Yop, chief architect of *juche* ideology and the highest ranking official yet to defect from North Korea, has stated that "the confrontation between North and South Korea is not a confrontation between socialism and capitalism but that of capitalism and feudalism."[28] The North Korean state is neo-traditionalist; Charles K. Armstrong describes North Korea as "the most successful example of the indigenization of Stalinism in the communist world." Armstrong argues, however, that neotraditional features have become progressively more pronounced since the dissolution of the Soviet Union.[29]

Most striking is the fact that any of the above mentioned identity terms and adjectives can be as easily applied to the North Korean state, regime, or system. This shows that North Korea has a relatively simple mono-organizational system with a low degree of institutionalization, where the boundaries among state, system, and regime have become blurred and overlapping—if not completely erased. The North Korean state is and becomes synonymous with the North Korean system as a whole. As if to render credence to Wada's characterization of North Korea as a "guerrilla-band state" (*yugekitai kokka*),[30] the Korean People's Army (KPA) has been proclaimed in recent years to be synonymous with the people, the state, and the party.[31]

The most salient feature of the North Korean system, however, is the deified role of the supreme leader, which brought about the supreme leader (*suryong*) system. Hwang Jang Yop characterizes the North Korean system

[28] Hwang's letter dated January 3, 1997, more than a month before actual defection, was passed on to Mr. X of South Korea and published in *Chosun Ilbo* on February 13, 1997.

[29] Charles Armstrong, "The Nature, Origins, and Development of the North Korean State," in *The North Korean System in the Post-Cold War Era*, ed. Samuel S. Kim (New York: Palgrave, 2001), 39–64.

[30] Wada Haruki, *Kita Chosen: yugekitai kokka no genzai* [North Korea: The Guerrilla-Band State's Current Situation] (Tokyo: Iwanami Shoten, 1998).

[31] *Rodong sinmun*, April 25, 1997, 4.

as "supreme leader absolutism" (*suryong choltae chuui*).[32] In the *suryong* system, the supreme ruler is greater than the state, as the latter depends on the former.[33]

In an age of expanding democratization, North Korea indeed displays all the trappings of fundamentalist theocracy. The leadership cult in the North Korean system is different from the cults of Mao or Stalin, surpassing them not only in persistence, intensity, and grandiosity but also in the stress on the "blood vein for the continuation of the revolution" from generation to generation. North Korea has even adopted its own so-called *juche* dynastic calendar, dating from the year of Kim Il-sung's birth (1912).

The new constitution was adopted by the first session of the tenth Supreme People's Assembly (SPA) on September 5, 1998. Unlike the 1972 socialist constitution, the newer version has a preamble that codifies the signature identity of the DPRK as a theocratic Kim Il-sung state: Kim Il-sung, "the founder of the DPRK and the socialist Korea," is "the sun of the nation" and "the eternal President of the Republic." The DPRK Socialist Constitution is the Kim Il-sung constitution.[34] Although nominally proposed by Kim Yong Nam (president of the Presidium of the SPA), the reelection of Kim Jong-il as chairman of the National Defense Commission (NDC) was legitimized by the father, as the son's "election" was "initiated and recommended by the great Kim Il-sung, the eternal leader of the Korean people in his lifetime."[35] The first session of the tenth SPA was said to be "an epochal occasion in firmly defending and exalting the *nature of our republic as the state of President Kim Il-sung*."[36]

To a significant extent the new Kim Il-sung constitution formalized the progressive shift of power—from the state to the party to the military—that had already taken place since the early 1990s. The Kim Il-sung constitution makes Kim Jong-il the head of state in practice (if not in theory) by making him the chairman of the NDC, the nerve center of a crisis-management garrison state. The SPA is still "the highest organ of State power in the DPRK" (Article 87) and the NDC is still "accountable to the SPA" (Article 105). Yet the ink was hardly dry before the new constitution was nullified by SPA Presidium President Kim Yong Nam, who declared: "The NDC

---

[32] Hwang Jang Yop, *Nanun yoksaui chili rul poattda* [I Have Witnessed Historical Truth] (Seoul: Hanul, 1999), 373.

[33] Dae-Sook Suh, "New Political Leadership," in Kim, *The North Korean System*, 65–86.

[34] For the text of the new Kim Il Sung Constitution, see *2004 Pukhan kaeyo* [North Korea Synopsis 2004] (Seoul: Ministry of Unification, December 2003), 479–80 (preamble), 479–503.

[35] "Kim Jong Il's election as NDC Chairman proposed," Korean Central News Agency (KCNA), September 5, 1998, http://www.kcna.co.jp/item/1998/9809/news09/05.htm.

[36] Ibid; and 2004 *Pukhan kaeyo*, 479–80.

chairmanship is the highest post of the state" and the chairman controls all of the political, military, and economic capabilities of the republic.[37] Even the Minister of National Defense is appointed or removed by the chairman of the NDC (Kim Jong-il), not by the premier.

The Kim Il-sung constitution makes some adjustments to the socialist command economy in three ways. First, the constitution acknowledges the range of "social cooperative organizations" that are allowed to possess such property as land, agricultural machinery, ships, and medium- to small-sized factories and enterprises (Article 22). Second, the constitution encourages "institutions, enterprises or associations" to establish and operate "equity and contractual joint-venture enterprises with corporations or individuals of foreign countries within a special economic zone" (Article 37). Third, the constitution grants citizens freedom to reside in and travel to any place (Article 75). Yet again these adjustments were immediately "amended" by reaffirming *juche* as the official ideology and backbone of the command economy. Reform and opening from the lips of imperialists were said to be nothing more than "honey-coated poison," and therefore the DPRK promised: "We will set ourselves against all attempts to induce us to join an 'integrated' world. We have nothing to 'reform' and 'open.'"[38] In sum, the defining characteristics of the North Korean system are the *suryong* system, *juche* ideology, the socialist command economy, and (more recently) the primacy of the NDC as the highest state organ and the nerve center of decisionmaking.

North Korean politics. These characteristic features constitute and function as the primary parameters of the possible and permissible for domestic politics in the DPRK. Process-level change is more frequent and more extensive than system-level change, just as foreign policy is more changeable than domestic policy.

The principle of "military-first politics" (*songun chongch'i*) holds that North Korea requires a military government capable of insuring system maintenance and survival, and this principle stands at the core of North Korean politics. The rapid rise of this approach reveals that the post–Kim Il-sung regime has been functioning on a crisis-management basis.[39] Despite requirements in the party charter (Article 21), the communist party-state

---

[37] *Rodong Sinmun*, September 6, 1998, 4.

[38] "Rodong Sinmun and Kunroja Call for Maintaining Independent National Economic Construction Line," KCNA, September 17, 1998, http://www.kcna.co.jp/index-e.htm.

[39] See, for example, Kim Jong-il's December 7, 1996 speech given at a secret meeting of party officials at Kim Il-sung University, "1996 nyon 12 wol Kim Il Sung Chonghap Taehak changrip 50 tol kinyom Kim Chong Il ui yonsolmun" [A Text of Kim Jong-il's Speech at the 50th Anniversary of the Foundation of the Kim Il-sung University, December 1996], *Wolgan Chosun*, April 1997, 306–17, especially 309.

has not convened its party congress since the Sixth Congress of the Korean Workers' Party (KWP) in 1980.[40] Nor have the Central Committee and the Politburo reportedly met, even though the party charter states that "the party Central Committee shall convene a plenary meeting of its own at least once every six months" (Article 24).[41] The DPRK political system no longer functions as a set of parallel vertical institutions (army, party, and state), but as a power system that radiates outward from Kim Jong-il as the "core" (*haeksim*). Political position in this power system depends on informal and often familial ties with the Great Leader.[42] Even after the Kim Il-sung Constitution of September 1998, which privileged the NDC and worked to formalize the organization of the government, the KWP remains last among the three realms of power in the political system.

The KWP seems to have taken on a role as an "ideological cheerleader" with the purpose of propagating and legitimizing the new principle of military-first politics. KWP statements reflect this role: "the military is the party, the people, and the nation," "our party's policy of giving priority to [the] army is invincible," and this is "the perfect mode of politics in our times." The military-first policy will prevent a collapse of the socialist system, we are told, even if the people are not prepared politically and ideologically: "This is a serious lesson drawn from the history of socialist politics in the twentieth century."[43]

In this ad hoc, vertical, secretive, and personalized style of politics, Kim Jong-il leads behind closed doors by formulating and developing policy through informal connections and channels rather than through the formal modes of party and government. It is believed that Kim Jong-il, however, uses both formal and informal means of maintaining his overall control of the system.[44] According to Ken Gause, Kim Jong-il's leadership style and the decisionmaking process do not fit the classical totalitarian (Stalinist) model. Kim Jong-il's North Korea has adopted "a hub-and-spoke approach"

---

[40] For the text of the Charter of the Korean Workers' Party (KWP), see *2004 Pukhan kaeyo* 504–29, especially 516 (Article 21) that stipulates that a Party Congress shall be held at least once every five years.

[41] See *2004 Pukhan kaeyo*, 517. According to Hwang Jang Yop, there has never been any official meeting or conference of any kind since Kim Il-sung died in mid-1994, even as Kim Jong-il carried out everything in secret: "He does everything secretly, behind closed doors, together with a handful of his closest advisers." See Olaf Jahn, "North Korea: Running against History," *Far Eastern Economic Review* (October 15, 1998): 30.

[42] See Samuel S. Kim, "North Korean Informal Politics," in *Informal Politics in East Asia*, ed. Lowell Dittmer, Haruhiro Fukui, and Peter N. S. Lee (New York: Cambridge University Press, 2000), 237–68.

[43] "WPK's Policy of Giving Priority to Army Is Invincible," KCNA, June 16, 1999, available on the KCNA website, http://www.kcna.co.jp/index-e.htm.

[44] *Tong-A Ilbo* (Seoul), February 14, 1996, 5.

to regime maintenance with the decisionmaking process including a system of checks and balances.[45]

The North Korean system of theocratic politics has experienced a rapid growth of incongruence in all four subsystems—political, ideological, economic, and cultural—that has accelerated the breakdown of system symmetry and expanded system dissonance. Alongside adverse external events, these trends have engendered a vicious cycle: rising duality in each subsystem has yielded increasing system incongruence, leading in turn to greater breakdown of symmetry between ideological and economic subsystems.[46] The demise of two overarching system goals—the promise of unification on North Korean terms and the promise of a socialist paradise—serves as evidence of this system incongruence.

North Korea's survival-centered grand strategy. Security, development, and legitimacy in the conduct of North Korean foreign policy remain inseparably linked, as clearly illustrated both in the U.S.-DPRK nuclear confrontation or negotiations and in Pyongyang's "package solution" proposal. Pyongyang's revised and downsized grand strategy is also closely keyed to and shaped by the triangulation of security, development, and legitimacy. Indeed, these three megacrises both frame and drive North Korea's survival-centered grand strategy in the post–Kim Il-sung era.[47]

The survival of post–Kim Il-sung North Korea in the post–Cold War era is something of a paradox. Several inter-related influences explain Pyongyang's surprising resilience and "the power of the weak" within the context of the nuclear confrontation with the United States. As a weaker state in this conflict, North Korea has used issue-specific and situation-specific power, which in turn has demanded a wide range of asymmetric resources, skills, and tactics in order to be credible. Foremost among these are North Korea's short distance from the field, its high-risk brinkmanship strategy, and its resolve, all of which have rendered far-stronger U.S. structural power less relevant and applicable.

The physical location of the DPRK is one of the most powerful elements of Pyongyang's survival strategy. Despite being "surrounded" by four great powers (China, Japan, Russia, and the United States) and confronting its southern rival, North Korea uses its home advantage to

---

[45] Ken E. Gause, *North Korean Civil-Military Trends: Military-First Politics to a Point* (Carlisle Barracks, PA: Strategic Studies Institute, 2006), 5.

[46] See Sung Chull Kim, "Development of Systemic Dissonance in North Korea," *Korean Journal of National Unification* 5 (1996): 83–109; Sung Chull Kim, *North Korea under Kim Jong Il: From Consolidation to Systemic Dissonance* (Albany: State University of New York Press, 2006); and Kim, "North Korean Informal Politics."

[47] Much of the material in this subsection is drawn from Samuel S. Kim, *North Korean Foreign Relations in the Post–Cold War World* (Carlisle, PA: Strategic Studies Institute, April 2007), 81–88.

play either brinkmanship games or the collapse card. This suggests a twist to the conventional realist wisdom that stronger states exert greater control than do weaker ones. In this case, where a smaller state occupies a position of strategic importance or where the locus of dispute is the smaller state's home ground, the weaker power can demonstrate bargaining power disproportionate to its aggregate structural power.[48] Three examples illustrate this process.

The first is that North Korea's geographical location at the heart of the strategic crossroads of Northeast Asia has enabled Pyongyang to exert disproportionate control during the negotiation process by constantly changing the rules of the game. North Korea's preference for direct bilateral negotiations with the United States is clear evidence of this. Second is Pyongyang's adroit use of its still considerable military resources. More than two-thirds of the DPRK's 700,000 troops, 8,000 artillery systems, and 2,000 tanks are forward deployed near the DMZ, just forty kilometers from Seoul and its 12 million people. Pyongyang's threats to turn Seoul into "a sea of fire" within minutes are serious. Third, North Korea's location as the locus of Northeast Asia's security complex provides Pyongyang the means to embroil any or all four great powers in a spiral of conflict escalation that each would prefer to sidestep. Pyongyang is able to use this to its advantage by threatening escalation to war, thereby reducing the relative power of its partners in the six-party talks process.

For the United States, this plays out in the lack of viable alternatives to negotiation. As a self-styled hermit kingdom, North Korea is far less susceptible to diplomatic efforts (such as sanctions) than more normal, non-pariah states would be. For China (and to a lesser extent for South Korea, Russia, and Japan), sanctions are even more disturbing given the possible outcomes they might engender, such as prompting North Korea to "go nuclear" or destabilizing the country to such an extent that millions of refugees would flee to neighboring China and Russia. Despite Pyongyang's growing difficulties, the collapse card has only increased North Korea's leverage.

Of course, a high-risk strategy without clear resolve or the capability to make credible threats would be ineffective in an asymmetrical negotiation. The loss of support from the Soviet Union and Russia's subsequent rapprochement with South Korea raised the salience of the nuclear issue for North Korea, which has used its nuclear weapons program as a cost-effective foreign policy tool. For Pyongyang, the nuclear program is "a military deterrent, an equalizer in national identity competition with South

---

[48] William Habeeb, *Power and Tactics in International Negotiation: How Weak Nations Bargain with Strong Nations* (Baltimore: The Johns Hopkins University Press, 1988), 130–31.

Korea, a bargaining chip for extracting economic concessions from the United States and China, and a cost-effective insurance policy for regime survival."[49]

The importance of a credible threat of military force to North Korea's survival strategy suggests that, without a comprehensive economic, security and legitimacy grand bargain package offer, Pyongyang is highly unlikely to abandon the nuclear program, a move that would only leave North Korea without the single most important lever in the six-party process. From Pyongyang's perspective, developing asymmetrical capabilities such as nuclear weapons and ballistic missiles affords the DPRK one of its few comparative advantages vis-à-vis South Korea.

In sum, North Korea's proximity to the field of play, brinkmanship and resolve, and military capabilities have allowed Pyongyang to exercise bargaining power disproportionate to its aggregate structural power in the nuclear crisis and six-party negotiations.

Given the 50-year history of distrust and hostility between North Korea and the United States, Pyongyang has little reason to trust Washington as these strategies play out. North Korean distrust only increased with the Bush administration's designation of the DPRK as a member of the "axis of evil." Yet as if to nod to the notion that nuclear deterrence would serve as the ultimate security guarantee for a weak state like North Korea through existential deterrence akin to a "barren survival,"[50] there has nonetheless been some evidence that North Korea is considering systemic reform over the current survival strategy. In July 2002, North Korea launched a series of economic reform measures emphasizing marketization, monetarization, decentralization, and attraction of foreign investment. With these reforms Pyongyang began to adjust its system of controlled prices, devalue the *won*, raise wages, reform the rationing system, open a "socialist goods trading market," give farmers limited property rights, and extend laws for special economic zones.[51] North Korea's negotiating strategy has thus changed from a zero-sum survival strategy to a more dynamic approach offering tangible concessions for system maintenance and survival.[52] In short, North Korea's survival-driven grand strategy is not carved in stone but subject to time-specific and situation-specific adaptation.

---

[49] Kim, *North Korean Foreign Relations in the Post–Cold War World*, 87.

[50] Victor D. Cha, "Making Sense of the Black Box: Hypotheses on Strategic Doctrine and the DPRK Threat," in Kim, *The North Korean System*, 180–81.

[51] See Marcus Noland, "Famine and Reform in North Korea," Institute for International Economics, Working Paper WP 03–5, July 2003.

[52] See Scott Snyder, "Negotiating Regime Survival in the Face of System Crisis," in Kim, *The North Korean System*, 157–76.

Policy Implications

What is most striking about the post–Cold War grand strategies of the two Koreas is not the centrality of the Big Four but rather the extent to which Washington's regime-change strategy and Beijing's mediation diplomacy have served as a kind of force-multiplier for catalyzing some major changes and shifts in Pyongyang and Seoul. Thanks to the Bush administration's hard-line strategy (until recently) and China's uncharacteristically proactive diplomacy in the latest U.S.-DPRK nuclear confrontation, North Korea has assembled three new life-supporting geopolitical patrons in Beijing, Seoul, and Moscow as well as a new pair of life-supporting geoeconomic patrons in Beijing and Seoul—even as South Korea has shifted away from the fear of allied abandonment to a new two-legged grand strategy. Contrary to the received realist wisdom that the Korean Peninsula still remains as the last Cold War stronghold, the peace process on the divided Korean Peninsula—a functional "peace-by-pieces" process—has continued to widen and deepen, largely unaffected by the on-again, off-again nuclear tensions.[53]

All three of North Korea's contiguous neighbors—China, Russia, and South Korea—strongly oppose Washington's regime-change strategy. Due to the second-term Bush administration's multiple challenges at home and abroad—e.g., Hurricane Katrina, a deepening quagmire in Iraq, and Republican defeat in the 2006 Congressional elections—Washington too has been forced to shift its diplomatic gears from the no direct negotiation stance to direct, behind-the scenes negotiations with Pyongyang in Berlin in early 2007. The new approach paved the way for the adoption of the February 13 Action Plan—officially known as "Initial Actions for the Implementation of the Joint Statement"—at the third session of the fifth round of the six-party talks held in Beijing from February 8–13, 2007.

Despite uncertain prospects for near-term movement on the reciprocal and simultaneous "action for action" implementation process, the six-party process does offer an opportunity to produce something larger than mere resolution of the specific issue of North Korea's nuclear program. Regional and global multilateralism are now an integral part of security thinking in Beijing, Moscow, and Seoul; such multilateralism is also a useful instrument

---

[53] Despite the many turns and twists, inter-Korean functional cooperation witnessed impressive accomplishments from 1999 to 2006: (1) inter-Korean trade increased from $333 million to $1.349 billion, (2) the number of South Koreans visiting North Korea increased twentyfold from 5,599 to 100,836, (3) more than 1.5 million South Koreans have visited Mount Kumgang in the North, (4) some 16,000 members of separated families have participated in reunions since the summit in 2000, (5) more than 15,000 North Koreans are now working at the South's Kaesong Industrial Complex located in the North, and (6) there have been 204 official talks between the two Koreas, including ministerial-level talks. See "7 Years After Joint Summit, North-South Relations at a Critical Juncture," *Hankyoreh*, Editorial, June 16, 2007, http://english.hani.co.kr/arti/english_edition/e_national/216235.html.

for the much needed conflict-management mechanisms in Northeast Asia. One of the key points in the February 13 Action Plan calls for a working group to discuss the creation of "a peace and security mechanism in Northeast Asia." The six-party process and rising multilateralism in both Beijing and Seoul open new pathways of forming and institutionalizing a truly Northeast Asian security regime by advancing greater institutionalization of the six-party process.

In both Seoul and Pyongyang, Washington is seen as part of both the Korean problem and the Korean solution. Given its history of involvement in the Korean Peninsula and the mutual security treaty with South Korea, the United States is now the most important external factor in both Korean states. Yet U.S. and Korean identities in the post–Cold War era have grated against one another. The U.S. identity as the world's sole superpower has come into conflict with the Korean one-nation ethnonational identity, a conflict fueled by the domestic politics of Washington, Pyongyang, and Seoul. Alongside an expansion of U.S. global activity, there has been a resurgence of the Korean nationalism that historically arose as an ideology of antiimperialism and anticolonialism. The new nationalism has served as a key determinant in shaping both inter-Korean relations and the relationship of both Koreas with the United States. Nonetheless, both despite and in conjunction with Pyongyang's decrying of U.S. unilateralism, Pyongyang's strategic thinking and behavior takes Washington as a mortal threat, an external life support system, or sometimes both.

Because so much of the U.S. perceptions of the levels of cooperativeness of other states is viewed through the Manichean lens of September 11, a danger exists in speeding up security-dilemma dynamics, perhaps even in transitioning Pyongyang's security-cum-survival strategy into more irreversible nuclear directions. The absence of any substantial U.S. security assurances would be used by hard-liners in Pyongyang as evidence of the failure of diplomacy in dealing with the world's lone superpower.

In both the academic world and the realm of policy and punditry, there is a tendency to forget that state intentions are often in flux and susceptible to the self-fulfilling-prophecy effects of the behavior of other states. In the policy world, the implications can lead to actions that produce the very outcomes they are designed to avoid. In no small part because of the severity (until recently) of U.S. demonization rhetoric, U.S.-DPRK relations have remained in a precarious balance. The United States is not entirely to blame, of course, as the DPRK's shrill confrontational rhetoric and nuclear brinkmanship certainly lend themselves to enflamed feelings of betrayal. With the combination of Manichean rhetoric from a unilateralist United States and the provocation of nuclear brinkmanship from a unilateral

Korea, however, the notion of a common security that can help bring at a long peace in Northeast Asia becomes completely overshadowed. Only by taking steps to revive the notion of common security, largely by addressing the issue of North Korea's own security-cum-survival, can U.S.-DPRK relations and Northeast Asian international relations come to rest on a more stable, safe, and sane footing.

Still, what complicates our understanding of the future of the Korean Peninsula is that all the countries involved have become moving targets on turbulent trajectories of domestic politics subject to competing and often contradictory pressures and forces. As noted in the preceding pages, top leaders in both Koreas will have a determinative role in the making of grand strategy. With recent reports of Kim Jong-il's declining health and potential succession power struggle looming in the North, and with South Korea and the United States on the cusp of presidential elections in December 2007 and November 2008, the future of the two Koreas' grand strategies cannot be predicted with confidence.

EXECUTIVE SUMMARY

This chapter examines Russia's political system, economy, and social conditions to assess whether Russia under Putin has the domestic foundations for a strong, strategic foreign policy.

MAIN ARGUMENT:

Russian grand strategy is derived from a domestic system that is fundamentally weak, corrupt, and unsustainable. The political system faces a period of uncertainty and potential instability with a presidential succession in March 2008. The increasingly state-controlled economy is booming but remains dependent on energy exports and is vulnerable to shocks. The economy has also failed to develop or sustain key sectors. Russian society acquiesces because Putin has delivered stability and generally improved living standards. The image of a powerful Russia rests on this fragile equilibrium, which is virtually certain to shift and is an inadequate basis for a truly strategic foreign policy.

POLICY IMPLICATIONS:

- Russian policy in Asia is tactical rather than strategic, missing opportunities to build long-term favorable relationships with Asia's rising powers. Fundamentally weak, Russia cannot effectively oppose U.S. policies or intentionally harm U.S. interests in Asia.

- Because the Putin leadership uses warnings of external threat to justify its control, the rhetoric and tone of the political process will likely worsen with the upcoming presidential succession. After March 2008 a new leadership may return to a more pragmatic policy.

- Since specific interests and tactics rather than grand strategy drive Russian policies in Asia, the U.S. may need to avoid actions that reinforce any anti-U.S. or balancing tendencies in Russia's relations in Asia.

Russia: The Domestic Sources of a Less-than-Grand Strategy

Celeste A. Wallander

If ever there were a country likely to be so tightly constrained and shaped by geopolitical circumstance and the international system that internal forces should be a weak factor in its grand strategy, that country would be Russia. Spanning the Eurasian land mass from Alaska to Finland, Russia borders or is a neighbor to almost every great or emerging power of the 21st century—the United States, China, Japan, India, Iran, and the European Union (EU). Russia also shares long and fragile borders with some of the world's most dangerous and insecure regions—the Caucasus, Central Asia, and South Asia. Because of its location, Russia should be acting carefully and strategically as a great power seeking to ensure its own survival. The enormous security demands arising from Russia's geopolitical location alone would seem to compel a multidimensional grand strategy of carefully allocating resources to manage security and economic relations to the west, east, and south. If ever there were a country that needed a Bismarck or a Brzezinski, Russia would be it.

Though no one has yet laid claim to a Bismarckian mantle, the current Russian leadership under President Vladimir Putin does assert that the state and economy are designed to provide the vast resources necessary for securing Russian national interests. Purporting to manage a political system that secures the interests of the nation in a dangerous international environment, the Putin leadership emphasizes inescapable geopolitical realities and global terrorism. At the same time this leadership draws

Celeste A. Wallander is Visiting Associate Professor at Georgetown University. She can be reached at <caw39@georgetown.edu>.

The author is grateful to Stephen Hanson, Brian Taylor, and two anonymous reviewers for helpful comments. Any errors of fact or analysis that remain are the author's alone.

attention to threats posed by the United States—U.S. unipolarity, supposed intent to weaken Russia through a strategy of encirclement, and obsession with democratization—that would dismantle the strong domestic political and economic order achieved in the past eight years.

The Putin leadership is correct in that the form of the country's politics, economics, and society determines Russia's capacity for power and ability to defend its national interests. If grand strategy is defined as the matching of interests and security requirements with the means and resources for achieving them, then maintaining domestic order is crucial for Russian strategy, grand or otherwise. The international strategic environment establishes geopolitical challenges facing Russia and the balance of power in which all states must operate, but Russia's capacity to meet them, and the specific form of its grand strategy, depend upon the country's domestic order.

This chapter begins with an overview of Russia's articulation of its grand strategy as developed in the past two years under Putin's leadership—Russia's strategic environment, national interests and the type of state and economy needed to secure them, and current policies. The next section then examines critically the Russian domestic system and the argument that the state and economy under Putin make Russia strong. The analysis then returns to Russian grand strategy and argues that it is neither grand, nor strategic, nor sustainable. Whether Russia will survive as a great power in 21st century Asia remains an open question. The factors that Russia's current leadership identifies as the source of its power—its state and economy—are also the source of its weakness and vulnerability as a strategic player in Asia.

Russian Grand Strategy

Russian grand strategy in the Putin period poses a striking contrast to that of the Yeltsin era. Under Yeltsin, Russia's strategy was to cope with the country's weakness by drawing closer to the United States and to Europe, liberalizing the state and economy in order to harness modern market forces, and renouncing nineteenth century geopolitical thinking that compelled Russia to control the policies of smaller neighbors.[1]

By the time Putin became president in 2000, two crucial foundations of Russian grand strategy had already shifted. First, the Russian economy had begun to grow without having had to attract foreign investment or

---

[1] For examples of the degree to which the Yeltsin leadership sought resources for foreign policy support of the United States, see Strobe Talbott, *The Russia Hand: A Memoir of Presidential Diplomacy* (New York: Random House, 2002).

conform to Western economic norms. The pursuit of Russia's national economic interests seemed to increase national power rather than leading to ever-greater subservience, as the Russian state managed the terms of its own engagement with the international economy. Putin "bowed to the imperatives of global economics, but…less in terms of enhancing national welfare than in terms of enhancing national power."[2] To rebuild Russia as a great power, the Putin leadership needed a stronger Russian state. In January 2000 Putin thus signed into law a national security concept that gives the Russian state a greater role in shaping the economy, safeguarding stability, and regulating social and political life.[3]

Second, Russia's assessment of the international environment and external threats to Russian security underwent substantial changes. Yeltsin's official policy had identified Russia's greatest threats as coming from within. Putin provided a substantial list of external threats, including weakened United Nations and Russian influence, military political blocs and alliances, foreign military bases or deployment of forces on Russia's borders, proliferation of WMD and their means of delivery, the escalation of conflicts in Eurasia, and territorial claims against Russia. The new national security concept also attributed the "distinctive quality" of Russian foreign policy to its "balance" between Europe and Asia.[4] Whether Putin's support of President Bush in the wake of September 11 was a mere interlude or lost opportunity, the U.S. decision to use military force against Iraq without UN Security Council approval reinforced a Russian strategy that sought to balance and constrain U.S. hegemony in a unipolar world.[5]

In the past two years this Russian assessment has evolved further, taking on an added dimension of threat assessment that is rooted in Russia's domestic politics and has implications for grand strategy. In his February 2007 speech at a yearly meeting of senior defense officials in Munich, Putin warned of the threat of U.S. unilateralism and "the uncontained hyper use of force," calling for a "reasonable balance" and reliance on the UN Security Council. Noting, in a more traditional geopolitical vein, that it is reasonable to expect that countries that are newly successful in the economic sphere will become important political powers in global affairs, Putin did not name,

---

[2] Robert Legvold, "Russian Foreign Policy During Periods of 'Great State Transformation,'" in *Russian Foreign Policy in the Twenty-First Century and the Shadow of the Past*, ed. Robert Legvold (New York: Columbia University Press, 2007), 98.

[3] See *2000 Russian National Security Concept*, Permanent Representation of the Russian Federation to the Council of Europe website, http://www.russiaeurope.mid.ru/russiastrat2000.html.

[4] Ibid.

[5] William C. Wohlforth, "Russia's Soft Balancing Act," in *Strategic Asia 2003–04: Fragility and Crisis*, ed. Richard J. Ellings and Aaron L. Friedberg (Seattle: The National Bureau of Asian Research), 165–79.

but obviously was referring to, Brazil, Russia, India, and China.[6] At a January 2007 meeting at the General Staff Academy concerning a new draft military doctrine, Chief of the General Staff General Yuri Baluyevsky declared: "The United States is aiming for world leadership, striving to establish itself in regions where Russia has traditionally maintained a presence."[7] The draft doctrine reportedly also identifies both the North Atlantic Treaty Organization's (NATO) involvement near Russian borders and the "spreading of hostile information about Russia's policies" as primary threats. These threats top the priority list, followed by terrorism and separatism— formerly the major preoccupations of Russian security policies. In his April 2007 State of the Union address, Putin denounced the deployment of U.S. missile defense facilities in Europe and called for a moratorium on the Conventional Armed Forces in Europe (CFE) Treaty, creating another stir in Western capitals.[8] In his speech for the Victory Day celebration in Moscow commemorating the 62nd anniversary of the defeat of Germany in World War II, Putin followed up the standard acknowledgement of allied cooperation with a warning to domestic and international audiences:

> We have a duty to remember that the causes of any war…have their roots in an ideology of confrontation and extremism…these threats are not becoming fewer but are only transforming and changing their appearance. These new threats, just as under the Third Reich, show the same contempt for human life and the same aspiration to establish an exclusive dictate over the world…only common responsibility and equal partnership can counter these challenges and enable us to join forces in resisting any attempts to unleash new armed conflicts and undermine global security.[9]

Although he subsequently denied it when Secretary of State Condoleezza Rice raised the issue during meetings in Moscow in late May 2007, clearly Putin was warning that the United States posed the kind of threat to international security, and to Russia, as had Hitler's Germany. In interviews before and during the June 2007 the group of eight (G-8)

---

[6] For the text of Vladimir Putin's speech, see "Speech at the 43rd Munich Conference on Security Policy, February 10, 2007," Munich Conference on Security Policy website, http://www.securityconference.de/konferenzen/rede.php?menu_presse=&menu_2007=&menu_konferenzen=&sprache=en&id=179&.

[7] For the full text of Baluyevsky's speech, see the Russian Ministry of Defense website, http://www.mil.ru/847/852/1153/1342/20922/index.shtml.

[8] For an English text of Putin's speech, see "Annual Address to the Federal Assembly," Kremlin website, http://www.kremlin.ru/eng/sdocs/themes.shtml?month=04&day=26&year=2007&prefix=&value_from=&value_to=&date=&type=&dayRequired=no&day_enable=true&Submit.x=9&Submit.y=9.

[9] For an English text of this speech, see "Speech at the Military Parade Celebrating the 62nd Anniversary of Victory in the Great Patriotic War," Kremlin website, http://www.kremlin.ru/eng/sdocs/themes.shtml?month=05&day=09&year=2007&prefix=&value_from=&value_to=&date=&type=&dayRequired=no&day_enable=true&Submit.x=9&Submit.y=7.

summit, Putin continued to emphasize the dangers an unbalanced and unconstrained United States poses in Europe and Asia. Subsequently toning down the rhetoric at a press conference wrapping up the summit, Putin called for cooperation and compromise and proposed a joint missile defense radar site at a Russian-leased base in Gabala, Azerbaijan.[10]

This rhetoric of the past two years raises an important question: why has contemporary Russian policy become so explicitly anti-U.S. and oppositional in tone and content? For years Putin has been warning of U.S. unilateralism and has been developing a multidimensional strategy with important countries in Europe and Eurasia. Yet, in the past two years Russian assessments of U.S. motivations and behavior have become much more strident and undiplomatic—particularly so in 2007.

Many analysts attribute the evolution of Russia's forceful criticism of U.S. (and increasingly European) foreign policy to the success of the Russian economy. Global energy prices have remained very high, and Russia continues to reap the economic benefits both of its resource endowment and its control of the geostrategic corridors for energy transport. In structural realist terms, with oil at a price of $70 per barrel Russia today has the resources to attempt to balance the United States, whereas weak and poor in the 1990s Russia had little option but to bandwagon with U.S. "hyper-power."

Policymakers and analysts also identify both Russia's consolidated state and the country's new wealth as conditions that have allowed the Putin leadership not only to strategically craft and implement policy but also to mobilize the resources of the country's burgeoning economy for strategic purposes. Unlike Yeltsin's Russia—with its liberalizing priorities, fractured politics, and state institutions beholden to oligarchic interests—Putin's Russia has a strong system at home that supports a strong policy abroad.[11]

Moreover, by 2007 the Russian elite was preoccupied by new threats: democratization and liberalization. Following the Rose Revolution in Georgia in 2003, the Orange Revolution in Ukraine in 2004, and the Tulip Revolution in Kyrgyzstan in 2005, the Russian leadership began to argue that U.S. (and Western) support for democratization poses a threat to Russia. The Putin leadership claims that democratization is meant to weaken the Russian state and reverse the successes of its policies, particularly in the economic sphere.[12] In his 2007 State of the Union address, Putin accused

---

[10] For Putin's interview with select press representatives before the 33rd the group of eight (G-8) summit, see the Kremlin website, http://www.kremlin.ru/eng/speeches/2007/06/04/2149_type82916_132716.shtml.

[11] On the contrasting conditions and their dynamics, see David McDonald, "Domestic Conjunctures, the Russian State, and the World Outside, 1700–2006," in *Russian Foreign Policy*, 145–203.

[12] Celeste A. Wallander, "Suspended Animation: the U.S. and Russia after the G-8," *Current History* 195, no. 693 (October 2006): 315–20.

foreign countries of hoping "to continue plundering our national wealth as they did in the past" and trying "to deprive our country of its economic and political independence."[13] This danger, structural unipolarity, and the U.S. military presence in Eurasia together constitute the primary threats to Russia's security as formulated in official policy.

The key, according to the Russian leadership, is that the country's more assertive, coherent, and seemingly successful strategy is due to the strengthened Russian state and economy. The Putin leadership argues that the United States seeks to weaken Russia and prevent it from balancing U.S. unipolarity by pushing for democratization, liberalization, and independent civil society and media. An analysis of how—and whether—the Russian state and economy have been strengthened follows below.

The Russian System

Politics: Institutions and Processes

Putin's Russia is less liberal and free—and its leadership less accountable to society—than seven years ago. First, Russia's political system is highly centralized. Although nominally a federation, Russia is in practical terms a unitary state. The president appoints the governors, the central government collects taxes and allocates resources to regional governments, and the central legislature is responsible for all important legislation. Though many local officials are elected, candidates not supported by the Kremlin rarely win and sometimes face obstacles to registering for campaigns or investigations into their taxes or finances. Given the extent of these central government controls, local and regional politics are effectively a matter of implementing national leadership policies.

Second, the Russian national legislative bodies are under effective presidential control. Members of the upper house of the legislature, the Federation Council, are no longer the elected representatives of Russia's regions; instead they are appointed by the regional governors and legislatures, who in turn hold office only with the support of the Russian president. The lower legislative house, the State Duma, is controlled by a two-thirds majority of United Russia, a party created by the Kremlin in 2001. United Russia has voter support largely because the party is associated with the popular president and enjoys favorable coverage from the state-controlled media. Nonetheless, there is evidence that election results in December 2003

---

[13] For the text of Putin's speech, see "Annual Address to the Federal Assembly," Kremlin website, http://www.kremlin.ru/eng/sdocs/themes.shtml?month=04&day=26&year=2007&prefix=&valu e_from=&value_to=&date=&type=&dayRequired=no&day_enable=true&Submit.x=9&Submit. y=9.

may have been falsified to exclude dissenting parties (particularly the liberal Yabloko) and favor the Kremlin-created quasi-opposition party Rodina. After the 2003 elections, the Kremlin-friendly Duma passed new rules that made registration much more difficult for opposition parties, raised the threshold for Duma representation from 5% to 7% of the national vote, and eliminated single-mandate district seats so that all Duma members must be chosen from national party lists.

Third, Russia's corrupt judicial system does not serve as a check or balance on the executive. Political authorities use the courts both to prosecute and imprison political opponents and to pressure business owners with threats of judicial action or serious judgments against their holdings so that state-controlled companies are able to acquire them. Court judgments enabled the state to take over Vladimir Gusinsky's NTV, Mikhail Khodorkovsky's Yukos oil firm, and, more recently, forced international investors to give up their majority stake in the Sakhalin-2 energy project.[14] Facing the threat of judgment, in June 2007 BP sold its investment in the TNK-BP joint venture for developing the Siberian Kovykta natural gas field to Gazprom in order to avoid being wholly expropriated.

Fourth, national media outlets are either controlled or thoroughly intimidated by the central state. In 2000 three national broadcast media networks were reporting on the government's actions, policies, and problems—albeit in a manner that was often biased and did not meet Western standards of professional journalism. The government has tamed two of these media outlets that were independent. A state-owned company acquired Boris Berezovsky's media empire after he supported a challenger to Putin in the March 2000 election. Gazprom, a state-controlled company, acquired NTV in 2001 after the brief imprisonment and subsequent self-imposed exile of its owner, Vladimir Gusinsky. The third national media outlet, RTR, was already under state control. As a result Russia now has no national outlet by which its citizens can obtain information about their government's performance or judge governmental claims about domestic and foreign policy. Since 2005 all major national newspapers (with the exception of *Novaya Gazeta*) have come under Kremlin or Kremlin-friendly control. The suspicious circumstances surrounding the deaths of high-profile independent investigative journalists Anna Politkovskaya and Ivan Safronov in the past year, as well as the beating and harassment of numerous other journalists in Russia, have created an intimidating atmosphere. Professional

[14] Robert Orttung, "Causes and Consequences of Corruption in Putin's Russia," Center for Strategic and International Studies, PONARS Policy Memo, no. 430, 2007, http://www.csis.org/media/csis/pubs/pm_0430.pdf.

media rights organizations see the violence as an attempt to discourage the kind of reporting necessary for government accountability.[15]

Fifth, and ultimately most important, the state is built on an enormous and largely under-appreciated expansion of the Federal Security Service (FSB), the successor agency to the KGB. Under Putin, the FSB "has both absorbed and colonized some of its key power ministry partners and rivals."[16] His former FSB colleagues have served not only as ministers and of defense and internal affairs but also in a number of key presidential administration positions. Former KGB and FSB officers have moved into business, often through appointments as senior management executives or as boardmembers of state-owned or -controlled companies. Whereas in the Soviet Union one had to be a loyal Communist Party member in order to gain a position in the state or industry, today the surest path to political or business success is either service in the intelligence bureaucracy or a connection to someone within the intelligence bureaucracy.

Even Kremlin supporters concede that Russia's political institutions are designed to control opposition and manage the outcome of its elections. The term "managed democracy" is appropriate: elections do not hold the government accountable to its citizens but instead serve as a tool to manage the political, economic, and social systems.[17] With an authoritarian system based on centralization and control, Russia is ruled by an elite that is not accountable to Russian society. Asserting that this strong state is necessary for stability, security, and prosperity, the leadership claims to exercise this control in pursuit of Russia's well-being.

Although institutions strongly shape the process, culture, norms, and expectations also affect how Russian politics really works. The political culture in Russia is one of patronage, corruption, and elite networks.[18] In many post-Soviet countries, government positions are used not to provide public service but rather to gain access to wealth and resources. Studies of corruption in Russia and other former Soviet countries find that, although

---

[15] "Call for International Support for Journalists and Human Rights Activists in Russia," Reporters Without Borders, May 15, 2007, http://www.rsf.org/article.php3?id_article=22158.

[16] Brian Taylor, "Power Surge? Russian Power Ministries from Yeltsin to Putin and Beyond," Center for Strategic and International Studies, PONARS Policy Memo, no. 414, 2006, 3, http://www.csis. org/media/csis/pubs/pm_0414.pdf. For the first serious scholarly article documenting the military and security service background of Putin's appointees, see Olga Kryshtanovskaya and Stephen White, "Putin's Militocracy," Post-Soviet Affairs 19, no. 4 (October–December 2003): 289–303.

[17] Neil Buckley, "Putin Aide Defends Russian Democracy," Financial Times, June 29, 2006, http:// www.ft.com/cms/s/f67c3f86-070b-11db-81d7-0000779e2340,dwp_uuid=3e7132ac-e41a-11da-8ced-0000779e2340.html.

[18] See "2006 Corruption Perceptions Index," Transparency International, http://www.transparency. org/news_room/in_focus/2006/cpi_2006__1/cpi_table; and Tom Parfitt, "Corrupt Bureaucrats Cost Russia £125bn a Year, Prosecutor Says," The Guardian, November 8, 2006, http://www. guardian.co.uk/russia/article/0,,1941743,00.html.

everyday interactions of administrative officials with citizens has in some cases declined, the problem of "state capture" (influencing the content of laws and rules) has in some respects worsened.[19]

The combination of Russia's non-democratic political institutions and the practices of patronage and corruption has led to the consolidation of patrimonial authoritarianism, a system in which the primary relationship in the system is that between patron and client.[20] Clients support patrons because patrons are able to create and control "rents"—wealth created by the political manipulation of markets.[21] Patrons create rents by using positions in the government to influence the content of laws and rules in favor of their clients and clans. Not merely a regrettable feature of an otherwise strong state, corruption in Russia is essential to the functioning of political power. Patrons are able to hold power because they can distribute wealth to their clans.[22] They are able to generate this wealth through political manipulation of businesses and economic transactions. If corruption and the ability to use position to control and distribute rents disappeared, patrons would lose the resources that gain them support, and thus their political power as well.

Accountability, rule of law, political competition, and transparency would prevent patrons from generating rents and distributing them to clients in return for political power. In order to sustain the system that keeps it in power, the Russian leadership must prevent competition, limit independent media, and enfeeble civil society and NGOs. The objective motivating the elite to maintain the system outlined in the previous section is not merely to make Russia strong in order to assert its role as a great power. The elite is also driven to secure its own power and control of the country's wealth and assets. Democracy and liberalization would bring transparency and accountability that threaten the system of power. Russia's leadership has created closed networks of mutual dependence and benefit, relying

---

[19] Stephen Knack, "Measuring Corruption in Eastern Europe and Central Asia," World Bank, Policy Research Working Paper, WPS3968, July 2006.

[20] This section draws on Celeste A. Wallander, "Russian Transimperialism and Its Implications," *Washington Quarterly* 30, no. 2 (Spring 2007): 107–22.

[21] On rents, see Clifford Gaddy and Barry Ickes, "Resource Rents and the Russian Economy," *Eurasian Geography and Economics* 46, no. 8 (December 2005): 559–83.

[22] See Thomas Graham, "Noviy rossiyskiy rezhim" [The New Russian Regime], *Nezavisimaya gazeta*, November 23, 1995. For an English edited version of this article, see Thomas Graham, "Who Rules Russia?" *Prospect Magazine*, January 1996, http://www.prospect-magazine.co.uk/article_details. php?id=4909.

on tightly knit clans with members either who served in the intelligence services or who worked with Putin during his time in St. Petersburg.[23]

Average Russians are largely aware of the degree of corruption in their country.[24] They are also aware that Russia is not a democracy: in a recent poll only 15% of Russian citizens said that Russia is a democracy.[25] Why then does the Russian populace seem to acquiesce? The reason Russians support their current leadership and are generally optimistic that their current economic situation will improve is because they are better off economically than a decade ago. According to studies of Russian public values and priorities, the Russian people are increasingly disaffected with political life but tolerate the political system as long as it provides order and acceptable socio-economic conditions. The legitimacy of the political system, in other words, is based on what the system provides, not what it is. Should the system fail to produce, the lack of accountability and responsiveness, as well as the pervasive cynicism of Russian citizens about their leaders, may expose the weakness underlying Putin's supposedly strong state.

Economics: Markets, Uncertainty, and the State

The Russian economy has grown some 60% since the 1998 economic crisis, with Russia's GDP reaching $733 billion ($1.723 trillion at purchasing power parity) at the end of 2006. The highest rates of growth, which occurred immediately following the 1998 crisis, were the result of devaluation and default. Since 2002, however, growth has been sustained by rising global energy prices. GDP growth in 2006 was 6.7%. Strong macro-economic policy established during Putin's first term, including reform of the tax system and the creation of a stabilization fund restricting government spending of high revenues from energy, has helped the leadership to manage the effects of a large trade surplus and rising demand. The government budget surplus in 2006 was 9% of GDP. The Russian government holds foreign reserves of $315 billion, largely from energy revenues. Inflation has been high (around 12% per year) but has remained within manageable levels. Russia has experienced a 50% reduction in its poverty rate and a 65% rise in personal income that has exceeded the

---

[23] For more on these clans and the members of the Russian state and business who belong to them, see Roman Shleynov, "Donoschiki snaryadov" [Informers of the Machinery], *Novaya gazeta*, April 26, 2007, http://www.novayagazeta.ru/data/2007/30/00.html; and Brian D. Taylor, *Russia's Power Ministries: Coercion and Commerce* (Syracuse: Institute for National Security and Terrorism of Syracuse University, 2007).

[24] Knack, "Measuring Corruption," 8–9.

[25] Vladimir Petukhov, "Democracy in Russia: No End of History in Sight," Russian Public Opinion Research Center, May 21, 2007, http://wciom.com/archives/thematic-archive/info-material/single/8225.html.

growth of GDP from 1998 to 2006.[26] Russia holds the world's largest natural gas reserves and ranks among the top ten in proven oil reserves.[27]

For at least three years, however, the World Bank's Russian Economic Reports have warned of falling industrial production and the extreme dependence of the economy on a few sectors, primarily natural resource extraction.[28] Manufacturing growth appears to have recovered to some degree in 2006, driven in part by genuine new demand and in part by factors specific to short-term conditions that are unlikely to be repeated.[29] Growth in both oil and natural gas production has flattened. The growth in Russian oil production since 1997 reflects re-establishing Soviet-era levels of oil production, rather than new investment or increased capacity. Energy and other raw materials account for 80% of Russian exports and 32% of government revenues. The largest new sources of economic growth in the Russian economy have been construction and non-tradables; this growth has been driven by consumer demand and energy investment, including a great deal of capital from abroad.[30] Illustrative is a quote by Clifford Gaddy, the leading U.S. expert on the Russian economy:

> People say: "But there's more there than just oil." Indeed, there is—more and more each year. The pillars support more. The visual image is a platform resting on the pillars...Piled on that platform, higher and higher, is business activity in retail, wholesale, consumer goods, construction, real estate. This is the "non-oil economy." So, yes, Russia's non-oil sectors are growing as a share of the total economy. Is oil then becoming less important for Russia? No. It is just the opposite. Oil becomes more important, because more businesses and more jobs depend on the flow from oil and gas.[31]

---

[26] Data from the Central Intelligence Agency, *The World Factbook 2007* (Washington, D.C.: Central Intelligence Agency, 2007), https://www.cia.gov/library/publications/the-world-factbook/index.html.

[27] On current Russian energy data, see the "Country Analysis Briefs: Russia," U.S. Department of Energy's Energy Information Administration website, http://www.eia.doe.gov/emeu/cabs/Russia/Background.html; and BP plc., "BP Statistical Review of World Energy June 2007," http://www.bp.com/productlanding.do?categoryId=6848&contentId=7033471.

[28] See "Russian Economic Reports," World Bank, http://web.worldbank.org/WBSITE/EXTERNAL/COUNTRIES/ECAEXT/RUSSIANFEDERATIONEXTN/0,,contentMDK:20888536~menuPK:2445695~pagePK:1497618~piPK:217854~theSitePK:305600,00.html.

[29] "Russian Economic Report #14," World Bank in Russia, June 2007, 2–5, http://web.worldbank.org/WBSITE/EXTERNAL/NEWS/0,,contentMDK:21362587~menuPK:64255468~pagePK:34370~piPK:34424~theSitePK:4607,00.html.

[30] Non-tradables are (primarily consumer-oriented) goods and services, including retail sales and entertainment, that are produced and consumed domestically and are not a close substitute for import goods.

[31] Clifford G. Gaddy, "The Russian Economy in the Year 2006," *Post-Soviet Affairs* 23, no.1 (January 2007): 2.

In the short term, there is good reason to expect continued growth. As long as global energy prices remain high, the enormous financial resources flowing into Russia will generate income that in turn creates demand in sectors such as services and consumption. In the medium to long term, however, Russia's fundamental economic weakness will be a very serious problem. Russia's resource boom is itself part of the problem. Because of the inflow of wealth and foreign investment in the energy sector, the Russian ruble continues to appreciate. Generally appropriate macro-economic policies designed to limit the effect of this inflow—especially including the creation of a stabilization fund for excess energy revenues—have not been sufficient. As a result Russian products unrelated to extractive industries are becoming more expensive, relative to imports, and less competitive internationally.[32] Strong export figures conceal both weak growth in export volume and rapidly growing imports.[33]

Furthermore, the basis for long-term sustainable growth is not being established in a period of prosperity. Energy prices may fall, depriving Russia of the flow of wealth that fuels consumption. Russia has far lower rates of investment in fixed capital, however, than necessary to diversify the economy, generate new sources of growth and wealth, and create sustainable development. Countries poised to transform booms into sustainable development—the familiar Asian success stories—typically have rates of fixed capital investment of 30–40% of GDP. Russia's nominal rate is about 18%, but the real rate (taking into account price differentials) is 9%.[34] Even compared to its post-Soviet neighbors, Russia has unimpressive growth rates and investment in fixed capital (see **Table 1**). Though growing, Russia is actually falling behind relative to many other countries pursuing the benefits of global trade, investment, and globalization.

FDI has grown substantially in the past two years, doubling from $15.9 billion in 2005 to $30 billion in 2006. Of the $9.8 billion FDI in the first quarter of 2007, however, $7.7 billion was FDI in the extractive industries. Only $0.7 billion (or 7%) of all FDI was in manufacturing, and half the manufacturing FDI was in food, drink, and tobacco.[35] Foreign capital is flowing in the form of loans to Russian businesses, portfolio investment, and direct investment in energy (where the Russian state allows it) and consumer goods and services. Russia is not, however, drawing foreign

---

[32] "Russian Economic Report #14," 6–8.

[33] Libor Krkosa, "Role of FDI in Russia's Economic Diversification" (points presented at the European Bank for Reconstruction and Development, Helsinki, May 21, 2007), http://www.oecd. org/dataoecd/56/7/38664146.pdf.

[34] Gaddy, "The Russian Economy," 6–7.

[35] "Russian Economic Report #14," 5.

TABLE 1   Comparative economic performance of select post-Soviet countries

Country	GDP growth (%)		Gross capital formation (% of GDP)		FDI net inflows (% of GDP)
	2005	2006	2005	2006	2005
Russia	6.4	6.7	20.9	18.2	2.0
Armenia	14.0	13.4	29.7	20.9	5.3
Azerbaijan	26.2	34.5	37.8	44.9	13.4
Belarus	9.2	9.9	29.6	25.9	1.0
Estonia	9.8	11.4	31.8	32.4	22.9
Georgia	9.3	8.0	26.3	30.0	7.0
Kazakhstan	9.7	10.6	27.0	27.0	3.0
Kyrgyzstan	-0.6	2.7	14.4	15.5	2.0
Latvia	10.2	11.9	34.2	31.4	5.0
Lithuania	7.5	10.3	25.0	23.0	4.0
Moldova	7.0	4.0	24.8	24.8	7.0
Tajikistan	7.5	7.0	14.3	19.9	2.0
Turkmenistan	N/A	6.0	23.0	28.8	2.0
Ukraine	2.6	7.1	19.2	22.9	9.4
Uzbekistan	7.0	7.3	23.1	N/A	0.0

SOURCE: World Bank, *World Development Indicators* (2006); and Central Intelligence Agency, *The World Factbook* (2007).

Investment in new technologies, manufacturing, and the cutting-edge sectors as would be expected of a 21st century great power.

The overall outlook for the economy, therefore, is ambiguous. On the one hand, growth rates are truly impressive, and revenues are enviable. Russian citizens have good reason to feel that they are better off now than a decade ago, and that they will be even better off in coming years. On the other hand, Russia's economy would not be able to sustain a shock or a drop in energy prices caused by a global recession or even slowing demand. The economy has not diversified and manufacturing capacity has disappeared over the past two decades. The lack of domestic or foreign investment in new sectors leaves Russia with little to build on. The weak banking system further constrains the potential for diversification by denying small and medium-sized enterprises sufficient assets to invest in new products or capacity.[36]

---

[36] Anders Aslund, "Putin's Decline and America's Response," Carnegie Endowment for International Peace, Policy Brief, no. 41, August 2005, 4.

The rule of law in Russia is weak, posing risks for business contracts. The legal system does not enforce or protect ownership and property rights.[37] Furthermore, the trends toward a strongly interventionist state, increased bureaucracy, and state takeovers in so-called strategic sectors (primarily energy and defense, but also some manufacturing such as automobiles) have discouraged foreign investment that would diversify the economy. Although foreign investment in Russia doubled from 2005 to 2006, the primary forms were (1) portfolio investment, which is easily redirected; (2) investment in the energy sector, for which international companies have little choice but to go where the energy resources are and accept the risk; and (3) established consumer goods enterprises, such as beverages and household products, that are not vulnerable to the ambitions of the Russian state.

In short, Russia is a market economy but not a liberal market economy. Profits are high because of high energy prices, not the underlying strength of the Russian economy. Foreign investors see Russia as posing acceptable risks for several reasons: energy prices are high, energy demand in Asia is rising, and instability in the Middle East and corruption in Nigeria and Venezuela make foreign investment difficult in those traditional energy-exporting regions. Despite the Russian state's increased ownership and control of energy companies (primarily via Gazprom and Rosneft), foreign investors have not abandoned the country. Shell, Mitsui, and Mitsubishi have remained, even after having to accept a 50% reduction of their share in the Sakhalin-2 project when the Russian government raised concerns about environmental impact. These foreign companies sold half of their holdings at favorable prices to Gazprom, apparently in return for Russian government support. TNK-BP agreed in June 2007 to sell Gazprom its stake in the Kovykta natural gas field in Siberia at a bargain price of (at most) 25% of its value. Under threat that its license might be revoked for non-

---

[37] "Russian Federation: Country Brief 2006," World Bank, http://web.worldbank.org/ WBSITE/EXTERNAL/COUNTRIES/ECAEXT/RUSSIANFEDERATIONEXTN/ 0,,contentMDK:21054807~menuPK:517666~pagePK:1497618~piPK:217854~theSitePK:3056 00,00.html#Economy.

performance, TNK-BP was reportedly relieved that its assets were not expropriated outright.[38]

Why is control of Russia's strategic sectors so important to the country's leadership? One explanation is consistent with the government's framing of its grand strategy: in order to realize and manage the wealth and power that derive from Russian national resources, the Russian state must own, or at least control, those resources. An examination of this explanation, however, reveals important inconsistencies.

First, the most mismanaged and unproductive enterprises in the Russian energy sector are those that are state-owned. Even as the Russian state has increased its ownership and control of the oil sector in the past four years, growth in oil production has slowed now to the point of having leveled off. In the natural gas sector, Gazprom has so mismanaged its investment and production that the company can no longer meet its domestic and international contractual commitments. Russia is able to supply its customers in Europe only by buying natural gas at a lower price from Turkmenistan (which at present has no alternative pipelines) and reselling it at a premium to European customers.[39]

Second, recent appointments suggest that the state's interest in taking control of the two energy giants was less a matter of ensuring stewardship and wealth for the Russian nation than of giving control to a closely-knit network of Putin's colleagues. If its goal in taking ownership were to realize the value of Russia's natural endowments for its citizens, the state would be expected to choose senior management officials who have substantial professional knowledge of the sectors, extensive experience in global business, or advanced training in economics and business. The chairman of the board of Rosneft, now Russia's largest oil company, is Igor Sechin, Deputy Chief of Staff of the Presidential Administration and former KGB colleague of President Putin. The chairman of the board of Gazprom, Dmitri Medvedev, was trained as a lawyer at St. Petersburg State University where

---

[38] "BP Could Lose Control of Russian Venture," *International Herald Tribune*, May 20, 2007, http://www.iht.com/articles/2007/05/20/business/bp.php; and "BP and TNK-BP Plan Strategic Alliance with Gazprom as TNK-BP Sells Its Stake in the Kovykta Gas Field," TNK-BP, Press Release, June 22, 2007, http://www.tnk-bp.com/press/releases/2007/6/70/. Both Sakhaliin-2 and the TNK-BP Kovykta project were viewed as being promising for major cooperative energy development between international energy companies and Russian enterprises. These projects would bring resources and technology to develop Russia's new field reserves, which are often in difficult places to access, such as Siberia and the ocean. In both cases, under pressure from the Russian state for environmental violations (Sakhalin) or non-performance (Kovykta), foreign investors faced complete loss of their assets and investment through questionable rulings of the Russian legal system. After Gazprom acquired a majority stake in Sakhalin, the environmental charges were dropped. TNK-BP was unable to fulfill its contracts to sell natural gas to China because Gazprom, which holds exclusive rights to export natural gas from Russia, refused to build the necessary pipeline.

[39] Henry Meyer, "Russia Wins New Natural Gas Deal, Undermining U.S. Plan," *International Herald Tribune*, May 14, 2007, http://www.iht.com/articles/2007/05/13/business/bxpipe.php.

he became a colleague of Putin, who brought him to Moscow to serve in his presidential administration in 1999. The choice of an intelligence service operative and a government lawyer for these corporate leadership positions seems to be based on loyalty to the president rather than on qualifications.

Such practices are more consistent with the model of patrimonial authoritarianism—and its accompanying elite and regime-based objectives—than with the objective of securing Russian national interests.[40] Evidence that Russia's major energy companies were being configured and used to serve national interests would include capital investments and active pursuit of foreign investment and technical know-how to expand Russian production and poise the country for integration into dynamic global markets. The appointment of Putin's trusted associates from the KGB and St. Petersburg as chairmen of these two enterprises vital to Russian power and prosperity is more consistent with a model based on narrow regime interests than national interests.

Society: Stability, Acquiescence, and Risk-Avoidance

Boris Yeltsin died on April 24, 2007. Despite the gestures of remembrance and respect that followed, Yeltsin remained deeply unpopular among Russians even at a moment when people tend to forget failures and foibles. According to polls conducted after his death, 80% of Russians believed Yeltsin had led Russia in the wrong direction.[41] Russians associate Yeltsin's democratization and liberalization with insecurity and loss, the 50% drop in GDP in the 1990s, armed confrontation in Moscow in 1993, foreign policy reversals such as NATO enlargement, the failed Chechen War (1994–96), and the terrorist attacks on Moscow apartments in 1999.

Under Putin's leadership, Russians have received what they wanted: security, stabilization, and an improvement in their daily lives. Reform and democracy have been thoroughly discredited in Russia. Russian polling data indicates that in principle Russian citizens want the freedoms and rights associated with liberalization, but not at the price of the democracy they believe they experienced in the 1990s. Russian citizens accept the leadership's argument for the necessity of placing limits on both society and the political sphere in order to avoid risky experiments in social, political, and economic

---

[40] Ian Bremmer and Samuel Charap, "The Siloviki: Who They Are and What They Want," *Washington Quarterly* 30, no. 1 (Winter 2006/2007): 83–92.

[41] Compare this figure to the negative evaluation of those polled regarding Stalin (48%) and Gorbachev, who Russians blame for destroying the Soviet Union (72%). "Epokha Yeltsina glazami Rossiyan" [The epoch of Yeltsin in the eyes of Russians]," Russian Public Opinion Research Center, April 25, 2007, http://wciom.ru/novosti/press-vypuski/press-vypusk/single/8078.html.

change.[42] Russian citizens are, however, educated, experienced, and modern. The general populace supports the Putin leadership but understands that the Russia's political system is corrupt and its elites are not accountable. If conditions were to worsen and Russian people were to stop believing that the future will be better, the citizenry might become less acquiescent.

Though the Putin leadership has delivered stability and economic growth, the government's claims to be effectively serving the basic needs of Russian society could at some point be undermined by a host of looming social problems. The most important indicator of a serious failure in social programs is Russia's demographic crisis: the Russian population, which numbered 141,378,000 in mid-2007, is declining by about 700,000 per year. Life expectancy for Russian males is 59 years and for females, 73 years. Russia has a birth rate of about 11 per 1,000 people, and a death rate of 16 per 1,000.[43] Russia differs, however, from other countries whose population growth is slowing or even declining. In such countries in Europe, the causes are advanced social conditions and opportunities for women that lead them to choose smaller families. Russia's population, however, is shrinking as a result of excess mortality and the ill-health of its male population. The excessive mortality rate among Russian men is due to cardiovascular disease, smoking, alcohol abuse, and poor diet.[44] Russia would have experienced a more serious population decline had it not been for the influx of ethnic Russian immigrants from other post-Soviet countries in the 1990s. Now that this migration has slowed, population decline is likely to accelerate in coming years as the effects of ill-health continue to take their toll.

Young Russian men are dying at a higher rate now than seven years ago at the start of Putin's presidency. The death rate for men ages 25 to 34 is five times that of most Western countries. The death rate for 30-year-old Russian men is now 48% higher before the advent of Putin's strong state and economy.[45] Alcohol abuse is a key factor in the high death rate for Russian men ages 25 to 34. Two other diseases that have become endemic in the Russian population—HIV/AIDS and drug-resistant tuberculosis (TB)—are

---

[42] One should keep in mind that measuring social support and public opinion is highly problematic in Russia given state control of the mass media and the elimination of genuine opposition political parties. The best way to think of evidence about current views in Russia society is that such views are genuinely held but may be volatile and subject to substantial change in light of new experience or information.

[43] See the Russia section of the Central Intelligence Agency, *The World Factbook 2007* (Washington, D.C.: Central Intelligence Agency, 2007).

[44] Nicholas Eberstadt, "The Russian Federation at the Dawn of the Twenty-First Century: Trapped in a Demographic Straitjacket," The National Bureau of Asian Research, *NBR Analysis* 15, no. 2, September 2004.

[45] Gaddy, "The Russian Economy," 8.

an even more serious threat that may kill an even larger number of younger Russian men as well as women. The effects of a further increase in mortality rates among the younger citizens—Russia's productive workforce—will likely last for decades. The growth rate of HIV infection in Russia has slowed somewhat, but this change has likely come about because the disease has moved from the population of commercial sex workers and intravenous drug users to the general population, where it is spread more often by heterosexual sex than by shared needles. Russia has 402,000 registered cases of HIV; the true number is estimated to be 1.3 million. One indication that the disease is now endemic in the Russian population is the increasing percentage of women in new cases registered: women comprised some 44% of the 40,000 cases reported in 2006.[46]

TB also poses a grave threat to Russian health in the long term. Although AIDS is deadly, its transmission is largely preventable. TB, however, is a highly infectious disease transmitted by airborne droplets. In the early 1990s the incidence rate of TB, following decades of decline, actually increased in Russia. Russia is now among the 22 countries with the highest incidence rates of TB in the world. Failures of the Russian health system in the 1990s allowed drug-resistant TB strains to develop and spread. These strains require longer and more expensive courses of treatment. A new strain of TB has appeared in Russia that is resistant to all known forms of treatment. Health monitoring programs are tracking the spread of this dangerous new strain both in Russian cities and abroad by those infected in Russia.[47]

The impact of HIV/AIDS and drug resistant TB on Russia's younger adult population could accelerate. Increasing mortality in younger age cohorts would also have a greater effect on the economy than the cardiovascular fatalities that affect men at the end of their working lives. A World Bank study projected that, because of the economic costs of HIV/AIDS, Russia's GDP in 2020 could be 10% lower than would otherwise be the case.[48]

Poverty and inequality are other important social issues that may lead Russian citizens to question the leadership's performance. Although Russia's poverty rate has declined as a result of the country's economic growth, inequality has grown. Moscow is aware of this problem, as evidenced in the

---

[46] "Number of HIV Cases Increasing in Russia, Health Official Says," *Kaisernetwork.org*, May 17, 2007, http://www.kaisernetwork.org/Daily_reports/rep_index.cfm?DR_ID=44962.

[47] Anya Andreyeva, "Drug Resistant TB Gains Strength in Russia," *NewsVOA.com*, March 21, 2007, http://www.voanews.com/english/archive/2007-03/2007-03-21-voa34.cfm.

[48] "The Economic Consequences of HIV in Russia," World Bank, Report, 2002, http://www.worldbank.org.ru.

government's "national projects" to improve pensions, housing, health, and education. First Deputy Prime Minister Dmitri Medvedev has been given the task of implementing these national projects to improve Russian lives.[49]

Widespread mass protests in January 2005 (against social benefits reform) and March 2006 (against housing reform) lend plausibility to the notion that social conditions could lead otherwise contented Russian citizens to question the Putin leadership.[50] The government's quick reversal of course in the face of the genuine popular protests suggests that the leadership understands the sources of its contingent legitimacy as well.

Many advanced modern societies face serious challenges in health, employment, and social services. What is problematic in Russia is the lack of political and societal mechanisms by which citizens can effectively make claims on their government. As a component of the government's efforts to prevent dissent or independent claims on the Russian state, the Putin leadership has worked to weaken civil society. The Kremlin correctly recognized that the success of citizen based protests against fraudulent elections in 2003 and 2004 (in Georgia and Ukraine, respectively) was largely due to the efforts of autonomous and well-organized civil society groups. The Putin leadership reacted by passing a series of laws restricting the operation of Russian NGOs and limiting rights of association and protest. In a very astute move, the Kremlin not only banned or made difficult the operation of authentic Russian NGOs but also created the Public Chamber—a state-friendly and state-funded body that manages civil society—as well as government financing for approved NGOs. The goal of these moves was to occupy the civic space with controlled representatives advancing acceptable messages.[51]

On the one hand, this is smart political management by the Kremlin insofar as these moves eliminate authentic or effective social opposition. On the other hand, this strategy creates a dangerous condition in which Russian citizens may become disaffected with government policies and performance but lack peaceful and legal outlets to express their opposition and press for change. By eliminating authentic independent political parties in favor of Kremlin-friendly "opposition parties" that do not challenge the current leadership, the Putin leadership is constructing a political system

---

[49] This development is widely viewed by Russian analysts as meant to position Medvedev as a contender to succeed Putin as president. Yaroslav Lissovolik, "Tackling the Problem of Income Inequality," *RussiaProfile.com*, May 14, 2007, http://russiaprofile.org/page.php?pageid=CDI+Russia+Profile+List&articleid=a1179156055.

[50] "Protest Movements Are Coordinating and Stepping Up Efforts," *RFE/RL Daily Report*, March 7, 2007, http://www.rferl.org/featuresarticle/2006/03/8da4cc95-c79a-46e4-bcd1-1019f3303091.html.

[51] "Putin Appoints First Members of Controversial Public Chamber," *Moscow News*, October 1, 2005, http://www.mosnews.com/news/2005/10/01/pubchamber.shtml.

that looks strong but is potentially unstable and fragile. If the only authentic opposition parties or NGOs are those on the fringe, what is left for Russian citizens who question the Putin regime's performance?

Ideas and Ideology

Given that Russia is the successor to a country whose politics and foreign policy were largely defined by ideology, Russia's politics and foreign policy have been less shaped by ideology than might be expected. With the collapse of the Soviet Union and delegitimation of the Communist Party and communist ideology, several potential sources for ideas emerged that would shape Russian values and perceptions of how the world works. The first was Westernization and liberalization of politics and economics—the variant initially embraced by Yeltsin and articulated by Russia's first post-Soviet foreign minister, Andrei Kozyrev.[52] As discussed earlier, the instabilities and economic collapse of the Yeltsin years delegitimated the ideology of Westernization for the vast majority of Russians.

An alternative ideology is Russian nationalism. Although a strong element in Russian politics and foreign policy throughout history, the modern role of nationalism has proved highly problematic. Given the ethnic and religious diversity of the country, ethnic definitions of Russia do not quite work. A "civic" definition of Russian nationalism—something akin to U.S. nationalism, which is not ethnically based—proved problematic as well because historic variants of Russian nationalism were rooted in the Russian Orthodox religion and thus too limited in scope for a modern all-encompassing Russian nationalism.[53] Another alternative rooted in Russian history was Eurasianism, an ideology with roots in the Russian Slavicist philosophy championed by Yeltsin's subsequent foreign minister, Yevgeniy Primakov. Eurasianism is an ideology rooted in Russia's geopolitical expanse, multi-regional scope, and special status as a country and culture bridging East and West. As a modern ideology, however, Eurasianism also is problematic; the traditional and geopolitical fundamentals of Eurasianism are a poor fit as a modern ideology for a Russia with ambitions to participate in a dynamic globalizing economy.[54] Putin may have been successful in making the case for both a strong Russian state and the need for vigilance

---

[52] Andrei Kozyrev, "Russia: A Chance for Survival," *Foreign Affairs* 71, no. 2 (Spring 1992): 1–16.

[53] Astrid S. Tuminez, *Russian Nationalism Since 1856* (New York: Rowman and Littlefield, 2000), 173–224.

[54] Dmitri Trenin, *The End of Eurasia: Russia on the Border between Geopolitics and Globalization* (Washington, D.C.: Carnegie Endowment for International Peace, 2001), chap. 7.

against external enemies, but even his concept of *gosudarstvennost'* ("stateness") is "fundamentally post-ideological."[55]

Early in his leadership, Putin favored pragmatism over ideology in domestic politics and foreign policy by focusing on growing the economy, creating stability and security, and finding like-minded partners internationally. Putin moved away from this approach in 2004 when, in the aftermath of the terrorist hostage-taking at a school in Beslan, he declared that Russia faced enemies abroad that sought to weaken the country from within.[56] Russian leaders had called upon other countries to join in multipolar balancing against U.S. power to restrain the United States from war in Iraq. Beginning in 2004, the Russian leadership became more focused on the idea that U.S. power would threaten its hold on power at home, as the Putin leadership saw a threat in the "color revolutions" in other post-Soviet states. What had been originally justified as "managed democracy" evolved—in the argument of Kremlin ideologist Vladislav Surkov—into "sovereign democracy," which he explained as a form of government that is defined and exercised by Russians alone, without control or influence by foreign countries or agents.[57] In Surkov's view, Russia must be sovereign and independent in order to be strong and stable and need not accept foreign countries' standards or definitions of democracy, the role of the state, or form of the economy. Indeed, as Putin stated in his May 9, 2007 Victory Day speech (cited earlier), non-Russians not only fail to understand what Russia needs or how the country works but also wish to weaken the country by forcing Russia to accept foreign definitions and standards.

Thus the key emergent ideology posits Russia as a great power: strong, sovereign, and built upon a centralized state that not only is autonomous from both foreign and internal influences (since Russians who do not support the ideology must be working for foreign powers) but also owns or controls most strategic sectors of the economy. Lilia Shevtsova, Russia's leading political analyst, sees a clear link between Russia's domestic system, its leadership's policies, and the concept of Russia as a great power. Shevstova notes that:

> the system of governance has acquired a new logic. Its main operating principles are: the subjugation of all branches of government to the executive;

---

[55] Stephen E. Hanson, "Russian Nationalism in a Post-Ideological Era," in *Russia Watch: Essays in Honor of George Kolt*, ed. Eugene B. Rumer and Celeste A. Wallander (Washington DC: Center for Strategic and International Studies Press, forthcoming 2007).

[56] Vadim Volkov, "Will the Kremlin Revive the Russian Idea?" Center for Strategic and International Studies, PONARS Policy Memo, no. 370, 2005, http://www.csis.org/media/csis/pubs/pm_0370.pdf.

[57] Edinnaya Rossiya, "Nasha rossiyskaya model demokratii nazyvayetsya 'suverennoy demokratiyey,'" [Our Russian Model of Democracy Is Called "Sovereign Democracy"], June 28, 2006, http://www.edinros.ru/news.html?id=114108.

the merger of political power and corporate ownership; the combination and incorporation of incompatible governing principles, thus preventing the formation of political alternatives to the regime; consensus among the political class and a portion of society on the need to maintain the status quo; political expediency as the driving force behind the regime's actions; and aspirations to great power status as a substitute for ideology.[58]

Whether this notion of Russia as a great power and sovereign democracy constitutes an ideology or is merely a rationalization is not important for the purposes of understanding the relationship between Russian grand strategy and domestic politics. Important for these purpose is the integrated whole that clearly emerges from the pieces: the Russian leadership's external threat assessment (U.S. power), internal threat assessment (foreign influence and meddling in Russia's politics and economy), and the need for a strong state and state-controlled economy to make the country a great power abroad and sovereign at home.

A Sustainable Equilibrium?

The Putin leadership has built a state and economy that enable the political leadership to control the country's vast wealth, minimize dissent and effective political opposition, and advance a more assertive and strategic foreign policy. Although the leadership appears to be in a favorable position, an exploration of Russia's domestic conditions and grand strategy over the coming years calls into question the leadership's ability to sustain this equilibrium.

Three weak points in the system threaten the equilibrium. The first is political. The Kremlin has created a system in which it controls power, the economy, society, media, dissent, and even manufactured "opposition" parties. The stakes in the system are very high and the president is the main power broker. Russia's political landscape lacks genuinely competitive parties or authentic societal interest groups but is strewn with competing clans that use their political power to gain wealth and use their wealth to hold political power.

The constitution does not allow Putin to run for a third term. With his second term as president set to end in March 2008, Putin will likely select his own successor, as Yeltsin did. Russians will likely vote for Putin's choice out of a desire for order and stability that is reinforced by state-controlled media. Whoever becomes successor will be able to sustain the current set of power and lucrative business relationships—or completely re-structure them and create entirely new configurations of winners and losers. Putin's choice,

---

[58] Lilia Shevtsova, "Russia's Ersatz Democracy," *Current History* 105, no. 693 (October 2006): 307.

therefore, will become a threat to and target of all the other clan interests. In the interest of preventing the political fratricide (and thus instability) that would ensue, Putin has not yet identified his designated successor.[59] Because of the lack of legitimate functioning political institutions, the political system that the Kremlin has built over the past seven years to create order, stability, and state power is potentially unstable and weak at moments of leadership transition.[60]

Second, Russia's economy is hardly the powerhouse that high energy prices and revenues make it appear, especially for a country with pretensions to great power status. Russia is losing its industrial base, and both the politicization of the economy and the weak rule of law and legal system have prevented the country from developing highly advanced technology sectors as India has done. An increasingly unfriendly reputation among foreign investors and relatively high costs of business have prevented Russia from building diverse low technology sectors as China has done. As long as energy prices remain high, revenues will flow in; yet if oil drops below $40 per barrel the revenue stream will be squeezed. Furthermore, because Russian oil and gas production is no longer rising, growth rates will depend on rising prices rather than increases in production. International demand has helped to sustain Russia's military and nuclear industries but has not driven them to develop new systems or technologies.[61] Despite high revenues, GDP growth, and the government's stabilization fund, Russian government spending on health, education, and pensions has decreased.[62] This suggests that Russia's wealth is not being invested to build a society or economy able to sustain long-term growth. Therefore, while the success of the Putin regime at home and abroad is by no means an illusion, this success is built on a shaky foundation that almost certainly will shift. The only question is how long the energy price boom will last.

Third, Russia's people likely will face additional hardship. It is unlikely that average Russian have seen the last of the social and economic dislocations they have endured in the fifteen years since the collapse of the

---

[59] Leon Aron, "The Vagaries of the Presidential Succession," American Enterprise Institute, Short Publication, Spring 2007.

[60] For a detailed analysis, see Stephn E. Hanson, "The Uncertain Future of Russia's Weak State Authoritarianism," *East European Politics and Societies* 21, no. 1 (2007): 67–81.

[61] Julian Cooper, "Developments in the Russian Arms Industry," in *SIPRI Yearbook: Armaments, Disarmament, and International Security 2006* (Oxford: Oxford University Press, 2006), http://yearbook2006.sipri.org/chap9/app9c; and Pavel Baev, "Russia's Military Part of Kremlin's Intrigues," Jamestown Foundation, Eurasia Daily Monitor 4, no. 5419, March 2007, http://www.jamestown.org/publications_details.php?volume_id=420&&issue_id=4040. For example, Russia has a new tank (the T-90) and new ICBM (the Topol-M), but their high price has meant that fewer have been procured and deployed than originally planned.

[62] Aron, "The Vagaries of the Presidential Succession," 5.

Soviet system. The income growth fueled by the energy boom has led to rising wages and improved lifestyles for the young and middle class in Moscow, St. Petersburg, and major regional cities. Yet the structural problems of long-term decline and failure to invest in human capital and social infrastructure to improve Russian lives are deeply rooted. The government has allowed these problems to worsen through neglect; soon this decay will begin to plague the daily lives of average citizens. Russia's urban and transportation infrastructure is crumbling. Unlike wealthy Russians, average citizens cannot send their children to private school to avoid the failing education system. Income inequality is growing. Unemployment ranges as high as 25% in many Russian regions, with youth unemployment in some regions as high as 93%.[63]

The accumulation of very serious long-term structural social problems, the inflexibility and brittleness of the political system, and the distorted and vulnerable nature of Russia's current economic windfall combine to create the potential for disequilibrium, social discontent, and political opposition outside peaceful institutional channels. Change challenges every country, but Russia at the end of the Putin era is especially vulnerable to economic and social shocks. Russia itself is unlikely to break apart, and we should not expect a hundred-year anniversary Russian Revolution. Yet the current equilibrium of a booming resource economy, complacent society, corrupt state, and ostensibly effective foreign policy strategy is not sustainable. The equilibrium will likely shift along the system's most vulnerable dimensions. In the short term, the political system is at risk because of upcoming elections and the succession crisis. In the medium term, the economy is most vulnerable because of the dependence on energy prices and weakness of non-energy sectors. In general, the current equilibrium of political control, economic boom, and strategic assertiveness is not a good basis for predicting Russia's role in Asia over the medium to long term.

Russian Grand Strategy Revisited

This analysis of Russia's domestic landscape requires a modification of the Russian government's version of Russian grand strategy. First, it is helpful to distinguish between the national interest and the interests of the regime. In democratic political systems, political institutions and processes make leaders accountable to voters and thus make government policy

---

[63] "Economic Growth Should Benefit Human Development in all Russia's Regions," UN Development Programme, Press Release, May 16, 2007, http://www.undp.ru/index.phtml?iso=RU&lid=1&cmd=news&id=388.

reflect societal preferences and interests.[64] Since Russia's political system is not democratic and the country's leaders are not effectively accountable, one could reasonably argue that leaders pursue their own interests—which may or may not coincide with society's. Rather than using the term "national interests" in the context of grand strategy, therefore, it is more accurate to refer to regime interests. As Dmitri Trenin notes, "Russia" stands for a small group of people who own the country and hold political power.[65]

What are the regime's interests and what are the resulting implications for international policy and strategy? The regime's interests are twofold: remaining in power and becoming wealthier. The two priorities are linked because political power is necessary to acquire and control Russia's lucrative economic sectors, and wealth is necessary to generate the rents that sustain patron-client relationships upon which power is based. As Trenin has noted, "private and corporate interests are behind most of Moscow's major policy decisions, as Russia is ruled by people who largely own it."[66]

Given the overwhelming dependence of the Russian economy on the export of a very narrow range of goods (oil and natural gas, nuclear technology, other raw materials, military armaments, and steel), Russia's political economic elite need international trade to retain power and access wealth. Russian grand strategy is therefore directed at increasing its participation in the international economy, but on terms that allow that elite to retain control of the state, economy, and society at home.

For the short and medium term, the Russian regime's main focus will be Europe and its post-Soviet neighbors. Most of Russia's lucrative business is currently with Western countries and companies. Rising energy demands in Asia may, however, change that calculation over the coming decades. Furthermore, because Russia cannot sell arms or nuclear technology to Europe, the Russian elite cannot ignore relations with Asian countries that are current or potential customers in these sectors. In 2005, EU countries accounted for 58% of Russian exports and 45% of its imports; post-Soviet countries, 16% of Russian exports and 19.5% of imports. By comparison, China accounted for just under 6% of Russian exports and 7.5% of its imports; Japan, 1.5% of Russian exports and 6% of its imports; South Korea, 1% of Russian exports and 4% of its imports; and India, under 1% in each category. The United States accounts for just 3% of Russian exports and 4.5% of its imports.[67]

---

[64] Robert Dahl, *Polyarchy* (New Haven: Yale University Press, 1971), 1.

[65] Dmitri Trenin, "Russia Redefines Itself and Its Relations with the West," *Washington Quarterly* 30, no. 2 (Spring 2007): 95–105.

[66] Ibid., 95.

[67] *Direction of Trade Statistics*, International Monetary Fund, 2006.

Were the Russian state pursuing national interests in stability and economic growth, one would expect Moscow to diversify the economy and particularly to increase foreign investment in order to develop modern sectors and technologies. Russia's economy is certainly growing; there is money to be made by foreign investors, and the resources generated by a booming economy have raised incomes. Russian citizens also have money to spend, fueling a boom in construction, consumer goods purchases, and demand for services. If Russia's economic boom, however, is to be the foundation for a strategic foreign and security policy and the power necessary to make Russia an equal of China, India, and the United States, then Russia needs an economy that competes and grows in advanced sectors, that develops new technologies in defense worthy of a global great power, and that invests in human capital and education.

Because of the legal and practical limits on foreign investment in Russia's most lucrative sectors discussed above, the country is not an especially attractive destination for FDI. In non-extractive industries, there are many other international opportunities for investment that are much more worthy of pursuit. Were the Russian leadership interested in strengthening the country by improving its economy, Moscow would create a favorable investment climate, diversify the economy, and increase production capacity in the energy sector. Instead, in the past two years the Russian government has excluded foreign investors and pressured those already in the country to cede controlling stakes to state companies.

This leads to a second important nuance of Russian grand strategy: the central importance of control, lack of transparency, and "sovereignty" in dealing with the outside world. Contrary to the Kremlin's official line, the countries best poised to be powerful in the 21st century are those states that are relatively open to globalization and that facilitate participation in the international economy by playing a regulatory and compensatory role. China and India have higher growth rates and seem poised to become the rising great powers of the 21st century largely because of their openness to private enterprise and international business. Iran, in contrast, will likely not realize its potential to be more than a regional power in the Middle East if the repressive domestic political economy prevents the country from pursuing globalization's opportunities.

An atmosphere of openness and transparency would pose a threat, however, to the Russian political system. These conditions would limit the Putin leadership's ability to determine the presidential successor and, as a result, the power of the new president to maintain a system in which state officials control national wealth and energy revenues. That Russia might view U.S. unipolarity and unilateralism as a potential threat to national interests is understandable—note that even many U.S. allies in Europe criticize and seek to contain or balance U.S. power. Western calls for democratization, liberalization, rule of law, and protection of property rights do not threaten Russian national interests. Such calls do, however, threaten Russian regime interests by exposing the current elite to the risk of losing power and control over the economy if Russia were to move in these directions.

The worsening of Russia's relations with Europe over the past year demonstrates that U.S. unipolarity or unilateralism are not the only threats to the Putin leadership. In previous years Putin sought European support for balancing the United States. By the summer of 2007, however, Russia had become embroiled in confrontations with the EU over a number of issues: Russia's energy policy, human rights record, and ban on Polish meat products; the suspicious murders of Russian journalists and regime critics; and Russia's bullying of Estonia (for transferring a Soviet war memorial from central Tallinn to a military cemetery). The EU is Russia's main trading partner and source of foreign investment, yet the Putin leadership has refused to compromise on control of the energy sector or to exercise moderation in relations with EU members. Confident of Russia's power and growing economy, and bolstered by the leverage the country's energy exports afford, the Putin leadership is willing to put negotiation of a special relationship with the EU at risk rather than make concessions.

Russia's interest in balancing U.S. power, promoting multipolarity, and developing ties with important Eurasian countries like China and Iran is best understood in the context of this fear of openness and transparency. Russia's strategy of balancing U.S. power and presence certainly makes sense in strictly geopolitical terms. Underlying this strategy, however, is the additional objective of creating a coalition of countries that share Russia's view of U.S. power, presence, and efforts to democratize and liberalize Eurasian countries as a threat.[68] Analysts often note that a rising China in Asia poses a threat to Russian security that is as great as, or greater than, that posed by the United States. Such an assessment would seem to argue against strategic cooperation between Moscow and Beijing. The threat posed by China, however, is a long-term national threat. If Russia's leadership sees the immediate threat being a U.S. security strategy that embraces democratization, then Moscow would naturally choose to seek

---

[68] Countries that Russia seeks to engage in efforts both to oppose U.S. interference in domestic affairs and to prevent export of color revolutions varies but usually includes China, the Central Asian states, Iran, and sometimes Venezuela.

out geopolitical partners (including China) that also oppose the U.S. "transformational" agenda.[69]

On the one hand, the current business interests of the Russian leadership draw Moscow toward Europe. On the other hand, the leadership's perception of the United States as a threat—for both geopolitical and internal political economic reasons—requires the Kremlin's grand strategy to have a Eurasian dimension. Russia's Asia strategy is a blend of geopolitics, specific business interests, and finding common cause against the threat posed by Western liberalization to the Russian elite's grasp on power.

The third nuance of Russia's grand strategy questions its "grandness." If grand strategy is defined as the matching of interests and security requirements within a given strategic environment with the means and resources available for achieving them, Russia does not have a grand strategy for two reasons. First, the government's objectives and interests are those of a narrow elite and do not constitute the strategic interests of a country facing a complicated and challenging 21st century. The government's threat analysis merely serves narrow interests. Putin and his government warn of foreign enemies in order to justify the consolidation of a non-democratic state at home—as did many Russian and Soviet leaders before them.[70] Second, even more importantly, the Russian elite's determination to control the state and economy for personal power and wealth is weakening the country and will leave Russia ill-equipped to meet the challenges of globalization and security realities in Eurasia in the coming century. The leadership's claims to great power status, like its warnings of threats from foreign enemies, are meant to justify the leadership's policies. These claims are not serious assessments of Russia's capabilities, strategic requirements, and geopolitical environment.

"Russia's self-image as a great power is a highly imaginative one that does not correspond to its actual power," concludes one leading expert on Russia's history of empire.[71] An expert on modern Russian foreign policy concurs:

> From Ivan to Putin Russia has worn its great power status on its sleeve, and, when it is called into question, its leaders and essayists sink into a narcissistic preoccupation with the country's decline...Only the Russians in moments of distress revert to an affectation of great-power standing—that is, to asserting

---

[69] On U.S. policy, see Condoleezza Rice, "Transformational Diplomacy" (speech given at Georgetown University, Washington, D.C., January 18, 2006), http://www.state.gov/secretary/rm/2006/59306.htm.

[70] Lawrence T. Caldwell, "Russian Concepts of National Security," in *Russian Foreign Policy*, 284.

[71] Ronald Suny, "Living in the Hood: Russia, Empire, and Old and New Neighbors," in *Russian Foreign Policy*, 68.

their natural right to the role and influence of a great power whether they have the wherewithal or not.[72]

The conclusion drawn from this alternative assessment of Russian domestic politics and grand strategy stands in sharp contrast to the image that the Kremlin has tried to advance in the past few years, and one that so many Western officials and analysts seem to have accepted without looking at the fundamentals of Russian interests and power. With a domestic landscape of patrimonial authoritarianism, centralized yet fragile political power, looming societal crises, and an economy increasingly reliant on selling whatever oil and gas can be pumped from aging fields, however, Russia is not poised to plan or execute the grand strategy of a Eurasian great power in the coming years. At best, a tactical Russia will survive its succession crisis in the next year and—if energy prices decline gradually and stabilize at a lower price—a new leadership will be encouraged to plan for an economy worthy of a great power. At worst, though, Russia may just be entering the next chapter in its long post-Soviet decline.

Implications for Asia

In March 2007 the Russian Foreign Ministry published a review of the country's foreign policy that had been prepared at the request of the president.[73] Three key opening paragraphs of this review are of particular note. First, the section on the Asia-Pacific attributes the strategic significance of the region to its role as the "locomotive" of the world economy, with lead roles played by China and India. Second, a section on major developments in the region identifies efforts by the United States to consolidate bilateral strategic alliances with Japan, South Korea, and Australia. Third, the review also notes both that Russia's primary interest in the region is the accelerated development of Siberia and the Russian Far East and that Russia's strategic goal is the formation of deep and balanced relations with countries in the region to guarantee long-term stability. These three elements encapsulate Russia's main concerns in Asia: (1) economics and growth, (2) security "architectures" and U.S. influence, and (3) the connection between internal and international stability.

China is central to these three concerns. Many analysts have noted Russia's ambivalence about China. On the one hand, Russia has reason to pursue closer ties and even a strategic partnership with its southern

---

[72] Robert Legvold, "Russian Foreign Policy," 114.

[73] "Obzor vneshney politiki rossiyskoy federatsii," no. 431, March 27, 2007, http://www.mid.ru/brp_4.nsf/sps?OpenView&Start=1.435&Count=30&Expand=1#1.

neighbor because China is a valuable trading partner, Asia's rising power, and a useful balance to U.S. power. On the other hand, China's power, geopolitical presence, and economic dynamism pose a potential threat that thereby limits the closeness of the relationship.[74] Among Russia's most salient concerns is Chinese immigration—though warnings of creeping Chinese territorial encroachment through legal and illegal immigration have proven overblown, Chinese immigrants continue to travel to and work in Russia's depopulating Far East where their presence draws constant attention and comment. After implementing a law to regulate migration in January 2007, the government reported the registration of 2 million Chinese migrants by May 2007. Such measures, however, will not eliminate the unease many Russians feel about China's "creeping colonization" of Russia's Far East.[75]

There are also serious constraints on Russian-Chinese economic cooperation. Increasing demand from China has contributed to the rise in global energy prices, which in turn has benefited Russia. Because of China's growing need for energy, Russia has become more important to China, and Russia—so dependent energy on exports—sees China as a potentially important customer. Yet Russia's interests as supplier and China's as customer are far from identical or even harmonious. As a consumer, China's interests are in long-term reliable supply and low prices.[76] The Russian government in contrast has an interest in high prices. By moving in 2007 to consolidate control over a number of energy corridors and pipelines, Russia was aiming in particular to prevent the diversification of pipelines from Central Asia. Russia must purchase Central Asian gas to fulfill European supply contracts and meet domestic demand and therefore needs to control the transit routes. In May 2007, Putin secured agreement with the presidents of Kazakhstan and Turkmenistan to build a new gas pipeline westward through Russian territory. Western commentary focused on how the deal thwarted U.S. efforts to make both the Central Asian suppliers and European consumers less dependent on Russia by encouraging alternative routes.[77] Putin's triumph appeared to be another success in his strategy of using energy both to exercise leverage over the West and Russia's post-Soviet

---

[74] See, for example, previous volumes in this series, especially Wohlforth, "Russia's Soft Balancing Act"; and Stephen E. Hanson, "Strategic Partner or Evil Empire?" in *Strategic Asia 2004–05: Confronting Terrorism in the Pursuit of Power*, ed. Ashley J. Tellis and Michael Wills (Seattle: The National Bureau of Asian Research, 2004), 183–85.

[75] Interfax, May 2, 2007; and "The 'Age of China' in Russia," *Gazeta.ru*, April 9, 2007.

[76] Erica Downs, "Energy Security Series: China," Brookings Institution, December 2006, 13–14, http://www3.brookings.edu/fp/research/energy/2006china.pdf.

[77] Ilan Greenberg, "Russia to Get Central Asian Pipeline," *New York Times*, May 13, 2007, http://www.nytimes.com/2007/05/13/world/europe/13putin.html?ex=1336708800&en=88b76ac3bf634c6d&ei=5088&partner=rssnyt&emc=rss.

neighbors and to enrich his network of compatriots in Russian government and business circles.

Russia's actions also dealt a great blow not only to Chinese energy security but also to Asian energy consumers in general. As long as the pipelines that carry Eurasian energy to global markets and consumers traverse the long and tortured routes west across Russia, China and other potential customers like India will be dependent on Russian policy. Clearly aware of this problem, China made a separate deal with Kazakhstan to build an oil pipeline between the two countries and has been pursuing plans for others. As a result, Russia's monopoly on Central Asian energy corridors may not ultimately be secure. Although suppliers and consumers may have common interests when their exchange is on a market basis, their relationship is more likely to be competitive (or even zero-sum) when power and politics enter the equation.

On the one hand, Putin's consolidation of state control over both Russia's energy sector and Central Asia's energy exports is shifting the Russia-China relationship from partnership back toward competition. On the other hand, the Russian regime's elevation of the U.S. threat over the past year has been an impetus for greater cooperation between Russia and China. From the Russian perspective, the June 2006 summit of the Shanghai Cooperation Organization (SCO)—which partners China, Russia, and the Central Asian states—was a success. The inclusion of India and Iran as observers supported Russia's framing of the SCO as an institution to advance multipolarity in Eurasia. A joint statement on the fifth anniversary of the founding of the SCO praised the organization for respecting the right of all countries to "safeguard nation unity and their national interests" and to "pursue particular models of development." The statement also cautioned that diversity in history and culture "should not be taken as pretexts to interfere in other countries' internal affairs."[78]

As a successful regional organization, the SCO lends support to the great power claims of the Russian leadership—particularly with regard to Russia's ability to partner with China in defining the organization. The SCO gives legitimacy both to the leadership's case that Russia is a great power and to its arguments in favor of a strong state with a direct role in the economy—and the recognition of this legitimacy by other important countries that also seek to balance and limit U.S. influence in Eurasia. Whether the SCO is fundamentally antithetical to Western interests or

---

[78] See "Declaration on the Fifth Anniversary of the Shanghai Cooperation Organization," Central People's Government of the PRC website, http://www.gov.cn/misc/2006-06/15/content_311283. htm.

will succeed is irrelevant.[79] The Russian leadership's policy is tactical, being meant to justify its control of state and economy at home in order to prevent either any challenge to its system of power or complications in preparing for the Putin succession. For the Russian leadership an SCO that demonstrates Eurasian agreement about the problem of U.S. presence and meddling and affirms the legitimacy of a strong state for stability may be merely a tactical victory, but it fits the timeframe of the March 2008 presidential elections and the protection of regime interests that define Russia's limited strategic vision.

Russia will not consider the lack of progress in relations with Japan as a great loss. For significant improvement, Russia would need to entertain concessions on the issue of the Northern Territories (or Kurile Islands). In keeping with its obsession of managing the process of leadership transition, the Putin leadership has justified eliminating independent political, business, and social forces by pointing to the need to build strength to be a great power once again. From the Russian perspective, great powers do not cede territory won in war. As a result, an improvement in Russian-Japanese relations in the coming year is unlikely. Another major obstacle in improving ties will be the chilly investment climate in Russia. Given the Russian government's successful pressure on Mitsui and Mitsubishi to accept minority ownership in the Sakhalin-2 oil and gas project, the Putin leadership clearly does not prioritize pursuing better relations through business ties.

Russian objectives toward North Korea and South Korea are still focused on preventing armed conflict (nuclear or otherwise) and enticing South Korean investment to bring resources to Russia's struggling Far East regions. The stakes in engaging Korea, and the incentives to do so, may shift when the Sakhalin energy projects begin to produce significant volumes, making export and transit routes more important.[80]

Russian relations with India are still based on the twin pillars of balancing regional political ambitions and commercial sales. Russia's potential as a global supplier of advanced nuclear reactor technologies and fuel cycle services has emerged as a new and interesting element in Russian analyses of India. Putin's January 2007 visit to India focused on the potential for such an expanded commercial nuclear trade and investment

[79] For two opposing views, see Oksana Antonenko, "The EU Should Not Ignore the Shanghai Co-operation Organisation," Centre for European Reform, Policy Brief, May 2007, http://www.cer.org.uk/pdf/policybrief_sco_web_11may07.pdf; and Ariel Cohen, "The U.S. Challenge at the Shanghai Summit," The Heritage Foundation, WebMemo, no. 1124, June 13, 2006, http://www.heritage.org/Research/RussiaandEurasia/wm1124.cfm.

[80] Gilbert Rozman, "Russia in Northeast Asia: In Search of A Strategy," in Levgold, *Russian Foreign Policy*, 365–66.

relationship, including an agreement on a $1.2 billion arms deal for Indian purchase of an aircraft carrier and MiG-29 fighters. Putin also suggested that Russia's nuclear agency was interested in building four additional nuclear power plants. The sudden interest may have been driven by the need to compete with U.S.-Indian relations, as analysts have suggested. The move was also consistent with Moscow's efforts to create a global energy supplier triad, augmenting Russia's importance on international oil and natural gas markets with nuclear energy. In April 2007 Putin signed a decree creating a commercial entity, AtomEnergoProm, to manage Russia's nuclear industry—its production and sales, both domestically and abroad—through a single company.[81]

The Russian military in Asia is in no better shape than it has been for the past few years.[82] In February 2007 Putin stated that the Intermediate Range Nuclear Forces (INF) Treaty no longer served Russian interests. A few days later General Yuri Baluyevsky said in an interview that Russia could withdraw from the treaty if Moscow had cause, which he said it did. The INF issue may be related to Russian criticism of U.S. plans to deploy limited missile defenses in Poland and the Czech Republic; a possible additional reason is to rebuild Russia's strategic nuclear deterrent capabilities in Asia. By complying with the INF, Russia has eliminated a large number of strategic missiles with flexible targeting distance.[83] Freed from INF restrictions, Russia could concentrate efforts on introducing a new generation of strategic nuclear weapons. Such a move would be consistent with the Russian military doctrine that a willingness and ability to use nuclear weapons can compensate for Russia's conventional military weakness. This revision in doctrine in 2000 was clearly related to the relative weakening of Russian military capabilities vis-à-vis NATO,[84] but the expansion of scenarios for nuclear use would also be as useful to the Russian military in Asia—if Russia had the available forces. Russia's intercontinental strategic forces currently match and balance U.S. forces and North American targets; introducing intermediate range missiles could allow for deterrence in Asia against rising powers. Although this strategy might seem to contradict Russia's current policy of eagerly providing support for annual SCO joint

---

[81] "Putin Orders Government to Restructure Nuclear Industry," *RIA/Novosti*, April 27, 2007, http://en.rian.ru/russia/20070427/64563510.html.

[82] See Stephen J. Blank, "Potemkin's Treadmill: Russian Military Modernization," in *Strategic Asia 2005–06: Military Modernization in an Era of Uncertainty*, ed. Ashley Tellis and Michael Wills (Seattle: The National Bureau of Asian Research, 2005), 175–205.

[83] Nathan Hughes and Peter Zeihan, "The INF Treaty: Implications of a Russian Withdrawal," Stratfor, February 20, 2007, [restricted access] http://www.stratfor.com/.

[84] Celeste A. Wallander, "Wary of the West: Russian Security Policy at the Millennium," *Arms Control Today* 37, no. 2 (March 2000): 10.

military exercises (with the most recent round held August 2007 in Russia's Ural mountains and focusing on counterterrorism), Russia is still far from forming a military alliance with China. Moscow's strategic ambivalence leaves Russian analysts preoccupied with deterrence scenarios in Asia as much as in the West.[85]

This may, however, be more strategic a vision than actually underlies Russian policy in Asia. Russian strategy in Asia in 2007 is not particularly ambitious in strategic terms. It is tempting to attempt to make strategic sense of Russia's engagement with China, focus on the SCO, leverage in the energy sphere, and active diplomacy against U.S. presence and meddling in Eurasia and Asia. Despite the dynamism, however, this activity does not add up to a grand strategy for managing either Asia's geopolitical realities and rapidly changing economic landscape or Russia's ultimate internal and international weakness. Russia has not pursued a policy of building multipolarity in order to limit the United States; if this were the case the country would have a strategy for pursuing economic relations and overcoming political differences with Japan. Nor has Putin crafted an Asian policy that leverages the region's wealth and dynamism to bring investment and an improvement in living standards to Russia's crumbling Far East. Russia appears poised to devote its Eurasian energy efforts merely to tying Central Asia more closely to European energy markets, rather than taking advantage of the geopolitical opportunity to advance regional integration with the global economy's "locomotives."

Implications for the United States

Until Russia's leadership succession occurs in March 2008, there is little basis in current Russian domestic conditions to expect a fundamental improvement in U.S.-Russian relations. The Russian leadership is vulnerable, the stakes are high, and the image of a hostile outside world with designs to weaken Russia justifies the actions of a political leadership that depends on control and unquestioned access to Russia's wealth. The leadership is flush with cash and this, together with recent diplomatic successes (such as the agreement on a Russia-Central Asian pipeline), deprives the United States of effective leverage over Moscow. As the Russian Duma elections (December 2007) and presidential elections near, the atmosphere of U.S.-Russian relations will likely worsen, given that the Putin leadership gains domestic support for the regime's authoritarianism

---

[85] Bobo Lo, "A Fine Balance—The Strange Case of Sino-Russian Relations," Institut Français des Relations Internationales, Russie Cei Visons, no. 1, April 2005, http://www.ifri.org/files/Russie/bobolo_anglais.pdf.

by claiming that the United States seeks to weaken and encircle Russia. To the extent that finding common cause against U.S. unipolarity and democratization plays a role in Russia's Eurasian policies, Moscow will likely to be calling for resistance to any expanded role by Washington in Russia's Asian diplomacy over the next year.

Being essentially tactical and driven by internal politics, however, such behavior by Russia is actually not particularly serious or threatening to the United States. Furthermore, this anti-U.S. posturing may be transitory. Despite warning of external threats and efforts to limit foreign involvement within Russia (whether in the form of funding for Russian NGOs or Western investors), even the Putin leadership has no real interest in serious confrontation. The current Russian leaders do have an interest in the wealth that globalization can bring. Once the Russian leadership has worked through the new alignment of patron-client relations following the succession crisis, another period of pragmatism in foreign policy may follow. The same sequence occurred following President Putin's accession in 2000–02.

Because Russian diplomacy and initiatives in Asia are primarily tactical, counteractions that would reinforce them would be counterproductive. There are no serious geopolitical motivations or Russian grand strategy to counter. There are, of course, long-term strategic trends that will shape Russian policy in the region. Most important of these will be Asia's growing demand for energy and Russia's potential to meet this demand. Although the current Russian leadership has not crafted an effective strategy for expanding energy production for Asian markets, the potential remains— primarily in the Sakhalin energy projects and in the massive Kovykta natural gas field. Structural realities will draw Moscow closer to Asia, even as Russian domestic weakness prevents the future leadership in Moscow from crafting an effective national strategy for maximizing the country's Asian energy potential.

The image of a strategic Russia in Asia is, however, without real foundation. Neither Russian capabilities nor a well-crafted grand strategy threaten U.S. stakes in Asia. After years of largely fruitless discussions with a Russian government that wants to retain control over energy fields and transit routes, China is already beginning to look elsewhere for energy. The SCO is a successful regional organization, but other than rhetoric against U.S. unilateralism and liberalization, the organization's successes do not threaten U.S. interests. Regional cooperation to counter terrorism is not contrary to U.S. interests in Eurasia, and Russian-Chinese military exercises within SCO remain largely symbolic. Given Russia's ongoing military decline, it would be extraordinary for Russian leaders to move toward any kind of military alliance with China in which Russia would be the weaker partner.

As India and China continue to grow by expanding manufacturing capacity, attracting foreign investment, and facilitating advanced technologies and industries, the hollowness of Russia's claims to being a great power will become more apparent by comparison. In 2002–03 Putin scored a major diplomatic victory in joining with France and Germany to forge a balancing coalition against the United States to oppose the war in Iraq. Four years later, this diplomatic coalition is in shambles. Russian-European relations are on a long slide, albeit one slowed by the willingness of many European elites to further increase Europe's energy dependence on Russian state-controlled companies. A grand strategy of geopolitical balancing, forging multipolarity, and achieving Russian great power status would have to be more long lasting and strategic to be worthy of the term.

Russia's foreign relations look increasingly tactical because Russian domestic policies are tactical, based on narrow interests, and dominated by short time horizons. The good news is that because of these domestic characteristics Russia does not pose a threatening strategic challenge to the United States in Asia akin to that the Soviet Union posed. Russia's less-than-grand strategy means that a new Cold War, whether global or in Asia, is unlikely.

Russia stills poses challenges to the United States in Asia, however. Moscow's tactical preoccupations create opportunities for Central Asian states, as well as China, to play their own Russian card in dealing with the United States. For example, with the Russian leadership willing to invest in their own corrupt resource-driven economies, Central Asian leaders have an easier time managing U.S. power and resisting U.S. policy preferences. Although the SCO is far from effective, alliances have been built on less. The potential, however slight, of an anti-American Eurasian alliance based upon the SCO still exists.

The largest strategic challenge Russia poses, however, is the country's fundamental weakness. Russia's domestic political system, economy, and society are fragile, unstable, and terribly burdened. Russian weakness does not mean U.S. power, and Russian insecurity or decline would not be a U.S. victory, despite what the Russian leadership seems to believe. Given changing power balances and relations throughout Asia, Russia's weak domestic conditions are a potential threat. A weak Russia can be a source of insecurity and instability as it would be less likely to maintain border security against terrorists or traffickers. A weak Russia, moreover, cannot be an effective partner against WMD proliferation. The United States needs to partner with a state that is both strong and effective in order to insure the security of nuclear, chemical, and biological weapon materials. Preparing to respond to the international reverberations of Russia's weakness is an important task facing the United States and countries in Europe and Asia.

Less likely—but still to be taken seriously—is the potential for political instability in connection with the succession crisis, social protests if the government cannot cushion the population from the collapse of social services, or economic difficulties in the face of falling energy prices or distorted development. Russia is unlikely to collapse or break apart. The country is, however, likely to face a new round of challenges arising from demographic decline, a vulnerable economy, and a society that has already been through a great deal. U.S. allies, partners, and even competitors across Asia—as well as Russia itself—share an interest in encouraging Russia to develop as a stable, secure, and coherent Eurasian country. For this to occur will require much better foundations than those Russia has in 2007.

EXECUTIVE SUMMARY

This chapter examines the positive and negative impact of democracy and internal change on the prospects for India's emergence as a great power.

MAIN ARGUMENT:

Rapid economic development has begun to improve India's relative standing in the international system, but weak national leadership, political fragmentation, and a defensive strategic culture suggest India might not be able to take full advantage of a positive international environment. Even suboptimal outcomes for India's grand strategy still might be large enough to make a difference to the evolution of the international system.

POLICY IMPLICATIONS:

- U.S. recognition that a rising India has no incentive to accept the status of a junior partner may help the effort to build enduring security cooperation with India. Leveraging the structural factors that are drawing India and the U.S. closer might be more effective than fitting India into a preconceived alliance framework.

- Assisting India in the economic reintegration of South Asia would create a new zone of stability and prosperity with the potential to influence the Middle East, Central Asia, and East Asia.

- India is driven by its own motivations to balance China in Asia. Strengthening India's power potential to achieve this aim should be a more attractive option for the U.S. than the direct containment of China.

- The current hands-off approach by the U.S. has made it possible for India to move forward on negotiations with Pakistan over Jammu and Kashmir. Active but discreet U.S. support to India-Pakistan rapprochement could help ease the legacy of Partition and help promote moderation and modernization among the 40% of the world's Muslims who live on the subcontinent.

Poised for Power: The Domestic Roots of India's Slow Rise

C. Raja Mohan

Perceptions of India as a rising power with significant potential to influence the balance of power in Asia and beyond began to take hold by the middle of the first decade of the 21st century. Yet many scholars familiar with the country's political evolution continue to doubt India's ability to emerge as a great world power. Pointing to previous unrealized strategic expectations and multiple domestic political and economic challenges, skeptics find reason to doubt that the gap between India's power potential and actual performance will narrow. This chapter, however, not only assumes that the past is not necessarily a guide to India's future as an international actor but also holds that all-pervasive change has been the principal feature of India's domestic environment and external behavior since the launch of economic reforms in 1991. Not all change, however, will facilitate India's rise; some changes might in fact constrain India's emergence as a great power. The objective of this chapter is to assess the consequences of domestic economic and political change on India's grand strategy.

Following the introduction, the second section of the chapter assesses the positive impact of India's accelerated economic growth rates of recent years on the country's international standing. Having broken out of a decades-long equilibrium of low economic growth, New Delhi has found extraordinary new opportunities for pursuing long-standing political objectives within the subcontinent, India's extended neighborhood (covering the Indian Ocean littoral and Afro-Asian region), and the international system as a whole. Average annual growth rates of 6% in the 1990s gave way

C. Raja Mohan is Professor at the S. Rajaratnam School of International Studies at Nanyang Technological University in Singapore. He can be reached at <iscrmohan@ntu.edu.sg>.

to higher growth rates of 8% by 2005. Sustained growth rates of more than 8% in the coming years could rapidly improve India's relative economic status and enhance the country's ability to influence the future regional and global balance of power.

At the heart of the perception of India's rise in the international system is the country's impressive economic performance. The sustainability of this higher growth path and the potential negative impact of many other internal changes (or the lack thereof) in India remain major concerns. The third section of the chapter therefore offers a brief overview of the Indian political system and analyzes four factors affecting India's ability to leverage its expanding international influence. The first of these factors is the continuing proliferation of Indian political parties and the inability of pan-Indian parties such as the Indian National Congress (known as the Congress Party) and the Hindu nationalist Bharatiya Janata Party (BJP) to establish national dominance. The second factor is the so-called democratic constraint on New Delhi's ability to pursue more far-reaching economic reforms that are the key to consolidating India's emergence as a major power. The third factor relates to the tight relationship of the Hindu-Muslim divide within India and the country's perennial confrontation with Pakistan, which has constituted a barrier to India's strategic freedom. The fourth factor is the persistence of a defensive strategic culture in the national security establishment that has impeded India's adaptation both to the changed external environment and to the country's own increased strength.

The fourth section of the chapter analyses the impact of these four domestic factors on India's five immediate strategic priorities. India's first priority is to break out of the historic "two-front" problem with China and Pakistan. Indian initiatives to resolve both the boundary dispute with China and the question of Jammu and Kashmir with Pakistan are potentially paradigm-breaking but remain vulnerable to domestic political dynamics. The second priority involves the redefinition of India's conventional military strategy by moving away from the traditional preoccupation with territorial defense toward the development of expeditionary capabilities. A third priority relates to the new possibilities for South Asian regional economic integration under India's leadership amid positive trends toward economic liberalization and accelerated growth across the region. The fourth priority is to balance the rise of China without undermining a Sino-Indian relationship that for the first time in decades has begun to demonstrate many positive features. India's fifth and most important strategic priority is to accelerate the construction of a security partnership with the United States, despite entrenched fears about losing its much-vaunted autonomy in foreign policy.

The chapter concludes with an assessment of the interplay between India's domestic politics and grand strategy and the resulting policy challenges for the United States over the coming years. India may never be able to demonstrate a clean or linear progression on economic reforms, but structural change in the Indian economy is occurring with many strategic consequences. At an ideological level, India's recent rapid growth surge has the potential to break the widely perceived negative relationship between democracy and development. In terms of global power distribution, even a slow pace of economic reform is likely to offer India a significant role in shaping the regional and global balance of power. Though the nature of India's domestic political discourse and the persistence of a defensive strategic culture will produce suboptimal outcomes in the international arena, the same can be said of the domestic politics of most major democracies. A slow and incremental restructuring of Indian security policies might present many complementary aspects for U.S. grand strategy. To realize the significant potential for strategic cooperation with India, however, the United States might need to avoid a unilateral definition of the terms and conditions of the relationship. Even a slowly rising India has no incentive to become a junior partner to the United States.

India's Grand Strategy

For the first time in the sixty years since independence, India appears well poised to realize some of its ambitious grand strategic objectives. These include sustaining economic and political primacy in the subcontinent, developing a capacity to balance other powers in the extended neighborhood of Asia and the Indian Ocean region, and gaining influence in the management of international peace and security. Although long animated by a special sense of its own destiny, India was prevented from realizing its grand strategic ambitions by three major constraints: the partition of the subcontinent on religious lines, the Cold War, and the country's enduring romance with socialism. With the Cold War having ended and fascination for socialism slowly yielding to an increasing respect for globalization, elimination of the third constraint—the debilitating consequences of the Partition—has emerged at the top of India's national agenda.[1]

Following the end of the Cold War and the launch of economic reforms in the early 1990s, India began to improve its standing in each of the three concentric circles of its external relations: the immediate neighborhood, the

---

[1] For a recent review of India's grand strategy, see C. Raja Mohan, "India and the Balance of Power," *Foreign Affairs* 85, no. 4 (July/August 2006): 17–32.

extended neighborhood, and the international system.[2] India's sustained high economic growth rates in the 1990s, averaging around 6% per annum, surpassed the economic performance of Pakistan, the country's traditional subcontinental rival, and held out the promise of arresting India's relative economic decline vis-à-vis China, a more consequential rival for influence in Asia and the world. This growth in turn has provided India the space and resources to re-establish its primacy on the subcontinent, to compete with China for influence in its extended neighborhood, and to begin substantive engagement with the great powers, especially the United States. Defying worldwide skepticism regarding India's ability to sustain annual growth rates above 6%, the country's economy was growing at approximately 8% per year by 2005 (see **Figure 1**). In an apparent structural shift to a higher growth path, India's 11th Five Year Plan (2007–12) sets an average growth rate of 9% as the target and suggests achieving a possible 10% annual growth rate at the end of the plan period.[3]

As India's economic growth acquires greater traction and pace, the potential consequences of this growth are becoming visible. Domestically, growth has raised hopes for a decisive break—within a generation—from the endemic and entrenched poverty that has long been a principal signifier of India.[4] In addition, accelerated economic growth has allowed India both to increase defense spending in the first years of the new century (ending a steep decline that began in the late 1980s) and to undertake plans for substantive military modernization.[5] Higher growth has also raised international expectations regarding India's economic performance. A 2003 Goldman Sachs study on Brazil, Russia, India, and China (the BRICs) was among the first to draw attention to India's growing economic prospects and potential to overtake the leading economies of the world.[6] As India's growth exceeded these initial expectations, a 2007 Goldman Sachs study revised these original projections, arguing that if India sustains an annual growth

---

[2] Ashley J. Tellis, "South Asia," in *Strategic Asia 2001–02: Power and Purpose*, ed. Richard J. Ellings and Aaron L. Friedberg (Seattle: The National Bureau of Asian Research, 2001), 248–53.

[3] Planning Commission, Government of India, *Towards Faster and More Inclusive Growth: An Approach to the 11th Five Year Plan* (New Delhi: December 2006), http://planningcommission.nic.in/plans/planrel/app11_16jan.pdf.

[4] Shantanayan Devarajan and Ijaz Nabi, "Economic Growth in South Asia: Promising, Un-equalizing…Sustainable?" World Bank, June 2006, http://siteresources.worldbank.org/SOUTHASIAEXT/Resources/South_Asia_growth_June_2006.pdf.

[5] See John H. Gill, "India and Pakistan: A Shift in the Military Calculus?" in *Strategic Asia 2005–06: Military Modernization in an Era of Uncertainty*, ed. Ashley J. Tellis and Michael Wills (Seattle: The National Bureau of Asian Research, 2005), 238–53.

[6] See Dominic Wilson and Roopa Purushottaman, "Dreaming with BRICs: The Path to 2050," Goldman Sachs, Global Economics Paper, no. 99, October 2003, http://www2.goldmansachs.com/insight/research/reports/99.pdf.

FIGURE 1   Annual percent change of India's GDP growth (in constant prices)

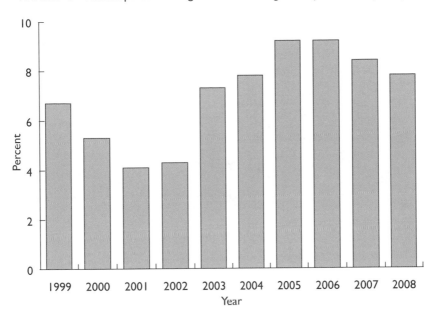

SOURCE: International Monetary Fund, World Economic Outlook Database, April 2007.

NOTE: The base year of national accounts is 1999–2000. Data for 2006 is an estimate. Data for 2007 and 2008 are projections.

rate of 6.9% between 2006 and 2020, India might be positioned to surpass the United States before 2050 to become the second-largest economy after China (See **Figure 2**).[7]

With the economy growing at a faster pace, India has already made significant diplomatic and strategic gains that are reflected in all three concentric circles of the country's grand strategy. In the outmost circle—relations with the great powers—these gains are evident in India's transformation of the tentative and difficult engagement that followed the controversial May 1998 nuclear tests into an intensive exercise that has led to the proclamation of strategic partnerships with China, Japan, the European Union (EU), and the United States. India's relationship with the

---

[7] See Tushar Poddar and Eva Yi, "India's Rising Growth Potential," Goldman Sachs, Global Economics Paper, no. 152, January 22, 2007, http://www.usindiafriendship.net/viewpoints1/Indias_Rising_Growth_Potential.pdf.

FIGURE 2   Comparative timeline for India's economy to surpass those of the G-7

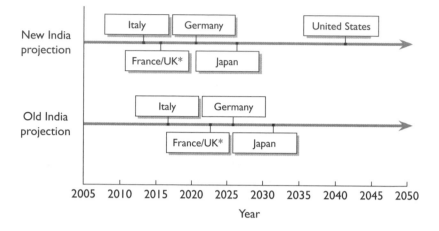

SOURCE: This figure is adapted from Tushar Poddar and Eva Yi, "India's Rising Growth Potential," Goldman Sachs, Global Economics Paper, no. 152, January 22, 2007, http://www.usindiafriendship.net/viewpoints1/Indias_Rising_Growth_Potential.pdf.

NOTE: Poddar and Yi note that the "new projections for India's potential growth envisage an average growth of 6.9% in 2006–2020…[and assume] the same exchange rate changes [until] 2050 as in the original BRICs projections. Under the original BRICs projection, India would become the third largest economy by 2050."

* In both the old and new projections, India's GDP (measured in dollars) will exceed that of the UK one year after surpassing that of France.

United States, however, has undergone the most expansive transformation. India's improved political relationship with the United States at the turn of the millennium acquired rapid momentum in the second term of the George W. Bush administration. President Bush's commitment to end the decades-long nuclear dispute with New Delhi by facilitating renewed international civilian nuclear cooperation has laid the basis for a historic change in the structure of Indo-U.S. relations.[8] U.S. enthusiasm for a new relationship with India has spurred other powers to emulate Washington. The EU has held an annual summit-level dialogue with India since 2000 with the aim of strengthening the bilateral partnership.[9] After years of a

---

[8] See C. Raja Mohan, *Impossible Allies: India, U.S. and the Global Nuclear Order* (New Delhi: India Research Press, 2006).

[9] See the European Commission, "The European Union and India: A Strategic Partnership for the 21st Century," Brussels, 2005, http://ec.europa.eu/external_relations/library/publications/25_india_brochure.pdf.

lukewarm attitude, Japan has now placed special emphasis on a strategic partnership with India that is focused on expanding economic, political, and military cooperation.[10] Even China, previously unwilling to see India as a potential factor in the regional security calculus, has begun to pay more attention to bilateral ties. During the 2005 and 2006 visits of Prime Minister Wen Jiabao and President Hu Jintao to New Delhi, the two sides affirmed their commitment to build a strategic partnership.[11]

Together with this frenetic multidirectional engagement with the great powers, India has embarked on a more intensive interaction with its extended neighborhood—the second concentric circle of New Delhi's grand strategy. Though China's new role in Africa has received considerable international attention, India has also been quietly stepping up its activity on the continent.[12] In the Persian Gulf, much international attention has focused on India's relationship with Iran, yet New Delhi has also rapidly expanded India's engagement with the Arab nations of the Gulf Cooperation Council. These nations have become a major market for Indian goods, home to nearly five million Indian migrant workers, and a source of energy resources and capital. India's traditionally cold relations with Saudi Arabia have begun to thaw with the first state visit to India in a half a century by King Abdullah in January 2006. Spurred by apprehensions concerning China's rise and growing maritime presence in the Indian Ocean, India has built stronger security partnerships—including access arrangements for its armed forces—with a number of countries in the littoral.[13] India's new influence is, however, most evident in East Asia. Notwithstanding China's reluctance to involve India in the new efforts to build an East Asian community, Japan, Indonesia, and Singapore successfully lobbied for India's inclusion in the East Asia Summit process that began in 2005.[14] That some of the key East and Southeast Asian nations were beginning to see India as a potential balancer to China marked an important diplomatic success in

---

[10] For the joint declaration issued by Manmohan Singh and Shinzo Abe, see "Joint Statement Towards India-Japan Strategic and Global Partnership," Ministry of External Affairs website, December 15, 2006, http://www.mea.gov.in/jshome.htm.

[11] See "Joint Statement of the Republic of India and People's Republic of China," April 11, 2005; and "Joint Declaration by the Republic of India and People's Republic of China," November 21, 2006. Both statements are available at http://www.mea.gov.in/jdhome.htm.

[12] See Francois Lafargue, "India: An African Power," Defense Nationale et Securite Collective, January 2007; and Sushant K. Singh, "India and West Africa: A Burgeoning Relationship," Chatham House, Africa Programme/Asia Programme, Briefing Paper, AFP BP 07/01, April 2007.

[13] See Donald Berlin, "India in the Indian Ocean," Naval War College Review 59, no. 2 (Spring 2006): 58–89.

[14] See Mohan J. Malik, "The East Asia Summit," Australian Journal of International Affairs 60, no. 2 (June 2006): 201–6.

India's renewed engagement of the region through its "look east" policy.[15] India has also been cautiously supportive of Tokyo's proposals for greater political cooperation between the major democracies of the Asia-Pacific: the United States, India, Japan, and Australia.

Within the immediate neighborhood, New Delhi for the first time is beginning to realize the opportunity that India's own rapid economic growth offers for reintegrating the post-Partition subcontinent economically and for reinforcing Indian political primacy in the region. India is now preparing to take the lead in promoting South Asian regional economic integration by skirting old political disputes, encouraging growth in the neighborhood, and making India an attractive regional economic partner. New Delhi now even supports the adoption of unilateral measures to help restore India's economic centrality to the region.[16] India's past attempts to exercise primacy in South Asia and to insulate the region from great power rivalry led to tensions with the West, China, and key players in India's extended neighborhood (such as Saudi Arabia). India's improved ties with the global powers, regional actors, and immediate neighbors now have become mutually reinforcing in a positive manner.

India's Political System

India's Domestic Politics: Institutions and Processes

The *Times of India* captured a new mood of Indian optimism with the publication of a series of articles entitled "India Poised" on January 1, 2007.[17] The "superpower obsession" of the Indian middle class, however, is often greeted with considerable Western skepticism. These skeptics point to the massive challenges of development that India faces. Suggesting that India is a long way from becoming a genuine great power, some observers insist that while perhaps able to resist extended pressure New Delhi is not capable of influencing the actions of others.[18]

---

[15] Most analysts of Indian foreign policy assess that the "look east" policy that was launched in the mid-1990s has been helpful in restoring India's traditionally strong ties with Southeast Asia. Some see the policy as part of India's attempt to reclaim a leadership of Asia that is rooted in the early foreign policy vision of independent India. For the latter assessment, see Christophe Jaffrelot, "India's Look East Policy: An Asianist Strategy in Perspective," *India Review* 2, no. 2 (April 2003): 35–68.

[16] See, for example, Prime Minister Manmohan Singh's offer of market access to its smaller neighbors without insisting on reciprocity at the 14th SAARC Summit in early 2007. "Prime Minister Manmohan Singh's Remarks at the 14th SAARC Summit," April 3, 2007, available on India's Ministry of External Affairs website, http://www.mea.gov.in/sshome.htm.

[17] Jaideep Bose, "India Poised: Make 2007 the Year of India," *Times of India*, January 1, 2007, 1.

[18] George Perkovich, "Is India a Major Power?" *Washington Quarterly* 27, no. 1 (Winter 2003–04): 129–44.

While acknowledging that India now enjoys a benign external environment conducive to the pursuit of India's developmental goals, Prime Minister Manmohan Singh recognizes that India's "real challenges are at home…it is our intention to deal with them as best as we can, within the constraints imposed by our polity."[19] This section focuses on the prime minister's understated reference to the "constraints imposed by our polity" on New Delhi's potential to transform India's regional and global standing. These constraints are deeply rooted in the structure of Indian politics. In 1947 the Indian national movement inherited a complex political legacy from the departing British colonial government. This structure included a variety of administrative forms: some territories directly ruled by British India, more than five hundred indirectly administered princely states, loosely administered frontier regions, and ill-defined boundaries. India's situation was further complicated by the linguistic, religious, ethnic, and social diversity of the country. Unifying India—so vulnerable to division—and welding it into a modern nation has been the state's overarching purpose since 1947.

The adoption of democracy as an organizing principle was both prudent and bold. Because of the country's diversity, only a form of governance based on the widest possible representation and consultation would be effective. At the same time, democracy made inevitable competitive mass politics that had the potential to reinforce centrifugal tendencies. The decision of India's founders to grant universal suffrage in an extremely poor and illiterate nation increased the role of populism and identity politics. This core contradiction, however, was managed with aplomb both by the Congress Party, which was the backbone of the national movement, and by the first prime minister, Jawaharalal Nehru. With the sole exception of the Emergency rule during 1975–77, democracy has not merely survived but has developed deep roots in modern Indian society. Over the last three decades most major political institutions in the nation—including the judiciary, the media, and civil society organizations—have contributed to the enrichment and deepening of Indian democracy.

A number of major areas of conflict continue to unfold within this democratic framework. One such conflict involves the relationship between the state and religion. India's founders recognized the importance of separating the two in the construction of a modern nation. Protecting the rights of the large Muslim minority has been a central challenge for independent India due to a number of factors: the partition of the subcontinent along religious lines, the perennial confrontation with

---

[19] "PM's address at 'The Economist' Round Table on India," March 13, 2007, available on the Prime Minister of India website, http://www.pmindia.nic.in/speeches.htm.

Pakistan, and the large number of Muslims that chose to remain in India after the Partition. Efforts to protect the rights of India's Muslim community have exposed the state to accusations regarding appeasement of religious minorities. Ever since the late 1980s the Hindu nationalist party BJP has successfully mobilized this sentiment, appealing to large sections of the majority Hindu community. The nature of Indian secularism has since become a major source of division within the Indian polity.

A second area of conflict is over the nature of Indian federalism. Although originally conceived as a "union of states," within the first four decades of independence India underwent a steady shift toward strengthening the center at the expense of the states. Several factors contributed to increased centralization and the weakening of federalism in India: preoccupation with national unification, the choice of state-led socialism as the economic strategy for development, and the dominance of the Congress Party. With the decline of the Congress Party since the late 1980s and the emergence of coalition governments at the national level, the role and influence of regional parties has steadily increased and contributed to the restoration of the federal character of India's polity.

The growing demands for social justice mark the third area of conflict in Indian politics. Attempts to overcome the deeply entrenched caste system has been an enduring theme of Indian politics. India's founders recognized the importance of integrating the Dalits (the "untouchable" castes) and marginalized tribal societies into the mainstream, but had to repeatedly extend affirmative action, which in turn drew demands for similar concessions from other so-called backward classes. The responsiveness of political parties to these demands from large groups of voters provoked a backlash from the upper castes of Indian society. Managing this tension has become a major preoccupation of Indian politics.

Finally, the Indian political classes since 1991 have needed to balance the traditional devotion to socialist ideas with new imperatives for economic liberalization and globalization. Although recognizing the importance of changing the national developmental strategy in favor of building liberal capitalism, all of the main political parties retain a profound reluctance to demonstrate open political commitment to reforms. The sections that follow examine how some of these factors might affect India's internal political evolution and external grand strategy in the coming years, organized around analysis of four specific issues: political fragmentation, the politics of economic reform, Hindu-Muslim divisions, and the persistence of a defensive strategic culture.

Political Fragmentation and National Purpose

Since the early 1990s Indian politics has undergone many structural changes including the increasing federalization of the polity, the transformation of the party system, the rise of coalition governments at the center, the decentralization of the economy, the federal government's growing role as a regulator, a social revolution marked by the assertion of lower castes, and the failure of extremism.[20] The core of these changes has been the decline of the "Congress system" that ruled uninterrupted at the national level for India's first three decades. The Congress Party managed a diverse national coalition that had a horizontal spread as well as a vertical reach.[21] The gradual breakdown of the Congress system from the late 1980s onward has not been accompanied by a similar dominance over national politics by any single party or political coalition. Instead, the trend has been toward the rise of strong regional parties and a new imperative for coalition governments at the national level.[22] Contrary to fears that coalition governments would result in instability at the center, at least three coalitions—led by Congress Party's P.V. Narasimha Rao (1991–96), Vajpayee (1998–99 and 1999–2004), and Manmohan Singh (2004–present)—have enjoyed substantive tenures.

The decline of one-party dominance over national life brought many other benefits. The excessive concentration of power in the hands of one party, and often in one individual leader as in the administrations of Indira Gandhi and Rajiv Gandhi, has yielded to a more consultative decisionmaking approach at the national level. The imperatives of power-sharing also encouraged better functioning of a cabinet system that had diminished effectiveness during the Indira and Rajiv years. In an era of economic reform, these changes have not only brought a new competition among states for investments but also placed greater pressures on state governments to undertake change.[23] The rise of the states has also begun to influence foreign and national security policies as local leaders push their respective popular agendas at the national level. Recognizing the benefits of restoring traditional links with neighboring Tibet, for example, the tiny state of Sikkim successfully pushed for a reopening of the Nathu La pass and

---

[20] Susane Hoeber Rudolph and Lloyd I. Rudolph, "New Dimensions of Indian Democracy," *Journal of Democracy* 13, no. 1 (January 2002): 52–66.

[21] See Rajni Kothari, "The Congress 'system' in India," *Asian Survey* 4, no. 12 (December 1964): 1161–73.

[22] For a survey of the evolution of the Indian political parties, see Peter Ronald deSouza and E. Sridharan, eds., *India's Political Parties* (New Delhi: Sage, 2006).

[23] See Aseema Sinha, "The Changing Political Economy of Federalism: A Historical and Institutionalist Approach," *India Review* 3, no. 1 (January 2004): 25–63.

is demanding greater contact and communication across the international border.[24] The government of Punjab likewise has helped expand the framework of engagement with Pakistan by promoting greater cross-border contact with neighboring West Punjab and highlighting the shared culture of "Punjabiyat."[25] Seeking to break out of their economic isolation, the states of India's northeast have become strong champions both of India's look east policy and of greater links to China and Southeast Asia.[26]

The many significant gains on the democratic front, however, have come at considerable cost. First, although having allowed for more democratic decisionmaking, power-sharing through coalitions at the national level has also tended to undermine the power of the prime minister. Prime ministerial powers have further eroded under the Congress government that has been in power since 2004. The prime minister has traditionally been the unchallenged leader of both the ruling party and the government, but the unprecedented power-sharing arrangement between party leader Sonia Gandhi and Prime Minister Manmohan Singh provides little incentive for even the Congress Party members of the cabinet to defer to the office of the prime minister. Strong bureaucratic institutions have also found it easy to resist political change. The Department of Atomic Energy has openly defied the attempts by the government to quickly implement the July 2005 nuclear agreement with the United States.[27] The Indian Army likewise was quite vehement in its opposition to attempts by the Congress government to settle the dispute with Pakistan over the Siachen glacier in Jammu and Kashmir.[28]

Second, the government has been reluctant to exercise foreign policy authority in the face of the strong political sentiments of its coalition allies in recent years. Domestic Tamil sentiments have always been a factor in India's approach to Sri Lanka, but both the recent BJP and the current Congress government have been apparently paralyzed by the fear of offending their alliance partners in Tamil Nadu in their approaches to the civil war in Sri Lanka.[29]

---

[24] See C. Raja Mohan, "Building a Gateway to Tibet," *The Hindu*, June 29, 2003, http://www.hinduonnet.com/thehindu/2003/06/29/stories/2003062902240900.htm.

[25] See C. Raja Mohan, "Punjabiyat and India-Pakistan Ties," *The Hindu*, February 16, 2004, http://www.hindu.com/2004/02/16/stories/2004021603711100.htm; and Alyssa Ayres, "A Cultural Path to Peace in South Asia," *World Policy Journal* 22, no. 4 (Winter 2005–06): 63–68.

[26] See "Gateway to the East: A Symposium on Northeast India and the Look East Policy," *Seminar*, no. 550, June 2005.

[27] See "Mumbai vs. Delhi," *Indian Express*, April 16, 2007, http://www.indianexpress.com/story/28428.html.

[28] "Army Not Out of Picture in Siachen Thaw," *Times of India*, January 16, 2007, http://timesofindia.indiatimes.com/articleshow/1208406.cms.

[29] See Nirupama Subramanian, "India and Sri Lanka: So Near, Yet So Far," *The Hindu*, December 28, 2005; and C. Raja Mohan, "UPA Watches as LTTE Flies High," *Indian Express*, March 28, 2007.

The third cost of weak central leadership has been a slow-down in the effective implementation of structural reforms and the conduct of foreign and national security policies. In sum, then, the lack of political coherence at the top has certainly limited India's ability both to take full advantage of an extraordinarily favorable international situation and to take timely and decisive steps. Yet at the same time, the success of very different coalition governments in effecting policy changes in an incremental manner has allowed many regional leaders to increasingly take on federal responsibilities. As a result, a broad sense of national purpose has begun to filter down to an expanding and widely dispersed political elite.

Economic Reform: The Democratic Constraint

All assessments of India's economic reform over the last two decades (and indeed regarding India's economic growth and political evolution since independence) inevitably confront the debate on democracy and development. Many historians, political scientists, and statesmen have long argued that wealth is a prerequisite for the construction of a democratic society and that democracies in developing states militate against the creation of prosperity.[30] Compared to the faster growth of the East Asian economies from the 1970s onward and the dramatic transformation of China since the 1980s, India's frustrating "Hindu growth rate" of just over 3% until the early 1980s has been widely seen as a confirmation of the difficulty inherent in engineering a rapid shift to economic prosperity in a democracy. India's impressive growth in the first decade of the 21st century, however, has opened the prospect of successfully challenging this widely accepted argument regarding the relationship between democracy and development. Singh in fact has often argued that democracy and development are indeed compatible.[31] Nonetheless the perception of a democratic constraint on India's rapid economic growth is widespread.

Irrespective of the deeper issue of the relationship between democracy and development, economic reformers in India face the genuine challenges of managing the tension between short-term pain and long-term gains, fending off pressures from sectoral interests, and limiting the electoral consequences of economic reforms. In order to cope with these

---

[30] See Jagdish Bhagawati, "New Thinking on Development," *Journal of Democracy* 6, no.5 (October 1995): 50–64.

[31] Singh, for example, has stated: "If more than a billion people can see their lives improving, living in an open society and in an open economy, the world will be a better place to live in. India's success will renew humanity's faith in liberal democracy, in the rule of law, in free and open societies. The 21st century will be a safer century if these values that we stand for find greater global endorsement," in "PM's address at 'The Economist' Round Table on India."

challenges, Indian policymakers have developed a range of stratagems. One strategy has been to focus on relatively easier reforms that do not have a direct impact on the population at large.[32] A second tactic has been introducing "reform by stealth."[33] This stratagem has involved manipulating the presentation of economic reforms by suggesting that the reforms were not significant departures from the status quo, dressing the reforms as pro-poor, and shifting the responsibility for implementation of the reforms to other levels, such as the state governments. A third aspect of India's reforms has been an emphasis on gradualism rather than on decisive shifts in policy. As one leading reformer has argued, the focus on incrementalism "took the form of first signaling the broad direction of reforms, which has usually been very clear, but leaving the detailed implementation to a more opportunistic process whereby the reforms are implemented at a pace that is politically feasible."[34]

Many attribute the slow pace of reform to the compulsions of electoral politics. Among the political class, the sense that resentment generated by economic reform would lead to loss of electoral support is strong, although the evidence for this connection is weak. Some observers attribute the electoral defeat of the BJP-led coalition in 2004 and the lack of resonance for the coalition's slogan "India Shining" to the unpopularity of economic reform. A leading Indian political analyst, for example, published this assessment:

> The verdict of Elections 2004 has done to economic reforms what a decade of intellectual criticism and popular agitations could not. It has halted the juggernaut of privatization, liberalization and globalization, sowed some seeds of doubt in the minds of the political class and has put, for once, the most hardcore liberalizers on the defensive.[35]

Although this assessment was based on a wide-ranging, post-poll survey (the National Election Study 2004), a causal link between economic reform and political defeat is hard to establish.

More germane is the question of whether economic reforms have helped improve living conditions for a broad segment of the population. All empirical data since the economic reform began suggests that India

---

[32] Ashutosh Varshney, "India's Democratic Challenge," *Foreign Affairs* 86, no. 2 (March/April 2007): 93–106.

[33] Rob Jenkins, *Democratic Politics and Economic Reform in India* (Cambridge: Cambridge University Press, 1999), 172–207.

[34] Montek Singh Ahluwalia, "Understanding India's Reform Trajectory: Trends and Future Challenges," *India Review* 3, no. 4 (October 2004): 270.

[35] Yogendra Yadav, "Economic Reforms in the Mirror of Public Opinion," *The Hindu*, June 13, 2004, http://www.hindu.com/2004/06/13/stories/2004061301681600.htm.

has made major progress in poverty reduction. The Indian government's periodic surveys of the population living below the poverty line have shown a consistent decline throughout the reform period—from 36% of the population in 1993–94 to 26% in 1999–2000 to 22% in 2004–05.[36] Though the trend is clear, the political class still finds it difficult to use this positive development to build support. Further, despite the absence of any convincing causal relationship between implementation of reforms and electoral success, or even between the economic performance of a government (either at the national or state level) and its electoral fortunes, the major parties exhibit little political will to take ownership of economic reform and project themselves as the agents of positive change. Although all parties at the national level and many at the regional level have found it necessary to embark upon reforms, very few leaders choose to present themselves as reformers.

This tendency can only be explained by some enduring elements of Indian political culture. Social democratic ideas have had powerful appeal for the political class throughout the evolution of the national movement and the construction of the modern Indian state. The relative success of the Soviet Union in comparison to the crisis-prone capitalist world during the inter-war period convinced many early Indian nationalists that state socialism was the most desirable foundation for India's economic development. The socialist ideal helped the Congress Party build stronger popular support, strengthen the nationalist coalition, and ward off internal political threats from the communist and socialist left. In the process, populism became a powerful force in Indian politics.[37] While a significant departure from this tradition is unlikely, neither can the prospects for the emergence of new political coalitions from the current upheavals in Indian politics be ruled out. Economic reform is unleashing historic changes in Indian society— accelerating social mobility, forcing the pace of urbanization, and making the under-privileged classes more politically assertive. Although at the national level the political elite is paralyzed by the fear of moving too far from the past socialist consensus, a large number of state leaders (including those of the Communist parties that are opposed to reform at the national level) have embarked on their own reforms and are becoming less bound by the rhetoric of the past. This in turn may open the door for very different future national coalitions that are able to combine the need for reform

---

[36] These figures have, however, been challenged by analysts who suggest the decline in poverty has been underestimated as well as by those who insist it has been overestimated. For a discussion of the controversy over the methodology of estimating poverty levels, see Mark Thirlwell, *Roaring Tiger or Lumbering Elephant: Assessing the Performance, Prospects and Problems of India's Development Model* (Sydney: Lowy Institute, August 2006), 14–15.

[37] See Narendra Subramanian, "Populism in India," *SAIS Review* 27, no. 1 (Winter/Spring 2007): 81–91.

with the imperatives of electoral politics. Moreover, even though the weak national consensus favoring rapid economic reform inhibits the country's growth, the incrementalism of reform will likely ensure greater stability in India's national development. If, as many believe, the acceleration of annual growth rates above 8% reflects a structural change in the country's economy, India's measured pace of reform is bound to produce extraordinary strategic opportunities for New Delhi and significant outcomes for the regional and global balance of power.

The Hindu-Muslim Divide

If accelerating economic growth is the most important factor for enhancing India's strategic influence in Asia and beyond, domestic Hindu-Muslim tensions remain the Indian state's single greatest vulnerability. On the one hand, failure to fully integrate the large Muslim minority into the national fabric has the potential to tear apart internal cohesion. On the other hand, successful accommodation of the Indian Muslim minority could have a powerful impact on religious extremism in South Asia and Islamist politics worldwide. Modernization of the 150-million strong Muslim community in India could transform the lives of nearly 40% of the world's Muslims residing in South Asia.

At the international level, two broad images of India and its Muslim population have emerged in the first decade of the 21st century. This first is the positive view that Indian democracy has managed successfully to insulate its large Muslim minority from the temptations of political terrorism.[38] This closely corresponds to the official narrative from New Delhi. The other image is sharply critical. Critics maintaining that Indian secularism has become hollow and New Delhi's claim to be a liberal democracy is dubious cite a number of developments as evidence: the steady rise of Hindu-Muslim rioting in India since the late 1960s, the rise of the BJP with an explicit hostility toward Muslims since the late 1980s, the inability of the Indian state to protect the Babri Mosque in Ayodhya in 1992, the Indian state's complicity with the local government in fomenting sustained attacks against Muslims in Gujarat, and the targeting of the Muslim minority in India's own war on terrorism.[39]

---

[38] Thomas L. Friedman, "Democracy Matters," *New York Times*, October 9, 2002.

[39] See Paul Brass, *The Production of Hindu Muslim Violence in Contemporary India* (Seattle: University of Washington Press, 2003); and Thomas Blom Hansen, *The Saffron Wave: Democracy and Hindu Nationalism in Modern India* (Princeton: Princeton University Press, 1999). For a selection of Indian writings, see Ashghar Ali Engineer, ed., *The Gujarat Carnage* (New Delhi: Orient Longman, 2002); and Siddharth Varadrarajan, ed., *Gujarat: The Making of a Tragedy* (New Delhi: Penguin, 2002).

Between the two sets of ideas that frame the intellectual discourse, a complex political dynamic on the Muslim issue is developing. Investigations into major terrorist incidents in Indian urban centers, including New Delhi and Mumbai during 2005 and 2006, indicate that Indian Muslims were indeed involved in supporting roles to the foreign militant organizations blamed for the attacks.[40] Studies have shown that some Indian Muslims are being radicalized by the intense anger over the Gujarat riots and a perception that the Indian state oppresses religious minorities. These studies also suggest that al Qaeda as well as Pakistan's Inter-Services Intelligence Agency might have begun to tap into the resentments of Indian Muslims.[41] At the other end of the spectrum is the view that the Indian state and civil society have not caved in to the Hindu extremism that was so brutally manifest in Gujarat. The Indian Central Election Commission prevented attempts by the Gujarat government to quickly rush toward elections in 2002 after the pogroms. The National Human Rights Commission investigated miscarriages of justice in Gujarat, and the Indian Supreme Court intervened to bring justice to the victims of the communal violence there. The vigorous and free Indian media was at the forefront of exposing the excesses of the Gujarat government. The reaction from various institutions in India to the Gujarat violence suggests that declarations that Indian secularism is dead are entirely premature.

As so very often occurs in India, an unexpected turn in politics changes the dynamics of larger trends that had been perceived as irreversible. The many observers who at the time thought the BJP-led National Democratic Alliance (NDA) coalition's victory in the 2004 general election was assured and that Hindu majoritarianism was unstoppable were proved hopelessly wrong by the results. The NDA's electoral defeat broke the momentum behind the forces of Hindu nationalism and exposed deep internal divisions among them. Even before the election, the incumbent prime minister, Atal Bihari Vajpayee who was projected to be leader of the NDA government, sought to distance himself both from the events in Gujarat and from his party's acquiescence to the open pursuit of confrontation with the Muslim population by that state's chief minister, Narendra Modi. To ensure a wider electoral base for the NDA, Vajpayee made a conscious effort to reach out to Muslim groups, especially those in north India.[42] After the election

---

[40] Somini Sengupta, "India Fears Some of its Muslims are Joining in Terrorism," *New York Times*, August 9, 2006.

[41] Arabinda Acharya, "The Changing Face of Muslim Terrorism in India," (unpublished paper, S. Rajaratnam School of International Studies, Singapore, 2007).

[42] See Niraja Gopal Jayal, "A Malevolent Embrace? The BJP and Muslims in the Parliamentary Election of 2004," *India Review* 3, no. 3 (July 2004): 183–209.

Vajpayee suggested that the attacks against Muslims in Gujarat were among the reasons for the coalition's defeat and argued that Modi should be removed.[43] The BJP was torn between returning to a stronger focus on Hindu nationalism and reaching out to the broader base needed to win the election. Confusion within the BJP on how to leverage religious nationalism was accompanied by declining political support in India's largest state, Uttar Pradesh. As the BJP stoked the fires of Hindu nationalism from the late 1980s, the party's share of the vote in Uttar Pradesh moved from 7.8% in the 1989 general election to a peak of 35.9% in the 1998 elections; by the 2007 elections to the Uttar Pradesh Assembly the figure had fallen to 16.9%.[44]

The left-of-center United Progressive Alliance coalition led by the Congress Party that came to power in 2004 began its administration by rewriting anti-terror legislation that tended to unfairly target Muslims. Even more importantly, the Congress government formed a committee led by former justice Rajinder Sachar to comprehensively examine the socio-economic circumstances faced by Muslims in India and suggest recommendations for dealing with the community's grievances.[45] Although aimed at promoting inclusiveness, enhancing diversity in a variety of spaces, and generating equality to reduce the sense of alienation, the Sachar Committee's recommendations emphasized general rather than community-specific initiatives. In terms of advancing the Indian debate on the Muslim question, the Sachar Committee was a landmark event. The scope and pace with which New Delhi will act on these recommendations is bound, however, by the political calculations of the ruling coalition and the assessment of the potential backlash from Hindu nationalist forces. There is no denying, however, the advent of a new phase in the politics of secularism, with a special focus on ameliorating conditions for Muslims rather than merely engaging in an ideological debate on secularism. Against this backdrop of increasing Muslim empowerment and declining Hindu extremism, the Congress-led government still was able to take advantage of the peace process with Pakistan initiated by the previous Vajpayee government. For the first time in decades a peace process with Pakistan has endured for over three years. Successful transformation of the peace process

---

[43] "Atal Blows Hot, Modi Catches Cold," *Times of India*, June 14, 2004.

[44] Yogendra Yadav and Sanjay Kumar, "Beyond the Blue: The Untold UP Story: BJP Decline, Congress Style," *Indian Express*, May 19, 2007, http://www.indianexpress.com/story/31272.html.

[45] See "Symposium on Sachar Committee Report," *Economic and Political Weekly* 42, no. 10 (March 10, 2007): 828–52.

into a historic reconciliation with Pakistan could also induce an enduring rapprochement between India's Hindus and Muslims.[46]

A Defensive Strategic Culture

The few extant studies on India's strategic culture emphasize New Delhi's defensive orientation inherited in part from the British Empire on the eve of Indian independence.[47] Having spent decades coping with the gap between ambitious national aspirations and a weak international standing, the Indian strategic establishment has become overly cautious and slow in responding to new geopolitical opportunities. Given India's economic performance since the 1980s and successful defiance of the world in conducting nuclear tests, the strategic establishment might reasonably have been expected to adopt a less defensive attitude and a vision to match India's potential for emergence as a great power. By mid-2007, however, indications suggest that India's transition to a nation capable of shaping the international system remains a work in progress. While there are many signs of new strategic thinking, old defensive attitudes persist.

India has clung to these defensive attitudes in part because of having needed, ever since the early 1990s, to confront directly many of the country's persistent vulnerabilities. New Delhi has needed to deal with external pressures to change India's internal economic orientation, attempts by the international system to limit India's nuclear and missile programs, and efforts by Pakistan to change the status quo in Jammu and Kashmir via support of cross-border terrorism. The Indian political establishment's quick mobilization of nationalist sentiment to ward of these external challenges has been entirely successful. The ultra-nationalist tendency left in the wake of such efforts has, however, limited the ability of weak national governments to pursue pragmatic accommodation with the external world.[48] For example, a strong nationalist reaction pushed back U.S. efforts to impose the Comprehensive Test Ban Treaty (CTBT) on India in the mid-1990s.[49] Yet the same nuclear nationalism obstructed efforts by the NDA government to bargain with the Clinton administration over India joining

---

[46] For a further discussion of the Indian-Pakistan peace process, see the fourth section of this chapter.

[47] George Tanham, "India's Strategic Thought: An Interpretative Essay," *Rand Report* (Santa Monica: Rand, 1992).

[48] C. Raja Mohan, "Perils of Ultra-Nationalism," *Seminar*, no. 569, January 2007.

[49] T.T. Poulose, *The CTBT and the Rise of Nuclear Nationalism in India* (New Delhi: Lancers Books, 1996).

the CTBT following the May 1998 nuclear tests.[50] Even in 2005, when the Bush administration offered far more attractive terms for a nuclear reconciliation, the Indian establishment remained deeply divided—with the Department of Atomic Energy raising a series of objections, some seemingly self-defeating.[51] After the technical objections of the Department of Atomic Energy were resolved in the negotiations with the United States, both the left and the right of the Indian political spectrum were unwilling to stop the ultra-nationalist attacks on the civil nuclear initiative with the United States.

Persistence in negotiations is an important trait in India's strategic behavior. Linked to this characteristic is an outlook of cultural superiority that "holds India's importance to be singular and self-evident, an entitlement and that does not need to be earned, proved or demonstrated."[52] India's complex negotiating style often degenerates into self-defeating sophistry that makes reaching closure difficult. New Delhi has not found an easy balance between negotiating firmly and finding pragmatic compromises.[53] This is certainly a tendency of most democracies, where the imperatives of domestic politics often prevail over the logic of external negotiation and where posturing often trumps the prospect of clinching a bargain. As India's opposition parties attempt to seize nationalist high ground during negotiations, sectoral interests exploit nationalist sentiments for their own ends—be it the reluctance of the business community to cede domestic economic space or the resistance of the bureaucracies (such as the Department of Atomic Energy) to change. Even when seeking fundamental change in a particular policy area the political leadership has faced continuous opposition from the national security bureaucracy.

As a result, attempts by the political establishment to reform the security sector have been less than successful. Following the nuclear tests, the NDA government formed the National Security Council (NSC) to better coordinate the formulation and implementation of external policies. Although the concept was debated for many decades, the eventual implementation of the NSC was not a smooth process.[54] The NDA

---

[50] See Strobe Talbott, *Engaging India: Diplomacy, Democracy and the Bomb* (Washington, D.C.: Brookings Institution, 2004).

[51] See C. Raja Mohan, *Impossible Allies*.

[52] Rodney Jones, "India's Strategic Culture," Science Application International Corporation, October 31, 2006, 7, http://www.dtra.mil/documents/asco/publications/comparitive_strategic_cultures_curriculum/case%20studies/India%20(Jones)%20final%2031%20Oct.pdf.

[53] Amrita Narlikar, "Peculiar Chauvinism or Strategic Calculation: Explaining the Negotiation Strategy of a Rising India," *International Affairs* 82, no. 1 (January 2006): 77–94.

[54] D. Shyam Babu, "India's National Security Council: Stuck in the Cradle," *Security Dialogue* 34, no. 2, (2003): 215–30.

government set up a committee of inquiry after a controversy arose over intelligence failures leading up to the 1999 Kargil War. The committee, headed by Krishnaswamy Subrahmanyam, called for a comprehensive overhaul of India's national security system.[55] Subrahmanyam, a long-time and vigorous advocate of the NSC, was deeply disappointed by the council's performance, noting that the "concept underlying the setting up of a National Security Council was that it should be the engine of long-term assessments and follow-up strategies. Unfortunately, though the NSC was set up in 1999, it did not make much headway in its role during the NDA regime."[56] Confrontations developed as individuals with strong personalities who became formulators and implementers of policy interacted with other decisionmakers. Such was the case with Brajesh Mishra, who held the combined offices of national security advisor and principal secretary to the prime minister during the BJP rule.[57] The Congress government, which succeeded that of the BJP, divided his former responsibilities across three positions—prime minister's principal secretary, national security advisor, and internal security advisor—a move that not only further weakened the direction of national security policy but failed to eliminate turf battles among agencies. Given the scale and depth of change needed to overhaul the security sector, New Delhi has far to go in developing an efficient national security system. Reforms in the security sector are less likely to be the product of a preconceived schema than the result of occasional initiatives from top leadership, the setting of new precedents, and an incremental approach to change in strategic policies.

Internal Politics and Grand Strategy

Given the historic structural changes underway in Indian society and polity, the gradual and painful process of democratic adaptation, and the absence of strong coherent strategic leadership, it would be tempting to conclude that the strategic consequences of India's internal change will be slow to materialize. Equally tempting would be to conclude that India remains an "emerging power" rather than a great power able to make a difference to the region and the world. The reality, however, is more complex. Despite the government's many vacillations in promoting economic

[55] Kargil Review Committee, *From Surprise to Reckoning: The Kargil Review Committee Report* (New Delhi: Sage, 2000).

[56] Krishnaswamy Subrahmanyam, "Emerging Power: Wanted Leaders with Vision," *The Tribune*, September 24, 2005, http://www.tribuneindia.com/2005/specials/tribune_125/main8.htm.

[57] It was an open secret that National Security Advisor Brajesh Mishra and Foreign Minister Jaswant Singh were at loggerheads on a range of issues during the NDA tenure.

reforms and frequent returns to socialist rhetoric, India's economic growth has acquired a momentum that has unleashed the energies of a vibrant private sector and raised the confidence of the middle class. This section will examine the implications of domestic change in five issue areas: war and peace, military doctrine, regional integration, coping with the rise of China, and building a security partnership with the United States. Progress in one or more of these areas, which would appear in any list of Indian strategic priorities, could considerably facilitate India's ascendancy. These areas, however, are also interrelated. Progress on some issues could either reinforce or retard advances in other directions. For example, greater cooperation with Washington improved the overall triangular relationship between India, Pakistan, and the United States but has begun to complicate Sino-Indian ties. Similarly, China's rising profile on the subcontinent has not only prompted India to take greater interest in regional integration but also intensified Sino-Indian rivalry.

War and Peace: Breaking Out of the Two-Front Problem

Engagement with the United States and the attempted nuclear reconciliation with the international community have preoccupied India's foreign policy discourse in recent years. The positive transformation of India's bilateral relations with two difficult neighbors, Pakistan and China, however, has received less attention in part because of the opaque nature of negotiations with these states.

Immediately after the May 1998 nuclear tests, the BJP leadership suggested that reaching final settlements on the Jammu and Kashmir question with Pakistan and the boundary dispute with China would now be important national security objectives.[58] Notwithstanding the Kargil War, military confrontation during 2002 over Pakistan's support to terrorism in India, a series of terrorist incidents nationwide, and intense wariness in the security establishment to engage Pakistan on the Kashmir dispute, both Vajpayee and Jaswant Singh actively pursued a peace process that has so far endured. A ceasefire along the international border and the contested international frontier in Jammu and Kashmir has held since the end of 2003. Since early 2004, India has engaged in sustained negotiations on all contentious issues. This longest uninterrupted engagement has brought rapid expansion of contact between peoples, opening of the border for the movement of people and goods (including in Jammu and Kashmir for the first time in many decades), and expansion of bilateral trade. Above

---

[58] See C. Raja Mohan, "India's Changing Territorial Diplomacy Towards China and Pakistan," *Strategic Analysis* 37, no. 1 (January–February 2007).

all, the peace process has led to the first serious negotiations on resolving the Kashmir dispute in more than four decades. Although a breakthrough remained elusive as of mid-2007, the two sides have agreed to a broad framework for Kashmir built around four principles: no change in the territorial disposition, an open border, significant political autonomy for the two parts of Kashmir, and a joint consultative mechanism between the two parts of Kashmir. Although the details of these four principles remain to be finalized, New Delhi and Islamabad have never seemed closer to a settlement.

In bilateral relations with China, New Delhi successfully resolved the dispute over the state of Sikkim, which was integrated into India in 1974, and has begun intensive negotiation on the boundary dispute. During his visit to Beijing in 2003, Vajpayee, departing from India's traditional approach to the boundary negotiations, agreed to negotiations based on "territorial give and take" rather than asserting that China was the aggressor and must vacate the disputed territories. The identification of a broad set of political parameters for the resolution of the boundary dispute marked the first success of this approach.[59] A more difficult negotiation on the nature of mutual territorial concessions has since followed.

Progress on the territorial disputes with Pakistan and China would not have been possible without India's acquisition of nuclear weapons. The nuclearization of South Asia gave India confidence that territorial disposition could not be changed by Pakistan and China through the use of force. The shifting balance of power between India on the one hand and Pakistan and China on the other has been even more significant. Owing to the rapid economic growth in recent years, India's relative power position vis-à-vis Pakistan has improved, and economic decline relative to China has been arrested.

Success in relations on either front, however, is not guaranteed. The absence of strong national leadership would also make it difficult for India to clinch bold decisions in the sensitive territorial negotiations with Pakistan and China. Opposition from the conservative national security establishment makes implementing necessary concessions toward Pakistan and China difficult. External circumstances could also derail reconciliation with both Pakistan and China. Increasing political instability in Pakistan, for example, could leave New Delhi without a strong interlocutor in Islamabad. Sections of the Pakistani army might also intensify support to

---

[59] "Agreement between the Government of the Republic of India and the Government of the People's Republic of China on the Political Parameters and the Guiding Principles for the Settlement of the India-China Boundary Question," April 11, 2005, available on India's Ministry of External Affairs website, http://www.mea.gov.in/.

terrorist groups in India. China will have to balance the tension between easing the consequences of India's two-front problem, on the one hand, and the perceived threat arising from New Delhi's enthusiasm for security partnerships with the United States and Japan, on the other. Both Beijing and Islamabad fully understand that a breakthrough in either or both territorial disputes could fundamentally alter the two-front problem that India has faced since independence. For that reason, neither Pakistan nor China might have the incentive to reach a full resolution. As India draws closer to the United States, for example, Beijing might feel compelled to strengthen China's strategic partnership with Pakistan. Yet irrespective of the outcomes, New Delhi's difficult negotiations with Islamabad and Beijing have altered the traditional national stances on both Kashmir and the China-India border dispute, opening space for more creative approaches. In confronting domestic resistance toward these difficult issues, Vajpayee and Singh have made moving toward resolution of these difficult issues easier for their successors.

Military Doctrine: Beyond Territorial Defense

The Kargil War and the trajectory of increased economic growth have generated strong domestic political support for a rapid military modernization of the Indian Armed Forces and reversed the decline in defense spending that occurred during the economic squeeze of the 1990s.[60] Now one of the largest defense markets worldwide, India has become an important arena of competition for the world's arms producers. The Bush administration's 2005 decision to encourage U.S. arms sales to India, part of a proclaimed intention to assist India's rise as a military power, has offered New Delhi an unprecedented opportunity to diversify its sources away from a traditional reliance on Russia.[61] This U.S. decision has also boosted India's ability to extract favorable terms on price, technology transfer, and offsets, as well as to promote the domestic defense industry (both the public and an incipient private sector).

India's nuclearization also has allowed the leadership to consider a shift in military doctrine away from the traditional obsession with territorial defense. In response to the post-nuclear military crises with Pakistan, the Indian Army first leaned toward the concept of a "limited war" under nuclear conditions but later adopted the "cold start" doctrine,

---

[60] See John H. Gill, "India and Pakistan: A Shift in the Military Calculus?" 237–67.

[61] See "Background Briefing by Administration Officials on U.S.-South Asia Relations," March 25, 2005, available on the U.S. Department of State website, http://www.state.gov/r/pa/prs/ps/2005/43853.htm.

which improved India's capabilities for a more rapid mobilization of forces to the Pakistan border.[62] Amid a cold peace with Pakistan and tranquility on the border with China, the army is beginning to debate the prospects for developing stronger expeditionary capabilities and deploying troops overseas. Although territorial defense and countering internal insurgencies have been the dominant preoccupations of the army since independence, surplus military capabilities have still allowed India to become one of the most important contributors to United Nations peacekeeping operations from the 1950s onward. India's attitude toward sending troops abroad has been plagued by a duality. On the one hand, New Delhi has rejected any attempt by the UN to constrain India's decisions to use force within the subcontinent; on the other hand, however, the government has demanded that any troop deployment beyond the subcontinent be done only under a UN mandate. The increasing interest of the United States in drawing the Indian Army into coalition operations has tested this attitude in recent years. Both the Vajpayee government's plans to send troops to Iraq in 2003 and the Manmohan Singh government's agreement in principle (in an Indo-U.S. framework for defense cooperation signed in 2005) to deploy troops in a coalition proved domestically controversial.[63]

The Indian security establishment's growing recognition that India's strategic interests lie far beyond the country's borders has been bolstered by expanding commercial (and particularly energy) interests in the country's extended neighborhood. Compelled by this awareness, New Delhi has considered the possibility of sending troops abroad outside the UN framework. Some senior government officials now argue that decisions on overseas troop deployment should be subject not to UN Security Council approval but to a national assessment of the costs and benefits.[64] When and where New Delhi deploys its troops overseas to defend India's interests are likely to be new questions confronting political leaders in the coming years. Even as the army is reviewing India's participation in peacekeeping operations, so has the navy begun to establish a higher profile in distant

---

[62] V.R. Raghavan, "Limited War and Nuclear Escalation in South Asia," *Nonproliferation Review* 8, no. 3 (Fall Winter 2001), http://cns.miis.edu/pubs/npr/vol08/83/abs83.htm. For an assessment of "cold start," see Subhash Kapila, "Indian Army Validates it Cold Start War Doctrine," South Asia Analysis Group, SAAG Paper, no. 1408, July 6, 2005, http://www.saag.org/papers15/paper1408.html.

[63] See C. Raja Mohan, *Impossible Allies*, 99–130.

[64] Author's discussion with senior officials in the Ministry of External Affairs, March 2007.

seas and the air force to emphasize the importance of operating beyond India's borders.[65]

Integrating the Periphery

Since the end of the Cold War, New Delhi has been preoccupied with sustaining India's political primacy in South Asia. Relations with most neighboring states had frayed considerably in the previous decades, but New Delhi has been prompted by successes in the 1990s to rethink India's approach to regionalism on the subcontinent. The simultaneous globalization of all South Asian countries has opened, at least in theory, the prospect of regional economic integration and reconstitution of India's primacy. After years of unproductive policies toward India's smaller neighbors, the political establishment is beginning to recognize New Delhi's own responsibility for improving the subcontinent's international relations. In 2005 then foreign secretary Shyam Saran stated that "the challenge for our diplomacy lies in convincing our neighbors that India is an opportunity not a threat, that far from being besieged by India, they have a vast, productive hinterland that would give their economies far greater opportunities for growth than if they were to rely on their domestic markets alone."[66] His successor, Shivshankar Menon, similarly argued for the creation of "vested interests in each other's stability and prosperity in the subcontinent" and indicated a new willingness to engage with India's neighbors without insisting on reciprocity.[67] Befriending the country's smaller neighbors runs counter both to the entrenched conservatism of India's security establishment and to the reluctance of the Indian commercial class to open up the domestic market to competition. As China's economic and security profile on the subcontinent begins to rise, however, Indian political leaders may face increasing domestic pressure to reclaim India's regional primacy, even through economic concessions to neighboring states if necessary. If India can successfully reintegrate the South Asian economies, which are currently among the fastest growing in the world, India's ability to shape the dynamics of the abutting regions—the Persian Gulf; Central Asia; Xinjiang, Tibet, and

---

[65] See for example, David Scott, "India's Grand Strategy for the Indian Ocean: Mahanian Visions," *Asia Pacific Review* 13, no. 2 (November 2006): 97–129. For a summary of the views expressed by Air Chief Marshal Shashindra Pal Tyagi, see "India's Strategic Environment and the Role of Military Power," Carnegie Endowment for International Peace, August 22, 2006, http://www.carnegieendowment.org/events/index.cfm?fa=eventDetail&id=908&&prog=zgp&proj=zsa.

[66] For a text of Shyam Saran's speech, see "India and its Neighbors," February 14, 2005, available at India's Ministry of External Affairs website, http://www.mea.gov.in.

[67] For a text of Foreign Secretary Shivshankar Menon's speech, see "The Challenges Ahead for India's Foreign Policy," April 10, 2007, available at India's Ministry of External Affairs website, http://www.mea.gov.in.

Yunnan provinces in China; Southeast Asia; and the island states of the Indian Ocean—will significantly increase. Simply stated, regional economic integration under India's leadership would imply a potential restoration of British India's expansive sphere of influence in Asia and the Indian Ocean.

India and China: Between Rivalry and Cooperation

The long-standing suspicion between India and China has begun to decline as the two develop more cooperative relations. Mutual competition, however, is still very much an element of Sino-Indian relations.[68] China plays several roles in Indian political discourse. In attacking opponents of economic reform, Indian reformers frequently cite China's economic growth rates, while China's more assertive behavior prompts strategic planners to argue the case for radically changing the country's security policy. Although both countries are expanding their strategic reach from the open seas to outer space, India's relations with China will not necessarily turn adversarial. The Sino-Indian relationship is likely to be characterized by enduring elements of rivalry and cooperation. To protect its own position, India will continue to put special emphasis on creating a "multipolar Asia" and sustaining a balance among all of the major powers.[69]

A number of internal and external factors may affect India's ability to manage the complex relationship with China. Though the attitudes of the business class toward China have undergone significant transformation—from the initial fear of being swamped by inexpensive Chinese goods to a new sense of the opportunities arising from the Chinese market—the national security establishment remains deeply suspicious of China and has sought to limit Chinese investment in sectors deemed sensitive. Meanwhile India's economic rise is raising new fears in Beijing over New Delhi's future international orientation. China is deeply concerned about the future of Tibet and India's potential to create trouble there. India, in turn, increasingly worries over the expanding Chinese influence in South Asia. Despite the two states' common desire for cooperative security, a strong potential for a deepening security dilemma between the two nations will persist.

---

[68] For a recent review of Sino-Indian relations, see Jing-dong Yuan, "The Dragon and the Elephant: Chinese Indian Relations in the 21st Century," *Washington Quarterly* 30, no. 3 (Summer 2007): 131–44.

[69] See Lisa Curtis, "India's Expanding Role in Asia: Adapting to Rising Power Status," Heritage Foundation, Backgrounder, no. 2008, February 2007, http://www.heritage.org/Research/AsiaandthePacific/bg2008.cfm.

Security Partnership with the United States

India's recent attitudes toward the United States have swung between expectations of a natural alliance between the two democracies to fears of subordination in a potential partnership with the world's sole superpower. Structural changes in the international system are driving India and the United States closer together, but many internal factors in both countries constrain the development of an explicit strategic partnership. Despite the best efforts of two successive governments in both Washington and New Delhi, old inhibitions continue. The consolidation of the Indo-U.S. partnership will likely depend on three important developments.

The first is implementation of the historic July 2005 nuclear deal.[70] Seeking to end nearly 35 years of nuclear disputes and provide a path toward stronger bonds of political cooperation, this agreement requires the United States to amend its domestic nonproliferation law and persuade the international community to modify the current nonproliferation regime in order to facilitate civilian nuclear cooperation with India. After the United States changed its domestic law at the end of 2006, Washington and New Delhi engaged in months of difficult and intensive negotiations to finalize the so-called 123 agreement (named after a section of the U.S. Atomic Energy Act) that defines the legal terms of nuclear cooperation. India's nuclear establishment was deeply concerned that the United States might continue to impose constraints on its freedom of action. Many of these fears were rooted in India's defensive strategic culture and a deep distrust of the United States inherited from the past. Although the nuclear agreement was conceived in order to remove this enduring distrust, such misgivings have instead prevented an early closure of the deal and facilitated the fomentation of all of India's traditional fears about the United States.

The second development lies in Indo-U.S. defense cooperation, which must evolve from military exchange programs and joint exercises to genuine cooperation in weapons supplies and technology transfer.[71] U.S. arms suppliers are hoping to secure major defense contracts in India, but the Indian defense establishment harbors doubts as to whether the United States will be a reliable supplier and whether Washington will in fact relax controls on military technology transfers. Finalizing and implementing the transfer of a major weapons system is key for the United States and India to build a long-term defense relationship.

---

[70] See C. Raja Mohan, *Impossible Allies*.

[71] See Stephen J. Blank, *Natural Allies? Regional Security in Asia and Prospects for Indo-American Strategic Cooperation* (Carlisle, PA: Army War College, 2005), http://www.strategicstudiesinstitute. army.mil/pubs/display.cfm?pubID=626.

The third development concerns bridging the significant differences in interests between India and the United States on the subcontinent and beyond. India's traditional resistance to external involvement in South Asia is slowly giving way to a form of security cooperation with other major powers—especially the United States, the European Union, and Japan—on regional security challenges, such as Nepal and Sri Lanka. Major differences remain, however, over Pakistan and Afghanistan. The United States welcomed India's role in the reconstruction of Afghanistan following the ouster of the Taliban but has been reluctant to see India take a political and security role there due to concerns over offending Pakistan. There is likewise an increasing convergence of Indian and U.S. interests in Southeast Asia and the Indian Ocean but little prospect of rapid development of a shared understanding on the Middle East. With its significant Muslim population, India is hesitant to identify with unpopular U.S. policies in the Middle East or take sides in the growing conflict between Washington and Tehran.

If in the near term these differences narrow, questions will continue regarding the possibility of a formal alliance between India and the United States. Two broad propositions are relevant here. The first is that India's primary objective is to emerge as an indispensable element to a balance of power in Asia. India is likely to pursue this objective irrespective of an alliance with the United States. The second proposition is that although cooperation with the United States could strengthen India's future options considerably, India is unlikely to become a junior partner in an alliance with the United States. The U.S. alliances with Japan and Britain will not prove feasible models for India's future. Neither is it likely that India will follow the example of France. The profound reluctance in New Delhi to enter into any unequal arrangements suggests that "strategic coordination" with the United States, i.e., something less than a formal alliance, is a more likely option.[72]

Conclusion

The recent pace of India's economic growth and the clear political will for deeper security cooperation with the United States have vindicated the Bush administration's judgments on the country's potential to emerge as a great power and the U.S. decision to invest significant political capital in transforming the bilateral relationship. Yet, lumbering elephant that it is, India is bound to test the patience of a U.S. strategic culture oriented

---

[72] For the idea of "strategic coordination" as different from formal alliance, see Ashley J. Tellis, *India as a New Global Power: An Action Agenda for the United States* (Washington, D.C.: Carnegie Endowment for International Peace, 2005).

toward the near term. To manage its own expectations of the bilateral relationship, the United States will need the patience to accept short-term disappointments in developing engagement with India. Although historic, the domestic economic and political changes taking place in India will necessarily unfold at their own pace. In some Asian governments external pressures often help force decisions; in India these pressures usually have the opposite effect. As in all democracies, domestic electoral calculations tend to override most other considerations. New Delhi's unfinished struggle with a legacy of socialism and the political compulsion to posture on equitable distribution will necessarily entail a slow implementation of the long overdue next generation of economic reforms. Yet unlike other democracies where change is often associated with a particular political party or leader, in India structural reforms to the economy and polity have been incrementally pursued by the political class as a whole. This process may lead to suboptimal outcomes, a price India will pay for democracy. The most consequential outcome, however, is that even the halting nature of India's reforms has set in motion the productive energies of the economy and has the potential to alter the global distribution of power over the long term. India's rapid economic growth could help alter the widely held perception that democracy and development are incompatible. The simultaneous deepening of democracy and expansion of prosperity in India will significantly boost U.S. values in the ideological battles of the 21st century. Indian success in integrating the country's Muslim population and reaching an enduring reconciliation with Pakistan will prove equally significant. If promoting democracy and modernizing Islamic societies remain two major priorities for the United States over the coming years, India's success on both fronts will vastly improve the prospects for the realization of these outcomes.

Absence of a strong national leadership, the persistence of a defensive strategic culture, and an entrenched suspicion of the outside world tend to slow India's transition from a self-perceived weak third world state to a great power that can shape the regional and international system. A lag between national potential and strategic performance is common among democratic powers. The history of the United States at the turn of the twentieth century illustrates the difficulty of developing a national security strategy commensurate with major economic capabilities. Delayed national responses to global and regional challenges, however, entail more than short-term opportunity costs; they also include a range of other penalties. That again is part of the nature of politics within democratic societies. Much like the isolationism and deep opposition to external entanglements that delayed the emergence of the United States as a great power in the first half of the twentieth century, India's political elite and strategic establishment might remain hesitant to undertake larger responsibilities as they battle their many inherited political demons.

On the positive side, India's political leadership, weak and constrained as it has been over the last two decades, has demonstrated the political will not only to take major strategic initiatives in the difficult relationships with the United States, China, and Pakistan but also to alter extant national policy consensus. Although the implementation of these initiatives has often met fierce resistance from bureaucratic and political opposition, the change in India's strategic orientation has been palpable. Moreover, the trajectory of change has survived frequent alterations in political dispensation at the national level. In building an enduring strategic partnership with India, the United States will have to overcome a lack of experience in dealing with other democracies as equals. India will not accept a subordinate strategic relationship with the United States, as West Europe and Japan were prepared to do after World War II. Setting India tests of loyalty and requiring demonstrations of formal solidarity will tend to be counterproductive. Pressed publicly by the U.S. leaders to fall in line with U.S. policy (for example, on Iran), the Indian political class will be compelled to affirm its unwillingness to be dictated to. Washington instead must credit New Delhi with the strategic intelligence to pursue India's own interests and effectively handle difficult situations. Recognizing the consequences of India's position on Iran for civilian nuclear cooperation with the United States, New Delhi without hesitation departed from tradition by voting against Iran twice in the International Atomic Energy Agency Board of Governors during 2005–06. Similarly, if ever forced to choose between Iran and the Arab Gulf, New Delhi would naturally align with the latter given India's huge stakes in the Gulf kingdoms. Respecting and working with India's political imperatives both to be and to be seen as an independent actor in world politics will offer richer rewards for U.S. policy over the long term. Although public attitudes in India toward the United States have begun to shift in a positive direction, the ambiguities in the minds of the national security elite might only be overcome through an extended period of strategic cooperation and coordination between the two nations.

STRATEGIC ASIA 2007–08

REGIONAL STUDIES

EXECUTIVE SUMMARY

This chapter analyzes the evolution of Bangladeshi and Pakistani domestic politics and the potential impact on their respective security, the security of India, and U.S. regional policy.

MAIN ARGUMENT:

Both Bangladesh and Pakistan are experiencing a weakening of their political parties, a growing assertiveness of their respective armies, an erosion of democracy, and a strengthening of Islamist organizations. Islamist organizations still depend on the army's goodwill in Pakistan but have emerged as kingmakers in Bangladesh, fulfilling the social role the state left empty. Both countries are at risk of becoming hubs of international terrorism as a result of increased political violence and Islamist militancy. Regionally, rapprochement between these two countries would be detrimental to India and beneficial to China, since Beijing could neutralize New Delhi through a series of bilateral alliances with countries on India's periphery.

POLICY IMPLICATIONS:

- If complacency or complicity of the Bangladeshi and Pakistani elites continues, both countries risk allowing a tiny minority—those identifying political Islam as their primary political identity—to ultimately determine both the bilateral relationship and the stability of the region.

- Even a low level of hostility between India and Bangladesh arising from Islamic activism on the border would likely strengthen relations between Dhaka and Beijing. China would benefit from an even more complete series of alliances in India's immediate neighborhood, de facto neutralizing New Delhi.

- Long-term U.S. interests would be better served by a genuine democratization process in both Pakistan and Bangladesh. Unless current U.S. policy toward Pakistan changes, Islamabad's increasing leverage will make it more difficult for the U.S. to apply pressures with regard to specific issues such as terrorism.

South Asia

Bangladesh and Pakistan: From Secession to Convergence?

Frédéric Grare

Bangladesh and Pakistan are in turmoil. Although for different reasons, both countries are experiencing a weakening of their political parties, a growing assertiveness of their armies, and an erosion of democracy. As a result, Islamist organizations are growing more powerful in both countries. Islamist organizations still depend on the army's goodwill in Pakistan. In Bangladesh, however, Islamist organizations have emerged as kingmakers, fulfilling the social role the state left empty. Political violence has increased and Islamist militancy is on the rise in both countries. Partly as a reaction, phenomena such as ethnic nationalism have reappeared in Pakistan. As a result, Bangladesh and Pakistan could become hubs of international terrorism.

In Bangladesh, corrupt and inefficient political practices have created a political vacuum that has been filled by Islamist parties that have used the polarization of the system to impose themselves as kingmakers. In Pakistan, the army has manipulated Islamist parties as a means to pressure the more mainstream political parties. This manipulation is also designed to influence Pakistan's foreign policy, both at the regional level (particularly toward Afghanistan and Kashmir) and at the global level (particularly using cooperation on the war on terrorism to leverage relations with the United States and Europe). Moreover, the risk remains that the Pakistani army may partially lose control of some of the extremist organizations it still supports. Finally joint activism of Bangladeshi and Pakistani Islamist organizations on the Bangladesh-India border could make them the vector of a new rapprochement between Dhaka and Islamabad.

Frédéric Grare is a visiting scholar at the Carnegie Endowment for International Peace. He can be reached at <fgrare@carnegieendowment.org>.

This chapter analyzes how changes in Bangladesh's and Pakistan's domestic politics have influenced their respective foreign policies. The chapter is divided into three sections. The first section analyzes Pakistan's and Bangladesh's grand strategies, describes their respective relations with India, and examines the consequences for each country's domestic politics. The second section examines the self-destructive tendencies apparent through the evolution of both countries' political systems and the role of their armies; a main focus of this section is on the use of Islamist organizations by other political forces and the resulting consequences for the nature of political violence. Finally, the third section assesses the impacts of these evolutions on the national and regional security of the main South Asian actors, including India, and resulting implications for U.S. policy.

Bangladesh's and Pakistan's Grand Strategies and Drivers of Political Change

Bangladesh's and Pakistan's grand strategies have several common characteristics but also major differences. For both countries, India is the key focal point. India's aspiration for regional leadership—fueled by the country's size, population, industrial and technological advancement, military power, and defense production—is viewed with suspicion by Dhaka and Islamabad. Both countries share an interest in preventing India from becoming too dominant (an outcome neither country is in a position to significantly influence) or, at the very least, from dictating terms to its smaller neighbors.

Although their respective relations with New Delhi are very different, both Bangladesh and Pakistan must seek out regional partners and allies to compensate for the asymmetry of power vis-à-vis India. Because Bangladesh owes its existence to the Indian intervention of 1971, Dhaka does not perceive India as an existential threat. Although Bangladesh needs to balance the power of its giant neighbor, Dhaka has not developed the same degree of aggressiveness toward New Delhi as Pakistan has. By contrast, the Pakistani leadership—particularly the military—is averse to a dominant India. Deeply resentful of India's role in the secession of East Pakistan, Pakistan still sees evidence that India has not yet accepted the partition of the subcontinent.

In terms of geography Bangladesh is nearly surrounded by India, except for an outlet through the Bay of Bengal in the south and a common border with Myanmar in the east. While good relations with India are thus imperative, Bangladesh must balance India's superior power by maintaining equally good relations with China and, despite painful memories, with

Pakistan. Overwhelmingly Muslim, Bangladesh enjoys good relations with the Muslim world. Going far beyond religious ties and cultural affinities, this Muslim inclination is a vital component of the country's integration within its regional environment, including Southeast Asia. This Muslim identity also helps Bangladesh overcome some of the geopolitical constraints already mentioned and guarantees continuous assistance from rich Muslim countries. With one of the highest population densities in the world, Bangladesh lacks land and natural resources, making economic development a domestic security imperative. The need for large scale economic assistance is therefore a component of the Bangladesh's grand strategy and a driver of the country's foreign policy. Consequently, non-alignment has long been the only strategy that would allow Bangladesh to reconcile the country's security imperatives with the need for economic development.[1]

Pakistan faces a security dilemma similar to that of Bangladesh. From the time of its formation in 1947, Pakistan was deeply divided. Early on, the Pakistani leadership played up the notion of the "Indian threat," hoping to use this as a powerful unifying factor that even Islam had been unable to provide. India soon seized the opportunity to exploit Pakistan's ethnic divisions, which were exacerbated by the dominance of the Punjabi in the Pakistani army and state bureaucracy. India not only used the Pushtunistan issue to put pressure on Pakistan in the late 1950s and during the 1960s by establishing an initially informal and later, after 1965, formal alliance with Afghanistan but also played a crucial role in securing Bangladesh's independence by providing military intervention in 1970–71.[2] The latter therefore underscores the essentially domestic character of Pakistan's vulnerabilities, in particular its ethnic divisions, which neither the systematic development of a popular perception of an Indian threat nor later policies of Islamization were ever able to fully balance.

This initial dilemma remained unchanged after 1971. The partitioning of Pakistan forced the leadership to develop somewhat problematic and artificial Middle Eastern and Central Asian identities. This development exposed the country to the additional hazards of these two regions' security problems, in the process drawing the inner divisions of the Muslim world into Pakistan. Sectarian movements and jihadist organizations became

---

[1] Dilara Choudhrury, "Bangladesh Foreign Policy Outlook: Regional and International Setting," in *South Asia and the World*, ed. Emajuddin Ahamed and Abul Kalam (Dhaka: Academic Publishers, 1992), 44–48.

[2] The Pushtunistan issue concerns the dispute between Afghanistan and Pakistan over the border and political status of territory in western Pakistan that is home to large Pushtun populations. Following Pakistan's independence in 1947 Afghanistan has refused to recognize the boundary established by the British colonial government, known as the Durand Line.

not only a source of Pakistan's fragility but also an instrument of foreign policy that Islamabad has exploited against India—similar to Islamabad's transformation of the Afghan conflict into a component of its India policy. In Kashmir, most terrorist operations have been conducted by four main jihadist organizations—Hizbul Mujahedin, Harkat-ul-Mujahedin, Lashkar-e-Toiba, and Jaish-e-Mohammad—that have operated under different names and often used the help of sectarian movements to carry out operations that the more Kashmiri-oriented organizations refuse to conduct.

Bangladesh's and Pakistan's grand strategies have mostly been antithetical. Through its non-aligned stance, Bangladesh has searched for a security that eluded Pakistan in its various alliances with the West.

Although the conflict between Pakistan and India centers on Kashmir, Islamabad's entire regional policy is articulated around the rejection of a regionally dominant India and the need to counterbalance India by any means possible. Beyond its involvement in Kashmir and support of separatist organizations, Pakistan gives expression to this policy in Afghanistan. Islamabad is working to keep India from becoming a dominant influence in Afghanistan in order to avoid having to face a double front in the event of conflict with India.

Pakistan, seeking a counterweight to India, is now tempted to exploit Bangladesh's need in a similar manner. Irrespective of Dhaka's official intentions, Islamabad's involvement in Bangladesh extends beyond Pakistani-Bangladeshi shared interests but—provided the intensity of the conflict remains low—without affecting Dhaka's fundamental interests. Pakistan is clearly attempting to recreate, through jihadist organizations, the strategic situation that existed before 1971 when India was sandwiched between East and West Pakistan. Pakistan's and Bangladesh's respective strategic partnerships with China are other important elements of convergence.

Governance, Stability, and Prospects for Democratization

The national elections, scheduled for 2007 in Bangladesh and 2008 in Pakistan, have the potential to deeply affect the political contours of the Indian subcontinent. In both countries the elections will occur against a background of sustained economic growth, growing army interference in politics, and increasing political violence. Analysis centers around the role of the political actors. In Pakistan the army continues to be a decisive factor. The Bangladeshi military, although still seeing itself as the protector of political order, could be tempted to return to power. In both countries the elite base is too narrow and self-centered to allow a real democratic culture to emerge. In the context of this democratic regression, Islamist parties (operating alone or in coordination with a major political actor) are only too willing to occupy the vacuum left by the decline of the political parties—and in doing so further amplify this vacuum.

Bangladesh's and Pakistan's Political Systems

Officially, Pakistan and Bangladesh are democracies fashioned, until recently, after the British model. Bangladesh's constitution defines the parliamentarian system under which the president, elected by the 300-seat parliament every five years, holds a largely ceremonial post and the prime minister holds the real power. A change instituted in 1996, however, has given the president considerably expanded powers during periods when the parliament is dissolved and a caretaker government assumes power temporarily to oversee general elections. The president now has control over the Ministry of Defence, the authority to declare a state of emergency, and the power to dismiss the chief advisor and other members of the caretaker government.[3] The prime minister is appointed by the president but must be a member of parliament (MP) and command a majority of MPs. The prime minister selects the ministers for appointment by the president. The cabinet is collectively responsible to the parliament. A supreme court guarantees fundamental rights as written in the constitution.

Although the current political system reflects the initial dispositions of the 1972 constitution, this was not always the case. In 1975 the fourth amendment created a presidential system, concentrating all powers in the office of the president, and effectively ended the independence of the judiciary. The restoration of democracy during the early 1990s, however, returned the system to a parliamentary democracy.

The political scene in Bangladesh is dominated by two major political parties: the Bangladesh Awami League (AL) and the Bangladesh Nationalist Party (BNP). The BNP is generally depicted as center-right, urban, anti-Indian, pro-Pakistani, and generally favored by the business community, in contrast to depictions of the AL as center-left, pro-Indian, rural, and popular with farmers.[4] In fact, both parties operate as federations of various interest groups. Their ideological differences matter little; mutual antagonism is really what generates most of their political differences. The AL and BNP are essentially electoral machines used to contest elections. In addition to these two major parties, close to one hundred other rather minor parties participate in political life.

---

[3] "Background Note: Bangladesh," U.S. Department of State website, September 2006, http://www.state.gov/r/pa/ei/bgn/3452.htm.

[4] "Bangladesh Today," International Crisis Group, Asia Report, no. 121, October 23, 2006, 3.

Pakistan initially had a parliamentary system very similar in form to the current system in Bangladesh. In 2004, however, Islamabad made the switch to a presidential system. Under the Legal Framework Ordinance the president has the power to remove the prime minister, is able to dismiss the parliament, and holds discretionary power to appoint a caretaker government. Similarly, governors in the provinces can, with presidential approval, dismiss the provincial assemblies.

The problem lies, however, not in the transition from a parliamentary to a presidential system—presidential systems exist elsewhere and are compatible with democracy—but in the total absence of checks and balances. The seventeenth amendment, introduced by the military regime, institutionalizes constant manipulation of the system by the army and a select group of benefiting elites.

Two national mainstream parties have traditionally dominated the political landscape in Pakistan: the center-left Pakistan People's Party (PPP) and the more conservative, pro-business Pakistan's Muslim League (PML). Both parties have generated splinter groups, which have often assumed the name of the original organization. Pakistan's political scene is also influenced by ethnic relations. Co-existing with national mainstream parties are regional parties, including the Pushtun Awami National Party (ANP), Balochistan National Party, Jamhoori Watan Party (JWP), Pustun Khwa Milli Awami Party (PMAP), and Muttahida Quami Movement (MQM). Religious political organizations such as the Jamaat-i-Islami or the Jamaat Ulema-e-Islam play a major role in Pakistani politics. The prominence of religious parties is due not so much to their electoral strength as to their having been the favorite tool of successive military regimes looking to control the political scene.

The Role of the Army in Bangladesh and Pakistan: Different Situations, Similar Trends

The role of the army in Bangladesh and Pakistan has been very similar. Both countries have extremely politicized and quasi-autarkic military institutions. Both countries have experienced military coups, with the military having been asked by the civilian government to intervene in response to a current crisis situation involving political opponents. In both countries, the military refused to relinquish power once the crisis was defused. How the military governments wielded their political power, however, has varied considerably in these two cases.

In 1975 Bangladesh's fourth amendment to the constitution created a presidential one-party system concentrating all power in the hands of

President Mujibur Rahman, a move sometimes qualified as a "constitutional coup." Soon thereafter, Bangladesh experienced its first military coup when General Zia-ur-Rahman seized power. After his death, civilians briefly returned to power but were ousted by General Ershad on March 24, 1982. The general was forced out of power in 1990.

Although having exercised no political responsibility since 1990, the Bangladeshi military might, following the Pakistani model, be tempted to first step in to preserve the political order and then retain power for itself. So far exercising its influence from behind the scenes, the army is still a major power in Bangladesh—leading many to speculate that it is simply a "sleeping tiger."[5]

The military does not yet seem ready to seize power. Following weeks of violent protests leading up to the 2007 national elections, Bangladesh's president sent soldiers onto the streets in December 2006. Even public sentiment seemed to have turned in favor of having the army stay in power and take control.[6] Currently the army seems satisfied with the role it has carved for itself over the years. The decision to exile leaders of the two mainstream parties in April 2007, however, effectively created a political leadership vacuum and may mark the beginning of a new era.

The behavior of the army in Bangladesh is influenced by three major considerations: the army's autonomy, budget, and prestige. Of these three considerations, prestige is probably the least problematic. The army enjoys social respect and international prestige for its contributions to UN peacekeeping missions. The combination of these three factors has resulted in increased professionalization of the military and its relative depoliticization.

Since Bangladesh's return to democracy, however, all successive governments have been careful not to antagonize the military. During the 1990s the Bangladeshi government decreased the army's budget to make allowance for meeting socio-economic objectives. Following a small increase in 1991–92, the budget decreased considerably until 1995 only to increase again between 1995 and 1997. This last increase occurred just before a new round of elections, as the army was called upon again to ensure the security of voters during the poll.[7]

---

[5] Jeremie Codron, "La Democratisation Elitaire du Bangladesh" [Elitist Democratization in Bangladesh], Institut d'Etudes Politiques de Paris, Memoire pour le DEA d'Analyse Comparative des Aires Politiques, 2002, 58, http://www.ceri-sciencespo.com/themes/asie/ceri/enseignements/memoire/codron.pdf.

[6] "Other Views: Deccan Herald, The Times, Daily Times," *International Herald Tribune*, December 15, 2006, http://www.iht.com/articles/2006/12/15/opinion/edother16.php.

[7] Codron, "La Democratisation Elitaire," 59.

Until January 11, 2007, links between the army and politics remained strong; paradoxically this could be seen as a guarantee that the military would not try to seize power again. Despite the myth that the BNP—founded by a general—was more attractive to the military, former officers could be found in all major parties, reflecting the actual diversity of political opinions within the armed forces. Yet each government sought to buy the allegiance of different factions of the military elite. The army was therefore "not a neutral institution. It [was] an instrument of power, a political resource that governments appropriated,"[8] but whose subordination could not be taken for granted. The government was influenced by the military, particularly in foreign policy and national security. Since 1991, however, conflicts between the military and civilian governments were resolved in favor of the government. The military therefore could not be considered a source of political instability. Rather than demonstrating the preeminence of civilian power, this indicated an implicit power-sharing agreement.

Since January 2007, however, the agenda of the military has been unclear. The army has clearly stated its intention to work through the political process. As observed by William Milam, a former U.S. ambassador to Bangladesh, "[the military] could decide to take only a short term agenda to restore stability and set up a certifiable free and fair election before a full return to civilian rule"[9] or could decide to retain power in the belief (or the pretense) that it is the only institution able to undertake the necessary political reforms in the country.

Since 1958 Pakistan's military has almost always been the dominant force in Pakistani politics. Over the years it has developed a "savior complex"—the firm belief that the military is the only institution able to run the country. The military's political power, however, is not purely the result of "necessity" but rather is due to a careful process of social engineering meant to erode the strength and cohesiveness of existing political forces while preventing new ones from emerging. The military has done so through the manipulation of religious symbols—trying successfully since independence to overcome ethnic identities and tribal allegiances in order to unite the country under the banner of Islam. In a constant game of divide and rule in pursuit of this goal, the military has often used political organizations (both secular and religious).

Religious organizations have always played a significant role in this process. Because these organizations confer credibility to the myth of an Islamist threat, they are the foil that legitimizes military power for the outside

---

[8] Codron, "La Democratisation Elitaire," 62.

[9] William B. Milam, "Bangladesh and the Burden of History," *Current History* 106, no. 699 (April 2007): 155.

world. Domestically they are used as a means of exerting pressure on other political organizations. According to the needs of the moment, the military can use religious organizations to form any specific alliance it believes suits its own interests. Being better served by a semblance of democracy, the military has never tried to eliminate the political organizations. Moreover, by keeping religious organizations weak but allowing them to compete in the political arena, the military insinuates itself as the indispensable arbiter of politics.

As a result the army's influence is now deeper than ever. The military not only holds power but also controls a number of economic institutions and the entire administration. The military sets the agenda of Pakistan's domestic and foreign policy, manipulating politics to maintain power while trying to establish Pakistan's influence in its immediate neighborhood, particularly with regard to India and Afghanistan.

To some extent, the difference in the relations of the Bangladeshi and Pakistani armies within their respective political spheres is one of degree rather than substance. The Bangladeshi army finds its relative absence from the political game more suitable for its own institutional interests. By contrast, the Pakistani army prefers assuming direct political power but has occasionally withdrawn behind the scenes, leaving to civilians the day-to-day burden of government while retaining for itself the main levers of power; the army might decide to assume direct political power again in the near future if domestic pressures become unbearable.

The Decline of Political Parties

Both Bangladesh and Pakistan have experienced a decline of their political parties. In both countries the responsibility for this decline is shared by the political parties themselves; in the case of Pakistan, the army, which sometimes intervened to compensate for the civilian incompetence it helped create, is also responsible.

Bangladeshi political parties have essentially themselves to blame. Both the center-right BNP and the center-left AL ideologues opted for patron-client relationships rather than internal democracy. Because both parties are outgrowths of the personalities of their respective leaders, leadership is highly personalized and monopolized by the founding dynasties. The BNP is led by Begum Khaleda Zia, widow of the former military dictator Zia-ur-Rahman. Sheikh Hasina Wajed, daughter of the assassinated Sheikh Mujibur Rahman, presides over the AL. The political disputes between the two parties are exacerbated by the mutual hatred between these two leaders.

Politics in Bangladesh is characterized by patronage and corruption. Short-term tactical and financial considerations outweigh any sense of duty to the nation. Corruption permeates all levels of society and often degenerates into criminalization, resulting in an increase of violence and continual human rights violations. This corruption has had a particularly blatant effect on local journalists, for whom it has become dangerous to investigate the nexus of politics, crime, and militancy.[10] As a result radical organizations have prospered, benefiting from the deficiencies of mainstream parties and encouraged by the reluctance of successive government to crack down on their activities.

Yet neither the political system nor the very imperfect democracy has entirely collapsed. While disillusionment is undoubtedly present, the Bangladeshi people still believe in the democratic process, even as the process is increasingly eroded by a corrosive political culture.

A similar phenomenon can be observed in Pakistan where dynastic politics, as much a reality as in Bangladesh, prevents true democratization of political organizations. The two largest mainstream parties, the PML-N (Pakistan's Muslim League faction led by Nawaz Sharif) and the PPP, have been dominated for decades by the Sharif and Bhutto families, respectively. All Pakistani political parties place great emphasis on personalized politics and individual leaders, and as a result, workers at the lower tiers often have little role in the making of party policies. The lack of internal democracy combined with poor governance during the "democratic" interim of the 1990s caused the gradual loss of credibility of electoral politics in the country. Internal deficiencies such as highly centralized decisionmaking structures, ineffective mechanisms to ensure party discipline, and lack of transparency also make the parties vulnerable to military intervention.[11]

Under the presidency of Pervez Musharraf, the military has been actively working to weaken the political parties. The constant pressure that security agencies place on the politicians, the exile of the mainstream parties' political leaders, and the permanent manipulation of the political game—including military-engineered defections through coercion whenever necessary—have weakened Pakistan's political parties to an almost unprecedented level. The Political Party Order of 2002, which replaced the Political Parties Act of 1962, barred both convicted criminals and those charged with a crime and failing to appear before the courts from standing

---

[10] "Bangladesh Today," 10.

[11] "Authoritarianism and Political Party Reform in Pakistan," International Crisis Group, Asia Report, no. 102, September 2005, 1.

for election.[12] Another example of the army's intervention in politics was the redefinition of the electoral districts in Balochistan and the North West Frontier Province (NWFP) to favor Islamist parties.

In Pakistan, as in Bangladesh, political parties have nonetheless kept their support despite these manipulations. The aspiration to democracy remains, as demonstrated by widespread backing for Chief Justice Iftikar Mohammed Chaudhry who was sacked by President Musharraf after denouncing the unconstitutionality of his holding the functions of both president and chief of army staff. The crisis demonstrated a difference of attitudes between the expectations of the majority of the population and their political elites. This underscores one of the major challenges for Pakistan's political parties: the growing disconnect between their support base and the leadership elites, who belong to the establishment. In that sense, the democratic challenge in Pakistan is as much sociological as it is political.

The Role of Islamist Organizations in Bangladesh and Pakistan

In both countries the decline of political parties has created a political vacuum that Islamist parties are keen to exploit. Yet the Islamists play different roles in Pakistan and Bangladesh. Although autonomous in both countries, the Islamist parties are manipulated in different ways by other political forces in Pakistan than in Bangladesh.

For their own benefit mainstream Bangladeshi parties have used Islamist parties as political allies. Two Islamist parties—the Jamaat-i-Islami and the Islami Oikkyo Jote (a united front for several small parties) participated in the government from 2001 to 2006. Long discredited for their collaboration with Pakistan during the 1971 war, these parties were reintroduced into the political game by Zia-ur-Rahman in his search for legitimacy and political support. The military dictator authorized Golam Azam, the Amir of the Jamaat-i-Islami who was exiled in Pakistan, to return to Bangladesh. He also amended the constitution, suppressing the term "secularism" from its preamble.

Despite their collusion with military governments, Bangladesh's Islamist parties opportunistically joined the anti-Ershad movement in 1990.[13] The

---

[12] See "Authoritarianism and Political Party Reform in Pakistan," 6. Clearly aimed at the exiled Benazir Bhutto, this text did not prevent sectarian leader Azam Tariq, who was then in jail for the charge of murder, from contesting the elections under state patronage.

[13] The anti-Ershad movement began in the early 1980s after the coup by General Ershad who toppled the elected civilian president, Abdus Sattar. The widow of assassinated military dictator Zia-ur-Rahman, Begum Khaleda Zia, assumed the leadership of the Bangladesh National Party created by her late husband. She was soon joined by other political parties as diverse as the secular Awami League and the Islamist Jamaat-i-Islami. Their repeated assaults from the mid-1980s until 1990 led to the fall of the Ershad government on December 6, 1990.

Jamaat-i-Islami formed an electoral alliance with the BNP, which emerged from the 1991 election with an absolute majority. The Jamaat-i-Islami, however, was itself able to secure 12% of the vote, becoming the fourth largest political organization in the parliament.

The deficiencies and self-interested behavior of the mainstream parties opened a political space for the Islamist parties, which were viewed as being much less corrupt than the mainstream parties. The Islamists' strong social agenda—particularly the Jamaat-i-Islami party's support of interest-free micro-credit, opposition to the dowry tradition, and focus on education—and genuine dedication to local communities garnered a relatively large constituency.

Since the reestablishment of democracy both mainstream parties, unable to secure power alone, have sought alliances of convenience. After forming alliances with the Jamaat-i-Islami and the Islami Oikkyo Jote, for example, the BNP came to power in 2001 thanks to Islamist support. The main opposition party, the AL, signed a memorandum of understanding with a small fundamentalist party, Khalaphat-e-Majlis, in December 2006.[14] As a result, Islamist parties have emerged as kingmakers in Bangladesh.

Islamist militancy in Bangladesh became a matter of international concern after the U.S. intervention in Afghanistan in October 2001, long before the Bangladeshi authorities openly acknowledged it as a problem. As early as October 2002, *Time* magazine warned that the arrival of Taliban and al Qaeda fighters from Afghanistan could turn Bangladesh into a new front in the U.S.-led war on terrorism.[15] Until very recently the ruling coalition of Prime Minister Khaleda Zia denied the existence of Islamist militancy in Bangladesh, terming it "hostile propaganda."[16] Only after a terrorist attack in August 2005 did the government began cracking down on selected individuals.

As a recent phenomenon in Bangladesh, Islamist militancy is a new version of the structural political violence that has plagued Bangladesh's political life since independence. The roots of Islamist militancy lie in the societal changes that began in the 1990s: urbanization, education, and the development of the middle class, amplified by the role of western NGOs whose emphasis on gender equality provided women access to new economic resources and micro-credit, reducing their dependence on local and religious

---

[14] Michael Connolly, "EuroLinks Daily View," *Wall Street Journal*, January 11, 2007, http://online. wsj.com/PA2VJBNA4R/article/SB116849321985073628-search.html?KEYWORDS=eurolinks &COLLECTION=wsjie/6month.

[15] "Bangladesh Today," 5.

[16] Sumit Ganguly, "The Rise of Islamist Militancy in Bangladesh," United States Institute for Peace, Special Report, no. 171, August 2006.

male authorities. Feeling marginalized, these traditional actors reacted accordingly. Their reaction was soon politicized, and the resulting anti-NGO movement quickly targeted the secular judicial system and "foreign" elements. This is the background against which jihadism developed.

The militant Islamist groups that have emerged in Bangladesh over the past several years are in no way monolithic, neither in composition nor in purpose. The Jamaat-ul-Mujahideen Bangladesh (JMB), supposedly the youth wing of the banned Harkat-ul-Jihad, first drew notice in 2002 and was banned in February 2005. The Jagrata Muslim Janata Bangladesh (JMJB), believed to have been formed in 1998 on the Taliban model, gained public attention in 2004 when it started killing members of the East Bengal Communist Party. Supposedly founded in 1992 with the assistance of Osama Bin Laden, the Harkat-ul-Jihad-Islami (HuJI) has aims to turn Bangladesh into Afghanistan. The Islami Chhatra Shibir is the student branch of the Jamaat-i-Islami Bangladesh. The Hizb-ut-Tahrir is only the Bangladeshi branch of the organization, which was founded in Jerusalem in 1953.[17]

These organizations are only the better known Islamist groups. Some are affiliated with specific political parties, some have no particular political affiliation. Many militant groups are small, poorly organized, and scattered or fractured. Bangladeshi Islamists, however, although essentially focused on their own country, "are indeed inspired by global causes and maintain a variety of international ties."[18]

Deobandi organizations are a recruitment source for the jihad, particularly in the south of the country. Deobandi madrasahs from the Chittagong region are said to have links with the famous Karachi-based Binori madrasah and the Harkat-ul-Jihad al-Islami in Pakistan. Though not exclusively imported to Bangladesh, militancy developed with the support of NGOs whose funding emanated from the Gulf countries of Saudi Arabia, Kuwait, and the United Arab Emirates. The JMB, for example, has since its creation in 1998 enjoyed relations with the Ahle Hadith Andolon Bangladesh (AHAB), itself evolved from a group created in 1978 in Bangladesh, the Ahle Hadith Jubo Sangho. Jihadists with a foreign background—often trained in Afghanistan and Pakistan and practicing a version of Islam relatively similar to the one of the Taliban—thus coexist with national militants trained entirely in Pakistan, either through deobandi, Alhe Hadith organizations, or the Jamaat-i-Islami.

Links to militant groups raise questions concerning the democratic credentials of the "institutional" Islamist parties. The major concern is that links to legitimate Islamist parties provide cover for underground

---

[17] Ganguly, "Islamic Militancy in Bangladesh," 6.

[18] "Bangladesh Today," 19.

organizations. Seven members of the Jamaat-ul-Mujahideen arrested after the 2005 bomb blasts had been members of the Jamaat-i-Islami or its student wing.[19]

The government and some mainstream parties, however, are ambivalent about their relations with Islamist militancy. The BNP has gone as far as cultivating some militant groups to counterbalance leftist groups. Under U.S. pressure, the government tracked down and arrested the leaders of the JMB and JMJB in March 2006, but many observers, both foreign and Bangladeshi, are skeptical of the authorities' resolve to tackle the issue. Previous arrests led to quick releases. This ultimately raises some worrying questions about the future of Bangladesh as a new sanctuary for Islamist terrorists.

In Pakistan, the Islamist parties have been turned by the military into a more potent political force than they would naturally have been in order to weaken the mainstream political parties. They are also used as a foil vis-à-vis the outside world to confer international legitimacy on military rule. The 2002 legislative elections were particularly significant in this regard. Thanks to the severe manipulations of the military dictatorship, the Muttahida Majlis-e-Amal (MMA), a coalition of six Islamist parties, won 11.1% of the votes for the National Assembly and was able to form a government in the two provinces adjacent to Afghanistan. The military establishment told the international community and the United States in particular that it was operating under Islamist threats and that some of the pressure on Pakistan had to be lifted. At the same time, the presence of a significant number of Islamist parliamentarians allowed the government to form the coalition it needed according to the circumstances. This led for example to the adoption of the seventeenth amendment, which changed the constitution to allow the president to dismiss the parliament and sack the prime minister, transforming the Pakistani political system from a parliamentary to a presidential system.

The significant development in Pakistan is not the emergence of militant organizations, which have been a part of the political scene for decades. Nor is it that these organizations, working in their own interests or as Pakistani military proxies, are operating in the various geopolitical hot spots on the subcontinent. Rather, the significance lies in a two-part dynamic: simultaneous with Pakistan's relative loss of control over some of these organizations, these organizations have been used as instruments for international blackmail.

Waziristan offers a good example of such a phenomenon. With Islamabad's complicity, a federally administered tribal area located along

---

[19] Ganguly, "Islamic Militancy in Bangladesh," 5.

the Afghan border (that during the Afghan jihad had been a launching pad for operations against Soviet forces) welcomed Afghan Taliban and al Qaeda members during the liberation of Afghanistan by the coalition forces. Not until 2002 did a reluctant Pakistan, under increasing U.S. pressure, begin to take action against the radical Islamists. Despite mobilizing some 80,000 regular troops in the area, Pakistan suffered considerable losses and, forced to negotiate with the Taliban, concluded two successive agreements in 2004 and 2006. The Pakistani government cannot be absolved of responsibility in the Talibanization of Waziristan; the government was complicit both in welcoming Taliban fleeing the U.S. intervention in Afghanistan and in the Islamist takeover of political power. Although the government has suffered a relative loss of control, reasons remain to suspect that Pakistan is not a passive victim of the Afghan situation but rather a continuing actor in the insurgency.

Equally problematic is Pakistan's policy toward international terrorism. Previously banned groups have been re-authorized under a new name. For example the Lashkar-e-Toiba, banned in January 2002, is now welcoming and training foreign militants. Islamabad cooperates against terrorism but always threatens, both implicitly and explicitly, to cease cooperation if not satisfied in other theaters such as Balochistan or Afghanistan.

This continued instrumentalization of Islamist militant groups, combined with a relative loss of control, increases the domestic pressures on Pakistani society and the polity. This situation also raises the risk of international terrorism and generates a pro-army reaction abroad.

Prospects for Political Reform in Bangladesh and Pakistan

In both countries the prospects for reform and democratization appear limited, although not completely closed. Of note in this regard are some striking similarities between Pakistan and Bangladesh.

The first similarity relates to each country's lack of acceptance and respect for democratic rule or even for the most basic component of democracy— the electoral process. In Bangladesh, despite three elections since the return to democracy, political parties still disagree over electoral issues. Election results are met with suspicion and the winners are systematically denied legitimacy by their opponents. Members of both parties complain that elections are dominated by "money and muscle" while "politically influenced killings frequently happen within and between parties."[20] The leadership of

---

[20] "Report of the National Democratic Institute (NDI) Pre-Election Delegation to Bangladesh's 2006/2007 Elections," National Democratic Institute for International Affairs, September 11, 2006, 4, http://www.accessdemocracy.org/library/2054_bd_finalstatement_091106.pdf.

these parties clearly bears direct responsibility for violence having become an acceptable political tool, even if they are not to blame for specific acts of violence. The existing culture of political violence will not change unless the leadership firmly resolves to improve the situation and restore discipline among party members. Despite an increasingly chaotic political situation in Bangladesh, such a shift seems unlikely. This creates space both for Islamist militancy and for military authoritarianism.

The situation in Pakistan is both similar to and different from the situation in Bangladesh. The situation in Pakistan—where the democratic culture of the political leadership (including that of the mainstream political parties) is quite superficial—is further complicated by the role of the army as a political actor. Political parties constantly (and correctly) blame the army and the intelligence agencies, in particular the so-called political wing of the Inter-Services Intelligence (ISI), for their constant interference in the political game. Yet leaders of all parties regularly call on the military leadership to act as a political arbiter and constantly question the legitimacy of the election winners. As a pledge not to repeat this practice, the two exiled ex-prime ministers Mian Nawaz Sharif and Benazir Bhutto signed the Charter for Democracy in May 2005. With the approach of the elections and the prospect of a return to power, however, this pledge has already been broken.

The lack of internal party democracy is also preventing renewal of party cadres at each level and might lead to political sclerosis. Paradoxically, the necessary democratization of Pakistan's political development, which would have to be imposed by the leadership, is unlikely to take place, as it would almost inevitably threaten the party elites' own position. The behavior of the political parties does not, however, diminish the responsibility of the army. The army pursues a constant policy of divide-and-rule by pressuring party cadres, exiling political leaders, and eroding the strength of mainstream organizations while reinforcing non-democratic forces such as Islamist organizations and other secular but totalitarian forces such as the MQM.

The actual and potential role of the international community in the democratization process is also critical for both Pakistan and Bangladesh. The international community has never played a major role in Bangladesh. Bangladesh has attracted little international visibility, with the exception of its participation in peacekeeping operations and in response to the natural catastrophes that regularly afflict the country. Bangladesh, never considered a threat, has been viewed internationally as an imperfect yet functional democracy where problems of development legitimately overshadowed other considerations.

The international community's attitudes toward Bangladesh could, however, change in response to the rise of Islamist militancy. The intent here is not to suggest that Bangladesh has direct responsibility for, or gives support to, militant groups. Rather, the goal is to emphasize that militancy is facilitated by political practices, such as those described above, that foster political ambivalence toward the problem and reluctance on the part of the leadership to combat it with the required determination. Moreover, given the gradual decline of the democratic institutions in both Pakistan and Bangladesh, it would make sense for the international community to place conditions on aid or use other pressures to influence political behaviors in these countries. Should militancy increase and internationalize, the international community may be tempted to welcome (or at least give consent to) a new military dictatorship in Bangladesh, similar to the prevailing scenario in Pakistan.

In Pakistan today the war on terrorism trumps any other consideration, including democracy—which is considered an important but distant objective. Such misplaced priorities persist even though the perpetuation of military power contributes to the problem of international terrorism and the continuing insurgency in Afghanistan. This situation allows the Pakistani military establishment to literally blackmail the international community by constantly recalibrating the level of its cooperation in the war on terrorism and Afghanistan.

Pakistan's fear of an Iranian- or Taliban-style Islamist regime has been a major reason underlying the country's refusal to actively promote democracy. Though largely unfounded, this fear forms part of the most effective propaganda of the Pakistani regime and may well be utilized for similar purposes in Bangladesh. Because the political vacuums in Pakistan and Bangladesh are not comparable to those in Arab regimes, Islamist parties in these two countries are not in a position to seize power through the electoral process. The political systems in both Pakistan and Bangladesh could, therefore, conceivably be reformed without the risk of their falling into the Islamist trap; democratization will not take place in either of the two countries, however, without external "incentives" that under present conditions are unlikely to be provided. In the absence of a genuine democratization process, the self-destructive tendencies of the two countries will be reinforced.

Uncertain Futures?

If complacency or complicity of the Bangladeshi and Pakistani elites continues, both countries risk letting a tiny minority—those for whom political Islam is their primary political identity—ultimately determine their country's external relations and the stability of the region.

In Bangladesh the key determinant will be the willingness and the ability of the political parties to reform themselves in order to address the actual needs and grievances of the population. This self-reform would require both a deeper acceptance of the rules of the political game and major internal reform—in other words, a change of political culture. The loss of credibility for Bangladeshi political parties, should they fail to reform, may gradually translate into increased legitimacy for Islamist organizations. With this new status, Islamist organizations could become kingmakers given that the two major political organizations would need to ally with them to form a parliamentary majority and govern. This development would likely lead to political instability that would be conducive to the development of radicalism. Another possibility—very real since December 2006—would be a direct or indirect takeover of the country by the Bangladeshi army following the Pakistani model, including the possible use of the Islamist organizations in a coup or the imposition of martial rule.

The key political driver in Pakistan is the army and the evolution of its role. To a large extent the future of the country will depend on the perpetuation of the army's hold on power. As long as the military remains in power, Pakistan will continue following the same foreign policy track and supporting militant Islamist groups (although this support may vary over time, according to the needs of the moment). This situation would continue to generate problems not only for Pakistan's neighbors (especially India and Afghanistan) but also for Pakistan itself. Although the army's continued hold on power would not likely destabilize the state, the constant harassment and weakening of the political parties would continue and the prospect for the reestablishment of genuine democracy would diminish.

Strategic Implications

Current political trends in Bangladesh and Pakistan could have serious regional and global security consequences.

Over the past six years both countries have witnessed an increase in indigenous Islamist terrorism. Sectarian violence is not a new phenomenon in Pakistan but has, according to reports by many observers, risen over the past few years. Militancy in both countries has indigenous origins that have been fed by regional conflicts, in particular by the situation in Afghanistan. The two countries diverge, however, in one important aspect. Since the early 1980s Pakistan has used Islamist violence as a foreign policy tool, most significantly in Kashmir and Afghanistan; yet despite alliances between mainstream political parties and Islamist organizations, Bangladesh to date has not had to resort to the same tactics.

Hubs of International Terrorism?

Bangladesh is at risk of becoming, like Pakistan, a hub of international terrorism. Pakistan is a key country for al Qaeda, which according to U.S. intelligence sources operates from Pakistan across the entire South Asian and Middle Eastern regions. Bangladesh may well become another haven for al Qaeda according to intelligence specialists, some of whom warn of Bangladesh becoming another sanctuary (like Lebanon and Gaza). Selig Harrison noted in August 2006 that "a growing fundamentalist movement linked to al Qaeda and Pakistani intelligence agencies is steadily converting the strategically located nation of Bangladesh into a new regional hub for terrorist operations that reach India and Southeast Asia."[21]

The likelihood of such a development is questioned by those who believe that Bangladesh's ethnic homogeneity and population density make it extremely difficult for any foreign group in the country to operate clandestinely. They further observe that Bangladeshi militants involved with the Taliban in Afghanistan were low-level operators lacking organizational capabilities. The development of local terrorist cells remains, however, a possibility that cannot be excluded a priori, particularly if the Bangladeshi government remains as complacent as it has to date.

The Regional Scenario

At the regional level, such developments could potentially lead to the creation of a new, although distant, front between India and Pakistan. Terrorist operations might conceivably be conducted from Bangladesh in cooperation with secessionist movements in northeastern India—as in Kashmir, although without the territorial claims that exist in that case. Pakistan's core concern would be to maintain pressure on India while continuing the current peace process with New Delhi. By helping Bangladeshi militants either directly or through Islamist allies, Pakistan would widen the front. Pakistan would thus be able to continue harassing India while maintaining plausible deniability. Pakistan could continue its proxy war against India while diminishing the risk of international isolation and condemnation. This could even be seen as an effective increase of its own strategic depth. The likelihood of such an outcome is greater if the

---

[21] Selig Harrison, "A New Hub for Terrorism? In Bangladesh, an Islamic Movement with Al-Qaeda Ties Is on the Rise," *Washington Post*, August 2, 2006.

BNP, which is more pro-Pakistani and more accommodating of Islamist sentiment, wins the elections.

There are partial indications that this scenario is already playing out. Both the HuJI and the Islami Chhatra Shibir are suspected of having links to Pakistan's ISI. The HuJI is also said to have helped the United Liberation Front of Assam establish training camps in the Chittagong Hill Tract, next to the Indian state of Tripura.[22] A March 2006 bombing in Varanasi, India had reported links with the HuJI.[23]

After the July 11, 2006 bomb blasts that killed 200 people in Mumbai, the Indian authorities arrested a number of individuals with ties to terrorist groups in Bangladesh and Nepal "who were directly or indirectly linked to Pakistan." These allegations were, however, denied by both Pakistan and Bangladesh.[24]

Although government spokesmen in New Delhi and in Indian state capitals have argued that Bangladesh's Directorate General of Field Intelligence (DGFI) is actively working with Pakistan's ISI to destabilize India's northeast, the BNP or the Bangladeshi authorities in general are unlikely to act as an accomplice to Pakistani operations in the area.[25] Bangladesh will more likely give Islamist organizations the kind of leeway that would allow these organizations to be used by the Pakistani intelligence agencies. Of course the possible eventual success of the peace process in Kashmir would make this kind of consideration irrelevant. Nothing to date, however, indicates that such a peace is close. Therefore Pakistan will likely keep its last bargaining assets as long as possible.

Given the seemingly extensive links between Islamist groups in Bangladesh and Pakistan, Bangladeshi activism in northeast India could allow Pakistan to continue its harassment of India while diffusing international pressure on Islamabad resulting from Pakistani militancy in Kashmir. In such a scenario, deniability would be easier and Islamabad might envisage signing a peace treaty with India regarding Kashmir.

Both Pakistan and Bangladesh use (or accept the use of) their geographical proximity and ethno-religious affinities with parts of India to affect India's domestic, ethnic, religious, and political relationships, thus helping secessionist movements within India. By doing so, the two countries help bring adverse external forces into the subcontinent, creating a risk of instability for India's security environment.

---

[22] Ganguly, "Islamic Militancy in Bangladesh," 7.

[23] Bruce Vaughn, "Bangladesh: Background and U.S. Relations," Congressional Research Service Report for Congress, RL33646, September 7, 2006, 10.

[24] Ibid.

[25] Ganguly, "Islamic Militancy in Bangladesh," 7.

India's Reactions to the Political Decline in Bangladesh and Pakistan

While the consequences of the political decline in Bangladesh and Pakistan will be different, India will probably look for some cautious accommodation with the powers in place, dealing with whatever government emerges in both countries.

Many contentious issues remain between India and Bangladesh. In particular, two issues may cause a source of friction with Bangladesh and cause political problems in India if the Bangladeshi political system continues to decline. Should Bangladesh either gradually fall into political chaos or fall under some form of military dictatorship, illegal migration to India may increase. The number of illegal Bangladeshi immigrants to India has been a matter of debate for years. The question is not whether the number is "tolerable" by India. Rather, the issue is the popular reaction to increased immigration pressures particularly if, due to an increase of Bangladeshi Islamist militancy, this population is associated by some segments of the Indian population with terrorism.

Moreover, the blame game over cross-border militancy could intensify if the political situation degenerates in Bangladesh. India and Bangladesh regularly accuse each other of harboring insurgents. New Delhi accuses Bangladesh of providing sanctuary to the United Liberation Front of Assam and the National Socialist Council of Nagaland (NSCN), while Dhaka blames India for sheltering the Shadin Bangabhumi Andolon (SBA) and the United People's Democratic Front (UPDF) as well as criminals wanted in Bangladesh.[26] If a weak government in Dhaka sought legitimacy in strong nationalist rhetoric, mutual accusation could intensify and relations degenerate.

India's interests lie in a politically stable Bangladesh, but New Delhi will remain cautious not to antagonize or weaken any Bangladeshi government. New Delhi must navigate between its publicly declared support for an early return to democracy in Dhaka and the importance of developing a working relationship with whoever holds power there, including the present caretaker government.

New Delhi's position will remain even more ambivalent with regard to the situation in Pakistan, where a result of political decline is a stronger army. While the perpetrator of a number of terrorist acts in Kashmir, the Pakistani army is the only real possible guarantor of an eventual peace agreement, however imperfect. India would undoubtedly prefer a democratic civilian government. Past Pakistani civilian governments were almost always willing to conduct a more peaceful foreign policy toward India. Military

---

[26] Imtiaz Ahmed, "The Indo-Bangla SAARC Puzzle," *Himal Southasian*, March 2007, http://www.himalmag.com/2007/march/cover4.htm.

governments have been more aggressive—the most spectacular recent example being the 1999 Kargil War, when groups comprised of jihadis and Pakistani regular troops occupied the hills over the Indian city of Kargil only a few months after the prime ministers of India and Pakistan signed the Lahore declaration committing the two countries to a peace process.

Both the Kargil episode and the nine-month stand-off along the Indo-Pakistani border, which followed the December 13, 2001 terrorist attack against the Indian parliament in New Delhi, proved that disputes between the two nuclear powers could not be resolved militarily as either large-scale or limited conventional war would considerably increase the risk of a nuclear conflagration in the subcontinent. No matter how slow the pace of the ongoing "peace process" is, engaging Pakistan therefore remains the only viable policy option for New Delhi. India will likely thus maintain a working relationship with Pakistan's military governments.

Implications for the United States

Should they continue, these trends in Pakistan and Bangladesh will affect U.S. regional and global interests on several levels.

Unless the United States changes the course of its policy toward Pakistan, relations with Islamabad will become increasingly difficult to manage. Structural dependence will remain. Pakistan will be increasingly able to leverage its cooperation on any U.S. proposal to gain leeway on its own more crucial objectives. As the number of such objectives rise—for example if Pakistan redefines itself as a "frontline state" in a covert war against Iran—so will Pakistan's bargaining power. As the trade-offs increase, the United States will have more difficulty applying pressures on specific issues such as terrorism.

Moreover, should the Pakistani army retain power U.S. interests would inevitably be affected as well. As the legitimacy of the regime diminishes, so will the popularity of its main sponsor. As a result anti-U.S. sentiment would likely increase, making both the war on terrorism and the fight against the Taliban more difficult. This development in turn would limit NATO's effectiveness in the area, raising questions about the organization's ability to conduct operations outside Europe.

A Pakistani rapprochement with the Bangladeshi government, or even simply with Bangladeshi groups, that allowed Pakistan to operate along the India-Bangladesh border would make matters even more complex. Such a development would allow Pakistan to maintain the same kind of pressures on India as it has with Kashmir. Pakistan would be able to train Bangladeshi Islamist militants in Pakistan without concern for potential spillover effects for Bangladesh. This situation would have contradictory consequences for Pakistan. Although such a development would necessitate changes in U.S. policy vis-à-vis Pakistan, Islamabad could deflect pressure to dismantle its terrorist infrastructure by moving the infrastructure to Bangladesh. Direct responsibility for terrorist acts also would be more difficult to determine.

The probability of such a scenario would increase if the military returned to power in Dhaka. Military governments under Zia and Ershad had close ties with the Pakistani military. Civilian governments would, however, not be a significant impediment for Islamabad. Given the authorities' complacency toward both Islamist parties and Islamist militancy, these governments could develop direct relations with Islamist militant groups along the border, irrespective of the party in power (although likely more easily with the pro-Pakistan BNP).

The possible developments described above would benefit China, as even a low level of hostility between India and Bangladesh from Islamist militancy on the border would most likely strengthen relations between Dhaka and Beijing. China would benefit by forming a series of alliances in India's immediate neighborhood from Islamabad to Rangoon, de facto neutralizing New Delhi. As a result India would be less useful as an ally for the United States as New Delhi would have more difficulty projecting power internationally due to constant aggressive harassment on its borders.

In both Bangladesh and Pakistan, long-term U.S. interests would be better served by a genuine democratization process. For Pakistan, the question is now whether even short-term interests would benefit from the same process. The return of civilian government to Islamabad would not eliminate all uncertainties. If the past is any indication, however, such a return would diminish the likelihood of an aggressive foreign policy and possibly prove more accommodating for ethnic minorities, leading to greater social stability. The key issue would be the ability of Pakistani political parties to enlarge their limited political space and consolidate power while simultaneously democratizing the country. Ultimately a democratized Pakistani government would probably prove more efficient in mobilizing the population in the war on terrorism.

EXECUTIVE SUMMARY

This chapter examines the impact of political change in Southeast Asia on U.S. strategic alliances as the U.S. and ASEAN cope with the security implications of China's rise for the regional balance of power.

MAIN ARGUMENT:
U.S. grand strategy in Southeast Asia is focused on maintaining the regional balance of power, which historically has meant a preponderance of U.S. power. To do so at the time when China's rise is creating region-wide strategic uncertainty, the U.S. must adapt to alterations in the local balance caused by domestic political change within key states. The Philippines and Thailand—U.S. traditional allies—face crises of government legitimacy and military professionalism. Indonesia, Southeast Asia's rising power, is forming a new strategic partnership with the U.S. Also emerging as a dynamic regional actor, Vietnam sees its relationship with the U.S. as a hedging strategy against China. U.S. relations with Indonesia and Vietnam may be the key points for regional balancing following the war on terrorism.

POLICY IMPLICATIONS:
- Both the relevance of U.S. traditional Southeast Asian alliances and expenditure of political capital in maintaining them warrant broad consideration in the context of China's rise.

- Security relations with the Philippines and Thailand would benefit from careful managment to ensure that the U.S. is not perceived as a "regime enabler" in the future.

- Indonesia's "strategic partnership" with the U.S. will need approval through Indonesian democratic parliamentary and electoral processes. This will require U.S. appreciation of the country's Muslim and nationalist sensitivities.

- The U.S. would best be sensitive to the constraints China places on how far and fast Vietnam can deepen a security relationship with the U.S.

Political Change in Southeast Asia: Challenges for U.S. Strategy

Donald E. Weatherbee

For both the United States and the countries of Southeast Asia, the central regional strategic issue is coping with the rise of China. Since 2001, while the United States has been preoccupied with the war on terrorism, an emerging China has pursued an agenda in Southeast Asia that some analysts have seen as rivaling the United States in a zero-sum game for influence. China's rise has been peaceful, characterized by intensive diplomatic exchange and building economic relationships. China's rise is occurring in a peaceful, politically stable, and open regional strategic environment that has to date favored the interests of the countries of the region, China, and the United States. No evidence indicates that a fundamental reordering of strategic orientations in the region is taking place.

The United States and the Association of Southeast Asian Nations (ASEAN, an intergovernmental organization that encompasses all of the states of the region except East Timor) have worked to foster cooperation with China in areas of mutual interest, including security. Strategic planners, however, must consider possible future divergent interests that would disrupt the prevailing order. A hostile U.S.-China relationship accompanied by Chinese efforts to challenge the U.S. security presence in the subregion would be a strategic nightmare for Southeast Asia. As the Pentagon's 2006 *Quadrennial Defense Review Report* (QDR) states, "of the major and emerging powers, China has the greatest potential to compete militarily with the United States and field disruptive military technologies that could over time offset U.S. traditional military advantages absent U.S.

Donald E. Weatherbee is the Donald S. Russell Distinguished Professor Emeritus at the University of South Carolina. He can be reached at <donald.e.weatherbee@verizon.net>.

counter strategies."[1] The QDR goes on to point out that "the pace and scope of China's military build-up already puts regional military balances at risk."[2] That pace is accelerating. As a result Southeast Asian countries are concerned over China's long-range ambitions in the region and the integrity of the U.S. security commitment.

The current regional strategic setting is usually, but inaccurately, described as a balance of power. In fact, the United States remains preponderant in the distribution of power. U.S. bilateral alliances with Thailand and the Philippines and the de facto alliance with Singapore are still at the heart of Southeast Asia's "security architecture," to use the category of security cooperation and coordination examined by Nick Bisley elsewhere in this volume. In some respects a relic of the Cold War, this traditional alliance system remains the backbone of U.S. strategic posture in the region. Other regional bilateral strategic partnerships, military access agreements, military exercising networks, and military assistance and training programs augment this system. Despite criticism from Muslim groups, Malaysia has no plans to scale down military cooperation with the United States. Instead the country is, in the words of the Malaysian defense minister, "looking for avenues to increase the cooperation."[3] The United States initiated a peacekeeping training program for the Cambodian military after that country became eligible for U.S. military assistance in 2005 by signing an agreement on U.S. immunity from the International Criminal Court.[4] Ties with Indonesia and Vietnam are, however, the most strategically important regional security links for the United States beyond those with the traditional allies.

The U.S. "hub and spoke" security network in Southeast Asia together with its deployable strategic reach from Northeast Asia and the Pacific give the United States a unique regional security presence as a great power. The United States considers its security ties in Southeast Asia to be vitally important. A major focus and goal of the U.S. Pacific Command (PACOM), moreover, is the "advancing of regional security cooperation and engagement" so as to "facilitate situations in which future security

---

[1] U.S. Department of Defense, *Quadrennial Defense Review Report*, February 6, 2006, 29, http://www.defenselink.mil/pubs/pdfs/QDR20060203.pdf.

[2] Ibid.

[3] "Malaysia's Defense Chief Says No Easing of Military Ties with U.S.," *AntaraNews*, April 16, 2007, http://www.antara.co.id/en/arc/2007/4/16/malaysias-defense-chief-says-no-easing-of-military-ties-with-us/.

[4] "Memorandum for the Secretary of State Waiving Prohibition on U.S. Military Assistance with Respect to Cambodia," White House, Press Release, August 2, 2005, http://www.whitehouse.gov/news/releases/2005/08/20050802-5.html.

challenges can be met through strong regional cooperation and capacity."[5] This security cooperation and engagement, however, will continue to be on a bilateral basis. Although Southeast Asian states agree that a U.S. strategic presence is necessary to balance China, there is no collective framework to incorporate that presence in any operational way. ASEAN's vision of a "security community" does not include a pan-ASEAN military cooperation system—let alone one linked to the United States. For the ASEAN states, the consultative multilateral mechanisms such as the ASEAN Regional Forum (ARF) or the ASEAN +1 partnership meetings do not constitute a basis for strategic hedging. These mechanisms are designed to keep extraregional powers involved, rather than affect the region's military balance.

Given that there is little prospect for a multilateral and multidimensional regional security architecture emerging in Southeast Asia, maintaining the current stable U.S.-supported strategic setting will require more than simply adapting and adjusting to the rise of China. Also of importance is the continued cooperation and engagement by the United States with key Southeast Asian states to secure local strategic goals. The quality and intensity of each particular U.S. relationship will also depend on the domestic political conditions in the partner state. The direction and pace of domestic political change in each country will affect not only bilateral interactions with the United States but also the regional balance of power itself. The war on terrorism and the search for coalition partners in Iraq have masked recent strategy-relevant alterations in the local Southeast Asian domestic political landscape.

The pages to follow will first argue that political instability compounded by institutional problems within their respective militaries may diminish the strategic value of the Philippines and Thailand—the traditional U.S. alliance partners. This chapter then proposes that Indonesia and Vietnam are emerging as strategically important to the United States. Their choices regarding cooperation and engagement will affect the regional balance of power. As the traditional partners in the U.S. hub and spoke regional security system become less important to the balance of power, a new local security architecture may emerge in which the United States is an element but not necessarily the hub.

---

[5] William Fallon, testimony before the House Armed Services Committee, Washington, D.C., March 7, 2007, http://armedservices.house.gov/pdfs/FCPACOM030707/Fallon_Testimony030707.pdf.

The Philippines: Marcos Redux?

The Philippines is the oldest strategic ally of the United States in Southeast Asia. The then secretary of state Colin Powell underlined the continuing relevance of this security link in 2002, when he stated that the "alliance between the United States and the Philippines has been a bulwark of freedom and stability in the Asia-Pacific region."[6] While the benefits of the alliance for the United States have been in the Asian regional setting, the benefits for the Philippines have been domestic. The alliance has bolstered the will and capacity of the Armed Forces of the Philippines (AFP) in two counterinsurgency campaigns: one against the Communist Party of the Philippines/New People's Army (CPP/NPA), the only remaining communist insurgency in Southeast Asia, and the other against a decades-old Muslim revolt in the south, led by the Moro Islamic Liberation Front (MILF) and, at its radical margins, the Abu Sayyaf Group (ASG). More problematically for the United States, the close security relationship also has the effect of demonstrating U.S. support for politically beleaguered President Gloria Macapagal-Arroyo. The current partnership is one between the United States and a Philippine government of questionable legitimacy, reliant on the support of the military, and resistant to reform—as was the case during former president Ferdinand Marcos' rule. If the degradation of democratic norms in the Philippines continues, the United States will need to reassess at some point the Philippines' strategic value as a contributor to peace, stability, and democracy in Southeast Asia.

The democratic presidential succession that followed the Marcos period came to an end in 2001 when supporters of the then vice president, Gloria Macapagal-Arroyo, toppled the popularly elected president, Joseph Estrada, a charismatic former movie star and man of the masses. Estrada's administration was plagued by accusations of corruption and criminality. When efforts to impeach him failed, Arroyo's forces mounted mass demonstrations that they called EDSA II, likening them to the earlier popular revolt against Marcos.[7] In an important echo of the original EDSA movement, the military openly swung their support behind Arroyo. Claiming that the welfare of the people overrode the constitution, the Supreme Court declared the presidency vacant and swore in Arroyo on January 20, 2001. Though acknowledging Estrada's democratic mandate, the United States countenanced the irregular transfer of power, explaining that

---

[6] "Joint Press Conference with Philippine Foreign Affairs Secretary Blas F. Ople," U.S. Department of State, August 3, 2002, http://www.state.gov/secretary/former/powell/remarks/2002/12434.htm.

[7] EDSA (Epifanio de los Santos Avenue) refers to the site of mostly non-violent mass demonstrations that led to the subsequent downfall of Marcos in 1986.

"it is in [the U.S.] interest to look to the future, not the past."[8] In the view of Estrada supporters, Arroyo had stolen the presidency. To them, Estrada had been a champion of the urban poor and rural peasantry. Arroyo, in contrast, came from the traditional ruling oligarchy. In May 2001, Arroyo sent troops into the street to quell demonstrations against her allegedly illegal seizure of power.

Any qualms the United States might have had about Arroyo's ascension were put to rest by Philippine assistance in the war on terrorism. Arroyo was the first Southeast Asian leader to contact President George W. Bush after September 11 to offer support. Her administration characterized the counterinsurgency campaigns against the CPP/NPA and Islamist separatists as part of the battle against terrorism. The pay-off for the Philippines has been a massive reinvestment by the United States in U.S. security interests there. A 1999 Visiting Forces Agreement (VFA) pushed through the Philippine Senate by Estrada had already partially filled the bilateral security vacuum and the military to-military relationship that had followed the 1992 closure of U.S. bases in the country. In the war on terrorism, the Philippines outstrips by far all other Southeast Asian aid recipients in every category of military assistance.[9]

In recognition of the alliance's strength and vitality, in 2003 Bush designated the Philippines a "major non-NATO ally."[10] With the VFA in place, joint exercising and training have been expanded, with the centerpiece being the annual Balikatan joint combined exercises.[11] The deployment since 2002 of a U.S. Joint Special Operations Task Force-Philippines (JSOTF-P) to the southern Philippines to assist and advise the AFP in the field against terrorists linked to al Qaeda and Jemaah Islamiyah (JI) has been perhaps most indicative of the new security relationship. According to counterinsurgency analysts, U.S. assistance has been the crucial factor in the better performance of the AFP in recent years.[12] Though technically acting

---

[8] Thomas Hubbard, testimony to the hearing The Philippines: Present Political Status and Its Role in the New Asia before the Subcommittee on East Asian and Pacific Affairs, Washington, D.C., March 6, 2001.

[9] "GMA Cites Benefits of Strong RP-U.S. Military Partnership," Office of the President of the Republic of the Philippines, Press Release, March 5, 2004, http://www.op.gov.ph/news.asp?newsid=4589.

[10] "Joint Statement between the United States of America and the Republic of the Philippines," U.S. Embassy in Manila, October 18, 2003, http://manila.usembassy.gov/wwwhr132.html.

[11] For discussion of U.S.-Philippine military-to-military relations, see Rommel C. Banlaoi, "The Role of Philippine-American Relations in the Global Campaign Against Terrorism: Implications for Regional Security," *Contemporary Southeast Asia* 24, no. 2 (August 2002): 405–22; and Renato Cruz De Castro, "Philippine Defense Policy in the 21st Century: Autonomous Defense or Back to the Alliance," *Pacific Affairs* 78, no. 3 (February 2005): 403–22.

[12] Donald Greenlees, "Philippine Military, with U.S. Help, Checks Rebels," *International Herald Tribune*, February 12, 2007.

only in an advisory capacity, the U.S. military has extended its involvement down to the battalion and company levels, at times blurring the distinction between advice and operational involvement. A perceived ambiguity in the U.S. role has led Filipino critics of the return of U.S combat forces to accuse the Arroyo government of flouting the constitution.[13] The 2002 signing of the Mutual Logistics Support Agreement further aroused nationalist apprehensions over U.S. involvement with the AFP. The agreement allowed the pre-positioning of U.S. supplies and equipment in the Philippines as well as U.S. access to Philippine facilities. A storm of protest resulted, and charges that the United States was looking for basing rights were vigorously denied by Manila and Washington. The domestic political implications of the enhanced military-to-military relations reached their height with the 2005 arrest and 2006 trial of four U.S. marines charged with rape. The legal and political tussle in the context of the VFA for custody of the accused servicemen rekindled the nationalist flames that had burned over the old military basing agreement. When Arroyo overrode judicial authorities in the case, she justified her decision as necessary to prevent further deterioration in the U.S.-Philippines strategic relationship.[14]

In an address to the Philippine Congress during his October 2003 state visit, Bush stated that the "U.S.-Philippines military alliance is a rock of stability in the Pacific."[15] The CPP/NPA and Muslim insurgencies are not, however, the only possible threats to that stability. The same types of social and political forces that ultimately brought down the Marcos regime are undermining the foundations of the Arroyo government. The tipping point came with the May 2004 presidential election. After Arroyo won by a close vote, accusations of massive fraud and systematic cheating began to swirl around the Arroyo camp.[16] The defeated candidate, Ferdinand Poe, appealed to the same electoral base as Estrada had. Again, the popular perception was that the traditional oligarchs had stolen the presidency from the people. Arroyo's approval ratings plunged to the lowest point any president

---

[13] An exposition of the domestic political issues raised by the JSOTF-P was published by the Philippines Center for Investigative Journalism (PCIJ). See Herbert Docena, "The U.S. Troops' 'Unconventional' Presence," Philippines Center for Investigative Journalism, PCIJ Special Feature, 2007, http://www.pcij.org/i-report/2007/us-troops.html.

[14] "Smith's Transfer to Avoid Erosion of RP's Strategic Relations with the U.S.-PGMA," Office of the President of the Republic of the Philippines, Press Release, January 2, 2007, http://www.op.gov.ph/news.asp?newsid=16858.

[15] "Remarks of the President to the Philippine Congress," White House, Office of the Press Secretary, Press Release, October 18, 2003, http://www.whitehouse.gov/news/releases/2003/10/20031018-12.html.

[16] Benjamin Muego, "The Philippines in 2004: A Gathering Storm," in Southeast Asian Affairs 2005, ed. Chin Kin Wah and Daljit Singh (Singapore: Institute of Southeast Asian Studies, 2005), 293–312.

had seen since the last year of the Marcos administration twenty years earlier. Demonstrations against her were dispelled by water cannons and truncheons. In the clamor, the military declared neutrality and adherence to the constitution. The Catholic Church meanwhile issued a pastoral letter stating that "like Pope Benedict XVI, we do not believe in the 'intrusion into politics on the part of the hierarchy'."[17] These stances were markedly different from the positions of the AFP and the Church during EDSA I and II, when they had intervened against the incumbent presidents.

Frustrated by the checks and balances of a tripartite governmental system, in 2005 Arroyo began to press aggressively for constitutional revision in a move termed Charter Change or, in popular parlance, Cha-Cha. Her goal was to shift to a unicameral parliamentary system by eliminating the Senate, which was dominated by her political opponents. When the Senate blocked her attempts, Arroyo threatened to employ extraconstitutional means to achieve her ends. What many Filipino democrats saw as an assault on the 1987 reform constitution was thus added to the constitutional coup and rigged elections in the litany of accusations directed against Arroyo. Efforts at impeachment were blocked in the Philippines House of Representatives. Nagging charges of corruption against her husband and son for receiving kickbacks from operators of the illegal *jueting* (numbers rackets) lotteries further damaged her standing. Even formerly staunch supporters of the president suggested that she should resign for the betterment of the country.

The crisis over Arroyo's battered presidency came to a head in February 2006. Fear that she was trying to reverse the democracy that had been won back from Marcos moved people again into the streets. As the twentieth anniversary of EDSA I approached, public unrest was coupled with rumors of a coup or the possible emergence of an EDSA III movement. Preemptively, Arroyo declared a state of national emergency. Proclamation No. 1017 of February 24, 2006, ostensibly issued to defend and preserve democracy, bore an eerie resemblance to Marcos' Proclamation No. 1021, which declared martial law in 1972.[18] Arroyo implemented her proclamation by issuing General Order No. 5 directing "the Armed Forces of the Philippines in the face of national emergency, to maintain public peace, order, and safety and to prevent and suppress lawless violence."[19] In response, the Catholic Bishop's

---

[17] Lorraine C. Salazar, "The Philippines: Crisis, Controversies, and Economic Resilience," in *Southeast Asian Affairs 2006*, ed. Daljit Singh and Lorraine C. Salazar (Singapore: Institute of Southeast Asian Studies, 2006), 230.

[18] For the full text of Proclamation No. 1017, see Office of the Press Secretary, Republic of the Philippines, February 24, 2006, http://www.news.ops.gov.ph/proc_no1017.htm.

[19] For the full text of General Order No. 5, see Office of the Press Secretary, Republic of the Philippines, February 24, 2006, http://www.news.ops.gov.ph/go_no5.htm.

Conference abandoned its neutrality and endorsed rallies against Cha-Cha. As her popular support melted away, Arroyo made a tactical retreat and put Cha-Cha on the backburner. Despite being temporarily stymied, the president promised that she would still pursue her commitment "with urgency and fervor."[20]

Any future success in Arroyo's pursuit of Cha-Cha and other parts of her legislative program would have required the emergence of a more amenable Congress from elections held in May 2007. As expected, her allies maintained control of the House of Representatives in district elections that were marred by violence, bribery, official misconduct, and military and police intimidation. In the Senate elections—which are nationwide and were widely viewed as a referendum on Arroyo's presidency—she suffered a crushing defeat. Half of the 24 Senate seats were up for election. Arroyo's opponents won 9 of the 12. Although Arroyo's continued control of the House of Representatives will assure the failure of any new impeachment effort, control of the Senate by her opponents presents major legislative hurdles to her programs and budgets. The manner in which Arroyo reacts to congressional stalemate and the degree to which a factionalized AFP will continue providing steadfast support to her incumbency will be major factors in determining Philippine political stability and the quality of Philippine-U.S. relations.

New indicators of political repression in the Philippines emerged in 2007. A package of antiterrorist laws called the Human Security Act was passed, giving the government greater powers to act preemptively against suspected terrorists and conspiracies. The opposition fears that Arroyo will use her new authority to stifle legitimate dissent. The UN Human Rights Commission's Special Rapporteur on Human Rights and Counterterrorism has called on the next Philippine Congress to repeal or amend the legislation, stating that the "overly broad definition" of terrorism was incompatible with the International Covenant on Civil and Political Rights and that "many provisions of the Human Security Act are not in accordance with international human rights standards."[21] The deployment of armed troops before the elections into some of Manila's poorest urban neighborhoods, termed "problematic areas" by the government, was even more immediately disturbing to Arroyo's opposition. Anti-Arroyo political activists viewed the military presence as coercive harassment. Despite hesitancy on the part of

---

[20] "PGMA's Speech during the 40th Anniversary of the Asian Development Bank (ADB)," Office of the President of the Republic of the Philippines, Press Release, December 19, 2006, http://www.ops.gov.ph/speeches2006/speech-2006_dec19.htm.

[21] "UN Rights Expert Calls on Philippines to Amend or Repeal Anti-terrorism Law," UN News Centre, March 12, 2007, http://www.un.org/apps/news/story.asp?NewsID=21827&Cr=philippine&Cr1.

some members of the administration over the this use of the AFP, Arroyo herself offered congratulations after visiting a detachment in Manila's Tondo slum, telling the soldiers to keep up the good work.[22]

The credibility of the AFP is also at risk. The international reputation of the Arroyo presidency has been marred by a pattern of extrajudicial killings that, since 2001, has taken the lives of journalists, human rights activists, labor leaders, leftist politicians, community activists, and others who have been characterized as possible communist sympathizers. In claims supported by Amnesty International, Philippine human rights organizations have documented 836 murders, 357 attacks in which the wounded escaped, and 196 missing persons.[23] Reporting on a March 2007 investigation of the problem, UN Human Rights Commission's Special Rapporteur on Extrajudicial, Summary or Arbitrary Executions Philip Alston pointed out that it was not only the specific numbers that mattered, but the corrosive impact of the killings was also important in many ways: "it intimidates vast numbers of civil society actors, it sends a message of vulnerability to all but the most well connected, and it severely undermines the political discourse which is central to a resolution of the problems confronting this country."[24] In his initial presentation to the Human Rights Commission, Alston laid the blame on the military, corroborating the charges that had been brought by both Filipino and non-Filipino human rights groups.

Arroyo's own investigative commission, the Melo Commission, which depended only on official sources, concluded that the killings were a fact and that the military could be culpable; a conclusion that the AFP chief of staff claimed was strained and unfair.[25] This latter comment seems to confirm that the military, in the words of Alston, is "in a state of almost total denial" over the killings.[26] The European Union (EU) has also expressed misgivings. According to the EU's representative to the Philippines, although government action has been promised, no measures have actually

[22] Alcuin Papa, "Arroyo OKs Troops in the City," *Philippine Daily Inquirer*, April 1, 2007.

[23] Mari Hilao-Enriquez, testimony to the hearing Extrajudicial Killings in the Philippines: Strategies to End the Violence before the Senate Subcommittee on East Asian and Pacific Affairs, Washington, D.C., March 14, 2007, http://www.senate.gov/~foreign/testimony/2007/ EnriquezTestimony070314.pdf.

[24] "UN Special Rapporteur on Extrajudicial, Summary or Arbitrary Executions Ends Philippine Visit," United Nations in the Philippines, February 21, 2007, http://www.un.org.ph/Resourcehub-news.html.

[25] For a digest of the Melo Report by the U.S. Embassy in Manila, see http://108113015.onlinehome. us/embassy_update_03.pdf.

[26] "Alston: Govt Reaction to Visit 'Deeply Schizophrenic,'" *Philippine Daily Inquirer*, March 28, 2007.

been taken: "The point is that the killings have continued."[27] The issue of military complicity in extrajudicial killings and human rights abuse may lead to challenges to Arroyo and the AFP in the Philippine Senate.

The United States acknowledges that at the top the responsibility lies with Arroyo. Answering questions from the U.S. Senate committee investigating the killings, Deputy Assistant Secretary of State for East Asian and Pacific Affairs Eric John acknowledged that:

> the chain of command for the security forces leads to the president of the Republic of the Philippines. That does not mean they are operating under orders. But as the ultimate authority in the chain of command, she has to take the steps to stop any involvement by members of the security forces.[28]

Yet there has been no accountability at any level of the military to date. Arroyo's growing dependence on the military to sustain her government makes it unlikely that she will take any action other than eventually finding scapegoats in the lower ranks. Doing anything more would risk altering the terms of her alliance with the military, which have included impunity for military misdeeds.

The political trajectory of the Arroyo-AFP axis is a key challenge for U.S.-Philippine relations. Even with the U.S. partnership, the modernization of the AFP is still a work in progress that suffers from intractable issues of professionalism. Numerous investigations of corruption in the senior ranks have found kickbacks from ransoms paid to kidnappers and the skimming of funds from U.S. assistance. The AFP leadership is rife with factionalism. Coup-makers have been treated leniently by their civilian overseers for fear of military retaliation. Although Arroyo and her supporters in the AFP have attempted to purge anti-Arroyo elements, the possibility of another coup remains lurking in the background. Because of the pattern of democratic and human rights abuses, rights activists in the Philippines and the United States are calling for the United States to cut off military assistance. When asked about such a suspension, however, Deputy Assistant Secretary John responded that it would be "counterproductive" to U.S. efforts to influence change in the Philippines.[29]

---

[27] As quoted in Douglas Bakshian, "European Experts Offer Help to Philippines in Solving Extrajudicial Killings," *Voice of America* (VOA) News, June 18, 2007, http://www.voanews.com/english/2007-06-18-voa13.cfm.

[28] Eric John, testimony to the hearing Extrajudicial Killings in the Philippines: Strategies to End the Violence before the Senate Subcommittee on East Asian and Pacific Affairs, Washington, D.C., March 14, 2007, http://www.senate.gov/~foreign/testimony/2007/JohnTestimony070314.pdf.

[29] As quoted in Deborah Tate, "U.S. Senate Panel Focuses on Murders of Activists in Philippines," *VOA News*, March 14, 2007, http://www.voanews.com/english/archive/2007-03/2007-03-14-voa93.cfm.

To the United States one such possible counter-productive outcome may stem from concerns regarding the Sino-Philippine relationship. China is fostering closer relations with the Philippines without regard to issues of democracy, human rights, or military professionalism. In addition to its broad economic "peaceful development" agenda toward ASEAN in general, China also seems especially to be courting the Arroyo government in a balancing reaction to the heightened and renewed U.S. military engagement with the Philippines. The potential functional or technical benefits to the Philippines of any military relationship with China are limited, however, given the AFP's logistical tail to the United States. China has made three donations of military engineering equipment that, although perhaps symbolic, are not evidence of a real military assistance alternative for the Philippines. Australia, for example, is becoming a much more functionally valuable security partner than China, having recently signed a new security agreement with the Philippines. Overall there is little proof to suggest that the Philippines has a true China card to play beyond a hedging strategy to counter the leverage that the United States has in the bilateral security relationship. The U.S. Congress may become less reluctant to use that leverage in the future if the conditions of democracy in the Philippines continue to deteriorate.

Thailand: Back to an Undemocratic Future?

Thailand has been second only to the Philippines as a long-standing and dependable U.S. strategic ally in Southeast Asia. As with the Philippines, the Thai military's assault on democracy since September 2006 is straining the quality of the bilateral relationship. Thailand, under a series of military dictatorships, had opted to ally with the United States rather than to balance in the Cold War distribution of power. U.S. economic and military assistance was a material and political resource for the Thai military's authoritarian rule. During the Cold War the security value of the Thai alliance to the United States outweighed the costs of political association with a harsh military regime. In the present environment, however, faced by the prospect of the remilitarization of government in Thailand, the United States must reevaluate its strategic relationship with Thailand in the context of both the rise of China and Thailand's changed relations within ASEAN.

Since the end of the Cold War, security has remained an important element in the U.S.-Thai relationship. Thai ports and airfields have provided a basis for logistic support during the Persian Gulf War and current war in Iraq. Thailand made symbolic deployments of troops to Afghanistan and Iraq and became a close ally in the war on terrorism under Prime Minister

Thaksin Shinawatra. In recognition of the deepening and expanding security relationship, Bush designated Thailand a major non-NATO ally in December 2003.[30] Both Bush and Thaksin promised even greater cooperation on strategic and security issues.[31] In 2005, after more than half a century, the United States still viewed Thailand as a primary partner in maintaining strategic stability in Southeast Asia amid mounting great power competition for influence in the region.[32]

The political context of this strong bilateral defense relationship was drastically changed on September 19, 2006 when Royal Thai Army Commander in Chief General Sonthi Boonyaratglin led a coup overthrowing democratically elected Thaksin. The coup leaders declared martial law, and the 1997 constitution—the most democratic in Southeast Asia and the one that had truly empowered the Thai people—was discarded. When Thaksin's Thai Rak Thai (TRT) party won 376 of the 500 single-member constituency seats in the 2005 election, Thaksin formed the first majority parliamentary government in Thai history, allowing him to govern without a coalition. As a populist, Thaksin paid particular attention to the social and economic grievances of the rural Thais. Drawing upon this electoral base, he challenged entrenched urban Bangkok elites—the bureaucrats, military, royalists, and academics—who tended to view their power in the country's governance as an entitlement rather than as a democratic reward. In addition to his populism, Thaksin also had a self-aggrandizing policy and personal agenda.

The concentration of power in Thaksin's hands alarmed not only the customary stewards of Thai politics but also pro-democracy activists, who believed he had overridden constitutionally sanctioned institutions and mechanisms of checks and balances. As opposition to Thaksin's rule and the TRT's absolute majority in parliament mounted in Bangkok's political classes, in April 2006 Thaksin sought once more to demonstrate popular support by dissolving parliament and calling snap elections. Although the TRT again emerged with a majority, a boycott by the opposition resulted in unfilled parliamentary seats and the Constitutional Court invalidated the election. The Election Commission set new elections for November.

---

[30] "Bush Formally Designates Thailand as Major Non-NATO Ally," U.S. Embassy in Bangkok, Press Release, December 30, 2003, http://bangkok.usembassy.gov/relation/rel123003.htm.

[31] "Joint Statement between President George W. Bush and Prime Minister Thaksin Shinawatra," White House, Office of the Press Secretary, Press Release, September 19, 2005, www.whitehouse.gov/news/releases/2005/09/20050919-3.html.

[32] The background for this view is surveyed in Emma Chanlett-Avery, "Thailand: Background and U.S. Relations," Congressional Research Service, CRS Report for Congress, RL32593, September 6, 2005, http://fas.org/sgp/crs/row/RL32593.pdf.

Motivated by fear that the TRT would win again, in September 2006 the army declared martial law and shut down the political system.

The junta labeled itself the Council for National Security (CNS) and published a "white paper" justifying the coup in November 2006. The document was an indictment of Thaksin for abuses of power and various crimes.[33] One of the major charges, later withdrawn, was *lèse majesté* (an offense against the dignity of the reigning sovereign), a very serious crime in Thailand. Other charges of corruption and conflicts of interest had not been proven by mid-2007. The white paper also referenced several policy issues, the most serious of which was Thaksin's failure to resolve the violence of the growing Muslim separatist insurgency in Thailand's south. Unmentioned in the catalogue of Thaksin's failings, but also important, was the fact that he was not a member of the traditional political elite, which tended to view him with antipathetic disdain. In a certain sense, Thaksin was to the Thai ruling class what Estrada had been to its Filipino counterparts.

The United States quickly distanced itself from the coup. The White House expressed disappointment and called for the restoration of democracy, which "not only means elected government, but protected rights of citizens, including freedom of speech and assembly."[34] The State Department echoed the dismay, with its spokesperson stating that "there is no justification for a military coup in Thailand or in any place else."[35] The commander of PACOM termed the coup "unacceptable and not helpful" to U.S.-Thai security relations.[36] The immediate consequence for the bilateral relationship was the invocation of the provision of Section 508 of the Foreign Operations Act that prohibits the United States from financing any military assistance to a country whose elected government is deposed by a military coup or decree. With the exception of assistance to promote democratic elections or public participation in a democratic process, the funds by law cannot be restored until the president of the United States certifies that a democratically elected government is in place. The Section 508 sanction was applied to Thailand on September 28, 2006.[37] For FY 2006 and 2007, this has resulted in the reallocation of $35 million in assistance funds originally intended for Thailand.

[33] The white paper, entitled "Facts about Thailand's Administrative Reform on September 19, 2006," was published in an unofficial English translation by *The Nation* on November 26, 2006.

[34] "Press Gaggle by Tony Snow," White House, Office of the Press Secretary, September 9, 2006, http://www.whitehouse.gov/news/releases/2006/09/20060920-5.html.

[35] "Daily Press Briefing," U.S. Department of State, Press Release, September 20, 2006, http://www.state.gov/r/pa/prs/dpb/2006/72883.htm.

[36] Fallon, testimony before the House Armed Services Committee.

[37] "Daily Press Briefing," U.S. Department of State, September 28, 2006, http://www.state.gov/r/pa/prs/dpb/2006/73326.htm.

The status of the planned 2007 annual joint military exercise—Cobra Gold, the largest in Southeast Asia—remained in limbo until the quiet announcement in February 2007 that Cobra Gold would take place as scheduled in May. It was realized that even more so than military assistance suspension, cancelling the exercise could lead both to a major breach in U.S.-Thai relations and serious damage to U.S. regional strategy. The United States lacked a lever in its military-to-military relations similar to that which the United States had exercised over the Philippines when U.S. cancellation of Balikatan 2007 had forced Manila to give way on the VFA custody issue. Almost concurrent with Cobra Gold, a bill to strip Thailand of its major non-NATO ally status, the Thailand Democracy Act of 2007, was introduced in Congress in May.[38]

China showed its willingness to fish in troubled waters by promptly offering a military assistance package to compensate for the loss of U.S. funding. This gesture could be considered analogous to the offer of a rescue package by China to Thailand in the 1997 financial crisis after Washington snubbed Bangkok. Analysts have viewed Thailand as potentially susceptible to China's strategic influence ever since the Thai military's informal alliance with China during the Third Indochina War.[39] Much was made of the expression of appreciation for China's consistent support and understanding by junta-appointed Prime Minister Surayud Chulanont during a May 2007 visit to China. The visit could have been interpreted as a symbolic response to the U.S. and EU shunning of high-level contacts with the junta. The only major substantive outcome of the meeting was the formal signing of a five-year Joint Strategic Plan of Action that had been under negotiation since 2005 and initiated by Thaksin. Most of the functional areas for cooperation had already been addressed under existing bilateral mechanisms; the new agreement simply calls for expedited cooperation. The functional arrangements are in fact very similar to the bilateral partnerships that China has both with other ASEAN nations and with ASEAN as a whole.

Responding to domestic and foreign concerns about the restoration of constitutional, democratic rule, the junta quickly began writing a new constitution to provide the basis for new elections. The sympathies of the Constitution Drafting Committee were with the junta, which had chosen the committee chairman. The entire process took place under martial law and was closed, with press restrictions and a ban on political gatherings of five or more people in effect. In the interim the CNS installed a handpicked

---

[38] U.S. Congress, House, *Thailand Democracy Act of 2007*, H.R. 2382, 110th Cong., 1st sess., http://frwebgate.access.gpo.gov/cgi-bin/getdoc.cgi?dbname=110_cong_bills&docid=f:h2382ih.txt.pdf.

[39] Lawrence Grinter, "China, the United States, and Mainland Southeast Asia: Opportunism and the Limits of Power," *Contemporary Southeast Asia* 28, no. 3 (December 2006): 455–59.

"civilian" government, headed by former army commander in chief General Surayud, that has been singularly unsuccessful in managing the country. Observers have described the administration as incompetent and lacking vision.[40] The new government's economic policies—framed in the king-blessed ideology of a "sufficiency economy," rather than Thaksin's embrace of globalism—have been disastrous. Once the leader of Southeast Asia's "little tiger" economies, Thailand's growth rate now trails the region. The World Bank has dropped its growth rate prediction for Thailand in 2007 to 4.3%, only half that of Vietnam.[41] The World Bank's lead economist in Thailand attributed the poor performance to a "lack of policy clarity and policy direction."[42] Both poorly conceived capital controls and revisions to the investment law inspired by economic nationalism have eroded investor confidence. Political uncertainties have also caused investment to decline.

The inability of the junta to successfully tackle the violence in the country's four southern provinces with Muslim majorities has seriously undermined its credibility. Simmering for years, the sporadic acts of separatist violence that began in 2004 have grown into a full-scale insurgency in a familiar cycle of escalating conflict.[43] The deteriorating security condition in the south was a major catalyst for the coup, yet since the junta has taken charge the situation has worsened. The death toll by 2007 was over 2,300 and is climbing daily. A terrified Buddhist minority and an intimidated Muslim population are caught between the insurgents and the authorities. Critical elements of the government's social infrastructure—health workers, teachers, and local officials—are fleeing. The military force of 25 to 30 thousand soldiers and paramilitary rangers will be reinforced by mid-2007 with an additional 15 thousand troops. The army is considering stationing a mixed battalion of soldiers and paramilitary rangers in each of 33 districts in the south. Voices of those in government—including even the queen—have called for arming the Buddhist residents of the south. The crisis is deepening as local militias and vigilante groups form and sectarian lines harden. The junta's failure in the south has allowed the insurgents to gain the upper hand, thrown the army into disarray, and left the people of

---

[40] See, for example, Thepchai Yong, "Does the Government Have the Political Will to Live?" *The Nation*, March 20, 2007.

[41] "Thailand Economic Monitor (April 2007)," World Bank, http://siteresources.worldbank.org/INTTHAILAND/Resources/Economic-Monitor/2007april_tem_overview.pdf.

[42] As quoted in Parista Yuthamanop, "Policy Slips, Politics to Knock GDP," *Bangkok Post*, April 6, 2007.

[43] For a post-coup analysis of the situation in the south, see "Southern Thailand: The Impact of the Coup," International Crisis Group, Asia Report, no. 129, http://www.crisisgroup.org/home/index.cfm?l=1&id=4697; and Carin Zissis, "The Muslim Insurgency in Southern Thailand," Council on Foreign Relations, Backgrounder, February 1, 2007.

the region living in fear.[44] In short, as one headline captured the situation, there is "utter mayhem" in the south.[45]

In April 2007 the unveiling of the draft constitution confirmed civil society's fears that the proposed system would marginalize the Thai electorate by returning power to the bureaucratic-military-royalist elite. A new House of Representatives balanced by an unelected Senate seems designed to ensure a return to the pattern of weak governments that characterized the past. In this new framework real democratic political power would be diffused, guaranteeing that factionalized coalition governments would not be able to move in bold policy directions. Thaksin's TRT party, Thailand's largest, has been declared illegal and the party's senior politicians have been barred from politics for five years. This situation leaves the rural TRT voters—responsible in large part for delivering Thaksin his huge legislative majority—disenfranchised and available for political mobilization against the country's rulers. To the dismay of many Thai democrats—even those who had opposed Thaksin—the proposed new constitution would take politics back to a future of governmental instability with possible military interruptions. The new constitution will be presented for public acceptance or rejection in a national referendum in August, with national elections scheduled for December. General Sonthi, leader of the coup, preemptively warned that disturbances could lead to a state of emergency being reimposed—a euphemism for martial law—if politics grows turbulent and efforts are made to discredit the government and erode confidence in the CNS (and by extension the junta).[46] Sonthi has also sat in on cabinet meetings and has pressed Surayud to name a deputy prime minister responsible for security, presumably a high-ranking army officer.

The outcome of the "up or down" referendum cannot be predicted even though the junta has called for a full-court military press to assure an affirmative vote. Regardless of the outcome, however, the junta will be able to limit the democratic future of Thailand. Even if the new constitution is rejected, the junta can arbitrarily impose a constitution of its choosing by virtue of the terms of the interim constitution. Sonthi's public expressions of resolute firmness in suppressing dissent demonstrate recognition of mounting opposition toward the coup and pro-democracy sentiment. In this atmosphere any clash between the army and civilian opponents could ignite a firestorm of violence. Such was the experience of the last coup in Thailand

---

[44] This conclusion was drawn in an editorial, "Military Needs Dose of Its Own Medicine," *The Nation*, April 24, 2007.

[45] "Utter Mayhem in South," *The Nation*, February 20, 2007.

[46] "State of Emergency Still Possible: Sonthi," *The Nation*, April 19, 2007.

when riotous pro-democracy demonstrations in the spring of 1992 forced out the last military government led by General Suchinda Kraprayoon.

The junta has made clear that, whatever constitutionally managed form of democracy ensues, it intends to ensure the continuation of a strong military guiding hand in Thai politics. One of the first acts of the CNS was to push through the tame interim legislature an unprecedented increase in the military budget that has quadrupled since the coup. This funds an institution characterized by factions, corruption, and a lack of professionalism. The funds are not expected to trickle down to enhance the capabilities of the non-career soldiers deployed to the south—who are underpaid and poorly trained—let alone the paramilitary volunteer rangers who are becoming part of the problem there. The best military units are garrisoned in Bangkok and other key centers to ensure that the military can act quickly to put down civil unrest and maintain control. In addition to regular army units, the CNS has a 14,000-man "special operations" force under its direct control that was secretly deployed around the country in December 2006 to monitor and quell disturbances.[47]

The coordinating center for military suppression of civilian dissent is a revitalized Internal Security Operations Command (ISOC). ISOC is a post–Cold War successor to the Communist Suppression Operations Command (CSOC) that under Thailand's military dictatorships from 1966 to 1973 was the scourge of students, leftists, and democratic activists. Sonthi also heads the ISOC and is tipped to stay on as ISOC director when he retires from active duty army service in September. In anticipation of Sonthi's possible future ISOC service, the junta drafted a law in June 2007 giving ISOC sweeping new powers to handle future threats.[48] The junta also announced plans in March 2007 to name senior military officers as deputy governors for security affairs in all 76 provincial administrations to coordinate between military and provincial administrations.[49] The military deputy governors would report to ISOC, giving the army a basis for territorial authority. Those familiar with the control mechanisms over civil authority used by the Indonesian army during the Suharto regime will recognize this pattern. The United States has already indicated concern over the implications that the increased power of the military has for democracy.[50]

---

[47] "Secret Military Division Deployed," *The Nation*, December 27, 2006.

[48] "Cabinet Approves Security Bill," *Bangkok Post*, June 20, 2007.

[49] "CNS Moves to Tighten Army's Grip. Officers to Be Deputy Governors for Security," *Bangkok Post*, March 2, 2007; and "Sonthi Defends Move to Extend Army's Role," *Bangkok Post*, March 4, 2007.

[50] Eric G. John, "The Impact of Section 508 Sanctions on Thailand and Fiji: Helpful or Harmful to U.S. Relations?" testimony before the House Committee on Foreign Affairs Subcommittee on Asia, the Pacific, and the Global Environment, Washington, D.C., August 1, 2007, http://www.state/gpve/p/eap/rls/rm/2007/89924.htm.

The destabilizing political conflict in Thailand and the war in the south affect U.S. strategic planning. Under the new constitution, the military's power would be unchecked and independent of parliament. With their parochial nationalism and focus on safeguarding their own political and economic interests, Thailand's military leadership resembles the generals running Myanmar more than its own Thai democratic predecessors. During the preceding democratic governments, the United States had envisioned Thailand maintaining firm bilateral strategic ties while being the focal point of a stable Southeast Asian continental bloc in the increasingly liberal East Asian and global economies. This vision is dimming, however, in light of a militarized Thai future. Thailand's diplomacy is in shambles and the country's role in ASEAN diminished. The junta's insistence that the war in the south can be won without concessions is self-defeating. In sum, the junta seems overwhelmed by the challenges that face it. If the Thai army should use force, as it did in 1992, to put down opposition protest in the lead-up to implementing a new constitution and holding elections, Washington will not be able to maintain the type of relationship with Bangkok that has prevailed since 2001.

The prospect of a widening war in the south of Thailand is even more serious for long-range U.S. strategic interests. If the Thai military heeds angry Thai Buddhist voices for using greater force in its southern campaign, the reactions of Malaysia, Indonesia, and the Organization of the Islamic Conference could leave ASEAN in tatters. Thailand's relations with its Muslim neighbors are already strained by the army's tactics. The naming of retired general Pallop Pinmanee as ISOC's security advisor for the war in the south suggests that the junta is ready to abandon reconciliation. Pallop is notorious for his willingness to use force, including instigating the 2004 Krue Se mosque raid that killed 32 alleged insurgents and played a role in triggering the current crisis. Speaking of the insurgents in the south, Pallop stated: "If we cannot make them surrender, then we have no choice but to destroy them."[51] Any hint that the U.S.-Thailand strategic alliance is an enabling factor in the military campaign in the south would give further credence to the radical Islamist voices in the region that claim the U.S.-led war on terrorism is actually a war against Islam. There are already worrisome signs that the United States could become involved in the southern conflict. Expressing concern about the escalating insurgency in Thailand, the commanding general of the U.S. Special Operations Command Pacific (SOCPAC) suggested in April 2007 that, if asked, SOCPAC could help train

---

[51] As quoted in Thomas Fuller, "Thai Generals Ask Former Assassin to Be Security Advisor," *International Herald Tribune*, May 25, 2007.

and assist the Thai military.[52] Even if only a remote possibility, the idea of the introduction of a joint special operations force in Thailand similar to JSOTF-P would raise alarm throughout the Muslim world.

The impending question of royal succession is also in the background of any analysis of future stability in Thailand. The king's moral authority is very important, but given his advanced age (he is 80) and poor health, his influence may be transient. In previous crises the king has been able to gently intercede. Privy Councilor Prem Tinsulanond, former army chief and prime minister, is widely believed to be the current link between the palace and the junta. A period of royal transition would expose intra-elite conflicts over political power and succession as new allegiances and factions are formed. If there is a consolidation of democratic institutions beforehand, a softer landing may be possible.

Indonesia: A Rising Phoenix?

Indonesia stands out as a democratic success in Southeast Asia. As democracy is under attack in the Philippines and Thailand and states elsewhere in Southeast Asia show no signs of changing their semi-authoritarian ways, Indonesia is consolidating its democracy. Ten years after the fall of the Suharto regime, the country can now be described as a "normal developing democracy," with a vibrant and free civil society and an elected parliament, as well as having a president, Susilo Bambang Yudhoyono, with a reform agenda.[53] In contrast to the Philippines and Thailand, the military has returned to the barracks. The principles of civilian control over the military are clearly returning to a civil-military culture in transition.[54] Macroeconomic reforms have helped Indonesia's once-moribund economy achieve a growth rate projection of 6.3% for 2007–08.[55] The country has successfully completed IMF-supervised

---

[52] "U.S. Offer to Help Quell Islamic Insurgency in the South Rejected," *Straits Times Interactive*, April 19, 2007.

[53] For an overview of the democratization process in Indonesia, see Douglas E. Ramage, "Indonesia in 2006: Democracy First, Good Governance Later," *Southeast Asian Affairs 2007*, ed. Daljit Singh and Lorraine C. Salazar (Singapore: Institute of Southeast Asian Studies, 2007), 135–57.

[54] For the background on military reform, see John B. Haseman and Angel Rabasa, *The Military and Democracy in Indonesia: Challenges, Politics, and Power* (Santa Monica: The Rand Corporation, 2002). For an appraisal of what reforms are still needed, see Marcus Mietzner, "The Politics of Military Reform in Post-Suharto Indonesia: Elite Conflict, Nationalism, and Institutional Resistance," East-West Center Washington, D.C., Policy Studies, no. 23, 2006, http://www.eastwestcenter.org/fileadmin/stored/pdfs/PS023.pdf.

[55] "Indonesia: Economic and Social Update," World Bank, April 2007, http://siteresources.worldbank.org/INTINDONESIA/Resources/Country-Update/April_2007.pdf.

reforms and demonstrated economic confidence by terminating the Consultative Group on Indonesia donor consortium.

The state is politically stable despite sporadic ethnic disturbances. A memorandum of agreement to end the long separatist war in Aceh was signed by the government and the Free Aceh Movement (Gerakan Aceh Merdeka, or GAM) on August 15, 2005, putting an end to Indonesia's most urgent crisis. Indonesia's parliament passed a bill for the province to become autonomous in July 2006, and Aceh's voters chose a former GAM commander as their first directly elected governor the following December.[56] Yudhoyono's assertion of "democratic control" over the armed forces and police in order to ensure adherence to the terms of the peace agreement was an important element in the success of the peace process.[57] According to the U.S. ambassador, Lynn Pascoe, Indonesia under Yudhoyono has made "enormous strides" in the pursuit of counterterrorism.[58] In 2007 a series of arrests of top JI leaders effectively decapitated the organization. Though diffused and fragmented terrorist cells continue to exist and there are still outbreaks of sectarian violence in Poso and Ambon, the government has shown a willingness to intervene forcefully.

Indonesia under Yudhoyono seems finally poised to rise like a phoenix from the political ashes of the Suharto regime and the false starts of the early post-Suharto governments to assume a leading role in the region.[59] Indonesia's political stability, internal security, and improved economic performance together with the diminishing roles of potential regional rivals—particularly Thailand—provide a platform for Indonesia to reclaim its "strategic centrality" within Southeast Asia.[60] This centrality (a more neutral term than predominance) is based on a number of factors. Indonesia's population—the world's fourth largest and the largest in the

---

[56] "Aceh: A New Chance for Peace," International Crisis Group, Asia Briefing, no. 40, August 15, 2005; "Aceh: Now Comes the Hard Part," International Crisis Group, Asia Briefing, no. 48, March 29, 2006; and "Indonesia: How GAM Won in Aceh," International Crisis Group, Asia Briefing, no. 61, March 22, 2007. All Asia Briefings are available at http://www.crisisgroup.org/home/index.cfm?l=1&id=2959.

[57] Pieter Feith, "The Aceh Peace Process" (remarks by the Chief of the Aceh Monitoring Mission to the United States-Indonesia Society and the Department of Southeast Asian Studies of the Johns Hopkins University Nitze School of Advanced International Studies, November 9, 2006), http://www.usindo.org.

[58] Nancy-Amelia Collins, "Outgoing U.S. Ambassador to Indonesia Hails Good Relations between the Two Countries," VOA News, February 15, 2007, http://www.voanews.com/english/archive/2007-02/2007-02-15-voa23.cfm.

[59] Donald E. Weatherbee, "Indonesian Foreign Policy: A Wounded Phoenix," in Chin and Singh, Southeast Asian Affairs 2005, 150–70.

[60] The concept of Indonesia's "strategic centrality" was originally used by Anthony L. Smith, Strategic Centrality: Indonesia's Changing Role in ASEAN (Singapore: Institute of Southeast Asian Studies, 2000).

Muslim world—makes up more than half that of the entire Southeast Asia region. The country's geography gives it a command over the chokepoints on Asia's sea lanes to the Middle East and Europe. Indonesia holds an implicit veto over ASEAN and East Asian integration schemes. In dealing with neighboring states, the country has already shown itself not to be bashful in pressing its national interest. Jakarta successfully used economic pressure to force Singapore to link an extradition treaty to defense cooperation, while also employing diplomatic pressure to obtain a pledge from Canberra that Australia would not support the activities of separatist groups that might threaten Indonesia's sovereignty and territorial integrity. For Indonesia, this had special reference to Papua.

In returning to an important regional and international role, moreover, Indonesia is also finding a new, democratic, and liberal voice. As one long-time observer has noted, an Indonesia that is fully engaged internationally and espousing leadership will bring Southeast Asia's geopolitical "chemistry" back into balance.[61] Indonesia has again become Southeast Asia's pivotal state— a country poised at a critical point whose choices will strongly affect regional and even global security.[62] Indonesia's place in U.S. strategic thinking should be ultimately as a pivotal state in the regional balance of power—not simply as a key country in the war on terrorism.

Over the course of the evolution of their bilateral relationship the United States has had several different strategic perceptions of Indonesia. During the Cold War the United States viewed Indonesia under Sukarno as a threat to regional order and stability. The military-based Suharto regime was seen as an anticommunist pillar of stability and the key to restoring a favorable regional balance of power that had been unsettled by the potential regional threat of Soviet-backed Vietnam. U.S. strategic interests pushed concerns over the undemocratic qualities of Suharto's government and its human rights violations, particularly in East Timor, to the background. Yet human rights issues came to the fore in the post–Cold War environment. Outrage over Indonesia's human rights record in East Timor led Congress to restrict U.S. security assistance to Indonesia in 1992 and ultimately prohibit it altogether in 1999.

In the immediate post-Suharto era, however, U.S.-Indonesian relations entered a new phase. Though still interested in a politically stable Indonesia

---

[61] Michael Vatikiotis, "Susilo, Regional Affairs, and Lessons from Sukarno," *Jakarta Post*, November 3, 2004.

[62] The concept of pivotal state and the classification of Indonesia as a pivotal state were developed in John Bresnan, "Indonesia," in *The Pivotal States: A New Framework for U.S. Policy*, ed. Robert Chase, Emily Hill, and Paul Kennedy (New York: W. W. Norton, 1999), 15–39. In what was viewed as a bell-wether Jakarta gubernatorial election in August 2007, the candidate backed by nationalist and nonsectarian parties decisively defeated the candidate supported by the Islamists.

in the regional balance of power, ~~now the United States sought stability through fostering democratic transition and economic reform rather than through authoritarian rule~~. U.S. strategy has, after September 11, shifted again, with the focus now on Indonesia as a key country in the war on terrorism. The vast size of Indonesia's Muslim population, which has captivated U.S. security planners, has obscured three important political facts: ~~that Indonesia is a pluralist democracy, that radical Islamists do not have electoral strength,~~[63] ~~and that there is little public support for radical Islamist violence.~~[64]

~~The war on terrorism was the proximate spur to U.S.-Indonesian security rapprochement.~~ The first step was to restore normal military-to-military relations. At a May 2005 meeting Yudhoyono and Bush agreed that "normal military relations would be in the interests of both parties."[65] Washington waived the final restrictions on security assistance in January 2006. The United States and Indonesia have since resumed a full agenda of security interactions, including training and joint exercises. Garuda Shield 2007—the first brigade-level army-to-army joint exercise between the two states since 1997—was held in West Java in April.[66] An annual U.S.-Indonesia security dialogue now takes place between the U.S. Department of Defense and the Indonesian Ministry of Defense, as well as a working-level U.S.-Indonesia bilateral defense discussion. As a hint of future possibilities, Bush and Yudhoyono agreed to explore the possibility of a Status of Forces Agreement at their November 2006 meeting in Jakarta. The two states decided to consider a possible defense cooperation agreement at the fifth security dialogue in April 2007.[67] ~~Normalized security relations and counterterrorism cooperation now form the basis for what the United States terms a "strategic partnership."~~[68] On an official visit to Indonesia in March 2006 Secretary of State Condoleezza Rice placed the bilateral relationship in

---

[63] Polling data from 2006 indicates a sharp decline in support for the explicitly Islamist parties that collectively won less than 10% of the votes in 2004. "Prospek Islam Politik di Indonesia," Lembaga Survei Indonesia, October 10, 2006, http://www.lsi.or.id/riset/143/prospek-islam-politik-di-indonesia.

[64] Indonesian attitudes toward terrorism have been measured in the Pew Global Attitudes Project's recent annual surveys available at http://www.pewresearchcenter.org.

[65] "Joint Statement between the United States of America and the Republic of Indonesia," White House, Office of the Press Secretary, May 25, 2005, http://www.whitehouse.gov/news/releases/2005/05/20050525-11.html.

[66] "Garuda Shield 2007 Scheduled for Kick-off," U.S. Army, Pacific Public Affairs Office, http://www.usarpac.army.mil/news/GS2007.asp.

[67] "Joint Statement between the United States and the Republic of Indonesia," White House, Office of the Press Secretary, November 20, 2006, http://www.whitehouse.gov/news/releases/2006/11/20061120-3.html.

[68] Eric G. John, "The U.S. and Indonesia: Toward a Strategic Partnership" (speech delivered to the United States-Indonesian Society, Washington, D.C., December 20, 2005).

the context of a "growing strategic partnership and strategic relationship."[69] In a 2007 joint statement, Indonesia and the United States have agreed "to expand and deepen cooperation based on strategic partnership."[70]

Indonesian officials also clearly value the strategic presence of the United States as important to both Indonesia and the region. The partnership is based on the convergence of specific interests: the defeat of radical Islamist terrorists, the consolidation of a democratic Indonesia, open economic regionalism in Southeast Asia, and a continuing strategic role for the United States in the regional balance of power. The evolving U.S.-Indonesian security relationship is one of shared interests and substantive ties. The relationship far surpasses the essentially rhetorical invocations of security cooperation and consultation in the Sino-Indonesian relationship, which Indonesia perceives as having a more symbolic value as a hedge than operational utility. Jakarta has also reached out regionally for enhanced defense cooperation, although not as part of a hedging strategy. Indonesia has concluded new security pacts with Australia and Singapore and initiated military exercises with India. As Indonesia builds ties regionally upon its own stability, the country may develop the capacity to become the ASEAN focal point for a regional balance in which Indonesia becomes a hub among its security partners rather than merely being a spoke emanating from the U.S. center.

The convergence of some specific interests underpinning the U.S.-Indonesian strategic partnership does not, however, imply the complete congruence of national interests in areas of strategic concern. As a rising middle power with its own international agenda and a free and active foreign policy, Indonesia has a strategic vision that diverges from that of the United States across a range of interest areas. Jakarta views with suspicion what it considers to be great power unilateralism in global affairs by the United States. Indonesia also insists on a just and equitable peace process in the Middle East on terms that Israel and the United States find unacceptable.

In reacting to the idea of a strategic partnership with the United States, a leading Indonesian foreign policy analyst noted that it was important for both countries "to really understand the ground rules for strategic partnership, because the price of failure would be serious for Indonesia, the region, and, not least, for the U.S."[71] If it is to be structured symmetrically, a partnership has reciprocal privileges and obligations. Indonesia insists

---

[69] "Remarks with Indonesia's Foreign Minister Noer Hasan Wirajuda," U.S. Department of State, March 14, 2006, http://www.state.gov/secretary/rm/2006/63087.htm.

[70] "Joint Statement Indonesia—United States Security Dialogue V," U.S. Embassy, Press Release, April 19, 2007, http://www.usembassyjakarta.org/press_rel/joint_statement_defence.html.

[71] Bantarto Bandoro, "Is RI-U.S. Partnership a Strategic Alliance?" *Jakarta Post*, November 16, 2006.

that the country's autonomy and independence be respected. Indonesia's vote for a UN resolution sanctioning Iran in March 2007, for example, illustrates Indonesian sensitivity to partnering with the United States. Muslim politicians and academics criticized the government for giving way to Western pressure and not supporting Iran. The vote was important to the United States and it was well known that Jakarta was under heavy pressure to vote with the United States. Bush spoke to Yudhoyono over the telephone and Rice had a face-to-face meeting with her Indonesian counterpart. Many Indonesians concluded that Indonesia's strategic partnership had affected Indonesian policy, making the country overly dependent on the United States and unable to risk offending Washington by acting independently on the issue of Iran.[72] The foreign minister made a semi-apology, expressing his hope that the people "not merely consider [the vote] as a betrayal toward Iran or as support for Israel and the U.S. or the West."[73] The government sought to repair the domestic damage by later blocking the adoption of a French-initiated UN Security Council statement that denounced Iranian president Mahmoud Ahmadinejad's call for the collapse of Israel.

Indonesian public discontent with the government's vote on the Iran resolution and linkage of that vote to the country's dependent position in the strategic partnership with the United States is revealing. This criticism reflects the difficulties that democracies—in being accountable to elected representatives and a voting public—have in managing conflicting interests while maintaining a controversial strategic partnership. This is particularly true in Indonesia, where there is widespread and deep opposition to the U.S. role in the Middle East in general and the war in Iraq in particular. The Yudhoyono government has so far given priority to Indonesia's long-term strategic interests in the bilateral relationship with the United States and has contained political backlash in parliament and on the streets. The government's own initiatives, no matter how tenuous, to obtain a seat at the Arab-Israeli peace process as a large Muslim nation distant from the conflict is part of this political containment strategy to proactively divorce Indonesian policy from that of the United States. Problematically Yudhoyono's need to renew his presidential mandate and parliamentary coalition majority in the 2009 national elections may require the government to further distance itself from a perceived U.S. embrace. Former Indonesian president Habibie's foreign policy advisor has suggested that the role of the public in the current U.S.-Indonesia security relationship may be the

---

[72] Abdul Khalik, "RI Slammed over Iran Resolution," *Jakarta Post*, March 25, 2007.

[73] "Minister Denies RI Was Pressured by West to Support Sanctions on Iran," *AntaraNews*, March 27, 2007, http://www.antara.co.id.

reverse of that during the Suharto era.[74] Opposition to bilateral security ties with Suharto's regime came from U.S. public opinion, NGOs, and members of Congress concerned over human rights violations in Timor. Opposition to the strategic partnership today comes from Indonesian Muslim public organizations and members of parliament upset by the U.S.-led war in Iraq. The pressure on the U.S. government to sever the relationship in the former case was eventually successful. NGO and congressional support of secessionist efforts in Papua could even further arouse Indonesian nationalism by compromising U.S. support of Indonesia's sovereignty and territorial integrity.[75]

Vietnam: Waiting in the Wings?

Although not an ally, a strategic partner, or a democracy, Vietnam is nevertheless emerging as an increasingly important actor in the regional balance of power. Like its ASEAN partners, Vietnam is improving relations with the United States in order to strengthen national capabilities and hedge against China. As a result of geographic location, two millennia of history, and previous bilateral conflicts, Vietnam's strategic outlook is dominated by China perhaps more than that of any other country in Southeast Asia. Unchangeable asymmetries in size and capabilities shape the geopolitical and geostrategic context of the relationship.[76] Previously, Vietnam had relied on the Soviet Union as a security patron. Without that option today, Vietnam has adopted a mix of strategies to manage the relationship with China ranging from balancing to deference.[77] Engagement and interdependence, both within ASEAN and through multiple ASEAN +1 structures, have been particularly important in placing Vietnam's relationship with China in a broader regional framework. Hanoi sees itself as a bridge between ASEAN and China. Even though a general sense of friendship and cooperation prevails in the frequent official Sino-Vietnamese interactions, old frictions still irritate the relationship. For instance, Vietnam and China are still at

[74] Dewi Fortuna Anwar, "United States and Indonesia: Bilateral Relations and External Factors" (keynote address to a conference of the Johns Hopkins University Nitze School of Advanced International Studies and the United States-Indonesian Society, Embassy of Indonesia, Washington, D.C., April 19, 2007).

[75] "New Head of Asia Panel on U.S. Congress Champions Self-determination for Papua," *Jakarta Post*, January 24, 2007; and Donald E. Weatherbee, "Yellow Light for Indonesia," Pacific Forum CSIS, PacNet, no. 4, February 1, 2007, http://www.csis.org/media/pubs/csis/pubs.pac0704.pdf.

[76] Brantley Womack, *China and Vietnam: The Politics of Asymmetry* (New York: Cambridge University Press, 2006).

[77] Alexander L. Vuving, "Strategy and Evolution of Vietnam's China Policy," *Asian Survey* 46, no. 6 (November/December 2006): 805–24.

odds over sovereignty and jurisdictional control in the contested South China Sea.[78] The July 2007 Chinese attack on Vietnamese fishing vessels was another example of China's intimidating posture toward Vietnamese presence in disputed areas.

Vietnam is also shoring up its contiguous continental flanks by deepening economic and political engagement in Cambodia and Laos, both of which are also targets of Chinese economic and political penetration. The heightened Vietnamese visibility in Indochina contrasts with the relative isolation of Thailand under the junta following the collapse of Thaksin's version of a Bangkok-centered local hegemony. Vietnamese invocations of the historical links between Vietnam and the ruling governments in Cambodia and Laos are of particular interest. Hanoi has affirmed "traditional friendly political relations and the closeness in terms of geography of Vietnam and Cambodia as well as the traditional solidarity between the two people."[79] Harking back to Ho Chi Minh and the days of the Vietminh-Pathet Lao alliance, the current Vietnamese and Lao administrations still speak in terms of the traditional friendship, special solidarity, and comprehensive cooperation that is being "unceasingly consolidated and developed in both scale and depth," including in security, national defense, and external relations.[80]

Vietnam's rapid economic growth, exceeding 8% annually for the past three years, has contributed to the country's increasing capability to promote its national interests internationally. The country has moved into the ranks of the other Southeast Asian little tigers. A World Bank expert on Vietnam stated that "there is probably no other country in the world that, over the past 15 years, has moved its development so far and so fast."[81] Full normalization of relations with the United States and increasing access to U.S. markets and investment have been important factors enhancing the diplomatic and economic capabilities of Vietnam. U.S.-Vietnamese two-way trade has increased by 50% since 2001, reaching $9.7 billion in 2006. Sino-Vietnamese trade, in contrast, is not expected to reach $10 billion until 2010.[82] The United States is Vietnam's top export market. The establishment of Permanent Normal Trade Relations (PNTR) status for Vietnam by the

---

[78] Stein Tønnesson, "Vietnam's Objectives in the South China Sea: National or Regional Security," *Contemporary Southeast Asia* 22, no. 1 (April 2000): 199–220.

[79] "President's Visit Helps Boost Vietnam-Cambodia Economic Ties," *VietnamNet*, February 3, 2007, http://english.vietnamnet.vn.

[80] "Vietnam and Laos Issue Joint Communiqué," *Nhan Dan*, February 8, 2007.

[81] Klaus Rohland, former World Bank Vietnam country director, as quoted in "New Five Year Plan for Vietnam," World Bank, http://www.wordbank.org.

[82] "Vietnam, China to Eclipse $10bn in Trade Value by 2010," *Thanh Nien News*, October 6, 2006.

United States in December 2006, together with Vietnam's accession to the World Trade Organization (WTO) in January 2007, provided the basis for launching negotiations in March 2007 to conclude a U.S.-Vietnam Trade and Investment Framework Agreement (TIFA) that will spur even faster expansion of trade and investment.[83] The United States is also a major investor in Vietnam: investment reached $4 billion in 2006 and is forecast to double to $8 billion in 2007.[84] Counting both direct and indirect investment through third countries, the United States is the fifth largest investor in Vietnam. U.S.-Vietnamese political rapprochement, embodied in a succession of high-level exchanges, has accompanied the burgeoning U.S. economic presence in Vietnam. Bush visited Hanoi in 2006 and Vietnam's president, Nguyen Minh Triet, reciprocated in June 2007 with the first post-normalization trip to the United States by a Vietnamese head of state, during which the concluded TIFA was quickly signed.

Though overshadowed by the booming U.S. economic participation in Vietnam, Washington and Hanoi have also quietly begun to construct a third pillar on which a comprehensive and stable bilateral relationship that adds to the regional balance of power can be built. Although defense-related links are still modest in scope, the two countries are moving to establish a security relationship "at a measured pace comfortable to both sides," according to the commander of PACOM on a 2006 visit to Vietnam.[85] During then secretary of defense Donald Rumsfeld's June 2006 visit to Hanoi the Vietnamese agreed to step up "exchanges at all levels of the military."[86] The decision to lift the long-standing arms embargo on Vietnam also seemed to indicate where Vietnam might fit into Washington's strategic vision. In the December 2006 memorandum to the secretary of state authorizing sales, Bush stated that "[the] furnishing of defense articles and defense services to Vietnam will strengthen the security of the United States and promote world peace."[87] This major step toward normalizing military-to-military relations has seemingly clear implications. As one security analyst has concluded, "lifting the arms embargo indicates that the U.S. is

---

[83] "U.S. Trade Representative Schwab Meets with Vietnamese Deputy Prime Minister Pham Gia Khiem," Office of the United States Trade Representative, Press Release, March 19, 2007, http://www.ustr.gov/Document_Library/Press_Releases/2007/March/US_Trade_Representative_Schwab_Meets_with_Vietnamese_Deputy_Prime_Minister_Pham_Gia_Khiem.html.

[84] These are figures cited by U.S. Ambassador to Vietnam Michael Marine in "U.S. Investment in Vietnam Likely $8 bln for 2007," *Thanh Nien News*, April 5, 2007.

[85] "Fallon: U.S., Vietnam Steadily Rebuilding Military Ties," *Navy Times*, July 20, 2006.

[86] Michael R. Gordon, "Rumsfeld, Visiting Vietnam, Seals Accord to Deepen Military Cooperation," *New York Times*, June 6, 2006.

[87] "Memorandum for the Secretary of State," White House, December 29, 2006, http://www.whitehouse.gov/news/releases/2006/12/20061229-6.html.

taking Vietnam seriously as an element in the Asian security equation."[88] Another veteran Vietnam watcher echoed this view, noting that though the economic side of the U.S.-Vietnamese relationship is prominent, "the strategic side is much more important."[89]

Domestic politics, however, could still complicate how far and fast Washington can go in furthering the bilateral strategic relationship. During Vietnam's campaign for PNTR and WTO membership, Hanoi was forced to adjust its policies in order to accommodate criticism of the country's human and civil rights record (in particular on religious freedom and the treatment of ethnic minorities) as part of the diplomatic bargain for joining the global economic club. Vietnamese suppression of political dissent and restrictions on NGOs following the PNTR and WTO agreements have led to charges that the United States was double-crossed.[90] Human and civil rights reform is a continuing issue in U.S.-Vietnamese diplomatic exchanges, and the topic of Vietnam's rights record is very much alive in the U.S. Congress. In May 2007 the House of Representatives passed by a vote of 404 to 0 House Resolution 243 demanding both the immediate and unconditional release of all Vietnamese political prisoners and prisoners of conscience and compliance with internationally recognized standards for basic freedoms and human rights.[91] Hanoi is acutely aware of U.S. concerns in this area. Vietnam released several dissidents before Triet left for his visit to the United States. Bush and congressional figures raised the topics of human rights and democracy in meetings with Triet. The Vietnamese president has articulated a willingness to increase dialogue on the issue, accompanied by "a determination not to let the differences affect the two countries' overall larger interests."[92] From Vietnam's vantage point, one of those interests is balancing China. Speaking of the necessity of a strong U.S.-Vietnam relationship, a leading Vietnamese economist stated: "If not, the big neighbor to the north could try to push harder on Vietnam. And this is not good for the stability of the region and not good at all for Vietnam."[93]

---

[88] Marvin Ott, as quoted in "U.S.-Viet Ties Get Boost with End to Ban on Arms Sales," *Straits Times*, February 3, 2007.

[89] Carl Thayer, as quoted in "Vietnam Has High Hopes for President's Meetings in Washington," *VOA News*, June 20, 2007.

[90] Shawn W. Crispin, "Hanoi's Double-cross on Democracy," *Asia Times*, March 30, 2007.

[91] "House Passes Smith's Resolution Calling for Human Rights Reform in Vietnam," Congressman Chris Smith website, May 2, 2007, http://chrissmith.house.gov/News/DocumentSingle.aspx?DocumentID=64172.

[92] "President Bush Welcomes President Nguyen Minh Triet of Vietnam to the White House," White House, Office of the Press Secretary, Press Release, June 22, 2007, www.whitehouse.gov/news/releases/2007/06/20070622-2.html.

[93] Le Dang Doanh, as quoted in Seth Mydans, "Hanoi Leader Braces for U.S. Critics," *International Herald Tribune*, June 13, 2007.

He might have added that Chinese pressure on Vietnam would also not be good for the interests of the United States in the region.

Conclusion: A New Distribution of Power in Southeast Asia

There is a widespread perception in Southeast Asia that the war on terrorism has pushed other U.S. interests in the region to the background. Many argue that the priority given to the war on terrorism has caused the United States to fall behind China in terms of regional influence because China has pursued a broad political and economic offensive strategy in the region. As one of Southeast Asia's most accomplished diplomatists has noted, "The U.S. is losing the competition for influence in Southeast Asia. The winner, at least for the time being, is the People's Republic of China."[94] Beijing's offers of limited military cooperation and assistance indicate a desire both to add a military and strategic presence to the mix of its Southeast Asian overtures and to carve out a nexus of security relationships.[95] China's limited military-to-military interactions in Southeast Asia do not, however, begin to approach the intensity and depth of those of the United States—which are essentially clientage in the Philippines, dependence in Thailand, and based elsewhere on technological and interoperability preferences. Chinese security assistance to the region will not displace such close U.S.-Southeast Asian military relations.

Rather than pursuing a regional arrangement in which either China or the United States is predominant, ASEAN is instead seeking regional stability in which both great powers are stakeholders. Accepting China's rise and the prospect of a greater Chinese power presence in the region as facts, ASEAN's strategy does not seek to contain China. At the same time, ASEAN also wants to ensure that U.S. attention and commitment to the region does not waver should the war on terrorism wane. From ASEAN's perspective, the balance of power in Southeast Asia after the war on terrorism is concluded will require even deeper U.S. regional engagement and closer bilateral ties across the spectrum of political, economic, and security interests. In this framework, traditional U.S. military alliances with the Philippines and Thailand are decreasingly relevant to the strategic problems posed by China. By supporting militaries that are obstacles

---

[94] Tommy Koh, "America's Role in Asia: What Does Southeast Asia Want from Washington?" Pacific Forum CSIS, PacNet, no. 53, December 21, 2004, http://www.csis.org/media/csis/pubs/pac0453.pdf.

[95] David Fullbrook, "China's Strategic Southeast Asian Embrace," Asia Times, February 21, 2007.

to democratic development, these traditional alliances in fact may be counter-productive.

Though security ties with Indonesia and Vietnam do not match those of traditional U.S. allies, continuing to enhance these relationships would add to the capabilities of Southeast Asia's two major rising states. As discussed above, Indonesia is also looking beyond the United States for potential security partners, establishing its own network of ties. This emerging network has the potential to transform fragmented but shared security concerns in the heart of ASEAN into nascent coordinated security mechanisms to address local strategic problems, such as the security of the Strait of Malacca. Indonesia, Singapore, and Malaysia, and to a lesser extent Thailand are already creating multilateral mechanisms that both task the littoral states with enforcement and engage the United States, Japan, India, China, and Australia in technological, logistic, and financial assistance.

The parallel emergence of Vietnam's efforts to hedge and balance China along with Indonesia's new international confidence suggest a possible future regional security structure in which Vietnam in the north and Indonesia in the south are the two strong poles of a regional balance. Indonesia had actually envisioned just such an environment in the 1980s, objecting to a China-supported ASEAN policy of crippling Vietnam. Indonesia preferred Vietnam to be a potential ASEAN strategic ally in a balance of power strategy against China rather than a weak gateway for Chinese expansion into Southeast Asia.

The focus in this chapter has been on four key ASEAN actors in the Southeast Asian strategic balance. The Philippines and Thailand maintain strategic relationships with the United States that have roots in the past but uncertain futures. Indonesia and Vietnam, however, have overcome their histories and are emerging as vital participants in the future balance of power in Southeast Asia. Though the U.S. security links still follow the hub and spoke system, ASEAN does not constitute an alliance "wheel." ASEAN has presented no framework of its own within which U.S. policy can function on a region-wide basis. In coping with the rise of China over the long term, ASEAN may need to seek more than mere U.S. engagement if "engagement" means only politically vulnerable bilateral ties without regional coherence or integration. ASEAN, or some states in Southeast Asia, may find it necessary to rethink the nature of an ASEAN security community in terms of both deepening intra-ASEAN relations and of managing extraregional great power relations. An ASEAN security community in which China and the United States are members could provide a framework to address the local strategic goals of these two powers in a stable, peaceful balance of power.[96] Until there is an alternative, the traditional system will persist. In the current Southeast Asian system, however, it is important that the United States give a higher priority to the future than to the past in its strategic alliances.

---

[96] On the issues surrounding such potential security architectures, see Nick Bisley's chapter in this volume.

EXECUTIVE SUMMARY

This chapter studies the evolution of the foreign policies of Central Asia's states, focusing on Kazakhstan and Uzbekistan.

MAIN ARGUMENT:

The newly independent states of Central Asia are institutionally weak and surrounded by larger regional powers. Foreign policies in the region generally aim to maintain balance among great powers and to ensure regime security. Russian and Chinese influence is strong and supportive of the latter, but the quest for balance spurs the development of ties to the U.S. and other powers. Pressure for democratization accompanies these relations with the West, which need to be treated with care by U.S. policymakers.

POLICY IMPLICATIONS:

- Promoting security, reliable supplies of energy, and good governance are the primary U.S. interests in the region. Though widely viewed as mutually contradictory, these objectives are only achievable in the long term if pursued in concert.

- Informal politics is a key element in the domestic and foreign policies of Central Asian states. Strengthening formal institutions is, therefore, a compelling priority for the U.S., as is seeking a better understanding of informal power structures.

- The "color revolutions," though beneficial to the countries that underwent them, have had negative consequences both for U.S. interests in Central Asia and for broader democratic reform. By injecting an ideological element into regional politics, these revolutions have increased Russian and Chinese influence and weakened the U.S. position. Uzbekistan stands out as the primary example.

- Strategic thinking and long-term policies toward the region that inspire confidence and predictability would restore U.S. influence. Calibrating the democracy promotion agenda to the strategic realities of the region would help state-building efforts and dialogue on a wide range of issues.

Finding Balance: The Foreign Policies of Central Asia's States

Svante E. Cornell

Upon independence in 1991, the five states of post-Soviet Central Asia were confronted with the entire battery of institution-building tasks normally associated with post-colonial environments. These new states found themselves in a much more challenging geopolitical position than most post-colonial states. In addition to being new and institutionally weak, the Central Asian states are relatively small and are surrounded by Eurasia's most powerful countries. Central Asian governments have responded to this environment by seeking to strengthen their sovereignty through balancing the interests of external powers. At the same time these governments have worked to safeguard stability by controlling the pace of internal political change.

State-building processes initially led Central Asia's rulers to look inward. Over time increasingly consolidated statehood gradually enabled these states to pursue more independent foreign policies. Against the backdrop of this broader regional trend, however, diverging domestic political and economic realities have strongly affected the choices these rulers have made for their countries' external relations. The contrasting evolutions of Kazakhstan and Uzbekistan, the region's two most important states, are particularly noteworthy in this context. Foreign policies of the two countries have developed in nearly opposite directions, mirroring differences in their domestic development.

Svante E. Cornell is Research Director of the Central Asia-Caucasus Institute and Silk Road Studies Program. He can be reached at <scornell@silkroadstudies.org>.

In the mid-1990s Uzbekistan sought to launch itself into the role of a regional power.[1] Economic stability undergirded Tashkent's ambitions to play an independent role both by balancing Russian influence with ties to the United States and by exerting influence over smaller neighbors. This strategy intensified following September 11, 2001 when Uzbekistan seemed to achieve its aim of forging a strategic partnership with the United States. By 2005, however, Tashkent had abruptly cut ties to Washington, expelled the U.S. military base from its territory, and re-embraced Moscow's leading role in Eurasian security affairs.[2] This u-turn betrayed a reactive approach, which stemmed from a growing sense of domestic insecurity.

In contrast, Kazakhstan was initially concerned with its large Russian minority and 2,000-mile border with Russia. Rapid economic liberalization accelerated the short-term economic difficulties generated by the collapse of the Soviet Union.[3] The Kazakh leadership mostly kept a low profile in international issues and refrained from challenging Russia. By the mid-2000s, however, the situation had changed. The infrastructure associated with the earlier economic reforms led to an oil boom. Growing domestic stability and economic growth enabled Kazakhstan to begin to formulate a distinctively independent foreign policy based on achieving balance in relations with the great powers.

Nevertheless, two main concerns apparently guide both countries' foreign policies as well as those of the other states in the region. One concern is the strength of their newly won independence as evidenced by their attempt to maximize freedom of maneuver by broadening the scope of their foreign relations. A second is the maintenance of internal stability and regime security (concepts the ruling elites understand as synonymous), as evidenced by efforts to prevent the rise of various domestic and transnational opponents—including legitimate opposition forces, criminal groups, and Islamic radicals.

These considerations pose a dilemma for the rulers of Central Asia. Foreign policies oriented toward Russia and China would increase regime security for these rulers but at the cost of an independent foreign policy. Happy to support the internal stability of the governments of Central Asia, Moscow and Beijing care little about the domestic policies of the states in this region. Russia and China are, however, also working more closely together

---

[1] S. Frederick Starr, "Making Eurasia Stable," *Foreign Affairs* 75, no. 1 (January/February 1996): 80–92.

[2] John C. K. Daly, Kurt H. Meppen, Vladimir Socor, and S. Frederick Starr, *Anatomy of a Crisis: U.S.-Uzbekistan Relations, 2001–2005*, Silk Road Paper, February 2006 (Washington, D.C.: Central Asia-Caucasus Institute & Silk Road Studies Program, 2006).

[3] Sally Cummings, *Kazakhstan: Power and the Elite* (London: IB Tauris, 2005), 21–26; and Richard Pomfret, *The Central Asian Economies Since Independence* (Princeton: Princeton University Press, 2006), 40–60.

to minimize the influence of the West—and thus would only support states in the region that toe this line. A Western orientation, on the other hand, would allow the regional governments to broaden the scope of their foreign relations and avoid total dependence on their larger neighbors—but at the cost of regime security. Improving relations with the West, and especially with the United States, would entail exposing the Central Asian states to the Western democracy promotion agenda. Rulers in the region increasingly understand this agenda as a threat to their continued hold on power.

This Central Asian dilemma in turn translates into a complex environment for the formulation of U.S. policies toward the region. U.S. interests fall into three main categories: security and strategic access, the westward export of the Caspian region's energy resources, and internal reform in the mainly authoritarian countries of the region. The United States faces the task of building a coherent policy that makes these interests compatible rather than contradictory

This chapter begins by describing the state structures and political systems of Central Asia in order to provide an understanding of the political realities influencing foreign policy. Analysis of the external environment of the region, with particular attention given to the influence of the western democracy agenda, then follows. The chapter ends by detailing the interaction of foreign and domestic policies in the region and concludes by drawing policy implications for the United States.

State Structure and Political Systems

The domestic determinants of foreign policy in Central Asia are tightly linked to the recent nature of statehood in the region, with Central Asian states having only appeared as independent entities on the world map in 1991. The most salient characteristic of the region's states is their institutional weakness, which stems from the immense economic and social problems that accompanied the transition from Soviet rule. Worth remembering is that no state, emirate, or principality had ever existed with the name, or even roughly the same borders, of the current five post-Soviet Central Asian states.

The Challenge of Independence

The territorial entities that now constitute the states of Central Asia were created somewhat arbitrarily by the Soviet central government in the 1920s and 1930s. The borders often ignored ethnic, linguistic, economic, topographic, and geographic realities. All states of the region are multiethnic; some have substantial concentrated groups of ethnic minorities. Soviet borders made little sense, especially in the Ferghana Valley, historically a single economic and cultural unit dominated by the Uzbeks. Uzbekistan, Kyrgyzstan, and Tajikistan divide the area, but each country is seasonally cut off from its valley territory. This division had negligible effects during the Soviet period, when administrative borders did not impede communications or transportation. Since independence, however, borders have acquired real importance. With the emergence of militant Islamist movements in the late 1990s, many borders were closed and even mined, most extensively by Uzbekistan. The networks of roads, railroads, and power and gas distribution centers had been laid out with little heed to borders, however, interlinking the regional states in ways that limited their economic sovereignty. Individual governments perceived this cross-border network as a threat to their independent development and each built separate infrastructure networks entirely within its own national border. Though reducing dependence on each others' consent or cooperation, the creation of these national networks diverted the use of scarce resources.

In economic terms, the Soviet Union's command economy and cotton monoculture forced several regional states to import foodstuffs, making them ill-prepared for integration into the world economy. That these states are far from world markets adds a "distance tariff" to the region.[4] These economic challenges have been further exacerbated by the ongoing unrest in Afghanistan and the region's unnatural economic dependence on Russia.

Central Asia does have rich hydrocarbon and water resources, but the unequal distribution is a major problem. Almost all hydrocarbons are located in Kazakhstan, Uzbekistan, and Turkmenistan, and almost all water originates from sources in Kyrgyzstan and Tajikistan. In Soviet times, during the hot summers the eastern states delivered water to the farmlands downstream, emptying reservoirs that could otherwise have been used for electricity generation. The oil and gas producers to the west in return delivered energy to their eastern neighbors in the cold winters at nominal cost. After independence, however, oil and gas producers often succumbed to the temptation of charging for energy while refusing to pay for water—thereby generating substantial tension.

These factors, combined with a lack of historical legitimacy, induced an acute sense of vulnerability on the part of the region's leaders. Central Asian states were generally against the dissolution of the Soviet Union for good reason. Kazakh leader Nursultan Nazarbayev, for one, frantically

---

[4] S. Frederick Starr, "The War against Terrorism and U.S. Bilateral Relations with the Nations of Central Asia," testimony before the Senate Committee on Foreign Relations and the Subcommittee on Central Asia and the South Caucasus, Washington, D.C., December 13, 2001.

tried to achieve a reformed union.[5] Central Asia's rulers at first faced independence with a mix of reluctance, anticipation, and concern for the viability of their states.

Evolution of Political Systems

The above conditions presented significant challenges to the development of both the functioning market economies and the democratic rule of law. The Central Asian states were in an unenviable position to conform to the so-called transition paradigm that strongly influenced Western understanding of, and policies toward, countries "in transition" in the 1990s. The paradigm's central assumption—that "any country moving away from dictatorial rule can be considered a country in transition toward democracy"—may have been accurate in Central and Eastern Europe.[6] In Central Asia, however, the socialist state system was replaced not by democratic governance but by other forms of authoritarian or semi-authoritarian government. Western observers failed to "give significant attention to the challenge of a society trying to democratize while it is grappling with the reality of building a state from scratch or coping with an existent but largely nonfunctional state."[7]

In place of the transition paradigm, a new literature in political science is now emerging to understand the variety of new regime types, none of which neatly fit standard ideals of dictatorship or democracy.[8] Central Asian states offer political scientists a virtual laboratory for examining different semi-authoritarian forms of government. These states share a commitment to political reform that is tenuous at best. Only in Tajikistan did competition of any significant magnitude take place following a (short-lived) period of liberalization in 1990–91; this experiment ended, however, in civil war and the eventual restoration of authoritarian rule.[9] In Kyrgyzstan, less-extensive leadership changes occurred—first in the late Soviet era and again following riots in March 2005—with most of the ruling elite surviving the changes at the top. In Kazakhstan, Turkmenistan, and Uzbekistan Communist Party first secretaries stayed securely at the helm

---

[5] H. Plater-Zyberk, *Kazakhstan: Security & Defence Challenges* (Camberley: Defence Academy of the United Kingdom Conflict Studies Research Centre, September 2002), 1.

[6] Quote taken from Thomas Carothers, "The End of the Transition Paradigm," *Journal of Democracy* 13, no. 1 (2002): 8.

[7] Carothers, "The End of the Transition Paradigm," 8–9.

[8] Larry Diamond, "Thinking about Hybrid Regimes," *Journal of Democracy* 13, no. 2 (2002): 21–35.

[9] Sergey Gretsky, "Civil War in Tajikistan: Causes, Development and Prospects for Peace," in *Central Asia: Conflict, Revolution, and Change*, ed. Roald Sagdeev and Susan Eisenhower (Washington, D.C.: Center for Political and Strategic Studies, 1995).

of their respective republics long after independence. With the 2006 death of Turkmenistan's president Saparmurad Niyazov, Kazakhstan's Nazarbayev and Uzbekistan's Islam Karimov are the sole Soviet-era leaders to remain in their posts. Though much of the older political elite is still in place, younger and more progressive forces have gradually taken up positions of influence across the region. This process is currently underway in Kazakhstan and has already occurred in Uzbekistan, although there has been a backlash in the last few years in the latter case.

A key—yet often overlooked—similarity among the Central Asian states is the salience of informal networks of power, which remain more important than formal institutions. All countries have what Frederick Starr calls "politics A" and "politics B"—the former referring to the overt, formalized political system, and the latter pointing to informal relations and factors not usually seen by the public.[10] Such informal networks and structures are relatively more important in developing or transitional countries with low levels of experience in independent politics, lesser cohesion in society, low acceptance of state authority, and weak governing institutions—exactly the situation in Central Asia. As one scholar has described, Central Asian politics are characterized by a "persistence of traditional societies with their pre-national patriotisms and the presence, under the umbrella of the nation-state, of lively subnational and regional realities." These subnational groups are often referred to as "clans."[11] Given the variety of sub-state social identities, the term "solidarity groups" is more accurate.[12] Three different types of groups exist. One consists of the traditionally nomadic tribes such as the Kazakhs, Kyrgyz, and Turkmen. A second includes networks that are regionally rather than network-based and that reflect traditional pre-Soviet power centers. The third category bases its power on control over economic resources, such as cotton, oil, or other industries; these groups overlap with the tribal and regional networks.[13] Unlike Russia's oligarchs, who emerged primarily following the Soviet collapse, Central Asia's networks were firmly grounded before the dissolution of the Soviet Union, or even earlier.

---

[10] S. Frederick Starr, *Clans, Authoritarian Rulers, and Parliaments in Central Asia*, Silk Road Paper, June 2006 (Washington, D.C.: Central Asia-Caucasus Institute & Silk Road Studies Program, 2006), 10–12.

[11] Donald S. Carlisle, "Geopolitics and Ethnic Problems of Uzbekistan and Its Neighbours," in *Muslim Eurasia: Conflicting Legacies*, ed. Yaacov Ro'i (London: Frank Cass, 1995), 73; Kathleen Collins, "The Logic of Clan Politics: Evidence from the Central Asian Trajectories," *World Politics* 56, no. 2 (2004): 224–61; Edward Schatz, *Modern Clan Politics: The Power Of "Blood" In Kazakhstan and Beyond* (Seattle: University of Washington Press, 2004); and Adrienne Lynn Edgar, *Tribal Nation: The Making of Soviet Turkmenistan* (Princeton: Princeton University Press, 2004).

[12] Vitaly V. Naumkin, "Uzbekistan's State-building Fatigue," *Washington Quarterly* 29, no. 3 (Summer 2006): 127–40.

[13] Starr, *Clans, Authoritarian Rulers, and Parliaments in Central Asia*, 7–8.

Presiding over the formal institutions of the state and faced with few checks and balances, Central Asia's authoritarian rulers appear in control. These leaders do not, however, have similar sway over the tribal, regional, or economy-based power brokers who exert a substantial pressure upon policymaking in the country. This is particularly true in the case of foreign economic relations—as opposition to market reforms often comes from those controlling important economic sectors. Numerous elite groups also maintain contacts in Russia, which influences their views on foreign policy and provides Moscow with a lobby within Central Asian countries that is separate from the official, institutionalized foreign policymaking process. The influence of regional and economic elites also contributes to the growing fusion of political and economic power characteristic of many post-Soviet states.

Each Central Asian state grapples with problems of identity that reinforce these strong subnational solidarity groups. Identification with a nation-state remains relatively weak in Central Asia, further weakening central governmental authority and bolstering regional power-brokers. All governments have engaged in nation-building, digging into the past for historical precedent and legitimization of the existence of the nation and the rule of the government. Each government produced a nationalism designed to unify the population around leadership of the government.

These similarities in domestic political development have contributed to the gravitation of Central Asian states toward a range of semi-authoritarian to authoritarian systems, with differences between states being only a matter of degree and not nature. Economic development, however, has been more divergent, with Kazakhstan's success having been as remarkable as Uzbekistan's stagnation.

Kazakhstan: From Bicommunal Society under the Russian Shadow to Success Story

In the early days of independence, Kazakhstan was one of the most fragile states of Central Asia. One regional expert has termed Kazakhstan "an accidental country, a nation that was carved out of a Soviet republic whose boundaries were never intended to be those of an independent state."[14] Indeed, Kazakhstan was the last and most reluctant republic of the Soviet Union to embrace independence and the only Soviet republic whose titular population formed less than half of the republic's population.

---

[14] Martha Brill Olcott, "Democratization and the Growth of Political Participation in Kazakhstan," in *Conflict, Cleavage and Change in Central Asia and the Caucasus*, ed. Karen Dawisha and Bruce Parrott (New York: Cambridge University Press, 1997), 201.

Kazakhstan's leader, Nursultan Nazarbayev, had been a leading advocate of saving—but reforming—the Soviet Union. After independence, Nazarbayev became one of the foremost champions of integration in the post-Soviet space. The main challenge facing the new country was demography—as Kazakhs only slightly outnumbered the Russian minority that dominated the five northern provinces of the country and the capital, Almaty.

Almaty had been one of the first trouble spots of the perestroika era. Riots erupted there in 1986 when Soviet authorities replaced long-time Kazakh leader Dinmukhamed Kunaev with an ethnic Russian. The move was a departure from standard Soviet practices—natives headed the bureaucracy in almost all other administrative units. The riots demonstrated the potential of ethnicity as a mobilizing factor in Kazakhstan. Political movements based on Russian and Kazakh nationalism emerged in the following years. Boris Yeltsin's suggestion that Kazakhstan's northern provinces be incorporated into Russia, as well as subsequent Russian steps to make the protection of ethnic Russians abroad state policy, further aggravated ethnic tensions.[15] The double threat of a bifurcated society and the Russian "shadow" forced Kazakhstan to walk a tightrope to ensure survival and sovereignty.

Internally, Kazakhstan suffered stronger controversies over the form of government than did most other regional states. Tensions between the parliament and the president exploded into the open in 1994, when the parliament overtly challenged the president's powers. Nazarbayev was opposed largely by Slavs from the north and Kazakhs from the west, who resented the dominance of the large eastern informal networks—known as "hordes" in the Kazakh context—that they saw Nazarbayev as representing. This risked leading Kazakhstan down the road of a constitutional and political crisis. Nevertheless, Nazarbayev disbanded parliament in 1995, a bold move that formed the decisive step in moving Kazakhstan toward a presidential republic. Similar to what was ongoing in most post-Soviet states at the time, this development increased political stability but did so at the cost of democratic development.

Political difficulties also affected economic policy. In the mid-1990s Kazakhstan compared poorly even to Uzbekistan in terms of economic reform. Flawed privatization processes generated a great deal of controversy and led to the replacement of at least one prime minister. Nevertheless, Kazakhstan was able to capitalize on its oil and gas resources, the largest in the region, by signing several development agreements.

Nazarbayev's family also gained increasing clout in Kazakhstan public life during this period. His daughters Dariga and Dinara, and

---

[15] Dilip Hiro, *Between Marx and Muhammad: The Changing Face of Central Asia* (London: HarperCollins, 1994), 118–19.

their respective husbands Rakhat Aliyev and Timur Kulibayev, became towering figures in Kazakhstan's media, banking, and energy sectors. Kazakhstan is perhaps the only Central Asian country where individuals not deeply connected with politics have been able to amass significant fortunes. The increasing domination of the Nazarbayev family demonstrated, however, the importance the Kazakhstan leadership attached to key sectors of the economy.

The late 1990s proved a turning point for Kazakhstan. The leadership of the country gradually succeeded, despite long odds, in building a sovereign nation state run mainly by Kazakhs and with a prominent position for Kazakh language and culture—without triggering conflict with the Russian minority. Kazakhstan strongly supported integration within the Commonwealth of Independent States (CIS), but insisted on cooperating on equal terms with Russia and other members.[16] Moreover, the Kazakh leadership took the bold step of moving the capital from Almaty in the very southwest to the town of Aqmola (subsequently renamed Astana) in the north, at least in part in order to assert control over the northern areas of the country. By bringing the seat of government closer to the northern, predominantly Russian-populated provinces, the move is likely to contribute in the long run to evening out demographic imbalances in the country. As for the economy, oil-led growth began to accelerate in the early years of the new century. Kazakhstan capitalized on this opportunity by developing the leading banking sector in Central Asia and pushing through reforms that had lagged in the 1990s.

Affluence rapidly differentiated Kazakhstan from the rest of the region in economic terms. A GDP larger than that of all other Central Asian states combined has clearly increased Kazakhstan's sense of security. Economic growth has reduced frustration and apprehension among the ethnic Russian minority and weakened the increasingly marginalized political opposition. Moreover, prosperity has blunted the appeal of radical Islamism; Kazakhstan has clearly not faced this threat to the same extent that Uzbekistan, Tajikistan, and Kyrgyzstan have.

In the realm of politics, Kazakhstan has held several competitive elections, though the executive remains dominant over the electoral process. The electoral process has improved over the past several elections. Nazarbayev's decision to hold elections to choose regional leaders is an important political reform. Though yet unfulfilled, the commitment stands in stark contrast to recent developments in Russia—where power is increasingly centralized and regional leaders are appointed.

---

[16] Martha Brill Olcott, *Kazakhstan: Unfulfilled Promise* (Washington, D.C.: Carnegie Endowment for International Peace, 2002), 19.

Kazakhstan's economic development and internal stability, second to none in the region, have allowed Astana to make a claim for regional leadership in the past several years. Only five years ago that title would have been reserved for Uzbekistan. In terms of international standing and growing prosperity, Kazakhstan is leading the way in the region. Uzbek president Islam Karimov's reported awe in visiting the new Kazakh capital at Astana in 2006 well illustrates the dramatic reversal in fortunes of these two countries.[17]

Kazakhstan does face the danger of the "resource curse"—oil wealth could still undermine the non-oil economy and distort the political system. Nevertheless, Kazakhstan has clearly come a long way since its extremely tenuous position in the early 1990s, when the continued existence and independence of the country were very uncertain. Oil is a leading reason for Kazakhstan's remarkable progress. Much credit must also go, however, to the Kazakh leadership for successfully carrying out the difficult balancing act.

Uzbekistan: The Challenges of Unrest Next Door and Radical Islam

Prior to Russia's conquest of Central Asia in the late nineteenth century, three historical centers of power had existed in Central Asia: the Emirates of Bukhara, Khiva, and Kokand. The 1924–25 national delimitation of Central Asia grouped the lands of all three, and a population almost as large as all other republics combined into the newly created republic of Uzbekistan. The country hence emerged as the most important republic in Central Asia, and has maintained this position after independence. Indeed, the Soviet leadership acknowledged Uzbekistan's predominant role in Central Asia encouraging Uzbekistan to "relate" to Central Asia's other republics as Moscow "relates" to Uzbekistan.[18] Uzbekistan received most of the industrial investments that went to the region. The republic produced more than half of the Soviet Union's cotton and large quantities of natural gas and oil. Uzbekistan upon the dissolution of the Soviet Union also inherited more military equipment, enabling the newly independent state quickly to build the most potent army in the region.[19]

In addition to these advantages, however, independence also left Uzbekistan with serious weaknesses. Much of the countryside was poor, and Soviet rule had exacerbated growing regional disparities through the

---

[17] Marat Yermukanov, "Islam Karimov Asks for Kazakh Investment to Bolster Uzbek Economy," *Central Asia-Caucasus Analyst* 8, no. 18 (September 20, 2006).

[18] Mikhaile Kalinin, *Izbrannye Proizvedeniia, Tom I (1917–1925)* [Selected Works, Vol. I (1917–1925)] (Moscow: 1960), 630, quoted in Donald S. Carlisle, "Geopolitics and Ethnic Problems of Uzbekistan and Its Neighbors," 77.

[19] Pomfret, *The Central Asian Economies since Independence*, 25.

promotion of region-based Uzbek elites. Prior to independence, natives of Samarkand and Tashkent had gradually concentrated political and economic power, sidelining hitherto influential elites from the populous Ferghana Valley. Cotton, energy, and other industries had meanwhile provided power bases for a network of economic elites that intersected with the regional groupings. Following independence, these entrenched interest groups vigorously resisted economic reforms. The cotton "barons," for instance, have maintained a system of practically indentured low-cost labor—providing social stability and considerable profit in the short term, but at the cost of foregoing obvious potential improvements in efficiency.

Domestic political conflict in Uzbekistan has been more tumultuous than in Kazakhstan. A substantial revival of ethnic nationalism targeted Russians, Meskhetian Turks, Koreans, and other minorities. A clearly discernible revival of radical Islamic movements, most active in the conservative Ferghana Valley that is home to a quarter of the country's population, emerged. In the city of Namangan, a group split off from the all-union Islamic Renaissance Party to form the Adolat (Justice) Party and demanded the creation of an Islamic state. The party's leaders attempted, sometimes successfully, to take over the roles of local government and law enforcement bodies—even going so far as to receive emissaries from Saudi Arabian religious charities.[20] When civil war erupted in Tajikistan in 1992 the government mustered the courage to crack down on the radicals. The Islamists fled, but only to join other radical Islamists participating in the conflict in Tajikistan. Meanwhile, another civil war intensified on the southern border of Uzbekistan in Afghanistan.

The Uzbek leadership believed they had narrowly avoided civil war by cracking down on radical movements before the Islamists became strong enough to overpower the fledgling institutions of the Uzbek state, as occurred in Tajikistan. This perception of vulnerability colored the entire Uzbek state-building process, strengthening the hand of those seeking to centralize power and restrict the liberalization process first introduced in the late Soviet era. Thus Uzbekistan began, earlier than its neighbors, to restrict political freedoms, undermine and eventually ban opposition movements, and retrench state control over the economy.[21] President

---

[20] Vitaly V. Naumkin, "Militant Islam in Central Asia: The Case of the Islamic Movement in Uzbekistan," Berkeley Program in Soviet and Post-Soviet Studies, Working Paper Series, Spring 2003, 20–21; and Michael Fredholm, *Uzbekistan and the Threat from Islamic Extremism*, no. K39 (Sandhurst: Royal Military Academy of the United Kingdom Conflict Studies Research Centre, March 2003), 4.

[21] William Friedman, "Political Developments in Uzbekistan: Democratization?" in Dawisha and Parrott, *Conflict, Cleavage and Change in Central Asia and the Caucasus*, 384–93.

Karimov himself openly made the case that Uzbekistan had to build its economy and institutions prior to implementing democracy.[22]

Uzbekistan has not, however, been without internal debates on domestic politics; these discussions have just never been held publicly. Reformist forces did develop in, and eventually control, the ministries of defense and foreign affairs. From these institutional bases the reformers sought to push the president to liberalize the country's political system and facilitate improved relations with the West. The limited political thaws that have intermittently occurred in Uzbekistan are testimony to the influence of these progressive forces. Yet the so-called power ministries—such as those of interior and national security—have long acted (and often in tandem with informal vested interests) as powerful brakes on any liberalization.

Regardless, opinion polls throughout the 1990s demonstrated that President Karimov's rhetoric of sustaining order and preventing instability and chaos received considerable backing among the Uzbek population. By a large margin Uzbeks appeared to continue to favor stability, even at the cost of political freedoms.[23] Uzbekistan's success in avoiding the economic collapse that befell virtually all post-Soviet states was an important factor in this regard. Uzbekistan experienced the smallest reduction in GDP after independence of any other former Soviet state. As a consequence, Uzbekistan maintained a relatively unreformed economy, only gradually introducing very moderate economic reforms in the mid to late 1990s.[24]

As the 1990s drew to a close, Uzbekistan seemed firmly established as the regional leader in Central Asia. Though authoritarian, the country was politically as well as economically stable. Uzbekistan also appeared to be the only country in the region to assume an independent and proactive international role. Uzbekistan's progressive forces had even established good relations with the United States and undertaken the most comprehensive military reforms in the former Soviet Union. Yet the situation would soon change for the worse. Unwillingness to reform resulted in gradual economic stagnation just as the leadership of Kazakhstan was embarking on a reform program. Meanwhile, the Uzbek Islamic militants moved to Afghanistan where the Taliban was now extending its power to the northern areas. The Islamic Movement of Uzbekistan (IMU) was formally founded in Kabul in 1998. In February 1999 a series of bomb explosions rocked Tashkent and

---

[22] Islam Karimov, *Uzbekistan on the Threshold of the Twenty-First Century* (Surrey: Curzon Press, 1997).

[23] Timur Dadabaev, "Public Confidence, Trust and Participation in Post-Soviet Central Asia," *Central Asia-Caucasus Analyst* 8, no. 11 (May 31, 2006).

[24] For an overview of Uzbekistan's economic policies, see Pomfret, *Central Asian Economies*, 23–39.

almost killed Karimov. That same summer (as well as the next) the IMU used bases in Tajikistan to attack areas in Kyrgyzstan and Uzbekistan.[25]

Uzbekistan reacted by turning inward out of concern for the stability and security of both nation and regime. Uzbekistan decided to close and mine its Ferghana Valley borders with Tajikistan and Kyrgyzstan, despite the resulting extremely negative impact on local communities dependent on cross-border linkages in this maze of borders and territorial enclaves. On the domestic front Tashkent intensified its campaign against Islamic extremists, adopting a blanket strategy that often led to persecution of all Islamic movements not under state control. This campaign especially targeted more extremist Islamic sects termed as "Wahhabists" in a wholesale manner by the Uzbek authorities.[26] This harsh government repression of Islamic movements continued, even after the IMU—which had posed the greatest threat to Uzbekistan's security—was decimated in Afghanistan following the September 11 attacks.[27] Some of these groups, such as Hizb-ut-Tahrir, have become radicalized. As regional expert Zeyno Baran has argued, this group now "operates as an ideological vanguard that supports and encourages terrorist acts."[28] As a result of these policies Uzbekistan has remained among the least reformed countries in Eurasia in both political and economic terms. For Uzbekistan this lack of reform has led not only to complications in international affairs (as explained below) but also to increasing stagnation in the early 21st century. Meanwhile the growing influence of solidarity groups on the Uzbek political and economic system is paralyzing government and making reforms difficult. Extensive purges of the progressive and pro-Western forces that dominated the ministries of foreign affairs and defense accompanied the collapse of U.S.-Uzbekistan relations in 2005, allowing the repressive forces more closely affiliated with informal power structures to dominate the agenda. Concomitantly, public dissatisfaction has grown considerably in recent years in response to the country's economic stagnation and the increasing arbitrariness of

[25] Svante E. Cornell, "Narcotics, Radicalism and Armed Conflict in Central Asia: The Islamic Movement of Uzbekistan," *Terrorism and Political Violence* 17, no. 3 (2005): 577–97.

[26] Adeeb Khalid, "A Secular Islam: Nation, State and Religion in Uzbekistan," *International Journal of Middle Eastern Studies* 35, no. 4 (November 2003): 573–98.

[27] Hizb-ut-Tahrir claims both to be non-violent and to seek to change society through peaceful means. The ideology that lies at its base is, however, by no means non-violent. Harshly anti-Semitic, the group's beliefs are fundamentally opposed to liberal democracy. See Zeyno Baran, *Hizb-ut-Tahrir: Islam's Political Insurgency* (Washington, D.C.: Nixon Center, 2004).

[28] Zeyno Baran, "Radical Islamists in Central Asia," in *Current Trends in Islamic Ideology*, ed. Hillel Fradkin, Hussain Haqqani, and Eric Brown (Washington, D.C.: Hudson Institute, 2005), 42. See also Zeyno Baran, S. Frederick Starr, and Svante E. Cornell, *Islamic Radicalism in Central Asia and the Caucasus: Implications for the EU*, Silk Road Paper, June 2006 (Washington, D.C.: Central Asia-Caucasus Institute & Silk Road Studies Program, 2006).

government policy. Uzbekistan once portrayed itself as a bastion of stability but now is apparently becoming increasingly unstable—a development that holds important consequences for the region.

Regional Politics: The Structure of Instability

Central Asia's regional politics are based on several factors. At the foundation lie the Central Asian states' threat perceptions with regard to each other, great powers, or transnational threats such as Islamic radicalism and drug trafficking.[29] Two factors have, however, contributed to the sustained instability in the region's international affairs. The first factor is the interplay of small states with regional powers, as well as the impact on the region of the inter-relationships among these powers. A second factor is Western states' growing insistence on freedom and democracy which, given the authoritarian environment of Central Asia's setting, has upset the predominantly realpolitik character of the region's international affairs.

Small States and Regional Powers

As noted earlier, Central Asia's states are small relative to their larger and more powerful neighbors. This power imbalance is exacerbated by the Central Asian states' weakness and lack of mechanisms for regional cooperation.[30] Moreover, regional politics remain fluid and unpredictable.[31] Many states, neighboring as well as further afield, have developed interests in Central Asia. Despite its geopolitical location, however, Central Asia is not central to the interests of any of these states, whose main priorities lie elsewhere. Although Central Asia briefly occupied a place of importance on the U.S. agenda between 2001 and 2003, that agenda changed after the invasion of Iraq. China is far more concerned with Taiwan and the Korean peninsula. Even Russia, despite its historical influence and interests in Central Asia, is more preoccupied with the Caucasus and Russian relations with the West (though Russia remains the country with the most interest in the region). Smaller powers such as Iran, India, and Turkey also have other concerns that trump Central Asia in their considerations. As a result the policies of most powers in the region are characterized by irregular efforts

---

[29] Svante E. Cornell, "Regional Perspectives on Military and Economic Security in the Caucasus and Central Asia," The National Bureau of Asian Research, *NBR Analysis* 14, no. 3 (October 2003).

[30] Niklas L. P. Swanström, "The Prospects for Multilateral Conflict Prevention and Regional Cooperation in Central Asia," *Central Asian Survey* 23, no. 1 (March 2004): 41–53.

[31] Svante E. Cornell, "The United States and Central Asia: In the Steppes to Stay?" *Cambridge Review of International Affairs* 17, no. 2 (Summer 2004): 239–54.

or short-term initiatives rather than consistent strategies. A stable regional environment has yet to emerge.[32]

For most of the 1990s, no power had the capacity or desire to play a dominant role in Central Asian politics. Russia's influence gradually waned despite President Vladimir Putin's renewed efforts to assert a role for Moscow as the primary arbiter of regional affairs.[33] Turkey and Iran sought to exercise influence in the region in the early 1990s, ultimately realizing, however, that they lacked the necessary resources.[34] China has silently increased its influence in the region since the mid 1990s but has not developed a dominant influence on any particular country.[35] The support of Pakistan for the Taliban visibly failed to accomplish Pakistan's dual goals of ensuring a pliant Afghan government and securing access to Central Asia.[36] Attempts by India to expand political influence in Central Asia, meanwhile, remain limited as a result of India's geographic distance from the region.[37]

Regional arrangements proved unsuccessful. Russian and Chinese interlocutors sought to employ the "Shanghai mechanism," originally conceived in 1995 to resolve border conflicts between the Soviet successor states and China, in order to establish a Central Asia collective security framework in 2001.[38] Though the regional states joined the revamped Shanghai Cooperation Organization (SCO), Central Asian nations were reluctant to be subsumed by the organization. The weakness of this Chinese-Russian mechanism is best illustrated by the speed and openness with which the Central Asian states welcomed U.S. forces on their territory following the attacks of September 11. Unlike the SCO, which offered little in terms of economic aid or military protection, new partnerships with Washington provided Central Asian regimes with enhanced security and a concomitant broadening of their foreign relations. The failure of the United

---

[32] S. Frederick Starr, Charles J. Fairbanks, Richard Nelson, and Kenneth Weisbrode, *A Strategic Assessment of Central Eurasia* (Washington, D.C.: Atlantic Council and Central Asia-Caucasus Institute, 2001).

[33] Martha Brill Olcott, "Taking Stock of Central Asia," *Journal of International Affairs* 56, no. 2 (Spring 2003): 4.

[34] Svante Cornell and Maria Sultan, "The New Geopolitics of Central Eurasia," *Marco Polo Magazine*, no. 5–6 (Winter 2000–2001); and Svante E. Cornell, "Regional Politics in Central Asia: The Changing Roles of Iran, Turkey, Pakistan," in *India and Central Asia: Building Linkages in an Age of Turbulence*, ed. Indranil Banerjee (Middlesex: Brunel Academic Publishers, 2004).

[35] Niklas L. P. Swanström, "China and Central Asia: A New Great Game or Traditional Vassal Relations?" *Journal of Contemporary China* 14, no. 45 (November 2005): 569–84.

[36] Imtiaz Gul, *The Unholy Nexus: Pak-Afghan Relations under the Taliban* (Lahore: Vanguard, 2002).

[37] Stephen J. Blank, "India's Rising Profile in Central Asia," *Comparative Strategy* 22, no. 2 (April–June 2003): 139–57; and Juli MacDonald, "Rethinking India's and Pakistan's Regional Intent," The National Bureau of Asian Research, NBR Analysis 14, no. 4, November 2003.

[38] Stephen Blank, "The Shanghai Cooperative Organization: A Post-Mortem," *Nordic Institute of Asian Studies Newsletter*, no. 3 (2002): 12–13.

States to sustain engagement with the region has, however, led Moscow and Beijing to redevelop the SCO and use it as a vehicle for minimizing Western interests in the region.[39]

On a deeper level, these constantly changing priorities and capacities have generated a structural instability. The current constellation of forces in and around Central Asia has produced a zero-sum jockeying for power. A mechanism for cooperation based on mutual restraint and including all major powers—the United States, Europe, and Japan, as well as neighboring countries—is necessary to address this instability. The prospects for such a structure to emerge in the short term are, however, extremely low.

U.S. Interests in Central Asia: Contradictory or Compatible?

U.S. interests in Central Asia are diverse, falling roughly into three categories: security, energy and trade, and governance. Security interests stem from the realization that the United States is engaged in a "long war" against Islamic radicalism. Preserving strategic access to Central Asia and developing security ties with the states of the region have become important priorities in this conflict. Secondly, the United States has long worked for the westward export of the Caspian region's energy resources, both for the sake of sustaining the independence and sovereignty of the regional states and in view of their effect on regional and global energy markets. As energy markets tightened and oil prices soared, this gradually became an even more important issue. Aside from energy, the United States has also promoted the development of continental trade in the region.[40] Governance interests, lastly, include a consistent U.S. emphasis on internal reform in the mainly authoritarian Central Asian countries. Both principle and pragmatism have contributed to this objective. Support for democratization and human rights has become a moral element of Western foreign policy, shared by both the United States and the European Union (EU). Moreover, democratization is increasingly understood as a means to address perceived root causes of terrorism such as socio-economic backwardness and political repression.

U.S. policymakers have nevertheless failed to overcome a perception that these objectives are inherently contradictory. After September 11, for instance, many at home and abroad strongly criticized Washington for once again allying with dictators out of narrow U.S. security purposes and thereby ignoring human rights and democracy. These contradictions are

---

[39] Vladimir Socor, "The Unfolding of the U.S.-Uzbekistan Crisis," in Daly et al., *Anatomy of a Crisis*, 44–65.

[40] S. Frederick Starr, ed., *The New Silk Roads: Transport and Trade in Greater Central Asia* (Washington, D.C.: Central Asia-Caucasus Institute, 2007), 5–31.

more imagined than real, however. The argument that interests in security and energy are harmful to reform and democratization stems from a view of the governments of the region as monolithic and authoritarian—ignoring the array of forces, as described above, that influence the Central Asian regimes. This same view has led European and U.S. policymakers to focus on bringing about change by supporting NGOs, rather than by working with government offices themselves. Representatives of the media and human rights communities in particular often view cooperation with and assistance to governments as strengthening authoritarian rule. By the same token, critics see Western interests in energy or security as providing the regional governments with leverage and instruments to withstand pressures for reform and sustain authoritarian rule.

In practice, however, all governments of the region include a mixture of forces favoring reform and forces favoring authoritarian rule. The latter are often deeply corrupt or controlled by special interest groups, reinforcing the authoritarian tendencies of opponents of reform. Because of the Western emphasis on democracy, transparency, and openness, those benefiting from corruption are typically opponents of a Western orientation. These groups tend to favor instead a closer relationship with Russia, which pays little attention to a government's domestic characteristics. On the other hand, advocates of reform are typically pro-Western, seeing in Western institutions the tools, assistance, and guidance necessary for meaningful reform. Support for these pro-reform groups has enabled them to exert a positive influence on governance by promoting reform or checking the influence of repressive forces. The considerable worsening of the already precarious human rights situation in Uzbekistan in 2005–06, for instance, coincided with a purge of pro-Western forces from that country's government.

The dilemma the United States is said to face, therefore, is a false one. An approach that treats U.S. interests in security, energy, and governance as contradictory is a self-fulfilling prophecy that in fact undermines each goal. Interest in democratization, for instance, has led the United States and Europe to support civil society as a counterweight to authoritarian rule. Meanwhile, the West has ignored or shunned work with state institutions, considering them corrupt or work with them impossible. Even before the "freedom agenda" grew in force with the Eurasian color revolutions, the Central Asian ruling elites increasingly perceived these policies as antagonistic. Policies intended to encourage democratization consequently had the perverse effects of undermining the progressive forces in government that constituted the best hope both for gradual political and economic reform and for strengthening the very autocratic forces that Western policies were designed to counter. Non-governmental (and some governmental) groups in the West have a strong tendency to see isolation, exclusion, and finger-pointing as the preferred ways to deal with authoritarian governments. By undermining both progressive forces in government and Western influence, such methods are in effect the surest ways to bring about the victory of authoritarian-minded forces in countries such as those of Central Asia. The timing of the emergence of the "freedom agenda"—just as President Putin has consolidated his increasingly authoritarian presidency—has further undermined the chances for successful democratization.

An Authoritarian Neighborhood and the Democracy Agenda

Pragmatic calculations of self-interest have been the primary determinant of Central Asian politics. The realist understanding of international affairs is, therefore, particularly relevant. External powers and regional states all have based their policies on their self-perceived national interests. Ideology has had very little influence on the region—especially during the 1990s, but also in the first years following the events of September 11. Emphasizing domestic governance, human rights, and democratic reforms in their relationships with the region, Western powers, and especially the United States, have always balanced such factors with national interests in security, energy, or other issues. Because the West had limited interests and influence in the region during this time period, however, the emphasis on democracy and governance did not upset international relations in the region. Central Asian regimes did not perceive these policies as a threat to either stability or regime security. As a result, democratization was neither an asset nor a liability for the United States in its relationship with Central Asia.

This was to change following the turn of the century, however, for two major reasons. The first was Vladimir Putin's presidency in Russia. Whereas his predecessor Boris Yeltsin had been a convinced democrat, Putin soon after taking power showed himself to be an equally convinced autocrat. Although Yeltsin had not made democracy an element of Russian foreign policy in the region, his democratic credentials had helped reform movements and democratic forces in Central Asia. Under Putin's authoritarian rule Russia ceased to be a model of development for democrats in Central Asia. Russia's growing authoritarianism instead emboldened Central Asian rulers to increase their authoritarian practices. These rulers also valued the predictability of Putin's policies as compared to Yeltsin's.[41] The second factor was the onset of color revolutions in the

---

[41] Sally N. Cummings, "Happier Bedfellows? Russia and Central Asia under Putin," *Asian Affairs* 32, no. 2 (2001): 149.

former Soviet Union. Coinciding with a growing focus on the promotion
of democracy and freedom in U.S. foreign policy, these revolutions
introduced a strong ideological element into Central Asian politics.

The democracy agenda, of course, has long been a factor in U.S.
foreign policy.[42] A growing focus on democracy was clearly visible in the
Bush administration's policies from 2003 onward.[43] This "Bush Doctrine"
particularly affected the post-Soviet space through the color revolutions,
beginning in Georgia in 2003. Georgia's "Rose Revolution" was widely
seen as a U.S.-sponsored revolution, made possible through the work of
various U.S.-funded NGOs. This event upset post-Soviet leaders, such as
Kyrgyzstan's weakened president Askar Akayev; the United States, however,
seemed happy to take some credit. The Georgian revolution initially seemed
to be an isolated event. The "Orange Revolution," led by Viktor Yuschenko,
that prevented the Ukrainian leadership under Leonid Kuchma from
securing the election of a designated successor indicated that the events in
Tbilisi were not isolated. The collapse of the Akayev regime a few months
later, which forced Akayev to flee the country, put the entire region on high
alert. Led by President Putin, leaders across the region began restricting the
activities of NGOs working on democratization and human rights issues,
as well as all groups with foreign funding more generally. Democracy
promotion increasingly came to be seen as an alien, externally induced
phenomenon rather than a domestically rooted process.[44] This backlash
swept across Central Asia, ironically joined by the new government in
Kyrgyzstan, which soon felt as weak and vulnerable as the ousted Akayev
regime had.

Suddenly, ideology had mixed with realpolitik. Central Asian rulers
no longer perceived the United States as simply supporting improvements
in governance and gradual democratization. The U.S. goal now appeared
instead to be regime change—the removal, with the help of U.S. funding,
of some rulers in order to replace them with other, more pro-Western
ones. The domestic roots of these upheavals and the limited nature of the
support they received from abroad mattered little; the Bush administration
heaped praise on revolutionary governments, often for good reason, while
Russian leaders actively portrayed the United States as the architect of the
revolutions. Gradually, the region's leaders—conflating their regime security
with stability—began to view the influence of the United States in the region

[42] Michael McFaul, "Democracy Promotion as a World Value," *Washington Quarterly* 28, no. 1 (2006): 147–63.

[43] Jonathan Monets, "The Roots of the Bush Doctrine," *International Security* 29, no. 4 (2005): 112–56.

[44] Thomas Carothers, "The Backlash against Democracy Promotion," *Foreign Affairs* 85, no. 2 (2006): 55–68.

as a destabilizing factor.[45] In associating these revolutions with the United States, the Central Asian governments came to fundamentally reappraise U.S. trustworthiness.

Putin capitalized on these fears by offering Russian support as a bulwark against regime change promoted by the West. As Pavel Baev has noted, Russian foreign policy under Putin, previously based only on energy politics and counterterrorism, now added a third, "counter-revolutionary" leg, with the goal of "preserving authoritarian regimes in post-Soviet state."[46] Putin enlisted Beijing to help Moscow rapidly revamp the SCO as an institution through which common positions could be announced and Central Asian leaders could be persuaded to follow Russian regional leadership. Through the SCO Moscow and Beijing worked successfully for the removal of the U.S. base in Uzbekistan in 2005 and almost succeeded in achieving the same outcome in Kyrgyzstan.[47]

The juxtaposition of ideology and realpolitik in Central Asia has been tremendously detrimental both to U.S. interests and to the cause of democracy and good governance in Central Asia more broadly. On the one hand, the United States has lost much of the influence and goodwill that Washington had built up in the region in the aftermath of the events of September 11. U.S. policymakers have now been relegated to reacting to the policy initiatives brought forward by Moscow and Beijing. On the other hand, the West has been powerless to halt the backlash against pro-democracy NGOs in the region and beyond. The mistrust between Central Asian governments and the politically active civil societies in the region is greater than ever. In this context the interaction of domestic and foreign policies in Central Asia is of the utmost importance.

Domestic and Foreign Policies: Interaction

Domestic and foreign policies are interlinked to varying degrees in all of the states of Central Asia. The considerable economic interests and the perceptions of the aims of foreign powers of the various elite groups shape these groups' priorities and the foreign policy decisions of the states themselves. As will be described below, the backlash against U.S. interests may have peaked. Washington's efforts to rebuild confidence and Moscow's

---

[45] Boasts of a "mission accomplished" by the Freedom House director in Bishkek upon President Akayev's hurried escape from Kyrgyzstan did not help the perception of the United States in the region. Richard Spencer, "Quiet American Behind Tulip Revolution," *Daily Telegraph*, April 2, 2005.

[46] Pavel K. Baev, "Turning Counter-Terrorism into Counter-Revolution: Russia Focuses on Kazakhstan and Engages Turkmenistan," *European Security* 15, no. 1 (March 2006): 4.

[47] For details of this episode, see Daly et al., *Anatomy of a Crisis*.

overreaching have led the Central Asian states to seek balance once again and overcome their suspicions of U.S. ambitions in the region.

Uzbekistan's U-Turns

The most dramatic shifts in Central Asian politics involve Uzbekistan. Tashkent has long been known to make abrupt reversals on a variety of issues. To take just one example, Uzbekistan left the Russian-led Collective Security Treaty in 1999 only to join immediately the pro-Western GUAM alliance,[48] then suspended its activities with GUAM in 2002 and officially quit in early May 2005. Events in 2005 trumped these turns, however. The U.S.-Uzbekistan relationship had been faltering for a considerable time. In 2004 the United States decertified Uzbekistan for not making progress on human rights and political reform and thus cut assistance to the country. The Uzbek government then brutally cracked down on an upheaval in the Ferghana Valley city of Andijan in May 2005, where at least 180 people and possibly many more were killed. The Andijan events were rapidly defined by the international media as a "massacre" of unarmed civilians. Nevertheless, the events remain highly controversial. Many Western observers, especially in the human rights community, maintain that the government opened fire unprovoked. These critics insist that the victims were unarmed protestors, unaffiliated with any radical groups.[49] Other scholars view the event as being much more complex. Without denying or excusing the excessive use of force by the Uzbek authorities, these observers nevertheless argue that the protestors were armed, began their uprising with an attack on a government arms deport, and used civilians as human shields. Moreover, these scholars argue that strong indications suggest the protestors were members of militant Islamic organizations.[50]

Andijan turned out to be a watershed moment in Uzbek foreign policy. Growing criticism from the United States and Europe, demands for an international investigation, and targeted sanctions imposed on Uzbekistan all combined to push Uzbekistan's relations with the West to

[48] The GUAM alliance consists of Georgia, Ukraine, Azerbaijan, and Moldova.

[49] "Uzbekistan: The Andijon Uprising," International Crisis Group, Asia Briefing no. 38, May 25, 2005; and Rachel Denber, ed., "'Bullets Were Falling Like Rain': The Andijan Massacre, May 13, 2005," Human Rights Watch 17, no. 5, June 2005.

[50] Shirin Akiner, *Violence in Andijan: An Independent Assessment*, Silk Road Paper, July 2005, (Washington, D.C.: Central Asia-Caucasus Institute & Silk Road Studies Program, 2005), 14, 17, 21, 27–29; John C. K. Daly, "The Andijan Disturbances and their Implications," *Central Asia-Caucasus Analyst* 6, no. 3 (June 29, 2005); Margarita Assenova, "Uzbekistan Is Running Out of Time," *Internationale Politik* (Fall 2005); Baran et al., *Islamic Radicalism in Central Asia and the Caucasus*; and Abdumannob Polat, "Reassessing Andijan: The Road to Restoring U.S.-Uzbek Relations," Jamestown Foundation, Occasional Paper, June 2007.

the breaking point. The United States had supported the transfer to other countries of Andijan refugees who had been sheltering in Kyrgyzstan; this support infuriated the Uzbek authorities, who argued that the refugees included armed militants. On July 29 the Uzbek government informed U.S. embassy in Tashkent that U.S. troops would be required to vacate the Kharshi-Khanabad (K2) airbase near the Afghan border within 180 days, effectively severing the U.S.-Uzbekistan strategic partnership that had been signed in 2002. Russia and Uzbekistan signed an alliance treaty on November 14—seven days before the U.S. flag was lowered from the K2 base.[51] Tashkent spared no efforts to reverse its long-standing foreign policy of distancing itself from Moscow. In the following months, Tashkent acceded to the two most important Russian-led multilateral organizations in the region, joining the Eurasian Economic Community (EurAsEC) in January 2006 and the Collective Security Treaty Organization (CSTO) in June of the same year.[52] The Uzbek government also opened the country to Russian investment. A deal with Gazprom allowed the Russian state-owned natural gas monopoly to develop some of Uzbekistan's largest gas fields. Another agreement committed Uzbekistan to sell gas to Russia at the steeply discounted price of $80 per thousand cubic meters. Russia, meanwhile, sells gas to Europe for three times as much and purchases gas from even Turkmenistan at a higher price.[53]

These bold steps have worked to reverse the course of a decade and a half of Uzbek foreign policy. Since this new direction was taken, Tashkent has apparently sought to restore some balance in Uzbekistan's foreign relations. Uzbekistan has reached out to Europe and quietly attempted to rebuild ties to the United States. Visitors to Uzbekistan now report a widespread feeling that the government, including President Karimov personally, reacted emotionally and in an exaggerated manner to U.S. actions in 2005 and early 2006. Nevertheless the prospects for a restoration of relations are slim as long as Karimov's government stays in place.

Tashkent's decisions during this period are difficult to understand. As scholar Gregory Gleason has noted, the "about-face was not caused by any single incident but was the result of a cumulative series of events that culminated in the spring of 2005." After the color revolutions:

> Karimov realized that he was facing two starkly different choices. He could out-compete the democratic "color revolutions" by introducing serious governance

---

[51] Socor, "The Unfolding of the U.S.-Uzbekistan Crisis," 61.

[52] The CSTO is the successor organization to the Collective Security Treaty that Uzbekistan had left in 1999. "CSTO Readmits Uzbekistan as Full-Fledged Member: Putin," *People's Daily Online*, June 24, 2006, http://english.people.com.cn/200606/24/eng20060624_276876.html.

[53] Daly et al., *Anatomy of a Crisis*, 108.

reforms, or he could try to enlist the help of outside allies to strengthen his regime...enlisting new allies to prop up the regime would entail a complete reversal of Uzbekistan's foreign policy. Karimov chose the latter course.[54]

Indeed, this conflation of national and regime interests explains a great deal of Uzbek foreign policy in this period. The ruling elite that comprise an authoritarian regime commonly view societal interests and their own interests as identical.[55] This view perhaps stems from a ruling elite belief that they are the only force capable of formulating and defending the interests of the nation; the regime thus believes that if they were removed from power disaster would ensue for the country. More pragmatically, the regime could simply be seeking to safeguard the profits of its position or fear the consequences of losing power.[56] In reality, these two categories of motivation may be impossible to separate.

In the case of Uzbekistan the government's foreign policy until 2005, although occasionally capricious, nevertheless derived from a stable understanding of the national interests of the country. In the interest of achieving independence and sovereignty, Uzbekistan crafted a policy of developing close ties with the United States in order to balance pressure from Moscow. The government followed its policy meticulously, despite occasional setbacks. For example in 1999 after Washington failed to provide Tashkent with the assistance he had requested Karimov turned to Moscow, but only after having signed partnership deals with China as a demonstration that Uzbekistan was a regional player with other options available.[57] Notwithstanding the occasional disappointment, the Uzbek leadership persevered in its quest for balance. Even before September 11, the government took every opportunity to seek closer ties with the West. The government's decisions in 2005, however, diverge completely from this pattern. Tashkent's move toward Moscow appears irrational and emotional. In return for little visible benefit, Uzbekistan sacrificed important elements of sovereignty (the energy sector for example) and contradicted a foreign policy that had previously been rather effective. EurAsEC will benefit Uzbekistan's economy little; the CSTO, meanwhile, does little to enhance Uzbekistan's security.

---

[54] Gregory Gleason, "The Uzbek Expulsion of U.S. Forces and Realignment in Central Asia," *Problems of Post-Communism* 53, no. 2 (March/April 2006): 50.

[55] See Bruce Bueno de Mesquita and James Lee Ray, "The National Interest versus Individual Political Ambition: Democracy, Autocracy, and the Reciprocation of Force and Violence in Militarized Interstate Disputes," in *The Scourge of War: New Extensions of an Old Problem*, ed. Paul Diehl (Ann Arbor: University of Michigan Press, 2004), 94–119.

[56] Shahram Akbarzadeh, "Uzbekistan and the United States: Friends or Foes?" *Middle East Policy* 14, no. 1 (Spring 2007).

[57] Svante E. Cornell, "Uzbekistan: A Regional Player in Eurasian Geopolitics," *European Security* 9, no. 2 (Summer 2000): 115–40.

The only plausible explanation based on the information available is that the Karimov regime saw its linkage with the United States as a threat either to Uzbekistan's national security or to its own regime security—or to both. There were rumors circulating in Tashkent in 2005 that U.S. officials had met and struck a deal with the IMU in Afghanistan; though sounding absurd, these rumors do support the former explanation. While these rumors are wildly unlikely, given that the IMU is allied with al Qaeda, parts of the Uzbek security apparatus apparently believed them—or at least used them for ulterior motives. Intelligence services hostile to the presence of the United States in Central Asia were likely responsible for spreading the misinformation. Why the rumors were believed in Tashkent despite being so illogical is unclear. If Tashkent indeed saw the Andijan uprising as a harbinger of Islamic rebellion, it must also have assumed, perhaps erroneously, that the United States had enough intelligence on the issue to come to the same conclusion. Though requiring a leap of logic, such a series of interpretations could, in the absence of honest dialogue and mutual confidence, have led Tashkent to conclude that Washington indeed had subversive intentions that would harm the sovereignty and independence of Uzbekistan in addition to the regime's security.

The alternative interpretation is that Tashkent perceived Washington's support for democratic revolutions in Eurasia as an implicit declaration of war against all authoritarian regimes such as itself. This interpretation would explain the excessive leaps toward Moscow that Tashkent took in 2005 and 2006. Alignment with Russia may have been determined more by the ruling elite's needs for regime security than by its understanding of Uzbekistan's national security. In the final analysis, it will likely be years before the true thinking behind Uzbekistan's u-turn in 2005 is understood. A likely explanation, however, is that more narrow interests than those of Uzbekistan as a state affected the decisions.

Kazakhstan's Balancing

Kazakhstan began its course as an independent state by relying on relations with Moscow. As noted above, the Kazakhstan elite perceived Moscow as a threat to the independence of Kazakhstan and aligned with Moscow in order to reduce this threat.[58] Under the leadership of long-time foreign minister Kassymzhomart Tokayev, however, Kazakhstan established a policy based on the Uzbek model of balancing Russian dominance in order to safeguard and consolidate independence. Kazakhstan did so in a more long-term, methodic, and less confrontational manner than Uzbekistan.

---

[58] See, for example, Olcott, *Kazakhstan: Unfulfilled Promise*.

In what Starr has called a "characteristic combination of eagerness and prudence," Kazakhstan began to develop relations with China.[59] Resilient suspicion and fear of China, stemming partly from ethnic tensions and partly from continued fear of Maoist encroachment, were still persistent among the Kazakh elite. Nevertheless, as Nazarbayev explained in the chapter on national security in his text *Kazakhstan 2030*:

> To ensure our independence and territorial integrity, we must be a strong state and maintain friendly relations with our neighbours, which is why we shall develop and consolidate relations of confidence and equality with our closest and historically equal neighbour—Russia. Likewise we shall develop just as confident and good-neighbourly relations with the PRC [People's Republic of China] on a mutually advantageous basis. Kazakhstan welcomes the policy pursued by China for it *is aimed against hegemonism* and favours friendship with neighbouring countries.[60]

The description of China as an anti-hegemonic power is a clear indication of the balancing act that Nazarbayev was proposing; in the Central Asian context, hegemony can only be understood as referring to Russian domination. Kazakhstan has continuously developed its relationship with its great eastern neighbor, despite simultaneous concerns of possible Chinese economic domination of the region in the long term. Meanwhile, Kazakhstan took on an active role in Asia, for example by hosting initiatives on confidence-building. In 1997 Tokayev explicitly used the term "balance" in describing Kazakhstan's foreign relations, noting the strategic relationships with both Russia and China. Following this, Kazakhstan sought to broaden its energy security by agreeing to and eventually building (against Moscow's will) an oil pipeline to China, completed in 2005. Gradually, and without the use of harsh rhetoric, Kazakhstan asserted its independence. Starr offers the following analysis:

> The challenge for Astana is to balance [the multiple strategic partnerships] in ways that are mutually beneficial, that minimize or curtail the worst tendencies of each partner, and that in the end strengthen the sovereignty and independence of Kazakhstan itself. Because each strategic partner is seen as complementary to the other, both relationships, and the relation between them, must be based on trust. All this requires delicacy and art.[61]

Developments in the late 1990s certainly created difficulties for the strategy of Nazarbayev and Tokayev. Though Kazakhstan had embraced

---

[59] S. Frederick Starr, "Kazakhstan's Security Strategy: A Model for Central Asia?" *Central Asia Affairs*, no. 3, (January 2007): 4.

[60] See "Kazakhstan 2030," Embassy of Kazakhstan to the United States and Canada website, http://kazakhembus.com/Kazakhstan2030.html; emphasis added.

[61] Starr, "Kazakhstan's Security Strategy: A Model for Central Asia?" 8.

the Shanghai forum and later the SCO as a Chinese-led initiative, rapprochement between Moscow and Beijing allowed the two great powers to coordinate joint policies toward the region—effectively reducing the utility of relations with China as a balancer to Russia, at least for the short term. This led Kazakhstan to more actively seek to develop ties with the West, despite much-publicized allegations of high-level corruption that constrained U.S.-Kazakh relations.[62] Indeed, Kazakhstan moved rapidly, even before September 11, to develop its relationship with the West. By adding a third strategic partnership, one with the United States, Astana sought to add a third balancing force to its foreign policy.[63] Following September 11, Kazakhstan expressed support for the United States and offered the use of its airspace, though geographical distance from Afghanistan ensured that the question of a U.S. military base was not seriously broached. Moreover, despite continuing involvement in the CSTO and SCO, Kazakhstan was also the only Central Asian state to develop a relationship with the North Atlantic Treaty Organization (NATO) to the point of submitting an Individual Partnership Action Plan, accepted in January 2006.[64] (Uzbekistan had initiated but never completed this process, cutting most of its links to NATO in 2005.) Kazakhstan also supported U.S.-sponsored efforts to advance trade and transportation through Afghanistan in a north-south direction.[65]

The color revolutions proved the same shock for Astana as they did for Tashkent. Like that of Uzbekistan, the Kazakh elite has also been accused of placing private interests over national interests in foreign policymaking.[66] Astana's reaction to the events nevertheless diverged strongly from Tashkent's. On the one hand, Nazarbayev's government clearly was concerned by the developments; several analysts noted a slide toward positions espoused by Moscow and Beijing.[67] Kazakhstan also intensified

---

[62] See, for example, Seymour M. Hersh, "The Price of Oil," *New Yorker*, July 9, 2001.

[63] Starr, "Kazakhstan's Security Strategy: A Model for Central Asia?" 9.

[64] See Roger McDermott, "Kazakhstan's Partnership with NATO: Strengths, Limits and Prognosis," *China and Eurasia Forum Quarterly* 5, no. 1 (February 2007): 7–20.

[65] Niklas Norling, ed., "First Kabul Conference on Partnership, Trade and Development in Greater Central Asia," Central Asia-Caucasus Institute & Silk Road Studies Program, Conference Report, April 2006, 8–12.

[66] Tor Bukvoll, "Astana's Privatised Independence: Private and National Interests in the Foreign Policy of Nursultan Nazarbayev," *Nationalities Papers* 32, no. 3 (September 2004).

[67] Pavel Baev, "Turning Counter-terrorism into Counter-revolution," 11; and Stephen Blank, "Kazakhstan's Foreign Policy in a Time of Turmoil," *Eurasia Insight*, April 27, 2005.

efforts to develop relations with the United States, however.[68] A series of reciprocal visits illustrates these efforts: Foreign Minister Tokayev visited the United States in September 2002 and again in early September 2006, U.S. Secretary of State Condoleezza Rice visited Astana in October 2005, U.S. Vice President Dick Cheney visited Astana in May 2006, and President Nazarbayev visited Washington in September 2006. Astana also worked quietly but consistently to develop multiple options for energy resource exports. One example is plans to export both oil and gas through the Baku-Tbilisi-Ceyhan pipeline (a U.S.-supported project completed in 2005) initially by barges but holding the option of a Trans-Caspian pipeline open in the longer term.

The policies of Uzbekistan and Kazakhstan have diverged primarily in the nature of the strategic partnerships the two countries have built. Uzbekistan has pursued more antagonistic and exclusive relations: when the country leaned toward the West, Uzbek relations with Russia soured and rhetoric against Russian ambitions grew fairly loud. Conversely, Uzbekistan leaned increasingly on Russia as relations with the United States worsened and anti-American diatribes from Tashkent grew louder. The pursuit of good relations with any one great power for Tashkent has come at the expense of relations with another. Kazakhstan has pursued a different policy, seeking inclusive and compatible relationships with the three great powers of most consequence in the region. Kazakhstan has built ties with the United States in tandem with, rather than at the expense of, ties with Russia. Both foreign policies seek balance, albeit in different manners.

Several factors account for these differences. First of all, no incident similar to that at Andijan occurred in Kazakhstan; in general, the internal threats to the Kazakh ruling elite are much less acute. Kazakhstan's form of government is among the most open in Central Asia. Though Kazakhstan's multi-party elections allow opposition parties to participate, the elections have never been termed free or fair by the international community and substantial problems in terms of political freedoms and human rights remain. Nevertheless, Kazakhstan compares favorably to its neighbors on this count. The comparatively lower level of repression is itself a consequence of the lower level of threats perceived by the ruling elite. Secondly, following the debacle that its relationship with Uzbekistan had become, the United States moved quickly to retain whatever U.S. influence still remained in Central Asia. Defense Secretary Donald Rumsfeld, for instance, traveled

---

[68] See, for example, Kanat Saudabayev, "Kazakhstan and the United States: Growing Partnership for Security and Prosperity," *American Foreign Policy Interests* 27, no. 3 (February 2005): 185–88; and Kassymzhomart Tokayev, "Kazakhstan: From Renouncing Nuclear Weapons to Building Democracy," *American Foreign Policy Interests* 26, no. 2 (April 2004): 93–97.

to Kyrgyzstan to save the Manas air base. Even more significant was Cheney's visit to Astana following on the heels of a long-expected invitation to Azerbaijan's president Ilham Aliyev to visit Washington. These events, culminating in Nazarbayev's Washington visit, signified the understanding of the United States that reaching out to semi-authoritarian leaders in the region was now necessary to preserve U.S. presence in the region; Kazakhstan was the major beneficiary of this realization.

Kazakhstan and Azerbaijan were both able to maintain such close ties to the United States only because the ruling elites felt secure enough not to allow fears of purportedly U.S.-sponsored color revolutions guide their thinking. Indeed, relatively stable domestic situations and popular regimes have been the primary factors leading these states to press for engagement with the United States. The benefits of engagement, in turn, allowed pro-Western forces in Astana as well as in Baku to prevail over pro-Russian forces in each government.

As noted above, the contrast between Kazakhstan and other post-Soviet states is striking. Tashkent pursued a policy of balance between great powers in the negative sense of the term. Uzbek policies toward Moscow were harsh and confrontational, as were those of Georgia in the Caucasus. The sovereignty and independence of both states had been subjected to the most assertive Russian pressure in their respective regions. The failure of both states to build relations with Moscow nevertheless entailed dependence on another foreign power, in this case the United States. The Karimov government, however, failed to understand that U.S. support at the level needed to balance Russia would require Uzbek domestic reform—at least for U.S. domestic reasons, if nothing else. The Nazarbayev government, on the other hand, was able to portray itself as a more acceptable partner to the West. Kazakhstan sought to build a balance between great powers in the positive sense of the term. Friendly relations with the great powers did not come at the cost of compromise on issues of sovereignty and independence.

The Others: Kyrgyzstan's Chaos, Turkmenistan's Neutrality, and Tajikistan's Belated Emergence

In this sense, the foreign policies of the two heavyweights of Central Asia have evolved in opposing directions. The smaller states of the region face a more complicated situation because of their weakness and relative poverty. Turkmenistan, somewhat of an outlier, has chosen to ally with no one. This policy of positive neutrality aims for balance by avoiding the creation of a need to balance against any particular state. Three factors make this possible: an isolated geographic location, energy resources, and the total control by the state over society. Isolation both from Russia and the major trouble-spots of southeastern Central Asia ensured that the security concerns of Turkmenistan were much less serious than those of Kyrgyzstan, Tajikistan, or Uzbekistan. Nevertheless, maintaining positive relations with all Afghan governments (including the Taliban), as Ashgabat has, required considerable diplomatic skill. Energy resources and a small population have meanwhile enabled the Turkmen government to eschew regional economic cooperation and develop a more autarkic economy. Finally, the high level of repression in the country, exceeding even that of Uzbekistan, has ensured that few if any threats from society have emerged. Because Turkmenistan does not offer competitive elections, there has been little risk of a color revolution. It remains to be seen, however, whether the Turkmen leadership will be able to stick to a policy of neutrality. The death of eccentric ruler Saparmurad Niyazov in December 2006 and discord between other regional powers over Uzbek energy resources are both potentially destabilizing factors.

Kyrgyzstan and Tajikistan are in many ways similar: they are small, weak, mountainous, and contain sections of the Ferghana Valley. These states also face similar security challenges of Islamic radicalism, internal turmoil between stark regional divisions, and the rapidly growing problem of drug trafficking from Afghanistan that both strengthens violent non-state actors and criminalizes the state apparatus.[69] Naturally, there are important differences, however. Because of the border it shares with Afghanistan, Tajikistan is much more embroiled in Afghan affairs. Civil war has not only weakened the state severely but also provided the incumbent government with considerable latitude—the population will tolerate substantial excesses to avoid a renewed conflict. Tajikistan has become increasingly stable in recent years as a result. In Kyrgyzstan, on the other hand, erstwhile political stability evaporated early in the first decade of the 21st century, leaving little of the country's early mantle as the "Switzerland of Central Asia." Perhaps the weakest governing elite in Central Asia, Kyrgyzstan is constantly torn by in-fighting, enjoys little popular legitimacy, and faces a strong but undisciplined opposition split along regional lines.

In foreign policy the two countries have pursued a Russia-first approach stemming very much from their weakness and fear of potential threats emanating from Afghanistan and China. The Tajik government relied on support from Moscow to survive the civil war. Both current and

---

[69] Svante E. Cornell and Niklas L. P. Swanström, "The Eurasian Drug Trade: A Challenge to Regional Security," *Problems of Post-Communism* 53, no. 4 (July 2006): 10–28; and Erica Marat, *The State-Crime Nexus in Central Asia: State Weakness, Organized Crime, and Corruption in Kyrgyzstan and Tajikistan*, Silk Road Paper, October 2006 (Washington, D.C.: Central Asia-Caucasus Institute & Silk Road Studies Program, 2006).

former elites in Kyrgyzstan meanwhile look to Moscow for protection—though Russia's help provided little solace for Akayev in the face of the Tulip Revolution. Nevertheless, even these weak states are unwilling to compromise on their sovereignty. The Kyrgyz government faces the most difficult situation, hosting the only remaining U.S. military base in Central Asia and a Russian base less than forty miles away. When Moscow and Beijing capitalized on the U.S.-Uzbek rift to end U.S. presence in Uzbekistan, the two also pressured the new president of Kyrgyzstan, Kurmanbek Bakiyev, to evict the United States. Kyrgyz officials appeared to agree both to Russian demands that Kyrgyzstan expel U.S. troops and to Washington's demands to allow U.S. troops to remain as long as operations in Afghanistan warranted. Eventually, the Kyrgyz government pushed for a multifold hike in the rent paid by the United States for use of the base, obtained essentially through blackmail.

As for Tajikistan, the regime's growing sense of confidence has enabled it to branch out in its foreign relations. President Imomali Rakhmonov opened Tajikistan's first embassy in Washington and joined the Partnership for Peace in 2002. Though symbolic, these steps demonstrate a greater independence than had been apparent in the 1990s, when Tajikistan seemed little more than a Russian vassal in foreign policy matters. Moreover, Tajikistan has worked hard to develop ties with Asian countries. India, for one, has gained a military presence in the country.[70] Tajikistan has also shown greater assertiveness in dealings with Moscow regarding the Russian military presence in the country.

Both Kyrgyzstan and Tajikistan are, despite their weakness, pursuing policies of balance. As Starr observes, however, these countries have done so in an ad hoc manner, never developing or implementing coherent strategies to guide their foreign policies. Instead, Kyrgyzstan and Tajikistan operate in a reactive manner, often improvising to maximize their gains.[71]

Central Asia's Future and U.S. Interests

U.S. future relations with, and access to, Central Asia will largely depend on the ability to formulate a long-term strategy toward the region that incorporates and balances its three sets of interests in the region in a predictable and durable manner. The low ebb of current U.S. influence in Central Asia relates much to Washington's lack of a comprehensive and coordinated strategy. This lack of a clear strategy has enabled policies that

---

[70] Sudha Ramachandran, "India Makes a Soft Landing in Tajikistan," *Asia Times*, March 3, 2007.

[71] Starr, "Kazakhstan's Security Strategy: A Model for Central Asia?" 13–14.

have tended to alienate Central Asian states and have undermined U.S. influence over the policy directions of these countries.

Of course, the Central Asian states themselves will play an important role in determining their bilateral relations with Washington—and in this context the maintenance of positive U.S. relations with Kazakhstan is of key importance. Though U.S. relations with Uzbekistan have the potential for further development, risks are also present. On the U.S. side, Washington's attention span is an important concern, especially given that the outcome of the upcoming presidential election could lead to a change in priorities. On the Kazakh side, in order to develop relations with the United States the government must check the temptation arising from the recent oil bonanza to stall reforms. The length of President Nazarbayev's tenure in power is another concern. As for Uzbekistan, a rapid restoration of the relationship to its previous level is difficult to imagine. A new administration in Washington or in Tashkent could make improved ties a greater possibility, though without the revision of fundamental elements of Uzbek domestic policy a good relationship is unlikely to develop.

Designing policies toward these and other Central Asian states will require a more nuanced view of the Central Asian political scene. Understanding the formal and informal structures in the policymaking environments of these states will be key. U.S. efforts to strengthen formal institutions will be necessary to keep the influence of unpredictable informal structures in check.

The waning of the color revolutions is a positive factor for the United States. Though beneficial for Georgia and Ukraine, these movements caused severe collateral damage to U.S. interests in Central Asia. Washington now has an opportunity both to re-calibrate the democracy promotion agenda to the strategic realities of the region and to mitigate the inadvertent counterproductive effects of policies over the past years. Shifting the emphasis to state-building efforts and to developing dialogue on a wide range of issues (though primarily the three discussed above) would go a long way toward this goal.

Engagement through the development of broad-based relations in multiple fields would provide the best course of action for the long-term strengthening of sovereignty, governance, and democracy. If Western governments view relations in different sectors as complementary rather than conflicting, relations in the energy and security spheres could have important and positive effects on internal reform in the states of the region. Increased energy and security cooperation can be used to develop tighter institutional and bilateral links between the Central Asian countries and the

United States. If used properly these links can in turn be used as a tool to nudge the states gradually in the direction of reform.

Clearly, interests in security or energy should not be allowed to stifle U.S. support for democratic and institutional reform in the region—yet neither should excessive demands for Central Asian countries to achieve overnight a level of democracy comparable to leading Western states at the expense of legitimate security and energy interests or the development of trade relations. It is in the interest of the United States to advance these three issues in parallel, without allowing one to take precedence over the other. Only by the simultaneous promotion of governance, energy, and security interests can the United States succeed in striking a balance among them and thereby contribute to its own security and development as well as to that of the countries of the region.

STRATEGIC ASIA 2007–08

SPECIAL STUDIES

EXECUTIVE SUMMARY

This chapter examines the domestic sources and dynamics of Iran's nuclear program and the implications for Iran's future political orientation.

MAIN ARGUMENTS:
Domestic concerns drive Iran's nuclear program and will determine the program's direction. International pressure will stimulate domestic debate and reappraisal of the regime's plan of action, yet whether such pressure will change Iran's nuclear trajectory before enrichment is mastered remains uncertain. The manner in which the nuclear issue is resolved will determine Iran's future path, both domestically and internationally.

POLICY IMPLICATIONS:
- Keeping a UN coalition intact entails a slow diplomatic pace. If UN sanctions prove inadequate, the U.S. may need to build a broad informal coalition, carefully coordinating with European and Asian states.

- A technical solution to the nuclear issue may necessitate the U.S. devising a comprehensive package to address the broader issues of Iran's "behavior change." Calling for a "regime change" will not encourage Iran to be flexible. Stimulating a fundamental reappraisal of the program within Iran requires both raising the foreign policy costs of such a program and offering generous incentives to make critics of current policy more credible domestically.

- If Iran persists with enrichment, the U.S. will need a containment and deterrence strategy, which would imply closer cooperation with the Gulf Cooperation Council states as well as with Russia and European countries.

- Although a "squeeze" strategy is more effective than confrontation, the U.S. would best be prepared for regional fallout from exercising an ultimate military strike option.

- The major Asian states are affected by Iran's nuclear ambitions to differing degrees. Major economic investments in Iran from Asia, however, will not likely be forthcoming until the nuclear issue is resolved.

Iran: Domestic Politics and Nuclear Choices

Shahram Chubin

Iran's quest for a nuclear capability is the product of domestic politics and the demands of revolutionary legitimacy rather than a strategic imperative. Like those of other states, Iran's motivations for embarking on a nuclear trajectory are multiple and include prestige, status, and security. Yet the persistent motivator behind Iran's nuclear program—and the one most likely to condition the program's pace and eventual shape—is domestic politics. This chapter contends that the direction of Iran's domestic evolution (and the country's external orientation) will determine both whether Iran will accept constraints on its nuclear program and the program's ultimate form. The analysis presented here argues that, apart from broad generalizations, the so-called national consensus in Iran is largely fictive and obscures a basic schism, particularly among the country's elites. On one level, the nuclear issue symbolizes a desire shared by both the elites and public to raise Iran's power and status. Yet on a more profound level, the nuclear issue hides differences both over what type of society Iran should strive to become (pluralistic and open versus fundamentalist and closed) and how the country should relate to the rest of the world (as a normal state versus as a revolutionary state). This leads to two very different notions regarding the uses of a nuclear option. The first notion is that a nuclear capability is a means to regularize Iran's relations with the world, embracing both globalization and domestic reform. The second notion is that a nuclear capability can be used to both deal with the world from a position of power and to perpetuate a vision of Iran as a model of a

Shahram Chubin is Director of Studies at the Geneva Centre for Security Policy. He can be reached at <s.chubin@gcsp.ch>.

revolutionary and anti-Western state. Thus, many different visions of Iran, the country's international role, and the utility of a nuclear capability lie behind the vaunted consensus on the nuclear program. When discussing the factionalism and political infighting, which often relate to tactics and tone, it is also important to recognize the limits imposed on explicit criticism of this issue. Given the restricted nature of the "debate," it is difficult to assess whether there is room for compromise with those who support a "nuclear rights" rubric short of allowing Iran to develop the full fuel cycle. Populist Mahmoud Ahmadinejad's appropriation of the nuclear question as a partisan issue has further politicized the debate, exacerbating factional differences and making a solution based on compromise more difficult.

Iran's ultimate aims for the nuclear program, as well as the program's eventual stopping point, are not clear even to Iranians. A nuclear option within the Treaty on the Non-Proliferation of Nuclear Weapons (NPT) may be preferable to one faction yet inadequate to another; for one group a nuclear option is a bargaining chip, while for another it is an equalizer. Measures that condemn or isolate Iran without threats and overt interference and that impose economic costs on pursuing the program will stimulate greater internal debate about the country's proper course. Such measures might slow—even reorient—the program. The critical question, however, is whether the timeframe of Iran's technical progress and that of political sanctions (and suspension) can be synchronized. If not, the emergence of a nuclear Iran will ultimately consolidate the regime's hard-liners and profoundly destabilize the immediate region and Asia.

This chapter examines the political and strategic context of the nuclear program first by examining Iran's self image, grand strategy, and view of the world in general and Asia in particular. The second section analyzes the origins and motivations influencing the program, the relationship between the program and Iranian nationalism with reference to the role of public opinion and debate, and decisionmaking and the vested interests behind the program. The role of factionalism and domestic politics in the nuclear program is examined here. The third section addresses the political dynamics and Iran's options. In noting the uncertainties surrounding Iran's ultimate intentions and the current status of the program, this section argues that external powers have the ability to influence the program's direction through pressure and inducement, while Iran's strategic options are limited. This section also looks at the role of Asia in determining the future outcome of Iran's nuclear program. Lastly, in the conclusion the chapter examines Iran's strategic options and draws implications from this analysis for U.S. policy toward Iran.

The Islamic Republic and the World

The External Environment and Grand Strategy

As often follows great revolutions, Iran has an ambivalent view of the world, seeing it as hostile, yet simultaneously demanding international recognition and promoting itself as a model for others. Iran's quest for status, influence, and respect implies that the country is asserting its own path and independence.

Rejecting the international system as unjust and overly influenced by the United States, Iran has developed a deep distrust of normal diplomacy and international institutions (seemingly proven by the failure by the international community to act against Iraqi aggression in 1980). In the early period of the revolution Iran sought to distance itself from the major powers and, by seeking to export its revolution and the use of terrorism as a political instrument, provoked a coalition of Arab states against it. Notwithstanding uneven relations with its neighbors and their allies, Iran sees itself as a victim of the manipulations and interference of other states—both currently and historically. Feelings of grievance and injury are matched by a sense of entitlement and thwarted ambition.[1]

The external environment is thus seen as an arena of both danger and opportunity. The United States is the barrier to Iran's ambitions of becoming both the "natural" hegemon in the Persian Gulf and the dominant power in the prevailing regional order.[2] In this view, the U.S. threat has recently increased because current U.S. policies have positioned the United States as a major local player. Iran sees the U.S. presence as intended both to extend control over regional resources and to buttress local clients, such as Israel. Declared policies of "regime change" add to Iran's insecurity, notwithstanding the U.S. entanglement in Iraq. Additionally, Tehran is convinced of undying U.S. hostility in part because Washington has never recognized Iran's revolution. Iran sees the United States as having a new strategy that seeks to stir up ethnic tensions on Iran's periphery (Kurdistan, Azerbaijan, and Baluchistan) while promoting and aggravating sectarian differences within the region.

The security of the regime—the "Islamic system"—remains Iran's overriding priority that determines all other policies and requires Iran to actively explore all available options. Iran's grand strategy has focused on reducing U.S. power in the region by organizing the region against the United States. Given its military weakness, however, Iran's strategy has

---

[1] Ali Larijani, speech given at the Middle East Center, Tehran, October 27, 2005 and reprinted in *Journal of European Society for Iranian Studies*, no. 1 (Winter 2005): 125–31.

[2] See Ray Takeyh, *Hidden Iran* (New York: Times Books, 2006), 61.

been indirect, leveraging regional conflicts and instabilities to pressure the United States and its allies. Entailing a posture of "forward defense," Iran uses this spoiler strategy by investing assets wherever possible—in Palestine with Hamas and Islamic Jihad, in Lebanon with Hezbollah, in Afghanistan with both the government and anti-government forces, and with diverse Shi'a and Sunni elements in Iraq that include the Mahdi army, Supreme Islamic Iraqi Council, and the insurgency.

Where the rejectionist front has little support among governments in the region, Iran can appeal to popular opinion in Arab countries. Here Iran can invoke its own revolutionary model and experience in battling against superior odds in the Iran-Iraq War. That struggle strengthened the regime internally, fusing self-reliance, nationalism, and revolutionary pride, as well as confirming the need for military preparedness to avoid technical surprises (such as Saddam Hussein's use of chemical weapons). The war has passed into the realm of myth—its values of resistance and martyrdom are constantly celebrated and reaffirmed; Iran now claims that its experience is applicable to others, for example invoking Hezbollah's model of resistance as its own.

Iran's regional activism and claims to a larger constituency serves the regime's interests by both pointing to the continued validity of its revolutionary stances and promoting a sense of embattlement that serves to suppress domestic debate about Iran's course. Iran's isolation is thus welcomed as proof of its moral stature and integrity; officials dismiss hardship and sanctions as the price of independence.

Mahmoud Ahmadinejad's administration is exceptional not in its perception of a hostile world but in its confrontational rhetoric and activism. His constituency represents the second generation of the revolution—drawn from the Islamic Revolutionary Guards Corp (IRGC) and its paramilitary counterpart the Basij—which espouses "Iran's longstanding goals" and welcomes confrontation if only to prove its revolutionary credentials.[3] Foreign policy is thus very much an extension of domestic politics.

Since the revolution Iran has learned from experience that when domestic problems (notably ones of an economic nature) are intractable, the most convenient and plausible excuse is to attribute such difficulties to foreign machinations and threats. Foreign hostility provides a clear excuse from the mundane concerns of economic performance and has so far proven unfailingly successful as a diversion.

Iranian public opinion overwhelmingly supports an active role for Iran in the world (86%) and believes that Iran's "influence in the world"

---

[3] See John Negroponte, "Annual Threat Assessment of the Director of National Intelligence," statement to the Senate Select Committee on Intelligence, January 11, 2007, 6.

is positive (83%).[4] Although most Iranians believe that Iran is entitled to respect and aspirations of equality, there is no evidence of a new infusion of revolutionary spirit. There is likely a disconnect between the revolutionary government of 2005 and a society experiencing post-revolutionary exhaustion, political apathy, and a need to focus on basic economic and social welfare issues.

Broadly stated, Iran's strategy lends itself to two approaches regarding the nuclear issue. One is to seek to cut a deal with the United States, trusting in enough mutual interests to fashion a durable agreement. The other is to confront the United States with enough power to make Washington reconsider its policies. The first approach implies Iran's willingness both to moderate the country's revolutionary ambitions in the region and to temper independence with greater engagement. The second approach insists on Iran's taking its own path, resisting pressures, and compelling others to accept the country on its own terms. These two approaches are reflected in the principal factions on the nuclear issue and also have different implications for domestic politics—one based on calm and orderly debate and the other on mobilization and a siege mentality.

Asia in Iran's Grand Strategy

Iran has found little regional resonance for its campaign to replace the U.S. presence with an indigenous security architecture in the Persian Gulf. With its traditional westward orientation effectively blocked, Iran has sought Asian support. Under the Shah tentative steps were taken in relations toward India and China. Later Iran's goals and nuclear ambitions put Tehran at odds with the European Union (EU) as well as with the states of the Gulf Cooperation Council (GCC). During the Iran-Iraq War sanctions and embargoes limited Iran's access to arms and spare parts, forcing a shift to China, North Korea, and Russia that has since continued, with Asia replacing the West as the source of Iran's conventional arms and missiles. In the 1990s Iran continued "looking east" as much to diversify political relations and reduce dependence on the West as from any economic incentive. The direction of Iran's oil exports also began to shift toward the East during this period.[5]

---

[4] "Public Opinion in Iran and America on Key International Issues," WorldPublicOpinion.org (conducted in partnership with Search for Common Ground and Knowledge Networks), January 24, 2007, http://www.worldpublicopinion.org/pipa/pdf/jan07/Iran_Jan07_rpt.pdf.

[5] Japan, China, South Korea, and India respectively are Iran's main energy export markets. In 2004–05 Asia accounted for 50% of Iranian crude exports (versus Western Europe at 30%). See Fereidun Fesharaki, "Energy Issues in Iran" (paper presented at the Oil and Money Conference, London, September 2006), 3.

The Khatami presidency (1997–2005) placed priority on normalization of relations first with GCC states and then with Europe. Relations with Asia, particularly India, were not neglected, however. Replacing Khatami in 2005, Ahmadinejad made a more deliberate effort to cultivate Asia as an alternative to the West. This strategy has involved leveraging Iran's energy resources in order to consolidate alliances.[6] Reflected in its obtaining observer status in the Shanghai Cooperation Organization in June 2006 and in the South Asian Association for Regional Cooperation in April 2007, Iran's aim has been to drive a wedge between the Asian and Western states, especially the UN Security Council (UNSC) members, in terms of dealing with Iran's nuclear program. Iran's belief that dangling trade incentives before the key Asian states would allow Tehran to buy their support has proven mistaken and seems to reflect an exaggerated sense of self-importance.[7] These reversals, however, have not prevented Iran's continued attempts to play the commercial card by insisting that the nuclear issue is not "political."

Iran has misjudged its own importance as a strategic ally and market as well as its ability to divide and play the great powers against each other. Although Asia remains an option for support that could be cemented by trade, investment, and even strategic cooperation (especially with India), all of these possibilities will remain curtailed as long as the nuclear crisis persists.

The Domestic Politics of Nuclear Decisions

The Origins, Motives, and Rationales for the Nuclear Program

States rarely embark on a nuclear program with only one aim—energy, security, and status may all be considerations. An evolving context, different leaders, and changing priorities all complicate an assessment of the "real" motives behind the program. First cancelled by the revolutionary authorities, Iran's nuclear program was revived in 1985 during the war with Iraq. The rationale for the program, which first revolved around the sunk costs in the Bushehr reactor, shifted to energy diversification in the 1990s. Since then, motivations such as the need for energy security, control over the full fuel cycle, and the aim of eventually becoming a supplier of enrichment services have been stressed. Mastery of enrichment has also been depicted

---

[6] Jad Mouwad, "Iran Uses Its Oil Assets to Create Alliances," *New York Times*, April 30, 2005.

[7] Critics within Iran have noted this strategy's limits, with one suggesting that Iran treat the votes of India, China, and Russia as a "barometer for assessing Iran's present position in the world." *E'temad* website on September 26, 2005, available though BBC Monitoring, September 27, 2005.

by officials both as opening the way for Iran to enter the circle of advanced scientific powers and as a type of self-reliance.[8]

Characterized by persistence and incrementalism rather than urgent strategic necessity, Iran's nuclear program was far from being a crash program during the period from 1986 to 2003. Investment continued nonetheless encompassing various presidencies and stages of war and reconstruction. Significantly, the program accelerated in 1999 at a time when U.S.-Iran relations were less strained and Saddam Hussein was boxed in by UN inspections.[9] The rhythm of the program corresponded with the availability of suppliers, relying first on China, then on A.Q. Khan, and later on Iran's own progress in mastering the technology. An example of Sagan's "solution searching for a problem," the program reflects no clear or consistent rationale.[10]

What of the officially stated energy rationale as motivation? It is true that nuclear energy is experiencing a resurgence as a clean source of energy with fewer adverse effects on climate change than other sources. Diversification of energy sources is also prudent for a country that cannot indefinitely rely on indigenous resources due to a growing population and rising domestic consumption. Yet Iran's explanation for the quest for the full fuel cycle—that nuclear power would make Iran self sufficient for energy and allow the country to compete in the global market for supplying enriched fuel—is much weaker. Iran does not have indigenous uranium and will always be dependent on imports. At this stage in development enrichment makes no economic sense for Iran and will not do so until the country has approximately a dozen reactors. Taken together with its refusal to consider suspension, Tehran's insistence on urgently mastering the full cycle raises the question of whether there is another motive. Complicating the issue further is Tehran's secrecy, cat-and-mouse games with the International Atomic Energy Agency (IAEA), and deliberate cultivation of ambiguity regarding joining the nuclear club.[11] Iran's stated aims are hardly plausible

---

[8] Hossein Faqihiyan, Director-General of Nuclear Fuel Production Company and deputy to the Atomic Energy Organization of Iran (AEOI), was cited by a daily newspaper as stating: "If today we insist on having [the] fuel cycle, [it] is because we want to generate scientific creativity and innovation inside the country…Big powers want to prevent the developing countries from gaining these abilities. Having a nuclear fuel cycle significantly helps a country to reach stable development." *Farhang-e Ashti* on May 4, 2006, available through BBC Monitoring, May 10, 2006.

[9] See Hasan Rowhani, interview with Fars News Agency on May 12, 2006, available through BBC Monitoring, May 14, 2006. For background, see Shahram Chubin, *Iran's Nuclear Ambitions* (Washington, D.C.: Carnegie Endowment, 2006).

[10] Scott Sagan, "Why Do States Build Nuclear Weapons? Three Models in Search of a Bomb," *International Security* 21, no. 3 (Winter 1996–97): 65.

[11] See Chubin, *Iran's Nuclear Ambitions*, 63–80; and Mark Fitzpatrick, "Assessing Iran's Nuclear Programme," *Survival* 48, no. 3 (Autumn 2006): 5–26.

or credible in light of other evidence, most notably the secrecy surrounding Iran's enrichment activities that were brought to light in 2002.

None of this would be necessary if the program was indeed motivated by an above-board energy rationale. By insisting that its "rights" (i.e., right to peaceful uses of nuclear energy as a signatory under the NPT) include enrichment, Iran is seeking to exploit this gap in the treaty (while remaining within the NPT); Iran's goal is clearly to move as far as possible toward achieving the capability to produce weapons-grade fissile material.[12] Iran has had reasons to seek a hedge, most notably against Saddam Hussein during the Iran-Iraq War. More recently the U.S. presence in the region has given Tehran cause for seeking some type of deterrent, especially following the introduction of the phrase "regime change" into the U.S. lexicon in 2002. Iran's access to conventional arms is both limited and costly, so a focus on missiles and WMD has appeared attractive. Likewise, an equalizer might be seen as a necessary insurance policy. Iran's own regional policies—which tend to antagonize or frighten its neighbors, leaving Tehran isolated—lead to a further rationale for weapons to counter the self-induced sense of siege.

Frustrated nationalism and aspirations for regional influence are additional reasons for Iran to seek such capabilities. A nuclear-capable state can expect to be listened to more attentively and consulted regularly. By the mid-1990s Iran's regime had lost support for its revolutionary values. Having failed to deliver economic gains, the regime had no performance legitimacy on which to fall back. The nuclear program was clearly intended to serve this purpose—to boost the regime's support base and legitimacy.[13]

If Iran's motives for nuclear technology are both shifting and multiple, and the program is faltering, how determined is Iran to acquire a nuclear capability? Is the decision to "go nuclear" reversible and sensitive to costs and inducements? Iran's program has been undertaken for reasons that are as much motivated by grandeur and influence as by concrete security concerns.[14] Implicit in Iran's rationale is the assumption of increased influence. The nature of both the program and of Iranian diplomacy since 2003 suggest that Iran does not have a predetermined end in mind, for the

---

[12] For similar analysis, see Shahram Chubin, "Does Iran Want Nuclear Weapons?" *Survival* 37, no. 1 (Spring 1995): 81–104; Fitzpatrick, "Assessing Iran's Nuclear Programme," 5–26; and Shahram Chubin, *Whither Iran? Domestic Reform and Security Policy*, Adelphi Paper 342, (Oxford: Oxford University Press for the International Institute of Strategic Studies, 2002): 76–78.

[13] See also Chubin, "Does Iran Want Nuclear Weapons?"; Chubin, "Whither Iran?"; and Mohsen Sazegara, "The Point of No Return," The Washington Institute for Near East Policy, *Policy Focus*, no. 54, April 2006, 7, 10.

[14] Iran corresponds to Sagan's third model where symbols and status rather than security or particular interest groups account for the existence of the program. See Sagan, "Why Do States Build Nuclear Weapons?" 78.

sake of which it is willing to accept any cost. Instead, Iran appears to be testing the resolve of the international community, waiting to see the world's reaction to Tehran's provocations before deciding on an ultimate end point. Iran would like to create a *fait accompli* yet, absent an overriding security imperative, Iran's decision to pursue a nuclear capability appears flexible in principle and open to being delayed or even reversed. For this change to occur, however, the price of continuing to develop a nuclear capability will need to outweigh that of stopping the program. Because public opinion is not united on this issue and political dynamics within Iran are not all aligned in support of current policy, unacceptable costs will prove to be measures that threaten the regime's control of power—measures that generate significant popular discontent. This logic implies, therefore, that the international community will need to demonstrate unity in implementing sanctions that hurt the government and the citizenry.

Nationalism and Public Opinion: The Nuclear Issue in Context

By creating a sense of embattlement and protracted crises, Tehran has used external threats in order to keep the populace mobilized and unified behind the regime and reduce scope for criticism or domestic debate. Iranian politics remain intensely parochial and doctrinal, focused on the minutia of factional debates and maneuvers. Such characteristics obscure and distort the regime's understanding of international concerns and account for Tehran's systematic misjudgment evident in the nuclear case.[15]

The Iranian regime has invested the nuclear issue with a great deal of symbolism, treating the country's accession to the ranks of states that have mastered nuclear technology as something even more significant— the arrival of Iran as a great power in its own right. By equating science, technology, and power with peaceful nuclear power, the regime has depicted Iran's progress toward entry into an "exclusive club."[16] The leadership is convinced that attaining an enrichment capability will unlock untold riches and assure regime security.[17] Supreme Leader Ali Khamenei, for example, has stated that "the nuclear issue is not…just of concern today. It is an issue

---

[15] Iran has misjudged the possibility of dividing the EU-3 (Germany, Britain, and France) from the United States, the likelihood of referral to the UNSC and a UNSC sanctions resolution, and the probability of a military strike. Finally, in the author's view, Tehran misjudges the utility of nuclear weapons.

[16] "World Must Accept Iran's Entry into the Nuclear Club—Hasan Rowhani," Vision of the Islamic Republic of Iran Network 1 on March 7, 2004, available through BBC Monitoring, March 8, 2004; and "Rafsanjani Says Iran Expected to Join Club of Nuclear States," Islamic Republic News Agency (IRNA) website on December 3, 2004, available though BBC Monitoring, December 4, 2004.

[17] See Mohammed ElBaradei interview in Daniel Dombey, "Pressure Mounts on Iran over Its Nuclear Programme," *Financial Times*, February 21, 2007, 3.

for…the country's future. It is an issue that concerns the country's destiny."[18] By elevating the issue, the nuclear question becomes one that transcends politics, factions, or diplomacy. Hence Iran is naturally likely to resist efforts that hinder its progress and render the country dependent.[19]

Hard-line newspapers such as *Keyhan* that have quasi-official status have more leeway in their editorials than their dwindling and intimidated reformist counterparts. This imbalance sets the tone for—and skews—the public "debate." Public opinion is deceptive on the nuclear issue, being supportive of Iran's rights yet not keen to suffer economically or politically from confrontation with the international community. The more educated are also skeptical of the regime's intentions. Aware of this, Iran's leaders have made no effort to promote debate or discussion on its approach to the nuclear question. Framing the issue as one of rights, denial, double standards, respect, and dictation, the regime has played on the sense of Iran's victimization and historical grievance among the populace.[20]

Outsiders erroneously tend to see Iranians as all having the same opinions on the nuclear issue. True, the issue has become a litmus test of nationalism. Most Iranians accept the proposition that the nuclear issue reflects general discrimination against Iran obtaining all advanced technology, not just nuclear.[21] Some see the issue as fundamentally related to "the way that world powers view the nature of Iran's regime."[22] For others the nuclear issue is intrinsically linked both to the type of state Iran is and seeks to become and to the type of relations Tehran seeks with other states.[23] Most Iranians support the quest for status, respect, and aspirations for a broader regional role. They see advanced technology, scientific progress, and independence as linked and desirable. On one level, therefore, there is national consensus on Iran's nuclear program. At this level it is a unifying platform for the regime—one that is fully exploited. Beyond this level, however, unity fractures. Official polls do suggest that approximately 80% of the populace is supportive of the program; such polls do not reveal,

---

[18] Cited by Voice of the Islamic Republic of Iran, February 17, 2007, available through BBC Monitoring, February 19, 2007.

[19] Text of report in English by IRNA on February 4, 2007, available through BBC Monitoring, February 4, 2007.

[20] See Gareth Smyth, "Fundamentalists, Pragmatists and the Rights of the Nation: Iranian Politics and the Nuclear Confrontation," *Century Foundation Report*, December 15, 2006.

[21] Larijani has referred to the desire to keep Iran as an industrial backwater. Interview in *Financial Times*, January 23, 2006, 4.

[22] See *Jomhuri-ye Eslami* website on December 1, 2005, available through BBC Monitoring, December 28, 2005.

[23] See Ahmad Shirzad, *E'temad* website on December 25, 2005, available through BBC Monitoring, January 5, 2006.

however, how the questions that elicit such overwhelming support are phrased. Given the gap between state and society, support for the program would be carefully conditioned too if the proposition that it might help in the consolidation of the current regime was added in the question poll.[24]

An informed debate about energy rationale in the context of alternative policies and options has never been encouraged. Until 2002 public opinion was neither a driver nor a constraint on nuclear development and popular will remains clearly a background factor in decisionmaking on nuclear policy. Public dissatisfaction with the costs of the program or sanctions associated with it, however, cannot be ignored. Both hard-liners and pragmatists have invoked public opinion as an important consideration in pursuing the program. The latter group, appealing generally to the middle class, cautions that the danger and costs of pursuing a confrontational policy are likely to weaken the regime. Pragmatists fear risk of a rapid economic crash with consequent damage to the regime if the current course is pursued. The second broad grouping, made up of conservatives and appealing largely to fundamentalists, having manipulated the issue themselves now feel constrained by public opinion against retreat.[25]

Nationalism is accompanied by the demand for economic development—the principal concern for most Iranians—which the nuclear program potentially threatens.[26] Where public support and consensus on this program's continuation clearly fade is in terms of the resulting sanctions, loss of investment confidence, capital flight, and international estrangement.[27]

---

[24] See also Michael Herzog, "Iranian Public Opinion on the Nuclear Program," Washington Institute for Near East Policy, Policy Focus, no. 56, June 2006, 4–5; and Karim Sajadpour, "How Relevant Is the Iranian Street?" *Washington Quarterly* 30, no. 1 (2007): 151–62.

[25] Chen Kane, "Nuclear Decision Making in Iran: A Rare Glimpse," Crown Center for Middle East Studies at Brandeis University, Middle East Brief, no. 5, May 2006.

[26] See Tellier, "The Iranian Moment," 15, 23; Sajadpour, "How Relevant is the Iranian Street?" 151–62; and Naghmeh Sohrabi, "Conservatives, Neoconservatives and Reformists: Iran After the Election of Mahmud Ahmadinejad," Crown Center for Middle East Studies at Brandeis University, Middle East Brief, no. 4, April 2006.

[27] See especially Shahram Chubin and Robert S. Litwak, "Debating Iran's Nuclear Aspirations," *Washington Quarterly* 26, no. 4 (2003): 104–7; Herzog, "Iranian Public Opinion on the Nuclear Program"; and Mahan Abdin, "Public Opinion and the Nuclear Standoff," Mideast Mirror 1, no. 2 (April/May 2006). A Zogby/Readers Digest poll reports that 41% of Iranians put reforming the economy before having a nuclear capability (27%). See "Zogby International Poll of Iranians Reveals a Society in Flux", July 13, 2006, http://www.zogby.com/news/ReadNews.dbm?ID=1147. A more recent poll reports that 84% of Iranians think it is very important for Iran to have a full fuel cycle and 89% for Iran to have a nuclear energy program. See "Public Opinion in Iran and America on Key International Issues."

Nuclear Decisionmaking

Policy reflects narrower institutional and political considerations as well. The broad political context and climate necessarily affect decisions. **Figure 1** provides an approximate schematic reflecting Iran's opaque nuclear decisionmaking structure. Just as Iranian opinion is not monolithic, nuclear decisionmaking is not the product of a unitary system; decisionmaking reflects institutional inputs and interest group biases. In addition the supreme leader's "soundings" among his clerical network (in Qom and elsewhere) and the primacy of informal networks and procedures are as influential as formal organograms.[28]

Despite claims that the system of government has popular support, Iran's administration operates in near secrecy. An unelected and unaccountable cabal makes sensitive decisions without acting transparently, obscuring its actions even from the legislature (the Majlis). The nuclear program, especially its secret components, has been the domain of a small group of people, among whom former president Hashemi Rafsanjani (now head of the influential Expediency Council) is the most prominent. It is likely that the leaders of the Atomic Energy Organization of Iran (AEOI), the longstanding members of the Supreme National Security Council (SNSC) such as Hasan Rowhani, former IRGC commander Mohsen Reza'i, and former foreign minister Ali Akbar Velayati have had knowledge of the program. Parts of the IRGC have been responsible for the security of installations. Until mid-2002 there was little discussion and no indication of a debate over the nuclear program, nuclear weapons, or current and future strategy. In 2003 experts complained of being excluded from participating in elite discussions, which they perceived to be taking place within a "security halo" and with little reference to the economic feasibility of the proposed program.[29]

Among the inputs into decisions are interested parties such as the AEOI, which looks to its own institutional interests and is a strong supporter of the nuclear program. The AEOI provides input on the technical side, points to valuable experience acquired, and underscores the costs of a long suspension of activities in terms of morale and attrition of scientific personnel.

---

[28] See Amir Ali Nourbakhsh, "Iran's Foreign Policy & its Key Decision Makers," Payvand's Iran News website (originally written for the Tharwa Project), April 25, 2005, http://www.payvand.com/news/05/apr/1188.html; and Mohsen Sazegara, "Iran: Toward a Fourth Republic?" Washington Institute for Near East Policy, Policy Watch, no. 1001, 2005.

[29] "Iranian MP Proposes Nuclear Energy Plant Rethink," Yas-e Now website on December 8, 2003, available through BBC Monitoring, December 9, 2003. Nur Pir-Mozen, a Majlis Deputy and nuclear specialist, observed that "We still do not know what has been going on in Bushehr for the past thirty years." "Majlis Deputy Questions Spending on Nuclear Power Plant," *Mardom-Salari* website on October 5, 2005, available through BBC Monitoring, October 7, 2005.

FIGURE 1   Institutional flow of decisionmaking in Iran

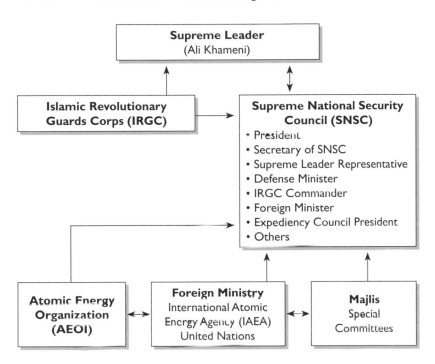

NOTE: Iranian politics are highly informal and personal; institutional influence depends largely on personal ties.

The Foreign Ministry and SNSC argue the costs of estrangement and confrontation with Europe and the IAEA, as well as point to international obligations. The appointment of Rowhani, longstanding secretary of the SNSC and pragmatist, as chief nuclear negotiator in 2003 was in itself a significant choice indicative of the prevailing political environment at the time. With the entrance of a more conservative and hard-line government in August 2005, the composition of the SNSC leadership accordingly changed, as did the negotiating team and the principal negotiator (with Larijani replacing Rowhani).

Establishing consensus is a form of self-protection for the elite, implying collective decisionmaking and responsibility with little room for opting out or criticism. Such use of consensus also serves as a safety net for particularly contentious topics—such as reversing course on the nuclear program—while also acting as insurance against foreign exploitation of internal differences.

The default position on national security issues remains hard line (under the more pragmatic Khatami presidency even Khatami himself was marginalized on security issues). The supreme leader, who has the final word, is said to balance factional demands, but as arbiter it is unclear whether he follows or forms the prevailing consensus. Although he appears comfortable with hard-liners, ambiguity over Khamenei's role in consensus-building has made Iran's foreign and security policies seem incoherent.[30] Increasingly Khamenei is being upstaged by President Ahmadinejad, a populist whom Khamenei is reluctant to overrule or discipline.[31] This complex political situation, taken together with the nuclear program's momentum, indicates that obtaining a reversal or freeze will be more difficult, requiring the type of decisive decisionmaking foreign to Khamenei.[32]

Vested Interests and the Nuclear Program

Although officially denied, alongside the ostensible energy rationale there is a security motive for the nuclear program. Both of the strongest supporters of the program, the AEOI and the IRGC, also have vested organizational interests in the program, although their interests are neither identical nor their political weight equal.

Iran envisages an ambitious nuclear energy program that includes approximately a dozen reactors generating about 10,000 megawatts (MW).[33] To become fully self-reliant in energy, Iran plans to master all aspects of nuclear energy from extraction through enrichment.[34] As a result, there has been parallel growth of constituencies and bureaucracies

---

[30] Ali Gheissari and Vali Nasr, "The Conservative Consolidation in Iran," *Survival* 47, no. 2 (2005): 176.

[31] See Bernard Hourcade, "Iran's Internal Security Challenges" in Walter Posch, ed., "Iranian Challenges," Chaillot Paper 89 (Paris: EU Institute for Security Studies, 2006): 57.

[32] See Marie Claude Decamps, "L'Iran veut negocier sur la dossier nucleaire sans perdre la face," [Iran Wants to Negotiate the Nuclear Issue without Loss of Face] *Le Monde*, March 9, 2007, 1.

[33] The figures vary from ten to twenty reactors and between 7,000 MW and 10,000 MW. See "Iran Experts Say Nuclear Power Necessary for Electricity Generation," Vision of the Islamic Republic of Iran Network 1 on June 13, 2004, available through BBC Monitoring, June 14, 2004; "Majlis Deputy Says Iran Needs Nine More Nuclear Power Plants," Voice of the Islamic Republic of Iran on October 25, 2004, available through BBC Monitoring, October 26, 2004; and "Iran Majlis Studying Proposals on Construction of 20 Nuclear Power Plants—MP," Mehr News Agency on January 30, 2005, available through BBC Monitoring, February 1, 2005.

[34] Deputy Head of the AEOI Mohammad Saidi, "Nuclear Energy Top Priority in Iran's Nuclear Programme—Official," IRNA on March 22, 2005, available through BBC Monitoring, March 23, 2005; and Elaine Sciolino, "Iran and the US Have One Thing in Common," *International Herald Tribune*, March 23, 2005, 4.

that will benefit from the program.[35] The AEOI is clearly one of the main beneficiaries of the program's ambitious scope. By furnishing technical input in the process, the organization has an enormous stake in the program and nuclear policy in general.

The AEOI's opposition to freezing enrichment is due in part to the potential impact on retaining and employing scientific personnel.[36] One expert has argued that the costs of suspension are, at minimum, the loss of $5 billion and failure of fifteen years of effort. Stopping and restarting the spinning of centrifuges is technically demanding at Iran's current level of capability and will likely lead to crashes and costly delays to the program. From a technical standpoint, the argument is that the elimination of any one of the five phases of nuclear production "will render all other phases and the efforts of scientists in past years ineffective."[37]

The AEOI argues for an unconstrained program on security grounds as well, claiming that "if we do not produce nuclear fuel inside our country, they will use fuel as leverage to threaten our independence and territorial integrity in the future."[38] Gholam Reza Aghazadeh, head of the AEOI, tirelessly promotes the program and compares the quest for indigenous enrichment with the need for food self-sufficiency. By not being subject to political turnover, the AEOI has special clout within the decisionmaking process that comes from having a steadfast position, consistent line, and a constant presence.[39]

Growing political and economic influence make the IRGC a formidable policy actor with security as well as commercial interests.[40] Most analysts

---

[35] See Takeyh, *Hidden Iran*, 139–40, 154, 156. He notes that some 250 scientists wrote a letter urging the government not to cede its rights to technology.

[36] See comments by AEOI Chief Aghazadeh in "Iran's Atomic Energy Chief Says Suspension of Uranium Enrichment Problematic," Iranian Students News Agency (ISNA) on December 12, 2003, available through BBC Monitoring, December 12, 2003. On the retention of personnel indispensable for further nuclear progress, see comments by Aghazadeh in "Iranian Officials Discuss Ways to Retain Nuclear Scientists," *Shargh* website on December 16, 2004, available through BBC Monitoring, December 20, 2004.

[37] See "Cessation of Iran's Enrichment Programme Not an Option—Agency," *Baztab* website on March 30, 2005, available through BBC Monitoring, April 1, 2005.

[38] AEOI Deputy Director Mohammad Sai'di, Mehr News Agency (in English), January 17, 2007, available through BBC Monitoring, January 18, 2007.

[39] See ISNA website, March 7, 2007, available through BBC Monitoring, March 8, 2007. For the continuity of the AEOI in decisionmaking, see ISNA on April 17, 2007, available through BBC Monitoring, April 18, 2007.

[40] Commercial interests also make the IRGC reluctant to normalize relations with the West. See Karim Sadjadpour interview: "Revolutionary Guards Have a Financial Interest in Keeping Iran Isolated," *New York Times*, May 29, 2007, http://www.nytimes.com/cfr/world/slot1_20070529. html?pagewanted=print.

believe that the IRGC is the strongest lobby for a nuclear option.[41] Tasked formally with the "defense of the revolution" (as opposed to territorial or national defense) the IRGC has been put in charge of the missile force and nuclear installations yet its mission and accountability remain opaque. Iran's nuclear program, both ambitious and expensive, yields opportunities for graft, and the IRGC's security role has been eclipsed by its commercial activities. Together with affiliates, the IRGC has become an economic force by winning over $5 billion in no-bid contracts from the government.[42] These unusual commercial activities are paralleled by black market smuggling of subsidized oil for export and other questionably legal activities.[43]

The increasing role of the IRGC in Iran's politics is another source of concern. Of 152 new members elected to the Majlis in February 2004, 91 had IRGC backgrounds. A further 34 former IRGC officers hold senior-level posts in the government.[44] In the June 2005 presidential elections, there were 3 other candidates from the IRGC besides Ahmadinejad. The growing dominance of the IRGC and intelligence officials in government could open the country to a new militarism.[45] Both by not answering to authority and by interpreting issues of great concern in a unilateral manner, the IRGC is acting like a "state within a state."[46] The IRGC's autonomy and insulation from government control obfuscate whether particular activities reflect the "decentralized nature of power" in Iran or are in fact extensions of government policy. For example, attributing responsibility for the Qods Brigade's activities in Iraq to the Iranian leadership has been difficult. Recent behavior suggests that the IRGC is not "afraid of provoking a crisis."[47] This was illustrated in February 2007 when IRGC elements were reported to have secretly painted their emblem on the side of a U.S. warship.[48] A similar

---

[41] Ray Takeyh, "Understanding the Iran Crisis," testimony before the U.S. House Committee on Foreign Affairs, Washington, D.C., January 31, 2007.

[42] "Iran: Ahmadinejad's Tumultuous Presidency," International Crisis Group, Middle East Briefing no. 21, February 6, 2007, 12–14.

[43] Abbas Milani, "Understanding the Iran Crisis," testimony before the U.S. House Committee on Foreign Affairs, Washington, D.C., January 31, 2007, 8–9.

[44] Figures quoted from Judith Yaphe and Charles Lutes, "Reassessing the Implications of a Nuclear Iran," Institute for Strategic Studies at the National Defense University, McNair Paper, no. 69, 2005, 6.

[45] See Bill Sami'i, "The Military-Mullah Complex: The Militarization of Iranian Politics," Weekly Standard, May 14, 2005; and Mohsen Sazegara, "The New Iranian Government: Resurrecting Past Errors," The Washington Institute for Near East Policy, Policy Watch, no. 1013, July 2005.

[46] Ali M. Ansari, Confronting Iran (New York: Basic Books, 2006): 218–20.

[47] The phrase is Ansari's; see Ansari, Confronting Iran.

[48] See the report in Keyhan website on February 14, 2007, available through BBC Monitoring, February 15, 2007.

example took place in March 2007 when the IRGC took prisoner fifteen British sailors, who were later released.[49]

Since the debate among the leadership over nuclear weapons is not accessible, we can only conjecture about the role of the IRGC in such a debate. As the custodians of the related missile technology, the IRGC does support military technologies that have equalizing or "short-cut" capabilities. Support for the nuclear program is an outgrowth of experience with missiles and chemical weapons in the Iran-Iraq War. A nuclear missile option could serve both as a deterrent and as a means to project power and influence regionally. During the last phase of the Iran-Iraq War, IRGC Commander Reza'i argued that Iran could not hope to win the war without nuclear weapons.[50] The nuclear option would also, importantly, reinforce the IRGC vis-à-vis the larger regular armed forces. Apart from demonstrating skepticism toward arms control agreements, the IRGC has not publicly expressed an institutional view about nuclear weapons. Like other hard-liners in the regime, however, it has supported the nuclear program. In private, and in the SNSC, the IRGC may be expected to strongly favor pressing forward with the nuclear program with minimum constraints.

The Nuclear Debate and Political Factionalism

From the outset of the revolution, Iran's political power structure has been diffuse and decentralized. As a consequence, domestic politics are volatile and produce inconsistent policies that often appear to have resulted from a game of tug-of-war. Behind common support for the "system," strenuous political infighting is the norm. This often bitter rivalry has largely been over turf and patronage (i.e., power) rather than differences of principle. Iran's current political structure is also polarized between those who want Iran to liberalize and those who see liberalization as undermining their power. Given that the top-heavy state is providing subsidies it cannot afford, the regime is unable to make necessary economic reforms and instead relies on short-term solutions that only aggravate an accumulating number of problems.[51]

---

[49] Besides retaliation for U.S. arrests of Iranian soldiers in Iraq, the most plausible explanation for this episode is that it was political diversion for the unpopularity of the regime. See Juan Cole, "Iran's New Hostage Crisis," Salon.com website, April 3, 2007, http://www.salon.com/opinion/feature/2007/04/03/iran/.

[50] See Najmeh Bozorghmehr, "Nuclear Row Sparks Echoes of Iran's Brutal War with Iraq," *Financial Times*, October 26, 2006, 5; and Rasool Nafisi, "The Khomeini Letter: Is Rafsanjani Warning the Hardliners?" at http://www.iranian.com/RasoolNafisi/2006/October/Nuclear/index.html.

[51] See Parvin Alizadeh, "Iran's Quandary: Economic Reform and the 'Structural Trap,'" *Brown Journal of World Affairs* 9, no. 2 (Winter/Spring 2003): 267–81; and Elliot Hen-Tov, "Understanding Iran's New Authoritarianism," *Washington Quarterly* 30, no.1 (Winter 2006–07): 163–79.

In Iran "national interest" is an elusive term. Among Iran's elite, there are major differences over whether it is time for Iran to set aside its revolutionary past and normalize foreign relations or continue its global defiance and revolutionary stance. This rift is reflected in the nuclear issue and has the potential to be the deciding factor in the future course of Iran. Rowhani, a pragmatic conservative close to both Rafsanjani and Khatami, has made clear that split opinions among the elite over the nuclear issue stem from "divisions and disagreements [that] are far wider and deeper than what the ordinary members of the public can see" and arise from differences on what he terms "certain fundamental issues and premises."[52] This is an authoritative and revealing statement, confirming both that political factionalism is significant and that the disparity of approaches toward the nuclear issue reflect much broader differences regarding Iran's evolution and role in the world.

Rowhani has also set the nuclear issue in a wider context, noting that the "Libyan model" did not imply merely giving up centrifuges but also meant moving toward recognition of Israel and "cutting off relations with the liberation movements in the world."[53] Rowhani did not reject this "behavior change" option that implies normalizing relations with the United States; rather he sought to point to this as one option.

Differences over the nuclear issue reflect varying perspectives regarding what type of relations should Tehran have with Washington. Whereas Iran's pragmatic conservatives seek normalization with Washington as the culmination of the revolution, opponents see engagement and compromise with the United States as delegitimizing the revolution.[54] These schisms tend to divide the elite into several, sometimes overlapping, categories.

First, reformists generally support the nuclear program but see going nuclear as one option among several technologies, rather than as the holy grail. This group does not wish to see Iran's nuclear pursuits lead to further estrangement from the international community.[55]

Second, there are two sets of conservatives—pragmatic/traditional (which include Rafsanjani and Rowhani) and ideological (such as

---

[52] "Ex-Nuclear Chief Criticizes 'Ideological' Impact on Foreign Policy," *E'temad* website on July 23, 2006, available through BBC Monitoring, July 25, 2006.

[53] Quoted on *E'temad* website on February 23, 2006, available through BBC Monitoring, February 26, 2006. These excerpts are from a speech given by Rohwani in autumn 2005 that was referenced in the Rahbord, the quarterly journal of the Strategic Studies Centre of the Assembly of Experts.

[54] For an analysis of these differences and efforts by the conservatives to sabotage normalization under Rafsanjani and Khatami, see Ansari, *Confronting Iran*, 142, 179, 189, 202–13, 223.

[55] See "Critics of Nuclear Policy Must Be Allowed to Express Views," *Aftab-e Yazd*, December 3, 2005, available through BBC Monitoring, December 14, 2005. A reformist candidate for president in 2005 called for suspension of enrichment activities, see *Keyhan* website on April 19, 2005, available through BBC Monitoring, April 21, 2005.

Ahmadinejad). These two sets appear to agree on the need for a nuclear weapons option, but differ over the means and price of achieving it. In reality, however, these two groups actually seek different ends. The pragmatic conservatives resemble the reformists and seek power in order to cut a deal and normalize foreign relations, while the ideological conservatives shun a deal and want to impose power over the region and beyond.[56]

Both reformists and pragmatic conservatives also seek a larger regional role for Iran and view the United States as a potential obstacle. While believing that an enhanced nuclear capability would strengthen Iran's regional power and that "the enemy would not like Iran to play such a role," these groups do *not* see this as preventing a full normalization with the United States and engagement with the world.[57] The reformists and pragmatic conservatives thus see a change in Iran's overall orientation as a prelude to guaranteeing Iran's security and interests.

By contrast, ideological conservatives view the acquisition of a nuclear option not as a bargaining card but as an equalizer with which to confront the United States. Ahmadinejad's policy of "active diplomacy" seeks to increase power, not just to survive but also to impose Iranian power on the international community. Larijani has stated that in order to resist U.S. pressure, "[Iran must use its] prominent geopolitical position...[and] find a way to be able to take the country's level and status to a point so as to automatically solve [the country's] national security problem, otherwise this pressure factor will always weigh upon [Iran]." Similarly, he has also stated that "if Iran becomes atomic Iran, no longer will anyone dare challenge it, because they would have to pay too high a price."[58] Hence, from this perspective, the priority is acquiring technology rather than reassuring the international community. To Larijani mention of security guarantees is demeaning: "Iran does not need these kinds of condescending guarantees and it is fairly capable of protecting itself." Proponents of this view argue that Iran does not need either technology or status conferred on it; Iran is prepared to seize them by its own efforts.[59] Larijani sees North Korea's

[56] Some analysts believe all factions want nuclear weapons and differ only on the pace of the program, associated costs, and international sensitivities, rather than on ultimate aims. This author disagrees with such an assessment.

[57] Hasan Rowhani, "Iran Needs to Counter 'Multi-Dimensional' Threat from West," text of report in English, IRNA, January 14, 2006.

[58] Larijani to IRGC Commanders, *Farhang-e Ashti* website on November 30, 2005, available through BBC Monitoring, December 12, 2005. On Iran's geopolitical position, see "Iran's Security Chief Explains Tehran's Nuclear Strategy in TV Interview," Vision of Islamic Republic of Iran Network 2 on January 2, 2006, available through BBC Monitoring, January 3, 2006.

[59] "US Firms Not Welcomed to Join Iran's Enrichment plan—Larijani," Mehr News Agency on December 13, 2005, available through BBC Monitoring, December 14, 2005.

implacability as a model for Iran—sooner or later the West will have to concede to Iran's nuclear status.[60]

Such differences in goals are also reflected in approaches these groups take toward nuclear diplomacy. The pragmatic conservatives who controlled negotiations from 2003 to 2005 were under constant pressure from the ideological faction. The pragmatic conservatives were open to compromise when necessary (such as in the Tehran and Paris agreements in 2003 and 2004 respectively) and sought to limit the fallout from Iran's program. Sensitive both to international opinion and to the potential costs of a disruption of relations, this group was willing to suspend enrichment activities and accept constraints (the NPT's Additional Protocol) in order to appear reasonable and cooperative. To bridge the gap between Iran's desire for technology (to "not give up our rights") and development, and to avoid a crisis, Iranian negotiators relied on confidence-building measures, but with only mixed success.[61] Although seeking to enhance power, the pragmatists were unwilling to take a confrontational manner and left open the possibility of a grand bargain—an accommodation across the board that would see Iran's interests and security guaranteed in exchange for both a normalization of relations and moderation of behavior.

At home the pragmatists were put on the political defensive regarding their negotiations with the EU-3 (Germany, Britain, and France). They countered that without flexibility they would come to a crisis point with the IAEA and "the great contracts that Iran signed with [IAEA] countries in the field of oil and gas would have been impossible."[62] The message of this group was clear: Iran should not cause a crisis over the enrichment issue that would impair the country's overall development prospects. This view held by Rowhani and Rafsanjani, however, is not shared by some in Iran who would prefer a crisis, enabling them to make a point of principle by stopping such interaction.[63]

The pragmatists' approach became the target of sustained criticism from the ideological conservatives who took control following the rigged

[60] Nazila Fathi and Michael Slackman, "Iran's President Rolls Back the Clock," *International Herald Tribune*, December 21, 2005, 4.

[61] Rowhani, "Iran's Security Chief Rejects IAEA Demand to Suspend Enrichment," Islamic Republic of Iran News Network on September 19, 2004, available through BBC Monitoring, September 20, 2004.

[62] Negotiations helped create the atmosphere for long-term gas contracts with India, China, Pakistan, and the United Arab Emirates. See Hossein Mousavian, "EU Waiting for New Iranian Government to Proceed with Talks—Official," IRNA on July 17, 2005, available through BBC Monitoring, July 18, 2005.

[63] Representative of this viewpoint is Mohsen Reza'i, the Secretary of the Expediency Council, "Failure to Close Iran Nuclear File at IAEA Risks Paris Deal—Iran Official," ISNA on November 21, 2004, available through BBC Monitoring, November 24, 2004.

Majlis elections in 2004. Playing to Iranian nationalism, they criticized the reformists as being duped by European negotiators.[64] The election made it even more imperative for the new conservative government to use foreign policy issues as a smokescreen.[65] With the further consolidation of conservative power resulting from Ahmadinejad's presidential victory in June 2005, the government made a renewed effort to depict its predecessors as having been soft in defending the nation's rights.[66] Ideological conservatives welcome confrontation, seeing Iran's geopolitical position as providing a number of important advantages. Increased oil income in recent years serves both to fund an "activist" policy and to buffer the effects of possible sanctions. These assets, it is assumed, will also give Iran the means to successfully divide Russia and China from the West.

The pragmatic conservatives have cautioned against this approach, judging that it is prone both to overestimating Iran's power and centrality and to misjudging the external world. Rafsanjani has called for "serious prudence," and Rowhani noted that in barely three months the new government had twice managed to provoke serious discussions of referral to the UNSC and had once been the object of a critical Security Council statement.[67] Within six months the new government had precipitated a referral to the UNSC, something its predecessor had avoided for thee years.

Ahmadinejad and the Politics of Nuclear Populism

Following Ahmadinejad's assumption of the presidency, the nuclear project designed to legitimize the regime under a national banner was now appropriated by a single faction. Ahmadinejad inflated the stakes and outbid political rivals in his support for the program. Between 2005 and 2007 the "right to acquire technology" shifted almost imperceptibly into the "right to acquire the fuel cycle."

In his frequent forays into the provinces, Ahmadinejad hammered home the slogan that Iran insist on its nuclear rights, encouraging his audience at each stop to chant the refrain in unison. In appropriating the nuclear issue, the president spoke over the head of the supreme leader and undercut his chief nuclear negotiator Ali Larijani. Where foreign affairs were concerned,

---

[64] Nazila Fathi, "Iran Snubs European Plan," *New York Times*, May 18, 2006.

[65] See especially Ansari, *Confronting Iran*, 174–75, 209, 216.

[66] See Farideh Farhi, "Iran's Nuclear File: The Uncertain Endgame," *Middle East Report Online*, October 24, 2005, http://www.merip.org/mero/mero102405.html.

[67] "Iran's Rafsanjani Defends Nuclear 'Right' Calls for Prudence," Vision of Islamic Republic of Iran Network 1 on January 11, 2006, available through BBC Monitoring, January 12, 2006; and "New Government Depicts 'harsh image' of Iran—Rowhani," report by Fars News Agency on November 15, 2005, available through BBC Monitoring, November 17, 2005.

Ahmadinejad came into power with an attitude rather than a strategy. His foreign policy was "shaped in response to other Iranian factions."[68]

By insisting on Iran's rights, untrammeled and without compromise, Ahmadinejad harkened back to the early days of the revolution. Ahmadinejad sought to differentiate himself from his predecessors in all areas—economics and politics, domestic and foreign policy. He insisted that Iran would not consider suspending enrichment and would instead accelerate the nuclear program.[69] He told audiences that "access to nuclear know-how was the key to national development and the preservation of Iranian civilization" and that it would be worth "stopping everything else for ten years" to concentrate only on nuclear energy.[70] To buttress this uncompromising stance, Ahmadinejad created a special stamp marking the nuclear program and encouraged students both to prepare petitions protesting UNSC resolutions and to form human chains around the Bushehr reactor.[71] He accused his critics "of not aligning themselves with the people" and of propagating "a culture of compromise."[72]

In seeking to strengthen support for his presidency, Ahmadinejad upped the ante by "daring other significant players to publicly oppose hardline stances that [Ahmadinejad] drapes under the mantle of ideological purity."[73] At the same time he gambled that his use of the nuclear issue and the appeal of his revolutionary slogans would attract a powerful domestic constituency that would outweigh those seeking to temper Iran's revolutionary impulses in favor of pragmatic accommodation.[74]

As long as Iran suffered no serious costs from this approach, Ahmadinejad's political rivals were cowed into silence. The emotional nationalism inherent in his hard-line stance made appeals to moderation a losing proposition politically. With the passage of the unanimous UNSC Resolution 1737 on December 23, 2006, however, this state of affairs began to shift. The resolution was weak in itself, but it was adopted under

---

[68] Alireza Haghighi and Victoria Tahmasebi, "The 'Velvet Revolution' of Iranian Puritan Hardliners: Mahmoud Ahmadinejad's Rise to Power," *International Journal* 61, no. 4 (Autumn 2006): 970.

[69] Islamic Republic of Iran News Network on February 11, 2007, available through BBC Monitoring, February 12, 2007.

[70] See respectively speech, IRNA on February 22, 2007, available through BBC Monitoring, February 23, 2007; and ISNA website, February 21, 2007, available through BBC Monitoring, February 22, 2007.

[71] IRNA on February 10, 2007, available through BBC Monitoring, February 11, 2007; Voice of Islamic Republic of Iran on February 5, 2007, available though BBC Monitoring, February 6, 2007; and IRNA on February 10, 2007, available through BBC Monitoring, February 11, 2007.

[72] ISNA on February 23, 2007, available though BBC Monitoring, February 24, 2007.

[73] "Iran: Ahmadinejad's Tumultuous Presidency," 21.

[74] Ahmadinejad's support base can be found in the rural poor, IRGC, and the Basij militia.

Chapter VII of the UN Charter, which meant that Iran constituted a threat to international peace and security and that additional measures would be taken. This created consternation in Iran when taken together with U.S. measures—such as both "informal sanctions" targeting the dollar-based transactions of some Iranian banks and more robust military posturing with the deployment of a second carrier task force to the Persian Gulf in January 2007. Prospects of a U.S. military strike and tighter sanctions affecting the population emboldened Ahmadinejad's rivals to respond. The passage of a second UNSC resolution in March 2007 increased the pressure on Iran with the imposition of sanctions more specifically targeted against the nuclear program, dual-use technology, the missile industry, and specific individuals associated with these programs, notably from the IRGC.

Criticisms of the president have focused as much on his style as his policy. Reformists have not been alone in finding his rabble-rousing dangerous "and fearful that populism could lead, as before, to dictatorship."[75] The pragmatist coalition saw Ahmadinejad's grandstanding as a diversion from Iran's real problems.

Reformist movements have been more scathing in their critique, noting that the principal issue was how to achieve Iran's nuclear rights while protecting Iran's economic interests and system of government against damage.[76] Some have made comprehensive criticisms of the government's approach to nuclear policy.[77] Ahmadinejad's defiant statement that "the train of the Iranian nation is without brakes or reverse gear" elicited the rejoinder that "in the real world a train without brakes needs to be repaired....One can only reach one's destination on a train that is not faulty."[78]

A source close to the supreme leader noted that the government after two years had failed to ameliorate and seemed insensitive to the people's economic plight. The source concluded that "the government should not

---

[75] Ansari, *Confronting Iran*, 162.

[76] See *Aftab-e Yazd* website on February 6, 2007, available through BBC Monitoring, February 12, 2007; and *Emrooz* website on January 6, 2007, cited in Y. Mansharof, "Iranian Domestic Criticism of Iran's Nuclear Strategy," Middle East Media Research Institute, Inquiry and Analysis Series, no. 317, January 24, 2007.

[77] See especially the statement of Mojahedin of Islamic Revolution: "The Nuclear Crisis: The Consequences and Proposed Solutions," as cited on the *Asr-e Now* website on February 19, 2007, available through BBC Monitoring, February 23, 2007; and the "Nehzat Azadi [Freedom Party] Urged Diplomacy," *E'temad* website on January 21, 2007, available though BBC Monitoring, January 24, 2007.

[78] The first quotation is cited in Daniel Dombey, "'No Brakes, No Reverse' on Iran Nuclear Plans," *Financial Times*, February 26, 2007, 4. The second quote was made in the text of a party statement by Gholamali Dehqan, spokesman for the Moderation and Development Party, Iranian Labour News Agency website on February 26, 2007, available through BBC Monitoring, February 27, 2007.

forget that one cannot fight on a hundred fronts simultaneously."[79] A senior cleric added that "one cannot govern a country on slogans."[80]

Despite the regime's insistence on the priority attached to the nuclear issue—and irrespective of the Iranian public's willingness to suffer hardships in order to attain their nuclear rights—the leadership is sensitive to the mood of the people. For ordinary Iranians basic economic and social welfare issues are more pressing concerns than notional nuclear rights. "The world is focused on our so-called nuclear bomb but the only bomb on the point of explosion is that of our economy."[81] As the regime has become aware of the serious international and domestic ramifications of Ahmadinejad's strategy to manipulate the issue at home, the priority has shifted from regime legitimation to damage control.

This section has argued that under Ahmadinejad the instrumentalization of the nuclear issue for domestic purposes among various political factions has reached a new level. His defiant stance, though congenial to hard-liners, has not produced tangible results and risks eliciting a political backlash, particularly if and as the costs of confrontation rise. If Ahmadinejad successfully calls the bluff of the international community, however, he will emerge strengthened from the confrontation. Iran's domestic evolution and international orientation are thus at stake in the outcome of the nuclear dispute.

Political Dynamics and Strategic Choices

Uncertainties Surrounding Iran's Nuclear Program

Iran's nuclear program shows all the indicators of, at a minimum, seeking a nuclear weapons option. A number of uncertainties exist, however, about key elements of the program including Iran's aims and technical capabilities (as well as possible clandestine facilities) and how sensitive Iran might be to outside pressure.

Iran does not appear to have made a definitive decision to acquire nuclear weapons. Despite an interest in weaponization that is evident in the missile program and research, it seems more likely that Iran seeks a nuclear weapons option, something short of an operational capability. Following the "Japan model" would enable Iran to stay within the formal limits of the NPT while giving Tehran the means to "break out" in a strategic emergency.

---

[79] Mehdi Mohammadi, *Keyhan* website, January 17, 2007.

[80] Hossein Ali Montazeri, quoted in "Mahmoud Ahmadinejad plus en plus critique" [Ahmadinejad More and More Criticized], *Le Monde*, January 25, 2007, 4.

[81] Quoted in Marie Claude Descamps, "Ahmadinejad, le grand frere du peuple" [Ahmadinejad, the People's Elder Brother], *Le Monde*, March 15, 2007, 3.

Mastery of the full fuel cycle would arguably give Iran the strategic benefits of a nuclear weapon without its opprobrium.

The distinction between actual weaponization and a latent capability to weaponize may be too fine or narrow to be an attractive basis for policy. If international efforts to prevent Iran's mastery of the fuel cycle fail, however, this distinction may be the only basis for policy in practical terms and would refocus efforts on how to deter or prevent Iran from assuming an overt nuclear weapons posture.[82] Apart from the nature of Iran's ultimate aims and flexibility, there is also uncertainty about the technical timeframe—it is unclear how far Iran's program has advanced and therefore to what extent Iran is vulnerable.

Iran's leaders exploit ambiguity and indirection regarding their nuclear weapons intentions. As long as ambitions for weapons ambitions are denied, there cannot be an official debate about nuclear strategy; allusions, however, are frequent. A senior official has stated that "the nuclear program is not about the bomb it's about power" while another has told the IRGC that in a military context "the country is on the threshold of a leap forward due to access to nuclear technology and other major achievements of our specialists."[83] Press commentary is even less reserved, boasting that by accelerating the production of centrifuges, Iran "will have nuclear deterrence in six months."[84] Nonetheless, Iran still apparently seeks a nuclear capability within the NPT, making use of ambiguity while blunting opposition to enrichment.[85]

The Current State of Affairs

Iran rebuffed an offer by the EU-3 in June 2005 to enter into broad negotiations in exchange for a freeze on enrichment by Iran. The permanent five members of the UNSC and Germany (P5+1) made another offer in June 2006. This second offer, which involved the United States for the first time, was for Tehran to enter into negotiations with the prospect of gaining access to technology (including nuclear), on the condition that Iran cease all uranium enrichment and related activities prior to such negotiations. The Western offer included the lifting of sanctions and a number of other

---

[82] See Mark Fitzpatrick, "Can Iran's Nuclear Capability Be Kept Latent?" *Survival* 49, no. 1 (Spring 2007).

[83] See Christiane Amanpour, "Iranian Official Offers Glimpse from Within: A Desire for US Ally," http://www.cnn.com/2007/WORLD/meast/02/21/btsc.iran.amanpour/index.html; and Fars News Agency on February 21, 2007, available through BBC Monitoring, February 22, 2007.

[84] Hoseyn Allahkaram, commentary on "Nuclear Strategy," *E'temad* website on January 23, 2007, available through BBC Monitoring, January 24, 2007.

[85] For a discussion, see Avner Cohen, "The Nuclear Ambiguity Route," *Haaretz*, February 12, 2007, http://www.serve.com/vanunu/20070212haaretz.html.

inducements. Iran rejected the precondition. After a delay the UNSC moved toward sanctions.

Iran failed to comply both with the December 2006 UNSC Resolution 1737 that required Tehran to halt uranium enrichment and with a second similar resolution voted on in March 2007 that gave Iran a deadline of sixty days to do so. The second resolution issued sanctions on technology acquisition as well as individuals involved in the nuclear and missile programs. Iran responded by curtailing the access of IAEA inspectors to the country's nuclear facilities. Although currently limited, the sanctions can be expected to increase and hurt more over time. Iran insists, however, that ceasing enrichment cannot be a precondition for negotiations. Iran's response has been to try to accelerate its enrichment by running as many centrifuges as it can continuously.

Iran's reluctance to consider a freeze is understandable. Restarting enrichment may be more politically and diplomatically provocative once Iran accedes to a freeze, even one that is only temporary. A stoppage would delay and might hurt the program technically and, on the home front, the Iranian government would be forced to respond to its critics by explaining why its vaunted activist (i.e., confrontational) policy failed to produce more than the policy of its comparatively conciliatory predecessor. Above all, a suspension runs counter to Iran's efforts to progress far enough for Tehran to argue that its mastery of the fuel cycle is irreversible—a *fait accompli* and new baseline that would need to be recognized.

Iran is therefore playing for time by attempting to divide the P5+1 while offering to negotiate without preconditions in order to demonstrate political goodwill. Iran wants the issue removed from the UNSC, which Tehran sees as political (i.e., dominated by the United States), and returned to the more technical IAEA. To encourage this shift in responsibility, Tehran is toying with the prospect of accepting the Additional Protocol to the NPT and being more cooperative with the agency.[86]

Putting aside the question of preconditions and the sequencing of procedures, there are several technical solutions and options on the table for resolving the nuclear dispute:

---

[86] See Ali Larijani's comments on the ISNA website on February 27, 2007, available through BBC Monitoring, February 28, 2007.

- The P5+1 has proposed immediate suspension of all Iranian enrichment activities for the duration of negotiations, which would be followed by discussions on guaranteeing foreign fuel supplies for Iran's nuclear needs and technical assistance with those needs once Iran agrees to forgo mastering the fuel cycle. In principle this idea is compatible with the Russian and IAEA proposals.

- The Russian proposal is to have Iran invest as a full partner in enrichment facilities in Russia with guarantees that Russia will supply fuel to meet Iran's needs. Under this scenario Iran might maintain its own pilot facilities. Iran has neither accepted nor rejected this proposal, which is incompatible with Tehran's insistence on self-reliance.

- The IAEA and others have argued that there is a need both for multinational or regional fuel centers that would provide enrichment services for states needing fuel for their reactors and for full guarantees for the security of supply and protection against price manipulation.

- Iran insists on enrichment facilities within the country. Tehran proposes that in order to keep enrichment at the level useful for reactors (less than 5%) but below a weapons-grade level, Iran is prepared both to enhance IAEA inspections and to accept an international consortium (i.e., foreign countries and investors) that could be reassured of the country's activities through participation.[87]

Iran's key consideration is to continue its enrichment activities inside the country and assure its own future supplies. At a minimum, this strategy entails continuing research and some domestic enrichment activities (such as a pilot project). Tehran might consider suspension but will find it more difficult to accept dismantling existing facilities. As a result Tehran has every incentive to ensure that any agreed freeze occurs once Iran has achieved a level of ability that includes mastery of the fuel cycle. Hence Iran's interest lies in resisting or delaying suspension until Tehran can demonstrate a level of progress that is irreversible.

The West's critical consideration is to ensure that Iran's indigenous enrichment capabilities are minimal to none. This imperative arises because monitoring and guaranteeing the peaceful intent of a pilot plant or continued research on the fuel cycle would be difficult, even at a low level of production. Hence the West prefers that Iran completely renounce

---

[87] Larijani made this suggestion to Javier Solana in autumn 2006, but the West did not show much interest. See report by Islamic Republic of Iran News Network on February 25, 2007, available through BBC Monitoring, February 27, 2007.

enrichment and is unwilling to support any enrichment within Iran under Iranian control.

The Nuclear Timeline

A diplomatic agreement reconciling or modifying these approaches will depend in part on the timeline of Iran's mastery of the technology. Iran has a strong incentive to overplay the program's advances in order to underscore the futility of trying to turn back progress on Iran's "nativization" of the technology. By capitalizing on uncertainties over this issue, however, Tehran risks increasing the concerns of outside powers, likely resulting in stronger measures to be taken against Iran. Estimates vary on the time available before Iran's nuclear program becomes fully capable. Broadly, Iran may be able to produce enough enriched uranium for a single weapon within two to three years. In order to achieve sustained production of highly enriched uranium, not to mention an integrated weapon tied to a delivery system rather than merely a crude bomb, Iran would require a longer timeline, closer to the five to ten years suggested by official U.S. sources.[88] These estimates are based on projections of indigenous capability from known facilities and do not take into account either clandestine facilities or access to fissile material from abroad.

Having installed 1,312 centrifuges and with its target of 3,000 within reach, Iran was a "matter of months away" from completing the next phase of its nuclear program as of mid-2007.[89] The target of 50,000 centrifuges for industrial-scale enrichment is still further in the future. Most estimates suggest that once 3,000 centrifuges are successfully installed and begin operating it will take at least another one to two years before Iran will be able to produce enough material for one nuclear bomb.[90] Iran has encountered numerous technical difficulties that have delayed its program, including lack of access to outside expertise and technology, deficiencies in the complex production and engineering processes, lack of maraging steel,

---

[88] CIA estimate in August 2005 cited in Dafna Linzer, "Iran Is Judged 10 Years from Nuclear Bomb," *Washington Post*, August 2, 2005, A1. Robert Gates acknowledges variations in U.S. intelligence estimates from "late 2008–09" to 2015 for Iran to have a nuclear weapon. See Daniel Dombey and Stephen Fidler, "Strains Grow Over Strategy to Rein in Iran," *Financial Times*, June 4, 2007, 4.

[89] Despite slippage in meeting this target, a leaked IAEA letter suggested Iran's acceleration of its program. See Daniel Dombey, "Uranium Enrichment in 'full swing,'" *Financial Times*, April 20, 2007, 5. David Sanger, "Atomic Agency Confirms Advances by Iran's Nuclear Program," *New York Times*, April 19, 2007, http://www.nytimes.com/2007/04/19/world/middleeast/19nukes.html?ex=1 334635200&en=eb8cfdc190e67053&ei=5088&partner=rs.

[90] See David Albright, "Iran's Nuclear Program: Status and Uncertainties," testimony before the U.S. House Committee on Foreign Affairs, Subcommittee on Middle East and Asia, Washington, D.C., March 15, 2007.

failure-prone technology, and inadequate systems integration.[91] Mastery of the technology, however, would imply a point of no return.[92] That domestic political reasons have spurred Ahmadinejad toward political posturing on Iran's progress only increases uncertainty about Iran's actual progress.[93]

As a leaked internal EU paper concluded, the ability to master the necessary technology seems to be restraining Iran more than any diplomatic pressure or package that has yet been devised.[94] The indisputable fact is that Iran "has made serious progress in its ability to enrich uranium. We are therefore working within some fairly serious time constraints."[95] The questions for the West are three-fold: whether Tehran would be amenable to an incentive package that is properly and systematically applied, how susceptible to pressure is the government, and how set is the decision to seek a nuclear option.

External Influences on Iran's Choices

The timelines of Iran's progress toward a nuclear option, however approximate, and diplomatic prevention measures need to be synchronized. An estimate of three to five years still leaves scope for diplomacy. Tehran has been surprised by referral to the UNSC, the accompanying resolutions, and UNSC refusal to exclude the possibility of using force. The sanctions resolutions, though tempered for maximum political consensus, steadily expand the list of individuals and institutions affected. The limited sanctions have already had a disproportionate effect in a number of ways. They have both demonstrated unity among the principal powers and sent Tehran the message that Iran should not count on eluding penalties and should expect that the international community will take further measures against Iran. This squeeze, as opposed to a confrontational approach, is a well-suited action to take against Iran because it makes it harder for the regime to rally and mobilize the support of constituents. Though limited, the measures

[91] Peter Beaumont, "Nuclear Plans in Chaos as Iran Leader Flounders," *Observer*, January 28, 2007.

[92] M. ElBaradei has suggested that Iran could have 3,000 centrifuges installed by August 2007 and 8,000 by the end of 2007. See David Sanger, "Atomic Official Issues Stern Warning on Iran," *International Herald Tribune*, June 13, 2007, 8; and Daniel Dombey and Fidelius Schmidt, "Iran Moves Ahead with Nuclear Programme," *Financial Times*, May 24, 2007, 7.

[93] William Broad and David Sanger, "More Bluster than Menace?" *International Herald Tribune*, February 5, 2007, 5.

[94] Daniel Dombey and Fidelius Schmid, "Too Late to Halt Iran's N-bomb, EU Is Told," *Financial Times*, February 13, 2007, 1.

[95] *Iranwatch*, interview with William Tobey, Deputy Administrator for Defense Nuclear Nonproliferation at National Nuclear Security Administration, U.S. Department of Energy, January 17, 2007, http://www.iranwatch.org/ourpubs/roundtables/interview-tobey-030207.htm.

have at the same time added to the sense of government bungling and a "general insecurity about economic viability."[96]

Led by the United States, the international effort to target institutions related to Iran's nuclear and missile programs is intended to create delays and impose costs on continuation of these programs, implicitly threatening that these costs will incrementally increase. This effort is intended to encourage debate and reconsideration of policy within Iran. The U.S. view is that, even after the first resolution, the "extraordinary set of moves" have "put the Iranians on their back foot." The United States seeks to increase Iran's economic isolation by encouraging states to take unilateral steps not necessarily tied to the timetable or precise wording of UN resolutions.[97] For example, though balking at U.S. leadership and the timetable, Russia has delayed the provision of fuel and completion of the Bushehr reactor, adding to Tehran's sense of siege.

That sanctions are notorious for taking time to work and can be resisted or undermined when there is little international solidarity does not render them universally ineffective.[98] In this case international consensus and stigmatization, even quite apart from the costs imposed, send Iran a powerful message. Unlike Iraq under Saddam Hussein, Iran's regime cannot dismiss the consequences of sanctions and let them fall on the populace; Tehran remains sensitive to public opinion. Smart sanctions targeting either the regime directly or elements involved with the programs are a useful starting point; if this approach proves insufficient, however, devising measures that directly affect the citizenry may be necessary to generate more traction.

The most obvious indicators of Iran's economic failure are the decline in per capita income since 1979, the consistently high rates of inflation and unemployment, the near complete dependence on oil income, and the bloated and often unaccountable state sector. The state's inability to reduce food and oil subsidies—amounting to $25 billion annually—reflects a structural economic problem that resists short-term and fluctuating expedients, such as increasing government spending when oil prices rise. The cessation of foreign credits and investment, plus the increased cost of doing business, will contribute to the increasing malaise, especially

---

[96] See David Ignatieff, "Signals from Tehran," *Washington Post*, February 23, 2007, 19.

[97] Nicholas Burns, "Global Leadership Series: A Conversation on U.S.-Europe Cooperation on Issues Beyond Europe" (remarks presented at the Atlantic Council of the United States, Washington, D.C., February 21, 2007), 12, 39, http://www.acus.org/docs/070221-NICHOLAS_BURNS-Atlantic%20Council.pdf.

[98] See Bruce Jentleson, "Sanctions against Iran: Key Issues," New York, Century Foundation, February 2007.

as oil revenues dip or decline and government spending reduces the oil contingency fund for future investment.[99]

The most vulnerable point of Iran's economy is the oil sector. Oil price fluctuations in both directions make planning difficult, and diversification has lagged. Without consistent access to foreign technology and investment, the needed investment and exploration to assure a steady level of production has been erratic. Lacking indigenous refinery capacity, Iran is forced to import 40% of its domestic gasoline needs, which is especially costly because domestic prices are heavily subsidized; this need to import energy could be an obvious eventual target for sanctions. Although nothing is inevitable about declining oil production, Iran will need to make some strategic choices about avoiding further sanctions and encouraging greater investment if Tehran is to avoid these projections.[100]

Supreme Leader Khamenei admitted that "economic developments since the victory of the Islamic revolution in 1979 have not matched the deep socio-political developments in the country."[101] One of the constant dilemmas of the leadership is recognition that the regime's legitimacy can be challenged if the economy continues to underperform, but the necessary deep structural reforms are not feasible with the current power structure. Critics of the president find it relatively easy to attack his economic policies, including the failure to privatize and the short-term expedients that ignore planning.[102] More direct criticism comes from others who stress that the country's economic plight and public dissatisfaction stem from specific policies and are aggravated by economic sanctions.

The president's efforts to dismiss the impact of sanctions have not been generally shared. Iran's oil minister admitted financing oil projects has not gone smoothly.[103] A parliamentary report—which estimated the cost of

[99] See Patrick Clawson, "Hanging Tough on Iran," *Policywatch* 1194, Washington Institute for Near East Studies, February 9, 2007; Barbara Slavin, "Iran's Economic Conditions Deteriorate," *USA Today*, February 27, 2007; and Marc Shulman, "Iran's Economic House of Cards," American Future web log, http://americanfuture.net/?p=2597.

[100] For two views see Roger Stern, "The Iranian Petroleum Crisis and United States National Security," *Proceedings of the National Academy of Sciences of the USA* (PNAS) 104, no. 1 (January 2, 2007), http://www.pnas.org/cgi/doi/10.1073/pnas.0603903104; and Fereidun Fesharaki, "Iran Petroleum Crisis Claims 'fundamentally unsound,'" *Middle East Economic Survey*, January 15, 2007. See also Jad Mouawad, "Iran Feels the Squeeze of Western Pressure," *International Herald Tribune*, February 13, 2007, 1, 8.

[101] Cited by Vision of the Islamic Republic of Iran News Network 1 on February 28, 2007, available through BBC Monitoring, March 2, 2007.

[102] See ISNA on February 25, 2007, available through BBC Monitoring, February 26, 2007; and Abbas Abdi, "Retrogression of the Economy," *E'temad* website on February 19, 2007, available through BBC Monitoring, February 20, 2007.

[103] See Najmeh Bozorgmehr and Roula Khalaf, "Tehran Admits Sanctions Are Hurting Oil Sector Investment," *Financial Times*, December 21, 2006, 1.

sanctions to be $1.5–2 billion per year—warned of a potential for the country to destabilize and argued that Iran should make diplomatic efforts to avoid sanctions.[104] The government seriously considered rationing oil consumption or introducing a two-tier market for prices—a shift indicating that past practices and prospective stringencies may be on a collision course.[105]

Asia and a Nuclear Iran

Asia has played an underappreciated role in Iran's strategic thinking; similarly Asian states have an underacknowledged role in supporting Iran's nuclear program and will be important in any resolution of the nuclear crisis. China, Pakistan, and Russia all supplied Iran with sensitive nuclear technology in the 1980s and 1990s. The first two of these states were not members of the NPT (China only joined the NPT regime in 1992). In all three states, companies, governments, and non-state entities were involved in technology transfer, most notably A. Q. Khan from Pakistan. Chinese assistance included training and technology, Russia built the power reactor at Bushehr with one thousand of its own technicians at the cost of $800 million, and Pakistani assistance included technology, plans, and expertise. Pakistan's assistance has been the most damaging in terms of accelerating Iran's program and the oddest in that this assistance was extended when official relations were at their worst.[106]

In every case this cooperation was halted or limited by U.S. pressure—but this pressure was clearly not the only cause.[107] Asian states began to have their own concerns. Despite sympathy for Iran (particularly in India), in September 2005 Asian states voted in the IAEA Board to report Iran for non-compliance to the UNSC. Russia and China have voted twice in the UNSC for sanctions against Iran to be imposed until Tehran ends uranium enrichment, and Indonesia and Qatar (as rotating members of the UNSC) also voted against Iran in the March 2007 resolution.

Of the Asian states, Pakistan would be the most directly threatened by a nuclear Iran, even if bilateral relations improve from their current parlous state. First, a new nuclear neighbor would complicate Pakistan's

---

[104]   *Le Monde* reported on this leaked Majlis report. See Laurent Zecchini, "L'embargo qui fait peur a Teheran," [The Embargo Which Frightens Iran], *Le Monde*, January 21–22, 2007, 3.

[105]   See William Sam'i, "Iran Considers Gasoline Rationing," *Weekly Standard*, February 7, 2007.

[106]   See David Albright and Corey Hinderstein, "Unravelling the A.Q. Khan and Future Proliferation Networks," *Washington Quarterly* 28, no. 2 (Spring 2005): 111–28; on China, see Kenneth Katzman, "Iran: US Policy Concerns and Policy Responses," Congressional Research Service, CRS Report for Congress, RL 32048, November 1, 2006, 37–38.

[107]   Pressure of course continues especially where companies continue their activities. For recent examples, see "US Imposes Sanctions to Stop Weapon Sales," *International Herald Tribune*, April 24, 2007, 6.

strategic calculations and raise the necessity of planning for a two-front war. Pakistan's concern would be even greater if Iran's relations with India continue to grow. Second, a nuclear Iran would unsettle the GCC states (especially Saudi Arabia), which would look to Pakistan for reassurance. Third, a nuclear Iran might emerge in the context of increased sectarian rivalry—including even polarization in the Middle East.[108] (The situation in Iraq has aggravated sectarian tensions which have spilled over into regional politics.) Convinced that Iran seeks nuclear weapons without cause, Pakistan is especially concerned that the current crisis might lead to military action, which would aggravate sectarian divisions throughout the region.[109] The emergence of a nuclear Iran—also resisted by the country's Arab Sunni neighbors—in an environment of strong sectarian tensions could deepen regional polarization if Iran is the possessor of a "Shi'a bomb" in opposition to Pakistan's "Sunni bomb."

India is also averse to a nuclear Iran. Prime Minister Manmohan Singh told the Indian parliament that it was not in India's interest to have a "nuclear-armed Iran."[110] This reaction is in part due to the way Iran has sought to circumvent the NPT to which Tehran freely adhered.[111] India resists any comparison between itself and Iran, arguing that India is a "responsible nuclear power" that adheres to international obligations and that other countries should do the same.[112] India shares with China and Russia a perception that "a nuclear Iran is a threat to its long-term strategic interests."[113] New Delhi will therefore work to prevent Iran's nuclear break-out while seeking to maintain good ties with Tehran.

China and Russia have both sought to distinguish themselves from the United States by excluding the military option and emphasizing diplomacy. Neither of the two powers is very optimistic about the ultimate outcome; both have tried to reason with Tehran while supporting international sanctions. China especially is concerned that a military strike against Iran could lead to a prolonged round of hostilities that would jeopardize the oil

[108] Vali Nasr, "Regional Implications of the Shi'a Revival in Iraq," *Washington Quarterly* 27, no. 3 (Summer 2004): 7–24.

[109] See Qazi Hussain Ahmed, "Possible US Attack on Iran and Pakistan," *Naw'a-i wagt* website on March 3, 2007, available though BBC Monitoring, March 28, 2007.

[110] PTI news agency, July 23, 2006.

[111] Sheele Bhatt, interview with K. Subrahmanyam, "No American Can Treat India Like a Pet," October 11, 2005, http://www.rediff.com/news/2005/oct/11inter.htm.

[112] "Iran Pulls Up Indo-US N-deal, India Replies," Express News Service, January 17, 2006, http://www.expressindia.com/fullstory.php?newsid=61506.

[113] P. R. Kumaraswamy, "Will Mottaki Have the Answers?" *Indian Express*, July 17, 2006, http://www.indianexpress.com/story/8644.html.

supplies on which its economy and hence own political stability are based.[114] More broadly, in a region of such geopolitical importance a nuclear Iran hostile to the United States could lead to additional instability. Iran would frighten smaller states and cast a shadow over regional politics as long as perennial rivalries persist. This scenario would not be in the interest of any Asian state. Also destabilizing for Asia would be if a nuclear Iran led to a further scramble for nuclear arms.

None of the major Asian states supports the idea of a nuclear Iran, and no state wants to choose between Iran and the United States. Each of the Asian states—especially China, India, and Pakistan—has cross-cutting interests in region, such as trade and investment with the GCC states, that they do not want to jeopardize. Hence the reaction of Iran's major Asian partners to the nuclear crisis has been to delay or slow commitments and investments, leaving the door open for expansion in the future.[115]

Conclusions

Iran's Strategic Options

It is impossible to predict the outcome of the current crisis and determine answers to whether a diplomatic solution that limits Iran's nuclear potential is possible or whether Iran will seek a weapons capability. If Iran does seek a nuclear weapons capability, questions remain over not only whether Tehran will do so overtly or prefer a latent (or virtual) capability, but also in what timeframe this might unfold. The consequences of and responses to the emergence of an overtly nuclear-capable Iran will differ from those of an Iran that stays within the NPT. In either scenario the NPT will be weakened and regional states will not be slow to respond. Iran's strategy may include playing on the ambiguity over its program precisely to inhibit responses while maximizing benefits.[116]

Tehran's strategic options are cloudy. Iran is unlikely to benefit from becoming a Shi'a hegemon in the region, which would only increase the suspicions of its Arab neighbors.[117] Promoting anti-Americanism, appealing to Arab public opinion, and funding obstructionism toward Israel are short-

---

[114] Michael Vatikiotis, "The Conflict That Stalks Asia," *International Herald Tribune*, February 2, 2007, http://www.iht.com/articles/2007/02/02/opinion/edvatik.php?page=2.

[115] Carola Hoyos, "Lure of Iran Gas Puts Energy-hungry Asian Companies in Hot Seat," *Financial Times*, May 10, 2007, 2.

[116] See Mehdi Mohammadi on "Strategic Ambiguity," *Keyhan* website on April 10, 2007, available through BBC Monitoring, April 13, 2007.

[117] As the nuclear crisis has unfolded since 2003 the states most directly affected in the region have begun to hedge by looking anew at nuclear technology, ostensibly for energy purposes.

term policies rather than a long-term strategy. Already these policies have sparked cohesion among the Arab states and pushed them to craft overtures to Israel. As long as the nuclear crisis is unresolved, support from Asia looks no more promising. Once the crisis is surmounted, Tehran could develop important strategic relations with New Delhi and Beijing, diversifying Iran's sources of technology and arms and expanding its markets.

Iran's basic strategic choice is between continuing revolutionary agitation, on the one hand, and recognizing the value of becoming a normal state, on the other. Once the leadership decides that the regime can survive normalcy and engagement with the world, the stage will be set for a strategic rapprochement with the West. Engagement rather than conflict and confrontation will then be seen as satisfying Iran's strategic priority of regime survival and perpetuation.

The key variable affecting Iran's decisions on the nuclear issue is the impact sanctions and isolation might have on both public discontent and support for the regime. Strong international consensus to increase the pressure on Iran will make Tehran pause to reflect on its actions as the sanctions bite. A critical variable here is the timeframe for the nuclear program's advancement required to make a nuclear option achievable and practically resistant to outside sanctions. In addition, although the regime is sensitive to popular discontent, it is not in any danger of imminent reversal.[118]

Strong external pressures, weak oil prices, and domestic discontent could lead to a reversal of the program's direction and a willingness to negotiate a delay or freeze. Conversely a strong oil market and feeble international consensus could result in an acceleration of the program. Explicit and credible military threats cut two ways: they give diplomats reasons to deflect such threats by offering compromises while simultaneously increasing the incentives for developing a military deterrent.

Moving toward an overt weapons program and withdrawal from the NPT would only accentuate Iran's isolation. Iran's ambiguity concerning its nuclear ambitions reflects genuine uncertainty regarding the country's own ultimate goals. Iran needs to decide whether there is enough urgency to continue to defy the international community or whether defusing the crisis would be more in the country's interests. Given the status motivations behind the program, Tehran should be receptive to policies that seek to give Iran the respect, equality, and security it seeks. Iran would then be more inclined to slow its program and keep its capability virtual. Dialogue,

---

[118] Because of "the intricate interconnections between political actors and interests, stability in Iran is not a function of how many people support or oppose the regime, but rather the intensity of that support or opposition." Hisham Sallam, Andrew Mandlebaum, and Robert Grace, "Who Rules Ahmadinejad's Iran?" United States Institute of Peace Briefing, April 2007, http://www.usip.org/pubs/usipeace_briefings/2007/0412_ahmadinejad_iran.html.

incentives, and security assurances all have important roles in influencing Iran's strategic choices. Yet to ensure that these are not seen as acts of desperation, the international community will first have to demonstrate a willingness to assess the crisis from a position of strength, after which magnanimity and flexibility will be essential.

Iran will be influenced by the degree to which the United States regains its standing and leverage in the region, the degree to which the UNSC and others (such as the EU, Japan, and India) remain united, the demands of its own economy, and finally the speed with which its mastery of the full fuel cycle develops or languishes. In order to influence the debate inside Iran, the United States must influence the broader debate and not just that over the nuclear program. Washington would benefit from helping shape the debate on how Iran should be as a state and how Tehran should pursue foreign relations.

Should Iran accept "the Libyan model," this scenario would imply a change in domestic politics that shifts power from the hard-line constituency to the middle classes, students, and commercial elements. It is difficult to see the beneficiaries of the current system giving up their privileges voluntarily. Such a long overdue transition has encountered obstacles whenever attempted before (such as by Rafsanjani and Khatami). For these reasons domestic and factional politics will determine the fate of this latest episode in the program as well.

Implications for U.S. Interests

Whether Iran goes overtly nuclear or develops the latent capability to do so, the United States will be called to assist in limiting the repercussions. This task will be a complicated one in a regional context where Shi'a Islam is emerging as a dynamic new political factor. Broadly there are three related options available to pursue: prevention, freeze, and containment.

Prevention. Diplomacy and sanctions have been applied toward the cause of prevention. Maintaining the broad international coalition and incrementally ratcheting up sanctions (both formally by the UNSC and unilaterally by states) together aim to raise the costs of continuing enrichment to Iran. If both these efforts continue and if Iran takes several years to master enrichment, the heavy costs to Iran's economy and populace may encourage a debate over the wisdom of Tehran's policy. Such debate has already begun among the elite and may result in some adjustment in policy (possibly even including a limited freeze). The program's momentum and driving political factors and interests, however, make such an outcome unlikely unless the costs and benefits of a freeze are stark and credible.

Counting on Iran's continued inability to master enrichment in the near-to mid-term is a weak basis for policy. A technical solution to the nuclear issue will not eliminate the problem. The United States should use the time before Iran obtains fuel cycle mastery to encourage a strategic reappraisal within Iran. To accomplish this, the United States will need to be willing to respect Iran's interests in exchange for responsible behavior. The United States would need to drop the lexicon that promotes regime change, substitute policy and behavior change, and facilitate such change with a handsome package of inducements. Far from rewarding bad behavior, this approach would shift Iran's domestic debate and make continuing on a radical course an unpopular option.

Freeze. If Iran persists, deflects pressure, and moves to large-scale enrichment, the United States will need to shift to a policy that seeks to freeze existing capabilities in order to eventually see the program rollback, preferably voluntarily. This situation implies acceptance of Iran possessing some enrichment capacity in exchange for more intrusive inspections. Keeping Iran's capability latent is part of this strategy. The assumption behind a freeze is that time may work in favor either of more moderate voices emerging in Iran or that in time U.S.-Iranian relations may experience a thaw that allows the issue to be better managed.

For a freeze strategy to be effective, Washington will need to mobilize the region against Tehran in order to demonstrate the associated costs for Iran of its current course. Efforts to this end have already begun.[119] U.S. policy could seek to neutralize or offset any prospective benefit a nuclear Iran might gain, including Patriot missile defenses, increased military presence, and more explicit security assurances to regional allies (such as Turkey and Persian Gulf partners). The United States is planning to position anti-missile defenses in Europe to counter the threat from Iran, a move that has evoked protests from Russia. Close coordination with Europe will clearly be necessary.

Containment. The last U.S. policy option is acquiescence over a nuclear Iran with a strategy that contains and deters this new nuclear power. This approach would entail consideration of what would constitute a credible security deterrent regarding Iran, both technically (e.g., smaller warheads) and politically (e.g., greater forward and regional deployment). One of the key questions in this scenario is whether the uncertainty that is supposed to work in favor of deterrence would do so here. A nuclear Iran also raises complications for Israel and U.S. policy toward that state.

---

[119] Another role for the regional states might be in promoting a regional fuel bank, enabling Iran to climb down from its insistence on unilateral enrichment.

In the final analysis, the issue of Iran's nuclear ambitions cannot be divorced from the nature of Iran's regime and its overall goals. A technical solution to the nuclear issue may buy time that can be used to deal with related issues or provide the basis for an overall accommodation. Failure to arrest Iran's nuclear ambitions, however, will surely result in a continuation of the regime's radical and hard-line course of action and the consolidation of power.

EXECUTIVE SUMMARY

This chapter examines the current status and possible evolution of Asian efforts to develop cooperative multilateral approaches to regional security.

MAIN ARGUMENT:

- Asian states participate in a complex array of multilateral, bilateral, and unilateral mechanisms to advance their security interests. Despite the recent growth in multilateral processes, most states still focus the majority of their bureaucratic and fiscal resources on bilateral and unilateral military approaches.

- Asia's current political and strategic circumstances preclude the possibility of applying a strongly institutionalized European approach to the construction of a regional security architecture.

- Palpable mistrust among the major powers and divergent views as to the nature and character of the key threats the region faces block efforts to make any meaningful change to regional security policy.

POLICY IMPLICATIONS:

- The most significant barriers to the creation of a more effective regional security architecture are the entrenched sense of mistrust and suspicion among the major powers and divergent conceptions of the nature and character of security threats.

- The recent growth in multilateralism reflects a clear demand for more cooperative approaches to regional security. The U.S. has an opportunity to capitalize on this interest in ways that can advance its interests.

- The U.S. will not be well served over the medium to longer term by maintaining the bilateral military structure of its presence in Asia.

- Asia's proliferation of regional institutions and multilateral processes hinder effective policy cooperation. States attempting to construct a regional architecture would best be mindful of this problem and either reform existing institutions or find a better division of labor among existing entities.

Asian Security Architectures

Nick Bisley

For the bulk of the post-1945 period, security policy in Asia followed traditional patterns. Faced with a complex strategic setting in which the global dynamics of Cold War rivalry intersected with conflicts deriving from the legacy of European colonialism, states overwhelmingly sought to secure their national interests through alliances and self-help strategies. Since the mid-1990s, states have supplemented these traditional approaches with an expanding range of cooperative security initiatives in response to the changing geopolitical landscape, the increasing dynamism and interdependence of the region's economies, and the rise of new security challenges such as transnational terrorism, infectious diseases, and pollution. Despite exploration of more multilateral approaches to securing national interests, most states continue to make self-help strategies and alliances the central focus of security policy. Yet the persistent view that the security environment demands more than the current arrangements leads many scholars and analysts to argue that an effective multilateral security architecture would be a better option. Driving this view are: (1) the recognition that the present period is one of power transition—associated historically with instability—and that more coordination is needed to minimize the destabilizing effects of change and (2) the realization that globalization broadens the range and reach of security challenges, most of which require multilateral cooperation and policy coordination if they are to be avoided or their effects mitigated.

Nick Bisley is Senior Lecturer and Director of the Graduate Program in Diplomacy and Trade in the Graduate School of Business, Monash University. He can be contacted at <nicholas.bisley@buseco. monash.edu.au>.

The author wishes to thank the anonymous referees for their very helpful comments and suggestions on earlier versions of this chapter and Stephanie Renzi for her excellent research assistance.

This chapter examines the current state and possible future trajectory of efforts to create an Asian security architecture. Asia presently has a fractured security architecture; however, moving beyond the status quo, while beneficial to U.S. interests, will be difficult. The problems are challenging but not insurmountable. Undertaking efforts to build a workable security architecture would advance U.S. interests in the region—even though full implementation of such a system would be a long way off.

The chapter is in five sections. The first briefly discusses the idea of a security architecture and defines the term. The second section considers the European experience vis-à-vis the current Asian situation, arguing that Europe's multilayered system of security and governance has some relevance for Asia, but the security setting in Asia prevents replication of the European system. A comparison of the European and Asian circumstances also reveals the structural sources of existing weaknesses in the regional security architecture. The third section surveys the current range of security mechanisms in the region and argues not only that Asia has a fractured architecture but also that the present order is in a state of flux in which current security arrangements are likely to change over the medium and long term. Thus the next five years or so will be important in determining the shape of things to come. Given this transitional situation, the fourth section presents different forms that a more coherent security architecture might take and considers their plausibility. The chapter concludes that while a feasible and effective region-wide security architecture may be difficult to imagine in the short term, there are good reasons for the United States to take a broader approach to its security interests in Asia and to adopt a more multidimensional approach to advancing these interests.

Security Architecture: Meaning and Concepts

Unlike concepts with a settled meaning, such as a security community[1] or multilateralism,[2] the idea of a "security architecture" is somewhat opaque. Use of the architectural metaphor to describe forms of international cooperation and coordination emerged from the calls to reform international financial governance in the wake of the 1997–98

---

[1] See Karl Wolfgang Deutsch, Sidney A. Burell, and Robert A. Kann, *Political Community and the North Atlantic Area* (Princeton: Princeton University Press, 1957).

[2] John Gerrard Ruggie, "Multilateralism: Anatomy of an Institution," in *Multilateralism Matters: The Theory and Praxis of an Institutional Form*, ed. John Gerrard Ruggie (New York: Columbia University Press, 1993), 3–47.

international financial crises.[3] The metaphor conveys not just the sum of cooperative measures but also the concerted, multifaceted effort required to cope with the complex problems of international economic governance. That this idea appeals to security policymakers and scholars is no surprise. Just as international finance has diverse strands (both public and private) and thus requires distinct mechanisms to keep the system as a whole stable, international security is increasingly perceived as a complex and multidimensional proposition. Whereas in the past states viewed the military and ideological challenges of other states as the exclusive source of serious threats, today states see these challenges as only one part of a complex matrix of transnational, social, economic, and environmental threats to national well-being. This complexity, many feel, is better dealt with through the creation of a security architecture.

The Idea of a Security Architecture

Of the range of security policies and institutions dotting the landscape of world politics, only the set established in Europe presently appears to qualify as a security architecture. Aside from being the only security architecture of substance, what makes it of particular interest is the capacity of the European system to quell geopolitical tensions while also coordinating responses to humanitarian crises, to consolidate democratic transitions, and to construct a sense of trust and common cause among a diverse and once antagonistic group of states. The European architecture is comprised of an institutional core centered on the collective defense commitments of the North Atlantic Treaty Organization (NATO). This core is supplemented by a series of cooperative and collaborative measures including the European Union's (EU) common foreign and security policy, the Organization for Security and Co-operation in Europe (OSCE), and the Council of Europe. The European architecture takes a generally inclusive approach to security challenges and has a multidimensional conception of security matched with a capacity to respond to these challenges with a wide array of policy tools.[4] At the core of Europe's security structure is a sense of shared interests, values, and perception of common threats. This multilayered system relies on a series of often overlapping institutions and mechanisms that provide

---

[3] For example, Barry J. Eichengreen, *Toward a New International Financial Architecture: A Practical post-Asia Agenda* (Washington, D.C.: Institute for International Economics, 1999).

[4] On the generally inclusive approach, see Celeste A. Wallander and Robert O. Keohane, "Risk, Threat and Security Institutions," in *Imperfect Unions: Security Institutions Over Time and Space,* ed. Helga A. Haftendorn, Robert O. Keohane, and Celeste A. Wallander (Oxford: Oxford University Press, 1999), 24–29.

a complex and fairly robust method for securing human communities in Europe.

This distinctive security system emerged as a result of a number of unique European developments. First, the Cold War brought U.S. military power to Europe and provided an external security guarantee over a long period of time that was crucial to dampening European mutual mistrust. Second, the external threat of the Soviet geopolitical and ideological challenge further focused European policymakers both on the shared character of the security threats and on Western Europe's underlying political, strategic, and economic common interests. Third, the manner of the Cold War's conclusion—the disappearance of the Soviet challenge and incorporation of most states in Central and Eastern Europe into the liberal international system—placed the common interests and values of Western European states at the heart of a new and more geographically expansive European order. These developments, alongside the growth of the European Union, were crucial not only to creating a sense of shared threats and common interests and values but also to the establishment of policy mechanisms the European states need to protect their interests in a globalizing world. Although having began as a military alliance, the European security architecture in its current form transcends the original exclusionary system's singular focus on military responses to security.

The notion of a security architecture can, of course, refer to a wide range of security mechanisms and approaches. For example, the term can refer to a multistate alliance system governed by a traditional collective security logic in which common values and ideas would receive no support and the shared conventional national interests of the alliance members would remain the focus of concern. This chapter takes the view that the term should be used to refer to a distinct practice of international security and not simply as a new label for an existing practice. Thus, security architecture here refers to a reasonably coherent association of international institutions, dialogue forums, and other mechanisms that collectively work to secure a defined geopolitical space. This space is the product of a broader set of shared interests and values together with a common sense of risks and threats among participants in the association.

This fairly expansive and liberal conception places cooperative commitments and shared values and interests at its core. The focus of this chapter therefore is on self-conscious efforts to foster a range of institutional mechanisms to secure the peoples of Asia through cooperative interstate relations. The underlying purpose of an architecture is to reduce security threats and, in doing so, transform the interests and identities of Asian states and societies. An architecture should not require those changes to come into being. Rather, an architecture could underwrite regional stability through the coordination of state policy involving: (1) states seeking cooperation to mitigate the effects of globalization, (2) major powers seeking to reduce the risks of conflict, and (3) the dominant power (the United States) seeking to reduce the risk premium of states moving away from the status quo. Put plainly, more than a reflection of the "realities of power" as some realists insist, a security architecture is a set of institutional mechanisms for facilitating interstate cooperation to cope with both traditional and new threats to human communities.

The Security Setting: Asian and European Circumstances

A feature of recent scholarly debate about Asian security is an argument about the relevance of the European historical experience. Some argue that, sitting uneasily within the existing power structure, Asia's rising powers are likely to follow the example of European great-power rivalry and war.[5] Others assert that because of Asia's unique circumstances the region is unlikely to follow the European experience.[6] Although the policy relevance of historical parallels is open to debate, there is merit in comparing the two regions. Notwithstanding some important commonalities, a range of significant obstacles in Asia—impediments that European states either do not face or have overcome make the development of an effective Asian security architecture, at least along European lines, unlikely in the short to medium term.

This section examines the differing security settings of Europe and Asia, both drawing attention to the challenges of trying to transpose the European approach in Asia and highlighting the sources of the ongoing difficulties existing Asian security cooperation faces. The section looks at the geopolitical setting, the diversity of security challenges experienced by Asian states, the vastly different perceptions of threats, the role of the United States, and the very different approaches to sovereignty and the role of nationalism in Europe and Asia.

---

[5] For example, see Aaron Friedberg, "Will Europe's Past Be Asia's Future?" *Survival* 42, no. 3 (Autumn 2000) 147–60; and John J. Mearsheimer, *The Tragedy of Great Power Politics* (New York: W. W. Norton & Company, 2001), chap. 10.

[6] David C. Kang, "Getting Asia Wrong: The Need for New Analytic Frameworks," *International Security* 27, no. 4 (Spring 2003): 57–85.

The Geopolitical Setting

The geographic scope and geopolitical diversity of Asia, along with the wide range of socio-economic circumstances among societies in the region, raise a host of strategic issues with which any putative security architecture must grapple. Foremost amongst these issues is the tremendous variety of security challenges facing Asia's subregions. Uncertainty and mistrust dog relations among the major powers in East Asia, nuclear proliferation and regime stability are the key concerns on the Korean Peninsula, and the increasing military capabilities of China and Japan make all of East Asia uneasy. For Southeast Asian states the primary concerns are transnational problems such as terrorism, secessionism, low-intensity cross-border conflicts, and crime. Western Pacific states are suffering a range of crises in governance and state capacity with significant regional security consequences. The Central Asian states of the former Soviet Union face threats that derive from weak states and porous borders—Islamist extremists, organized crime, and domestic instability. In South Asia, India-Pakistan tensions predominate, but civil wars and low-intensity conflicts continue to bedevil Sri Lanka and Nepal. Pressure is mounting against efforts by NATO to stabilize post-Taliban Afghanistan.

One key aspect of the European security system is a robust sense of trust shared by its participants. Even Russia, the only significant European power that is uncomfortable with the European architecture, has, in the NATO-Russia Council, a formal relationship with and stake in the system.[7] In Asia the central feature of the strategic setting is the ongoing uncertainty, mistrust, and at times outright antagonism between the major powers. Although the People's Republic of China (PRC) has been undertaking a diplomatic "charm offensive" as part of a broader normalization of its foreign policy, the country's relations with Japan and the United States remain mistrustful.[8] Despite a superficial cordiality, U.S.-China relations are characterized by a strong sense of mutual suspicion. Acrimonious Sino-Japanese strategic relations belie the close economic linkages of these two states. Although having helped to ease relations, recent bilateral summits have not really addressed the root of mutual antagonism. In South Asia important steps have improved the tone and tenor of relations between India and Pakistan, but friction between the two states—due to entrenched differences on Kashmir stemming from continued militancy and mutual mistrust—remains an enduring feature of Asia's strategic setting.

---

[7] In the past two years this relationship has deteriorated considerably.

[8] On the "charm offensive," see David Shambaugh, "China Engages Asia: Reshaping the Regional Order," *International Security* 29, no. 3, (Winter 2004/05): 64–99.

A second aspect of the European architecture is a settled sense of the key risks and threats Europe faces. The majority of European states are part of a common alliance system and do not perceive interstate military conflict in Europe as realistic in the short or long term. Human security challenges and broader disturbances to global security pose the primary threats to these states. The EU's 2003 European Security Strategy identifies terrorism, proliferation of WMD, regional conflicts, state failure, and organized crime as the central threats.[9] In comparison, the security setting in Asia involves traditional interstate rivalries, unresolved territorial disputes, and transnational threats that unfold in various ways across the region.

The differences between Europe and Asia extend beyond the sharp contrast in their respective security problems. Perceptions of the character and origins of the threats to regional security differ as well. For example, while cautious in public, leaders in the United States and Japan perceive China's economic rise and military modernization not only as a threat to the East Asian strategic balance but also as a longer-term challenge to their regional, and indeed global, interests. As Kenneth Lieberthal points out in his contribution to this volume, China's leadership characterizes the same underlying trends as part of a "peaceful development" and has adopted a "new security concept" that articulates a commitment to a shared view of the region's security threats.[10] Moreover, Beijing perceives an anti-China mind-set in the United States as the primary source of threat.[11] Although the PRC and other states in the region share some common threat assessments (e.g., over terrorism), China's security policy and the regional response to it represent a classical security dilemma at work. That is, the various parties have very different perceptions of the motives and purposes of their own and others' defense policies and act on an assumption that the defense policies of other states are inherently threatening. This trend can be seen in other parts of Asia, most obviously among India and Pakistan. At the same time, as many of the chapters in this volume attest, perceptions in Central Asia of the sources and character of security threats (e.g., radical Islam and drug trafficking) are different from perceptions in Southeast Asia, where internal state coherence and maritime security are of primary concern.

Any Asian security architecture must cope with two formidable challenges. The architecture must be able to incorporate a vast range

---

[9] Javier Solana, *A Secure Europe in a Better World: European Security Strategy* (Brussels: European Union Institute for European Studies, 2003), 3–5, http://www.iss-eu.org/solana/solanae.pdf.

[10] See also Guangkai Xiong, "The New Security Concept Initiated by China," *International Strategic Studies*, Beijing, Series 65.3, 2002, cited in David L. Shambaugh, *Power Shift: China and Asia's New Dynamics* (Berkeley: University of California Press, 2006), 361.

[11] On this point, see Evelyn Goh, "The US-China Relationship and Asia-Pacific Security: Negotiating Change," *Asian Security* 1, no. 3 (September 2005): 216–44.

of security threats—from interstate rivalry and territorial disputes to transnational crime—as well as overcome the tremendous gulf of opinion among regional powers over the kinds of risks the region faces. If a security architecture requires a consensus about the nature of security risks and the policies to respond to those risks, then Asia clearly falls short.

External Power

One of the striking similarities in European and Asian security is the role played by the United States in underwriting stability in both regions. This security anchor is of more recent provenance in Asia and is primarily focused on East Asia. Nevertheless, the forward projection of U.S. power has secured geopolitical stability in the past 25 years or so in both regions. This similarity belies some important differences in the manner of projecting power and the underlying purpose of so doing.

In Asia, U.S. military power is organized through a set of bilateral alliances and alignments, the most important feature of which is the forward deployment of significant military assets in Japan and South Korea.[12] The bilateral structure provides the United States with greater autonomy than a multilateral approach and reflects the region's complexities.[13] The European posture is almost the reverse, involving a multilateral alliance system with an integrated command structure backed up by a range of multilayered governance mechanisms that the United States has supported over a long period of time. NATO has evolved to become both a means to deter military aggression against member states and a coordination and cooperation center for members to raise security issues of common concern and coordinate any joint action.

Initially a function of Europe's inability to defend itself, the U.S. presence in Europe remains unchanged in more recent times because European powers have been unwilling to undertake sufficient defense spending to change this. In Asia the United States does not underwrite a mutual security system but is a stabilizing force in a mistrustful region. The U.S. presence deters China from using force against Taiwan and keeps Japan from assuming a greater military role. If the United States is thought to be needed in Europe because the European states will not spend enough, the United States is needed in Asia to make sure Asian states do not spend too much.

---

[12] For an overview, see Robert G. Sutter, *The United States and East Asia: Dynamics and Implications* (Lanham, MD: Rowman & Littlefield Publishers, 2002).

[13] On its historical origins, see Christopher Hemmer and Peter Katzenstein, "Why Is There No NATO in Asia? Collective Identity, Regionalism, and the Origins of Multilateralism," *International Organization* 56, no. 3 (Summer 2002): 575–609.

Although Washington participates in multilateral dialogue and ad hoc cooperation on issues such as piracy and counterterrorism, the bilateral alliances are the most important feature of U.S. Asia policy. The series of bilateral arrangements, however, is a fairly blunt security instrument whose central component is deterrence based on the credible threat of the use of force. Alternative actions, while possible, are not integrated and often lack the political heft that better coordination would provide. In Europe the range of policy options is much broader: NATO has mechanisms linking military, diplomatic, and humanitarian action, and a range of non-NATO groups also contribute to security efforts. Although in both regions the United States underwrites security and through this promotes regional cooperation, there are important differences in the form and function of U.S. power projection in Europe and Asia.

Sovereignty and Nationalism

A final point of contrast between the European and Asian security settings lies in Asia's quite different attitudes toward sovereignty and nationalism, which constrain efforts to create a workable security architecture. European states have famously taken a flexible view of sovereignty: they have modified principles of sovereign equality in the EU's voting procedures, created a single economic space, and given up large swathes of policymaking autonomy, most notably among those that have adopted the Euro and have opened internal borders.[14] Not only the old European powers but also many of the newly independent states of Eastern Europe and the former Soviet Union have adopted this approach to sovereignty with remarkable swiftness.

In contrast, Asian attitudes are just as famously committed to a much more orthodox approach to political authority. While happy to commit to interstate agreements to serve their economic interests (such as joining the World Trade Organization), many Asian states are reluctant to go any further. With the activities of the European Commission firmly in mind, the Association of Southeast Asian Nations (ASEAN) and the Asia-Pacific Economic Cooperation (APEC) deliberately neutered their secretariats so as to limit organizational autonomy. Describing Asian states as sovereignty absolutists overstates the case; these states are, however, still very protective of the principles of equality, autonomy, and exclusive authority that European practices of sovereignty have diluted.

---

[14] See William Wallace, "The Sharing of Sovereignty: The European Paradox," *Political Studies* 47, no. 3 (1999): 503–21.

In both Europe and Asia nationalism is an important political force. Although viewing Europe as a post-nationalist utopia and Asia as home to backward-looking demagogues would be wrong, recognizing the decidedly different role of nationalism in the two regions' efforts to construct regional institutions is important. The motivating idea (often forgotten today) behind European integration was to prevent nationalism from leading to war.[15] A central feature, among other factors that drove the formation of the European communities, was a concerted effort to institutionalize mechanisms for diluting the functional capacity of nationalism to lead to interstate conflict. Asia's recent embrace of regionalism has involved not only a commitment to a fairly strict interpretation of sovereignty but also the use of regional institutions as tools to reinforce and advance nationalist projects and statist conceptions of economic development.[16]

Although multidimensional and widely supported, the European security architecture is not flawless. European shortcomings in the face of the long-running break-up of Yugoslavia are well known. Moreover, while Western and Central Europe are secure, states and societies on the periphery do not benefit from the architecture's securing force to anywhere near the same degree. For example, the eastern reaches of Turkey, a NATO member, are insecure and have become decidedly more so since the 2003 Iraq intervention.

A number of factors should curb any optimism about Asia's ability to replicate the European architecture—the geopolitical setting, the divergent opinions on common risks and threats, the attitude toward regional cooperation, and the different role that the United States plays in Asia—all of which fly in the face of the conditions that have been key to European success. It is safe to say that Europe's present is not going to be Asia's future; but to assume, therefore, that Asia's future will necessarily be Europe's past would be a mistake.

Asian Security Architectures: Current Status

In spite of the region's circumstances, Asia has begun to adopt aspects of security multilateralism with some enthusiasm. From the formation of the ASEAN Regional Forum (ARF) to security cooperation at APEC, aspects of an embryonic architecture are increasingly evident. The region now has three modes of security policy: (1) a set of traditional military approaches

---

[15] See Desmond Dinan, *Ever Closer Union: An Introduction of European Integration* (Boulder: Lynne Rienner Publishers, 2005), chap. 1.

[16] Baogang He, "East Asian Ideas of Regionalism: A Normative Critique," *Australian Journal of International Affairs* 58, no. 1 (March 2004): 105–25.

dominated by U.S. bilateral alliances; (2) a series of ongoing and broadly focused multilateral efforts comprising intergovernmental and unofficial "Track II" discussions, and (3) a number of bilateral and multilateral mechanisms designed to deal with specific problems or functional issue areas. This section examines these developments and considers the way in which they operate to produce a fractured regional security architecture. Although multilateral efforts have undergone remarkable expansion, their capacity to deliver substantive policy cooperation has thus far been limited.

Traditional Approaches

As discussed above, the central feature of Asian security consists of both the bilateral military alliances the United States has with Japan, South Korea, and Australia and the tacit commitments the United States has to Taiwan, the Philippines, Singapore, and Thailand. Formed during the Cold War, these alliances have survived the region's recent geopolitical and geoeconomic transformation largely intact.[17] They underwrite regional security and stability and are increasingly explicitly described as serving this purpose.[18] Beyond their primary deterrence function, these alliances not only reduce the risks that states might seek to alter the region's strategic balance but also secure the sealines of communication (SLOC) that are vital to regional prosperity.

In East Asia both the PRC and the Democratic People's Republic of Korea (DPRK, or North Korea) structure their traditional military security policy on self-help principles. Each country maintains sufficient military capacity to defend its vital interests or, at the very least, make any potential aggressor pay a high price for intervention. In Southeast Asia, as noted elsewhere in this volume, the primary focus of traditional approaches is on internal state cohesion, and in South and Central Asia self-help military approaches are the order of the day. From a bureaucratic and fiscal point of view, Asian states devote the highest priority in their defense and security policies to traditional military approaches run either through bilateral alliances or on a self-reliance basis.

---

[17] See Roger Buckley, *The United States in the Asia-Pacific since 1945* (Cambridge: Cambridge University Press, 2002).

[18] See, for example, the language in "Joint Statement of the Security Consultative Committee, Alliance Transformation: Advancing United States-Japan Security and Defense Cooperation, May 1, 2007," available on the Ministry of Foreign Affairs of Japan website, http://www.mofa.go.jp/region/n-america/us/security/scc/joint0705.html.

Nascent Security Multilateralism

This emphasis on bilateral alliances and self-reliance may lead analysis to overlook the expansion of Asian security multilateralism at both intergovernmental and informal Track II levels. This section first discusses ARF, APEC, the South Asian Association for Regional Cooperation (SAARC), and the Shanghai Cooperation Organization (SCO) and then examines new dialogue forums and the growth in informal security dialogues and other Track II processes.

In the 1994 formation of ARF, ASEAN created a geographically expansive security dialogue forum with three underlying objectives.[19] The first was to shape the security policies of the major powers, primarily by locking in U.S. interests in Asia at a time when Washington's commitment to the region was in doubt, and to draw an emerging China into a regional multilateral process. The second objective—stemming from the recognition by ASEAN states that their security setting was increasingly shaped by forces outside Southeast Asia—was to use opportunities that ARF might provide to influence this environment. ASEAN's third objective was to use ARF for developing cooperative responses to emerging transnational security challenges.[20] Initially aiming to promote dialogue on political and security issues of common concern, in 1995 ARF established a framework structure and planned a three-stage evolution.[21] Although having achieved some success—ARF has enhanced mutual trust and is thought to have been key to the change in China's posture on security dialogues—the evolution of the institution has stalled.[22] ARF is unable to discuss several of the region's most significant security issues, most notably Taiwan. Increasingly, the appeal of ARF—that it travels at a pace all member states find comfortable and operates on the principle of consensus—is becoming a source of frustration for many member states. Key parties are becoming disengaged from the process, most evident in the relatively low level of representation sent by some countries, including the United States. These shortcomings

---

[19] The current membership includes Australia, Bangladesh, Brunei, Cambodia, Canada, China, the European Union, India, Indonesia, Japan, North Korea, South Korea, Laos, Malaysia, Myanmar, Mongolia, New Zealand, Pakistan, Papua New Guinea, the Philippines, Russia, Singapore, Thailand, East Timor, the United States, and Vietnam.

[20] On the formation of the ARF, see Michael Leifer, *The ASEAN Regional Forum*, Adelphi Paper 302 (London: Oxford University Press for the International Institute for Strategic Studies, 1996).

[21] Secretariat of the Association of the Southeast Asian Nations, "The ASEAN Regional Forum: A Concept Paper," http://www.aseansec.org/3635.htm.

[22] See Akiko Fukushima, "The ASEAN Regional Forum," in *The Regional Organizations of the Asia-Pacific: Exploring Institutional Change*, ed. Michael Wesley (Basingstoke: Palgrave Macmillan, 2003), 76–95, 89–90.

notwithstanding, ARF is the most expansive multilateral security institution within Asia.

APEC, which held its first meeting in 1989 and expanded rapidly through the 1990s, was intended both to promote growth and development in the region through economic cooperation and to enhance trade liberalization in line with General Agreement on Tariffs and Trade (GATT) principles.[23] During the first years of the organization, APEC members sought to keep political and security matters outside the forum, with most seeing a division of labor between APEC and the ARF. Faced with the broader failure of its trade liberalization ambitions, its haplessness during and after the Asian financial crisis, and the impossibility of keeping economic and security matters separate, however, APEC has begun to develop a small but significant security cooperation dimension.[24] The annual leaders' meetings have proven to be an effective means for discussing areas of common concern and prompting action. Agreements reached at the 1999 Auckland summit paved the way for the East Timor intervention, and the 2001 summit served both to ease tensions between the United States and China following the EP-3 spy plane incident and to provide a clear pan-regional condemnation of terrorism. More recently APEC has adopted a Secure Trade in the APEC Region (STAR) initiative aimed at improving security for maritime shipping, particularly from the threat posed by terrorists.[25] In the ongoing discussions on how to reinvigorate APEC, members have expressed interest in adding resource and energy security as a further APEC competence.

The 1985 establishment of SAARC was an effort to foster intraregional trade and investment through international cooperation as part of a broader effort to advance regional welfare and thereby reduce South Asia's interstate and transnational conflicts.[26] SAARC is generally regarded as an ineffective institution despite an extensive array of meetings, working groups, and summits. This failure is primarily due to the lingering mistrust between the region's two biggest powers and the broader lack of

---

[23] See John Ravenhill, *APEC and the Construction of Pacific Rim Regionalism* (Cambridge: Cambridge University Press, 2001). Its member economies are Australia, Brunei, Canada, Chile, the People's Republic of China, Hong Kong SAR, Indonesia, Japan, South Korea, Malaysia, Mexico, New Zealand, Papua New Guinea, Peru, the Philippines, Russia, Singapore, Chinese Taipei, Thailand, the United States, and Vietnam.

[24] Nick Bisley, "APEC and Security Cooperation in the Asia-Pacific," in *People, States and Regions*, ed. Anne Hammerstad (Johannesburg: South African Institute of International Affairs, 2005), 225–49.

[25] See John Ravenhill, "Mission Creep or Mission Impossible: APEC and Security," in *Reassessing Security Cooperation in the Asia-Pacific: Competition, Congruence and Transformation*, ed. Amitav Acharya and Evelyn Goh (Cambridge: MIT Press, 2007).

[26] The present membership is Bangladesh, Bhutan, India, Maldives, Nepal, Pakistan, and Sri Lanka.

administrative capacity that many members face. India and Pakistan have always been hesitant participants in the organization, the creation of which was driven largely by Bangladesh. SAARC's primary focus has been to increase regional trade, yet problems such as non-compatible comparative advantage, lack of surplus productive capacity, and poor infrastructure have kept achievement on this front to a minimum.[27] Members are interested in addressing SAARC's shortcomings, but disputes continue to limit regional cooperation despite efforts to excise contentious areas from discussion.[28] SAARC's present contributions to security are minimal, although the 2004 Additional Protocol to its 1987 Regional Convention on the Suppression of Terrorism indicates some cooperation in targeting international financing of terrorism.[29] Although the edifice of SAARC could contribute to regional security, as yet this potential remains largely unrealized.

In 2001 China formed the SCO as the successor organization to the Shanghai Five grouping established in 1996.[30] As part of a broader effort by China to stabilize its borderlands and project influence in Central Asia, an area of vital strategic interest, the primary concern of the SCO was demilitarization of the former Soviet borders.[31] In recent years the grouping has turned its attention to counterterrorism, drug trafficking, and trade liberalization. The Regional Anti-Terrorist Structure (RATS), primarily an information-sharing mechanism, is generally regarded as having been reasonably successful in reducing transnational terrorism in Central Asia.[32] The SCO recently has become a vehicle for geopolitical posturing and has been involved in several less than subtle moves against U.S. interests, most notably in supporting Uzbekistan's closure of U.S. bases and increasing ties with Iran. That said, hawkish interpretations of the SCO as an embryonic Warsaw Pact seem wide of the mark. Though primarily a dialogue body, the organization not only has played an important role in coordinating

---

[27] A. R. Kemal, Musleh-ud Din, Kalbe Abbas, and Usman Qadir, "A Plan to Strengthen Regional Trade Cooperation in South Asia," in *Trade, Finance and Investment in South Asia*, ed. T. N. Srinivasn (Oxford: Berghan Books, 2006), 239–319.

[28] See discussion in Faizal Yahya, "Pakistan, SAARC and ASEAN Relations," *Contemporary Southeast Asia* 26, no. 2 (August 2004): 346–75.

[29] See "Additional Protocol to the SAARC Regional Convention on the Suppression of Terrorism," available on the South Asian Association for Regional Cooperation (SAARC) website, http://www.saarc-sec.org/main.php?id=11&t=3.2.

[30] Members include China, Russia, Kazakhstan, Tajikistan, Kyrgyzstan, and Uzbekistan. Presently, Mongolia, Iran, India, and Pakistan have formal observer status.

[31] "Declaration on the Establishment of the Shanghai Cooperation Organization," Shanghai Cooperation Organization, Press Release, June 15, 2001, http://www.sectsco.org/html/00088.html.

[32] Kevin Sheives, "China Turns West: Beijing's Contemporary Strategy towards Central Asia," *Pacific Affairs* 79, no. 2 (Summer 2006): 205–24.

counterterrorism cooperation but also is increasing military cooperation through joint maneuvers, intelligence sharing, and counterterrorism joint-action.[33] Appearing to work reasonably effectively as a dialogue and cooperation forum on areas in which there is consensus (such as counterterrorism and secessionism), the SCO is, however, decidedly less effective in other areas (such as trade and investment facilitation). Moreover, the underlying tension between China and Russia acts as an impediment to any significant institutionalization of security cooperation, although some scholars point out the increasing chance that the SCO will become the basis of a gas cartel along the lines of OPEC (the Organization of the Petroleum Exporting Countries), the petroleum cartel.[34]

Asian states clearly have a considerable appetite for security dialogue. Some observers see the growth in range and scope of these bodies as potentially counterproductive.[35] Beyond APEC and the ARF, three further venues for multilateral security dialogue have emerged in recent years: ASEAN +3,[36] the Shangri-La Dialogue, and the East Asia Summit (EAS).

ASEAN +3, created following the first Europe-Asia Meeting in 1996 as a response to regional demand for economic cooperation, has instigated a number of policy measures, most notably the Chiang Mai Initiative and discussion around an East Asian Free Trade Agreement.[37] Although its primary concern is economic, ASEAN +3 has (in contrast to APEC) from the outset made political and security dialogue an explicit focus of its work. Dialogue occurs at many levels. In 2004 ASEAN +3 began to focus on transnational crime, targeting eight areas for specific attention: terrorism, illicit drug trafficking, trafficking in persons, sea piracy, arms smuggling, money laundering, international economic crime, and cyber crime.[38] At its January 2007 summit, ASEAN +3 not only made commitments to cooperate on infectious disease prevention and energy security but also gave

---

[33] Rollie Lal, *Central Asia and Its Asian Neighbors: Security and Commerce at the Crossroads* (Santa Monica: Rand Corporation, 2006), 7.

[34] Stephen Blank, "The Shanghai Cooperation Organization as an 'Energy Club': Portents for the Future," Central-Asia Caucasus Analyst, Bi-Weekly Briefing 8, no. 19, October, 2006, http://www.cacianalyst.org/newsite/files/20061004Analyst.pdf.

[35] Allen Gyngell, "Design Faults: The Asia-Pacific's Regional Architecture," Sydney, Lowy Institute for International Policy, Lowy Institute Policy Brief, July 2007, http://www.lowyinstitute.org/Publication.asp?pid=638.

[36] The ten ASEAN states plus China, South Korea, and Japan.

[37] See Richard Stubbs, "ASEAN Plus Three: Emerging East Asian Regionalism?" *Asian Survey* 42, no. 3 (May–June 2002), 440–55.

[38] "Joint Communiqué of the First ASEAN Plus Three Ministerial Meeting on Transnational Crime," Association for Southeast Asian Nations, January 10, 2004, http://www.aseansec.org/15645.htm.

diplomatic support to the six-party talks in Korea.[39] ASEAN +3 members see the group as a central mechanism in the emerging regional architecture, and China prefers to direct its East Asian regional commitments through ASEAN +3.

The Shangri-La Dialogue, convened in Singapore since 2002, is an annual meeting of defense ministers, military and civilian officials, advisors, and academic experts organized by the London-based International Institute for Strategic Studies.[40] This dialogue provides an informal environment in which defense and security policymakers and scholars can discuss a wide range of security matters. Beyond confidence building and communication, the dialogue allows for corridor diplomacy without the media glare that higher-profile meetings garner and provides a venue for diplomatic signaling on defense and security matters. The Shangri-La Dialogue is increasingly recognized as playing an important role in the region's multilateral security efforts.

The object of the EAS, which held its first meeting in December 2005 and its second in January 2007, is to further regional political and economic cooperation.[41] The declaration made at the first summit clearly identifies political and security dialogue as central to the organization's purpose.[42] Growing regional support for the idea of an East Asian Community could be realized through the EAS. The creation of an East Asian Community would, if achieved, generate political and security spillovers from economic collaboration. For example, Malaysian Prime Minister Abdullah Badawi has called for the creation of a functional East Asian community whereby increasing economic integration would transform state interests and thus heighten political and security cooperation and regional stability.[43] As a group whose membership is intended to reduce China's influence and to broaden the geographic scope and political focus of regional institutions beyond ASEAN +3,

---

[39] See "Chairman's Statement of the Tenth ASEAN Plus Three Summit," Cebu, Philippines, January 14, 2007, available on the Ministry of Foreign Affairs of Japan website, http://www.mofa.go.jp/region/asia-paci/asean/conference/asean3/state0701.html.

[40] Governmental representatives come from Australia, Bangladesh, Brunei, Cambodia, Canada, China, France, India, Indonesia, Japan, Malaysia, Mongolia, Myanmar, New Zealand, Pakistan, the Philippines, Republic of Korea, Singapore, Sri Lanka, Thailand, Timor-Leste, the United Kingdom, the United States, and Vietnam.

[41] Participants include the ASEAN +3 members plus India, Australia, and New Zealand.

[42] "Kuala Lumpur Declaration on the East Asia Summit," Association for Southeast Asian Nations, December 14, 2005, http://www.aseansec.org/18098.htm.

[43] Dato' Seri Abdullah Ahmad Badawi, "Towards an Integrated East Asia Community," address to the Second East Asia Forum, Kuala Lumpur, December 6, 2004, http://www.pmo.gov.my/WebNotesApp/pmmain.nsf/75b3202912e2d4f6482570c400031dbc/f78c2c8eaada406648256f6300118854?OpenDocument.

both EAS and its attempt at community building appear to be prompting some institutional competition in the region.[44] Although revealing more about the differences among the EAS membership regarding purpose and organizational process, the two summits also indicate a commitment to discuss political, defense, and security matters in a multilateral forum.[45]

Asia generally, and East Asia specifically, has witnessed an explosion of Track II processes in recent years with nearly 150 Track II meetings or discussions on East Asian security in 2004 and a similar number in 2005.[46] Track II refers to "unofficial activities, involving academics, think-tank researchers, journalists and former officials, as well as current officials participating in their private capacities."[47] In contrast to broader civil society matters, these initiatives have some means to feed into official policymaking mechanisms. Among the more notable mechanisms are the Council on Security and Cooperation in the Asia-Pacific (CSCAP),[48] the ASEAN-Institute of Strategic and International Studies (ASEAN-ISIS) Roundtable, and the recently established Network of East Asian Think-Tanks (NEAT).[49] Although often criticized as ineffective talk shops, Track II processes are commended by supporters for a range of contributions. For example, Track II processes are credited with drawing attention to common regional interests and mitigating the military bias of conventional approaches as well as providing means for the development of regional cooperation through channels for alternative diplomatic routes and contributing to novel policy developments by offering mechanisms to test their plausibility.[50] The perceived relative success has come with a price: as Track II bodies become more influential, governments have tried to constrain their activities. For example, CSCAP is finding discussion about Taiwan, and the participation of Taiwanese scholars, increasingly problematic.

---

[44] See Mohan Malik, "The East Asian Summit," *Australian Journal of International Affairs* 60, no. 2 (June 2006): 207–11.

[45] On the difference, see Hadi Soesastro, "The East Asia Summit and East Asian Community Building," Global Economic Review [forthcoming, 2007].

[46] Japan Centre for International Exchange (JCIE) runs an ongoing report series, "Dialogue and Research Monitor: Towards Community Building in East Asia," that produces biannual reports on Track II meetings. For 2004 and 2005 meeting reports see "Inventory of Meetings in 2004" and "Inventory of Meetings in 2005" on the JCIE website, http://www.jcie.or.jp/drm/Jan2004/track2.html.

[47] Desmond Ball, Anthony Milner, and Brendan Taylor, "Track 2 Security Dialogue in the Asia-Pacific: Reflections and Future Directions," *Asian Security* 2, no. 3 (August 2006): 174–88.

[48] On CSCAP, see Desmond Ball, *The Council for Security and Cooperation in the Asia-Pacific: Its Record and Prospects* (Canberra: Australian National University, 2000).

[49] NEAT is a China-led network that supports the ASEAN +3 grouping.

[50] See Brian L. Job, "Track 2 Diplomacy: Ideational Contribution to the Evolving Asian Security Order," in *Asian Security Order: Instrumental and Normative Features*, ed. Muthiah Alagappa (Stanford: Stanford University Press, 2002), 241–79.

Functional Security Mechanisms

The third category of Asian security cooperation is a group of ad hoc functional mechanisms. Unlike the institutions and open-ended dialogue processes, these mechanisms focus on one issue area or attempt to resolve a particular crisis. In response to the challenges of transnational terrorism, many Asian states have undertaken bilateral and multilateral counterterrorism initiatives. From bilateral agreements, such as those signed between Australia and Indonesia, to multilateral commitments such as the 2001 ASEAN counterterrorism declaration, the post-2001 threat of transnational terrorism has prompted an unprecedented degree of cooperation and coordination among Asian states.[51] A second area of cooperation relates to attempts to prevent WMD proliferation. In Asia the United States has found relatively good support for the Proliferation Security Initiative (PSI). Although the PSI is not organized around a treaty or an institution, Singapore, Thailand, Canada, Australia, Russia, Japan, and New Zealand participate in joint PSI-related military exercises and, it is assumed, will be involved in future interdictions.[52] Other Asian states are being actively courted by the United States, including Cambodia, China, India, Indonesia, Malaysia, Pakistan, South Korea, and Vietnam, although not many are likely to participate in a maritime interdiction system that has an uncertain status in international law.

The Five Power Defence Arrangements (FPDA) in Southeast Asia have recently taken on new life.[53] The original purpose of the FPDA, which was established in 1971, was to underwrite the security of post-colonial Malaysia and Singapore, which until recently involved a range of political and strategic dialogues and regular military exercises involving the five member states.[54] In June 2004, FPDA members announced an effort to revitalize the organization and broaden its focus from the joint security of Malaysia and Singapore to include cooperation on new security threats and terrorism.[55] This event is notable in its presaging of multilateral cooperation across one of the most important and vulnerable SLOCs.

---

[51] See Seng Tan and Kumar Ramakrishna, "Interstate and Intrastate Dynamics in Southeast Asia's War on Terror," *SAIS Review* 24, no.1 (Winter 2004): 91–105.

[52] See Mark J. Valencia, *The Proliferation Security Initiative: Making Waves in Asia*, Adelphi Paper 376 (London: Routledge and International Institute for Strategic Studies, 2005).

[53] The five are Britain, Australia, New Zealand, Malaysia, and Singapore.

[54] Damon Bristow, "The Five Power Defence Arrangements: Southeast Asia's Unknown Regional Security Organization," *Contemporary Southeast Asia* 27, no. 1 (April 2005): 1–20.

[55] "2nd FPDA Defence Ministers' Informal Meeting," Singapore Ministry of Defence, Press Release, June 7, 2004, http://www.mindef.gov.sg/imindef/news_and_events/nr/2004/jun/07jun04_nr.html.

Finally, the shortcomings of the range of bilateral approaches to North Korea, most notably the 1994 Agreed Framework, have turned the attention of policymakers to multilateral means to resolve the long-standing nuclear problems on the Korean Peninsula.[56] On China's initiative, the six-party talks were first held in Beijing in August 2003 subsequent to the October 2002 breakdown of the Agreed Framework. These talks involve all of the parties who have significant interests at stake in the peninsula meeting at a senior level on a regular basis. The intent of this multilateral approach to the ongoing nuclear crisis was threefold: (1) to establish a means for overcoming U.S. refusal to negotiate bilaterally with the DPRK, (2) to develop a more effective carrot-and-stick diplomatic framework in which the United States and its allies were matched by China and Russia, and (3) to more effectively monitor and enforce any agreement. The nuclear test of October 9, 2006, seemed to spell failure for the talks, yet the February 2007 agreement committing North Korea to undertake a disarmament process has breathed fresh life into not only the talks but also the prospects of multilateralism in Northeast Asia, where it has hitherto been almost entirely absent.[57]

Asian Security Architecture: A Fractured System

The considerable array of institutional, ad hoc, and unofficial groupings and processes in Asia promote various dimensions of and visions for regional security. Despite this profusion of forums, indeed in some respects because of it, the region lacks a coherent association of security measures that collectively advance a common goal. A view of Asia as having, at best, even a partial security architecture is called into question by the significant degree of mistrust that persists across the region—mistrust that makes for an architecture that is more fractured than partial. That said, existing forums and processes do offer glimpses of what a more inclusive and coherent architecture might look like: such an architecture might have a membership like the ARF or APEC, processes like the six-party talks, and a conception of security as articulated by CSCAP.

Despite the wide range of security dialogue forums available to them, Asian states continue to see anything more than talk as imposing unacceptable constraints on security options. The existing institutionalized

---

[56] While the Korean Peninsula Energy Development Organization involved South Korea, the United States, Japan, and the European Union, it was the product of a bilateral process. See Peter Van Ness, "The North Korean Nuclear Crisis: Four-plus-Two—An Idea Whose Time Has Come," Department of International Relations, Australian National University, 2003, http://rspas.anu.edu.au/ir/pubs/keynotes/documents/Keynotes-4.pdf.

[57] See Samuel S. Kim, ed., The International Relations of Northeast Asia (Lanham, MD: Rowman and Littlefield, 2004).

cooperation not only is weak and highly uneven both in geographic distribution and in issue area but also fails to have much purchase in the security policies of most Asian states. The most effective forms of multilateral cooperation have been in the ad hoc bodies, which appear to hold the most promise for any future developments.

A consequence of the uncoordinated expansion in the number as well as the scope of activities of many regional security processes is a lack of clear division of labor between the processes and a considerable overlap in the membership and agendas of many groupings. For example, all members of the East Asia Summit are members of the ARF and, with the exception of India, are also members of APEC. The overlap is in part due to some groupings latching onto new developments in order to reinvigorate themselves, but it is also the result of a good deal of uncertainty as to the most appropriate venue for such discussions. At present each grouping is devoting time and resources to attempts at developing mechanisms for dealing with matters such as counterterrorism, energy, and resource security, but with little coordination. As a result discussion at best is inefficient and at worst allows for competitive regionalism that not only saps political capital but can undermine the benefits that institutionalized cooperation promises.

Growth in cooperative efforts and the revitalization of older groupings are, however, indicative of the demand across Asia for means to deal with a complex and rapidly changing security environment. This tendency is fuelled by a growing awareness that the region requires old-fashioned military approaches as well as newer cooperative measures. It is also the product of a sense of power transition, with its attendant fragilities, leading many to conclude that the political and strategic role of the United States is unlikely to unfold in the coming 5 to 10 years as it has over the past 25. Asian states are thus turning increasingly to multilateral and cooperative approaches, as evident in the rapid rise of the SCO, the formation of the EAS, the attempts to reinvigorate the FPDA, and the efforts to transform the six-party talks into an ongoing Northeast Asian security mechanism.[58] The current fractured architecture is unlikely to be the institutional setting over the medium and longer term. The next five years thus present a distinct opportunity to match the demand for change with a more effective and coherent security architecture. Pasting a European model over the top of the existing setting will not be possible, but a different architecture of regional security—and one that better secures the region and U.S. interests and values—is possible. This architecture could be achieved in four different ways, as discussed below.

---

[58] "North Korea—Denuclearization Plan," U.S. Department of State, Press Release, February 13, 2007, http://www.state.gov/r/pa/prs/ps/2007/february/80479.htm.

Alternative Security Systems

Alternative I: From Six-Party Talks to a Northeast Asian Security Regime

Change. Since the inception of the six-party talks, scholars and analysts have been debating the possibilities of transforming the framework from an ad hoc process into an institutional means to stabilize one of the more volatile parts of the international system.[59] The February 2007 agreement established five working groups to advance the commitments made by the parties. The fifth working group, chaired by Russia, is tasked with examining the creation of a Northeast Asia Peace and Security Mechanism. How exactly this will develop is unclear, but all the key parties are supportive of the broader thrust.[60] Most likely beginning as a regular contact group or dialogue forum for areas of common concern, the group would be tasked first with building a sense of trust among the six parties and then with establishing procedures for dealing with crises as they might emerge. Such a new mechanism would fill an important gap in the regional security setting.

Consequences. Beyond providing a means for resolving the long-running standoff over North Korean nuclear ambitions, a mechanism that builds trust in Northeast Asia is badly needed not only because of the high level of tensions but also because of the significant benefits that increased trust between China, Japan, the United States, and Russia in Northeast Asia can have elsewhere in the region. Moreover, all parties recognize that, in the longer run, the DPRK regime is unsustainable. At some point in the future, the six parties will have to deal with the end of Korean Workers' Party rule—whether through regime change, integration with South Korea, or collapse. Having an institutional framework through which to conduct dealings related to this event is an important step to minimizing its negative regional consequences. A six-party framework might also be the most politically palatable way of dealing with the ongoing difficulties posed by Taiwan.

Plausibility. Given its recent relative success, there is a very real chance that an institutional dialogue body will come out of the six-party process. There is diplomatic support for this development among five of the powers as well as strong Track II backing. Key to the creation of a new institution will be capitalizing on the momentum of the six-party talks and establishing

---

[59] See, for example, Ian Bremmer, Choi Sung-hong, and Yoriko Kawaguchi, "A New Forum for Peace," *National Interest* 82 (Winter 2005/2006): 107–12.

[60] See comments by the Russian chair Aleksandr Lyuskov, "Russia Looks Forward to Chairing North Korea Working Group," ITAR-TASS News Agency, March 1, 2007.

a framework while political interests in Tokyo, Washington, and Beijing are conducive. An institutionalized dialogue forum would greatly benefit the United States, U.S. allies, and their shared interests. Whether such a body could successfully create a greater sense of common cause among the major powers of East Asia is difficult to ascertain, but the best chance to achieve such a long-term goal is with this framework, and the next twelve months or so provide a unique opportunity to set the process in motion.

Alternative II: A Pan-Asian Security Community

Change. When the ARF was first established, some hoped that the dialogue forum would develop into a security community. In the classical definition, a security community is a condition that generates the expectation that problems among its members will be peacefully resolved. Among ARF members, a number of important changes would need to occur for this condition to exist, the most important of which is that the major powers would stop thinking of one another as threats to their respective interests. For this to occur, these powers would need not only to make significant changes to the balance and planned use of military force in the region but also to accept existing geopolitical realities (such as the division of Kashmir and Taiwan's de facto independence).

Consequences. The emergence of a genuine security community would be of profound importance to regional stability. Such a development would underwrite increased economic growth and reinforce Asia's dominance of the global economy. Equally, the creation of this community would have important reverberations for the geopolitical stability of Europe and the Middle East, enhance the prospects of a more effective UN Security Council, and burnish the legitimacy of the U.S. global role.

Plausibility. The region would need to travel a considerable distance to achieve a pan-Asian security community. Arguably further away than in 1994, such a community is highly unlikely to be realized given the shortcomings of the ARF, the growing rivalry among the major powers, and the tendency of many key powers to see military mechanisms as the most appropriate means to resolving security problems. Unsurprisingly, member states exhibit little diplomatic enthusiasm for realizing the potential of the ARF; importantly, activity at CSCAP—the ARF's Track II organization—reflects much more limited ambitions, with discussion focusing on more immediate and incremental mechanisms for building trust and enhancing cooperation.

Alternative III: A Multilateral U.S. Alliance System

Change. In spite of the 1995 and 1998 Nye Reports that reaffirmed a long-term commitment to the bilateral alliances, recognition is increasing on both sides of the Pacific that this structure is not especially well-suited to the rapidly changing regional circumstances. This third scenario involves changing the projection of U.S. military power from its current bilateral structure into an integrated multilateral alliance system. Focusing primarily on the military stabilization of the region through a coordinated collective defense mechanism integrated into U.S. global strategy, the policy tools of this system would be designed to counter the challenges of traditional interstate military threats. Beyond maintaining the current deterrence and balancing role played by the bilateral system, the intent of this system would be to limit the military influence of Russia and China and to maintain the military preponderance of the United States, thus advancing the interests of the United States and its allies. Such an approach would require several controversial changes, most notably the military normalization of Japan, the acceptance of this normalization by South Korea and others in the region, the political and operational inclusion of India in the U.S. fold, and the reorganization of U.S. military assets to reflect the increased role played by regional powers. The aim of such a change would be to reduce the dependence of the allies on U.S. military power, to increase the political and strategic weight of each member in its respective subregion, and to increase the ability to respond swiftly to changing regional military circumstances without jeopardizing U.S. global strategy.

Consequences. First, the development of a multilateral U.S. alliance system would harden attitudes in China and Russia toward the United States and its alliance partners, prompting both to expand military spending. Although unlikely given the degree of acrimony between the two and the unwillingness of either to be a junior partner, such a move might even drive China and Russia into a counterbalancing alliance. Second, development of such a system would force regional powers to clearly choose sides and, in many cases, to dump current hedging strategies. Third, the region would become less dependent on the United States, therefore reducing U.S. costs but with the accompanying risk of reduced U.S. influence. A multilateral U.S. alliance system would provide little more than the present system with regard to non-military security challenges and quite probably would undermine many of the dialogue processes (such as ARF and EAS) that are trying to take steps to deal with these challenges.

Plausibility. While a full transformation to a multilateral U.S. alliance system is not plausible in the next five years, this scenario is not unrealistic, and some trends are already moving in this direction. Australia and

Japan signed a security declaration in March 2007, and the United States, Japan, and Australia have established a ministerial-level trilateral security dialogue.[61] Demand is coming from the region and from Washington to involve India in bilateral and multilateral moves, and Japan is normalizing its foreign and security policy. There is also support in a number of influential think-tanks in the region, most clearly articulated in Japan and Australia, for a multilateral U.S. alliance system. Of the different scenarios set out in this chapter, this scenario is the most likely to come to fruition over the medium term, yet one that also has some significant and disturbing shortcomings.

Alternative IV: A Multidimensional Asian Security Mechanism

Change. One further evolution of the U.S. role in Asia that has not received much attention at the official level is the substantial transformation of the U.S. presence from a bilateral military alliance system organized on a hub-and-spoke model into a multilateral and multidimensional security mechanism. This mechanism would be an expansion of the political and diplomatic function of the U.S. alliance system outlined above with a broadened security concept and operational capacities. Rather than having only a military-balancing function, this multidimensional security mechanism would have substantial diplomatic, political, and logistical capacities that would operate alongside a multilateral military alliance.

The mechanism would provide four key functions: (1) collective defense of all members, (2) peacekeeping and peacemaking operations in and around the region, (3) humanitarian operations, and (4) a political and diplomatic coordination role. The institution would be organized around a conception of security that encompasses both traditional and new threats. For example, the institution would have a capacity not only to provide a military stabilizing role but also to organize regional responses to humanitarian crises, organized crime, and piracy. This mechanism would require the creation of a political and military headquarters with permanent ambassador-level representation, a secretariat, and a leadership role for the institution along the lines of a secretary-general.

One model for such a system comes from the expanded and operationally transformed NATO. Originally a traditional collective defense alliance, since the late 1990s NATO has significantly transformed its function to include humanitarian operations, political support, and

---

[61] On the declaration, see "Australia-Japan Joint Declaration on Security Cooperation," March 13, 2007, available on the Australian Government Department of Foreign Affairs and Trade website, http://www.dfat.gov.au/geo/japan/aus_jap_security_dec.html.

out-of-theater peacekeeping roles.[62] The creation of a new, NATO-like mechanism in Asia would involve a range of significant changes, including a marked increase in the strategic role and weight of the allied countries, reduced U.S. autonomy, and a significant change in the structure, purposes, and distribution of U.S. military power.

Consequences. Such a significant departure from the traditional way of doing things in the region would have both benefits and costs. The creation of such an institution would allow allies to act more effectively in response to regional crises and to better coordinate their diplomatic efforts. A multidimensional Asian security mechanism would provide an improved fit between security policy and the regional context as well as greater policy flexibility and a wider range of policy options for responding to security challenges while reducing the economic and political costs the United States shoulders for Asian stability. As the new NATO has shown, such a grouping can not only play an important role in consolidating democratic transitions but also build trust. This type of security mechanism also might be a more effective means to assuage regional concerns about Japan's military normalization.

Such an approach, however, is not without its problems. Most obviously, partners would need to bear considerably higher defense and security costs than they presently do. The "easy riding" many currently enjoy would not be sustainable.[63] Because the PRC would likely feel targeted and respond in a defensive fashion, the group would need to make efforts to assuage China in the short term through careful and sustained diplomacy. Over the longer term the PRC should be offered a stake in the system. Initially, this could involve something akin to the NATO-Russia Council that would create formal processes for regular dialogue, representation, and information sharing. Ultimately, the PRC's interests, and those of a putative multidimensional security mechanism, are not diametrically opposed; thus the system should leave open the very real possibility of Chinese membership. Moreover, because planning for the PRC's participation is not unrealistic given that China's key priorities require regional stability, creating an inclusive Asian security architecture in the long term should be a fundamental priority. As with any such institution, a multidimensional Asian security mechanism would not only significantly constrain the diplomatic flexibility of members but also have

---

[62] See Wallander and Keohane, "Risk, Threat and Security Institutions." For a recent discussion of this in relation to the "war on terror," see Renée de Nevers, "NATO's International Security Role in the Terrorist Era," *International Security* 31, no. 4 (Spring 2007): 34–66.

[63] "Easy riding" (as opposed to "free riding") refers to the situation in which the beneficiaries of the public goods contribute only a small proportion of their costs.

its own share of the broader problems of multilateralism, such as slow decisionmaking and institutional inefficiencies.

Plausibility. The evolution of the bilateral commitments in Asia into a multidimensional security system is, at present, fairly unlikely. Such a move is a radical departure from Washington's approach and one for which key allies have little appetite. That said, this scenario has been a topic of Track II discussion and has received some support. Supporters argue that this option presents the best long-term means to respond to the blend of old and new challenges facing the region. Regional policymakers should not let lack of support for this approach in the short term, however, lead them to rule it out of the plausible options available to them.

Conclusions

First, there is little or no chance that a pan-Asian security architecture akin to Europe's will come into being in the short to medium term. Those with ambitions to create aspects of a security architecture will need to focus on subregions and should avoid mimicking the European approach. Recognizing that the current European system took decades to develop and did not take on its multidimensional function until after 1991, supporters of such a system in Asia should not be unduly pessimistic about the region's chances to create a security architecture over the longer term.

Second, Asia presently has too many institutions and processes associated with security cooperation. This is more problematic at the official level (arguably a proliferation of Track II efforts is a strength, not a weakness). Dialogue, although almost always a good thing, may in this instance be reaching the point of diminishing returns. The current spectrum of venues for security discussion is too broad; the multitude of efforts clogs state bureaucracies and reduces the efficacy and policy influence of the process itself. Policymakers wishing to advance cooperative approaches to Asian security would be more effective if their efforts did not add to this institutional clutter. Building a security architecture through transformation of existing institutions, alliances, or dialogue forums is more likely to be successful than building from the ground up because existing entities have an organizational framework as well as bureaucratic and political capital that are easier to drawn upon.

A number of more general comments about the prospects of security cooperation are also worth noting. The very uneven character of the region's security setting and the changing circumstances relating both to globalization and shifting power configurations are prompting a range of efforts to pursue more multilateral and cooperative approaches to security.

Yet none of these efforts are making much headway in spite of the palpable demand for action. A number of pressing problems continue to block the creation of new approaches to regional security, leading not only to the perpetuation of bilateral and self-help military approaches to security policy but also the very meager achievements of those multilateral efforts that have thus far been tried. The absence of trust that besets the region, and particularly the mistrust that is most palpable among the major powers, is the biggest stumbling block to any efforts to transform the basic structures of regional security. This obstacle manifests itself most clearly in the preference that Asian states have for maintaining the current military and strategic balance. These states fear that any new regional order would be worse than the status quo and are concerned about the risks and potential costs of the transition to a new order.

Additionally, most states are still heavily influenced by divergent perceptions of the sources of insecurity in the region and in many cases pursue a security policy that is redolent of classical security-dilemma thinking. International cooperation, whether political, economic, or strategic, requires a considerable degree of leadership, which is decidedly lacking in Asia. Finally, these circumstances breed a heavy bureaucratic inertia in policy thinking and development as well as in budgetary allocation. Without room for ideas and the resources to pursue them, international security cooperation, always a fairly expensive business, has little chance to move forward in the region.

A number of steps can be taken to overcome these not inconsiderable impediments. First, any efforts to build an Asian security architecture require a marked increase in trust among the major powers in order to reduce the costs that fears of transition impose. Thus significant diplomatic effort is needed to reduce the sense of mistrust and to promote a sense of common cause among the key powers in the region. Second, the level of regional demand and the extent to which globalization is increasing the areas of shared interest among the region's major powers can provide a foundation for creating political will and breaking bureaucratic inertia. No state has the luxury of believing that status quo thinking is appropriate to advancing its interests, yet the security policies of most Asian states show little evidence of the level of policy creativity that the contemporary circumstances warrant.

The United States is not immune to this preference for the status quo. Yet it is increasingly clear that U.S. interests are not best advanced through a Cold War conception of regional security with its bilateral political infrastructure. There are two reasons for this. First, the geopolitical circumstances that drove the bilateral approach are undergoing change:

China's economic growth is prompting a significant military modernization, Japan is actively pursuing a more normal foreign and defense policy posture, and both India and Russia have a newly found strategic weight. More important, the intentions and interests of many powers have changed quite substantially in recent years. This development is most obvious both in the constructive diplomatic role that China is playing in the region and in the region's growing economic interdependence. The idea that the region's circumstances demand a set of bilateral military alliances to contain key powers and deter military ambition is increasingly out of step with the political reality.

Second, as made abundantly clear by events in Korea and South Asia as well as by the ongoing problems in Southeast Asia and the Western Pacific, the bilateral military system is of little use for the most pressing security issues and problems. As Kenneth Lieberthal's chapter in this volume makes clear, the risks and consequences of domestic problems in China for regional security and stability are greater and more plausible than an international conflict over Taiwan. For such problems, the bilateral military alliances are of little help. The general support for the current approach derived from a belief that U.S. power and the U.S. bilateral framework are an effective and politically palatable means to maintain regional security. This belief is beginning to weaken.

A change in approach to Asian security would appear to present a number of advantages for the United States. Transformation of the alliances into a multilateral and multidimensional security organization can provide a means to strike the necessary balance between the demands for traditional military responses and the more unconventional security challenges U.S. interests face in Asia. Such an ambition is a longer-term proposition. In the short term, U.S. efforts to support the transformation of the six-party talks into a Northeast Asian security regime can foster trust among key East Asian powers and create a forum for the states to develop cooperative approaches to their many shared interests, such as energy security and the security of East Asian SLOCs. Moreover, Washington would advance its own short- and long-term interests by re-energizing U.S. commitment to existing cooperative measures and helping to revitalize regional interest in ARF through high-level participation and the leadership of new initiatives. To help advance these goals the United States also could encourage a more open multilateralism among its alliance partners, such as that seen in the recent security declaration signed between Japan and Australia. The United States could take a further step in this direction by encouraging a similar South Korea-Japan agreement and a quadrilateral security ministerial meeting involving Japan, the United States, Australia, and South Korea.

As hinted at earlier in this chapter, changes in security policy are not cost-free, and moves away from the status quo will carry some risk, especially from a China that perceives any changes to be inherently destabilizing. Policymakers could, however, take some heart and some courage from China's surprisingly muted diplomatic response to the Australia-Japan security declaration. The PRC is increasingly pragmatic in its foreign and security policy dealings, and the political and diplomatic risks of change are not as great as they once were.

The creation of a European-style security community is unlikely over the next five to ten years. Asia may not have a security architecture worthy of the name, and achieving one might at first glance appear an impossibility; but U.S. and regional interests will benefit in the short term if the United States begins to lead efforts to create a multilateral security institution over the longer term. Embarking on this path will, however, require diplomatic and political efforts to build trust, to reduce security dilemmas, and to increase bureaucratic capacity. If the United States does not meet regional demands for more effective security cooperation, then Washington risks damaging its interests and surrendering its long-held position of regional leadership.

EXECUTIVE SUMMARY

This chapter examines the implications of environmental degradation and resource decline in Asia for U.S. security interests and policy in the region.

MAIN ARGUMENT:
Asia suffers widespread environmental degradation and resource decline that undermine economic and human security and can impact more traditional security concerns. Conflict between states is unlikely to result, but environmental degradation could be a factor in social stress, communal violence, and political disaffection and instability. Responses in the region to environmental insecurities have been uneven, marked by material and political difficulties and by policy failure.

POLICY IMPLICATIONS:
- U.S. strategic policy (which in the sense explored here includes aid and environmental policies) would benefit from accounting more fully and effectively for negative environmental trends in Asia that can undermine U.S. policy goals of promoting regional stability, fostering democracy, and encouraging human prosperity.

- The most effective U.S. policy responses to environmental security challenges in Asia would focus on the causes of environmental degradation. In foreign aid policy, this will involve project and program support for environmental mitigation, environmental protection, and environmental resilience activities across a range of policy concerns, not simply energy and climate change.

- Support for environmental policies can deliver political and security benefits to the U.S., possibly offsetting other tensions in bilateral and regional relationships. The U.S. will, however, need to be seen by the region as a collaborative partner rather than pursuing its own policy interests.

- U.S. environmental security leadership in the region will be strengthened as Washington takes further action to reduce the U.S. contribution to environmental degradation that has global reach.

Environmental (In)security in Asia: Challenging U.S. Interests

Lorraine Elliott

In its 2004 report entitled *A More Secure World: Our Shared Responsibility*, the United Nations Secretary-General's High-Level Panel on Threats, Challenges and Change proclaimed that the "biggest security threats...extend to environmental degradation."[1] Following similarly authoritative predecessors—including the UN Security Council, NATO, and the Millennium Summit of the UN General Assembly—the High-Level Panel expressed concern regarding the impact of environmental degradation on global peace and security. Just before the 2002 World Summit on Sustainable Development in Johannesburg, U.S. Secretary of State Colin Powell proclaimed that "sustainable development [is]...a security imperative." He argued that "poverty, destruction of the environment, degradation and despair are destroyers of people, of societies, of nations, a cause of instability...that can destabilize countries, and even destabilize entire regions."[2] In April 2007 the UN Security Council held its first ever debate on the security consequences of global warming.

Taking these concerns as its cue, this chapter examines the security implications of environmental degradation and resource decline for countries in Asia, for the region as a whole, and for the United States as

Lorraine Elliott is Senior Fellow in the Department of International Relations at the Australian National University. She can be reached at <lorraine.elliott@anu.edu.au>.

[1] United Nations Secretary-General's High-Level Panel on Threats, Challenges and Change, *A More Secure World: Our Shared Responsibility* (New York: United Nations Department of Public Information, 2004), 1.

[2] Colin L. Powell, "Making Sustainable Development Work: Governance, Finance and Public-Private Cooperation" (remarks at State Department conference, Meridian International Center, Washington, D.C., July 12, 2002), http://www.state.gov/secretary/former/powell/remarks/2002/11822.htm.

a key strategic and political actor in the region. This chapter argues that environmental security should not be conceptualized solely through the lens of realist orthodoxies that focus on instability and conflict but should also incorporate human and environmental insecurities. Nor should the term be defined only by concerns about climate change and energy that have become prominent in U.S. security policy discourses.[3] The chapter also assesses the potential for cooperation and conflict over environmental degradation and resource scarcities. It suggests that conflict is a more complicated issue than some analyses predict and argues that cooperation presents a more strategic response to key environmental security challenges in the region.

This chapter is divided into five sections. The first section reviews the intellectual and policy context animating environmental security as a form of non-traditional security. It takes as its starting point continuing debate over the answers both to the security problematic—security for whom and from what—and to the related question about what it means to be secure in a globalized world. To assess likely policy implications, section one identifies nine propositions examining the connection between environmental degradation and security. The second section outlines the most salient environmental challenges facing the Asia-Pacific region. The third section suggests how environmental degradation and environmental change may create actual security challenges for the region. The fourth section outlines regional responses to environmental (in)security, offering explanations both for the weak securitization of the Asia-Pacific's environmental challenges and for the limited institutionalization of environmental policy responses. The final section considers possible implications for three categories of U.S. policy: strategic, foreign aid, and environmental.

Environmental Security: New Concept for Old Problems?

Environmental security is a comparatively new term in the environmental and security lexicon, though the challenges it responds to are not.[4] The term's conceptual genesis is a result both of the rethinking of security following the end of the Cold War and of concerns stemming from globalization and modernity, sometimes encapsulated in the concept of a

---

[3] Most notably in the 2006 National Security Strategy and the 2007 report prepared by a panel of senior retired U.S. generals and admirals for the Center for Naval Analysis. See "National Security and the Threat of Climate Change," CNA Corporation, April 2007.

[4] The literature on environmental security is extensive. The following provide useful explorations of the various interpretations and contestations surrounding the term and its policy implications: Simon Dalby, *Environmental Security* (Minneapolis: University of Minnesota Press, 2002); Jon Barnett, *The Meaning of Environmental Security* (London: Zed Books, 2001); and Lorraine Elliott, *The Global Politics of the Environment* (New York: New York University Press, 2004), chap. 9.

"world risk society."[5] Traditional concerns focused on the security of states from external military threat in responding to the questions "security for whom (the 'referent') and from what"; in a world risk society these concerns seemed limited in scope or even counter-productive in their purpose.

Environmental security fits within two sometimes competing approaches to a non-traditional response to these security questions. The first approach is confined to a concern with non-traditional threats to traditional "referent objects" (i.e., states). Commentators have posited environmental degradation as a factor in the more "traditional indicators of insecurity—violent conflict and the outbreak of war."[6] In one of the most pessimistic but widely-read expositions of this position, Robert Kaplan argued that:

> [environmental degradation will be] the national-security issue of the early twenty-first century. The political and strategic impact of surging populations, spreading disease, deforestation and soil erosion, water depletion, air pollution, and, possibly, rising sea levels in critical, overcrowded regions like the Nile Delta and Bangladesh—developments that will prompt mass migrations and, in turn, incite group conflicts—will be the core foreign-policy challenge from which most others will ultimately emanate.[7]

The second broad approach to environmental security anticipates not just non-traditional threats but also non-traditional security referents. Environmental degradation is understood as part of a suite of challenges to the security of people, communities, ecosystems, and possibly even non-human species. The Commission on Global Governance reported that "threats to the earth's life support systems [along with] extreme economic deprivation, the proliferation of conventional small arms, the terrorising of civilian populations by domestic factions and gross violations of human rights…challenge the security of people far more than the threat of external aggression."[8] This is a human security approach, articulated initially by the UN Development Programme (UNDP) as a universal, people-centered concern with "human life and dignity" and an antidote to conventional views of security that had "for too long…been shaped by the potential for conflict between states…equated with…threats to a country's borders."[9]

---

[5] Ulrich Beck, *World Risk Society* (Cambridge: Polity Press, 1999).

[6] Paul F. Diehl, "Environmental Conflict: An Introduction," *Journal of Peace Research* 35, no. 3 (May 1998): 275.

[7] Robert Kaplan, "The Coming Anarchy," *The Atlantic Monthly* 273, no. 2 (February 1994): 58.

[8] Commission on Global Governance, *Our Global Neighbourhood* (Oxford: Oxford University Press, 1995), 79.

[9] UN Development Programme (UNDP), *Human Development Report 1994* (New York: Oxford University Press, 1994), 22, 3.

These themes have been taken up by both policymakers and scholars, the former usually making broad pronouncements about ecological damage as a new risk for stability and the latter seeking to develop more thoughtful conceptualizations based on empirical investigation or critical narrative.[10]

These two broad approaches have generated at least nine propositions about how environmental degradation poses a security problem. The first, most orthodox proposition is that environmental degradation and resource scarcity is a likely cause of conflict between states—although water, arable land, fish stocks, or differences in environmental endowment are as likely to be the new strategic resources as are the "old" strategic resources such as oil. The second proposition connects the environment and security by focusing on resources and environmental services as a weapon of war. The deliberate burning of oil wells and leaking of oil during the first Gulf War is perhaps the most notable recent example of this, with the use of defoliants in Southeast Asia during the Vietnam War providing a more regional example. From this follows the third proposition: environmental security includes the unintended environmental consequences of war and conflict. These concerns have become central to the work undertaken by the UN Environment Programme's (UNEP) Post-Conflict Assessment Unit in conjunction with HABITAT (the UN Human Settlements Programme). The fourth proposition relates to concerns about the stability of inter-state relations rather than the environmental consequences of instability, suggesting that whereas outright war over scarce environmental resources is unlikely, diplomatic tensions and stand-off short of war are not. Tensions may arise, for instance, over cross-border illegal resource extraction (on land and at sea) or the deliberate or unintended dispersal or dumping of wastes and pollutants. Such circumstances can have the potential for some type of military involvement, as examples from Asia later in this chapter will demonstrate. The fifth proposition, and to some extent the main motivation behind Kaplan's analysis, is that environmental degradation and resource scarcity will contribute directly or indirectly to civil turmoil, a breakdown in societal relations, and enforced movement of people—an outcome thought more likely in already fragile or failing states.

The remaining propositions move more firmly into the realm of "non-traditional" security referents: economies, people, and communities. The sixth articulation of a link between the environment and security is

---

[10] On the former, see UN General Assembly, *An Agenda for Peace: Preventive Diplomacy,* Peacemaking and Peace-keeping, UN General Assembly Resolution 47120B, June 17, 1992, http://www.un.org/documents/ga/res/47/a47r/20.htm; and "The Alliance's Strategic Concept," NATO, Press Release, April 24, 1999, http://www.nato.int/docu/pr/1999/p99-065e.htm. For examples of the latter, see Thomas F. Homer-Dixon, Environment, Scarcity, and Violence (Princeton: Princeton University Press, 2001); and sources in footnote 4.

concerned with economic security. In this proposition, environmental degradation changes the productive landscape and compromises economic security for both people and countries, particularly in developing countries. Loss of income and the indirect, often discounted, costs of resource depletion undermine economic sectors such as agriculture and other forms of primary production. Pollution intensifies demands on health and productivity sectors while also stretching public budgets. The economic security consequences of global problems such as climate change will be felt disproportionately by poorer countries for whom levels of economic development are also key indicators of state and societal security. The seventh proposition explores how environmental degradation and resource depletion are connected in often complex ways with other non-traditional security threats. Globally, transnational environmental crime—such as illegal logging, wildlife smuggling, and the black markets in ozone-depleting substances (ODS) and hazardous wastes—constitute illegal economies of similar value to those in arms and drugs sales and with similar levels of organized criminal activity. The habitat-changing consequences of environmental degradation may also influence disease vectors, possibly contributing to the pandemics that are now taken as serious security threats. The eighth proposition linking the environment and security is a more explicit human security one. The UNDP approach argues that environmental security is about the "basic question of human survival on an environmentally fragile planet."[11] The final proposition is that, in its most fundamental condition, environmental security must be about security of and for the environment, based on the reasoning that if the environment is not secure, then no other forms of security can be guaranteed. For this reason, the next section examines environmental degradation in Asia before exploring how these problems might generate different kinds of security challenges, informed by the propositions outlined here.

Environmental Degradation in Asia

Almost ten years ago the Asian Development Bank (ADB) reported that Asia had become "dirtier, less ecologically diverse and more environmentally vulnerable."[12] In 2001 the ADB maintained its position, arguing that environmental degradation in the region was

---

[11] UNDP, *Human Development Report 1994*, 2.

[12] Asian Development Bank (ADB), *Emerging Asia: Changes and Challenges* (Manila: ADB, 1997), 199.

"pervasive, accelerating and unabated."[13] In 2006 UNEP reported some "encouraging signs" that governments in the region were responding to population pressures and "extremely rapid economic growth" in dealing with environmental problems.[14] Despite this optimism, environmental degradation in Asia remains a serious problem with multiple drivers. In 2005 the Fifth Ministerial Conference on Environment and Development in Asia and the Pacific identified six key threats to environmental sustainability in the region: industrialization, expansion and intensification of agricultural production, consumption patterns, urbanization, increased energy demand, and pressure on water supplies.[15] Together, rapid economic growth and industrialization have been a major cause of environmental degradation and resource scarcity in Asia. The region's political economy is characterized by increasing rates of consumption, growing urban populations, rapid increases in energy demands, and changing relations of production. International trade in primary resources—timber, energy resources, and agricultural products—remains a key feature of economies in the region. These are sectors that rely on extraction and production practices that are often environmentally damaging. Between 1995 and 2002, industrial production in Asia also increased, by almost 40% (compared with a world average increase of 23%). The fastest growing areas of production were in "highly polluting industries that often use outdated technologies and operate under pollution control regimes that have little or no enforcement."[16] As a result, Asia's use of world ecological capacity has grown from 15% in 1961 to 40%

---

[13] ADB, *Asian Environment Outlook 2001* (Manila: ADB, 2001), 4.

[14] UN Environment Programme (UNEP), *Global Environment Outlook Yearbook 2006: An Overview of Our Changing Environment* (Nairobi: UNEP Department of Early Warning and Assessment, 2006), 18.

[15] UN Economic and Social Commission for Asia and the Pacific (ESCAP), "Review of the State of the Environment in Asia and the Pacific 2005" (paper prepared for the Preparatory Meeting of Senior Officials for the Ministerial Conference on Environment and Development in Asia and the Pacific, Seoul, South Korea March 4, 2005), http://www.unescap.org/mced/documents/presession/english/SOMCED5_1E_SOE.pdf.

[16] ESCAP, "Achieving Environmentally Sustainable Economic Growth in Asia and the Pacific" (theme paper prepared for the fifth Ministerial Conference on Environment and Development in Asia and the Pacific, Seoul, South Korea, March 3, 2005), 3, http://www.unescap.org/mced/documents/presession/english/SOMCED5_7E_Theme_Paper.pdf.

in 2001. The region's ecological footprint is now more than one-and-a-half times its own biological capacity.[17]

In response to urban, industrial, and agricultural needs, demand for key environmental goods such as energy and water is growing faster than supply. Per capita access to energy falls far below the global average, and by 2020 energy consumption is anticipated to increase threefold over 1990 levels.[18] Few countries in the region are self-sufficient in energy. Investment in regional power projects, electricity purchase agreements, and the construction of hydro-dams has been reinvigorated after the temporary halt wrought by the Asian financial crisis. The unintended consequences of these projects, however, will include environmental degradation and social dislocation. In Asia, per capita water availability is declining, equal to only half the global average in 2005. Almost 700 million people in the region do not have sustainable access to safe water supplies,[19] though substantial disparities often exist between rural and urban dwellers. Where solid data is available, the statistics for urban water-access coverage in the region are encouraging, with many countries—even developing ones—rating 90% coverage or higher. Rural coverage, on the other hand, is frequently poor.[20]

With few exceptions, the rate of population growth in the region has slowed significantly. Driven by the pull factor of urban-based industrialization and the push factor of rural poverty, however, the region's population is becoming increasingly urban. By 2020 more than half of Asia's population will live in urban areas, a threefold increase over 1990.[21] Urban infrastructure is often stressed beyond capacity, sometimes to the point of dysfunction. The political economy of agriculture is also changing, with permanent, commercialized, and more intensive agriculture favored

---

[17] Mathis Wackernagel, Justin Kitzes, Deborah Cheng, Steven Goldfinger, James Espinas, Dan Moran, Chad Monfreda, Jonathan Loh, Dermot O'Gorman, and Idy Wong, *Asia-Pacific 2005: The Ecological Footprint and Natural Wealth* (Cambridge: World Wide Fund for Nature and Global Footprint Network, 2005), 3, 8. This report includes Australia and New Zealand in its definition of the Asia-Pacific. The ecological footprint is a measure of the biologically productive area needed both to produce the resources consumed and to absorb the wastes generated by a population unit (for example an individual, city, or country). Ecological or biological capacity refers to the ability of an ecosystem to continue to produce resources and environmental services in order to maintain its current condition.

[18] For information on current access to energy, see ESCAP, "Achieving Environmentally Sustainable Economic Growth in Asia and the Pacific," 4.

[19] ADB, *Asia Water Watch 2015* (Manila: ADB, 2006), 9. These figures do include Central Asia. ESCAP puts the figure at 665 million; see ESCAP, *State of the Environment in Asia and the Pacific 2005: Synthesis* (Bangkok: ESCAP, 2006), 2.

[20] Based on 2002 data, rural coverage is at 30% for Mongolia, 40% for Myanmar, 59% for China, and in the mid-60% range for Indonesia and Vietnam. For data compiled from WHO and UNICEF, see ADB, "Improved Water Supply and Sanitation Coverage for Countries in Asia and the Pacific," http://www.adb.org/Water/Indicators/MDG-7/Table-01.pdf.

[21] ESCAP, *State of the Environment in Asia and the Pacific 2005* (Bangkok: ESCAP, 2006), 87.

over shifting cultivation. Village-based permanent agriculture can be less stressful on the land in situations where shifting agriculture has been overly exploitative of forest lands and where supplementary activities, such as hunting and gathering or off-farm employment, are limited.[22] Increases in agricultural production, however, have relied on intensive agriculture and a high-intensity use of pesticides and fertilizers at levels exceeding the world average.[23] Many Asian countries suffer severe land degradation and the overall region has less arable land per capita than the global average. Over one-third of the region's population lives in areas vulnerable to drought and desertification.[24] Intensive agriculture and high levels of agrochemical use have resulted in "salinized, acidified and waterlogged soils with reduced fertility."[25] India, for example, is now estimated to have reached the limits of the productive potential of agricultural land. The potential for expansion of China's productive land is also limited. As a whole, the region has become a net importer rather than exporter of food. Food security problems have been exacerbated by the over-exploitation of fish stocks, one of the region's main sources of protein. In the 1980s marine fish production grew at a faster rate in Asia than elsewhere in the world. This has resulted in the over-exploitation and near collapse of many fish stocks, a situation compounded by illegal fishing. Many countries in the region have pursued aquaculture (or fish farming) to compensate for loss of marine fisheries and Asian countries now dominate world production. Aquaculture, however, causes substantial environmental degradation and loss of breeding grounds for wild fish stocks through the "destruction of mangrove forests, conversion of wetland habitats, introduction of exotic species, increased use of chemicals ...degradation of water quality, and discharge of nutrients and other wastes."[26]

Per capita forest cover in the Asia-Pacific is somewhat lower than the global average and deforestation rates are much higher—approximately 1.2% to 1.8% of forest cover is lost in the region annually, compared with the global rate of about 0.23%. Less than 20% of the region's original

[22] See K. Rerkasem and B. Rerkasem, "Montane Mainland Southeast Asia: Agroecosystems in Transition," Global Environmental Change 5, no. 4 (1995): 313–22.

[23] ESCAP, "Achieving Environmentally Sustainable Economic Growth in Asia and the Pacific," 4.

[24] UNEP, Global Environmental Outlook 2000 (London: Earthscan, 1999), 76.

[25] UNEP, Asia-Pacific Environment Outlook 2 (Bangkok: UNEP Regional Office Asia Pacific, 2001), 14.

[26] Ibid., 28. Because approximately one-third of the conventional fish catch is used for fish meal and fish oil to feed farmed fish, the impact of aquaculture on wild fish stocks is exacerbated further. See ESCAP, State of the Environment, 84.

frontier forest area remains.[27] The environmental consequences of forest loss include land degradation, soil and coastal erosion, and damaged ecological functioning of rivers and waterways. While the data is uneven, loss of forest cover is generally thought to be a factor in groundwater depletion, water run-off, and problems of flooding and landslides. Over-exploitation of forests also creates negative feedback demands, placing further pressure on scarce resources. As wood processing becomes a sunset industry, for example, demands increase for more cleared forest to enable plantation cultivation of crops such as palm oil, tea, and citrus.

Air pollution is a serious problem for the region's urban agglomerations, with many exceeding the World Health Organization's (WHO) recommended safe limits of suspended particulates, sulphur dioxide, and nitrogen oxide. Coal, which generates about 40% of commercial energy production and is also a fuel source in rural areas, is a major contributor to local pollution and high levels of sulphur dioxide emissions. Indoor air pollution is another common problem that results from using biofuels (wood, dung, and crop residue) as a major energy source in poorer urban and rural households. The region's rivers and water sources are vulnerable to pollution from agricultural and industrial run-off, with some river ecosystems now so biologically compromised as to be effectively "dead." The Yangtze River, for example, one of the region's most important river systems, is reported as seriously and largely irreversibly polluted.[28]

The region is vulnerable to high levels of illegal resource activity and environmental crime. Illegal logging is a major cause of deforestation. Estimates suggest that between 50% and 90% of the timber cut in parts of Southeast Asia, for example, is "stolen" and then smuggled across borders. This is a problem within the region—China, for example, constitutes a major market for illegal Southeast Asian timber. Illegal timber is, however, also reprocessed ("laundered") and exported to the United States and Europe. Illegal wildlife trade is a second substantial illicit economy in the region, driven by the traditional Asian medicine market, consumer demand for "exotics" (including bush-meat, pashmina shawls, and individuals of rare plant and animal species) and demand from zoos and research laboratories. The Asia-Pacific is a hub for the global black market in ODS. China is a major source, Southeast Asia a key trade route, and the United States a major market for illicit ODS.

---

[27] See UNEP, *Asia-Pacific Environment Outlook* 2, 17–18; and Food and Agricultural Organization (FAO), Global Forest Resources Assessment 2005 (Rome: FAO, 2006), 18. Reforestation efforts in China contributed to an aggregate gain in forest cover in Asia overall, even though most countries experienced continuing forest losses.

[28] "Report: Yangtze Waters Worsening", *China Daily*, April 15, 2007, http://www.chinadaily.com.cn/china/2007-04/15/content_850842.htm.

As well as being problems in common, the environmental problems outlined here (and this is not an exhaustive list) also have quite specific transboundary dimensions. Pollutants and waste are displaced and dispersed across borders through the atmosphere, river systems, and coastal or ocean currents. Transboundary air pollution is a serious challenge for the region with consequences for human health, agriculture, and climate. Many Southeast Asian countries battle "the haze" from land-clearing fires in Indonesia, which remain a regular occurrence despite zero-burning laws. Extensive parts of South Asia suffer from the dense particulate haze known as the "Asian Brown Cloud" and transboundary acid rain and "yellow sand" are serious problems in Northeast Asia. Resource depletion becomes transboundary through activities such as illegal logging, species smuggling, and illegal, unregulated, and unreported fishing (known as IUU in official lexicon). Environmental degradation and resource exploitation are also driven by transboundary economic demands (i.e., economic demands that originate directly or indirectly outside the borders of the state in which exploitation takes place). In normal terms, this is simply a function of a trade-driven regional and global economy. These economic demands, however, also reflect a political economy that enables some countries in the region to sustain their own resources and ecosystems at the expense of others by externalizing their environmental costs. For example, Peter Dauvergne has persuasively shown that Japan's demand for timber products is a major contributor to deforestation in the region.[29] Logging bans in China, combined with the removal of tariffs on the import of logs, have mobilized Chinese companies to expand their logging activities, at least some of which are illegal, into Southeast Asia.

The most globalized environmental challenge facing countries in the region is climate change. Climate change will force countries around the globe to deal with a host of problems:

- rises in sea-levels, coastal erosion, and changing patterns of glacial melt in the Himalayas

- changes in weather patterns and precipitation, a likely increase in extreme weather and "natural disaster" events

- changes to growing seasons and agricultural yield, loss of coastal farmlands, and reduction in food production

- variations in the availability of already scarce freshwater, pollution of freshwater aquifers, and threats to biodiversity

---

[29] Peter Dauvergne, *Shadows in the Forest: Japan and the Politics of Timber in Southeast Asia* (Cambridge: MIT Press, 1997).

- an increased likelihood of vector-borne infectious diseases such as malaria, dengue fever, and schistosomiasis, possibly to epidemic proportions

As a result of increased energy demands and the rapid expansion of transportation (including private vehicles), carbon dioxide emissions have risen more rapidly in Asia than in other parts of the world. In gross national terms, China and India are major global emitters. In per capita terms, however, these two states continue to rank much lower than the industrialized countries, with the region's overall emissions still less than 20% of OECD average emissions.[30]

Environmental Challenges as Security Challenges

The environmental concerns outlined in the previous section pose challenges to be taken seriously in the broader security terms outlined earlier in this chapter. Environmental degradation is playing or has the potential to play a role in maldevelopment and the weakness of regional economies, political instability and social stress within countries, tensions in relationships between countries, and the continuing vulnerability of people and their communities to loss of livelihood, poverty, hunger, disease, and death.

Though at times unimaginative, the more conventional approaches to environmental security explored in the first section rely on assumptions concerning the links between resource scarcity, environmental degradation, and forms of conflict or political instability. In some versions, environmental degradation and resource depletion are a potential cause of conflict. In others, they are the consequence, whether intended or unintended. Though Asia has a legacy of suffering the environmental consequences of war, a quick review of the environmental legacy of conflict will suffice for the purposes of this chapter. The historical detritus is best exemplified in the use of defoliants in Vietnam during the U.S. campaign and in the limits that unexploded ordnance and landmines continue to impose on sustainable development and economic as well as social recovery in Cambodia and Laos. Resources and the environment have also been exploited in other ways in conflict situations. In the 1970s illegal logging and timber smuggling across the Thai-Cambodian border generated income for the Khmer Rouge in Cambodia. The same type of activity is now a major source of funds for both sides of conflict between the Burmese regime and insurgent groups.

---

[30] UNEP, *Asia-Pacific Environment Outlook*, 33.

The evidence on how ceasefire agreements affect environmental concerns is mixed. Some reports suggest that in Burma, for example, illegal logging and smuggling have actually increased during ceasefires as both sides have easier access to forest lands for illegal harvesting.[31] Global Witness, however, has reported that under a ceasefire agreement in northern Burma there has been a near standstill in logging in both regime-controlled areas and those controlled by Kachin state groups.[32]

The conflict-model of environmental security remains the dominant paradigm amid concerns over "troubling prospects"[33] or "likely future conflict."[34] Yet many commentators argue that the probability of resources or environmental degradation in the region being the primary cause of conflict between countries is low. War is strategically ineffective and potentially counterproductive as a means to gain or maintain access to scarce resources, even those technically "renewable" resources such as water, timber, fish, and arable land. War is particularly ineffective when the causes of scarcity and environmental degradation have transboundary dimensions—much of the literature suggests that scarcity is just as likely to encourage diplomatic resolutions to conflicts and cooperative management of shared resources.[35] This fact does not, however, discount the possibility of heightened tensions, stand-offs, or skirmishes between states over important resource issues, especially when influenced by other political disputes. Nor does it preclude deployment of military and security forces in patrolling land and maritime boundaries and territories against resource "incursion." Incursion in this instance could include activities within one country that affect environmental quality in another, the environmental (and political) vulnerabilities of land and maritime border regions, and competition over access to resources and environmental services. The "threat" arises

---

[31] Kirk Talbott and Melissa Brown, "Forest Plunder in Southeast Asia: An Environmental Security Nexus in Burma and Cambodia," Woodrow Wilson International Center, Environmental Change and Security Project Report, No. 4 (Spring 1998): 54.

[32] "China Border Logjam: The Beginning or the End of Action against Illegal Timber Exports in Northern Burma?" Global Witness, Press Release, January 23, 2006, http://www.globalwitness.org/press_releases/display2.php?id=327.

[33] James A. Winnefeld and Mary E. Morris, Where Environmental Concerns and Security Strategies Meet (Santa Monica: RAND, 1994), 65.

[34] Lim Teck Ghee and Mark J. Valencia, "Introduction," in Conflict over Natural Resources in Southeast Asia and the Pacific, ed. Lim Teck Ghee and Mark J. Valencia (Singapore: Oxford University Press, 1990), 3.

[35] See Alan Dupont, The Environment and Security in Pacific Asia (Oxford: Oxford University Press, 1998); Mikkal E. Herberg, "Energy: Asia's Energy Insecurity—Cooperation or Conflict," in Strategic Asia 2004–05: Confronting Terrorism in the Pursuit of Power, ed. Ashley J. Tellis and Michael Wills (Seattle: The National Bureau of Asian Research, 2004); and Jason Hunter, "Tumen River Area Development Program and Transboundary Water Pollution" (background paper prepared for ESENA Workshop: Energy-Related Marine Issues in the Sea of Japan, Tokyo, July 11–12, 1998), http://www.nautilus.org/archives/papers/enviro/hunter_tumen.html.

not primarily from challenges to territory but to sovereignty—testing a government's authority over resources and ability to control and manage borders against unwanted material flows both inward (such as pollutants) and outward (resources such as timber and fish).

Three versions of the "strategic" resource issue are most relevant here. The first, and one of particular concern to U.S. policymakers, is energy.[36] The heavy reliance by many countries in the region on imported energy sources makes securing new energy reserves and maintaining control over existing ones vital. The South China Sea, in particular, is one area where energy conflict is thought possible, even though the extent of actual energy reserves is unknown and the technology for exploitation expensive. For net importers of oil—Japan, the Philippines, South Korea, and Taiwan—the security of locally sourced supplies is crucial. For established producers and exporters of oil and gas, such as Brunei, Indonesia, and Malaysia, the South China Sea presents further commercial opportunities. While energy is not the only driver of competition for sovereignty over small uninhabited islands and rocks in the Spratly and Paracel Island groups, concerns regarding access to energy resources and reliability of supply have given the various claimants (Taiwan, China, Vietnam, the Philippines, Brunei, and Malaysia) few incentives to relinquish their claims. Public statements from the People's Liberation Army of China expressing determination to protect any possible reserves from what it calls the "predatory advances" of other states have only added to the complexity of the situation, despite doubts regarding China's ability to project serious maritime or commercial power into the South China Sea.[37] Sovereignty is also contested over the potentially energy-rich Diaoyu/Senkaku islands that are claimed by Japan, China, and Taiwan, with periodic eruptions of tensions and military posturing.

Fish stocks, a second strategic resource, constitute an exemplar case of disputes over access to and authority over resources that are "interactive with...threat perceptions."[38] Maintaining access to fishing grounds and seeking to deny such access to others, except in strict accordance with international law, has become an important security concern. Illegal fishing is a continual source of tension between Thailand and its neighbors, particularly Malaysia, and has involved naval and border patrol activity on both sides. In Northeast Asia, shots have been exchanged between North

---

[36] For a more detailed analysis of the implications of energy security for the United States, see Herberg, "Asia's Energy Insecurity."

[37] See Dupont, *Environment and Security in Pacific Asia*, 31.

[38] N. Ganesan, "Illegal Fishing and Illegal Migration in Thailand's Bilateral Relations with Malaysia and Myanmar," in *Non-Traditional Security Issues in Southeast Asia*, ed. Andrew T. H. Tan and J. D. Ken Boutin (Singapore: Institute of Defence and Strategic Studies and Select Books, 2001), 520.

Korean naval vessels and Chinese fishing trawlers and between Chinese and South Korean fishing trawlers. Russia and South Korea have, at times, both placed their navies on alert in the face of illegal fishing activity.

The third strategic resource is water. Most serious commentators have rejected the likelihood of "water-wars" between countries. Although transboundary water resources present problems, evidence from Asia (including South Asia) suggests that as water resource problems increase, governments are usually driven to cooperative, rather than competitive, management regimes. Diplomatic tensions over riparian rights are another matter, particularly regarding water held in transboundary and shared water systems. For example, despite the efforts of the Mekong River Commission, Laos' and Vietnam's claims to exploit the resources of their respective stretches of the Mekong as they see fit—for hydropower and water management—are a source of friction with Cambodia, which falls almost entirely within the river basin and relies heavily on the quality of river flow for irrigation and rice production. In addition, states downstream from the PRC are concerned about the impacts of China's various projects to dredge and dam the upper reaches of the Mekong on their own water resources, the ecology of the river basin, flood and siltation patterns, salinity, and freshwater fishing. Transboundary river pollution—caused by such problems as agricultural run-off, industrial chemical waste, and the dumping of mine tailings—has become another source of dispute in Northeast Asia, particularly between Russia and China.

Similar political tensions also arise over transboundary pollutants. The haze in Southeast Asia has been a persistent source of friction between Indonesia and neighboring countries whose health, agriculture, and tourism sectors have suffered from an environmental problem not of their own making. The Indonesian government is perceived to have been far too slow both in implementing policies to prevent the fires that are the cause of the haze and in prosecuting the perpetrators. In Japan and South Korea, the negative impacts of acid rain on agricultural yields and human health have created tension with China. This is not inter-state security in the traditional sense. In Asia, however—where diplomatic relationships are still hostage to recent history—tensions over environmental degradation and resource exploitation (particularly when the latter is done illicitly) can lead to a "blame game" and become a proxy for other political differences. As noted elsewhere in this chapter, however, governments have also sought to find cooperative solutions to problems such as haze, acid rain, and river pollution.

This "multiplier effect" also works within countries. Grievances over issues such as land tenure or riparian rights can escalate tensions within communities over scarce resources, especially when these resources are tied to traditional livelihoods. In Thailand, for example, conflict has erupted in Klong Tha Chin Bay and Songkhla Bay between inshore communities and commercial vessels over nocturnal anchovy fishing. Communal violence in Kalimantan between the Dayak peoples and the migrant Madurese has an environmental and resource dimension as the Dayak peoples are slowly dispossessed of their traditional access to land, forest resources, and livelihood. Water insecurities—such as competing and unmet demand for water or inequal distribution of scarce water resources—could lead to social conflict within countries. Local stresses and conflicts may lead to more open political instability if governments are unable to respond to resource and environmental demands. Strategic analysts have identified Nepal, Indonesia, and the Philippines as examples of how unsustainable resource use, mismanagement, and environmental degradation can drive instability and insurgency "on a par with ethnic and religious issues."[39] The UN Economic and Social Commission for Asia and the Pacific (ESCAP) reports that large-scale electricity generation projects have been a source of social conflict in China, India, and Thailand.[40] Environmental degradation and pollution are another factor in growing social unrest in China, a problem made more complicated by disputes over land tenure and rural poverty.[41] These issues also filter into a traditional state-security model when governments use force or the apparatus of the state to respond to challenges to authority. Extreme vulnerability to environmental degradation and increased reliance on food and energy imports could also affect the geo-strategic balance in the region if that vulnerability becomes a key variable in governments' loss of political legitimacy or in state collapse or failure.

Economic Security

Environmental degradation is closely bound to economic security. As the Asian financial crisis in the late 1990s demonstrated, economic stability and economic growth of individual countries is central to regional security. Stability and growth are assumed to have a stabilizing effect on regional security because they establish the conditions for mutual economic engagement and interdependence. Poorer countries, on the other hand, are

---

[39] See the executive summary of the conference "Environment and Security in the Asia-Pacific 2002" organized by the Asia-Pacific Center for Security Studies, November 19–21, 2002, http://www.apcss.org/core/Conference/CR_ES/021119-21ES.htm.

[40] ESCAP, *State of the Environment*, 52.

[41] See Kenneth Lieberthal's chapter on China in this volume. See also Thomas Lum, "Social Unrest in China," Congressional Research Service, CRS Report for Congress, RL33416, May 8, 2006, http://www.fas.org/sgp/crs/row/RL33416.pdf.

generally perceived as more prone to state collapse. Yet economic growth places enormous pressure on the region's environmental carrying capacity. Stresses on the environment in turn place constraints on long-term economic growth.

The economic insecurities of environmental degradation should not be downplayed. In the region environmental decline costs countries an average of 3% to 8% of annual GDP.[42] A doubling of atmospheric carbon dioxide is estimated to cost ASEAN countries between 2.1% and 8.6% of GDP, much higher than the world estimate of 1.4% to 1.9%.[43] The World Bank calculates that pollution-related health costs could be as much as 15% to 18% of urban income and up to 7% of GDP in some parts of the region.[44] A few examples from the litany of costs summarized by the ADB continue this depressing picture: productivity losses in China from land degradation, water shortages, and loss of wetlands are possibly as much as 7% of GDP; the health effects of particulate and lead pollution in Thailand are estimated at 2% of GDP; and health impacts of air and water pollution and productivity losses from soil erosion and deforestation in Pakistan constitute about 3% of GDP.[45] Economic growth generates other kinds of environment-related costs as well. One estimate holds, for example, that by 2025, the cost of managing the solid waste products of industrialization could increase to as much as $50 billion a year (double 1999 costs).[46] Economic costs from environmental degradation also become important as conventional security concerns when they contribute to or raise concerns over other forms of national or regional instability. For example, Pakistan already faces a precarious socio-economic situation that could be made worse by the economic burden of environmental degradation.[47] China's economic situation, which is being undermined by environmental decline, is considered crucial not just to domestic social-political stability but also to regional economic growth and stability.[48]

---

[42] J. Barkenbus, "APEC and the Environment: Civil Society in an Age of Globalization," East-West Center, AsiaPacific Issues, no. 51, 2001, 2. For useful summaries of estimated environmental costs in selected countries in the region, see Raghbendra Jha, "Alleviating Environmental Degradation in the Asia-Pacific Region: International Cooperation and the Role of Issue-Linkage" in *Regional Integration in the Asia Pacific: Issues and Prospects*, ed. Barrie Stevens and Randall Holden (Paris: OECD, 2005).

[43] ASEAN Secretariat, *ASEAN Report to the World Summit on Sustainable Development* (Jakarta: ASEAN Secretariat, 2002), 40.

[44] Cited in M. A. Bengwayan "Deaths and Illnesses from Pollution in Asia Increasing," *Earth Times*, March 11, 2000, www.earthtimes.org.

[45] ADB, *Asian Environment Outlook 2001*, 12.

[46] World Bank estimates cited in ESCAP, *State of the Environment*, 5.

[47] See Frédéric Grare's chapter on South Asia in this volume.

[48] See Kenneth Lieberthal's chapter on China in this volume.

Human Security

The human security consequences of environmental degradation need to be assessed with two things in mind. First, for people and communities, freedom from want and harm is as much a measure of regional and global security as freedom from fear. In the final analysis, a country or region in which people are not economically, socially, and environmentally secure in their daily lives cannot be said to be "secure." Second, in often complicated ways, human insecurities and social stresses are tied up with more conventional interpretations of state and regional security. The environmental externalities of unsustainable development have direct consequences for the security of people and communities in the region, who ultimately bear the cost of environmental harm through increased vulnerability, poverty, and ill health. Environmental decline and resource depletion sustain poverty in Asia where almost one-quarter of the population still lives on less than $1 a day, even though absolute poverty has declined. The poor in both urban and rural areas remain the most disadvantaged and impoverished by environmental degradation, pollution, and resource depletion because they are the least able to buy their way out of its consequences—a challenge that the ADB refers to as "environmental poverty."[49] Environmental degradation results in food-production shortfalls, food insecurity, poverty, and conflict over land tenure. Mortality rates from ambient and indoor air pollution, along with the incidence of chronic respiratory illness, are increasing. Solid waste and effluent pollution of water causes health problems ranging from diarrhea and dysentery to cholera and typhoid. Dirty water and poor sanitation result in over a half-million infant deaths a year in the region. Food insecurity is a real-life consequence of over-fishing and intensification of agriculture. Communities are dislocated by the environmental consequences of development projects. Indigenous peoples are displaced culturally and physically from their land. Environmental degradation and resource loss impels internal migration when local ecosystems can no longer support even subsistence lifestyles. Environmental degradation undermines the integrity of ecosystems that can help to protect people in the face of natural disasters such as flooding or tsunami.

The human security aspects of environmental change are also tied to the challenges of social (in)equity that in turn can feed into more explicit social grievances. The problem is not merely that the poor are affected by most of the environmental problems, but that they are affected disproportionately.

---

[49] See ADB, *Environmental Poverty: New Perspectives and Implications for Sustainable Development in Asia and the Pacific* (Manila: ADB, 2007).

In rural areas they are more dependent on the natural resources that are being depleted or degraded—forest, fisheries, and water. In urban areas, the poor live in conditions with minimal sanitation and limited access to clean water. They are more likely to live in or close to heavily industrialized areas that generate air and water pollution. The poor are also often the most vulnerable to environmental management strategies. Utilizing market value to allocate water resources can price the poor out of that market. Building dams to improve water management can exacerbate rather than reduce inequities if people are forcibly relocated or if changes to river ecology and flow undermine local subsistence agriculture or artisanal fisheries. Sustainable economic growth that minimizes environmental costs—i.e., environmental security in the positive sense—is still a weak measure of human and national security if distributive concerns are not properly taken into account. As explored above, these kinds of environmental and resource inequities are a growing factor in social conflict and political instability both within countries and, potentially, across the region. Policies addressing environmental "poverty [and] social inequality" can help to build the "conditions for stability and peace—even in those situations where there is no immediate or clear threat of violence."[50] This suggests that in order to enhance national and regional security, development must be more than environmentally sustainable; it must also be socially just.

Managing Environmental (In)security: Regional Responses

Regional capacity to respond to these various environmental security challenges will have implications for U.S. interests in maintaining and enhancing regional stability and therefore for U.S. policy responses. The discussion in the previous section suggests several conclusions. The first is that prolonged military conflict between states over resources or environmental degradation is unlikely. Second, the occasional use of military capabilities to protect resources or to prevent environmental degradation is possible, although this is most likely to be for patrolling and interdiction purposes (e.g., illegal fishing and logging). Third, if conflict is an outcome of resource scarcity or environmental degradation, then conflict is more

---

[50] Simon Tay, "Preventive Diplomacy and the ASEAN Regional Forum: Principles and Possibilities" (paper prepared for the ASEAN Regional Forum (ARF) Track II Conference on Preventive Diplomacy, Singapore, September 9–11, 1997). This paper was reproduced in Desmond Ball and Amitav Acharya, eds., *The Next Stage: Preventive Diplomacy and Security Cooperation in the Asia-Pacific Region* (Canberra: Strategic and Defence Studies Centre, 1999), 121.

likely to occur within a country, particularly between competing users or in the context of broader political and social grievances.

Cooperative response strategies in the region (explored in more detail below) involve not only governments but also private actors including NGOs, grassroots movements, scientific bodies, and corporate interests. Such responses provide a more effective way of dealing with environmental security challenges for several reasons. Overcoming environmental insecurities is the key to averting other forms of threat and insecurity explored earlier in this chapter. From an environmental perspective, many of the problems outlined in the second section cannot be managed easily by states unilaterally. Where pollutants or environmental resources cross borders—through dispersal, dumping, or illegal practices—cooperation is required among the various states involved. Cooperative regional responses also help to reduce the transaction costs of addressing environmental problems within countries by facilitating information gathering and data-sharing as well as the exchange of knowledge and expertise. From a security perspective, cooperation on environmental security has further benefits. It can contribute to trust-building within the region, helping to establish a cooperative mind-set on an issue perceived to be less politically-charged than other issue-areas.

The importance of cooperation is repeatedly stressed in regional and U.S. policy statements on non-traditional security and environmental degradation. The regional record on this, however, is mixed. The complexities of the environmental security agenda in the Asia-Pacific, ranging across both traditional and non-traditional concerns, are recognized in the region's security proclamations, yet with little real conviction and not much effective policy response. The problems of environmental degradation have also been well-acknowledged in various forums on environmental protection and sustainable development. Nevertheless, implementation of both national and regional environmental and sustainable development policy is uneven and, as this chapter has shown, serious environmental security problems remain.

The ASEAN Regional Forum (ARF), the region's principal mechanism for security dialogue, has offered a view of comprehensive security that includes economic and social aspects and recognizes that environmental degradation and resource scarcity have security implications. The ARF's three regional security policy conferences to date have, in some form, all "acknowledged the existence of or emergence of some threats to peace in the form of...non-traditional issues" which demand a "holistic and comprehensive approach."[51] The 2005 ARF seminar on enhancing cooperation in the field of non-traditional security issues noted that non-traditional security issues including environmental degradation have "in varying degrees, posed threats to the stability and development of the Asia-Pacific region."[52] Individual governments have also given passing attention to environmental threats. China's 2006 national defense white paper, for example, observes that security issues related to environmental degradation are becoming more damaging in nature.[53] The Republic of Korea's contribution to the ARF's "Annual Security Outlook 2005" discusses "newly emerging non-traditional kinds of threats [including] environmental hazards" as a "challenge to stability in the region."[54] Despite these declaratory observations, environmental concerns are rarely addressed in any substantive detail compared to other forms of non-traditional security such as terrorism, trafficking, maritime security, and pandemic disease. Although ARF seminars have suggested that environmental degradation is an area in which preventive diplomacy practices are relevant, the ARF has yet to hold a dedicated seminar or working group on environmental security. ASEAN and China's memorandum of understanding in 2004 regarding cooperation in the field of non-traditional security contains nothing on environmental issues.[55] Compared with other forms of non-traditional security, there is little real attention in official circles to environmental degradation as a regional security concern.[56]

---

[51] See the Chairman's Summary of the second ASEAN Regional Forum Regional Security Policy Conference, Vientiane, Laos, May 19, 2005, para. 6 and 22. This document, in PDF format, can be found via http://www.aseanregionalforum.org/PublicLibrary/ARFChairmansStatementsandReports/tabid/66/Default.aspx.

[52] See the Chair's Summary Report of the ARF Seminar on Enhancing Cooperation in the Field of Non-Traditional Security Issues, March 7–8, 2005, Sanya, China, para. 4, http://www.aseansec.org/arf/12arf/Chairs-Sanya-7-8March05.pdf. See also similar comments in the Co-Chair's Summary Report of the Meeting of the ARF Inter-sessional Support Group on Confidence Building Measures and Preventive Diplomacy, Manila, Philippines, March 1–3, 2006.

[53] Information Office of the State Council, China's National Defense in 2006 (Beijing, December 29, 2006), http://english.people.com.cn/whitepaper/defense2006/defense2006(1).html.

[54] ARF, "Annual Security Outlook 2005" (report prepared for the Twelfth ASEAN Regional Forum, Vientiane, Laos, 2005), 73, http://www.aseanregionalforum.org/Portals/0/aso-2005.pdf.

[55] Memorandum of Understanding between the Governments of the Member Countries of the Association of Southeast Asian Nations (ASEAN) and the Government of the People's Republic of China on Cooperation in the Field of Non-Traditional Security Issues, Bangkok, 10 January 2004, available on the ASEAN website, http://www.aseansec.org/15647.htm.

[56] Some sectors of the scholarly and "Track II" community in the region have sought to address this knowledge gap. Environmental security concerns have been on the agenda of the annual ASEAN-ISIS Asia-Pacific Roundtable, explored in the non-traditional security project coordinated by the Institute for Defence and Strategic Studies in Singapore, and examined in the work of the Consortium of Non-Traditional Security Studies in Asia network hosted by the Rajaratnam School of International Studies at Nanyang Technological University in Singapore. The United Nations University in Tokyo and the Japan Center for International Exchange have also sponsored some work in this area.

Environmental "threats" are rarely recognized as human security problems. As some member countries read "human security" as shorthand for intervention in human rights, the ARF does not use the term. The problem, however, is more than language. As Tan argues, human security discourse in Asia is state-centric because "it is deployed for the ongoing inscription or production of the state as an ontological entity."[57] Human insecurity is usually presented in official discourse as a problem not because of the implications for people, but because such insecurity can destabilize the state or impede economic progress. Nevertheless, not all noteworthy regional commentators are reluctant to use the term. Speaking on Southeast Asia's security environment at the First Plenary Meeting of the ARF's Experts and Eminent Persons, Mohamed Jawhar Hassan took the firm position that "human security issues are arguably the greatest security challenge for Southeast Asia" and are "at the core of national security concerns." He went on to say that "improving human security should be the primary concern of the ARF and ASEAN."[58] The most outspoken governments on human security have been Thailand (at least under previous administrations) and Japan. In the ARF's "Annual Security Outlook 2005," Thailand reported that it had "consistently advocated the promotion of human security…as an appropriate approach to dealing with the growing scope of security challenges, particularly those from the non-traditional sector."[59] Japan's commitment to human security has extended to sponsorship of the Trust Fund for Human Security established in the UN Secretariat. Through this mechanism and the Japan Fund for Global Environment, Japan has funded many human and environmental security projects focusing on local-level responses to insecurity challenges in various Asian countries.[60]

If there seems to be little meaningful action in the security sector to address environmental security, more is occurring in the environmental sector. The problem here, however, is not so much lack of recognition of the problems but rather lack of effective implementation of policy. All Asia-Pacific countries now have a ministry or an executive-level agency responsible for environmental protection and sustainable development. Many countries

[57] Tan See Seng, *Human Security: Discourse, Statecraft, Emancipation* (Singapore: Institute of Defence and Strategic Studies, 2001), 2; and Dewi Fortuna Anwar, "Human Security: An Intractable Problem in Asia," in *Asian Security Order: Instrumental and Normative Features*, ed. Muthiah Alagappa (Stanford: Stanford University Press, 2003), 536–70.

[58] Mohamed Jawhar Hassan, "Security Environment in Southeast Asia," (paper presented at ASEAN Regional Forum, The First Plenary Meeting of Experts and Eminent Persons, Jeju Island, Republic of Korea, June 29–30, 2006) 2–3, http://www.isis.org.my/files/bfpss/Security%20Environment%20in%20Southeast%20Asia.pdf.

[59] ARF, "Annual Security Outlook 2005," 96.

[60] Japan links its environmental development assistance program specifically to its human security agenda.

have either established or are in the process of establishing some form of a national council on sustainable development.[61] In addition to developing bureaucratic structures, governments have also enacted a remarkable suite of specific legislative initiatives including land laws, regulations on protected areas, water pollution, waste management, environmental impact assessment, national forestry plans, biodiversity and wildlife inventories, targets to phase out lead in petrol, and clean river programs.[62]

Regional institutions also pay considerable political attention to the environment. ASEAN has declared a "clean and green" Southeast Asia as a key objective of the ASEAN Vision 2020. The Ministerial Declaration and Regional Implementation Plan for Sustainable Development in Asia and the Pacific 2006, supported by the Seoul Initiative on Environmentally Sustainable Economic Growth, calls for regional commitment to the "green growth" paradigm. Though not all legally binding, cooperative regional or subregional agreements exist on such issue areas as regional seas, haze, transboundary pollution, fisheries, flora and fauna, dust and sandstorms, and integrated river basin management.[63] Northeast Asian countries cooperate on an acid deposition monitoring program and senior officials now meet regularly on environmental concerns. The South Asia Co-operative Environment Programme (SACEP) has fostered a number of regional agreements including the Malé Declaration on Control and Prevention of Air Pollution and its Likely Transboundary Effects for South Asia. Southeast Asia has strategic plans of action on the environment (although the last one, which expired in 2004, has been partly overtaken by the Hanoi Plan of Action as part of the ASEAN Vision 2020) and a range of

---

[61] By August 2004, eighteen countries in the region covered by ESCAP (including Australia and New Zealand) were in the process of implementing National Sustainable Development Strategies (NSDS), up from only five in 2003. The most recent information on the ESCAP's website, based on governmental self-reporting to the UN's Department of Economic and Social Affairs, suggests that most countries in South Asia (with the exception of Sri Lanka) do not yet have NSDS. No information was available from Vietnam, North Korea, Laos, and Cambodia; see the NSDS map at: http://www.un.org/esa/sustdev/natlinfo/nsds/nsdsMap.htm.

[62] For a useful summary of national initiatives, see UNEP, *Asia-Pacific Environment Outlook* 2, chap. 3; and Alan Khee-Jin Tan, "Environmental Laws and Institutions in Southeast Asia: A Review of Recent Developments," *Singapore Yearbook of International Law*, 8 (2004): 177–92.

[63] A select example of regional arrangements for environmental management includes: UNEP's East Asia Regional Seas Programme (established in 1981); the Coordinating Body for the Seas of East Asia (COBSEA) which oversees the East Asian Seas Action Plan; the Partnership for Environmental Management in the Seas of East Asia (PEMSEA); the UN project Reversing Environmental Degradation Trends in the South China Sea and the Gulf of Thailand (SCS); ASEAN's Cooperation Plan on Transboundary Pollution (1995), Regional Haze Action Plan (1997), and Agreement on Transboundary Haze Pollution (2002); ASEAN's Agreement on the Conservation of Nature and Natural Resources (1985); the Asia-Pacific Fishery Commission; the Acid Deposition Monitoring Network in East Asia; the Agreement on the Network of Aquaculture Centres in Asia and the Pacific; the Mekong River Commission and its various programs on integrated river basin management and integrated mountain development; and ASEAN's Wildlife Enforcement Network.

specific regional programs, projects, and networks on coastal and marine environments, criteria and indicators for the sustainable management of natural tropical forests, biodiversity conservation, wildlife smuggling, and environmental education.

To succeed as an environmental security strategy, cooperation must deliver outcomes in environmental protection and sustainable resource management. There has been national and regional progress in dealing with some environmental problems. For example, national cleaner production programs have succeeded in reducing local emissions in parts of China, Indonesia, South Korea, and Vietnam. Regional efforts have increased the number of interdictions of illegally smuggled ODS. Coverage of protected areas in the region has grown. The role that civil society has played in environmental policymaking and community-based management initiatives has increased, albeit unevenly across the region. Yet as the second section of this chapter has shown, none of the environmental problems confronting the region have been entirely or successfully resolved. Indeed, ESCAP reports that virtually no developing country in the region is on track to meet the targets and indicators set out in the seventh Millennium Development Goal of ensuring environmental sustainability.[64]

Explanations for limited progress focus on three problems. The first problem is a lack of material resources in terms of technology, funds, and human capacity (including expertise and know-how). This also makes it difficult to develop accepted indicators for assessing the impact of national programs and regional agreements. The environmental sector is usually under-funded and under-staffed, particularly compared with the security sector. The ADB estimates that countries in the Asia-Pacific spend on average between 1% and 2% of GDP on environmental protection compared with defense budgets up to 6%. Traditional security budgets thus surpass environmental security budgets by about three to one. Environment budgets, the ADB suggests, should be at least 7% of GDP.[65] The second problem is political. Regional institutions are generally weak in conformity with the so-called ASEAN-way: the norm of giving priority to sovereignty, non-interference, and non-confrontational diplomacy in the Asia-Pacific. Although considerable emphasis is placed on the advantages of cooperation to address the region's environmental security challenges, cooperation on environmental issues has been a matter of taking slow steps rather than institutionalizing authoritative regional organizations. The third suite of problems falls broadly under the heading of policy failure.

---

[64] ESCAP, *State of the Environment*, chap. 5.

[65] ADB, *Asian Environment Outlook 2001*, 24.

Despite a commitment from all governments that development should be environmentally sustainable, environmental protection goals are rarely prioritized over development or trade objectives. In human security terms, poverty alleviation is often narrowly pursued in terms of economic growth, potentially undermining rather than enhancing social equity and access to resources and ecosystem services that is part of the environmental security equation. Policies that pursue economic security can clearly undermine both human and environmental security.

Implications for U.S. Interests and Policy

According to the U.S. Department of State, U.S. security interests in the Asia-Pacific include "promoting regional stability, fostering democracy and human rights, encouraging economic prosperity, [and] furthering cooperation on fighting transnational issues and international crime."[66] Should the trends described in this chapter continue, environmental degradation and resource scarcity will undermine that U.S. security vision by making vulnerable the stability of political relationships between and among countries, by exacerbating social grievances and human insecurities within countries, and by their impact on economic development, trade, and resource security. National security efforts should strive to "protect stability where it exists and…instill it where it does not."[67] The best strategy for preventing forms of instability with environmental and resource components is to assist countries in the region to overcome environmental degradation and resource decline. This strategy has implications for U.S. policy in three broad areas: strategic policy (including energy policy), aid policy, and environmental policy.

In strategic terms, environmental insecurity and instability in the region could not only compromise U.S. security policy interests as described above but, in a worse case scenario, could involve the United States by requiring U.S. forces to "provide stability before conditions worsen…or undertake stability and reconstruction efforts…to avert further disaster and reconstitute a stable environment."[68] Though unlikely to be the single or predominant driver, environment-related internal grievances and disputes could contribute to a complicated matrix of factors that could undermine the political legitimacy of countries in transition to democracy

---

[66] See "Regional Topics" on the U.S. Department of State website, http://www.state.gov/p/eap/regional/.

[67] "National Security and the Threat of Climate Change," 13.

[68] Ibid., 6. On page 46 the report recommended that the administration should "evaluate the capacity of the military and other institutions to respond to the consequences of climate change."

or destabilize the region's larger powers such as China or Indonesia. Given that environment-related poverty can play a role in political disaffection, there are also somewhat opaque links to the war on terrorism. Climate change, for example, has been specifically identified as having a multiplier effect on other political, social, and economic stresses, leading to a possible rise in extremism in situations where governments have limited ability to cope.[69] U.S. interests (to say nothing of those of local people) could also be threatened if governments in the region use internal security mechanisms or exceptional measures to respond to environment-related grievances. Those interests would also be in jeopardy if violence is used to push through development and investment projects in the face of opposition on environmental grounds. Where environmental problems have global reach, those problems will also affect the United Sates itself. For example, the United States is not immune to the impacts of climate change. Disasters of nature in other parts of the world increase demands on the United States for emergency assistance. An increase in vector-borne diseases may well have consequences for health security in the United States. An increase in the movement of peoples that results from climate change or other serious environmental decline may place refugee demands on the United States.

This line of thinking suggests that U.S. strategic policy will need to recognize and account for these concerns more fully. Neither the 2002 or 2006 National Security Strategy devotes much attention to environmental issues, referring only in general terms both to energy security (especially in the context of U.S.-China relations) and to environmental degradation as a challenge of globalization. While U.S. government representatives have welcomed the ARF's emphasis on non-traditional security, this has usually been limited to support for prevention efforts on terrorism, pandemics, and WMD proliferation. The Clinton administration's 1998 U.S. Security Strategy for the East Asia-Pacific region—which was more explicit in addressing environmental security as a form of transnational security and in confirming the importance of political and economic development assistance in addressing the root causes of such challenges— has not been updated.[70] Non-traditional security concerns, including environmental ones, do however continue to be the subject of discussion at various seminars held by defense department think-tanks and the regional

---

[69] "National Security and the Threat of Climate Change," 6.

[70] A copy of this document is still available on the website of the U.S. Embassy in Thailand at: http://bangkok.usembassy.gov/services/docs/reports/ussec.htm. For an excellent overview of current U.S. "environmental security" policy, see Rita Taurek and Geoffrey D. Dabelko, "Profile of the United States" in *Inventory of Environment and Security Policies and Practices*, ed. Ronald A. Kingham (The Hague: Institute for Environmental Security, 2006), 113–22, http://www.environsecurity.org/ges/inventory/IESPP_Full_Report.pdf.

command structures such as Pacific Command and Central Command. Responsibility for the more conventional aspects of environmental security policy has been assigned to USAID's Office of Conflict Management and Mitigation (CMM), which has produced a series of toolkits for field staff on resource and conflict issues, including water, land, and forests.[71]

Resource issues in Asia have the potential to complicate U.S. energy policy, which is intent on reducing reliance on energy sources from regions of instability. Indeed, energy and climate change appear to be the environmental security issues that most concern U.S. decisionmakers. These are continuing themes in the Sino-U.S. Strategic Economic Dialogues, which met for the first time in December 2006 and again in May 2007. In January 2007 the Speaker of the House of Representatives appointed a Select Committee on Energy Independence and Global Warming to investigate the national security impacts of these problems. A bipartisan bill introduced into the Senate on March 28, 2007 called for a National Intelligence Estimate "on the anticipated geopolitical effects of global climate change and the implications of such effects on the national security of the United States."[72]

Environmental security concerns in the region have implications for more than simply strategic policy. While policy initiatives must recognize the various forms of insecurity that can result from environmental challenges, the most effective security response is to focus on the causes rather than symptoms. If U.S. policymakers are concerned that weak regional responses to environmental degradation could lead to instability, then it is in U.S. interests to expand existing project and program support for the efforts already underway in Asia-Pacific countries to mitigate the impacts of environmental degradation. Through financial, technological, and capacity-building assistance, U.S. support will strengthen national and regional resilience to environmental degradation and will enhance regional abilities to implement effective environmental protection and sustainable development policies. This points to the importance of continuing budgetary commitments to USAID to support the agency's regional environmental and development missions and its work with stakeholders from the local to regional level in Asia.[73] This moves "security policy" into the realm of aid policy and suggests a more explicit role for USAID in particular as a partner in U.S. policy dialogues with Asia on non-traditional security. If

---

[71] See "Conflict Management: Natural Resources and Conflict" on the USAID's website, http://www. usaid.gov/our_work/cross-cutting_programs/conflict/focus_areas/natural_resources.html.

[72] *Global Climate Change Security Oversight Act*, S 1018, 110th Cong., 1st sess., *Congressional Record*, no. 54, (June 4, 2007): S4059–S4061.

[73] More information on USAID's mission in Asia can be found on their website: http://usaid.eco-asia.org/.

environmental development assistance is to be strengthened further, then this may also involve support for the efforts of other government agencies in strengthening networks and partnerships on environmental protection as well as support for those U.S.-based private organizations, NGOs, universities, and state and local governments that are involved in policy development, capacity building, and environmental monitoring and repair in Asia.[74]

Given the range of problems outlined in this chapter, environmental security policy should not be limited to energy and climate change, important though those issues are. U.S. environmental security interests are likely to be served most effectively by strengthening and expanding environmental aid to and cooperation with Asian countries on a range of issue areas, including water, pollution, land degradation, biodiversity, and deforestation. Policy toward environmental security challenges will be stronger if approached in inter-sectoral terms to ensure that it is coherent and comprehensive rather than sectoral or piecemeal. For example, the Singapore-U.S. Free Trade Agreement has been criticized as making it easier to launder and smuggle illegally sourced timber into the United States, running counter to policy objectives under the President's Initiative Against Illegal Logging announced in July 2003.[75]

Support for environmental security policies in the region can deliver other political and security benefits to the United States, possibly offsetting tensions in other aspects of bilateral or regional relationships. The United States, however, will need to position itself as a collaborative partner supporting the environment and sustainable development priorities of the region rather than pursuing policies that are perceived to meet only its own environmental and security concerns. The United States would not benefit by being seen as hectoring regional partners on their environmental policy. This is particularly important given the widely held view (not always expressed in official communications) that the United States is an

---

[74] Constraints of space make it impossible to give any detail on the extent of involvement of U.S.-based public and private agencies and organizations who are involved in building capacity for environmental policy and protection in Asia. A few examples will give a flavor of the extent of this involvement. Government agencies include the U.S. Fish and Wildlife Service, the Bureau of Oceans and International Environmental and Science Affairs of the Department of State, and the U.S. Environment Protection Agency. NGOs and private agencies include the Asia Foundation, Conservation International, WildAid, and the Environmental Investigation Agency (U.S.). The Memorandum of Understanding on Cooperation in Decision-Making on Integrated Transboundary River Management, signed in 2004 between the Mekong River Commission, the Mississippi River Basin Alliance and the University of Minnesota Water Resources Center, shows how bodies working at a variety of levels seek collaboration to develop capacity building and information exchange partnerships.

[75] See "Singapore's Illegal Timber Trade and the U.S.-Singapore Free Trade Agreement," Energy Investigation Agency and Telapak, May 2003, http://www.eia-international.org/files/reports54-1.pdf.

environmental laggard that demands action from countries within the region but will not commit fully to its own responsibilities as a major global polluter.[76] The tension between U.S. demands that developing countries commit to pollution targets (such as those in the Kyoto Protocol) and developing countries' demands that the United States take seriously the principle of common but differentiated responsibilities will not be easily resolved.[77] The implication for U.S. policy is that action addressing Asian governments' perceptions and concerns will help strengthen the conditions for U.S. leadership in the region on environmental security challenges.

In summary, environmental insecurity complicates regional security and stability. This finding is central to U.S. interests in Asia that focus on enhancing stability where it exists and seeking to instill it where it does not. If these concerns and objectives are taken seriously, U.S. security practice will benefit from anticipating and understanding the full range of environmental insecurity problems. Equally important, U.S. security interests will benefit from providing material resources, program support, and policy expertise to assist Asian efforts to manage environmental degradation and resource decline that will otherwise undermine human security, constrain economic security, and lead to social conflict, violence, and instability.

---

[76] One criticism leveled at the Asia-Pacific Partnership on Clean Development and Climate—in which the United States is a lead partner—is that it criticizes regional countries for their growing emissions but does little to acknowledge the contribution of U.S. emissions to the global problem.

[77] The common but differentiated responsibilities principle was articulated in principle seven of the Rio Declaration adopted at the 1992 United Nations Conference on Environment and Development and codified in a number of multilateral environmental agreements. In brief, it reflects a political bargain between developed and developing countries by which "developed countries acknowledge the responsibility that they bear in the international pursuit of sustainable development in view of the pressures their societies place on the global environment and of the technologies and financial resources they command."

STRATEGIC ASIA 2007–08

INDICATORS

TABLE OF CONTENTS

Economies

Trade

Investment

Population and Society

Politics and International Relations

Energy

Defense Spending

Conventional Military Capabilities

Weapons of Mass Destruction

Space Programs

Strategic Asia
by the Numbers

The following twenty pages contain tables and figures drawn from NBR's Strategic Asia database and its sources. This appendix consists of 24 tables covering: economic growth, trade, and foreign investment; population size, urbanization, and unemployment; politics and international relations; energy consumption; and armed forces, defense spending, conventional military capabilities, weapons of mass destruction, and space programs. The data sets presented here summarize the critical trends in the region and changes underway in the balance of power in Asia.

The Strategic Asia database contains additional data for all 37 countries in Strategic Asia. Hosted on the program's website (http://strategicasia.nbr.org), the database is a repository for authoritative data for every year since 1990, and is continually updated. The 70 strategic indicators are arranged in 10 broad thematic areas: economy, finance, trade and investment, government spending, population, energy and environment, communications and transportation, armed forces, weapons of mass destruction, and politics and international relations. The Strategic Asia database was developed with .NET, Microsoft's XML-based platform, which allows users to dynamically link to all or part of the Strategic Asia data set and facilitates easy data sharing. The database also includes additional links that allow users to seamlessly access related online resources.

The information for *Strategic Asia by the Numbers* was compiled by Strategic Asia research assistants Michael Jones and Stephanie Renzi.

Economies

In 2006 the developing economies of Asia grew at their fastest pace in over a decade, with an average growth rate of 8.3%. China and India were at the forefront of this growth. Energy-exporting economies in Asia—particularly Russia and Kazakhstan—also experienced strong growth due to rising oil and gas prices. The economic growth rates in Southeast Asia were mixed due to high inflation and unfavorable investment climates in several key countries.

- Despite concerns that China's economy could overheat, China's GDP grew at 10.5% in 2006, the highest rate since 1995.

- India's economy grew at a rate of 8.5%. In 2005 India overtook South Korea as the world's fifth-largest economy.

- The Japanese economy continues to enjoy a gradual but steady recovery, registering 2.8% growth in 2006. Despite rising domestic demand, a slightly lower growth rate of 2.7% is projected for 2007.

- High interest rates and inflation in Indonesia have curbed consumer spending and investments and affected economic stability.

TABLE 1   Gross domestic product

	GDP ($bn constant 2000)				Rank	
	1990	2000	2005	2004–05 growth (%)	1990	2005
United States	7,055.0	9,764.8	11,046.4	3.2	1	1
Japan	4,111.3	4,649.6	4,992.8	2.6	2	2
China	444.6	1,198.5	1,889.9	10.2	4	3
Canada	535.6	714.5	809.5	2.9	3	4
India	269.4	460.2	644.1	9.2	8	5
South Korea	283.6	511.7	637.9	4.0	6	6
Australia	280.5	399.7	468.4	2.8	7	7
Taiwan	–	321.3	365.8	4.1	–	8
Russia	385.9	259.7	349.9	6.4	5	9
Hong Kong	108.4	168.8	207.9	7.3	10	10
Indonesia	109.2	165.0	207.7	5.6	9	11
Thailand	79.4	122.7	156.8	4.5	11	12
Malaysia	45.5	90.3	112.5	5.2	13	13
Singapore	44.7	92.7	112.2	6.4	14	14
Philippines	55.8	75.4	93.7	5.0	12	15
World	23,996.7	31,756.0	36,352.1	3.5	N/A	N/A

SOURCE: World Bank, *World Development Indicators*, 2007; and (data for Taiwan) Central Bank of China, "Annual Report," 2006.
NOTE: These values show GDP converted from domestic currencies using 2000 exchange rates. Figures for Taiwan are calculated using the average exchange rate for 2000. Dash indicates that no data is available.

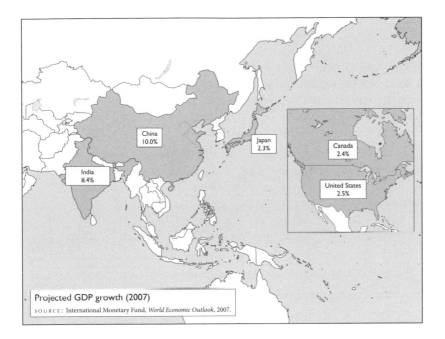

Projected GDP growth (2007)

SOURCE: International Monetary Fund, *World Economic Outlook*, 2007.

TABLE 2   GDP growth and inflation rate

	GDP growth (%)			Inflation rate (%)		
	1990–99	2000–04	2005–06	1990–99	2000–04	2005–06
United States	2.6	3.0	3.5	3.0	2.5	2.9
Japan	1.5	1.3	2.8	1.3	-0.5	0.0
China	9.3	8.4	9.8	7.4	0.8	1.7
Canada	2.1	3.0	2.9	2.1	2.4	2.1
India	4.8	5.7	8.1	10.0	5.0	4.8
South Korea	6.2	5.7	4.4	5.6	3.0	2.5
Australia	3.4	3.9	2.7	2.6	2.1	3.3
Taiwan	5.8	3.4	4.1	3.2	0.6	1.7
Russia	-6.6	5.7	6.5	34.8	15.9	11.3
Hong Kong	3.5	4.6	6.6	6.8	0.4	1.6
Indonesia	3.6	4.1	5.5	19.3	9.1	11.9
Thailand	5.1	4.7	4.7	5.1	1.8	4.8
Malaysia	6.6	5.0	5.4	10.5	1.5	3.4
Singapore	6.9	3.8	6.9	2.0	1.0	0.7
Philippines	2.7	4.2	5.3	9.2	4.5	6.9

SOURCE: Central Intelligence Agency, *The World Factbook*, 1990–2007.

Trade

Led by China's export growth, the developing economies of Asia are experiencing a widening trade surplus with the rest of the world. Intraregional trade now accounts for approximately 40% of total Asian exports. The Middle East, Africa, and Latin America are increasingly important trading partners for Asia, not only as sources of natural resources but also as export markets for consumer goods.

- Though still subject to Congressional approval, the United States and South Korea negotiated an FTA that would eliminate trade barriers— mainly in the agriculture, automotive, and apparel sectors.

- Both India and China are engaged in FTA negotiations with the Gulf Cooperation Council. China-GCC trade grew at an average rate of 40% from 1999 to 2005, reaching $33.8 billion. Trade between India and the GCC rose to nearly $25 billion in 2006, excluding energy imports.

- Increased exports in 2006 transformed Thailand's long-time trade deficit into a trade surplus, due to increased demand for the country's agricultural products, electronics, and other manufactured goods.

TABLE 3   Trade flow

	Trade flow ($bn constant 2000)				Rank	
	1990	2000	2005	2004–05 growth (%)	1990	2005
United States	1,159.6	2,572.1	2,837.1	9.0	1	1
China	129.9	530.2	1,405.1	18.4	6	2
Japan	649.4	957.6	1,149.3	9.6	2	3
Hong Kong	197.3	475.3	718.4	9.5	5	4
Canada	296.3	617.4	644.0	6.2	4	5
South Korea	118.0	401.6	630.4	7.8	7	6
Russia	305.9	176.8	318.8	11.0	3	7
India	39.8	130.5	280.3	22.0	13	8
Malaysia	67.0	206.7	269.7	8.4	10	9
Australia	88.1	178.0	221.4	8.6	8	10
Thailand	68.3	153.3	210.9	6.8	9	11
Indonesia	66.2	117.9	160.4	10.3	11	12
Philippines	42.8	82.7	105.4	3.3	12	13
Vietnam	4.1	35.1	76.6	17.1	15	14
New Zealand	21.6	36.6	47.4	10.0	14	15
World	8,328.2	15,957.1	21,000.2	7.5	N/A	N/A

SOURCE: World Bank, *World Development Indicators*, 2007.
NOTE: Data for United States, Japan, Canada, Australia, and New Zealand is for 2004 rather than 2005. World total for 2005 is an estimate. No comparable data from *World Development Indicators* is available for Singapore or Taiwan.

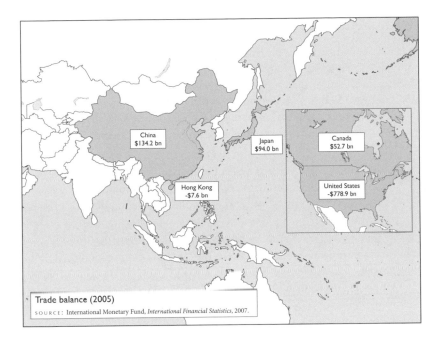

Trade balance (2005)

SOURCE: International Monetary Fund, *International Financial Statistics*, 2007.

TABLE 4   Export partners

	Exports ($bn) 2006	Export destinations (top three partners in 2006 with percentage share of total exports)
United States	1,024.0	Canada (22%), Mexico (13%), Japan (6%)
China	974.0	U.S. (21%), Hong Kong (16%), Japan (10%)
Japan	590.3	U.S. (23%), China (14%), South Korea (8%)
Hong Kong	611.6	China (47%), U.S. (15%), Japan (5%)
Canada	405.0	U.S. (82%), UK (2%), Japan (2%)
South Korea	326.0	China (25%), U.S. (13%), Japan (8%)

SOURCE: Central Intelligence Agency, *The World Factbook*, 2007.

TABLE 5   Import partners

	Imports ($bn) 2006	Import origins (top three partners in 2006 with percentage share of total imports)
United States	1,869.0	Canada (16%), China (16%), Mexico (10%)
China	777.9	Japan (15%), South Korea (11%), Taiwan (11%)
Japan	524.1	China (21%), U.S. (12%), Saudi Arabia (6%)
Hong Kong	329.8	China (46%), Japan (10%), Taiwan (8%)
Canada	353.2	U.S. (55%), China (9%), Mexico (4%)
South Korea	309.3	Japan (17%), China (15%), U.S. (11%)

SOURCE: Central Intelligence Agency, *The World Factbook*, 2007.

Investment

Asia remains a major destination for inward FDI, especially in financial services and high technology industries. Attracting $78.1 billion in foreign investments, China was the world's third-largest recipient of FDI in 2006. Asia's outward FDI was also strong, reaching $90 billion in 2006. Africa and Latin America are receiving growing investments from Asia, mainly because of their natural resources but also increasingly in the manufacturing and services sectors.

- China increased outward investments sixfold in 2005. In 2006 China's outward FDI was equal to $17.8 billion. Many of China's outward investments are cross-border merger and acquisition deals.

- FDI into the United States has slowly recovered since September 11, reaching $183.6 billion in 2006. Most inward FDI, however, comes from European states, such as the Netherlands, France, and the UK.

- Following the 2004 U.S.-Singapore FTA, Singapore has become the third-largest recipient of U.S. investment in the Asia-Pacific, behind Australia and Japan.

TABLE 6   Flow of foreign direct investment

	FDI inflows ($bn)				Rank	
	1990	2000	2005	2004–05 growth (%)	1990	2005
United States	48.5	321.3	109.8	-18.0	1	1
China	3.5	38.4	79.1	44.0	4	2
Hong Kong	–	61.9	33.6	0.0	–	3
Canada	7.6	66.1	29.1	–	2	4
Singapore	5.6	16.5	20.1	35.0	3	5
Russia	–	2.7	12.8	-17.0	–	6
Thailand	2.4	3.4	9.0	53.0	5	7
India	–	3.6	6.6	21.0	–	8
Indonesia	1.1	4.6	5.3	177.0	9	9
South Korea	0.8	9.3	4.3	-53.0	11	10
Malaysia	2.3	3.8	4.0	-14.0	6	11
Japan	1.8	8.2	3.2	-59.0	7	12
Pakistan	0.2	0.3	2.2	97.0	10	13
New Zealand	1.7	4.0	2.0	-21.0	8	14
Kazakhstan	–	1.3	2.0	-52.0	–	15
World	202.3	1,896.1	1,114.1	22.4	N/A	N/A

SOURCE: International Monetary Fund, *International Financial Statistics*, 2007; and (data on India for 2005) United Nations Conference on Trade and Development, *World Investment Report*, 2007.
NOTE: Dash indicates that no data is available.

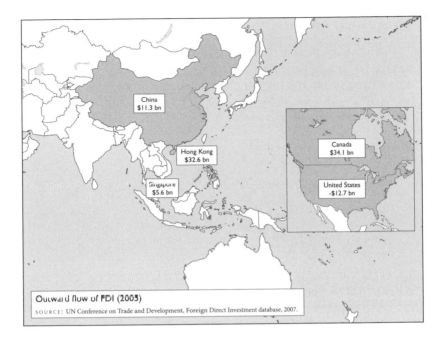

China
$11.3 bn

Hong Kong
$32.6 bn

Singapore
$5.6 bn

Canada
$34.1 bn

United States
-$12.7 bn

Outward flow of FDI (2005)

SOURCE: UN Conference on Trade and Development, Foreign Direct Investment database, 2007.

TABLE 7 Origins of FDI

	Origins of FDI (leading countries of origin for inward investment in 2005)
United States	UK, Netherlands, Japan
China	Hong Kong, Virgin Islands, Japan
Hong Kong	China, Netherlands, U.S.
Canada	U.S., UK, France
Singapore	EU, U.S., Japan
Russia	UK, Netherlands, Luxembourg
Thailand	UK, Japan, U.S.
India	Mauritius, U.S., Japan
Indonesia	Malaysia, Singapore, Seychelles
South Korea	EU, U.S., Japan
Malaysia	U.S., Singapore, Netherlands
Japan	Netherlands, Cayman Islands, Hong Kong
Pakistan	United Arab Emirates, U.S., UK
New Zealand	Australia, U.S., UK
Kazakhstan	Netherlands, U.S., Japan

SOURCE: U.S. Department of Commerce, *Country Commercial Guides*, 2005 and 2006; and *Economist Intelligence Unit*, 2006.
NOTE: Since data for FDI by country is not reported in a consistent form and varies across sources, this table shows only the main countries of origin for FDI and omits the values and percentage share.

Population and Society

Demographic transformations due to changing life expectancies, birth control policies, and patterns of urbanization throughout Asia are creating unprecedented social challenges for many Asian governments. Though cities account for less than 40% of the total population in both India and China, the speed of urbanization is placing considerable strain on government resources and social stability. Despite economic growth, poverty, widening income inequalities, and lack of social services remain problems in many states.

- As a result of Japan's aging population and prolonged low birth rates, the country will increasingly need to consider immigration to sustain its labor force.

- Russia is facing a demographic crisis due to its low birth rate and high mortality rate. Poverty, alcoholism, disease, stress, and other afflictions have particularly affected working-age males. Male life expectancy is approximately 58 years, which is below the pension age.

- An estimated 8.6 million people were living with HIV in Asia in 2006, including 960,000 people who became newly infected in the past year.

TABLE 8   Population

	Population (m)				Rank	
	1990	2000	2005	2004–05 growth (%)	1990	2005
China	1,135.2	1,262.6	1,304.5	0.6	1	1
India	849.5	1,015.9	1,094.6	1.4	2	2
United States	249.6	282.2	296.4	0.9	3	3
Indonesia	178.2	206.3	220.6	1.4	4	4
Pakistan	108.0	138.1	155.8	2.4	7	5
Russia	148.3	146.3	143.1	-0.5	5	6
Bangladesh	104.0	128.9	141.8	1.8	8	7
Japan	123.5	126.9	127.8	0.0	6	8
Vietnam	66.2	78.5	83.1	1.1	9	9
Philippines	61.1	75.8	83.1	1.8	10	10
Thailand	54.6	61.4	64.2	0.8	11	11
Myanmar	40.8	47.7	50.5	1.0	13	12
South Korea	42.9	47.0	48.3	0.4	12	13
Canada	27.8	30.8	32.3	1.0	14	14
Nepal	19.1	24.4	27.1	1.9	15	15
World	5,256.3	6,059.5	6,437.7	1.2	N/A	N/A

SOURCE: World Bank, *World Development Indicators*, 2007.

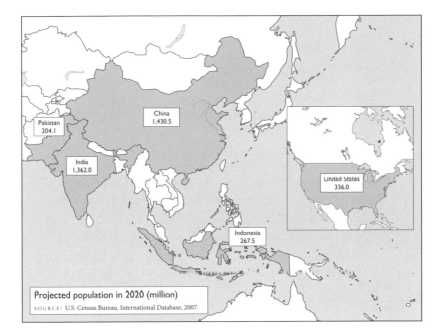

Projected population in 2020 (million)

SOURCE: U.S. Census Bureau, International Database, 2007.

TABLE 9   Urbanization and unemployment rate

	Urban population (m)			Unemployment (%)		
	1990	2000	2005	1990	2000	2005
China	311.0	452.0	527.0	2.5	3.1	4.2
India	216.6	281.4	314.1	–	4.3	5.0
United States	188.0	223.2	239.5	5.6	4.0	5.5
Indonesia	54.5	86.6	106.1	–	6.1	9.9
Pakistan	33.0	45.7	54.4	2.6	7.2	7.7
Russia	108.8	107.4	104.5	–	9.8	7.9
Bangladesh	20.6	29.9	35.6	1.9	3.3	–
Japan	78.0	82.7	84.1	2.1	4.8	4.7
Vietnam	13.4	19.1	21.9	–	–	–
Philippines	29.8	44.3	52.1	8.1	10.1	10.9
Thailand	16.1	19.1	20.7	2.2	2.4	–
Myanmar	10.1	13.4	15.5	0.0	–	–
South Korea	31.6	37.4	39.0	2.5	4.1	3.5
Canada	21.3	24.4	25.9	8.2	6.8	7.2
Nepal	1.7	3.3	4.3	–	–	–

SOURCE: World Bank, *World Development Indicators*, 2007.
NOTE: Unemployment figures are calculated by percentages of total work force. Dash indicates that no data is available.

Politics and International Relations

Leadership changes and political reforms altered the domestic political landscape of several countries in Asia in 2006–07. Military cooperation is on the rise and Northeast Asian nations have made goodwill gestures with neighboring countries to ease prevailing tensions. Although negotiations to resolve the North Korea nuclear dispute are in progress, uncertainties over North Korea's future will continue to keep neighboring countries on edge.

- Sino-Japanese relations have thawed considerably since Shinzo Abe became Japan's prime minister in September 2006. In a landmark speech to Japanese legislators, China's premier Wen Jiabao acknowledged Japan's apologies for its wartime aggression.

- Russian President Vladmir Putin will step down in March 2008, but he appears likely to play a decisive role in determining his successor.

- In advance of South Korea's 2008 presidential elections, polls suggest that the country favors the conservative Grand National Party.

- Saparmurat Niyazov, president of Turkmenistan, died in 2006 and was replaced by Gurbanguly Berimuhamedov.

TABLE 10 Political leadership

	Political leaders	Date assumed office	Next election
Australia	Prime Minister John W. Howard	March 1996	2008
Canada	Prime Minister Stephen Harper	February 2006	2011
China	President Hu Jintao	March 2003	N/A
India	Prime Minister Manmohan Singh	May 2004	2009
Indonesia	President Susilo Bambang Yudhoyono	October 2004	2009
Japan	Prime Minister Shinzo Abe	September 2006	2009
Kazakhstan	President Nursultan A. Nazarbayev	December 1991	2012
Malaysia	Prime Minister Abdullah bin Ahmad Badawi	October 2003	2009
Pakistan	President Pervez Musharraf	June 2001	2007
Philippines	President Gloria Macapagal-Arroyo	January 2001	2010
Russia	President Vladmir Vladimirovich Putin	May 2000	2008
South Korea	President Roh Moo-hyun	February 2003	2007
Taiwan	President Chen Shui-bian	May 2000	2008
Thailand	Interim Prime Minister Surayud Chulanont	September 2006	2007
United States	President George W. Bush	January 2001	2008

SOURCE: Central Intelligence Agency, *The World Factbook*, 2007.
NOTE: Thai prime minister Thaksin Shinawatra was overthrown in September 2006 in a coup led by General Sonthi Boonyaratglin. Thailand's military leaders suggest that the next general election will be held in December 2007. Table shows next election year in which the given leader may lose or retain his position. In some countries elections may be called before these years.

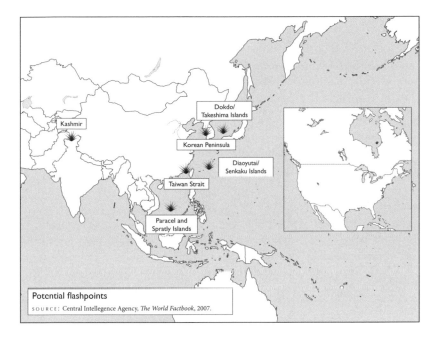

Potential flashpoints

SOURCE: Central Intellegence Agency, *The World Factbook*, 2007.

TABLE 11   Political rights, corruption, and globalization rankings

	Political rights score		Corruption score		Globalization index	
	2000	2006	2000	2006	2001	2006
Australia	1	1	8.3	8.7	23	8
Canada	1	1	9.2	8.5	10	6
China	7	7	3.1	3.3	47	51
India	2	2	2.8	3.3	48	61
Indonesia	3	2	1.7	2.4	38	60
Japan	1	1	6.4	7.6	29	28
Kazakhstan	6	6	3.0	2.6	–	–
Malaysia	5	4	4.8	5.0	20	19
Pakistan	6	6	–	2.2	–	56
Philippines	2	3	2.8	2.5	33	31
Russia	5	6	2.1	2.5	44	47
South Korea	2	1	4.0	5.1	31	29
Taiwan	1	1	5.5	5.9	–	35
Thailand	2	3	3.2	3.6	30	45
United States	1	1	7.8	7.3	12	3

SOURCE: Freedom House, *Freedom in the World*, 2001 and 2007, Transparency International, *Corruption Perceptions Index*, 2001 and 2006; and A. T. Kearney/Foreign Policy, *Globalization Index*, 2001 and 2006.
NOTE: Political rights = ability of the people to participate freely in the political process (1=most free/7=least free). Corruption = degree to which public official corruption is perceived to exist (1=most corrupt/10=most open). The globalization index tracks changes in economic integration, technological connectivity, personal contact, and political engagement (rank of 62 countries, 1=most globalized). Dash indicates that no data is available.

Energy

Rapid economic growth in Asia has kept energy demand at unprecedented highs in several countries, especially China and India. Elsewhere, growth in oil demand remains relatively flat. The high costs of natural gas, including investments for infrastructure, will keep coal the energy source of choice for China and India in the medium to long term.

- With growing state involvement in its oil and gas companies, Russia is aggressively seeking controlling stakes in previously foreign-led projects.

- Both China and India are courting Myanmar for access to its natural gas supplies. Russia is planning to help Myanmar build a nuclear research reactor and provide technical training.

- The International Energy Agency in 2007 stated that China may overtake the United States to become the world's largest emitter of carbon dioxide by 2008.

- Expiring contracts and volatile seasonal demand have led South Korea to increasingly rely on a growing LNG spot market to meet demand.

TABLE 12 Energy consumption

	Energy consumption (quadrillion Btu)				Rank	
	1990	2000	2006	2005–06 growth %	1990	2006
United States	78.0	91.7	92.3	-1.0	1	1
China	27.2	38.4	67.4	8.4	2	2
Russia	–	25.2	28.0	4.8	–	3
Japan	17.2	20.4	20.6	-0.4	3	4
India	7.7	12.7	16.8	5.4	5	5
Canada	9.8	11.5	12.8	1.7	4	6
South Korea	3.6	7.6	9.0	0.4	6	7
Australia	3.5	4.4	4.8	1.1	7	8
Indonesia	2.1	3.8	4.5	-0.3	8	9
Taiwan	2.0	3.8	4.5	2.7	9	10
Thailand	1.2	2.4	3.4	3.1	10	11
Malaysia	1.0	1.8	2.7	3.0	12	12
Kazakhstan	–	1.6	2.4	6.5	–	13
Pakistan	1.1	1.6	2.3	4.7	11	14
Uzbekistan	–	2.0	1.9	-1.0	–	15
World	322.7	369.4	428.1	2.4	N/A	N/A

SOURCE: BP plc., "BP Statistical Review of World Energy," June 2007.
NOTE: Dash indicates that no data is available.

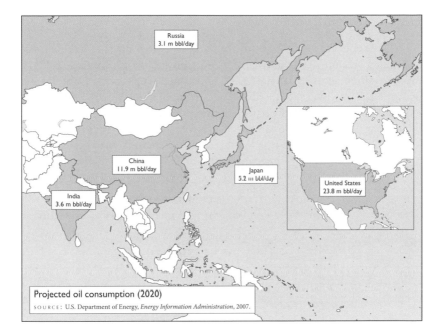

Projected oil consumption (2020)

SOURCE: U.S. Department of Energy, *Energy Information Administration*, 2007.

TABLE 13   Energy consumption by fuel type

	Energy consumption by fuel type, 2006 (%)				
	Oil	Gas	Coal	Nuclear	Hydro
United States	40.4	24.4	24.4	8.1	2.8
China	20.6	2.9	70.2	0.7	5.6
Russia	18.2	55.2	16.0	5.0	5.6
Japan	45.2	14.6	22.9	13.2	4.1
India	28.4	8.5	56.2	0.9	6.0
Canada	30.7	27.0	10.9	6.9	24.6
South Korea	46.7	13.6	24.3	14.9	0.5
Australia	33.4	21.3	42.3	0.0	3.0
Indonesia	42.6	31.2	24.2	0.0	2.0
Taiwan	46.2	9.5	34.8	7.9	1.6
Thailand	51.4	32.0	14.4	0.0	2.1
Malaysia	34.3	54.0	9.4	0.0	2.3
Kazakhstan	17.6	30.2	49.2	0.0	3.0
Pakistan	31.7	47.6	6.8	1.1	12.8
Uzbekistan	14.3	80.1	2.3	0.0	3.4

SOURCE: BP plc., "BP Statistical Review of World Energy," June 2007.
NOTE: Due to rounding, some totals may not add up to exactly 100%.

Defense Spending

Rising concerns over the future of the Korean Peninsula and the impact of China's rise on the regional balance of power are prompting military modernization across Northeast Asia. This is further exacerbated by Japan's fear of a rising China, South Korea's fear of militarized Japan, and China's fear of containment. As a result, all three countries are enhancing their defense capabilities. The possibility of a similar arms build-up in South Asia looms large as India bolsters its military capabilities and engages in strategic defense negotiations with the United States.

- China's official defense budget rose 14.7% to reach $35.3 billion in 2006. Beijing plans to increase its military spending by 17.8% in 2007, which would be the largest year-on-year increase in over a decade.

- Japan transformed the Japan Defense Agency into a formal ministry, giving the military new influence and greater organizational flexibility. Japan's defense expenditure, however, is expected to continue falling.

- Thailand's 2007 defense budget has quadrupled over the previous year to reach 115 billion baht.

TABLE 14 Total defense expenditure

	Expenditure ($bn)				Rank	
	1990	2000	2005	2004–05 growth (%)	1990	2005
United States	293.0	300.5	495.3	8.0	I	I
China	11.3	42.0	104.0	16.2	3	2
Russia	–	60.0	58.0	-2.8	–	3
Japan	28.7	45.6	43.9	-2.8	2	4
India	10.1	14.7	21.7	8.8	6	5
South Korea	10.6	12.8	20.3	18.6	4	6
Australia	7.3	7.1	15.6	10.6	8	7
Canada	10.3	8.1	12.8	10.3	5	8
Indonesia	1.6	1.5	8.4	10.1	12	9
Taiwan	8.7	17.6	8.0	5.5	7	10
Myanmar	0.9	2.1	6.9	15.2	13	11
Singapore	1.7	4.8	5.6	8.5	11	12
Pakistan	2.9	3.7	4.1	10.0	9	13
Vietnam	–	1.0	3.2	11.8	–	14
Malaysia	1.7	2.8	2.9	6.4	10	15
World	954.0	811.4	1,207.5	7.0	N/A	N/A

SOURCE: International Institute for Strategic Studies (IISS), *The Military Balance*, various editions; and (data for World in 1990) SASI Group and Mark Newman, "Military Spending 1990," 2006.
NOTE: Estimates for China vary widely. IISS reports that the 2005 value for China is a PPP estimate. Dash indicates that no data is available.

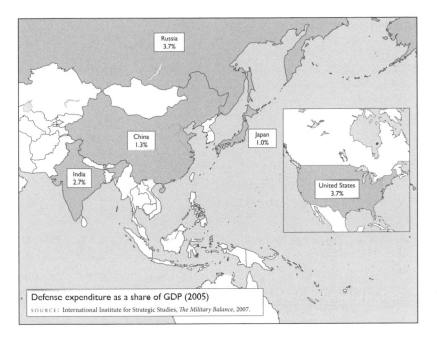

Defense expenditure as a share of GDP (2005)

SOURCE: International Institute for Strategic Studies, *The Military Balance*, 2007.

TABLE 15   Defense expenditure as share of GDP and CGE

	Defense expenditure as a share of GDP (%)			Defense expenditure as a share of CGE (%)		
	1990–99	2000–04	2005	1990–99	2000–04	2005
United States	4.2	3.4	3.7	18.5	17.3	19.3
China	5.2	3.9	1.3	28.3	19.4	–
Russia	7.6	4.5	3.7	26.1	18.4	18.8
Japan	1.0	1.0	1.0	5.7	–	–
India	2.9	2.9	2.7	13.7	14.4	–
South Korea	3.5	2.7	2.6	16.8	13.9	12.1
Australia	2.3	2.2	2.2	9.0	7.2	7.2
Canada	1.6	1.2	1.1	6.3	6.3	6.3
Indonesia	1.6	2.7	3.0	7.4	–	–
Taiwan	5.0	2.1	2.2	30.6	7.8	–
Myanmar	5.5	5.8	–	99.8	–	–
Singapore	5.1	5.0	4.8	21.9	29.3	–
Pakistan	6.8	4.1	3.7	26.9	25.3	23.1
Vietnam	6.7	7.2	6.0	11.2	–	–
Malaysia	2.5	2.2	–	13.0	10.9	–

SOURCE: International Institute for Strategic Studies (IISS), *The Military Balance*, various editions; Department of State, "World Military Expenditures and Arms Transfers," 2003; and World Bank, *World Development Indicators*, 2006.

NOTE: Data for some countries over certain periods is partial. IISS reports that the 2005 value for China is official budget figure at the official exchange rate. Dash indicates that no data is available.

Conventional Military Capabilities

Asia is one of the fastest-growing defense markets in the world, as many states replace or upgrade outdated hardware. Military modernization plans in countries such as Japan, China, and India are early indications of modest hedging strategies in the region. The United States will greatly affect the impetus for and outcome of these strategic decisions.

- China has been purchasing increasing numbers of fourth generation aircraft. By 2010, the PLAAF's fighter force will likely consist of between 1,500 and 2,000 aircraft, largely modified J-7s and J-8s, with most of the J-6s and early model J-7s retired from service.

- Rising insecurities over the future of the Korean Peninsula have caused South Korea to enhance its military modernization efforts and purchase several dozen combat aircraft. South Korea launched it first military communications satellite in August 2006.

- The U.S.-India Strategic Partnership and the U.S.-India Civil Nuclear Cooperation Agreement have set the stage for significantly upgrading India's military capabilities. Major multinational corporations are increasingly competing in India's growing defense market.

TABLE 16   Manpower

	Armed forces (th)				Rank	
	1990	2000	2007	2006–07 change (th)	1990	2007
China	3,030	2,470	2,255	0	2	1
United States	2,118	1,366	1,506	-40	3	2
India	1,262	1,303	1,316	-9	4	3
North Korea	1,111	1,082	1,106	0	5	4
Russia	3,988	1,004	1,027	0	1	5
South Korea	750	683	687	-1	7	6
Pakistan	550	612	619	0	8	7
Vietnam	1,052	484	455	0	6	8
Myanmar	230	344	375	-1	13	9
Thailand	283	301	307	0	10	10
Indonesia	283	297	302	0	10	11
Taiwan	370	370	290	0	9	12
Japan	249	237	240	-20	12	13
Sri Lanka	65	–	151	40	15	14
Bangladesh	103	137	127	1	14	15
World	26,605	22,237	19,801	-169	N/A	N/A

SOURCE: International Institute for Strategic Studies, *The Military Balance*, various editions.
NOTE: Active duty and military personnel only. Data value for Russia includes all territories of the Soviet Union. Dash indicates that no data is available.

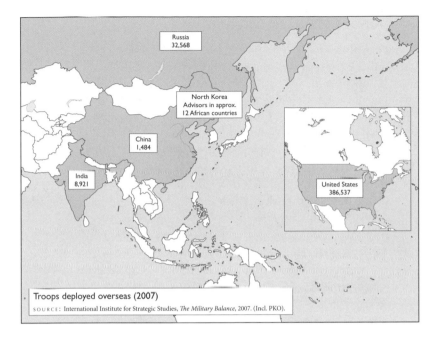

Troops deployed overseas (2007)

SOURCE: International Institute for Strategic Studies, *The Military Balance*, 2007. (Incl. PKO).

TABLE 17 Conventional warfare capabilities, 2006

	Tanks, APCs/LAVs, artillery	Combat aircraft	Principal surface combatants	Submarines
China	29,780	3,435	71	58
United States	15,758	4,016	118	72
India	17,660	886	54	16
North Korea	24,460	590	9	88
Russia	62,895	2,118	66	61
South Korea	15,584	556	43	20
Pakistan	8,018	343	7	7
Vietnam	6,355	221	11	2
Myanmar	968	125	3	0
Thailand	4,271	183	18	0
Indonesia	1,766	94	28	2
Taiwan	4,596	511	32	4
Japan	3,690	380	53	18
Sri Lanka	1,217	21	0	0
Bangladesh	590	62	5	0

SOURCE: International Institute for Strategic Studies, *The Military Balance*, 2006.

Weapons of Mass Destruction

North Korea's test of a nuclear device in October 2006 has increased the number of nuclear weapons–capable states in Asia to five and made the security dilemma in Northeast Asia more acute. Although Asian states are pursuing nuclear technologies for civil purposes, a secondary driver for these nuclear programs may be to serve as a future hedge should they feel threatened by WMD proliferation.

- Following international pressure (particularly from China), North Korea agreed to return to the six-party talks. The IAEA confirmed that North Korea had shut down the plutonium-producing facilities at the Yongbyon nuclear reactor in mid-July 2007 in exchange for 50,000 tons of heavy fuel oil.

- The five states of Central Asia signed the Central Asian Nuclear Weapons Free Zone (CANWFZ) treaty in September 2006, pledging not to develop, manufacture, stockpile, or store nuclear weapons.

- In April 2007 India tested the Agni-III, an intermediate-range ballistic missile capable of reaching Beijing and Shanghai.

TABLE 18   Nuclear weapons

	Nuclear weapons possession				Warheads
	1990	1995	2000	2006	2006
Russia	✓	✓	✓	✓	~16,000
United States	✓	✓	✓	✓	~10,300
China	✓	✓	✓	✓	410
India	✓	✓	✓	✓	70–110
Pakistan	–	–	✓	✓	50–110
North Korea	?	?	?	✓	~5–10

SOURCE: Carnegie Endowment for International Peace; and Monterey Institute of International Studies.
NOTE: Table shows confirmed (✓) and unconfirmed (?) possession of nuclear weapons. Dash indicates that no data is available.

TABLE 19   Intercontinental ballistic missiles

	Number of ICBMs			
	1990	1995	2000	2006
Russia	1,398	930	776	506
United States	1,000	580	550	550
China	8	17+	20+	46
India	–	–	–	–
Pakistan	–	–	–	–
North Korea	–	–	–	?

SOURCE: International Institute for Strategic Studies, *The Military Balance*, various editions.
NOTE: Dash indicates that no data is available. Question mark indicates unconfirmed possession of ICBMs.

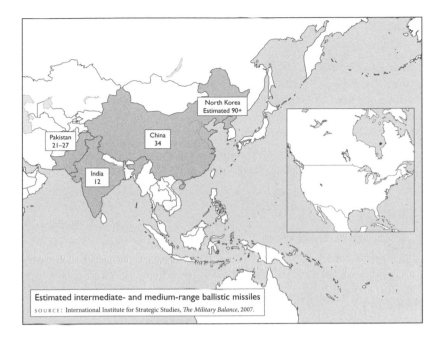

Estimated intermediate- and medium-range ballistic missiles
SOURCE: International Institute for Strategic Studies, *The Military Balance*, 2007.

TABLE 20   Nonproliferation treaties

	NPT	Additional Protocol	CTBT	CWC	BTWC
Russia	Ratified	Signatory	Ratified	Ratified	Ratified
United States	Ratified	Signatory	Signatory	Ratified	Ratified
China	Ratified	Ratified	Signatory	Ratified	Ratified
India	–	–	–	Ratified	Ratified
Pakistan	–	–	–	Ratified	Ratified
North Korea	Withdrew	–	–	–	Acceded

SOURCE: Nuclear Threat Initiative; and Monterey Institute of International Studies.
NOTE: NPT = Nonproliferation Treaty, CTBT = Comprehensive Test Ban Treaty, CWC = Chemical Weapons Convention, BTWC = Biological and Toxic Weapons Convention, Additional Protocol = IAEA Additional Protocol. Dash indicates non-participation.

TABLE 21   WMD export control regimes

	Nuclear Suppliers Group	Australia Group	Wassenaar Arrangement	Zangger Committee	MTCR
Russia	Member	–	Member	Member	Member
United States	Member	Member	Member	Member	Member
China	Member	**	–	Member	–
India	*	–	–	–	–
Pakistan	–	–	–	–	–
North Korea	–	–	–	–	–

SOURCE: Nuclear Threat Initiative; and Monterey Institute of International Studies.
NOTE: Dash indicates non-participation. Asterisk indicates India's membership is pending. Double asterisks indicate that China is not a member but has agreed to adhere to the group's guidelines.

Space Programs

Asia's space programs and plans came into the international spotlight following China's January 2007 anti-satellite (ASAT) weapons test. Asia's space activities—both military and commercial—have increased, and some states have plans to become commercial launching hubs. Both for China and for India, unmanned and manned missions to the moon are a priority for technological advancement and prestige value.

- China conducted a successful ASAT weapons test in January 2007, using a medium-range ballistic missile to destroy an inactive weather satellite.

- South Korea launched its fourth satellite (Koreasat-5) in August 2006. Although dual-purpose, Koreasat-5 is reported to be the first Korean satellite designed to secure military communications. South Korea's first space center on Naro Island in Goheung is also near completion.

- In 2007 India demonstrated its ability to launch commercial satellites into orbit with the successful launch of an Italian satellite.

- In 2006 Japan launched the second two of four indigenous intelligence-gathering satellites that are able to monitor any point on earth.

TABLE 22   Space programs

	Agency	Est. year	2006 budget ($m)	Satellite launch capability	Total satellites in orbit	Total space debris
Russia	RKA	1992	~1,300	yes	1,392	14,062
United States	NASA	1958	~17,000	yes	1,031	7,424
Japan	JAXA	2003	~2,000	yes	108	355
China	CNSA	1993	~500	yes	62	2,427
India	ISRO	1969	~800	yes	33	371
Canada	CSA	1990	~350	no	24	4
South Korea	KARI	1981	~150	in progress	11	0
Indonesia	LAPAN	1964	–	no	10	0
Thailand	GISTDA	2002	–	no	6	0
Malaysia	MNSA	2002	~25	no	4	0

SOURCE: CelesTrack, "SATCAT Boxscore," 2007; and NBR research team.
NOTE: Dash indicates that no data is available.

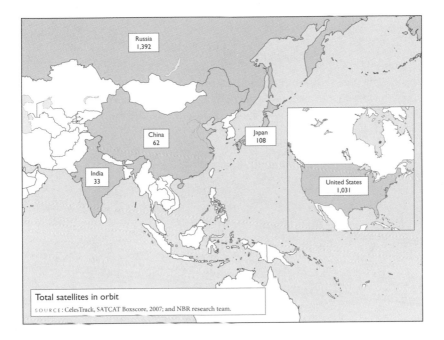

Total satellites in orbit
SOURCE: CelesTrack, SATCAT Boxscore, 2007; and NBR research team.

TABLE 23 Major launch sites

United States	Kennedy Space Center (FL), Cape Canaveral (CA), Vandenberg AFB (CA)
Japan	Tanegashima Space Center
Russia	Plesetsk Cosmodrome, Svobodnyy Cosmodrome, Baikonur Cosmodrome (Kazakhstan)
India	Satish Dhawan Space Centre (Sriharikota Island)
China	Jiuquan, Taiyuan, and Xichang satellite launch centers
South Korea	Naro Space Center (Goheung)

SOURCE: NBR research team.

TABLE 24 Operational military satellites

	No.	Comm.	Navigation	Meteor	Survey	Warning
United States	79	✓	✓	✓	✓	✓
Japan	4	–	–	–	✓	–
Russia	40	✓	✓	–	✓	✓
India	1	–	–	–	✓	–
China	18	✓	✓	–	✓	–
South Korea	1	–	–	–	✓	–

SOURCE: International Institute for Strategic Studies, *The Military Balance*, 2006; and NBR research team. Comm. = Communications, Meteor = Meteorology, Survey = Surveillance, and Warning = Early warning. Dash indicates no reported possession.

Index

Iran-Russia, 165, 169, 305, 321, 327, 332–33

Iran-United States, 318, 325; U.S. strategy toward, 323, 330, 336–38

Iraq, 95, 103, 245, 258, 350

Islami Chhatra Shibir, 223, 230

Islami Oikkyo Jote, 221–22

Islamic Movement of Uzbekistan (IMU), 279, 290

Islamic Renaissance Party, 277

Islamist radicalism: Bangladesh, 223, 227–29; Central Asia, 270, 275, 277–79, 282, 295; Pakistan, 213, 228–30

Israel, 35, 332–33, 257–58

Jagata Muslim Janata Bangladesh (JMJB), 223–24

Jaish-e-Mohammad, 214, 239, 254

Jamaat-i-Islami, 216, 221–24

Jamaat-ul-Mujahideen Bangladesh (JMB), 223–24

Jamaat Ulema-e-Islam, 216

Jamhoori Watan Party, 216

Japan, 16–17, 24; anti-terrorism law, 86, 97; Article 9 of the constitution, 95, 98–99, 110; Defense Agency, 87, 414; defense expenditure, 101–2; demographics, 408; economic growth, 402; economic reform, 92–93; electoral reform, 74–80; military capabilities, 346, 418; Ministry of Economy Trade and Industry (METI), 82, 103, 107; Ministry of International Trade and Industry (MITI), 82, 88; "normalization," 348, 363–65, 368; organized labor, 88–89; privatization of the postal system, 72, 78, 83–84, 94; regional security, 358, 361; Self Defense Forces, 87, 95, 98, 103; UN Security Council seat, 121; zoku (policy tribes), 78–79, 83

Japan-ASEAN, 93, 103, 108

Japan-Australia, 93, 105, 108, 363–64, 368

Japan-China, 32, 61, 105–6, 110; diplomatic relations, 96, 106, 410; strategic competitors, 35, 369

Japan Communist Party, 75

Japan-India, 93, 105, 181, 183

Japan-North Korea, 104–5

Japan-Russia, 170, 172

Japan Socialist Party (JSP), 72

Japan-South Korea, 105, 111; diplomatic relations, 125; security agreement, potential for, 368; trade, 123–24

Japan-United States, 91–93, 103–4; economic interdependence, 200; security cooperation, 100–1, 351; U.S. military bases, 236, 348; United States-Japan Security Treaty, 87

Karimov, Islam, 272, 276, 278, 288–89, 294

Kashmir, 178, 198–200, 214, 228; regional security, impact on, 346, 362

Kazakhstan, 18–19, 275–76; economics, 274–75; elite, 290, 293; energy resources, 274, 276, 291; Islamist radicalism, 275; political reforms, 272, 275, 293; regional leadership, 276; Russian minorities, 274; transition from Soviet rule, 274

Kazakhstan-China, 291–92

Kazakhstan-Russia, 168, 290–94

Kazakhstan-United States, 292–94, 297

KGB, 146, 154

Khalafat-e-Majlis, 222

Khamenei, Ali, 309, 314, 331

Kharshi-Khanabad (K2) airbase, 288

Khatami, Mohammed, 314, 318

Khodorkovsky, Mikhail, 145

Kim Dae Jung, 118–19, 121–22; policy toward North Korea, 124–26

Kim Il-sung, 114, 128–30

Kim Jong-il, 124, 128, 130–31, 136

Kim Yong Nam 128

Kim Young Sam, 121, 119

About the Authors

Nick Bisley (PhD, London School of Economics) is Senior Lecturer and Director of the Graduate Program in Diplomacy and Trade in the Graduate School of Business, Monash University, Australia. He is a member of the Council for Security and Cooperation in the Asia Pacific and has been involved with the training of senior defense and diplomatic personnel in Britain and Australia. Most recently this involved being Programme Director at the Centre for Defence and Strategic Studies in the Australian Defence College. He is the author of *Rethinking Globalization* (2007) and *The End of the Cold War and the Causes of Soviet Collapse* (2004), and he has published articles and chapters on a wide range of topics in international relations. His articles have appeared in such journals as *International Politics, International Relations of the Asia-Pacific,* and *Review of International Studies.* Dr. Bisley has a BA in History and Political Science from the University of Melbourne and an MSc and PhD in International Relations from the London School of Economics.

Shahram Chubin (PhD, Columbia University) is Director of Studies and Joint Course Director of the International Training Course in Security Policy at the Geneva Centre for Security Policy (GCSP). Born in Iran and educated in Britain and the United States, Dr. Chubin is a Swiss national. Before joining GCSP he taught at the Graduate Institute for International Studies in Geneva from 1981 to 1996. He has been Director of Regional Security Studies at the International Institute for Strategic Studies in London, and has been a fellow both at the Woodrow Wilson International Center for Scholars in Washington, D.C., and at the Carnegie Endowment for International Peace. Dr. Chubin has authored numerous publications on Iran and has published widely in such journals as *Foreign Affairs, Foreign Policy, International Security, Daedalus, The Middle East Journal, Survival,* and *The Washington Quarterly.* His recent publications include *Iran's Nuclear Ambition* (2006) and *Whither Iran? Reform, Domestic Policy and National Security,* Adelphi Paper no. 342 (2002).

Svante E. Cornell (PhD, Uppsala University) is Research Director of the Central Asia-Caucasus Institute and Silk Road Studies Program, a joint transatlantic research and policy center affiliated with the Paul H.

Nitze School of Advanced International Studies (SAIS) of Johns Hopkins University and the Stockholm-based Institute for Security and Development Policy. He is Associate Professor of Government at Uppsala University and Assistant Research Professor at SAIS. Previously Dr. Cornell taught at the Royal Swedish Military Academy and in 2002–03 served as Course Chair of Caucasus Area Studies at the Foreign Service Institute of the U.S. Department of State. His main areas of expertise are security issues, state-building, and transnational crime in Southwest and Central Asia, with a specific focus on the Caucasus. He is Editor of the *Central Asia-Caucasus Analyst* and of the Joint Center's *Silk Road Papers* series of occasional papers. Dr. Cornell is the author of four books, including *Azerbaijan Since Independence* (forthcoming) and *Small Nations and Great Powers* (2001), as well as co-editor of *The Baku-Tbilisi-Ceyhan Pipeline: Oil Window to the West* (with S. Frederick Starr, 2005). His articles have appeared in such journals as *World Politics*, *The Washington Quarterly*, *Current History*, *Journal of Democracy*, and *Europe-Asia Studies*.

Richard J. Ellings (PhD, University of Washington) is President and Co-founder of The National Bureau of Asian Research (NBR). He is also Affiliate Professor of International Studies at the Henry M. Jackson School of International Studies, University of Washington. Prior to serving with NBR, from 1986–89, he was Assistant Director and on the faculty of the Jackson School, where he received the Distinguished Teaching Award. He served as Legislative Assistant in the United States Senate, office of Senator Slade Gorton, in 1984 and 1985. Dr. Ellings is the author of *Embargoes and World Power: Lessons from American Foreign Policy* (1985); co-author of *Private Property and National Security* (1991); co-editor (with Aaron Friedberg) of *Strategic Asia 2003–04: Fragility and Crisis* (2003), *Strategic Asia 2002–03: Asian Aftershocks* (2002), and *Strategic Asia 2001–02: Power and Purpose* (2001); co-editor of *Korea's Future and the Great Powers* (with Nicholas Eberstadt, 2001) and *Southeast Asian Security in the New Millennium* (with Sheldon Simon, 1996); and the founding editor of the *NBR Analysis* publication series. He established the Strategic Asia Program and AccessAsia, the national clearinghouse that tracks specialists and their research on Asia.

Lorraine Elliott (PhD, Australian National University) is Senior Fellow in the Department of International Relations at the Australian National University (ANU). Her research focuses on global environmental politics, environmental security, and contemporary human security. Dr. Elliott was co-convenor of the Cosmopolitan Militaries Project at ANU. From September 2003 to 2005, Dr. Elliott was Reader in International Relations at the University of Warwick and Program Director of the Masters in International Relations program. She has held visiting fellowships at the Free University of Amsterdam, Balliol College at the University of Oxford, and the Asia Research Centre at the London School of Economics and Political Science. Dr. Elliott is a member of the Australian Committee of the Council for Security Cooperation in the Asia Pacific (CSCAP) and has been a visiting lecturer at military staff and defense colleges in both Australia and the United Kingdom. Her books include *Forces for Good: Cosmopolitan Militaries in the 21st Century* (co-edited with Graeme Cheeseman, 2005), *The Global Politics of the Environment* (2nd edition 2004, 1st edition 1998), and *International Environmental Politics: Protecting the Antarctic* (1994). As well as numerous book chapters, she has also published articles in *The Pacific Review*, *Global Society*, *Contemporary Security Policy*, and the *Australian Journal of International Affairs*.

Frédéric Grare (PhD, Graduate Institute of International Studies, Geneva) is a visiting scholar with the Carnegie Endowment for International Peace. Dr. Grare is a leading expert and writer on South Asia, having served most recently in the French embassy in Pakistan and, from 1999 to 2003, in New Delhi as Director of the Centre for Social Sciences and Humanities. Dr. Grare has written extensively on security issues, Islamist movements, and sectarian conflict in Pakistan and Afghanistan. He edited the volume *India, China, Russia: Intricacies of an Asian Triangle* (with Gilles Boquérat, 2003). His other works include *Pakistan and the Afghan Conflict, 1979–1985: At the Turn of the Cold War* (2003) and *Political Islam in the Indian Subcontinent: The Jamaat-i-Islami* (2001).

Samuel S. Kim (PhD, Columbia University) is Senior Research Scholar at Columbia University's Weatherhead East Asian Institute. He previously taught at Columbia University (1993–2006), Princeton University (1986–93), and the Foreign Affairs Institute in Beijing, China (1985–86). He is the author or editor of twenty-two books on East Asian international relations, Chinese and Korean foreign relations, and world order studies including: *The Two Koreas and the Great Powers* (2006), *The International Relations of Northeast Asia* (editor, 2004), *Korea's Democratization* (editor, 2003), *East Asia and Globalization* (editor, 2000), *Korea's Globalization* (editor, 2000), *North Korean Foreign Relations in the Post–Cold War Era* (editor, 1998), *The Quest for a Just World Order* (1984), and *China, the United Nations and World Order* (1979).

Kenneth Lieberthal (PhD, Columbia University) holds several positions at the University of Michigan: William Davidson Professor of Business Administration at the Ross School of Business, Arthur F. Thurnau Professor of Political Science, Distinguished Fellow and Director for China at the

William Davidson Institute, and Research Associate of the Center for Chinese Studies. In 2004 he received the University of Michigan's Distinguished Faculty Achievement Award. Dr. Lieberthal is also Nonresident Fellow at the Brookings Institution. He has consulted widely on Chinese and Asian affairs, including at the U.S. Departments of State, Defense, and Commerce; the World Bank; the Kettering Foundation; the Aspen Institute; the United Nations Association; and private sector corporations. Dr. Lieberthal served as Special Assistant to the President for National Security Affairs and Senior Director for Asia on the National Security Council from 1998 to 2000. Since 2004 he has served on the Department of Defense Joint Strategy Review Senior Review Panel. Dr. Lieberthal is Senior Director for Stonebridge International LLC and he serves as a member of the Board of Directors or Board of Advisors for many prominent organizations and universities dealing with China and Asia. He serves on the editorial boards of *Asia Policy, China: An International Journal, The China Quarterly, The China Economic Review, Foreign Policy Bulletin*, the *Journal of Contemporary China*, and the *Journal of International Business Education*. Dr. Lieberthal has written and edited nearly a dozen books and published approximately 60 articles.

Mike M. Mochizuki (PhD, Harvard University) holds the Japan-U.S. Relations Chair in Memory of Gaston Sigur at the Elliott School of International Affairs at George Washington University. He was Director of the Sigur Center for Asian Studies at George Washington University from 2001 to 2005. He also co-directs Memory and Reconciliation in the Asia-Pacific, a research and policy program of the Sigur Center. Previously he was a Senior Fellow at the Brookings Institution. Dr. Mochizuki has also held the following positions: Co-Director of the Center for Asia-Pacific Policy at RAND, Associate Professor of International Relations at the University of Southern California, and Assistant Professor of Political Science at Yale University. Dr. Mochizuki is a specialist of Japanese politics and foreign policy, U.S.-Japan relations, and East Asian security affairs. Two of his recent books include *Japan in International Politics: The Foreign Policies of an Adaptive State* (co-editor and author, 2007) and *The Okinawa Question and the U.S.-Japan Alliance* (co-editor and author, 2005). Dr. Mochizuki authored the Japan chapter in *Strategic Asia 2004–05: Confronting Terrorism in the Pursuit of Power*. He is currently completing a book entitled *A New Strategic Triangle: the U.S.-Japan Alliance and the Rise of China*.

C. Raja Mohan (PhD, Jawaharlal Nehru University) is currently a Professor at the S. Rajaratnam School of International Studies (formerly the Institute of Defence and Strategic Studies) at the Nanyang Technological University in Singapore. Previously he was Professor of South Asian Studies at the Jawaharlal

Nehru University in New Delhi. Dr. Mohan is one of India's leading columnists on international affairs and has been Strategic Affairs Editor of the *Indian Express* and *The Hindu*. He also served as a member of India's National Security Advisory Board between 1998 and 2000 and again from 2004 to 2006. His early career was spent as a Senior Fellow at the Institute for Defence Studies and Analyses in New Delhi, where his work related to arms control and international and regional security issues. Dr. Mohan's recent books include *Impossible Allies: Nuclear India, United States, and the Global Order* (2006) and *Crossing the Rubicon: The Shaping of India's New Foreign Policy* (2003).

Ashley J. Tellis (PhD, University of Chicago) is Senior Associate at the Carnegie Endowment for International Peace, specializing in international security, defense, and Asian strategic issues. He was recently on assignment to the U.S. Department of State as Senior Advisor to the Undersecretary of State for Political Affairs, during which time he was intimately involved in negotiating the civil nuclear agreement with India. He is Research Director of the Strategic Asia Program at NBR and co-editor (with Michael Wills) of *Strategic Asia 2006–07: Trade, Interdependence, and Security* (2006), *Strategic Asia 2005–06: Military Modernization in an Era of Uncertainty* (2005), and *Strategic Asia 2004–05: Confronting Terrorism in the Pursuit of Power* (2004). Previously he was commissioned into the Foreign Service and served as Senior Advisor to the Ambassador at the U.S. embassy in New Delhi. He also served on the National Security Council staff as Special Assistant to the President and Senior Director for Strategic Planning and Southwest Asia. Prior to his government service Dr. Tellis was Senior Policy Analyst at the RAND Corporation and Professor of Policy Analysis at the RAND Graduate School. He is the author of *India's Emerging Nuclear Posture* (2001) and co-author (with Michael D. Swaine) of *Interpreting China's Grand Strategy: Past, Present, and Future* (2000). His academic publications have also appeared in many edited volumes and journals.

Celeste A. Wallander (PhD, Yale University) is Visiting Associate Professor at Georgetown University. Dr. Wallander previously was Director and Senior Fellow of the Russia and Eurasia Program at the Center for Strategic and International Studies (2001–06), where she remains Senior Associate. She was Senior Fellow at the Council on Foreign Relations in Washington, D.C. (2000–01) and Associate Professor of Government at Harvard University (1989–2000). She is the founder and executive director of the Program on New Approaches to Russian Security. Her recent projects include work on U.S.-Russian security cooperation, the history of Russia and globalization, HIV/AIDS in Russia, and Ukrainian security relations. She is the author of over 70 scholarly and public interest publications, including a chapter entitled

"Global Challenges and Russian Foreign Policy" in *Russian Foreign Policy in the Twenty-First Century and the Shadow of the Past* (editor Robert Levgold, 2007). She is currently writing a book entitled *Geopolitics of Energy in Eurasia*. She often testifies before Congress and serves as a media analyst on Russia, Ukraine, Belarus, and Eurasian security issues. She has received fellowships from the National Science Foundation, the German Marshall Fund of the United States, and the National Council for Soviet and East European Research. She is a member of the Council on Foreign Relations.

Donald E. Weatherbee (PhD, Johns Hopkins School of Advanced International Studies) is the Donald S. Russell Distinguished Professor Emeritus at the University of South Carolina. Specializing in politics and international relations in Southeast Asia, he received his BA from Bates College and his MA and PhD from the School of Advanced International Studies (SAIS) at the Johns Hopkins University. He has held teaching and research appointments at universities and research centers in Indonesia, Singapore, Malaysia, Thailand, the United Kingdom, Germany, and the Netherlands, as well as at the U.S. Army War College. He was awarded the U.S. Army's Distinguished Civilian Service medal for his work on the post–Vietnam War strategic profile of Southeast Asia. He authored the chapter on Southeast Asia in *Strategic Asia 2006–07: Trade, Interdependence, and Security* (2006), and his most recent major publication is the book *International Relations in Southeast Asia: The Struggle for Autonomy* (2005).

Michael Wills is Director of Research and Operations and (until 2007) was Director of the Strategic Asia Program at The National Bureau of Asian Research. He is co-editor (with Ashley J. Tellis) of *Strategic Asia 2006–07: Trade, Interdependence, and Security* (2006), *Strategic Asia 2005–06: Military Modernization in an Era of Uncertainty* (2005), and *Strategic Asia 2004–05: Confronting Terrorism in the Pursuit of Power* (2004). He was a contributing editor to *Strategic Asia 2003–04: Fragility and Crisis* (2003) and *Strategic Asia 2002–03: Asian Aftershocks* (2002) and has served as technical editor on numerous books, including *China, the United States and South-East Asia: Contending Perspectives on Politics, Security and Economics* (2007), *Religion and Conflict in South and Southeast Asia: Disrupting Violence* (2006), *Strategic Asia 2001–02: Power and Purpose* (2001), and *The Many Faces of Asian Security* (2001). Before joining NBR, Mr. Wills worked at the Cambodia Development Resource Institute in Phnom Penh and, prior to that, with the international political and security risk management firm Control Risks Group in London. He holds a BA (Honors) in Chinese Studies from the University of Oxford.

About Strategic Asia

The **Strategic Asia Program** at The National Bureau of Asian Research (NBR) is a major ongoing research initiative that draws together top Asia studies specialists and international relations experts to assess the changing strategic environment in the Asia-Pacific. The Strategic Asia Program transcends traditional estimates of military balance by incorporating economic, political, and demographic data and by focusing on the strategies and perceptions that drive policy in the region. The program's integrated set of products and activities includes:

- an annual edited volume written by leading specialists

- an executive summary tailored for public and private sector decisionmakers and strategic planners

- an online database that tracks key strategic indicators

- briefings and presentations for government, business, and academe that are designed to foster in depth discussions revolving around major, relevant public issues

Special briefings are held for key committees of Congress and the executive branch, other government agencies, and the intelligence community. The principal audiences for the program's research findings are the U.S. policymaking and research communities, the media, the business community, and academe.

The Strategic Asia Program's online database contains an unprecedented selection of strategic indicators—economic, financial, military, technological, energy, political, and demographic—for all of the countries in the Asia-Pacific region. The database, together with previous volumes and executive summaries, are hosted on the Strategic Asia website at http://strategicasia.nbr.org.

Previous Strategic Asia Volumes

Over the past seven years this series has addressed how Asia is increasingly functioning as a zone of strategic interaction and contending with an uncertain balance of power. *Strategic Asia 2001–02: Power and Purpose* established a baseline assessment for understanding the strategies and interactions of the major states within the region—notably China, India, Japan, Russia, and South Korea. *Strategic Asia 2002–03: Asian Aftershocks* drew upon this baseline to analyze the changes in these states' grand strategies and relationships in the aftermath of the September 11, 2001 terrorist attacks. *Strategic Asia 2003–04: Fragility and Crisis* examined the fragile balance of power in Asia, drawing out the key domestic political and economic trends in Asian states supporting or undermining this tenuous equilibrium. Building upon established themes, *Strategic Asia 2004–05: Confronting Terrorism in the Pursuit of Power* explored the effect of the U.S.-led war on terrorism on the political, economic, social, and strategic transformations underway in Asia. *Strategic Asia 2005–06: Military Modernization in an Era of Uncertainty* appraised the progress of Asian military modernization programs and developed a touchstone to evaluate future military changes to the balance of power. *Strategic Asia 2006–07: Trade, Interdependence, and Security* examined how increasing levels of trade and changing trade relationships are affecting the balance of power and security in Asia.

Research and Management Team

The Strategic Asia research team consists of leading international relations and security specialists from universities and research institutions across the United States and around the world. A new research team is selected each year. The research team for 2007 is led by Ashley J. Tellis (Carnegie Endowment for International Peace). General John Shalikashvili (former Chairman of the Joint Chiefs of Staff), Aaron Friedberg (Princeton University and Strategic Asia's founding research director), and Richard Ellings (The National Bureau of Asian Research and Strategic Asia's founding program director) serve as senior advisors. Advising the program is the executive committee, composed of Herbert Ellison (University of Washington), Donald Emmerson (Stanford University), Francine Frankel (University of Pennsylvania), Mark Hamilton (University of Alaska), Kenneth Pyle (University of Washington), Richard Samuels (Massachusetts Institute of Technology), Robert Scalapino (University of California-Berkeley), Enders Wimbush (Hudson Institute), and William Wohlforth (Dartmouth College).

The Strategic Asia Program depends on a diverse funding base of foundations, government, and corporations, supplemented by income from publication sales. Support for the program in 2007 comes from the GE Foundation, Lynde and Harry Bradley Foundation, and National Nuclear Security Administration at the U.S. Department of Energy.

Attribution

Readers of Strategic Asia reports and visitors to the Strategic Asia website may use data, charts, graphs, and quotes from these sources without requesting permission from The National Bureau of Asian Research on the condition that they cite NBR *and* the appropriate primary source in any published work. No report, chapter, separate study, extensive text, or any other substantial part of the Strategic Asia Program's products may be reproduced without the written permission of The National Bureau of Asian Research. To request permission, please write to:

NBR Editor
The National Bureau of Asian Research
1215 Fourth Avenue, Suite 1600
Seattle, WA 98161
nbr@nbr.org.

The National Bureau of Asian Research

The National Bureau of Asian Research is a nonprofit, nonpartisan research institution dedicated to informing and strengthening policy in the Asia-Pacific. NBR conducts advanced independent research on strategic, political, economic, globalization, health, and energy issues affecting U.S. relations with Asia. Drawing upon an extensive network of the world's leading specialists and leveraging the latest technology, NBR bridges the academic, business, and policy arenas. The institution disseminates its research through briefings, publications, conferences, Congressional testimony, and email forums, and by collaborating with leading institutions worldwide. NBR also provides exceptional internship opportunities to graduate and undergraduate students for the purpose of attracting and training the next generation of Asia specialists. NBR was started in 1989 with a major grant from the Henry M. Jackson Foundation.